Vladimír Mařík   Jörg Müller
Michal Pěchouček (Eds.)

Multi-Agent Systems and Applications III

3rd International Central and Eastern European Conference
on Multi-Agent Systems, CEEMAS 2003
Prague, Czech Republic, June 16-18, 2003
Proceedings

Springer

Series Editors

Jaime G. Carbonell, Carnegie Mellon University, Pittsburgh, PA, USA
Jörg Siekmann, University of Saarland, Saarbrücken, Germany

Volume Editors

Vladimír Mařík
Michal Pěchouček
Czech Technical University
Faculty of Electrical Engineering, Dept. of Cybernetics
16627 Praha 6, Czech Republic
E-mail: marik/pechouc @labe.felk.cvut.cz

Jörg Müller
Siemens AG
CT, IC 6, Otto-Hahn-Ring 6, 81730 München, Germany
E-mail: joerg.p.mueller@siemens.com

Cataloging-in-Publication Data applied for

A catalog record for this book is available from the Library of Congress.

Bibliographic information published by Die Deutsche Bibliothek.
Die Deutsche Bibliothek lists this publication in the Deutsche Nationalbibliografie;
detailed bibliographic data is available in the Internet at <http://dnb.ddb.de>.

CR Subject Classification (1998): I.2.11, C.2.4, D.2, H.5.3, I.2

ISSN 0302-9743
ISBN 3-540-40450-3 Springer-Verlag Berlin Heidelberg New York

Springer-Verlag Berlin Heidelberg New York,
a member of BertelsmannSpringer Science+Business Media GmbH

http://www.springer.de

© Springer-Verlag Berlin Heidelberg 2003
Printed in Germany

Typesetting: Camera-ready by author, data conversion by DA-TeX Gerd Blumenstein
Printed on acid-free paper   SPIN: 10927878   06/3142   5 4 3 2 1 0

Lecture Notes in Artificial Intelligence   2691
Edited by J. G. Carbonell and J. Siekmann

Subseries of Lecture Notes in Computer Science

Springer
Berlin
Heidelberg
New York
Hong Kong
London
Milan
Paris
Tokyo

Preface

Recently, the area of agents and multi-agent systems has grown into a respected research field and a promising technology that has already been exploited in several industrial cases. There have been many novel methods, algorithms and theories investigated and formulated. These enrich and enhance classical software engineering and computer science, the areas of distributed systems and parallel computing, various fields of robotics, collaborative systems, Internet services and technologies, and grid computing, as well as knowledge management, computer-supported manufacturing or coalition formation and teamwork. Researchers have participated in a vast number of international and national research projects which have resulted in networks of excellence, thematic clusters and large-scale standardization efforts. Even though there has been noteworthy success in applying the research achievements of the areas of multi-agent systems and autonomous agents in design and manufacturing, transport and logistics, military and space applications, the tourism industry, e-commerce, and many other areas, there is still a gap between the state of the art achieved in the theoretical foundations of agent technologies and their potential for industry-wide deployment.

This volume continues in a successful series, "Multi-Agent Systems and Applications", of proceedings of important international events organized by the Gerstner Laboratory, CTU, Prague under EU support within the framework of the MIRACLE Center of Excellence project (IST No. ICA1-CT-2000-70002). The first volume in this series (LNAI vol. 2086) represented the proceedings of the Joint Summer School of ECCAI – 9th ACAI 2001 (*Advanced Course on Artificial Intelligence*) and AgentLink – 3rd EASSS 2001 (*European Agent Systems Summer School*) held in July 2001. The second volume (LNAI vol. 2322) contained selected papers from HoloMAS 2001 (2nd *International Workshop on Holonic and Multi-Agent Systems*) and AEMAS 2001 (*International Workshop on Adaptability and Embodiment Using Multi-Agent Systems*).

This volume represents the official proceedings of the CEEMAS 2003 "Central and Eastern Europe Multi-Agents Systems" international conference. After the success of two earlier workshops, namely CEEMAS 1999 (St. Petersburg, Russia) and CEEMAS 2001 (Cracow, Poland), CEEMAS 2003 took place in Prague, Czech Republic on June 16–18th, 2003, having been upgraded into a form of conference. CEEMAS 2003 was really a world-wide conference event. It brought together research scientists, academics, industrial experts and key decision-makers from all over the world in one location, where world-wide technological advances met the research potential of Central and Eastern European countries. The reputation of the conference has been enhanced by the three invited keynote speakers, namely Jeff Bradshaw (University of West Florida, USA), Austin Tate (University of Edinburgh, UK), and Onn Shehory (IBM Research Center, Haifa, Israel).

In this book we have managed to collect a selection of 58 high-quality papers (out of 109 excellent or very good submissions) as well as three contributions from the keynote speakers. The papers cover a wide range of technological areas in the field of agent technologies and multi-agent systems. There are theoretical papers providing formal models of various aspects of agents' individual and collective behavior as well as papers on agents' social behavior, meta-reasoning and reflectivity. The papers from well-known researchers are aimed at protocols, policies and inter-agent negotiations. The conference covered topics of planning, decision-making and coalition formation, but also adaptivity and evolution. A substantial part of the proceedings were devoted to agents' knowledge, ontologies and languages. The practical balance of the proceedings is provided by a selection of papers on applications of multi-agent systems in manufacturing, virtual enterprises, business processes, and the Internet.

We would like to thank all the contributors, PC members and referees (the full list is attached) for their outstanding contribution to the success of the CEEMAS conference. We are especially thankful to Jiří Hodík, Jaroslav Bárta and Aleš Říha for their technical support, to Milena Zeithamlová, Zuzana Hochmeisterová and Hana Krautwurmová for all their excellent organizational activities, and, finally, to Jiří Lažanský who carried out the main portion of the computer work related to the preparation of both the camera-ready and electronic versions of this volume.

April 2003   Vladimír Mařík
                                                              Jörg P. Müller
                                                           Michal Pěchouček

CEEMAS 2003

Third International/Central and Eastern European Conference
on Multi-Agent Systems

Multi-Agent Systems and Applications III

Prague, Czech Republic, June 16–18, 2003

Program Co-chairs

Vladimír Mařík   Czech Technical University, Czech Republic
Jörg Müller   Siemens AG, Germany
Michal Pěchouček   Czech Technical University, Czech Republic

Steering Committee

Barbara Dunin-Keplicz   Warsaw University, Poland
Vladimir Gorodetski   Russian Academy of Sciences, Russia
Michael Luck   University of Southampton, UK
Edward Nawarecki   University of Mining and Metallurgy, Poland

Program Committee

Stanislaw Ambroszkiewicz   Polish Academy of Sciences, Poland
Magnus Boman   Swedish Inst. of Computer Science, Sweden
Cristiano Castelfranchi   Italian National Research Council, Italy
Krzysztof Cetnarowicz   University of Mining and Metallurgy, Poland
Julius Csontó   Technical University of Košice, Slovakia
Grzegorz Dobrowolski   University of Mining and Metallurgy, Poland
Klaus Fischer   DFKI GmbH, Germany
Martyn Fletcher   Leeds Metropolitan University, UK
Roberto A. Flores   National Research Council, Italy
Piotr Gmytrasiewicz   University of Texas, USA
Wiebe van der Hoek   University of Utrecht, The Netherlands
Toru Ishida   Kyoto University, Japan
Jozef Kelemen   Silesian University, Czech Republic
Matthias Klusch   DFKI GmbH, Germany
Jiří Lažanský   Czech Technical University, Czech Republic
Viktor Mashkov   Ukrainian Academy of Sciences, Ukraine
Duncan McFarlane   Cambridge University, UK
László Monostori   Hungarian Academy of Sciences, Hungary
Marek Paralič   Technical University of Košice, Slovakia
Paolo Petta   Austrian Research Institute for AI, Austria

Leonard Popyack	Syracuse University, USA
Stefan Poslad	University of Westminster, UK
Robert Schaefer	Jagiellonian University, Poland
Onn Shehory	IBM Haifa Labs, Israel
Alexander Smirnov	Yaroslavl State University, Russia
Vadim Stefanuk	Russian Academy of Sciences, Russia
Olga Štěpánková	Czech Technical University, Czech Republic
Katia Sycara	Carnegie Mellon University, USA
Milind Tambe	University of Southern California, USA
Robert Tolksdorf	Freie Universität Berlin, Germany
Paul Valkenaers	KU Leuven, Belgium
József Váncza	Hungarian Academy of Sciences, Hungary
Rineke Verbrugge	University of Groningen, The Netherlands
Michael Wooldridge	University of Liverpool, UK
Steven Willmott	Swiss Federal Inst. of Technology, Switzerland

External Reviewers

Jaroslav Bárta	Lenka Lhotská	Viktor Skormin
Petr Bečvář	Filip Macůrek	Petr Šlechta
Robert W. Brennan	Petr Novák	Pavel Tichý
Michal Dobíšek	Marek Obitko	Jan Tožička
Jiří Hodík	Libor Přeučil	Tomáš Vlček
Petr Charvát	Aleš Říha	Jiří Vokřínek
Jiří Kubalík	Milan Rollo	Pavel Vrba

Organizing Committee

Hana Krautwurmová	Czech Technical University, Czech Republic
Jaroslav Bárta	Czech Technical University, Czech Republic
Jiří Hodík	Czech Technical University, Czech Republic
Aleš Říha	Czech Technical University, Czech Republic
Jiří Vokřínek	Czech Technical University, Czech Republic
Zuzana Hochmeisterová	Czech Technical University, Czech Republic
Milena Zeithamlová	Action M Agency, Czech Republic

Table of Contents

Coalitions

Evolution & Emergent Behavior

Platforms

Protocols

Security

Real-Time & Synchronization

Industrial Applications

E-business & Virtual Enterprises

Web & Mobile Agents

Making Agents Acceptable to People
Abstract of a Key-Note Speech

Jeffrey M. Bradshaw

Institute for Human and Machine Cognition, University of West Florida
jbradshaw@ai.uwf.edu

Because ever more powerful intelligent agents will interact with people in increasingly sophisticated and important ways, greater attention must be given to the technical and social aspects of how to make agents acceptable to people [4, p. 51]. The technical challenge is to devise a computational structure that guarantees that from the technical standpoint all is under control. We want to be able to help ensure the protection of agent state, the viability of agent communities, and the reliability of the resources on which they depend. To accomplish this, we must guarantee, insofar as is possible, that the autonomy of agents can always be bounded by explicit enforceable policy that can be continually adjusted to maximize the agents' effectiveness and safety in both human and computational environments. The social challenge is to ensure that agents and people interact gracefully and to provide reassurance to people that all is working according to plan. We want agents to be designed to fit well with how people actually work together. Explicit policies governing human-agent interaction, based on careful observation of work practice and an understanding of current social science research, can help assure that effective and natural coordination, appropriate levels and modalities of feedback, and adequate predictability and responsiveness to human control are maintained. These factors are key to providing the reassurance and trust that are the prerequisites to the widespread acceptance of agent technology for non-trivial applications.

The idea of building strong social laws into intelligent systems can be traced at least as far back as the 1940s to the science fiction writings of Isaac Asimov [1]. In his well-known stories of the succeeding decades he formulated a set of basic laws that were built deeply into the positronic-brain circuitry of each robot so that it was physically prevented from transgression. Though the laws were simple and few, the stories attempted to demonstrate just how difficult they were to apply in various real-world situations. In most situations, although the robots usually behaved "logically," they often failed to do the "right" thing— typically because the particular context of application required subtle adjustments of judgments on the part of the robot (e.g., determining which law took priority in a given situation, or what constituted helpful or harmful behavior.

In an insightful essay, Roger Clarke explores some of the implications of Asimov's stories about the laws of robotics for information technologists [3]. Weld and Etzioni [7] were the first to discuss the implications of Asimov's first law of robotics for agent researchers. Like most norm-based approaches described below (and unlike most policy-based approaches) the safety conditions are taken into account as part of the agents' own learning and planning processes rather than as part of the

V. Mařík et al. (Eds): CEEMAS 2003, LNAI 2691, pp. 1-3, 2003.

infrastructure. In an important response to Weld and Etzioni's "call to arms," Pynadath and Tambe [5] develop a hybrid approach that marries the agents' probabilistic reasoning about adjustable autonomy with hard safety constraints to generate "policies" governing the actions of agents. The approach assumes a set of homogeneous agents who are motivated to cooperate and follow optimally-generated policies.

Shoham and Tennenholtz [6] introduced the theme of social laws into the agent research community, where investigations have continued under two main headings: norms and policies. While sharing much in common with norm-based approaches, policy-based perspectives differ from them in subtle ways. In contrast to the relatively descriptive basis and self-chosen adoption (or rejection) of norms, policies tend to be seen as prescriptive and externally-imposed entities. Whereas norms in everyday life emerge gradually from group conventions and recurrent patterns of interaction, policies are consciously designed and put into and out of force at arbitrary times by virtue of explicitly-recognized authority. These differences are generally reflected in the way most policy-based approaches differ from norm-based ones with respect to three features. Policy-based approaches:

1. support dynamic runtime policy changes, and not merely static configurations determined in advance;
2. work involuntarily with respect to the agents, that is, without requiring the agents to consent or even be aware of the policies being enforced; thus aiming to guarantee that even the simplest agents can comply with policy; and
3. wherever possible they are enforced preemptively, preventing buggy or malicious agents from doing harm in advance rather than rewarding them or imposing sanctions on them after the fact.

In this talk, we outline our efforts to address some of the technical and social concerns about agent acceptability through the use of a policy-based approach as implemented in the KAoS framework. A more detailed discussion of these issues can be found in [2].

References

[1]   Asimov, I. (1942/1968). Runaround. In I. Asimov (Ed.), I, Robot. (pp. 33-51). London, England: Grafton Books. Originally published in Astounding Science Fiction, 1942, pp. 94-103.

[2]   Bradshaw, J. M., Beautement, P., Breedy, M. R., Bunch, L., Drakunov, S. V., Feltovich, P., Hoffman, R. R., Jeffers, R., Johnson, M., Kulkarni, S., Lott, J., Raj, A. K., Suri, N., & Uszok, A. (2003). Making agents acceptable to people. In N. Zhong & J. Liu (Ed.), Handbook of Intelligent Information Technology. Amsterdam, Holland: IOS Press.

[3]   Clarke, R. (1993-1994). Asimov's laws of robotics: Implications for information technology, Parts 1 and 2. IEEE Computer, December/January, 53-61/57-66.

[4]   Norman, D. A. (1997). How might people interact with agents? In J. M. Bradshaw (Ed.), Software Agents. (pp. 49-55). Cambridge, MA: The AAAI Press/The MIT Press.

[5]   Pynadath, D., & Tambe, M. (2001). Revisiting Asimov's first law: A response to the call to arms. Proceedings of ATAL 01.

[6]   Shoham, Y., & Tennenholtz, M. (1992). On the synthesis of useful social laws for artificial agent societies. Proceedings of the Tenth National Conference on Artificial Intelligence, (pp. 276-281). San Jose, CA.

[7]   Weld, D., & Etzioni, O. (1994). The firsts law of robotics: A call to arms. Proceedings of the National Conference on Artificial Intelligence (AAAI 94), (pp. 1042-1047).

Coalition Formation: Towards Feasible Solutions
Abstract of a Key-Note Speech

Onn Shehory

IBM Haifa Research Lab, Haifa University
Haifa 31905, ISRAEL
onn@il.ibm.com

Abstract. Coalition formation is an important cooperation method in multi-agent systems. Within coalitions, agents may be able to jointly perform tasks that they would otherwise be unable to perform, or will perform poorly. To allow agents to form coalitions, one should devise a coalition formation mechanism that includes a protocol as well as strategies to be implemented by the agents given the protocol. Coalition formation mechanisms proposed to date commonly provide these, however they include several restrictive assumptions, which do not hold in real-world domains where coalitions are necessary. In recent studies we have relaxed some of these assumptions to arrive at automated coalition formation mechanisms better suited for real domains.

A coalition is a set of agents that agree to cooperate to perform a task. Given N agents and k tasks, there are $k(2^N-1)$ different possible coalitions. The number of coalition configurations (that is, different partitions of the set of agents into coalitions) is of the order $O(N^{(N/2)})$. Given these, it is clear that when the number of agents is larger than a few dozens, an exhaustive search of the coalition configuration space is infeasible. Even if such a search is afforded, self-interested agents may have conflicting preferences over the possible outcomes of the search. Coalition formation is thus a difficult, complex task, nevertheless it is in many cases beneficial, as the gains from forming a coalition may surpass the costs of its formation.

When designers of agents attempt to provide their agents with a coalition formation mechanism, they need to address several issues:

- Given a set of tasks and a set of agents, which coalitions are those that an individual agent should attempt to form?
- Once the agent knows what coalitions it prefers to form, what mechanisms can it use for coalition formation?
- Given a specific coalition formation mechanism, what guarantees regarding efficiency and quality are provided?
- Once a coalition has formed, how should its members go about distribution of work/payoff?
- In times, it may be necessary to provide means for the agents to dissolve the coalitions they formed.

V. Mařík et al. (Eds): CEEMAS 2003, LNAI 2691, pp. 4-6, 2003.
© Springer-Verlag Berlin Heidelberg 2003

We have developed two mechanisms that address these issues, however relax some of the restrictive assumptions of classical coalition formation solutions. The first mechanism is aimed at a B2C wholesale market. In such markets, purchasing more of the same product reduces the price per unit, benefiting buyers. Nevertheless, sellers benefit as well from selling more goods and cutting marketing/distribution costs. However, buyers usually do not need large quantities, hence forming buyers' coalitions may be beneficial. We have devised a coalition formation mechanism for multiple purchasing agents in a wholesale environment which requires no explicit negotiation. Agents join coalitions by placing an order jointly with their coalition counterparts. They may leave to join a more beneficial coalition by withdrawing the order. We assume that agents know the retail price of the good they seek and the sites in which the good is sold, however they only know other agents they encounter by random. Following these assumptions and as a result of the simplicity of the mechanism, the communication and computation complexities are kept minimal. This is adequate for large-scale agent systems. We provide a formal, mathematical model of the behavior of the agents. This model allows quantitative analysis, predicting coalition formation attributes (e.g., number of coalitions, size distribution, gains, formation time). Based on this analysis, agent designers can tradeoff gains and execution time, thus beneficial, dynamic coalition formation is afforded. Additional details on this mechanism can be found in [1].

The second mechanism is aimed at a B2B RFP (Request For Proposal) market. In such markets, a requested product/service can typically be provided only by groups of suppliers, hence coalitions are a must. Additionally, one cannot assume complete information. Rather, agents value tasks individually and privately—resulting in multiple valuations of a specific task—and they do not know the value of a task to other agents, although they may have a rough idea of the value distribution of a task. Further, the coalition formation process, as an economic process, is bounded in time, and the value of a task is discounted as time elapses during the process. These assumptions are necessary for providing a solution applicable to a real-world coalition formation. The coalition formation mechanism we devise for this problem is comprised of two parts: a negotiation for coalition formation and an auction-like process for task allocation. The mechanism is monitored by a neutral third party manager. Agents send proposals for coalition formation to others via this manager. The decision upon task allocation to coalitions is later made by the manager as well. We have provided the agents with several strategies to be used in conjunction with the mechanism. Via experiments we were able to prove that two of these strategies are superior to the others and lead to coalitions where the average gain is close to the optimal gain computed centrally with complete information. Additional details on this mechanism can be found in [2].

In conclusion, we provide two mechanisms in which several restrictive assumptions of traditional coalition formation solutions are relaxed. By these relaxations we might be compromising gains and stability, nevertheless we arrive at solutions that are beneficial and in times are even close to optimal. These solutions are a step towards solutions for real domains; however further relaxation will be required in future work.

References

[1]   K. Lerman, O. Shehory, "Coalition formation for large-scale electronic markets", ICMAS'00, Boston, July 2000.

[2]   S. Kraus, O. Shehory, G. Taase, "Coalition formation with uncertain heterogeneous information", AAMAS'03, Melbourne, July 2003.

Coalition Task Support Using I-X and <I-N-C-A>

Austin Tate

Artificial Intelligence Applications Institute, University of Edinburgh
Appleton Tower, Crichton Street, Edinburgh EH8 9LE, UK
a.tate@ed.ac.uk
http://www.aiai.ed.ac.uk/project/ix/

Abstract. I-X is a research programme with a number of different aspects intended to create a well-founded approach to allow humans and computer systems to cooperate in the creation or modification of some product such as a design, physical entity or plan - i.e. it supports cooperative synthesis tasks. The I-X approach involves the use of shared models for task-directed cooperation between human and computer agents who are jointly exploring (via some, perhaps dynamically determined, process) a range of alternative options for the synthesis of an artifact such as a design or a plan (termed a product). The <I-N-C-A> (Issues - Nodes - Constraints - Annotations) ontology is used to represent a specific artifact as a set of constraints on the space of all possible artifacts in an application domain. It can be used to describe the requirements or specification to be achieved and the emerging description of the artifact itself. It can also describe the (perhaps dynamically generated) processes involved. I-X and |<I-N-C-A> have been applied to Coalition Task Support.

1 Introduction

I-X is a research programme with a number of different aspects intended to create a well-founded approach to allow humans and computer systems to cooperate in the creation or modification of some product or products such as documents, plans, designs or physical entities - i.e., it supports mixed-initiative synthesis tasks.

The I-X research draws on earlier work on Nonlin [1], O-Plan [2], [3], [4], [5], [6], Optimum-AIV [7], [8], <I-N-OVA> [9], [10] and the Enterprise Project [11], [12], [13] but seeks to make the framework generic and to clarify terminology, simplify the approach taken, and increase re-usability and applicability of the core ideas.

The I-X research programme includes the following threads or work areas:

1. **I-Core**, which is the core modular systems integration architecture.
2. **<I-N-C-A>**, which is an underlying ontology for synthesised artifacts.
3. **I-P²**, which are I-X Process Panels used to support user tasks and cooperation.

V. Mařík et al. (Eds): CEEMAS 2003, LNAI 2691, pp. 7-16, 2003.
© Springer-Verlag Berlin Heidelberg 2003

4. **I-Plan**, which is the I-X Planning System. This is also used within I-P2 and other applications as it provides generic facilities for supporting planning, process refinement, dynamic response to changing needs, etc.
5. **I-DE**, which is the I-X Domain Editor. This is itself an I-X application but is also used to create and maintain the domain models, including especially the process models and activity specifications used throughout I-X systems.
6. **I-Views**, which are viewers for processes and products, and which are employed in other applications of I-X. I-Views can be for a wide range of modalities of interface and types of user.
7. **I-Faces**, which are underlying support utilities to allow for the creation of user interfaces, inter-agent communications and repository access.
8. **I-X Applications** of the above threads in a variety of areas depending on our current collaborations. These include:

   - Coalition Operations (CoAX, CoSAR-TS)
   - Emergency and Unusual Procedure Assistance (I-Rescue)
   - Help Desk Support (I-Help)
   - Multi-Perspective Knowledge Modelling and Management (I-AKT)
   - Natural Language Presentations of Procedures and Plans (I-Tell)
   - Collaborative meeting and task support (I-Room, CoAKTinG).

9. **I-X Technology Transfer**, including work on standards committees.

2   I-X Approach

The I-X approach involves the use of shared models for task-directed cooperation between human and computer agents who are jointly exploring (via some predefined or dynamically created process) a range of alternative options for the synthesis of one or more artifacts such as a design or a plan (termed a product).

- An I-X system or agent has two cycles:
- Handle Issues (leading to the addition of Nodes especially, but also potentially further Issues, Constraints and Annotations)
- Respect Domain Constraints

An I-X system or agent carries out a (perhaps dynamically determined) process that leads to the production of (one or more alternative options for) a synthesised artifact.

I-X also involves a modular systems integration architecture that strongly parallels and supports the abstract view described. This is a Model - Viewer - Controller style of architecture. Plug-in components for Issue Handlers, Constraint Managers, I/O Handlers and Viewers allow for specific I-X systems to be created using this abstract architecture. More detail is available at the I-X web site - http://i-x.info.

3   <I-N-C-A> Ontology

<I-N-C-A> (Issues - Nodes - Constraints - Annotations) is the basis of the ontology that underpins the I-X approach, and provides the framework for the representation used to describe processes and process products within I-X systems and agents.

The forerunner of <I-N-C-A, <I-N-OVA> [9], when first designed, was intended to act as a bridge to improve dialogue between a number of communities working on formal planning theories, practical planning systems and systems engineering process management methodologies. It was intended to support new work then emerging on automatic manipulation of plans, human communication about plans, principled and reliable acquisition of plan information, and formal reasoning about plans. It has since been utilised as the basis for a number of research efforts, practical applications and emerging international standards for plan and process representations. For some of the history and relationships between earlier work in AI on plan representations, work from the process and design communities and the standards bodies, and the part that <I-N-OVA> played in this see [4].

At various stages of the development of the I-X research the typography for rendering <I-N-C-A> has varied as the components have received clarification. <I-N-CA> originally stood for Issues, Nodes, Critical and Auxiliary Constraints. The aspect of separating critical (shared communications) constraints from auxiliary (separately managed) constraints is still important within the I-X architecture, but is now considered a part of managing the "C" (constraints) component. The annotations were always present in the ontology and can be attached to all components, but the top level annotations capturing the rationale behind the synthesised product or the process/plan being described has required more prominence as the work has continued and as mixed-initiative and human communications aspects have become more important. Hence, the rendering <I-N-C-A> with the extra hyphen now stands for Issues, Nodes, Constraints and Annotations.

In <I-N-C-A>, both processes and process products are abstractly considered to be made up of a set of "Issues" which are associated with the processes or process products to represent potential requirements, questions raised as a result of analysis or critiquing, etc. They also contain "Nodes" (activities in a process, or parts of a physical product) which may have parts called sub-nodes making up a hierarchical description of the process or product. The nodes are related by a set of detailed "Constraints" of various kinds. Finally there can be "Annotations" related to the processes or products, which provide rationale, information and other useful descriptions. The I-X systems integration approach is based on the <I-N-C-A> Model of Synthesised Artifacts that provides it with a simple abstraction that provides an extremely flexible, extendable and intelligible representation of the processes and process products in I-X. It is well suited to communication between human and system agents engaged in some common task, each possibly taking the initiative over which parts they can handle at various stages.

3.1   Issues

The issues in the representation may state the outstanding questions to be handled and can represent unsatisfied objectives, questions raised as a result of analysis, etc. The I constraints can be thought of as implying potential further constraints which may have to be added into the design in future in order to address the outstanding issues. In work on I-X until recently, the issues had a task or activity orientation to them, being mostly concerned with actionable items referring to the process underway - i.e., actions in the process space. This is now not felt to be appropriate, and we are adopting the gIBIS orientation of expressing these issues as questions to be considered [14], [15]. This is advocated by the Questions - Options- Criteria approach [16] - itself used for rationale capture for plans and plan scheme libraries in our earlier work [17], [18] and similar to the mapping approaches used in Compendium [19].

3.2   Nodes

The nodes in the specifications describe components that are to be included in the design. Nodes can themselves be artifacts that can have their own structure with sub-nodes and other <I-N-C-A> described refinements associated with them.

The node constraints (these are of the form "include node") in the <I-N-C-A> model set the space within which an artifact may be further constrained. The "I" (issues) and "C" constraints restrict the artifacts within that space which are of interest.

Others have recognised the special nature of the inclusion of nodes (or activities) into a synthesised artifacts (or plan) compared to all the other constraints that may be described. In the planning domain, [20] differentiate Plan Modification Operators into "progressive refinements" which can introduce new actions into the plan, and "non-progressive refinements" which just partition the search space with existing sets of actions in the plan. They call the former genuine planning refinement operators, and think of the latter as providing the scheduling component.

3.3   Constraints

The constraints restrict the relationships between the nodes to describe only those artifacts within the design space that meet the requirements. The constraints may be split into "critical constraints" and "auxiliary constraints" depending on whether some constraint managers (solvers) can return them as "maybe" answers to indicate that the constraint being added to the model is okay so long as other critical constraints are imposed by other constraint managers. The maybe answer is expressed as a disjunction of conjunctions of such critical or shared constraints. More details on the "yes/no/maybe" constraint management approach used in I-X and the earlier O-Plan systems are available in [3].

The choice of which constraints are considered critical and which are considered as auxiliary is itself a decision for an application of I-X and specific decisions on how to split the management of constraints within such an application. It is not pre-determined for all applications. A temporal activity-based planner would normally have object/variable constraints (equality and inequality of objects) and some temporal constraints (maybe just the simple before{time-point1, time-point-2} constraint) as the critical constraints. But, in a 3D design or a configuration application object/variable and some other critical constraints (possibly spatial constraints) might be chosen. It depends on the nature of what is communicated between constraint managers in the application of the I-X architecture.

3.4   Annotations

The annotations add additional human-centric information or design and decision rationale to the information describing the artifact.

3.5   Observation

If we consider the process of planning as a large constraint satisfaction task, we may try to model this as a Constraint Satisfaction Problem (CSP) represented by a set of variables to which we have to give a consistent assignment of values. In this case we can note that the addition of new nodes ("include node" constraints in <I-N-C-A>) is the only constraint that can add variables dynamically to the CSP. The Issue (I) constraints may be separated into two kinds: those that may (directly or indirectly) add nodes to the product and those that cannot. The "I" constraints that lead to the inclusion of new nodes are of a different nature in the process to those that cannot.

4   Putting <I-N-C-A> to Use

<I-N-C-A> models are intended to support a number of different uses:

- for automatic and mixed-initiative generation and manipulation of plans and other synthesised artifacts and to act as an ontology to underpin such use;
- as a common basis for human and system communication about plans and other synthesised artifacts;
- as a target for principled and reliable acquisition of knowledge about synthesised artifacts such as plans, process models and process product information;
- to support formal reasoning about plans and other synthesised artifacts.

These cover both formal and practical requirements and encompass the requirements for use by both human and computer-based planning and design systems.

5   I-X Process Panels

We "deliver" useful functionality based on the <I-N-C-A> ontology via I-X Process Panels (I-P2). These support a user or collaborative users in selecting and carrying out "processes" and creating or modifying "process products". The aim of an I-X Process Panel (I-P2) is to act as an intelligent workflow support, reporting and messaging "catch all" for its user. It can act in conjunction with other panels for other users if desired.

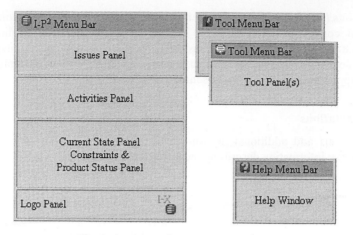

Fig. 1. Anatomy of an I-X Process Panel

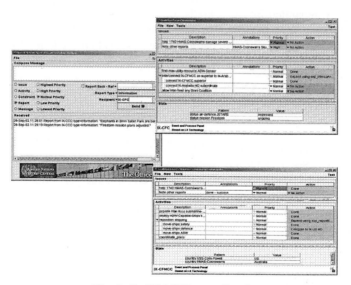

Fig. 2. CoAX I-X Process Panels

An I-X Process Panel:

- Can take requests to:
    - Handle an issue
    - Perform an activity
    - Add a constraint
    - Support an annotation
- Deals with these via:
    - Manual (user) activity

- o   Internal capabilities
- o   External capabilities (invoke or query/answer)
- o   Reroute or delegate to other panels or agents (pass)
- o   Plan and execute a composite of these capabilities (plan or expand)
- Receives reports and messages and, where possible, interprets them to:
  - o   Understand current status of issues, activities, constraints and annotations
  - o   Understand current world state, especially status of process products
  - o   Help control the situation
  - o   Improve annotations
- Copes with partial knowledge and can operate even where little or no pre-built knowledge of the domain is available.

6   Coalition Task Support

I-X and I-X Process Panels (I-P2) concepts have been demonstrated in a number realistic scenarios such as in Air Campaign Planning [21], Military Operations in Urban Terrain [22], the Coalition Agents eXperiment - CoAX [23], and Coalition Search and Rescue [24]. They are being considered for use in a number of future joint and multinational forces experiments and demonstrations.

7   Summary

I-X is aimed at supporting a range of collaborative mixed-initiative synthesis tasks - such as planning, design and configuration. It is intended to simplify and make more generic the component boundaries and naming conventions used in the construction of such systems and seeks to make the concepts more re-usable for a range of such tasks.

   I-X is based on the <I-N-C-A> constraint ontology - a powerful and extremely flexible representation of the products of the synthesis process that an I-X system supports. This represents a product as a set of constraints on the space of all possible products within the model of the domain that the I-X system has. This ontology relates well to emerging standards for process representation and interchange (e.g. in PIF, NIST PSL, DARPA SPAR).

   Both processes and process products are abstractly considered to be made up of a set of "Issues" which are associated with the processes or process products and may represent outstanding questions with respect to the products, unsatisfied requirements, problems raised as a result of analysis or critiquing, etc. They also contain "Nodes" (activities in a process, or parts of a process product) which may have parts called sub-nodes making up a hierarchical description of the process or product. The nodes are related by a set of detailed "Constraints" of various kinds. Finally there can be "Annotations" related to the processes or products, which provide rationale, information and other useful descriptions.

I-X and <I-N-C-A> have been utilized in a number of coalition cooperative task support scenarios in which the systems have to respond to dynamic events and changes of relationships between the agents involved.

Acknowledgements

Thanks to my co-workers on the I-X, CoAKTinG and CoSAR-TS projects at Edinburgh - especially Stuart Aitken, Jessica Chen-Burger, Clauirton de Siebra, Jeff Dalton, John Levine, Natasha Lino, Stephen Potter and Jussi Stader for discussions on the topic of this paper.

This material is based on research within the I-X and CoSAR-TS projects sponsored by the Defense Advanced Research Projects Agency (DARPA) and US Air Force Research Laboratory under agreement number F30602-03-2-0014 and under the Advanced Knowledge Technologies (AKT) Interdisciplinary Research Collaboration (IRC) and its Collaborative Advanced Knowledge Technologies in the Grid (CoAKTinG) project, which is sponsored by the UK Engineering and Physical Sciences Research Council under grant number GR/N15764/01. The AKT IRC comprises the Universities of Aberdeen, Edinburgh, Sheffield, Southampton and the Open University.

The U.S. Government, the University of Edinburgh, the AKT IRC research partners and sponsors are authorized to reproduce and distribute reprints and on-line copies for their purposes notwithstanding any copyright annotation hereon. The views and conclusions contained herein are those of the authors and should not be interpreted as necessarily representing the official policies or endorsements, either express or implied, of other parties.

References

[1]   Tate, A.: Generating Project Networks, Proceedings of the International Joint Conference on Artificial Intelligence (IJCAI-77), pp. 888-893, Cambridge, MA, USA, Morgan Kaufmann, (1977).

[2]   Currie, K.W. and Tate, A.: O-Plan: the Open Planning Architecture, Artificial Intelligence 52(1), Autumn 1991, North-Holland, (1991).

[3]   Tate, A.: Integrating Constraint Management into an AI Planner, Journal of Artificial Intelligence in Engineering, Vol. 9, No.3, pp. 221-228, (1995).

[4]   Tate, A.: Roots of SPAR, in Special Issue on Ontologies, Knowledge Engineering Review, Vol.13(1), March, 1998, Cambridge University Press, (1998).

[5]   Tate, A.: Intelligible AI Planning, in Proceedings of the Twentieth British Computer Society Special Group on Expert Systems International Conference on Knowledge Based Systems and Applied Artificial Intelligence, Cambridge, UK, December 2000.

[6]   Levine, J., Tate, A. and Dalton, J.: O-P3: Supporting the Planning Process using Open Planning Process Panels, IEEE Intelligent Systems, Vol. 15, No. 6, November/December 2000.

[7]   Aarup, M., Arentoft, M.M., Parrod, Y., Stokes, I., Vadon, H. and Stader, J.: Optimum-AIV: A Knowledge-Based Planning and Scheduling System for Spacecraft AIV, in Intelligent Scheduling (eds. Zweben, M. and Fox, M.S.), pp. 451-469, Morgan Kaufmann, (1994).

[8]   Tate, A. Responsive Planning and Scheduling Using AI Planning Techniques - Optimum-AIV, In Trends & Controversies - AI Planning Systems in the Real World, IEEE Expert: Intelligent Systems & their Applications, Vol. 11 No. 6, pp. 4-12, December 1996.

[9]   Tate, A.: The <I-N-OVA> Constraint Model of Plans, Proceedings of the Third International Conference on Artificial Intelligence Planning Systems, (ed. Drabble, B.), pp. 221-228, Edinburgh, UK, May 1996, AAAI Press, (1996).

[10]   Tate, A.: <I-N-OVA> and <I-N-CA> - Representing Plans and other Synthesized Artifacts as a Set of Constraints, AAAI-2000 Workshop on Representational Issues for Real-World Planning Systems, at the National Conference of the American Association of Artificial Intelligence (AAAI-2000), Austin, Texas, USA, August 2000.

[11]   Fraser, J. and Tate, A.: The Enterprise Tool Set - An Open Enterprise Architecture, Proceedings of the Workshop on Intelligent Manufacturing Systems, International Joint Conference on Artificial Intelligence (IJCAI-95), Montreal, Canada, August 1995.

[12]   Uschold, M., King, M., Moralee, S. and Zorgios, Y.: The Enterprise Ontology, in Special Issue on Ontologies, Knowledge Engineering Review, Vol.13(1), March, 1998, Cambridge University Press, (1998).

[13]   Stader, J.: Results of the Enterprise Project. In Proceedings of Expert Systems'96, the 16th Annual Conference of the British Computer Society Specialist Group on Expert Systems, Cambridge, UK, December 1996. See http://www.aiai.ed.ac.uk/project/enterprise/96-es96-enterprise.ps.gz, (1996).

[14]   Selvin, A.M.: Supporting Collaborative Analysis and Design with Hypertext Functionality, Journal of Digital information, Volume 1 Issue 4. See http://jodi.ecs.soton.ac.uk/Articles/v01/i04/Selvin/, (1999).

[15]   Conklin, J. Dialog Mapping: Reflections on an Industrial Strength Case Study. In: P.A. Kirschner, S.J. Buckingham Shum and C.S. Carr (Eds.), Visualizing Argumentation: Software Tools for Collaborative and Educational Sense-Making. Springer-Verlag: London, ISBN 1-85233-6641-1, pp. 117-136. See www.VisualizingArgumentation.info, (2003).

[16]   MacLean, A., Young, R., Bellotti, V. and Moran, T.: Design space analysis: Bridging from theory to practice via design rationale. In Proceedings of Esprit '91, pages 720-730, Brussels, November 1991.

[17]   Polyak, S. and Tate, A.: Rationale in Planning: Causality, Dependencies and Decisions, Knowledge Engineering Review, Vol.13(3), pp. 247-262, September, 1998, Cambridge University Press.
       See   http://www.aiai.ed.ac.uk/project/oplan/documents/1998/98-rationale.pdf, (1998).

[18] Polyak, S. and Tate, A.: A Common Process Ontology for Process-Centred Organisations, Knowledge based Systems, 2000. Earlier version by S. Polyak published as University of Edinburgh Department of Artificial Intelligence Research paper 930, 1998.
      See http://www.aiai.ed.ac.uk/project/oplan/documents/1999/99-sebpc-cpm.pdf, (1999).

[19] Selvin, A.M, Buckingham Shum, S.J., Sierhuis, M., Conklin, J., Zimmermann, B., Palus, C., Drath, W., Horth, D., Domingue, J., Motta, E. and Li, G. Compendium: Making Meetings into Knowledge Events, Knowledge Technologies 2001, Austin TX, USA, March 4-7, 2001.
      See http://www2.gca.org/knowledgetechnolgies/001/proceedings/ Conklin& Selvin%20Slides.pdf, (2001).

[20] Khambhampati, S. and Srivastava, B.: Unifying Classical Planning Approaches, Arizona State University ASU CSE TR 96-006, July 1996.

[21] Tate, A., Dalton, J. and Levine, J.: Generation of Multiple Qualitatively Different Plan Options, Fourth International Conference on AI Planning Systems (AIPS-98), Pittsburgh, PA, USA, June 1998.

[22] Tate, A., Levine, J., Dalton, J. and Nixon, A.: Task Achieving Agents on the World Wide Web, in Spinning the Semantic Web, Fensel, D., Hendler, J., Liebermann, H. and Wahlster, W. (eds.), MIT Press, (2003).

[23] Allsopp, D.N., Beautement, P., Bradshaw, J.M., Durfee, E.H., Kirton, M., Knoblock, C.A., Suri, N. and Tate, A. and Thompson, C.W.: Coalition Agents Experiment: Multi-Agent Co-operation in an International Coalition Setting, Special Issue on Knowledge Systems for Coalition Operations (KSCO), IEEE Intelligent Systems, Vol. 17 No. 3 pp. 26-35. May/June 2002.

[24] CoSAR-TS Team: Coalition Search and Rescue Task Support Project Web Site. http://www.aiai.ed.ac.uk/project/cosar-ts/, (2003).

Towards Motivation-Based Decisions
for Worth Goals

Steve J. Munroe[1], Michael Luck[1], and Mark d'Inverno[2]

[1] Electronics and Computer Science, University of Southampton, Southampton, UK
{sjm01r,mml}@ecs.soton.ac.uk
[2] Computer Science, University of Westminster, London, UK
dinverm@wmin.ac.uk

Abstract. In this paper we present a motivational mechanism to generate and determine the worth of goals and to represent various constraints involved in satisfying a goal. The work builds on the SMART agent framework and adds to the growing body of work that is attempting to extend the abilities of autonomous agents past the constraints of the traditional symbolic approaches to AI. The paper represents a first step in increasing an agent's autonomy in the domain of e-commerce, specifically enabling the agent to dynamically set issue parameters in relation to the importance of the issue and the effects of any existing constraints.

1   Introduction

Overcoming the limitations of symbolically based representations as used in intelligent agents, to cope with more realistic domains, is an area growing in size. Work from robotic control [14], design to criteria scheduling [19] and cognitive appraisal theory [16] all pertain to extending the abilities of computational agents into continuous, worth-oriented domains. Trading-off the satisfaction of multiple issues or goals in the context of conflicting constraints however, has had little attention as yet in the field of autonomous deliberative agents (cf. [17]), though work relevant to this exists in auctions in the case of multiple-issues (eg. [2]) and robotic control in the case of synthesising behaviour in the face of multiple constraints (eg. [14]). Traditional deliberative agent architectures (eg. [11]) tend to employ a static representation of preferences that an agent must try to satisfy with little or no room for adjusting them in the light of new information. Often it is not possible however, to fully satisfy existing goals in a particular environment and, lacking any way to relax goals, they are therefore likely to be dropped, and the associated utility gain lost.

Within the field of electronic commerce, recent advances in agents are allowing automation of many activities usually performed by humans. Agents are now able to use simple negotiation strategies in order to purchase a good or a service under conditions that best satisfy a user's preferences (eg. [8]). The dominant approach to the worth-oriented nature of such a domain is to use utility-based, selfish maximising agents (eg, [5]). However, take up of these new systems is

V. Mařík et al. (Eds): CEEMAS 2003, LNAI 2691, pp. 17–28, 2003.

generally limited to simple purchases over one *issue* such as price, in which user preferences are rigidly encoded, offering little opportunity for flexible yet robust adaptation to prevailing circumstances. It would be desirable to be able to combine both approaches to see how to increase an agent's autonomy with respect to making purchasing decisions in the face of dynamic environments and changing contexts.

Consider the task of keeping an inventory stocked with various items; the inventory keeper needs to decide *how much* of each good to buy whilst trying to satisfy certain constraints such as cost, urgency and demand for each item. All of these constraints should be factors in the final decision and the inventory keeper needs to discover the feasible goals available given the constraints. The problems in this situation consist of how to use information about the domain in order to dynamically set parameters associated with the preferences inside the agent, how to discover when one issue under consideration is more important than another and, finally, how to combine the varying importance of each issue under consideration into a coherent decision about what to do. There are many kinds of domains in which this may be done but, in this paper we focus on domains in which the agent needs to reason over *quantities* of a particular item though this can easily be reinterpreted as reasoning over levels of *quality* for say, service provision.

In this paper our approach uses the concept of motivation to combine the traditional notion of goals as state descriptions with the notion of the worth or utility of a goal. This allows us to give a different worth to a goal state depending on the current context and constraints. We describe a motivational mechanism capable of generating multiple goals, representing their worth in relation to each other and determining their parameters based on a number of constraints (also modelled as motivation). We begin by describing the basic underlying framework upon which this work is based, before describing the motivational mechanisms in detail. Then we begin a discussion on assigning worth to goals and constraints, its relation to motivation and the setting of goal parameters. After that we provide a worked example. The paper ends with a discussion of the approach.

2   Motivated Agents

In this work we adopt the SMART agent framework described in [4]. We also adopt the Z notation [15] which is based on set-theory and first order logic. Though we assume some familiarity with Z, the meaning should be clear. The arguments for Z are well-rehearsed (ie.[3]), and we omit further discussion.

We start by defining four primitives: *attributes*, *actions*, *goals* and *motivations*, which are used as the basis for development of the SMART agent framework. Formally, these primitives are specified as given sets, which means that we say nothing about how they might be represented for any particular system. Attributes are simply features of the world, and are the only characteristics that are manifest. Actions are operations that can add or remove attributes, goals are descriptions of states in terms of attributes that the agent would like to bring about and, finally, motivation is any desire or preference that can lead to the generation and adoption of goals and that affects the outcome of the reasoning or behavioural task intended to satisfy those goals [4].

[*Attribute, Action, Goal, Motivation*]

An agent is defined to be an entity with a set of attributes that describes its characteristics, a set of actions called *capabilities* that can be used to change the world and a set of goals that the agent wants to bring about, all of which are non-empty sets.

```
┌─ Agent ────────────────────────────────────────────
│   attributes : ℙ Attribute;  capabilities : ℙ Action
│   goals : ℙ Goal;  motivations : ℙ Motivation
│ ──────────────────────────────────────────────────
│   attributes ≠ ∅ ∧ capabilities ≠ ∅ ∧ goals ≠ ∅
└────────────────────────────────────────────────────
```

An autonomous agent is an agent with the additional constraint of a non-empty set of motivations.

$$Autonomousagent = [Agent \mid motivations \neq \varnothing]$$

Some of an autonomous agent's capabilities are perceptual capabilities by which attributes in the environment can be captured in the agent's *view* of the world which is defined as a set of attributes.

$$View == \mathbb{P}\,Attribute$$

We present the agent's perceptual capabilities in the schema, *AutonomousAgentPerception* below.

```
┌─ AutonomousAgentPerception ────────────────────────
│   View : ℙ Attribute
│
└────────────────────────────────────────────────────
```

The kinds of domains we are interested in are *worth-oriented domains* [13], where it is possible to assign a *worth value* to all possible states in relation to a goal. A *worth goal* is defined in a similar fashion to traditional AI state goals but we need to develop methods that can extract the extra information needed to reason about such domains. We thus define a worth goal (*WGoal*) to be the same as a state goal, i.e. in terms of state.

$$WGoal == State$$

3   Motivation

The notion of motivation is increasingly being used as the basis for control of autonomous agents. Indeed, motivation has already been investigated in terms of goal generation [4], proactive behaviour [10] and information processing [9]. Perhaps the predominant view is that of motivation as a means to enable agents to *generate* goals within, rather than *adopt* them from other agents [4]. Goals are generated from motivations, higher-level non-derivative components that characterise the nature of an agent. They can also be considered as the desires or preferences that affect the outcome of a given reasoning or behavioural task. In a computational context, we can imagine a robot that normally explores its environment in an effort to construct a map, but must sometimes recharge its batteries. These motivations of 'curiosity' and 'hunger' lead to the generation of specific goals at different times, with a changing balance of importance as time passes.

Like the traditional notion of utility, motivation places value on actions and world states, but is a more wide-ranging concept than utility. In the traditional view, an agent examines its options and chooses one with the highest utility. Whilst also performing this task, motivation is involved more intimately with the agent's decision-making process. A motivated agent has a dynamically changing internal environment, provided by motivations, that can influence its decisions. For example, in the presence of food, an agent may or may not choose to eat depending on the state of its internal environment (specifically its hunger motivation). In many systems, the utility for a given action or state is calculated in advance by the designer, but motivated agents can calculate utility on-the-fly based on weightings provided by their current motivational state.

We argue that the motivational approach offers a way to design more flexible agents that are able to act responsively within their sphere of concerns. More specifically, motivation offers a quantitative way for an agent to order a set of resource-conflicting goals in terms of importance within a given context. The actual ordering is therefore context-specific and changes with different sets of circumstances.

3.1   Intensity and Cues

In order to develop a computational model for motivation that can be manipulated and used in the way suggested above, we adopt the foundational work of d'Inverno and Luck [4] and Griffiths [6]. Much of what follows is based on this.

Motivation can be considered to be a dynamic control process [1], and the influence of a given motivation over an agent's decision-making can increase or decrease in response to changes in the environment or changes in the state of other motivations. We use the notion of *intensity* to capture this dynamic property. Intensity is here represented as a real valued number in the range [0,1] where 0 represents no intensity and 1 represents maximum intensity. The more intense a motivation, the more influence that motivation will exert over the decision-making process.

Thus, at any given time, each of an agent's motivations is characterised by an intensity that provides some indication of the motivation's appropriateness in the current environment. That is to say that when a motivation has high intensity, any goals generated should be highly *relevant* for the agent in the current environment. In order to achieve this, however, there must be some way of assessing the current environment in terms of relevance to motivations. The simplest way to achieve this is by attaching a set of *cues* to a motivation that determine when, and by how much, the motivation's intensity should be updated. These cues are similar to the *invocation conditions* of plans in BDI architectures [12].

In this way, a cue represents a *condition* which, when satisfied, results in a motivation's intensity being updated by some amount. This amount can either be fixed, or depend on some *measurement* of the environment. Each of these update methods calls for a different type of cue, called respectively *discrete* and *continuous*. In some cases, all an agent needs to know about a given world state in order to update its motivations is whether or not some proposition about the world state is true or false. *Discrete* cues provide this information to the agent. For example, a particular motivation may update its associated intensity by a fixed amount. Discrete cues represent sets of attributes and, as such, we can define them to contain a referent of type *attribute*:

$$DiscreteCue == \mathbb{P}_1\ Attribute$$

In the case of continuous cues an agent alters the intensity of its motivations in proportion to some measurement it takes from the environment. For example, an inventory agent may update its motivation to keep the inventory well stocked by an amount proportional to the amount by which a stock item has been depleted. Here, a continuous cue might return the current amount remaining associated with the cue referent. We define continuous cues similarly to discrete cues, but consider further effects later on.

$$ContinuousCue == \mathbb{P}_1\ Attribute$$

Thus, the set of cues attached to a motivation can be a combination of both types of cues and as such we define cues to be either discrete or continuous cues.

$$Cue ::= dcue\langle\!\langle DiscreteCue\rangle\!\rangle \mid ccue\langle\!\langle ContinuousCue\rangle\!\rangle$$

Motivation is considered to have seven basic components: a unique identifier; a current and maximum intensity value; a set of goals that can be used to mitigate the motivation; a set of cues that lead to updating motivational intensity; and a discrete effect function and a continuous effect function. In order to define motivation we also need to define $[RAT_0^1]$ as the rationals between 0 and 1, assuming basic arithmetic operations are applicable [18]. The schema below provides a formal definition.

WMotivation

$name : MotiveSym; \; currentintensity, maxintensity : RAT_0^1$
$goals : \mathbb{P} \; Goal; \; cues : \mathbb{P} \; Cue$
$discrete\_effect : Cue \to RAT_0^1$
$continuous\_effect : Cue \to View \to RAT_0^1$

---
dom $discrete\_effect \subseteq$ ran $dcue$ dom $continuous\_effect \subseteq$
    ran $ccue maxintensity \leq 1 currentintensity \leq maxintensity$

3.2 Updating Motivations

In order to update a motivation it is necessary to define update functions for both types of cue introduced above. Discrete cues are used in an update method called *discrete update* similar to Griffiths in [6], while continuous cues return update values that depend on measurements of the environment recorded through an agent's sensory processes; we refer to this update method as *measured update*. We explain each in turn below.

An agent's perceptual system forms a view of the environment that is composed of attributes. These attributes are checked against the cues attached to the agent's motivations to see if any cues are satisfied and, if so, the associated motivation is placed in the set of active motivations. To represent this formally, we define the function *selectActive*, which takes a state and set of motivations, and returns a set of motivations whose cues are satisfied.

$selectActive : View \to \mathbb{P} \; WMotivation \to \mathbb{P} \; WMotivation$

$\forall v : View; \; ms : \mathbb{P} \; WMotivation \bullet selectActive \; v \; ms =$
    $\{m : ms \mid (\exists \; cs : Cue \bullet cs \in m.cues \; \wedge$
    $(\bigcup \{m : m.cues \bullet (dcue \cup ccue)^{-1}m\} \subseteq v)) \bullet m\}$

We present discrete update as an axiomatic definition *dUpdate*. It takes a discrete cue of a motivation and increases its intensity to the minimum of either the maximum allowed intensity or the updated intensity of the motivation as determined by the value of its cue.

$dUpdate : Cue \to WMotivation \to WMotivation$

$\forall m : WMotivation; \; c : Cue \mid c \in (\text{ran } dcue) \wedge c \in m.cues \bullet$
    $dUpdate \; c \; m = (\mu \; new : WMotivation \mid new.currentintensity =$
    $\min \; (m.maxintensity, m.currentintensity + m.discrete\_effect \; c) \wedge$
    $new.goals = m.goals \wedge new.discrete\_effect = m.discrete\_effect \wedge$
    $new.continuous\_effect = m.continuous\_effect \wedge new.cues = m.cues \wedge$
    $new.name = m.name)$

We define the continuous update function similarly, though we leave out the predicate as it is similar to that for discrete update.

$cUpdate : Cue \to View \to WMotivation \to WMotivation$

Next, we state what happens when a discrete cue is processed. A cue is input and the agent's perception is changed indicated by the delta prefix to the *AutonomousAgentPerception* schema, the motivation associated with the cue is put into the class of active motivations using the *selectActive* function and is then updated using *dUpdate* function.

$$
\begin{array}{|l}
\underline{\quad ProcessDiscreteCue \rule{5cm}{0pt}} \\
cue? : Cue \\
\Delta AutonomousAgentPerception \\
wmotivations, wmotivations' : \mathbb{P}\ WMotivation \\
activatedmot, newmot : \mathbb{P}\ WMotivation \\
\hline
cue? \in (\mathrm{ran}\ dcue) \\
activatedmot = selectActive\ (dcue^{-1}\,cue?) \\
\quad wmotivations\ newmot = \{m : activatedmot \bullet dUpdate\ cue?\ m\} \\
wmotivations' = wmotivations \setminus activatedmot \cup newmot \\
\end{array}
$$

Continuous cues are treated similarly but with a modified third predicate. Here the motivation is updated using the *cUpdate* function.

$$wmotivations\ newmot = \{m : activatedmot \bullet cUpdate\ cue?\ view\ m\}$$

4 Worth-Goals and Motivation

Now that we have a more detailed understanding and model of motivation, we can return to a consideration of *goal parameters*, and investigate how they are related to motivations. In our work we use the concept of *worth* in two ways. First, we propose a mechanism by which the worth of a goal is dynamically set as a function of the intensity of the underlying motivation. In this way, the worth of a goal provides a way of choosing between competing goals. Second, we determine the worth of any state in relation to a goal through the use of a *metric* by which we can measure the *proximity* of an environmental state to a goal. In this way, it is possible to make judgements about the *relative* satisfaction an environmental state offers in satisfying a goal.

For example, an agent that is highly motivated to eat (i.e. its hunger motivation has high intensity) would assign high worth to any generated goals which, when satisfied, would mitigate its hunger. However, the very same goals would be assigned low worth if the hunger motivation of the agent was at low intensity. Thus the value or worth of a goal depends crucially on the underlying motivational intensity. Similarly, as the world state approximates the goal state (i.e of having eaten), it would receive a higher worth value. Below we show the signature of a function that calculates a goal's worth but omit details for space considerations.

$$Goalworth : WMotivation \to WGoal \to State \to RAT_0^1$$

In the above example however, the agent must also have a means to discover *how much* to eat. We refer to this as a *goal parameter*, and their values are also determined by the underlying motivation. Specifically, there must be some relation from the motivational intensity to the value placed on a goal parameter. For example, if an agent's hunger motivation was of high intensity then a parameter associated with a goal to eat could state that the agent eats a quantity close to the agent's eating capacity (we assume that parameters have a pre-defined range of acceptable values). Now, suppose that it is not possible to bring about the exact state defined by a goal, but only some approximation of it. How should one go about evaluating this state? The concept of a worth-oriented domain [13] allows for the development of a notion of *state-to-state proximity*, which can be represented by various metrics, depending on the scenario under consideration. For example, the proximity of the current state to the goal state above could be defined as the difference between the agent's current measure of satiation and the level defined in the goal's parameter.

By measuring the proximity of the current state to a goal state, we can assign a worth value to all states in relation to the goal. The effect of any given state on an underlying motivation is given by a *mitigation function*, which takes a goal, the associated motivation and the current world state defined as an agent's current view of the environment, and returns a value that is used to *mitigate* the intensity of the underlying motivation. States that completely match those defined by a goal should maximally satisfy, or mitigate, the associated motivation. Below we show the signature of the mitigation function but again omit details due to space considerations.

$$\mid \quad mitigate : WGoal \rightarrow View \rightarrow Motivation \rightarrow RAT_0^1$$

Of course, to achieve this it must be possible to determine suitable metrics within the domain over which such characteristics as goal parameters, and state-to-state proximity can be defined. For example, in describing the inventory scenario we need to represent the sets of items that are used to stock the inventory, such as batteries, transistors, etc. One of the goals of an agent could specify the amount of one type of item to buy, say batteries = 500. This numerical value is a *goal parameter*, and represents the *ideal* parameter value, but this is likely to be adjusted in the face of currently active constraints. By constructing environments with metrics of suitable granularity, it becomes possible to calculate the proximity of one state to another and, consequently, to calculate the worth of an environmental state in relation to a goal state in terms of their proximity. Thus, as well as specifying a goal as a collection of attributes with certain relations, it is necessary to define certain goal parameters which represent *ideal values* for a particular attribute defined in the goal. For example, an ideal value could simply refer to the *quantity* of some product, such as 300 transistors, or the *position* of some object, such as object a at location $20x$, $30y$. Alternatively, an ideal value could be defined over a collection of attributes, such as the *amount paid* for both batteries and transistors.

5   A Worked Example

Here we describe in detail the inventory example introduced above. An agent must keep track of the number of items in the inventory and purchase appropriate amounts of each as they are consumed. For simplicity we consider only two types of stock items, transistors and batteries. The *maximum quantity* of transistors and batteries is 100 each. The agent also values each transistor at $20 and each battery at $10.

The agent also has a number of constraints. The amount of stock stored can never exceed the *maximum available space*. There is also a *maximum monthly budget* for purchasing stock, and a *current budget*, which must never exceed the maximum. Over time, stock will be consumed and the inventory will become depleted. Suppose the agent has three motivations, one for economy m_e (a constraint motivation), which represents a concern over money spent; one for time m_t (another constraint motivation), which is related to how full the inventory is (the more empty the inventory is the *more urgent* is the need to restock it) and finally one to ensure that the inventory is kept well stocked, m_r (a re-stock motivation).

Each motivation has appropriate cues: m_e has a continuous cue whose referent is the state of the purchasing budget, where *lower* budget values bring about *higher* intensity levels. Conversely, the intensity of m_t is *increased* the *more empty* the inventory becomes, while m_r *increases* in proportion to the *declining* levels of each stock type remaining in the inventory. At a specified time the agent checks each of the stock types in the inventory, and their current level of depletion changes the intensity of m_r. In this example, the depletion of each type of stock has a simple additive effect, but it is easy to imagine that different types of item could have different intensity effects depending on the relative need for those products.

For example, at the start of the month the agent checks its inventory and sees that transistors and batteries have dropped below their respective maximum amounts. As a result the agent updates its motivation to restock each of the stock items. The motivations for economy and urgency are also updated. First, the quantity of stock left in the inventory is used to update the intensity of m_r. Let us suppose that the effect of the stock depletion leaves m_r with an intensity value of 0.3, and that to bring the stocks back up to quota the agent must buy 10 transistors and 5 batteries (where the values represent the goal parameters). Next, the available budget ($100) causes the m_e motivation to have an intensity of 0.2. Finally, m_t is updated by measuring the space left in the inventory. The store room has 10 m^2 of space left. The more space there is available the more urgent is the need to restock (as larger amounts take longer to process and install in the warehouse). Assume that the agent has only 10 hours in which to take delivery and install the required goods into the warehouse. Batteries take 1 hour per unit to process and transistors take 2 hours. Imagine that the intensity of m_t after calculating the space remaining is 0.5.

The cues determine the parameters of the agent's goals and the values taken on by the constraints. That is, exactly 10 batteries and 5 transistors are needed, but the total amount of time allocated for delivery of both batteries and transistors must not exceed 10 hours, and the total cost must not exceed \$100. It may not be the case, however, that the ideal values attached to the goal parameters can be satisfied given the constraints. Indeed, if the agent were to re-stock on all the batteries and transistors it needed, the processing time would reach 20 hours and the total cost would be \$250. Thus we need to discover the feasible goal parameter values given the constraints. However, we need to be certain to respect each motivation's relative importance. One way to proceed is first to order the concerns in terms of the intensity of their underlying motivations (which determines their importance), then satisfy the most important concern and then satisfy successively less important concerns, whilst at the same time not degrading the solution found in the preceding step. The time motivation has the highest intensity of 0.5 and thus its constraint is given the highest priority, followed by the re-stocking motivation, which has intensity of 0.3[1]. Finally, the economy motivation has the lowest intensity, 0.2, and its associated constraint is thus given the lowest priority. Mathematically, we can represent the problem as follows:

$$
\begin{aligned}
c_1 &: & x_1 + 2x_2 &\leq 10 \\
g_1 &: & x_1 &= 10 \\
g_2 &: & x_2 &= 5 \\
c_2 &: 20x_1 + 10x_2 &\leq 100
\end{aligned}
$$

We can now take these values and pass them to a goal programming (GP) algorithm (a form of mathematical programming, see [7]) which will return the *best* values for each of the concerns, where *best* refers to values that first satisfy the requirements of the highest priority concern and then lower priority concerns. In this case, the GP algorithm gives us the values of transistors (x_1) and batteries (x_2) as both 3. This result satisfies constraints c_1 and c_2 whilst minimally deviating from goals g_1 and g_2. The GP returns the values that at best satisfy the ideal values of each concern, or at worst minimally deviates from those values.

6   Discussion

This work adds to the growing body of work (eg. [1], [9], [14], [19]) that is attempting to extend the abilities of autonomous agents past the constraints of traditional symbolic approaches characteristic of most work on intelligent agents. The paper represents a first step in increasing an agent's autonomy in the domain of e-commerce, specifically in determining both a goal's *worth* and the effects of constraints on the parameters of a goal.

A motivational mechanism was presented that enables an agent to reason about and make decisions concerning multiple concerns in a worth-oriented domain. It describes a technique for updating motivational intensity levels using

---

[1] As stated above, we do not specify any difference in importance between batteries and transistors, so we prioritise the attached goals arbitrarily, but such a priority is possible (and indeed desirable) to accommodate.

a continuous measure of the environment. The mechanism also enables an agent to more flexibly respond to the prevailing context by varying the importance of a given goal in relation to other active goals. The mechanism also gives the agent the ability to discover optimal goal parameters such as ideal target value in the face of multiple constraints. The example presented in this paper has been implemented and we have shown that an agent with this mechanism can effectively deal with a number of resource conflicting goals. Future work will involve extensive empirical experimentation and evaluation. Limitations of this work include the inability of the model to deal with agent-to-agent interaction and the simplistic domain example. As such, we intend to extend the motivational mechanism to include social motivations and to improve the model to cope with the dynamic on-line determination of a variety of negotiation parameters.

References

[1] S. Allen. *Concern Processing in Autonomous Agents*, PhD Thesis, University of Birmingham, 2001.

[2] David, E and Azoulay-Schwartz, R and Kraus S. Protocols and Strategies for Automated Multi-Attribute Auctions, *ICMAS-2002 Fourth International Conference on MultiAgent Systems*, 2002.

[3] M. d'Inverno and M. Fisher and A. Lomuscio and M. Luck and M. de Rijke and M. Ryan and M. Wooldridge. Formalisms for Multi-Agent Systems. *KER*, 12:3, 1997.

[4] M. d'Inverno and M. Luck. *Understanding Agent Systems*. Springer-Verlag, 2001.

[5] P. Faratin and C. Sierra and N.R. Jennings. Negotiation Decision Functions for Autonomous Agents. *Journal of Robotics and Autonomous Systems*, 24:3-4, 159–182, 1998.

[6] Griffiths, N. *Motivated Cooperation*. PhD Thesis, University of Warwick, 2000.

[7] Ignizio, J.P. *Goal Programming and Extensions*. Lexington Books, 1976.

[8] N.R. Jennings and M. Wooldridge. *Applications of Agent Technology*. N.R. Jennings and M. Wooldridge (eds.), 1998.

[9] D. Moffat and N. Frijda. Where there's a will there's an agent. M. Wooldridge and N.R. Jennings (eds.) *Intelligent Agents: Theories, Architectures, and Languages*, LNAI Volume 890, 245–260, 1995.

[10] T.J. Norman and D. Long Goal creation in motivated agents. M. Wooldridge and N.R. Jennings (eds.) *Intelligent Agents: Theories, Architectures, and Languages* LNAI Volume 890, 277–290, 1995.

[11] Anand S. Rao AgentSpeak(L): BDI Agents Speak Out in a Logical Computable Language. W. van der Velde and J.W. Perram (eds.) *Agents Breaking Away* LNAI 1038, 42–55, 1996.

[12] Anand S. Rao and Michael P. Georgeff. BDI Agents: from theory to practice. 312–319. *Proceedings of the First International Conference on Multi-Agent Systems* ICMAS'95, 1995.

[13] Rosenschein, J.S. and Zlotkin, G. *Rules of Encounter: Designing Conventions for Automated Negotiation among Computers* MIT Press, 1994.

[14] E. Spier and D. McFarland. A Finer-Grained Motivational Model of Behaviour Sequencing. *In From Animals to Animats 4: Proceedings of SAB96*, 1996.

[15] Spivey, M. *The Z Notiation, 2nd ed.* Prentice Hall, Hemel Hempstead, 1992.

[16] A. Staller and P. Petta. Towards a tractable appraisal-based architecture In Ca namero, D.; Numaoka, C.; and Petta, P., eds., Workshop: Grounding Emotions in Adaptive Systems, 56–61. SAB'98: *From Animals to Animats*, 1998.

[17] Wagner T. *Toward Quantified, Organizationally Centered, Decision Making and Coordination.* PhD Thesis, University of Massac, 2000.

[18] Valentine, S. H. Bowen, J. P., Nicholls, J. E. (eds.) Putting Numbers into the mathematical toolkit. Z User Workshop, London 1992, *Workshops in Computing.* Berlin, 1993.

[19] T. Wagner and V. Lesser. Design-to-Criteria Scheduling: Real-Time Agent Control. *Proceedings of AAAI 2000 Spring Symposium on Real-Time Autonomous Systems.* 89-96, 2000.

Modal Structure for Agents Interaction Based on Concurrent Actions

Matías Alvarado[1] and Leonid Sheremetov[1,2]

[1] PIMAyC, Mexican Petroleum Institute
Eje Central Lázaro Cárdenas 152. Mexico, D.F., C.P. 07730
{matiasa,sher}@imp.mx
[2] St. Petersburg Institute
for Informatics and Automation of the Russian Academy of Sciences

Abstract. The central issue here is that individual agent actions interact. So, an action representation has to make these interactions explicit. The formalization of concurrent, parallel, and sequential actions as well as synchronous and asynchronous ones is introduced comparing it with existing proposals. Temporal modal logic formalism sets these different types of actions as particular cases of concurrent actions. This way the description and programming of diverse processes in distributed multi-agent systems can be made in an integrated fashion. The proposed model is illustrated through a multi-agent system for flexible manufacturing. TU Prolog is used to implement the developed formal model.

1   Introduction

A number of attempts made by researchers within DAI to develop formal models of real agents and multi-agent systems (MAS), usually try to achieve a balance in defining active and reactive behavior of agents; In other words, the balance between agent's knowledge and actions. A number of classic models of MAS consider actions simply as instant events resulting in the change that they produce in the environment and as a consequence in agent's beliefs [1, 2, 13]. System dynamics consists in updating of mental states of agents. For these types of models, dynamic logics can be used because there no need for the explicit representation of time intervals. By now, the coordinated behavior of agents involved in teamwork is considered, and concurrent actions are to be concerned [3, 4, 5, 6].

Recently, the fact that actions usually play a central role in formal models of agents, more research addresses the problem of representation of concurrent *interacting* actions [7]. The central issue here is that individual agent actions *do interact*. So, an action representation must make these interactions explicit and need to explicitly model different (discrete here) processes. In [8] we have presented the general framework for the logic of interaction. The central aspect, in which emphasis is made in this paper, is the way in which agents perform the actions. In this sense, it discusses differ-

V. Mařík et al. (Eds): CEEMAS 2003, LNAI 2691, pp. 29–39, 2003.
© Springer-Verlag Berlin Heidelberg 2003

ent aspects of this problem, such as synchronized and concurrent actions carried out by a single agent and by a group. Modal temporal logic formalism is used for action representation and modeling.

In the next Section the preliminary formal elements as well as the intuitions about actions are given to be captured by the definitions of the modal logic in Section 3. Section 4 is devoted to the description of the background model of the MAS as the interaction process played by agents within an interaction structure. The formalization of concurrent, parallel, and sequential actions as well as synchronous and asynchronous ones is presented in section 5, followed by the example. In discussion and conclusion section, presented approach is compared with existing proposals.

2   Intuitions about Actions and Semantics

First, we will attempt to describe the intuitions motivating the representation. Our representation is trying to capture the following properties of actions:

- Action is a way of classifying the different sorts of things that an agent can do to affect the world. By performing an action, an agent causes an event to occur, which defines the transition between states of the world.
- Time plays an essential role in any representation of actions. While some actions may be instantaneous, most occur over an interval of time. During this time, an action actually involves a wide range of different sub-actions, changing the world (state). Being related to the agent's goals (see below), we can consider this action as a single action. We call actions of this type, compound actions, and actions changing the state of the world from one time point to the next one, atomic actions.
- Actions are related with beliefs and goals such that beliefs establish the preconditions for actions execution. Goals result from the action execution and determine the post-conditions after the action realization.
- Actions are extended in time; that is why different actions may overlap in time and interact. We should be able to represent and reason about such complex interactions. These interactions can be associated both with the spatial as well as the temporal aspects of actions.

Based on these intuitions, basics of the formal definition, follows. Zero order logic formulas are obtained in the classical manner through logical connectives $\neg$, $\wedge$, $\vee$, $\rightarrow$, $\leftrightarrow$. The i agent's beliefs, goals and actions are modeled by the modal formulas $B_i\varphi$, $G_i\varphi$, $[do_i\ \alpha]\ \varphi$ and $[could_i\alpha]\varphi$, respectively meaning "i *believes* φ", "i *has the goal* φ", "i *do action* α *to achieve* φ" and "*if i could execute action* α *it would achieve goal* φ". Resulting modal language $\mathcal{L}$ is a subset of the closure of zero order logic language joined with these modal operators.

Modal logic syntax sets a Structure of Kripke having associated semantics of possible worlds. Let $Ag = \{1, 2\ldots, n\}$ be a set of symbols to denote *agents* and i, j $\in$ Ag, and let W be a set of worlds (interpretation in propositional logic). An agent i is defined by a 3-tuple $i = (B_i, G_i, X_i)$, where B_i are the agent's beliefs (pre-conditions), G_i

are the agent's goals (beliefs to achieve or post-conditions) and X_i are the actions that the agent could perform. Mental state of an agent is the 2-tuple of beliefs and goals (Bi, Gi). The formula φ is an i *belief* $B_i\varphi$ in the world s_0, if and only if it is true in all the possible worlds from s_0 by means of the partial relationship $R^{Bi} \subseteq W \times W$; Let T = $\{t_1, ..., t_m\}$ be the set of time points such that t, t' $\in$ T and $\propto$ a partial order over T such that t $\propto$ t' if and only if t' is posterior or equal to t. Thus, pair (T, $\propto$) is a flow of time [4] which determines a branching-time formalization. Intuitively, the flow of time can be seen as the *universal clock* with respect to every action occurs over the time.

3   Interaction Structure

The key notion of the structure is that defining the scenario to modeling agents' inter-actions, which can be played by individual or multiple agents; the purpose is to define the shared objectives, to indicate the ensuing organizational relationships between the participants, to set the channels through which interaction should occur, and to dictate the patterns of interchange that are appropriate. The change of the agent's state is through the realization of an action that carries out the agent's interaction in search of reaching its goal. This implies the balance between the mechanism of revision of be-liefs and the derived effects of the execution of the actions. Accompanying the inter-action definitions are the organization rules behind the scope of this article. The or-ganizational context shall be due by the interaction structure.

The elements playing a part in an interaction are the agent, the action and the goal to be achieved through the executed action by the agent. The 3-tuple (agent, action, goal) is named *interaction element*, so that I = Ag$\times$Ac$\times$G is the set of interaction ele-ments. One interaction is defined through:

-   I^n, n-Cartesian product of I
-   one time point t, and
-   the state where interaction elements interact

Thus, an *interaction* of n agents partaking it is modeled like an element of I^n, the agents, acting at the time t over state w.

Let $\Upsilon = I^n \times W \times T$ be an interaction structure, namely a Kripkean Structure mod-eling agent's beliefs, goals and actions. Modal formulas should be satisfied over the set of accessible worlds in accordance with the particular agent's beliefs, goals and actions relationships. The satisfaction definition of $B_i\varphi$ is as follows:

$$\Upsilon, s_0, t \models B_i\varphi \quad \text{iff} \quad \Upsilon, s, t' \models \varphi \text{ such that } (s_0, s) \in R^{Bi} \text{ and } t \propto t'.$$

The set of beliefs of agent *i* is denoted $B_i = \{B_i\varphi: \varphi$ is propositional formula$\}$. Par-tial relation of accessibility R^{Bi} is particular to agent i, so that different agents have different possible worlds and so different beliefs and goals. In a similar way, let $R^{Gi} \subseteq$ W$\times$W be a partial relation of accessibility between worlds concerning the agent i goals:

$$\Upsilon, s_0, t \models G_i \varphi \quad \text{iff} \quad \Upsilon, s, t' \models \varphi \text{ such that } (s_0, s) \in R^{Gi} \text{ and } t \propto t'$$

In order to introduce the modal action operator *do* next definitions are required. Let $A = \{a_1, \ldots, a_m\}$ be the set of atomic actions, whereas for compound action α, β sub-indexed if required are used; $|\alpha|$ denotes length of α. The action execution occurs between possible worlds (states) so that $R^{Doi} \subseteq W \times W$ is the relation of accessibility between states by realization of any α action by agent i. So, an atomic action execution do access from current state to a possible one, directly. Satisfaction definition for atomic action follows:

$$\Upsilon, s_0, t \models [do_i\ a]\varphi \quad \text{iff} \quad \Upsilon, s_0, t \models G_i\varphi, \quad \Upsilon, s, t' \models \varphi \text{ such that } (s_0, s) \in R^{Doi\ a} \text{ and } t \propto t'$$

For compound actions,

$$\Upsilon, s_0, t \models [do_i\ \alpha]\varphi \quad \text{iff} \quad \Upsilon, s_0, t \models G_i\varphi, \quad \Upsilon, s, t' \models \varphi \text{ such that } (s_0, s) \in R^{Doi\ \alpha} \text{ and } t \propto t'.$$

The accessibility relation R^{Doi} up to the type of actions could be reflexive, symmetric, asymmetric, serial, and/or transitive, etc.

Actions $a_1, \ldots, a_x$ denote the atoms composing α. Every atom action (doing access between direct possible worlds) over the flow of time extends from a time point t to one next t+1 (one *tick* of clock). Symbol s (or s_o) denotes an agent state whereas symbol ς the system state: at time t there can be different states s but only one ς. State ς includes beliefs and goals of agents playing roles inside interaction structure; respectively, they form the state's pre-conditions and post-conditions. Axioms for reasoning about agent beliefs compose KD45 structure. For reasoning about goals, axiom D is excluded. For nested beliefs (and goals) we have:

$$\Upsilon, s, t \models B_i(B_j)\varphi \quad \text{for i, j} \in Ag, \text{ and in general, } \Upsilon, s, t \models B_i(\wedge_{j \in Ag}, B_j\ \varphi_j)$$

In this paper, modal nesting for beliefs and goals, operators B and G respectively, defines a Noetherian structure so that infinite nesting is avoided. The perspective of partial relation of accessibility avoids problems of logic omniscience and ideal reasoning as much as the relation bounds the accessibility.

In the interaction structure, actions relay beliefs and goals as follows:

- Beliefs establishes the preconditions for actions execution
- Actions are executed given the preconditions
- Goals result from the action execution under given preconditions
- Goals determine the post-conditions after action realization

So, beliefs and goals match the states whereas actions are the transitions between them. Like an example of interactions, let $(i, \alpha, \varphi), (j, \beta, \psi) \in I$ be so that the interaction $((i, \alpha, \varphi), (j, \beta, \varphi), w, t)$ is between i executing α to achieve φ, with j that executes β to achieve ψ, in the world (state) w at the time t. Remark is that an (i, α, φ) it contains the elements that happen in the action operators *do*, namely, $[do_r\ \alpha]\varphi$.

4   Types of Actions

Let $\chi = \{a_1, \ldots, a_m\}$ be the set (alphabet) of atomic actions that can be executed in Υ by the agents. Let Σ be equal to χ joined with the logic connectives and the operators *seq* (sequential), *sync* (synchronization), *par* (parallel) and *conc* (concurrent), so that the language of actions is the Kleene star closure Σ^*. In the next Section, definitions of sequential, (a) synchronous, parallel and concurrent actions are introduced. Let $\alpha, \beta \in \Sigma^*$ be actions, either atomic or compound (possibly indexed), respectively executed by the agent i, $j \in A$. Let $t, t_1, t_2, \ldots, t_n \in T$ be time points. The special empty action formula ε do nothing spending one tick. It is assumed that different actions are executed by one agent or by different ones.

4.1   Sequential Actions

The action β is *sequential* with α, if and only if there is a possible world w' satisfying the post-conditions (end) of α and one w'' possible from w' satisfying the precondition of β. Formally:

$$\Upsilon,\varsigma_0,t \models [do_i \, \alpha]\varphi \; seq \; [do_j \, \beta]\psi \;\; \text{if and only if} \; \Upsilon,\varsigma_0,t \models [do_i \, \alpha]\varphi \; \text{and} \; \Upsilon,\varsigma',t_1 \models \varphi$$
$$\text{with} \; (\varsigma_0, \varsigma') \in R^{Doi}{}_\alpha \;\; \text{and} \; t \propto t_1,$$

and there are, a θ state with $\varsigma' \subseteq \theta$ and t_2 with $t_1 \propto t_2$ such that

$$\Upsilon,\theta,t_2 \models [do_j \, \beta]\psi \; \text{and} \; \Upsilon, \theta',t_3 \models \psi \; \text{with} \; (\theta, \theta') \in R^{Doj}{}_\beta \;\; \text{and} \; t_2 \propto t_3.$$

Definitions for synchronized and concurrent actions follow.

4.2   Synchronous and Asynchronous Actions

Action α is synchronous (*synch*) to β if and only if there is a time t such that either actions begin or finish at time t, or one finishes and the other begins at time t:

$$\Upsilon,\varsigma,t \models [do_i \, \alpha]\varphi \; synch \; [do_j \, \beta]\psi \;\; \text{if and only if} \; \Upsilon,\varsigma,t_0 \models [do_i \, \alpha]\varphi \; \text{and} \; \Upsilon,\varsigma',t_1 \models \varphi$$
$$\text{with} \; (\varsigma_0, \varsigma') \in R^{Doi}{}_\alpha \; \text{and} \; t_0 \propto t_1, \; \Upsilon,\theta, t_0' \models [do_j \, \beta]\psi \; \text{and} \; \Upsilon, \theta', t_1' \models \psi \; \text{with} \; (\theta, \theta')$$
$$\in R^{Doj}{}_\beta \; \text{and} \; t_0' \propto t_1', \; \text{such that} \; t = t_0 = t_0', \text{or} \; t = t_1 = t_1', \text{or} \; t = t_0' = t_1.$$

Notice that state of realization of actions is not relevant in definition of synchronized actions but only the time of beginning/ending of actions. Thus, either $\varsigma = \theta$ or not, $\varsigma' = \theta$ or not, or $\varsigma' = \theta'$ or not. This definition can be straight extended for n synchronized actions each one being performed by one (same or different) agent.

This definition of synchronized actions is general and abstract when making reference, exclusively, to the time in which the actions coincide, independently of the state in which they are executed. A particular case is when the synchronization happens in the same state. Example of synchronized actions is a career of relies and the Client-Server architecture, whose query-answer dynamic is sequential.

Action α_1 is asynchronous (*asynch*) to α_2 if and only if they are not synchronized. In agreement to synchronous actions definition, those are actions that do not have synchronous atomic actions at all. Formally, for n actions:

$$\Upsilon,\varsigma,t \models [do_i \, \alpha]\varphi \; asynch \; [do_j \, \beta]\psi \;\; \text{if and only if} \; \Upsilon,\varsigma,t_0 \models [do_i \, \alpha]\varphi \; \text{and} \; \Upsilon,\varsigma',t_1 \models \varphi$$
$$\text{with} \; (\varsigma_0, \varsigma') \in R^{Doi}{}_\alpha \; \text{and} \; t_0 \propto t_1, \; \Upsilon,\theta, t_0' \models [do_j \, \beta]\psi \; \text{and} \; \Upsilon, \theta', t_1' \models \psi \; \text{with} \; (\theta, \theta')$$
$$\in R^{Doj}{}_\beta \; \text{an} \; t_0' \propto t_1',$$

Let $\alpha = (a_1, a_2, ..., a_n)$ and $\beta = (b_1, b_2, ..., b_m)$ be compound actions, respectively with n and m atomic actions, $n, m \in N$.

4.3   Parallel Actions

Action α is parallel (*par*) to β, if and only if there are, respectively at least, one atomic action a_k of α and b_l of β such that a_i, is synchronous to b_j .

$\Upsilon, \varsigma, t \models [do_i \alpha]\varphi$ *par* $[do_j \beta]\psi$ if and only if there are states and times $\Upsilon, \varsigma_k, t_k \models [do_i a_k]\varphi_k$ and $\Upsilon, \theta_l, t_l \models [do_j b_l]\psi_l$ such that $\Upsilon, \varsigma_k', t_k' \models \varphi$ and $\Upsilon, \theta_1', t_1' \models \psi_l$ with $(\varsigma_k, \varsigma_k') \in R^{Doi}_{ak}, (\theta_l, \theta_l') \in R^{Doj}_{bl}, t \propto t_k \propto t_k'$ and $t \propto t_l \propto t_l'$ but $t_k = t_l,$ and $t_k' = t_l'$.

Definition of parallel actions extends the synchronous actions definition. States of execution of each action could be the same for both, as a particular case, but different in general. Again, the time point in which actions are executed is essential.

4.4   Concurrent Actions

Action α is concurrent (*conc*) to action β, iff there exists a possible world s such that both α and β post-conditions are satisfied in s. It means that the execution of their final atomic actions and the intended common goals are fulfilled in the same common state:

$$\Upsilon, \varsigma, t \models [do_i \alpha]\varphi \ conc \ [do_j \beta]\psi \ \ \text{iif there are states } \theta_1, \theta_2 \text{ with } \varsigma \subseteq \theta_1 \text{ and } \varsigma \subseteq \theta_2$$
$$\text{such that } \Upsilon, \theta_1, t_1 \models [do_i \alpha]\varphi, \Upsilon, \theta_2, t_2 \models [do_j \beta]\psi \text{ such that } \Upsilon, s, t' \models \varphi \wedge \psi \text{ with } (\theta_1, s) \in R^{Doi}_\alpha \text{ and } (\theta_2, s) \in R^{Doj}_\beta.$$

Concerning time points, it could happen that $t' = t_1 = t_2$, but this is not a general case. It could happen also that $t' = t_1$ but $t_2 \propto t'$ or that $t' = t_2$ but $t_1 \propto t'$. It means that concurrent actions concern with the achievement of a common state regardless the time points, this state is achieved. This definition can be straight extended to n concurrent actions, which could be realized by one, two or n different agents.

4.5   Remarks

The main observation concerns with the temporal *versus* spatial nature of the actions' coordination. Temporal coordination applies to (a)synchronous and parallel actions; essentially the state where it happens does not actually matter. It is the time point of coordination that determines synchronicity or parallelism. On the other hand, sequentially and concurrency deal with spatiality and do not mind the temporal point where coordination happens. Having a fear distinction of these concepts -both essentials at any computer process- combination of them follows in an integrated fashion.

Spatial coordination with respect to the clock:

- Sequential actions can be synchronous or asynchronous.
- Concurrent actions can be synchronous or asynchronous.
- Sequential actions are not parallel.
- Temporal coordination over states.
- Some synchronous actions are parallel.

- Asynchronous actions are not parallel, neither vice versa.
- Parallel actions are synchronous.
- Synchronous actions can be (but not necessarily) concurrent, and vice versa.
- Asynchronous actions can be (but not necessarily) concurrent, and vice versa.
- Parallel actions can be (but not necessarily) concurrent, and vice versa.

We can observe that extension of concurrency definition is possible by considering *concurrency in time*. This way, synchronicity and parallelism might be considered as temporal concurrency at times t and t' according to definitions given above. As remarked (spatial) concurrency could be synchronous or asynchronous. Moreover, as far as the empty action $\varepsilon \in \Sigma^*$ occurs spending one *tick* of the clock in its execution of nothing, it is always possible (if needed) to synchronize concurrent asynchronous actions. The applicability of this formalism is shown in the next Section considering the example of the manufacturing system control.

5   Case Study: Production Line

The considered domain is of a flexible manufacturing line. The process of manufacturing involves a basic numbers of parts (A, B, C), such that operations O1..., O9 are executed by the machines M1 to M9. The operations operate over a component or assemble different parts in order to produce a new component. The final products are composition of a sequence of operations.

The agent oriented approach in the task deployment is the following: each manufactured part is represented by an autonomous agent having the goal to achieve the end of the manufacturing line, by specific actions carried out over it. Also, one agent represents each machine. The main agents' goal is to get the maximum utility, to choose what kind of component can be accepted, and the time order of operations execution. When one specific agent component needs some operation it should negotiate with an agent machine, able to do the required operation. The simple agents being components of complex ones should coordinate their actions in order to get to the machine assembling them at the right (same) time, so that joined agents' efforts produce a new component. When the components are joined this way a new organizational structure emerges to represent a product. Agent interactions are modeled by the following expresions (Table 1).Each o_n denotes the n-th operation in some machine. System goals and preconditions are defined as follows:

Preconditions: $\forall i \Rightarrow agent(i) \rightarrow B_i \neg done(o_n)$ where o_n, denote the n-th operation

Goals: $\forall i \Rightarrow agent(i) \rightarrow B_i done(o_n)$ where o_n, denote the n-th operation

The implementation is developed using JADE Agent Plataform. On the other hand, Prolog is used to implement the agent's reasoning and planning elements used in the interaction process. Due to the fact that each agent is implemented as a Java thread, the interaction between agents exploits the *Synchronous N Transport Protocol* as a medium for message interchange. In addition, the own interpreter of the Interaction Logic, namely, a set of Prolog predicates that captures the formalism developed in this paper, has been developed and used.

Table 1. Expresions in logic of interaction for the system interaction

Product	Expresion in LI
1	$\forall_{in} agente(i_n) \Rightarrow M, q_n \mapsto [do_{i1} \quad o9]seq([do_{i2} \quad o7]par([do_{i3} \quad o6]seq([do_{i4} \quad o5]seq ([do_{i5} \quad o3]par[do_{i6} \quad o1])))$
2	$\forall_{in} agente(i_n) \Rightarrow M, q_n \mapsto [do_{i1} \quad o9]seq([do_{i2} \quad o8]par([do_{i3} \quad o6]seq([do_{i4} \quad o5]seq ([do_{i5} \quad o4]par[do_{i6} \quad o2])))$
3	$\forall_{in} agente(i_n) \Rightarrow M, q_n \mapsto [do_{i1} \quad o9]seq([do_{i2} \quad o7]par([do_{i3} \quad o6]seq([do_{i4} \quad o5]seq ([do_{i5} \quad o4]par[do_{i6} \quad o1])))$
4	$\forall_{in} agente(i_n) \Rightarrow M, q_n \mapsto [do_{i1} \quad o9]seq([do_{i2} \quad o8]par([do_{i3} \quad o6]seq([do_{i4} \quad o5]seq ([do_{i5} \quad o3]par[do_{i6} \quad o2])))$
5	$\forall_{in} agente(i_n) \Rightarrow M, q_n \mapsto [do_{i1} \quad o9]seq([do_{i2} \quad o8]par([do_{i3} \quad o6]seq([do_{i4} \quad o5]seq ([do_{i5} \quad o3]par[do_{i6} \quad o2])))$
6	$\forall_{in} agente(i_n) \Rightarrow M, q_n \mapsto [do_{i1} \quad o9]seq([do_{i2} \quad o8]par([do_{i3} \quad o6]seq([do_{i4} \quad o5]seq ([do_{i5} \quad o4]par[do_{i6} \quad o1])))$
7	$\forall_{in} agente(i_n) \Rightarrow M, q_n \mapsto [do_{i1} \quad o9]seq([do_{i2} \quad o7]par([do_{i3} \quad o6]seq([do_{i4} \quad o5]seq ([do_{i5} \quad o4]par[do_{i6} \quad o2])))$
8	$\forall_{in} agente(i_n) \Rightarrow M, q_n \mapsto [do_{i1} \quad o9]seq([do_{i2} \quad o7]par([do_{i3} \quad o6]seq([do_{i4} \quad o5]seq ([do_{i5} \quad o3]par[do_{i6} \quad o2])))$

6   Discussion and Conclusions

Representing and reasoning about the dynamic aspects of the world, primarily about actions and events is a problem of interest to many different disciplines. Agent-based computing has been interested in such problems to model the reasoning of intelligent agents as they plan to act in the world and to reason about causal effects in the world, support prediction, planning and explanation tasks in individual and group fashion. A number of approaches have been proposed for concurrent action representation and reasoning on them.

The predominant models of action are the situation calculus using syntactic approach, many-sorted first order logic and it's subsets, where concurrent action representation is based on a single action entity and the definition of an operator for simultaneously performing actions [2, 3]. Concurrent actions are also the focus of multi-agent planning approaches in order to produce coordinated multiagent plans. For these purposes STRIPS representation, joint intention and SharedPlan theories are used [9, 10, 11].

In _Semantic Language_ (SL) logical propositions are expressed in logic of mental attitudes and actions, formalized in a first order modal language with identity (see [12]). In GrAPL (Group Agent Programming Language), agents communicate synchronously to dynamically form groups that are synchronized in certain actions [13]. Agents negotiate about the restrictions on group actions. The restrictions are logical formulas, prescribing properties of the parameters of the action.

Most of these approaches are based on the paradigm of state space. As shown in [7], these approaches have weak temporal models, and thus either cannot handle the arising problems or require dramatic extensions. In the real world, actions occur over intervals of time, and cannot be reduced to some set of properties holding at instantaneous points in time, as treated by the models of dynamic logics [4]. Representation of actions as instantaneous events has two consequences. First, there is no provision for asserting what is true while an action is in execution. Second, since the state descriptions do not include information about action occurrences, such systems can not represent the situation where one action occurs while some other event or action is occurring. This paper has focused on the second aspect of the action representation. Furthermore, if one of these formalisms is extended in this way, the temporal logic part will dominate and the original formalism plays little role in the solution. That is why, in areas like formal verification and specification languages, representation of events and action based on temporal logic has been developed, following either liner or branching time approaches. The use of temporal logics to describe interactions among agents can be found in [4, 7]. In those works, while defining simultaneous actions, the authors are more interested in actions that have additional effects that neither one would have individually. On the other hand, we are more interested in the synchronization aspects of concurrent and that interacting actions.

In distributed systems while modeling synchronization aspects, the emphasis is in sub-processes of a process [14]. The compilation mechanisms later distribute these sequential - parallel - concurrent sub-processes among one (by means of interleaving) or several processors for execution; so the formalization seeks to capture and to specify these aspects. From the perspective of SMA as a methodology, architecture and language for applications that support the collaboration among highly complex organizations, the focus resides in: (i) the modeling of high level interactions, (ii) the specification of the organization of the interactions, and (iii) the languages for the expression of the interactions.

We consider that the specifications of interaction structure of Section 3 together with the formalization of concurrent actions (sequential, synchronous, asynchronous and parallel) of Section 4, offers the possibility to define and control agent actions in MAS. This formal account is fear to be implemented to deal with autonomous agents as illustrated in Section 5. The execution of concurrent actions is made to a certain extent in imperative way without offering any mechanism to negotiate the tasks that each agent will execute. In this work, though BDI agents are considered, agents beliefs and goals seems not to be taken into account. However, to this respect it can be said that in the action [doα]φ, the fact that an agent has the intention of carrying out the action to meet his goals and can do it according to his beliefs is implicit. Another aspect deals with the omnipotencience of agents in an ideal world, that is to say, for the model to be realistic it is necessity to deal with the possibility of *failure* in the execution of an action. However, the semantics of [doα]φ implies that to be true, it is necessary to arrive to a state where φ is valid and therefore this indicates that *do* was successful in the execution.

One problem usually seen with the BDI theory is that it has two-dimensional semantics (world and time) due to combination of modalities with the temporal operators. As shown in [15, 4], these problems partially can be avoided and a BDI logic can be treated as a epistemic logic for verification, or as an epistemic logic of tractable MAS planning [5]. In all these approaches, concurrency of actions is inherent to the issues they deal with.

Acknowledgements

This research support was by the CONACyT, Mexico, project 31851-A, and by the IMP project D.00006 "Distributed Intelligent Computing". The authors thank to W. Van Der Hoek and Macario Hernández for their helpful comments about this work.

References

[1]   Joseph Y. Halpern, Yoav Shoham. A Propositional Modal Logic of Time Intervals. Proceedings 1st Annual IEEE Symp. on Logic in Computer Science. Pp. 279-292, 1986.

[2]   V. Lifschitz. Toward a metatheory of action. Proc. of the 2nd Intl. Conf. On Principles of knowledge representation and reasoning (Eds. J. Allen, R. Fikes, E. Sandewall), 1991, p.376-387.

[3]   M. Soutchanski and E. Ternovskaia, Logical Formalization of Concurrent Actions for Multi-Agent Systems, In Proc. of ECAI'94 Workshop "Intelligent Agents: Theories, Architectures, and Languages", LNAI, vol. 890, Springer-Verlag, Berlin, 1995 .

[4]   Engelfriet J., Treur, J. and Jonker, C. Verification of Multi-Agent System in Temporal Multi-Epistemic Logic, In *Handbook of Defeasible Reasoning and Uncertainty Management Systems*, Vol 7: Agents-Based Defeasible Control in Dynamic Environments, Meyer, J. J and Treur, J (Eds.). Kluwer Academic Publishers, September 2002.

[5]   Van der Hoek, W. and Wooldridge, M., Tractable Multiagent Planning for Epistemic Goals, In Autonomous Agents and Multiagent Systems, AAMAS 2002, ACM Press, Part 3, pp 1167 – 1174.

[6]   Pynadath, D. and Tambe, M. An automated teamwork infrastructure for heterogeneous software agents and humans, *Journal of Autonomous Agents and Multiagent Systems*, 2002.

[7]   Allen J., F. and Ferguson G. Actions and events in interval temporal logic. Journal of Logic and Computation, 4(5):531--579, 1994.

[8]   Matias Alvarado, Leonid Cheremetov, E. German, and E. Alva, Logic of Interaction for Multiagent System, C. Coello et. Al., (Eds.) MICAI 2002: Advances in Artificial Intelligence, *Lecture Notes in Artificial Intelligence,* Springer Verlag, 2313: 387-400, 2002.

[9]   M. Tambe. Towards Flexible Teamwork. Journal of AI Research, 7(1997), 83-124.

[10]   Craig Boutilier and Ronen I. Brafman Planning with Concurrent Interacting Actions. In Proceedings of the 14th National Conference on Artificial Intelligence (AAAI-97) (1997).

[11]   Kumar, Sanjeev, Huber, Marcus J., Mcgee, David R.M., Cohen, Philip R., Levesque, Hector J.L. Semantics Of Agent Communication Languages For Group Interaction, In *Proc. Of Aaai-2000 Conference*, Austin, Tx, Aug. 2000, 42-47.

[12]   Sadek M.D. Attitudes mentales et interaction rationnelle: vers une théorie for-
        melle de la communication. *Thèse de Doctorat Informatique, Université de
        Rennes I,* France, 1991.
[13]   De Vries, W., de Boer, F., Hindriks, K., Van der Hoek, W., and Meyer, J. A
        Programming Language for coordinating group actions, In B. Dunin-Keplicz,
        E. Nawarecki (Eds.): From Theory to Practice in Multi-Agent Systems. *LNAI,*
        Springer Verlag, 2296: 313-321, 2002.
[14]   Chen, X & De Giacomo, G. Reasoning about Nondeterministic and Concurrent
        Actions: A Process Álgera Approach. Artificial Intelligence 107(1): 63-98
        (1999).
[15]   Schild, K. On the Relationship Between BDI Logics and Standard Logics of
        Concurrency. *Autonomous Agents and Multiagent Systems,* 3, 259-283, 2000.

A Multi-agent Modal Language for Concurrency with Non-communicating Agents

Stefano Borgo[1,2]

[1] Computer Science, Indiana University
Bloomington, IN 47405 (USA)
[2] LACL, Université de Paris XII
94010 Creteil Cedex (FR)
stborgo@indiana.edu

Abstract. We introduce a formal language for multi-agent systems based on new modal operators. The modal operators express concurrency at the syntactic level. Operators containing quantifiers describe the evolution of a system where each agent has knowledge of other agents' attitude toward a goal but not of their actions. This result is obtained without introducing standard epistemic operators. The semantics presents a mixture of Tarskian and game-theoretical elements. We apply game-theory to interpret the quantified modalities and to determine which information is available to the agents as well as their reasoning capabilities.

Keywords: Modal logic, multi-agent systems, independence, concurrency, game-theoretic semantics

1 Introduction

Nowadays, multi-agent systems [6, 13] are at the center of many research areas like computer science, philosophy, mathematics, linguistics, social science, and economics. The approaches to *multi-agent systems* (*MAS*) vary considerably in these areas but even if one limits the analysis to logical systems, one finds that different languages are applied to very similar problems. Generally speaking, these languages contain a variety of modal operators; epistemic operators are included to express the knowledge of the agents, deontic operators to express obligations, and so on. It is now common to find complex languages for multi-agent systems with the result that we need to deal with complex and different structures for phenomena that do not seem very different. This highlights, we believe, a need for logical tools explicitly developed to describe multi-agent systems.

Starting from this observation, in [3] we motivated the introduction of a new modal language for multi-agents systems and described in details the propositional system with its main properties.

In this paper, we continue to develop this approach introducing one quantified extension of the propositional system. Our aim is to present a new expressive

V. Mařík et al. (Eds): CEEMAS 2003, LNAI 2691, pp. 40–50, 2003.

tool, namely quantified modalities, that can deal with some features peculiar to any system with several entities like software agents, biological substances, or human beings. We hope to obtain a language which, using only one type of operator, can already express many features of systems in *MAS*, in particular concurrency and information independence among the agents. The formalism, it is believed, is well suited for description of agents and multi-agent systems properties as well as for reasoning within such systems.

Such a language may provide the starting point for the development of uniform languages for *MAS*. In this way it may become possible to reduce the number of modalities in the language thereby avoiding the need for combining operators from disparate logical approaches (dynamic, temporal, deontic, epistemic logic and the like). Indeed, it is well known that the formal interaction of these operators is often quite complex [2].

The formalism we are going to introduce describes an evolving system with a fixed number of independent agents. We do not give a precise definition of agent. For our purposes, it suffices to say that an *agent* is a rational and autonomous entity that has the power to choose and execute actions. Our notion of rational agent is deliberately broad. (It includes computational and human agents as well as biological substances.) By *state* of the system we refer to the usual notion of global state. The system state is not partitioned with respect to the agents, i.e., there are no "local" states for individual agents. Time is not considered explicitly and there is no reasoning about history. The formalism considers only the present state and the future.

For lack of space, in this paper we are not going to attempt a deductive characterization of the language nor to provide applications of the formalism.

In section 2 we give an example to show the potentiality of the formalism. Section 3 presents one quantified modal logic based on the operators introduced in the example. In the next section, we give the semantics. We conclude with a brief discussion of the literature in section 4.

2   A Guiding Example

Suppose that Friday morning Bill finally agreed to go tonight to a ballet that his wife Laure would love to see.

Since Bill is not interested in ballet, he would be happy to change the evening plans. However, he made a promise that if nothing comes up to prevent them from going, he will accompany her. According to his attitude, in the afternoon Bill does whatever he needs to do without thinking about the ballet. When he is with his wife Laure tonight, he will go with her to the ballet as agreed. Only some important problem could force him to change this schedule.

Laure loves ballets. She is enthusiastic about tonight's plan and she really wants to attend this one with Bill. Also, she is so into it that this afternoon she does everything she can think of to avoid possible obstacles. In particular, choosing what to do in the afternoon, she takes into account the fact that Bill is not enthusiastic as she is and so she cannot really count on him to avoid possible obstacles. However, she knows his attitude and, in particular, she knows he will not find any excuse tonight unless there is a problem (at that point unavoidable). Furthermore, as much as she loves Bill, she knows she will consent to do something different in the evening if, for some reason, Bill will not be able to attend the ballet.

This being the circumstances, we wonder how the situation evolves and if Bill and Laure will attend the ballet this Friday. Of course, for this we need to state the possible evolutions of the system and the actions available to our agents. To introduce these elements, we begin with an informal description of our quantified modal operators.

In order to state that Bill and Laure choose two successive actions with no knowledge of each other's choices, we write a 2×2 matrix with squared brackets like the following[1]

$$\begin{bmatrix} Q_1 x & Q_3 z \\ Q_2 y & Q_4 v \end{bmatrix} \text{ where } Q_i \text{ is either } \forall \text{ or } \exists \tag{1}$$

We use the first row to list in the right order the variables Bill has to instantiate (choose a value for them). In particular, first Bill chooses a value for x (in our example corresponding to what he does in the afternoon), then a value for z (in the example, his action for the evening). Similarly, the second row lists, in the right order, the variables reserved for Laure.

The intended reading is that Bill, while choosing an instance for x and z, has no knowledge of Laure's choices for y and v, and vice versa. The agents become aware of the effects of their combined actions only after both of them have chosen and executed their actions.

The situation of Bill and Laure is described by formula $\begin{bmatrix} \forall x & \exists z \\ \exists y & \forall v \end{bmatrix} \varphi$ where the first column is related to what the agents do in the afternoon, the latter to what they do in the evening (a column is a sort of time-step), and φ stands for "Bill and Laure attended the ballet".

The first row describes Bill's attitude during the day (not committed in the afternoon but wanting to please Laure in the evening doing everything he can to go to the ballet) while the other describes Laure's attitude (wanting to go in the afternoon but ready to give up in the evening to please Bill). Here we can recognize the specific role of existential and universal quantifiers. Roughly speaking, existential quantifiers mark entries where the agent chooses wanting to make φ true, i.e., looking for an action that leads to this result. The universal quantifiers, on the contrary, mark entries where agents choose with no commitment to the truth-value of φ, i.e., the agent can select any action. In general, it is intended that the agents choose and execute their actions simultaneously at each column.

---

[1] In general, we use a $2 \times n$ matrix for a sequence of n successive actions and a $k \times n$ matrix if the system has k agents.

We now introduce constant operators describing the possible evolutions of the system. Then, using this information, we discuss the options for Bill and Laure.

Suppose that the actions available to the agents are: $a \equiv$ "visiting Bill's parents", $b \equiv$ "going shopping", $c \equiv$ "working at the office", $d \equiv$ "going to the theater"; and that the possible combinations in the social environment are (these operators are possible instances of the quantified operator $\begin{bmatrix} \forall x & \exists z \\ \exists y & \forall v \end{bmatrix}$):

$$\begin{bmatrix} a & d \\ a & d \end{bmatrix}, \begin{bmatrix} a & d \\ b & d \end{bmatrix}, \begin{bmatrix} a & d \\ c & d \end{bmatrix}, \begin{bmatrix} b & d \\ a & d \end{bmatrix}, \begin{bmatrix} c & d \\ a & d \end{bmatrix}, \begin{bmatrix} a & b \\ a & d \end{bmatrix}, \begin{bmatrix} a & b \\ b & d \end{bmatrix},$$

$$\begin{bmatrix} a & b \\ c & d \end{bmatrix}, \begin{bmatrix} b & b \\ a & d \end{bmatrix}, \begin{bmatrix} c & b \\ a & d \end{bmatrix}, \begin{bmatrix} b & a \\ b & a \end{bmatrix}, \begin{bmatrix} c & a \\ c & a \end{bmatrix}, \begin{bmatrix} b & a \\ c & a \end{bmatrix}, \begin{bmatrix} c & a \\ b & a \end{bmatrix}$$

That is, if in the afternoon at least one of them goes for the traditional visit to Bill's parents on Friday (action a), then they are free to spend the evening by going to the theater or shopping together (actions b and d). However, if in the afternoon neither goes to pay a visit to Bill's parents, then they have both to go there for the evening. Furthermore, going to the theater is allowed in the evening but not in the afternoon, while working at the office is allowed in the afternoon only.

What should Laure choose to do in the afternoon? Since she wants to go to the theater together with Bill, she looks at the operators where the second column has only d's. There are five operators with this characteristic, these describe all the system evolutions compatible with Bill and Laure attending the ballet.

Certainly, Laure wants one of these to be used to instantiate the quantified modality. Among these five operators, the second and the third require Bill to perform action a in the afternoon. Since at least one of the entries in the first column has to be action a and since Laure cannot trust Bill to do it during the afternoon, she will do a herself. This means that she is going to choose a as value for y. Executing a in the afternoon, Laure restricts the possible instances to the following sublist $\begin{bmatrix} a & d \\ a & d \end{bmatrix}, \begin{bmatrix} b & d \\ a & d \end{bmatrix}, \begin{bmatrix} c & d \\ a & d \end{bmatrix} \begin{bmatrix} a & b \\ a & d \end{bmatrix}, \begin{bmatrix} b & b \\ a & d \end{bmatrix}, \begin{bmatrix} c & b \\ a & d \end{bmatrix}$.

Since Bill is willing to make formula φ true when choosing a value for z, he has to choose d if this is possible. Thus, Laure's first choice and Bill's second choice will necessarily isolate one instance for the quantified modal operator among these $\begin{bmatrix} a & d \\ a & d \end{bmatrix}, \begin{bmatrix} b & d \\ a & d \end{bmatrix}, \begin{bmatrix} c & d \\ a & d \end{bmatrix}$. That is, Laure has a strategy to reach her goal, no matter what Bill does in the afternoon.

Notice that the case presented above has several interesting features of multi-agent systems: concurrency, independence in choosing actions, knowledge of some behavioral factors, ignorance of other agents' actions, commitment (or indifference) to a goal, change of attitude toward a goal, and so on, and that these are all captured in the given setting by a unique quantified operator.

With operators like (1) we have enriched the meaning of the modal symbols '[' and ']' with respect to more traditional logics. In systems of modal logic, even elaborated as Dynamic Logic [7], brackets are used to represent grouping and are generally associated with the meaning of the necessity modality. In our formalism, the brackets mantain these roles and also receive an epistemic touch. In an operator of form $\begin{bmatrix} Q_1 x & Q_3 z \\ Q_2 y & Q_4 v \end{bmatrix}$, the brackets mark a situation where the agents perform a sequence of actions all the while receiving no feedback either about the evolution of the system or about other agents' actions. These brackets are like epistemic boundaries, and the agents, during the time spanned by the modal operator, act like isolated agents.

In the next section we formally introduce the language and its semantics. It is always assumed that actions in the same column of an operator are performed concurrently by different agents and all actions in the same row are executed, in the order they occur, by the same agent. In the rest of the paper, we posit a fixed number k of agents.

3 Multi-agent Basic Logic (MBL)

We fix countably many *constants* denoting actions $a_0, a_1, \ldots$, variables x_0, $x_1, \ldots$, and *atomic sentences* $p_0, p_1, \ldots$ *Const* is the set of constants in the language, *Var* the set of variables. (Sometimes we write $a, b, c, \ldots$ for arbitrary constants.)

Beside the propositional operators $\neg$ and $\rightarrow$ (from which $\vee, \wedge$, and $\leftrightarrow$ are defined in the usual way), there are unary (constant) modal operators (multi-agent operators). A *modal operator* $[M_n]$, where $n \geq 1$, is syntactically a matrix with k rows and n columns whose entries are constants. We call *cOP* the set of constant modal operators (from now on, all the operators and matrices have k rows unless otherwise stated, sometimes we drop the index n). Given any $k \times n$ ($n \geq 1$) matrix M, we write $[M]$ if it is in *cOP*.

We call *vOP* the set of all modal operators obtained from an operator in *cOP* putting at least one free variable in one entry of the operator but no quantified variables. We call *qOP* the set of all modal operators obtained from an operator in *cOP* $\cup$ *vOP* such that at least one entry contains one quantified variable. It is required that no variable, quantified or not, occurs more than once in an operator. Thus, operators in *vOP* are like operators in *cOP* with the only exception that some or all entries have form x_i. Instead, operators in *qOP* are like operators in *cOP* $\cup$ *vOP* with the only exception that some or all entries have form $\forall x_i$ or $\exists x_i$. When necessary, we refer to entries containing $\forall x_i$ or $\exists x_i$ as *quantified entries* while a *constant entry* is any entry containing a constant. Furthermore, we write $M(i, j)$ or $[M](i, j)$ for entry (i, j) in operator $[M]$. Operators in *qOP* are said *quantified* and operators in *vOP* are said *free*. *Constant* operators are the operators in *cOP*. Note that *cOP*, *vOP*, and *qOP* are pairwise disjoint. Finally, we put $OP = cOP \cup vOP \cup qOP$.

An operator $[A_n] \in cOP$ is said to be an *instance* of an operator $[M_n]$ if all the constants in $[M_n]$ match the constants in the corresponding entries of $[A_n]$. (We abuse the notation and sometimes talk of instances of matrices as well.)

For the sake of simplicity, in this paper we assume cOP is *total*, that is, it contains all possible operators with constants in *Const*. As a consequence, cOP is closed under juxtaposition: let $k = 2$ and $[A] = \begin{bmatrix} a_1 & a_3 \\ a_2 & a_4 \end{bmatrix}$, $[B] = \begin{bmatrix} a_5 \\ a_6 \end{bmatrix}$, then the juxtaposition of $[A]$ and $[B]$ is operator $[C] = [A \mid B] = \begin{bmatrix} a_1 & a_3 & a_5 \\ a_2 & a_4 & a_6 \end{bmatrix}$.

Formulas are inductively generated by the following clauses:

1. all atomic sentences are formulas
2. $\varphi \rightarrow \psi$ is a formula if φ and ψ are formulas
3. $y = z$ is a formula if y, z are constants or variables
4. $\neg\varphi$ is a formula if φ is a formula
5. $[M_n]\varphi$ is a formula if φ is a formula and $[M_n] \in OP$

The scope of a column operator is the formula to which it is applied and the scope of a quantifier in an operator is the same as the scope of the operator itself. An occurrence of a variable x is said to be *bound* in a formula φ if either it occurs quantified in a modal operator[2] or it lies within the scope of an operator where x occurs quantified. Otherwise, the occurrence is said to be *free*. A *sentence* is a *closed formula*, i.e., a formula with no free occurrences of variables.

A *model* for *MBL* is a 4-tuple $\langle W, P; \{R^{k \times n} \mid n \in N^+\}; [\![\cdot]\!] \rangle$ such that:

- W is a non-empty set of states;
- P is a set of actions in 1-1 correspondence with the constants of the language;
- for all $n \in N^+$ and for all matrices Γ, if there exists $[A] \in cOP$ with $\Gamma = [A]$ (see below), then $R^{k \times n}(\Gamma) \subseteq W \times W$ and, given $R^{k,n}(\Gamma)$ and $R^{k,m}(\Gamma')$, we have $R^{k,n}(\Gamma) \circ R^{k,m}(\Gamma') = R^{k \times (n+m)}(\Gamma \mid \Gamma')$;
- $[\![\cdot]\!]$ is a valuation function mapping atomic sentences to sets of states; distinct constants to distinct elements in P; operators $[A] = \begin{bmatrix} a_{1,1} & \cdots & a_{1,n} \\ \vdots & \cdots & \vdots \\ a_{k,1} & \cdots & a_{k,n} \end{bmatrix}$ to matrices $[\![\,[A]\,]\!] = \begin{pmatrix} [\![a_{1,1}]\!] & \cdots & [\![a_{1,n}]\!] \\ \vdots & \cdots & \vdots \\ [\![a_{k,1}]\!] & \cdots & [\![a_{k,n}]\!] \end{pmatrix}$. We write $[\![A]\!]$ for $[\![\,[A]\,]\!]$.

Given an environment $\Im$, that is, a function from variables to P, if $A = \begin{bmatrix} a_{1,1} & \cdots & a_{1,n} \\ \vdots & \cdots & \vdots \\ a_{k,1} & \cdots & a_{k,n} \end{bmatrix}$ is an element of vOP, we write $[\![\Im(A)]\!]$ for $\begin{pmatrix} b_{1,1} & \cdots & b_{1,n} \\ \vdots & \cdots & \vdots \\ b_{k,1} & \cdots & b_{k,n} \end{pmatrix}$, where $b_{i,j} = \Im(a_{i,j})$ if $a_{i,j}$ is a variable, $[\![a_{i,j}]\!]$ otherwise. Given a formula or operator χ, let χ_{sub} be obtained from χ substituting each free occurrence of a variable x (including those in modal operators) with constant a such that $\Im(x) = [\![a]\!]$.

---

[2] A quantified entry, for instance $\forall x_i$, in an operator stands for the quantified variable $\forall x_i$ as well as for a bound occurrence of x_i.

$$\begin{bmatrix} \forall x & \exists z & b \\ \exists y & a & \forall w \end{bmatrix} \; ; \quad \begin{bmatrix} \forall x & \exists z & b \\ \exists & a & \forall \end{bmatrix} , \quad \begin{bmatrix} \forall & \exists & b \\ \exists y & a & \forall w \end{bmatrix}$$

Fig. 1. A 3-column operator and the corresponding $M^{1,1}$, $M^{2,1}$ in the 2-game

k-Game Structure. Each formula with quantified operators receives a truth-value through a game, called k-game, played by the agents in the system. Here we describe the rules of the k-game.

Fix a model $\mathcal{M}$, a state s, an environment $\mathfrak{I}$. A k-game over sentence $[N_n]\psi$ is a sequence of choices that singles out a constant $k \times n$ operator. Let $([N_n]\psi)_{sub} = [M_n]\varphi$.

To begin the k-game, we fix k matrices $M^{1,1}, \ldots, M^{k,1}$, one matrix per agent, called *information-matrices*. In *MBL* an agent i knows only the attitude of other agents, thus at the beginning of the game $M^{i,1}$ (the matrix containing the information available to agent i) is as $[M_n]$ except that only the variables occurring in row i are shown; in other words, $M^{i,1}$ has all entries of row i and all constant entries as in $[M_n]$, but in the remaining entries it shows $\forall$ ($\exists$) where $[M_n]$ has $\forall x$ ($\exists x$), see Fig. 1. Also, put $\varphi^{i,1} = \varphi$ for all i.

The k-game in *MBL* begins with index $j = 1$ according to the rules given below. When all the choices for $(1, j), \ldots, (k, j)$ have been made, the index increases by one and the k-game continues according to the same rules. Let j be fixed. At entry (i, j), with $i = 1, \ldots, k$, agent i chooses a constant as follows:

– if entry (i, j) of $M^{i,j}$ is constant a, then agent i chooses a for (i, j). $M^{i,j+1}$ is put equal to $M^{i,j}$ and $\varphi^{i,j+1}$ equal to $\varphi^{i,j}$.
– if entry (i, j) of $M^{i,j}$ is $\forall x$ (or $\exists x$), agent i chooses a constant, say a, for x.[3] $M^{i,j+1}$ is put equal to $M^{i,j}$ with a substituted for $\forall x$ (or $\exists x$) and $\varphi^{i,j+1}$ is put equal to $\varphi^{i,j}$ with a substituted for the free occurrences of x.

Note that entry (i, j) of the information-matrix $M^{i,j}$ is always equal to entry (i, j) of $[M_n]$. Furthermore, $M^{i,j+1}$ is always equal to $M^{i,j}$ with the choice made for (i, j) shown. Formula $\varphi^{i,j}$ is used by agent i when deciding its j-th action. The formula represents the original φ as modified by previous choices made by agent i itself. Other agents' choices are not known by agent i and so they do not affect formula $\varphi^{i,j}$. This explains why only variables that occur in entries $(i, 1), \ldots, (i, j - 1)$ are instantiated in $\varphi^{i,j}$ by the corresponding values while other variables are left unchanged.

The k-game in *MBL* ends when $j = n + 1$. The *output* of the k-game is the unique constant operator A such that, for all i and j, $A(i, j)$ contains the choice made at (i, j) during the k-game.

There are a few issues pervading all of game-theory. Among these knowledge and memory are particularly important. These are key elements to understand

---

[3] The constant constrains the interpretation of $[M_n]$ and is used to instantiate all the occurrences of x in the scope of $[M_n]$, if any.

our semantics. In the framework presented here, the agent in charge of choosing for the given entry has perfect knowledge of the general elements of the k-game, that is, $\mathcal{M}$, s, $\mathfrak{S}$, and of all the information in $M^{i,j}$. Also, from the description above, each agent is perfectly aware of the changes due to its previous choices (through $\varphi^{i,j}$). These facts affect the agent strategy as we show next.

i-Strategies and Semantics. Having the structure of the k-game, we turn to the strategies for the agents, i.e., we explain how choices in quantified entries are made. A rational agent playing a k-game in *MBL* needs a *strategy*, that is, a rule telling at every step which choice(s) better fits its goal. Note that the strategy for agent i, or *i-strategy*, depends on the knowledge of agent i in the k-game.

In *MBL* we focus on choices for making a formula true. Thus, i-strategies in *MBL* define what to do at existentially quantified entries, i.e., where an agent has the (explicit) goal of making the formula true. Instead, at universally quantified entries we assume the agent chooses according to some unspecified goals. Not knowing these latter goals, we cannot characterize choises at universally quantified entries. We model this situation assuming that random choices are made at all entries containing an universal quantifier.

Given an instance $[A]$ for $[M]$, $[A](i, j)$ is said to *instantiate* variable x of $[M]$ if x occurs at $[M](i, j)$. Given a function f from *Const** (the set of finite sequences of constants) to *Const*, we write $[M]_f$ for the set of instances $[A]$ of $[M]$ such that for any existentially quantified entry $[M](h, h')$, $f(h, < a_1, \ldots, a_{h'-1} >) = [A](h, h')$ with $< a_1, \ldots, a_{h'-1} >$ the empty string for $h' = 1$ and $a_r = [A](h, r)$ for all $1 \leq r < h'$. (In other words, f says how to move at existential entries: it takes as arguments the row-index and any initial part of that row of $[A]$ and outputs the next value in that row.)

Fix $\mathcal{M}$, s, and $\mathfrak{S}$ and assume $\models_{MBL}$ has been defined on any formula $[A]\varphi$ with $[A] \in cOP \cup vOP$. An *i-strategy* for $[M]\varphi$ in *MBL*, with $[M] \in qOP$, is a function $f_i : Const^* \to Const$ such that for all $[A] \in [M]_{f_i}$, $\mathcal{M}, s, \mathfrak{S} \models_{MBL}$ $[A]\varphi^*$ where φ^* is obtained from φ as follows:
(a) any constant a of $[A]$ instantiating some variable x in row i of $[M]$ is substituted for all free occurrences of x in φ;
(b) if x occurs in $[M]$ at row j ($j \neq i$), then some constant a of $[A]$ instantiating a variable of $[M]$ not in row i is substituted for all free occurrences of x in φ.
Proviso: the overall number of variables for which a is substituted in φ cannot be higher than the total number of variables a itself instantiates in $[A]$.

The definition of i-strategy determines how an agent would play the k-game over $[M]\varphi$ if that very agent had to choose at *all* existential entries of $[M]$. (One can easily formulate a kind of k-game capturing this particular case.) Condition (a) forces any existentially quantified variable at row i of $[M]$ and its occurrences in φ to be correctly substituted by the corresponding value in $[A]$. Condition (b) ensures that the remaining variables are assigned some value that occurs in the output of the k-game. Each entry in the output $[A]$ can be associated with at most one variable in $[M]$ and, according to his information-matrix, our agent i

does not know which constant instantiates which variable, thus the extra proviso guarantees a meaningful substitution.

Given k functions $f_h : Const^* \to Const$, $[M]_{\{f_1,...,f_k\}}$ is the set of instances $[A]$ of $[M]$ such that for (i,j) existentially quantified entry of $[M]$, $f_i(i, < a_1, ..., a_{j-1} >) = [A](i,j)$ with $< a_1, ..., a_{j-1} >$ as in the description of i-strategy. (In short, function f_i is used at all existential entries of row i only, $1 \leq i \leq k$.)

The semantics for *MBL* is as follows:

1. $\mathcal{M}, s, \Im \models_{MBL} p_i$ if $s \in [\![p_i]\!]$
2. $\mathcal{M}, s, \Im \models_{MBL} t_1 = t_2$ if $\hat{t_1} = \hat{t_2}$ where $\hat{t}$ is $[\![t]\!]$ if $t \in Const$, $\Im(t)$ otherwise
3. $\mathcal{M}, s, \Im \models_{MBL} \varphi \to \psi$ if $\mathcal{M}, s, \Im \models_{MBL} \varphi$ implies $\mathcal{M}, s, \Im \models_{MBL} \psi$
4. $\mathcal{M}, s, \Im \models_{MBL} \neg\varphi$ if not $\mathcal{M}, s, \Im \models_{MBL} \varphi$
5. Let $[M] \in cOP \cup vOP$. $\mathcal{M}, s, \Im \models_{MBL} [M]\varphi$ if $(s, s') \in R^{k,n}([\![\Im(M)]\!])$ implies $\mathcal{M}, s', \Im \models_{MBL} \varphi$
6. Let $[M] \in qOP$. $\mathcal{M}, s, \Im \models_{MBL} [M]\varphi$ if both the following conditions hold:
    a) for all i there is an i-strategy for the k-game over $\mathcal{M}$, s, $\Im$, and $[M]\varphi$;
    b) for all sets $\{f_1, ..., f_k\}$ where f_r is a r-strategy as in a), $[M]_{\{f_1,...,f_k\}} \neq \emptyset$, and $[A] \in [M]_{\{f_1,...,f_k\}}$ implies $\mathcal{M}, s, \Im \models_{MBL} [A]\psi$ with ψ like φ except that all the occurrences of the variable in $[M](h,j)$ are substituted by constant $A(h,j)$ and all the free occurrences of some variable x not bounded in $[M]$ are substituted by constant a with $\Im(x) = [\![a]\!]$.

4   Related Work

Researchers in multi-agent systems have been developing tools for concurrency and information issues for several decades but only recently features of information independence and information sharing with a broad prospective have been considered. This happens in particular in systems where logic and game theory merge. In this respect, we have been influenced mostly by Henkin [8] and Hintikka [9]. Nevertheless, our quantified modalities differ from branching quantifiers as used in linguistics and logic: on the one hand the notions of player and agent are quite different, on the other hand the gist of k-games lies in the operators themselves and not in the formulas to which these are applied.

Several approaches tackle issues relevant to our work. We mention a few.

R. Parikh introduced *Game Logic* in [10] to reason about program correctness. This system shows how to construct complex games out of simpler ones and its semantics does not use the formal notion of game. M. Pauly developed this work further and also presented a new system called *Coalition Logic* [11]. Although not shown in this paper, our approach generalizes the idea behind both Game Logic and Coalition Logic providing tools for a finer analysis of games.

An extensive study of the relationship between logic, game theory, and language has been carried out by Ahti Pietarinen. The analysis of epistemic issues is central to his work [12] where he introduces multi-agent systems to capture multi-person (or multi-self) games like two-agent games with imperfect memory.

In comparison, our approach considers epistemic features only at the level of semantical parameters.

The logic *ATL* introduced by Alur et. al. in [1] can be captured in our language (dropping the temporal operators). *ATL* is a very interesting system with good deduction properties. Compared to our language, it cannot express multi-column operators with different quantifiers occurring in the same row. [4] presents an extension of modal logic along the lines of Hintikka's work on IF-logic. The semantics is given through "local states". Our system has similar features and is applicable to a wider class of agents including agents acting on each other like biological substances. In [5], a system called *IF modal logic* is introduced and interpreted over runs of particular transition systems. The resulting language is quite interesting. The link between equivalences induced by the logic and those provided by the model is still unclear.

Finally, we conclude by pointing out that full *MBL* is a very rich language in expressive power. Although clearly undecidable, there are several ways to extract manageable subsets. Furthermore, a logic system with the quantified modalities of sect. 3 can be associated to different k-games, agent strategies, or semantic clauses; thus it may enjoy different properties and describe a variety of multi-agent systems. One can also express cooperation and communication among agents tuning the notion of k-game accordingly. In short, the semantics we have associated with this language should be considered as one possibility among many. In the future, we plan to expand these observations and to study the proof-theoretical properties of the interpreted languages obtained in this way.

References

[1] R. Alur, T. Henzinger, and O. Kupferman. Alternating-time temporal logic. In de Roever W.-P., L. H., and P. A., editors, *Compositionality - The Significant Difference*, LNCS 1536, pages 23–60. Springer-Verlag, 1999.

[2] B. Bennett, C. Dixon, M. Fisher, U. Hustadt, E. Franconi, I. Horrocks, and M. De Rijke. Combinations of modal logics. *Artificial Intelligence Review*, 17(1), 2002.

[3] S. Borgo. Concurrency with partial information. In *CIMCA '03*, to appear, 2003.

[4] J. C. Bradfield. Independence: logics and concurrency. In *CSL'00*, LNCS 1862, pages 247–261, 2000.

[5] J. C. Bradfield and S. B. Fröschle. On logical and concurrent equivalences. *Electronic Notes in Theoretical Computer Science*, 52 (1), 2002.

[6] R. Fagin, J. Y. Halpern, Y. Moses, and M. Y. Vardi. *Reasoning about Knowledge*. MIT Press, 1995.

[7] D. Harel, D. Kozen, and J. Tiuryn. *Dynamic Logic*. MIT Press, 2000.

[8] L. Henkin. Some remarks on infinitely long formulas. In *Infinitistic Methods*, Pergamon Press, pages 167–183, 1961.

[9] J. Hintikka. *Principles of Mathematics Revisited*. Cambridge University Press, 1996.

[10] R. Parikh. The logic of games and its applications. *Annals of Discrete Mathematics*, 24, 1985.

[11] M. Pauly. A Modal Logic for Coalitional Power in Games. *J. of Logic and Computation*, 12(1):149–166, 2002.

[12] A. Pietarinen. Reasoning about focussed knowledge in multi-agent systems. In *Workshop on Cognitive Agents and Multi-Agent Interaction*, 2001.

[13] M. J. Wooldridge and N. R. Jennings. Intelligent agents: Theory and practice. *Know. Eng. Review*, 10(2):115–152, 1995.

Self-Synchronization of Cooperative Agents in a Distributed Environment*

Sergio Ilarri[1]**, Eduardo Mena[1], and Arantza Illarramendi[2]

[1] IIS Department, Univ. of Zaragoza
Maria de Luna 3, 50018 Zaragoza, Spain
{silarri,emena}@unizar.es
[2] LSI Department, Univ. of the Basque Country
Apdo. 649, 20080 Donostia, Spain
jipileca@si.ehu.es

Abstract. Multiagent systems have been widely used in applications that are inherently distributed such as information retrieval, network diagnosis, and distributed vehicle monitoring. The use of multiple cooperative agents offers some important advantages (such as parallelism, robustness and scalability) for those applications. However, the synchronization of those multiple agents is an important challenge, specially when they are executing on different computers.

In this paper we present a formal description of a mechanism based on deadline commitments to synchronize agents in a distributed application. In our proposal, agents synchronize themselves reacting to changes in the environment. The proposal considers a loose coupling among agents with the goal of maintaining the autonomy and independency of the involved agents.

Keywords: Coordinated behaviour, distributed cooperative agents

1 Introduction

Multiagent systems have been widely used in applications that are inherently distributed such as information retrieval [2], network diagnosis [1], and distributed vehicle monitoring [10, 3, 4, 9]. The use of multiple cooperative agents offers some important advantages (such as parallelism, robustness and scalability) for those applications. However, the synchronization of those multiple agents is an important challenge, specially when they are executing on different computers.

The synchronization techniques we describe in this paper are suitable to multi-agent applications that satisfy the following conditions:

1. *The main task is decomposed in several subtasks.* That is, an agent is in charge of performing such a main task. To achieve its goal, this agent creates

---

* This work was supported by the CICYT project TIC2001-0660 and the DGA project P084/2001.

** Work supported by the grant B132/2002 of the Aragón Government and the European Social Fund.

V. Mařík et al. (Eds): CEEMAS 2003, LNAI 2691, pp. 51–60, 2003.

as many agents as it needs, possibly in different computers. Each agent could create its own network of agents to achieve its own goal, and so on. Thus, agents are organized in a multi-layered, *hierarchical architecture*.

2. *Each task returns a certain result.* This could be a simple flag indicating success or failure, or information obtained from the environment. Agents at the bottom layer gets information from the environment to perform its tasks. Agents at an intermediate layer use the results received from its created agents as an input for their tasks. The process performs recursively until the root agent gets the final result of the main task (that will be shown to the user or stored for later use).

3. *The task must be performed periodically*, with a certain *execution frequency*, as the result of the task is based on data obtained from a dynamic environment, that changes along time.

In this paper we present a formal description of a mechanism based on deadline commitments to synchronize agents in a distributed application. In our proposal, agents synchronize themselves reacting to changes in the environment. The proposal considers a loose coupling among agents with the goal of maintaining the autonomy and independency of the involved agents. We also explain how to manage problems due to clock desynchronization and network delays, that could lead some agents to lose their deadline.

In Section 2 and Section 3 we explain our synchronization technique based on the use of deadlines. In Section 4 we describe how agents decide when they have to start their task. In Section 5 we describe some related work. Finally, some conclusions and future work are shown in Section 6.

2   Dealing with Deadlines

As explained in [6], it is necessary to coordinate the agents in a multi-agent application in order to avoid the generation of suboptimal solutions, the waste of computational/communication resources (due to the generation of redundant, unneeded or poorly timed results) and, in the worst case, the failure in getting a result or getting a wrong result.

We explain in this section the basics of the technique we propose to coordinate agents in a distributed application in an efficient way. The idea is that each agent must provide its creator agent with a result obtained as late as possible (in order to maximize the novelty of the data it considers to get that result) but within the required time (to return a new result with the required frequency).

To assure timely communications, *every agent in the network will be associated to a certain deadline that indicates the time at which a new result must be available to its creator agent.* The problem of keeping the final result up-to-date can be solved by the network of agents by communicating new results to the root agent *right before* a new result for the main task is required.

In Figure 1 we show how agents interact across layers. We focus on an intermediate agent at layer i, $Agent_i$, created by a certain $Agent_{i-1}$ at layer $i-1$. We

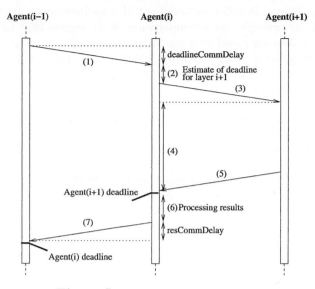

Fig. 1. Interactions among agents

explain the main steps to consider in order to manage deadlines: (1) $Agent_{i-1}$ communicates to $Agent_i$ the deadline for layer i; (2) $Agent_i$ receives its deadline and calculates the deadline of agents at layer $i+1$, by considering its own deadline and its estimated task delay; (3) $Agent_i$ communicates to agents at layer $i+1$ their deadline; (4) $Agent_i$ waits until the deadline of layer $i+1$ comes (to meet its own deadline, $Agent_i$ has to begin processing the received results right after they are obtained from layer $i+1$); (5) each $Agent_{i+1}$ sends its result to $Agent_i$; (6) $Agent_i$ processes the received results, and (7) $Agent_i$ sends its result to $Agent_{i-1}$. Agents at the lowest layer do not receive results from any agent, but they obtain data directly from the environment.

As mentioned before, every agent adopts a deadline-based approach to perform its task and communicate its result, instead of a waiting-based approach in which every agent would wait until it has received all the necessary results before processing them and communicating its own result. We consider that our solution has two major advantages:

- *A final result can be obtained despite partial failures in the system.* An agent can perform its task despite it has not received the result from some of its underlying agents, as using the last received result from such an agent could be a suitable approach in some applications.
- *A consistent snapshot of the environment is considered* by associating each agent with a time instant at which its task must finish. In this way, we synchronize the moment at which results from a certain layer are obtained. For example, let us consider a multiagent application whose goal is to get the average temperature of a campus by averaging temperatures obtained

by agents located in different buildings. If a waiting-based approach is used, we could, for example, get a temperature of 20 degrees that never happened before, because we could average temperatures measured at different time instants. In general, using a waiting-based approach it would be difficult that all the involved agents get their data within the same small time window (to get a consistent result).

To calculate deadlines, every agent must be aware of the time it needs to perform its tasks. The different types of delays in which an agent incurs are given by Definition 1 and Definition 2.

Definition 1. *We call* task delay *of an agent x at layer i created by a certain agent y at layer $i - 1$, to the time it spends performing the task of processing the results received from its underlying agents and communicating its own result to its creator agent:*

$$taskDelay_{x@i} = processDelay_{x@i} + resCommDelay_{y@i-1}^{x@i}$$

Definition 2. *We call* deadline change delay *of an agent x at layer i that creates several agents z at layer $i + 1$, to the time it spends performing the tasks it must do when there is a change in its delays; these tasks are the estimation of a new deadline for agents z and the communication of this deadline to agents z:*

$$deadlineChangeDelay_{x@i} = estimationDelay_{x@i} + deadlineCommDelay_{z@i+1}^{x@i}$$

Agents at the same layer can have different delays because they can execute on different computers. Besides, the delays can change along time: communication tasks can become more or less time expensive (as the size of the results to transmit can vary, the network load can change, etc.) and the time needed to perform the processing of results can also change (it could depend on the size of the results to process and even on its values). Thus, agents will keep track of the delays in which they incur in order to be able to estimate future delays. Based on its estimated delays, an agent will obtain the deadline of its underlying agents. In the following, we will use the $\hat{}$ symbol (e.g., $\widehat{taskDelay}_{x@i}$) to denote estimations of values.

Definition 3. *We call* absolute deadline *of an agent y at layer $i + 1$ to the time instant at which it should have made its result available to its creator agent x at layer i. It is given by:*

$$absDeadline_{y@i+1} = absDeadline_{x@i} - \widehat{taskDelay}_{x@i}$$

As agents in a multiagent system could execute on different computers[1], dealing with absolute deadlines would require to keep the internal clocks of these computers synchronized. We consider that this is a very strong requirement,

---

[1] Even they could move among computers, if they are mobile agents.

difficult to achieve in heterogeneous environments, specially when some of the computers to synchronize are wireless-connected. In the following, we will use a superscript like $x@i$ to indicate that a certain time instant is measured with regard to the computer clock where a certain agent x (at layer i) resides.

Definition 4. *The <u>clock shift</u> or desynchronization between the clocks of the computers where agents x (at layer i) and agent y (at layer j) reside, at a certain time instant t, is given by:*

$$shiftClock_{y@j}^{x@i} = t^{x@i} - t^{y@j}$$

Just a slight clock shift will make some agents to miss their deadlines, as they try to do their tasks as late as possible to maximize the novelty of the data they use in their tasks. Consequently, deadlines communicated among layers must be relative (e.g., "I want your result in ten seconds") rather than absolute (e.g., "I want your result ready at 13:05:20"). An agent calculates the relative deadline of its underlying agents as indicated in Definition 5.

Definition 5. *We call <u>relative deadline</u> of a certain agent y at layer $i+1$ to the time interval that will remain before the next absolute deadline of y comes once it receives this (relative) deadline from its creator agent x at layer i. It is given by:*

$$relDeadline_{y@i+1} = absDeadline_{y@i+1}^{x@i} - tDeadlineEst_{x@i}^{x@i} -$$
$$deadline\widehat{Change}Delay_{x@i}$$

where $tDeadlineEst_{x@i}$ denotes the time instant at which agent x (at layer i) starts estimating the relative deadline of its underlying agents.

3   Obtaining Absolute Deadlines from Relative Deadlines

As we have seen, deadlines are communicated in a relative manner. An agent will transform the relative deadline it receives into an absolute deadline in order to know the time instant at which it must finish its task. The transformation is performed as indicated in Definition 6.

Definition 6. *We call <u>absolute deadline estimation</u> to the way in which an agent y (at layer $i+1$) estimates its own absolute deadline from the relative deadline that it receives:*

$$\widehat{absDeadline}_{y@i+1}^{y@i+1} = tDeadlineRec_{y@i+1}^{y@i+1} + relDeadline_{y@i+1}$$

where $tDeadlineRec_{y@i+1}$ denotes the time instant at which agent y (at layer $i+1$) receives its relative deadline from its creator agent.

In Corollary 1 we prove that the formula given in Definition 6 is a good estimation of the absolute deadline of an agent.

Theorem 1. *The error in the absolute deadline considered by a certain agent equals the error committed by its creator agent when it estimated its deadline change delay.*

Proof. We will consider an agent y (at layer $i+1$) created by a certain agent x (at layer i). According to Definition 5, the relative deadline of agent y is calculated by agent x at time instant $tDeadlineEst$, as follows:

$$relDeadline_{y@i+1} = absDeadline^{x@i}_{\widehat{y@i+1}} - tDeadlineEst^{x@i}_{x@i} - \\ deadline\widehat{Change}Delay_{x@i}$$

According to Definition 4, we have:

$$tDeadlineRec^{y@i+1}_{y@i+1} = tDeadlineRec^{x@i}_{y@i+1} + shiftClock^{y@i+1}_{x@i}$$

The previous equality can be further decomposed by considering that agent y receives its new relative deadline after x has estimated such deadline and communicated it to y, that is:

$$tDeadlineRec^{x@i}_{y@i+1} = tDeadlineEst^{x@i}_{x@i} + deadlineChangeDelay_{x@i}$$

By Definition 4, we have:

$$absDeadline^{y@i+1}_{y@i+1} = absDeadline^{x@i}_{y@i+1} + shiftClock^{y@i+1}_{x@i}$$

By using the previous equalities in Definition 6, we obtain:

$$abs\widehat{Deadline}^{y@i+1}_{y@i+1} = absDeadline^{y@i+1}_{y@i+1} + \\ (deadlineChangeDelay_{x@i} - deadline\widehat{Change}Delay_{x@i})$$

$\square$

Corollary 1. *The absolute deadline estimation given by Definition 6 is a precise estimation of the absolute deadline of an agent (given by Definition 3), assuming that a precise estimation of the deadline change delay is provided.*

Proof. By hypothesis, it holds that

$$deadlineChangeDelay_{x@i} = deadline\widehat{Change}Delay_{x@i}$$

Thus, from Theorem 1:

$$abs\widehat{Deadline}^{y@i+1}_{y@i+1} = absDeadline^{y@i+1}_{y@i+1}$$

$\square$

4   Waiting the Deadline

We explain in this section how an agent determines how much time it has to wait before performing its tasks.

Definition 7. *We define the* spare time *of an agent y (at layer $i + 1$) at time instant t as the time interval that the agent will wait before performing its tasks. It is given by:*

$$spareTime^t_{y@i+1} = absDeadline^{y@i+1}_{y@i+1} - t^{y@i+1}_{y@i+1} - taskDelay_{y@i+1}$$

Definition 8. *We call* task finalization time *to the time instant at which an agent finishes its tasks (in a certain refreshment period), according to the computer clock where such an agent resides. If an agent y (at layer $i + 1$) waits T time units after time instant $t^{y@i+1}_{y@i+1}$ before performing its tasks, it holds:*

$$tEndTask^{y@i+1}_{y@i+1} = t^{y@i+1}_{y@i+1} + T + taskDelay_{y@i+1}$$

Proposition 1. *At time instant t, the maximum time interval that an agent y (at layer $i + 1$) can wait at time instant t before performing its task is given by $spareTime^t_{y@i+1}$ (see Definition 7).*

Proof. Let us assume that at instant $t^{y@i+1}_{y@i+1}$ the agent y waits T time units before performing its task. From Definition 7, we have:

$$absDeadline^{y@i+1}_{y@i+1} = t^{y@i+1}_{y@i+1} + spareTime^t_{y@i+1} + taskDelay_{y@i+1}$$

According to Definition 8, it holds:

$$tEndTask^{y@i+1}_{y@i+1} = t^{y@i+1}_{y@i+1} + T + taskDelay_{y@i+1}$$

To keep the agent from missing its deadline, it must hold:

$$tEndTask^{y@i+1}_{y@i+1} <= absDeadline^{y@i+1}_{y@i+1} \Longleftrightarrow$$
$$T \le spareTime^t_{y@i+1}$$

□

Corollary 2. *At time instant t, an agent y (at layer $i + 1$) must wait $spareTime^t_{y@i+1}$ (as defined in Definition 7) before performing its tasks.*

Proof. In order to consider data as new as possible, the agent must perform its task as late as possible. According to Proposition 1, the maximum amount of time that agent y can wait at time instant t before performing its tasks is $spareTime^t_{y@i+1}$. Consequently, that is exactly the time interval that the agent should wait.   □

Definition 9. *We define the estimated spare time of an agent y (at layer $i+1$) at time instant t as follows:*

$$spare\widehat{Time}^t_{y@i+1} = absDeadline^{y@i+1}_{y@i+1} - t^{y@i+1}_{y@i+1} - task\widehat{Delay}_{y@i+1}$$

Theorem 2. *The value of $spare\widehat{Time}^t_{y@i+1}$ (given by Definition 9) is a good approximation to $spareTime^t_{y@i+1}$ (given by Definition 7), assuming that a good estimation of the task delay is provided.*

Proof. A good estimation of delays implies that:

$$|taskDelay_{y@i+1} - task\widehat{Delay}_{y@i+1}| < \epsilon$$

for a small value of ϵ.

From Definition 7 and Definition 9, we have:

$$|spare\widehat{Time}^t_{y@i+1} - spareTime^t_{y@i+1}| = |taskDelay_{y@i+1} - task\widehat{Delay}_{y@i+1}|$$

Therefore:

$$|spare\widehat{Time}^t_{y@i+1} - spareTime^t_{y@i+1}| < \epsilon$$

$\square$

Proposition 2. *The estimation of delays must be pessimistic for the calculation of the estimated spare time of an agent, as otherwise an agent could miss its deadline.*

Proof. Let us consider an agent y at layer $i + 1$. According to Definition 8, and assuming that the agent waits its estimated spare time (as indicated by Corollary 2), it holds:

$$tEndTask^{y@i+1}_{y@i+1} = t^{y@i+1}_{y@i+1} + spare\widehat{Time}^t_{y@i+1} + taskDelay_{y@i+1}$$

From Definition 9, we have:

$$absDeadline^{y@i+1}_{y@i+1} = t^{y@i+1}_{y@i+1} + spare\widehat{Time}^t_{y@i+1} + task\widehat{Delay}_{y@i+1}$$

The agent will not miss its deadline iff:

$$tEndTask^{y@i+1}_{y@i+1} \leq absDeadline^{y@i+1}_{y@i+1} \iff taskDelay_{y@i+1} \leq task\widehat{Delay}_{y@i+1}$$

$\square$

Thus, an agent waits its spare time (estimated by the agent as shown in Definition 9) before performing its task. To avoid that a slight increase in the estimated delays makes an agent to miss its deadline, the agent could wait something less than what its estimated spare time indicates.

In Theorem 3 we prove that an agent should start processing the received results on the arrival of these results from its underlying agents. This is due to the fact that every agent performs its task as late as possible.

Theorem 3. *The time instant at which an agent x (at layer i) starts its task equals the deadline of its underlying agents y (at layer i + 1).*

Proof. Agent x starts its task after waiting its estimated spare time once it knows which its next deadline is, that is:

$$tStartTask_{x@i}^{x@i} = tDeadlineRec_{x@i}^{x@i} + \widehat{spareTime}_{x@i}$$

where, for the sake of readability, we have omitted the superscript for the spare time.

Using the formula given in Definition 9 with time instant $tDeadlineRec_{x@i}^{x@i}$, we get:

$$tStartTask_{x@i}^{x@i} = absDeadline_{x@i}^{x@i} - \widehat{taskDelay}_{x@i} = absDeadline_{y@i+1}^{x@i}$$

$\square$

5   Related Work

In [10, 9] a network of distributed sensors is used to track the location of moving objects by triangulating measures from three or more sensors. It is necessary that the measures obtained to triangulate a moving object's location refer to (approximately) the same (as recent as possible) time instant. They propose, as we do, an approach based on deadline commitments to reevaluate periodically the location. Although they mention the problem that would suppose to have desynchronized computers, no solution is proposed. Nevertheless, they tackle the problem in a more generic way, as negotiation among agents is considered instead of having agents with fixed roles.

In [7, 8], mobile agents are proposed as a mechanism to perform data integration in a distributed sensor network in an efficient way. However, as far as we know, they do not propose a mechanism to assure that the measures that they are integrating refer to (approximately) the same time instant.

6   Conclusions and Future Work

In this paper, we have provided a formal description of a mechanism based on deadline commitments to synchronize agents in a distributed application. The main features of our approach are the following:

- Agents adapt themselves to changes in the environment (changes in network or processing delays).
- A loose coupling among agents is considered, allowing them to work in an asynchronous and independent way.
- The system could work even when some agents in the system cannot do their tasks in time.

— Every agent performs its task as late as possible in order to consider data as recent as possible.

As future work, we plan to analyze how to deal with situations where the required execution frequency cannot be achieved. Some preliminary work for a specific application (a location-dependent query processor) is shown in [5]. We plan to study how to make good estimations of parameters such as the network delays by using past measured values.

References

[1] A. Bieszczad, T. White, and B. Pagurek. Mobile agents for network management. *IEEE Communications Surveys*, 1998.

[2] Brian Brewington, Robert Gray, Katsuhiro Moizumi, David Kotz, George Cybenko, and Daniela Rus. Mobile agents in distributed information retrieval. In Matthias Klusch, editor, *Intelligent Information Agents*. Springer-Verlag: Heidelberg, Germany, 1999.

[3] S. Ilarri, E. Mena, and A. Illarramendi. A system based on mobile agents for tracking objects in a location-dependent query processing environment. In *Twelfth International Workshop on Database and Expert Systems Applications (DEXA'2001), Fourth International Workshop Mobility in Databases and Distributed Systems (MDSS'2001), Munich (Germany)*, pages 577–581. IEEE Computer Society, ISBN 0-7695-1230-5, September 2001.

[4] S. Ilarri, E. Mena, and A. Illarramendi. Monitoring continuous location queries using mobile agents. In *Sixth East-European Conference on Advances in Databases and Information Systems (ADBIS'2002), Bratislava (Slovakia)*. Springer Verlag LNCS, September 2002.

[5] S. Ilarri, E. Mena, and A. Illarramendi. Dealing with continuous location-dependent queries: Just-in-time data refreshment. In *First IEEE Annual Conference on Pervasive Computing and Communications (PerCom), Dallas Fort-Worth (Texas)*. IEEE Computer Society, to appear, March 2003.

[6] Victor R. Lesser. Cooperative multiagent systems: A personal view of the state of the art. *Knowledge and Data Engineering*, 11(1):133–142, 1999.

[7] Hairong Qi, S. Sitharama Iyengar, and Krishnendu Chakrabarty. Distributed multi-resolution data integration using mobile agents. *IEEE Transactions on Systems, Man and Cybernetics (Part C):Applications and Reviews*, 31(3):383–391, August 2001.

[8] Hairong Qi, S. Sitharama Iyengar, and Krishnendu Chakrabarty. Multisensor data fusion in distributed sensor networks using mobile agents. In *Proc. Intl. Conf. Information Fusion*, pages 11–16, August 2001.

[9] Régis Vincent, Bryan Horling, Victor Lesser, and Thomas Wagner. Implementing soft real-time agent control. In Jörg P. Müller, Elisabeth Andre, Sandip Sen, and Claude Frasson, editors, *Proceedings of the Fifth International Conference on Autonomous Agents*, pages 355–362, Montreal, Canada, 2001. ACM Press.

[10] Regis Vincent, Bryan Horling, Roger Mailler, Jiaying Shen, Kyle Rawlins, and Victor Lesser. SPT: Distributed sensor network for real time tracking. In *Fifth International Conference on Autonomous Agents, Montreal (Canada)*, May 2001.

MIP-Nets: A Compositional Model of Multiagent Interaction

Sea Ling and Seng Wai Loke

School of Computer Science and Software Engineering
Monash University, P O Box 197, VIC 3145, Australia
{sling,swloke}@csse.monash.edu.au

Abstract. We show how to translate interaction protocols in AUML to equivalent Petri net specifications. A novelty of our approach is that the Petri nets are modular, clearly separating the protocol from the interaction behaviour of agents induced by their participation in the protocol, yet compositional. Our model can serve at least two purposes in multiagent systems engineering: firstly, specification and verification, and secondly, as a basis for synthesising skeleton code of interacting agents from specifications in the spirit of interaction-oriented programming.

1 Introduction

A number of interaction protocols have been proposed by FIPA,[1] whose purpose is to provide software standards for interacting agents. It has been proposed that each interaction protocol can be viewed as a pattern to be used as a "reusable aggregate of processing" [5]. In different problem domains, the pattern becomes a template that can be reused in such a way that the basic interaction and message sequencing remain the same while the agent roles and the message details will be modified to adapt to a different scenario. Such templates can be used by programmers as a guide when building their multiagent system.

However, it often requires clever and careful programming to ensure that agents built do implement a particular protocol. How can we build agents that conform to a given interaction protocol? The challenge grows when the agent has to interact with different parties using different protocols or sub-protocols. An approach is to start from specifications whose correctness have been verified, and then carefully derive (perhaps automatically) code from the specifications. Further debugging, if needed, can then be done as an additional step.

In this paper, we apply the Petri net formalism [14] to model interaction protocols, and show how our model can be used for analysing agent behaviours for correctness and for building agents that interact correctly. The use of Petri nets to model multiagent systems have been done in other recent work such as [7, 15, 12, 17]. However, we believe our approach is novel in the use of compositional Petri nets that are analogous to workflow nets [3], in clearly separating the pattern of interaction from agent behaviour that is induced by the interaction,

---

[1] http://www.fipa.org/

V. Mařík et al. (Eds): CEEMAS 2003, LNAI 2691, pp. 61–72, 2003.

and in our aim of engineering multiagent systems from patterns of interaction. By separating out the agent interaction behaviour, we hope to create specifications from which skeleton code can be created for agents that correctly work with the protocol. The skeleton code derived can then be fleshed out with application-specific code.

Our work begins with the simple observation that a given interaction protocol imposes particular constraints on the behaviour of participating agents. Informally but intuitively, an interaction protocol represented in AUML can be translated into a Petri net modelling the pattern of interaction [12], and each participating agents' (or agent roles') behaviour can be represented by a Petri net. The Petri net for each agent (or agent role) acts as a specification of the aspect of the agent's behaviour that is induced by their involvement in the interaction protocol. Such a specification is in the spirit of the agent skeletons proposed in [16], where a skeleton captures the interaction aspect of an agent (with respect to that protocol). Since Petri nets are used, it is natural to use existing Petri net analysis methods [14] to analyse and verify the correctness of specifications. Because we start from the interaction protocol, we can view our approach as being *interaction-oriented* [16], i.e. a multiagent system is constructed based on the interactions among agents.

The paper is organized as follows. Section 2 provides some background on Petri nets, defines a Petri net model of multiagent interactions and shows how interaction protocols can be represented in such models. Section 3 shows how the resulting Petri net model can be subject to Petri net analysis methods and discusses our approach of developing multiagent applications based on Petri net specifications obtained from AUML interaction protocol descriptions. Section 4 is the conclusion and future work.

2   Modelling Interactions with Petri Nets

2.1   Petri Net Preliminaries

This section provides some Petri net preliminaries which are used in subsequent definitions.

Petri nets [14] have been widely used for process specification and verification. A standard Petri net graph consists of *places* (represented by circles), *transitions* (represented by rectangles) and *arcs* (represented by arrows). Given a set of identifiers U, a *Petri net structure* or simply *net N* is a triple (P, T, F), where $P \subseteq U$ and $T \subseteq U$ are non-empty, finite disjoint sets of places and transitions respectively, and $F \subseteq (P \times T) \cup (T \times P)$, is the set of arcs (flow relation). The components of a net N are also denoted by P_N, T_N and F_N. A *path* of a net is a nonempty sequence $x_1 x_2 \ldots x_k (k \in \mathbb{N})$ of net elements which satisfies $(x_1, x_2), \ldots, (x_{k-1}, x_k) \in F$. It is *strongly connected* iff for every two net elements x, y there is a path leading from x to y. For some $x \in P \cup T$, the set $^\bullet x = \{y \mid (y, x) \in F\}$ is the *preset* of x and the set $x^\bullet = \{y \mid (x, y) \in F\}$ is the *postset* of x.

We can view places as describing the possible local system states or conditions, transitions as events which may modify the system state and arcs simply link a place to a transition or a transition to a place. In other words, an arc linking a place to a transition indicates from which local state can the event occur next, and an arc linking a transition to a place indicates the local state transformation induced by the event occurrence, if any.

At any time, a place contains zero or more *tokens*, drawn as black dots. The state M, referred to as *marking*, is the distribution of tokens over places. It is a mapping $M : P \rightarrow \mathbb{N}$. It will be represented as follows: for example, $2p_1 + p_2 + 3p_3$ denotes the state with 2 tokens in place p_1, 1 token in place p_2 and 3 tokens in p_3. If a place (condition) is marked with a token, the condition is true. A *Petri net system* is a pair (N, M_0) where N is a net structure and M_0 is a marking called the initial marking (initial state) of the system.

The dynamic behaviour of a Petri net is controlled by the firing rule. A transition can *fire* or an event can occur if there is at least one token in each of the transition's input places (i.e. the event's pre-conditions are true). This transition is then said to be *enabled*. An enabled transition fires by removing one token from all of its input places (pre-conditions) and depositing one token in each of its output places (post-conditions). This movement of tokens from place(s) to place(s) indicates a change of system states after the occurrence of the event. The notation $M_1 \overset{t}{\rightarrow} M_2$ denotes a transition t enabled in state M_1 and firing t in M_1 results in a new state M_2. If $M \overset{t_1}{\rightarrow} M_1 \overset{t_2}{\rightarrow} \cdots \overset{t_n}{\rightarrow} M_n$ are transition occurrences, then $\sigma = t_1 t_2 t_3 \cdots t_n$ is an occurrence sequence leading from M to M_n and we write $M \overset{\sigma}{\rightarrow} M_n$. M_n is *reachable* from M (we write $M \rightarrow^* M_n$) iff there is some firing sequence σ such that $M \overset{\sigma}{\rightarrow} M_n$. $[M\rangle$ represents the set of all reachable markings from M.

Some useful system properties have also been defined for Petri nets. A Petri net system is *live* if, for every marking M and every transition t, there is a marking $M' \in [M\rangle$ which enables t. The system is *bounded* if for every place p, there is a natural number n such that $M(p) \leq n$ for every reachable marking M. The system is *1-bounded* or *safe* if $n = 1$. Petri net analysis methods [14, 8] have been devised to check for these properties in system modelling.

2.2   Agent Nets

The behaviour of an agent can be modelled as a business process consisting of a set of coordinated tasks to be performed from start to finish. Specifically, a class of Petri nets called workflow net (WF-net) [2], used in business process modelling has been adapted for agent behaviour modelling. We call a Petri net that models an agent's behaviour an Agent net (A-net).

Definition 1. *A Petri net $A = (P, T, F)$ is an **Agent net (A-net)** iff:*

1. *A has two special places in and out, where $^\bullet in = \varnothing$ and $out^\bullet = \varnothing$; and*
2. *By adding a transition t^* to A, the short-circuited net $(P, T \cup \{t^*\}, F \cup \{(out, t^*), (t^*, in)\})$ must be strongly connected.*

In the context of agent systems, the first requirement states that the agent has a *start* state and an *end* state. The second requirement ensures that all places and transitions (or events) contribute to the overall behaviour of the agent. There are no "dangling" places and transitions. In Figure 2(a), there is one agent net on the right and one on the left, describing the behaviours of an initiator agent and a participant agent respectively.

2.3   Interaction Protocol Net (IP-Net)

On the left side of Figure 1 is a (chronological) sequence diagram which reproduces the FIPA specification of the Contract Net Interaction Protocol. The dotted box in the upper right corner indicates that this is a template with unbound parameters divided into three categories: role parameters, constraints and communication acts. The communication acts are represented by the arrows labelled with the names of the messages (instead of object-oriented style events in UML). In the protocol, a call-for-proposal (cfp) is sent by the initiator (the manager) to the participant (the contractor). Before reaching some deadline, the participant can either refuse, claim not-understood or propose by generating a proposal to perform a task. If a proposal is received by the initiator, the initiator can either reject-proposal or accept-proposal. After the proposal is accepted, the participant will perform the task till the end when another one of three message (failure, inform-done or inform-ref) has to be sent. It should be noted that for each agent, there are a number of vertical activation bars in the sequence diagram. Each bar represents a different agent role or a different processing thread of the agent. Intuitively, the separation of these bars allows an agent to have different lifelines. For example, after sending cfp at the end of a vertical bar, the initiator starts a new role or lifeline to accept a return message (refuse, not-understood or propose) from the participant. For the participant, the reception of cfp must be followed by the sending of one message at the end of the deadline on the same lifeline because these activities are constrained to occur on the same vertical bar. A protocol description in AUML can be translated to a Petri net model, as shown in Figure 1, called an Interaction Protocol net (IP-net), defined below. The translation process is similar to the one proposed in [12].

Definition 2. *A Petri net $IP = (P, T, F)$ is an* **Interaction Protocol net (IP-net)** *if and only if:*

1. *IP has a special transition $t^{in} \in T$ called the protocol input transition, such that $^\bullet t^{in} = \varnothing$;*
2. *IP has a special set of transitions T^{out}, such that for each $t \in T^{out}$, $t^\bullet = \varnothing$ and $t^{in} \notin T^{out}$;*
3. *there are two disjoint classes of transitions, namely $T^\alpha \subset T$ and $T^\beta \subset T$, such that $t^{in} \in T^\alpha$ and $T^{out} \subseteq T^\alpha \cup T^\beta$;*

In the definition, the protocol input transition t^{in} effectively starts a protocol with the view that every protocol is activated by firing a single transition t^{in}

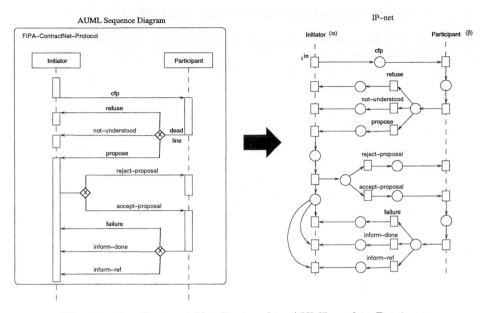

Fig. 1. The Contract Net Protocol in AUML and in Petri net

first. There are no other net elements before t^{in}. The IP-net terminates with a set of transitions T^{out} with no other net elements after each t in the set. In each IP-net, we can also distinguish two disjoint sets of transitions or events. Each set is related to one of the two agents (α and β) involved in the protocol. In Figure 1, intuitively, transitions in T^{α} and T^{β} are to be activated by the respective agents (α and β) through synchronisation. Note that t^{in} must be one of the initiator (α) agent, while the transitions in T^{out} can terminate in either α agent or β agent. Examples of T^{out} in the IP-net are those transitions on the dotted lines with no outgoing arcs.

In the protocol, an agent can have multiple lifelines or processing threads denoted by separate vertical bars. Messages can be sent and received within the same thread or in different threads independently according to the specification. We model such independence by having individual send and receive transitions in the IP-net. The initiator sends cfp via t^{in} independently of other events. However, if a proposal is received from the participant, the initiator must send reject-proposal or accept-proposal and wait to receive the message of failure, inform-done and inform-ref in the same thread (within the same vertical bar). This is the interpretation of the interaction protocol and it is reflected in the IP-net by enforcing these initiator transitions to be on the same processing thread.

2.4   Mutiagent Interaction Protocol Net (MIP-Net)

A multiagent system consists of a number of agents and a number of interaction protocols. Every pair of agents communicate with each other via one interaction protocol. This can be modelled by a Multiagent Interaction Protocol Net (MIP-net) which is a combination of A-nets and IP-nets using some synchronising elements. The following MIP-net definition is adapted from the definition of Interorganizational Workflow (IOWF) [3]. It should be noted that IOWF essentially combines several WF-nets describing processes from different organizations. In our work, we treat agents as individual processes and combine them with their interaction protocols to form a MIP-net.

Definition 3. *A* **Multiagent Interaction Protocol Net (MIP-net)** *is a tuple* $MIP = (A_1, A_2, \cdots, A_n, IP_1, IP_2, \cdots, IP_k, T_{SC}, SC)$, *such that:*

1. $n, k \in \mathbb{N}$, *where* n *is the number of A-nets and* k *is the number of IP-nets and* $n - 1 \leqslant k \leqslant n(n-1)/2$;
2. *for each* $i \in \{1, \cdots, n\}$: A_i *is an A-net with a start place* in_{A_i} *and an end place* out_{A_i};
3. *for each* $i \in \{1, \cdots, k\}$: IP_i *is an IP-net with a protocol input transition* $t_{IP_i}^{in}$ *and the transition sets* $T_{IP_i}^{\alpha}$ *and* $T_{IP_i}^{\beta}$;
4. T_{SC} *is the set of synchronous communication elements (fusion sets);*
5. $SC \subseteq T_{SC} \times T^{\diamond} \times T^{\square}$ *is the synchronous communication relationship, where*
$$T^{\square} = \bigcup_{i \in \{1, \cdots, n\}} T_{A_i}, \quad T^A = \bigcup_{i \in \{1, \cdots, k\}} T_{IP_i}^{\alpha}, \quad T^B = \bigcup_{i \in \{1, \cdots, k\}} T_{IP_i}^{\beta},$$
$T^{\diamond} = T^A \cup T^B$;
6. *for all* $t \in T_{SC}$, $\{(t', x, y) \in SC \mid t' = t\}$ *is a singleton;*
7. *for all* $(t_1, x_1, y_1), (t_2, x_2, y_2) \in SC$: *if* $t_1 \neq t_2$, *then* $x_1 \neq x_2 \wedge y_1 \neq y_2$.
8. *for all* $(t_1, x_1, y_1), (t_2, x_2, y_2) \in SC$: *if* y_1 *and* y_2 *are from the same A-net, then* $x_1 \in T_{IP}^{\alpha} \Rightarrow x_2 \notin T_{IP}^{\beta}$ *for a particular IP-net IP.*

Requirement 1 states the relationship between the number of protocols and the number of agents in the multiagent system, assuming that all agents must take part in communication with at least one other agent in the system. Requirements 2 and 3 defines all the A-nets and the IP-nets respectively.

A transition named t_{sc} in the set T_{SC} is the result of synchronising or "fusing" two transitions - one from the IP-net and one from the A-net - called a synchronous communication element. The relationship is defined by SC which is a set of triples, each consisting of the synchronous communication element and a pair of "fused" transitions. Requirement 6 and 7 state that for every synchronous communication element, there is only one unique element in SC and the pair of fused transitions are also unique. In other words, no already fused transition can be involved in other synchronous relationship. Requirement 8 states that every A-net will only synchronise with either the left (α) or the right side (β) of a particular IP-net.

The MIP-net in Figure 2(a) combines two A-nets with the IP-net in Figure 1 by synchronising pairs of appropriate transitions illustrated by the dotted lines. Note that each agent participates only with one side of the protocol. Note also that we consider only synchronous communications between transitions because it is more natural to assume that a task activated by an agent will immediately and synchronously trigger a corresponding activity (transition) in the protocol.

3 Verification of MIP-Nets

Like other existing Petri net work on multiagent systems [7, 12, 15, 17], one purpose of modelling multiagent systems in Petri nets is to make full use of the well-established analysis methods proposed for Petri nets. These methods are commonly used to detect the liveness and the boundedness properties of systems modelled [14]. We want to use Petri nets to provide a notion of correctness for multiagent systems and then to be able to verify and analyse multiagent systems.

Since A-nets are essentially modified WF-nets, the correctness of an A-net is defined similar to WF-net correctness, which is called *soundness*. It is defined based on the following behaviour. Informally, the behaviour of an agent modelled by an A-net is **sound** if and only if:

1. The agent is able to complete its tasks starting from *in* state and finishing at *out* state;
2. After completion, there is no more tasks left waiting to be completed in the A-net; and
3. Every defined task in the A-net must have a chance to be activated and completed.

It has been shown that workflow soundness is related to liveness and boundedness properties [2]. We can use the same theorem for agent soundness. Briefly, to decide whether $A = (P, T, F)$ is sound, we build an extended net $\bar{A}$ by adding an extra transition which connects the *out* place to the *in* place. Then $\bar{A}$ will be subject to traditional analysis methods for checking liveness and boundedness properties. Effectively, the theorem states that *an agent (or A-net A) is sound if and only if the Petri net system $(\bar{A}, in)$ is live and bounded.*

The two A-nets in Figure 2(a) are sound. However, the combination of these agents with an interaction protocol might be subject to protocol synchronization errors. The resulting MIP-net may not be "correct".

To verify whether a MIP-net is "correct", we modify the "unfolding" technique proposed for IOWF [3].

Definition 4. *Let $MIP = (A_1, A_2, \cdots, A_n, IP_1, IP_2, \cdots, IP_k, T_{SC}, SC)$ be a MIP-net. $U(MIP) = (P^U, T^U, F^U)$ is the **unfolding** of MIP where:*

1. $P^U = P_{A_1} \cup P_{A_2} \cup \cdots \cup P_{A_n} \cup P_{IP_1} \cup P_{IP_2} \cup \cdots \cup P_{IP_k} \cup \{i, o\}$;
2. $T^U = r(T^\square \cup T^\diamond) \cup T_{SC} \cup (\bigcup_{j \in \{1, \cdots, k\}} T_{IP_j} \setminus T^\diamond) \cup \{t_i, t_o\}$;
3. $\{i, o, t_i, t_o\} \cap \{P_{A_1} \cup \cdots \cup P_{A_n} \cup P_{IP_1} \cup \cdots \cup P_{IP_k} \cup T_{SC} \cup (\bigcup_{j \in \{1, \cdots, k\}} T_{IP_j} \setminus T^\diamond)\} = \varnothing$;
4. *r is the renaming function: $r(x) = t_{sc}$ if there is a $t_{sc} \in T_{SC}$ and $x, y \in \{T^\square \cup T^\diamond\}$ such that either $(t_{sc}, x, y) \in SC$ or $(t_{sc}, y, x) \in SC$. Otherwise, $r(x) = x$;*

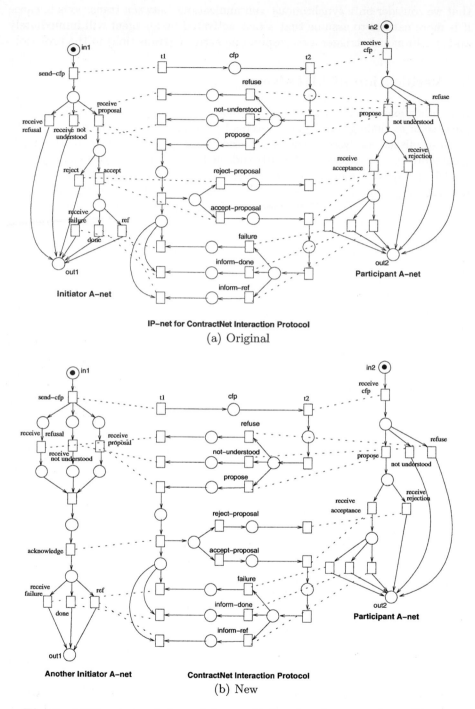

Fig. 2. MIP-nets, each formed by combining two A-nets and one IP-net

5. $F^{\square} = F_{A_1} \cup \cdots \cup F_{A_n} \cup F_{IP_1} \cup \cdots F_{IP_k}$.
   $F' = F^{\square} \cup \{(i, t_i), (t_o, o)\} \cup \{(t_i, in_{A_j}) \mid j \in \{1, \cdots, n\}\} \cup \{(out_{A_j}, t_o) \mid j \in \{1, \cdots, n\}\}$; and

6. $F^U = \{(r(x), r(y)) \mid (x, y) \in F'\}$.

The unfolding means to create a single, global A-net from the MIP-net by introducing two new transitions (t_i and t_o) and two new places (i and o). Effectively, place i and place o becomes the *in* and *out* places respectively of the global A-net. In Definition 4, requirements 1, 2 and 3 introduce the four new net elements. Requirements 4, 5 and 6 state that all the transition pairs undergoing IP-net and A-net synchronisation will be merged and given a new name by using the renaming function. The result of unfolding is a single Petri net which can then be subject to analysis, as mentioned previously. We define the soundness property of MIP-nets similar to IOWF-soundness [3].

Definition 5. *A MIP-net is sound if and only if every A-net in the system is sound and the unfolding of the MIP-net is also sound.*

As mentioned earlier, soundness can be verified by using Petri net methods to check for liveness and boundedness properties. After the MIP-net in Figure 2(a) is unfolded, the unfolding is found to be live and bounded. Since the two A-nets are also sound, the MIP-net is therefore sound, according to Definition 5.

So far, we have described a Petri net method to verify multiagent systems in which multiple agents are engaged in multiple interaction protocols. To summarise, the steps are: (1) Construct an A-net for each agent and an IP-net for each interaction protocol. (2) Combine the A-nets and the IP-nets to form a MIP-net. (3) Unfold the MIP-net. (4) Check the soundness of each A-net and of the unfolded MIP-net. If they are sound, then the system is sound.

To illustrate a particular use of the verification technique, we create the scenario that the initiator agent in Figure 2(a) decides to leave the interaction. A new initiator agent intends to take over the role of the previous agent. The result is a new MIP-net as shown in Figure 2(b). It can be shown that the A-nets are sound, but the unfolded MIP-net is not. Therefore, the MIP-net is not sound (Definition 5).

The reason why it is not sound is that the new initiator (on the left) implements its behaviour by creating three parallel threads to **receive refusal**, **receive not understood** and **receive proposal**, possibly to work in other systems, prior to joining the current protocol. The current system is no longer sound because the interaction protocol requires the joining initiator agent to accept only one of the three messages (a choice of three). To make the system sound, the new agent will have to adapt by changing its behaviour and therefore, needs to be re-programmed.

Given an interaction protocol, it is interesting to note that we can construct *minimal* A-nets to satisfy the protocol. The A-nets in Figure 2(a) are minimal (and have been derived by observing the structure of the IP-net). In other words, they provide the minimal number of receive/send transitions to synchronise correctly with the IP-net in Figure 1 and still ensure system soundness. From the

IP-net, the initiator is expected to have a transition (**send-cfp**) to synchronise with t^{in}, followed by three free-choice transitions (**receive refusal, receive not understood** and **receive proposal**) to accept one of the three possible messages. If a proposal is received (the third choice), it must be followed by an acknowledgement (**acknowledge**) and another one of three free-choice transitions (**receive failure, done** and **ref**) on the same lifeline. This is exactly as implemented for the initiator A-net and can be considered as the basis for the skeleton code of the initiator agent. Note that the A-net can be viewed as representing the agent role, rather than only the individual agent assuming the role. There might be multiple participant agents in a concrete realization of a multi-agent systems using the Contract Net protocol, and the participant A-net can be viewed as representing the class of participant agents.

We can modify the behaviour of the agent (and thus the skeleton code) by changing or enhancing the A-net with more transitions and places. Appropriate transformation rules must be followed to ensure that these changes will not affect the soundness of the agent and the entire system. An approach described in [4] for workflows and another describing agent subtyping relationship [10] can be adapted for changes in agent behaviour. In these approaches, the notion of behavioural equivalence and inheritance-preserving transformation rules have been defined. In A-nets and MIP-nets, we also need to preserve the correct order of activities. As an example, the new A-net in Figure 2(b) has not preserved the intended behaviour of the original A-net to ensure MIP-net soundness.

A-nets and IP-nets are also useful when reasoning with protocol enhancements and protocol compositions. One could model an enhancement of the Contract Net protocol with an IP-net and show that it is essentially equivalent (with some notion of bisimilarity) to the basic version. Domain independent enhancements to protocols can be similarly modelled - for example, to increase robustness when communicating over wireless environments. A composition of several protocols can be modelled by composing the associated IP-nets, after which the corresponding minimal A-nets can be derived.

Combining several A-nets and several IP-nets can be very complex, considering the size of the final MIP-net. Complexity issues have also been addressed for WF-nets and IOWF [1]. It has concluded that by restricting the Petri net models to free-choice nets, the analysis will be more efficient and the soundness property can be checked in polynomial time. These results can also be applied to A-nets and MIP-nets.

4   Conclusion

Earlier work [13, 9] on modelling multiagent systems using Petri nets exists in the literature. The general idea is to add intelligent elements and knowledge bases to existing formalisms. In [13], a class of object-oriented Petri nets is enhanced with other concepts to model intelligence in order to achieve the notion of agent-oriented programming.

More recent work focusing on agent interactions through interaction protocols has seen a type of Petri net called G-net extended to support agent modelling [17], whose extension is based on the BDI model. In [12], interaction protocols are translated to equivalent Petri net models so that they can be validated and analysed. Poutakidis et al. [15] used a different Petri net translation of the protocols to debug multiagent systems. In [10], the focus is on behavioural substitutability of agents participating in interaction protocols.

Our work on agent interactions has a different emphasis in that we intend to use Petri nets to develop minimal agent specifications using interaction protocols. Such a specification is in the spirit of the agent skeletons proposed in [16], where a skeleton captures the interaction aspect of an agent (with respect to that protocol). However, Singh's work [16] does not use Petri nets or AUML descriptions. We view IP-nets as template components which can be reused in different environments. In order to use or reuse the templates, agents must satisfy the requirements as stipulated in the interaction protocol and must adhere to (at least) the minimal expected behaviour.

In our earlier work [11], we modelled mobile agent itineraries with a type of Petri nets called Agent Itinerary (AI-) nets. An A-net models the interaction aspect of an agent (with respect to an interaction protocol) whereas an AI-net models the mobility aspect of an agent. The different aspects of an agent can be modelled and their consistency checked. The specifications can serve as basis for generating skeleton code for different aspects of agent behaviour (e.g., [6]).

There is no doubt that future work needs to address other issues common in multiagent systems, i.e., the intelligence and autonomous aspects of agent behaviour. The current MIP-net definitions need to be "upgraded" to high-level or coloured Petri nets to encompass true agent characteristics. These upgrades can be inspired from existing work mentioned previously. In addition, we are also working on analysis of non-functional properties such as performance and timing issues and timed commitments, using other advanced Petri nets such as timed Petri nets. Open protocols is also an area of concern where run-time verification of an agent's ability to undertake a protocol might be useful. We also need to extend our work to allow an agent to be engaged in several protocols at the same time, where the agent's interaction behaviour would then be a composition of the A-nets for each protocol engagement - this would also imply a cleaner separation between the concepts of agent and role than we have done here (where we assumed an agent takes up only one role).

References

[1] W. v. Aalst. Structural characterizations of sound workflow nets. Technical report, Computing Science Reports 96/23, Eindhoven University of Technology, Eindhoven, 1996.
[2] W. v. Aalst. The application of Petri nets to workflow management. *The Journal of Circuits, Systems and Computers*, 8(1):21–66, 1998.

[3] W. v. Aalst. Interorganizational workflows: An approach based on message sequence charts and Petri nets. *Systems Analysis - Modelling - Simulation*, 34(3):335–67, 1999.

[4] W. v. Aalst and T. Basten. Inheritance of workflows: an approach to tackling problems related to change. Technical report, Computing Science Reports 99/06, Eindhoven University of Technology, Eindhoven, 1999.

[5] B. Bauer, J. P. Müller, and J. Odell. Agent UML: A formalism for specifying multiagent interaction. In P. Ciancarini and M. Wooldridge, editors, *Agent-Oriented Software Engineering*, pages 91–103. Springer-Verlay, Berlin, 2001.

[6] S. Chachkov and D. Buchs. From formal specifications to ready-to-use software components: The concurrent object oriented petri net approach. In *Proceedings of the 2nd International Conference on Application of Concurrency to System Design (ACSD'01)*, pages 99–110, June 2001.

[7] R. Cost, Y. Chen, T. Finin, Y. Labrou, and Y. Peng. Modeling agent conversations with colored petri nets. In *Proc. 9th Int'l Joint Conference on Artificial Intelligence (IJCAI'99)*, 1999.

[8] J. Desel and J. Esparza. *Free Choice Petri Nets*. Cambridge University Press, 1995.

[9] J. M. Fernandes and O. Belo. Modeling multi-agent systems activities through colored Petri nets: An industrial production system case study. In *16th IASTED Int'l Conference on Applied Informatics (AI'98)*, pages 17–20, 1998.

[10] N. Hameurlain. Formal semantics for behavioural substitutability of agent components: Application to interaction protocols. In *2nd Int'l Workshop of Central and Eastern Europe on Multi-Agent Systems (CEEMAS'01)*, pages 131–40, 2002.

[11] S. Ling and S. Loke. Advanced petri nets for modelling mobile agent enabled interorganizational workflow. In *Proc. 9th Int'l Conference on Engineering of Computer-Based Systems (ECBS2002)*, pages 245–52, 2002.

[12] H. Mazouzi, A. El Fallah-Seghrouchni, and S. Haddad. Open protocol design for complex interactions in multiagent systems. In *1st Int'l Joint Conference on Autonomous Agents and Multi-Agent Systems (AAMAS'02)*, pages 517–25, 2002.

[13] D. Moldt and F. Wienberg. Multi-agent-systems based on coloured Petri nets. In *18th Int'l Conference on Application and Theory of Petri Nets 1997*, pages 82–101, 1997.

[14] T. Murata. Petri nets: Properties, analysis and applications. *Proceedings of the IEEE*, 77(4):541–80, April 1989.

[15] D. Poutakidis, L. Padgham, and M. Winikoff. Debugging multi-agent systems using design artifacts: The case of interaction protocols. In *Proc. 1st International Joint Conference on Autonomous Agents and Multi-Agent Systems (AAMAS 2002)*, 2002.

[16] M. Singh. Synthesizing coordination requirements for heterogeneous autonomous agents. *Autonomous Agents and Multi-Agent Systems*, 3(2):107–132, June 2000.

[17] H. Xu and S. M. Shatz. A framework for modeling agent-oriented software. In *21st Int'l Conference on Distributed Computing Systems (ICDCS-21)*, pages 57–64, 2001.

Calibrating Collective Commitments

Barbara Dunin-Kęplicz[1,2] and Rineke Verbrugge[3]

[1] Institute of Informatics, Warsaw University
Banacha 2, 02-097 Warsaw, Poland
keplicz@mimuw.edu.pl
[2] Institute of Computer Science, Polish Academy of Sciences
Ordona 21, 01-237 Warsaw, Poland
[3] Institute of Artificial Intelligence, University of Groningen
Grote Kruisstraat 2/1, 9712 TS Groningen, The Netherlands
rineke@ai.rug.nl

Abstract. In this paper we aim to formally model the strongest motivational attitude occurring in teamwork, *collective commitment*. First, building on our previous work, a logical framework is sketched in which social commitments and collective intentions are formalized. Then, different versions of collective commitments are given, reflecting different aspects of Cooperative Problem Solving, and applicable in different situations. The definitions differ with respect to the *aspects* of teamwork of which the agents involved are aware, and the *kind* of awareness present within a team. This way a kind of tuning mechanism is provided for the system developer to tune a version of collective commitment fitting the circumstances. Finally, a few exemplar versions of collective commitment resulting from instantiating the general tuning scheme are presented.

1 Introduction

Variety is the core of multiagent systems. This simple sentence expresses the many dimensions on which MAS is distinguished from distributed AI. The basic assumption underlying MAS is relaxing the constraints that were fixed before, in order to meet the needs of goal-directed behaviour in a dynamic and unpredictable environment. This is reflected in complex and possibly flexible patterns of interaction in MAS. Together with autonomy of agents and social structure of cooperative groups this determines the novelty of the agent-based approach.

A large share of this novelty pertains to the concept of motivational attitudes, i.e. intentions and commitments in Cooperative Problem Solving (CPS). What characterizes collective notions is an interplay between environmental and social aspects, which may become rather complex nowadays due to the increasing complexity of MAS. For example, when asking what it means for a group of agents to be *collectively committed* to do something, both circumstances in which the group is acting and properties of the organization it is part of, have to be taken into account. This implies the importance of differentiating the scope and strength of the notion of collective commitment. The resulting characteristics may differ significantly, and even become logically incomparable.

V. Mařík et al. (Eds): CEEMAS 2003, LNAI 2691, pp. 73–83, 2003.

The aim of this research is to formally model different aspects of collective commitments, including different scopes and degrees of awareness of cooperating agents. (The case of competition is not included.) The idea of a knob to be used to tune the nature of the commitment to the particular purpose seems to be both technically interesting and intuitively appealing. We intend to provide a sort of *tuning mechanism* which enables the system developer to *calibrate* a type of collective commitment fitting the circumstances, analogously to adjusting knobs on a sound system. The appropriate knobs, characterised in the sequel, belong to the device representing a general schema of collective commitment. The resulting notion of (group) commitment, described in multimodal logics, may then be naturally implemented in a created multiagent system. This way the tuning mechanism may be viewed as a bridge between theory and practice.

In order to illustrate the expressive power of such a sort of *tuning machine*, five definitions of commitments corresponding to different teamwork types occurring in practice are presented. Apparently, the entire spectrum of possibilities is much wider, due to the number of possibly independent choices to be made.

This work fits into a research program developed by the authors for a couple of years already (compare [3, 4, 2, 5]). It is based on a lot of previous research, extending and enhancing these results. The paper is structured in the following way. In section 2, individual and collective informational and motivational attitudes are briefly treated. The central section 3 explores different dimensions along which collective commitments may be tuned to fit both the organization and the environment. A general scheme is presented in a multi-modal language, and five different notions of collective commitment fitting to concrete organizational structures are presented in section 4. Finally, section 5 focuses on discussion.

2   Building Blocks of Collective Commitments

We propose the use of multi-modal logics to formalize agents' informational and motivational attitudes as well as actions they perform and their effects. In CPS, both motivational and informational attitudes are considered on the following three levels: individual, social and collective. The language, based on a finite set of agents, and its Kripke semantics have been defined in [5], which also presents axioms governing individual and collective beliefs, individual goals and intentions, and collective intentions. In this section, we repeat some notions important for the subject of the present paper. the set All motivational attitudes may be defined in two ways, namely with respect to propositions φ and with respect to actions α, depending on the need.

2.1   Individual and Collective Beliefs

To represent beliefs, we adopt a standard $KD45_n$-system for n agents as explained in [6], where we take $\mathrm{BEL}(i, \varphi)$ to have as intended meaning "agent i believes proposition φ".

One can define modal operators for group beliefs, in particular $E\text{-}BEL_G(\varphi)$ is meant to stand for "every agent in group G believes φ". The stronger operator *collective belief* $C\text{-}BEL_G(\varphi)$ is similar to the more usual one of common knowledge. $C\text{-}BEL_G(\varphi)$ is meant to be true if everyone in G believes φ, everyone in G believes that everyone in G believes φ, etc., as reflected by the following axioms and rule:

$E\text{-}BEL_G(\varphi) \leftrightarrow \bigwedge_{i \in G} BEL(i, \varphi)$

$C\text{-}BEL_G(\varphi) \rightarrow E\text{-}BEL_G(\varphi \wedge C\text{-}BEL_G(\varphi))$

from $\varphi \rightarrow E\text{-}BEL_G(\psi \wedge \varphi)$ infer $\varphi \rightarrow C\text{-}BEL_G(\psi)$ (Induction Rule).

The resulting axiom system governing individual and collective belief is called $KD45_n^C$ and is sound and complete w.r.t. the same Kripke models as $KD45_n$ (see [6, 8]).

Let $E\text{-}BEL_G^1(\varphi)$ be an abbreviation for $E\text{-}BEL_G(\varphi)$, and let $E\text{-}BEL_G^{k+1}(\varphi)$ for $k \geq 1$ be an abbreviation of $E\text{-}BEL_G(E\text{-}BEL_G^k(\varphi))$. Thus we have $\mathcal{M}, s \models C\text{-}BEL_G(\varphi)$ iff $\mathcal{M}, s \models E\text{-}BEL_G^k(\varphi)$ for all $k \geq 1$.

Degrees of Belief in a Group. It is well-known that for teamwork, as well as coordination, it often does not suffice that a group of agents all believe a certain proposition ($E\text{-}BEL_G(\psi)$), but they should collectively believe it ($C\text{-}BEL_G(\psi)$).

One advantage of collective belief over "everybody believes" is that if $C\text{-}BEL_G$ holds for ψ, then $C\text{-}BEL_G$ also holds for all logical consequences of ψ. Thus, agents reason in a similar way from ψ and collectively believe in this similar reasoning and the final conclusions. In short, one could say that collective belief is hard to achieve, but easy to understand.

In cases in which only $E\text{-}BEL_G(\psi)$ has been established, it is much more difficult for agents to maintain a model of the other team members with respect to ψ and its consequences. However, establishing $E\text{-}BEL_G(\psi)$ places much less constraints on the communication medium than $C\text{-}BEL_G(\psi)$ does. Thus, the system developer's decision about the level k of group belief ($E\text{-}BEL_G^k(\psi)$) to be established, hinges on determining a good balance between communication and reasoning taking into account a particular application.

2.2   Individual Motivational Attitudes

The key concept in the theory of practical reasoning is the one of *intention*. Intentions form a rather special consistent subset of an agent's goals, that the agent wants to focus on for the time being. Thus they create a screen of admissibility for the agent's further, possibly long-term, deliberation.

For the motivational operators GOAL and INT the axioms include the basic modal system K_n. In a BDI system, an agent's activity starts from goals. As the agent may have many different objectives, its goals need not be consistent with each other. Then, the agent chooses a consistent subset of its goals to be intentions. For more about individual goals and intentions, as well as axioms relating them with each other and beliefs, see [5].

2.3   Social Commitments

As Castelfranchi showed, it is important to distinguish between individual intentions, bilateral commitments, and collective motivational attitudes [1]. A social (bilateral) commitment is not as strong as a collective one, but stronger than an individual intention. If an agent commits to a second agent to do something, then the first agent should have the *intention* to do that. Moreover, the second one should be *interested* in the first one fulfilling its intention. These two conditions (inspired by [1]), need to be enhanced by the condition expressing the agents' awareness about the situation, i.e. about their individual attitudes. Such awareness is usually expressed in terms of collective belief. Here the defining axiom for social commitments is formulated with respect to actions:

$$\text{COMM}(i, j, \alpha) \leftrightarrow \text{INT}(i, \alpha) \wedge \text{GOAL}(j, done(i, \alpha)) \wedge$$
$$\text{C-BEL}_{\{i,j\}}(\text{INT}(i, \alpha) \wedge \text{GOAL}(j, done(i, \alpha)))$$

Here, $done(i, \alpha)$ means that agent i has just executed action α.

2.4   Collective Intentions

In this paper, we focus on strictly cooperative teams, which makes the definition of collective intention rather strong. In such teams, a necessary condition for a collective intention $\text{C-INT}_G(\varphi)$ is that all members of the team G have the associated individual intention $\text{INT}(i, \varphi)$ towards the goal φ. However, to exclude the case of competition between individuals or coalitions, all agents should also *intend* all members to have the associated individual intention, as well as the intention that all members have the individual intention, and so on; we call such a mutual intention $\text{M-INT}_G(\varphi)$. In the strong version of collective intention we assume that all members of the team are aware of this mutual intention, that is, they have a collective belief about this:

$\text{C-INT}_G(\varphi) \leftrightarrow \text{M-INT}_G(\varphi) \wedge \text{C-BEL}_G(\text{M-INT}_G(\varphi))$

Even though $\text{C-INT}_G(\varphi)$ seems to be an infinite concept, it may be established in practice in a finite number of steps [2]. For an alternative version of collective intention for environments where communication is hindered, see [5].

3   Tuning Machine for Collective Commitment

After a group is constituted on the basis of collective intention, another stage of CPS, namely plan formation is started, leading ultimately to a *collective commitment* between the team members. While a collective intention may be viewed as an inspiration for team activity, the collective commitment reflects the concrete manner of achieving the intended goal by the team. This concrete manner is provided by planning, and hinges on the allocation of actions according to an adopted plan. This allocation is concluded by agents accepting pairwise (i.e. social) commitments to realize their individual actions. This way, our approach to collective commitments is plan-based.

While investigating the calibration of group commitment to the particular purpose and the specific circumstances, we isolated and separately characterized invariant ingredients of collective commitments. These are:
- collective intention on which the team is built,
- degrees of belief in a team,
- different aspects of team awareness.

They may be viewed as three types of 'knobs' that are separately tuned in order to obtain a situation-sensitive notion of collective commitment of a desired strength. Before treating these 'knobs', we give a general schema for definining collective commitments. This generic schema together with a tuning mechanism may be viewed as a sort of *tuning machine* for creating collective commitments.

3.1   General Schema of Collective Commitment

In our generic description we will solely define basic ingredients constituting collective commitments, leaving room for case-specific extensions. The obligatory ingredients are related to different aspects of teamwork:

1. Mutual intention M-INT$_G(\varphi)$ between a group of agents.
   Let us stress the crucial role of mutual intention when creating a group: the team is *based* on this attitude, and exists as long as the mutual intention between team members exists. Thus, no teamwork is considered without a mutual intention among team members.
2. Social plan P on which a collective commitment will be based.
   The social plan provides a concrete manner for the team to collectively achieve the overall goal of the system, the object of their mutual intention. For a definition and examples of social plans, see [4].
3. Pairwise social commitments COMM(i, j, α) for actions from the plan.
   The group splits the tasks according to their social plan, and each agent takes on responsibility to do its part by accepting relevant social commitments.

Next to the above ingredients, different degrees of awareness about them may be present in a team. It may vary from the lack of any awareness to collective belief about the given aspect, as it was discussed before. Thus, a general schema covering different types of collective commitment is the following, where the conjuncts between curly brackets may be present or not, according to the position of the awareness 'knob' :

$$\text{C-COMM}_{G,P}(\varphi) \leftrightarrow$$
$$\text{M-INT}_G(\varphi)\ \{\wedge\ awareness_G(\text{M-INT}_G(\varphi))\}\ \wedge$$
$$constitute(\varphi, P)\ \{\wedge\ awareness_G(constitute(\varphi, P))\}\ \wedge$$
$$\bigwedge_{\alpha \in P}\ \bigvee_{i,j \in G}\ \text{COMM}(i, j, \alpha)\ \{\wedge\ awareness_G(\ \bigwedge_{\alpha \in P}\ \bigvee_{i,j \in G}\ \text{COMM}(i, j, \alpha))\}$$

In words, group G has a collective commitment to achieve overall goal φ based on social plan P (C-COMM$_{G,P}(\varphi)$) iff all of the following hold. The group mutually intends φ (with or without being aware); moreover, successful execution of social plan P leads to φ ($constitute(\varphi, P)$) (with or without the group being aware of this); and finally, for every one of the actions α from a plan P, there should be one agent in the group who is socially committed to at least one (mostly other) agent in the group to fulfil the action ($\text{COMM}(i, j, \alpha)$) (with or without the group being aware of this).

Instantiating the above schema corresponds to tuning the $awareness_G$-knobs from $\emptyset$, through individual beliefs and different degrees of E-BEL_G^k, to collective belief, and/or analogously for degrees of knowledge. These degrees have been discussed in subsection 2.1.

3.2   Different Aspects of Agents' Awareness

The notion of collective commitment, whatever strength of it is considered, combines essentially different aspects of teamwork: strictly technical ones related to social plans, as well as those related to agents' intentional stance. The latter concerns different aspects of awareness that appear in a group of agents in the course of CPS. The degree of this awareness, characterized in terms of different types of beliefs, may be different. In the sequel, the strongest version is considered, including collective belief about considered aspect of CPS. For this reason it is justified to speak about *collective awareness* in this context. In other circumstances, the degree of awareness can be weakened by using E-BEL_G (or another E-BEL_G^k) instead of C-BEL_G. Let us discuss the relevant aspects in detail.

1. Collective intention is the attitude constituting the group as a whole. Thus, it introduces (rather strong) collective awareness of the group as a cooperative team of agents. Formally this is expressed as a conjunct in the definition of collective intention:
   $\text{C-BEL}_G(\text{M-INT}_G(\varphi))$

2. When a team of agents exists, the next step is plan generation or adoption. Regardless of the method of arriving at this point, the type of awareness connected with this is collective awareness of the correctness of the plan with respect to the overall goal. Formally :
   $\text{C-BEL}_G(constitute(\varphi, P))$

3. When a plan as a recipe is in place, then the particular actions from it need to be allocated to particular team members in order to create pairwise social commitments between them. This way a social structure is built within a team, and the plan acquires the property of being social. The type of awareness connected with this phase may be twofold.

   (a) The first one is a collective awareness of the social structure in a team with respect to a given plan. This includes a *detailed* awareness of each social commitment involved. Formally:
   $\bigwedge_{\alpha \in P} \bigvee_{i,j \in G} \text{C-BEL}_G(\text{COMM}(i, j, \alpha))$
   This corresponds to the interpretation *de re*.

(b) The second one refers to a more *global* collective awareness of the social structure within the team, namely of the bare existence of social commitments with respect to a given social plan. Formally:

C-BEL$_G(\bigwedge_{\alpha \in P} \bigvee_{i,j \in G}$ COMM$(i, j, \alpha))$

This corresponds to the interpretation *de dicto*.

The distinction de re / de dicto stems from the philosophy of language [9]. A sentence of the form $\exists x$BEL$(j, A(x))$ is a *de re* belief attribution which relates j to a *res*, an individual that the belief is about. On the other hand, BEL$(j, \exists x A(x))$ is a *de dictum* belief attribution, relating j to a *dictum*, namely the proposition $\exists x A(x)$. This distinction is also fruitful for complex epistemic operators such as collective belief. Note that C-BEL$_G$ in (a) and (b) distributes over conjunction $(\bigwedge_{\alpha \in P})$, so that only the position of C-BEL$_G$ with respect to $\bigvee_{i,j \in G}$ matters.

The above aspects of awareness will be viewed as building blocks when distinguishing different strengths of collective commitments.

4   Different Notions of Collective Commitment

The following exemplar definitions are produced by keeping the *awareness$_G$*-knob fixed to a choice between $\emptyset$ and collective belief, and the knob for 'kind of mutual intention' fixed as the standard definition of subsection 2.4. We will start from the strongest form of collective commitment, fully reflecting the collective aspects of CPS. Subsequently, some underlying assumptions will be relaxed, leading ultimately to weaker notions of team and distributed commitment.

4.1   Robust Collective Commitment

Our discussion on different types on collective commitments will start from the two cases based on collective planning. Additionally, for every one of the actions α that occur in social plan P, there should be one agent in the group who is socially committed to at least one (mostly other) agent in the group to fulfil the action. Moreover, in a *robust collective commitment* (R-COMM$_{G,P}$), there is a detailed awareness of social commitments in the team:

$$R\text{-}COMM_{G,P}(\varphi) \leftrightarrow C\text{-}INT_G(\varphi) \wedge$$
$$constitute(\varphi, P) \wedge C\text{-}BEL_G(constitute(\varphi, P)) \wedge$$
$$\bigwedge_{\alpha \in P} \bigvee_{i,j \in G} COMM(i, j, \alpha) \wedge \bigwedge_{\alpha \in P} \bigvee_{i,j \in G} C\text{-}BEL_G(COMM(i, j, \alpha))$$

By the last conjunct, everybody's responsibility is public. The aspect of sharing responsibility is of crucial importance here. Among others it implies that there is no need for an initiator in such a team.

Example Robust collective commitment may be applicable in (small) companies where all team members involved are share-holders. Typically, planning is done collectively, whether from first principles or choosing from a plan library. Everybody's responsibility is public, because the social commitments are established publicly. In particular, when any form of revision is needed due to dynamic circumstances, the entire team may be collectively involved.

4.2   Strong Collective Commitment

In contrast to robust collective commitment, in the case of *strong collective commitment* (S-COMM$_{G,P}$), there is a global awareness about particular social commitments, but the group as a whole believes that things are under control, i.e., that every part of the plan is within somebody's responsibility:

$$\text{S-COMM}_{G,P}(\varphi) \leftrightarrow \text{C-INT}_G(\varphi) \wedge$$
$$constitute(\varphi, P) \wedge \text{C-BEL}_G(constitute(\varphi, P)) \wedge$$
$$\bigwedge_{\alpha \in P} \bigvee_{i,j \in G} \text{COMM}(i,j,\alpha) \wedge \text{C-BEL}_G(\bigwedge_{\alpha \in P} \bigvee_{i,j \in G} \text{COMM}(i,j,\alpha))$$

As the reponsibility is not shared due to the lack of detailed awareness in the last conjunct, the case of a team leader or initiator fits here. Also, as pairwise social commitments are not collectively known, they cannot be collectively revised when such a need appears.

Example Strong collective commitment may be applicable in companies with one or more leaders and rather separate subteams. Typically, planning is done collectively. However, establishing bilateral commitments is not done publicly in the whole team, but in subgroups. Sometimes this suffices, and it is sometimes preferable in order not to waste energy.

4.3   Weak Collective Commitment

In the weaker cases of collective commitment, the degree of team awareness is even more limited. When the plan as a whole is not known to the team, for example, if no collective decision making is assumed, there is no awareness that the plan leads to proper realization of the goal (C-BEL$_G$ $constitute(\varphi, P)$ is not in place). In this case we deal with a *weak collective commitment* (W-COMM$_{G,P}$):

$$\text{W-COMM}_{G,P}(\varphi) \leftrightarrow \text{C-INT}_G(\varphi) \wedge constitute(\varphi, P) \wedge$$
$$\bigwedge_{\alpha \in P} \bigvee_{i,j \in G} \text{COMM}(i,j,\alpha) \wedge \text{C-BEL}_G(\bigwedge_{\alpha \in P} \bigvee_{i,j \in G} \text{COMM}(i,j,\alpha))$$

In this case, the team knows the overall goal, but does not know details of the plan: there is no collective awareness of the plan's correctness. Apparently, also in this case no collective revision of social commitments may take place.

Example Weak collective commitment may be applicable in companies with a dedicated planner or planning department. Typically, the planner individually does believe in the plan's correctness $constitute(\varphi, P)$, and this may suffice.

4.4   Team Commitment

In the case of *team commitment* (T-COMM$_{G,P}$) agents remain aware solely about their piece of work, without any orientation about involvement of others. In this situation, there is no collective belief that all actions have been adopted by other committed members, but a team as a structure still exists :

$$\text{T-COMM}_{G,P}(\varphi) \leftrightarrow \text{C-INT}_G(\varphi) \land constitute(\varphi, P) \land \bigwedge_{\alpha \in P} \bigvee_{i,j \in G} \text{COMM}(i, j, \alpha)$$

Because of the presence of collective intention, the overall goal and composition of the team are collectively believed. Planning is not at all collective: it may be that even task division is not public; this is often done on purpose. Thus, distribution of social commitments cannot be public either.

Example Team commitment may be applicable in companies assigning limited trust to its employees. Information about the precise involvement of colleagues and other aspects of the plan may be confidential.

4.5   Distributed Commitment

The last case distinguished here is *distributed commitment* (D-COMM$_{G,P}$). It deals with the situation when agents' awareness is even more restricted: they may not even know the overall goal, only their share in an 'undefined' project:

$$\text{D-COMM}_{G,P}(\varphi) \leftrightarrow constitute(\varphi, P) \land \bigwedge_{\alpha \in P} \bigvee_{i,j \in G} \text{COMM}(i, j, \alpha).$$

This means that no 'real' team of cooperating agents is created, so that no collective intention C-INT$_G$ is in place. Instead, a rather loosely coupled group of agents works in a distributed manner without autonomous involvement in the project to be realized.

Example Distributed commitment may be applicable in companies contracting out some labour to outsiders. The overall goal and the group of agents involved may be classified information, e.g. in order to avoid competition.

5   Discussion and Conclusions

We have incrementally built a static theory of CPS, starting from individual intentions, through social commitments, leading ultimately to collective intentions and collective commitments. All these notions are defined in multi-modal logics with clear semantics (cf. [5]), comprising a descriptive view on collective commitments. In contrast to [3], we do not give one iron-clad definition of collective commitment here. Instead, we provide a sort of tuning mechanism for the system developer to calibrate an appropriate type of collective commitment, taking into account both the circumstances in which a group is acting, for example possibilities of communication, as well as organizational structure. The multi-modal logic framework allows to express subtle aspects of CPS, modeling different situations occurring in practical domains.

The definitions of collective commitments are not overloaded, and therefore easy to understand and to use. Some other approaches to collective commitments (see e.g. [7, 10]) introduce other aspects of collective attitudes, not treated here. For example, Wooldridge and Jennings consider triggers for commitment adoption formulated as preconditions [10]. If needed, these may be incorporated into our framework as well by adding an extra axiom. Note that in contrast to other approaches ([10, 7]), the collective commitment is not iron-clad: it may vary in order to adapt to changing circumstances, in such a way that the collective intention on which it is based can still be reached. Thus, our approach is especially strong when replanning is needed. Using our definitions of collective commitment it is often sufficient to revise some of the pairwise social commitments, instead of involving the entire team in the replanning process.

Acknowledgments

We would like to thank Cristiano Castelfranchi, Keith Clark, Rino Falcone, and Andrew Jones for fruitful discussions. This work is supported by the Polish KBN Grant 7T11C 006 20 and by the EU funded ALFEBIITE++ project.

References

[1] C. Castelfranchi. Commitments: From individual intentions to groups and organizations. In V. Lesser, editor, *Proceedings First International Conference on Multi-Agent Systems*, pages 41–48, San Francisco, 1995. AAAI-Press and MIT Press.

[2] F. Dignum, B. Dunin-Kęplicz, and R. Verbrugge. Creating collective intention through dialogue. *Logic Journal of the IGPL*, 9:145–158, 2001.

[3] B. Dunin-Kęplicz and R. Verbrugge. Collective commitments. In M. Tokoro, editor, *Proceedings Second International Conference on Multi-Agent Systems*, pages 56–63, Menlo Park (CA), 1996. AAAI-Press.

[4] B. Dunin-Kęplicz and R. Verbrugge. A reconfiguration algorithm for distributed problem solving. *Electronic Modeling*, 22:68 – 86, 2000.

[5] B. Dunin-Kęplicz and R. Verbrugge. Collective intentions. *Fundamenta Informaticae*, 51(3):271–295, 2002.

[6] R. Fagin, J. Halpern, Y. Moses, and M. Vardi. *Reasoning about Knowledge*. MIT Press, Cambridge, MA, 1995.

[7] H. Levesque, P. Cohen, and J. Nunes. On acting together. In *Proceedings Eighth National Conference on AI (AAAI90)*, pages 94–99, Menlo Park (CA), Cambridge (MA), 1990. AAAI-Press and MIT Press.

[8] J.-J. C. Meyer and W. van der Hoek. *Epistemic Logic for AI and Theoretical Computer Science.* Cambridge University Press, Cambridge, 1995.

[9] W. Quine. Quantifiers and propositional attitudes. *Journal of Philosophy,* 53:177–187, 1956.

[10] M. Wooldridge and N. Jennings. Cooperative problem solving. *Journal of Logic and Computation,* 9:563–592, 1999.

Abstract Architecture for Meta-reasoning in Multi-agent Systems

Michal Pěchouček[1], Olga Štěpánková[1,2],
Vladimír Mařík[1,2], and Jaroslav Bárta[2]

[1] Gerstner Laboratory, Czech Technical University in Prague
Technicka 2, 166 27, Prague 6, Czech Republic
{pechouc,step,marik}@labe.felk.cvut.cz
[2] Center of Applied Cybernetics, Czech Technical University in Prague
Technicka 2, 166 27, Prague 6, Czech Republic
barta@labe.felk.cvut.cz
http://gerstner.felk.cvut.cz

Abstract. Agent's meta-reasoning is a computational process that implements agent's capability to reason on a higher level about another agents or a community of agents. There is a potential for meta-reasoning in multi-agent systems. Meta-reasoning can be used for reconstructing agents' private knowledge, their mental states and for prediction of their future courses of action. Meta-agents should have the capability to reason about incomplete or imprecise information. Unlike the ordinary agents, the meta-agent may contemplate about the community of agents as a whole and is expected to contribute to agent's operation efficiency improvement. This contribution suggests a theoretical specification of an abstract reasoning and knowledge representation architecture for the meta-reasoning agents and discusses/categorizes the related computational processes.

1 Introduction

Multi-agent systems are collections of autonomous, heterogeneous agents with specialized functionalities. The agents are usually able to carry out collective decision making, share resources, integrate services or just collaboratively seek for specific information. The possible application domains of such multi-agent systems are e.g. production planning and scheduling, supply chain management, simulation of virtual enterprisers, or coalition formation processes. Distributed problem solving architectures provide important features, e.g. capability to find 'reasonably-good' solutions efficiently, robustness and a very high degree of fault-tolerance, reconfigurability capabilities, "openness' of the community to integrate new agents or to replace the disappearing, etc.

As the agents cannot access computational models of the other agents (unlike objects in software engineering), no agent can be sure (cannot prove in advance) the resulting behavior of the other agent. Therefore, unexpected, emergent patterns of agent-to-agent interaction and of the behavior of multi-agent system as

V. Mařík et al. (Eds): CEEMAS 2003, LNAI 2691, pp. 84–99, 2003.

a whole are expected to appear. Thus we may see that the simple multi-agent system lacks the self-explanation capacity, the capability to improve its behavior with time, to self-organize its functionality, to perform self-diagnostics, etc.

We suggest the concept of a meta-reasoning agent (*meta-agent*) as a reflective component of a multi-agent system. The goal of the meta-agents is to evaluate the activities of individual agents from the global perspective, to understand the behavior of the community, explain it and provide recommendations for its improvement. The meta-agent is not an inevitable component of a multi-agent community. Had it failed to operate or been overloaded, the community of agents is not affected.

In this contribution we neither describe implementation of a meta-reasoning agent nor we give full details of the encapsulated meta-reasoning methods. Instead, we try to present, on a formal and theoretical level, an abstract knowledge and reasoning architecture of a meta-agent. However, it should be noted that this article covers a part of the research which will result in a full implementation of the meta-agents using different meta-reasoning methods.

2   Shortly about Meta-reasoning and Meta-agents

We refer to meta-reasoning as an agent's capability to reason about the knowledge, mental states and reasoning processes of other members of the multi-agent community. We will refer to **object agents** which are subject of another agent's meta-reasoning process. Meta-reasoning can be carried out either by the object agent or by a specific agent - **meta-agent**, whose role is to carry out the meta-reasoning related process only.

Meta-reasoning is an important and inseparable part of reflective behavior of a multi-agent system [14]. If we require any computational system to be reflective, it needs to be able to reason about itself, its knowledge, problem solving strategies, scope of competence or record of past behavior. A reflective system consists of object-level components and a reflective component. Reflection in any computational system relies on self-representation:

- **meta-representation** - a model of the object-level part of the system,
- **meta-reasoning** - a capability to manipulate with the meta-representation and
- **causal connection** - which makes the meta-reasoning model to comply with object-level part of the system. [16, 9].

The causal connection consist of an introspective integrity and an introspective force. While the former updates the model, the latter changes the system. Introspective integrity in multi-agent systems relies primarily on the monitoring process and collecting information about the object agents. The set of new facts that meta-reasoning detects, is exploited within the introspective force phase. In this phase, the meta-reasoning agent affects the community by sending messages, affecting the environment, or constructing new agents. This phase, which is also referred to as a community revision phase, may result in knowledge revision of object agents' knowledge.

According to the role/contribution of the object agents to the meta-reasoning process we distinguish between two different types of meta-reasoning:

- **collaborative meta-reasoning**: In this case, the object agents are aware of being monitored, which is what they agree with and support. The purpose of collaborative meta-reasoning is very often an improvement of the object-agents' collective behavior. We distinguish also between two types of collaborativness: (i) by providing knowledge about the object agents' internal states to the meta-reasoning agent, (ii) by providing copies of the communicated messages to the meta-reasoning agent.
  By this the object agents take part in the meta-reasoning process.
- **non-collaborative meta-reasoning**: In this case, the object-agents do not want to be monitored and are not supporting the meta-reasoning process. The meta-reasoning agent is supposed to use different techniques rather than rely on the object agents to provide copies of their communication.

2.1   Meta-agents

Many researchers have approached the problem of meta-agency from different points of view. Very often the agents, that reason or maintain knowledge about the community of object agents, are linked to the agents' interaction platform (e.g. *facilitators*, which play the role of communication interfaces among collaborating agents [11] or DF and AMS components in FIPA that administer the white-page and yellow-page list of agent). However, meta-reasoning can be implemented also by loosely coupled agents such as *brokers*, which are responsible for finding the best possible addressee of the transmitted message [15], *matchmakers* which also suggest cooperation patterns that may be equally used in the future [2], or *mediators*, which besides facilitating, brokering and matchmaking coordinate the agents by suggesting and promoting new cooperation patterns among them [15]. If these agents are tightly connected to the implementation platform, they have been classified as *middle agents* [18].

Unlike the middle agents, the meta-agent is a loosely coupled agent that does not facilitate any functionality that is inevitable for operation of the object-agents. As any other reflective component of a computational system, the meta-agent is connected with the object level part of the system via causal connections (introspective integrity and introspective force [9]). This is not the case of the agents listed in the previous paragraph as they take an active (irreplaceable) role in the agent's operation. The meta-agent observes the behavior of the community and tries to draw some assumptions about the agents' behavior. This type of meta-agent can use certain type of domain-relevant knowledge to help the other agents to make optimal decisions and therefore improve the performance of the multi-agent system as a whole. By introducing the concept of the meta-agent, one may get an overall view of the community's functionality. The use of multiple meta-agents avoids making the meta-reasoning process too fragile by relying on a single independent meta-agent, which can become a bottleneck of the process of meta-reasoning.

According to an impact that has the meta-agent on the community of agents we distinguish between:

- **passive meta-agent**: In this case, the meta-agent has no impact on the object agents and does not intervene in the object agents' operation. This instance of meta-reasoning is used primarily for purposes of visualization, explanation and simulation.
- **active meta-agent**: In this case, the meta-agent reflects back the results of the meta-reasoning process and makes an attempt to influence the object agents' community by revising their knowledge, commitments and intentions. This instance of meta-reasoning is used for constructing adaptive and reflective multi-agent systems.

3   Meta-agent Reasoning Architecture

The central point of the meta-agent's operation is an appropriate syntactic model (a set of true formulas) of the community. This model has to be expressed in an appropriate language of adequate granularity. For any reasonable manipulation with the model we need to specify the relevant semantic properties of the object-level community it is supposed to model. This is what we will refer to as the **background knowledge – bk**. In the simplest case, this is a theory in the first order logic.

According to the model of social knowledge [10], the **agent's social neighborhood** $\mu(A)$ is a collection of agents that are subject of agent's A meta-reasoning processes. While $\mu^+(A)$ is a set of agents, which are monitored by the agent A, $\mu^-(A)$ is a set all agents that monitor the agent A. Provided that m denotes a meta-agent, we can say that:

$$\forall m \in \mu^-(A) : A \in \mu^+(m). \tag{1}$$

However, in the multi-agent environment it is hard to implement a mutually shared knowledge structure that would represent agent's social neighborhood. This is why each agent maintains its social neighborhood by itself in a special knowledge structure – *acquaintance model* (see [10]). Therefore, we shall interpret the set μ^+ as a collection of agents that the agent A intentionally monitors, and the set μ^- as a collection of agents about which the agent A knows that they monitor it.

Under such interpretation, the formula (1) is true in both the collaborative and the non-collaborative environments, while the inverse formula $\forall A \in \mu^+(m) : m \in \mu^-(A)$ is true in a collaborative environment only (as there may exist agents which are monitored and they do not know about it).

Let us define the model of the object-level community as a set of true facts about the respective agents. As we admit the meta-agent to be mistaken we do not require necessarily truthfulness of these facts, while we want the meta-agent

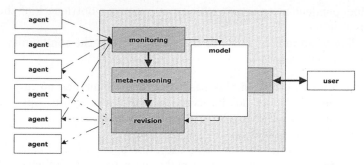

Fig. 1. Meta-Reasoning Architecture - A Process View

to believe in their truthfulness. We will collect the fact that the meta-agent m knows about the agent A into a belief-set bel_m^A.

The model, managed by the meta-agent m, is then a set as follows:

$$\mathsf{model}(m) = \bigcup_{A \in \mu^+(m)} \mathsf{bel}_m^A. \qquad (2)$$

Let $\Im$ be a set of all true formulae that we can make about the object-agents' community. The model provides the meta-agent with the facts that are true provided that:

$$\forall A \in \mu(m)^+ : \forall \varphi \in \mathsf{bel}_m^A : \varphi \in \Im. \qquad (3)$$

Provided that φ_A denotes a formula expressing true property of the agent A we may say that the model mirrors precisely the object-level community provided

$$\forall A \in \mu(m)^+ : \forall \varphi_A \in \Im : \varphi \in \mathsf{bel}_m^A. \qquad (4)$$

Now let us briefly mention how the model may be constructed and exploited. The meta-reasoning process in a multi-agent system is built upon three mutually interconnected computational processes:

1. **monitoring** – process that makes sure that the meta-agent knows the most it can get from monitoring the community of object agents. This process builds basics of the **model**(m) – model of the community and implements the introspective integrity (in the sense of [9]). The monitoring process preserves truthfulness of the model, while it cannot usually assure perfectness of the model.
2. **reasoning** – this process manipulates the model of the community so that true facts (other than monitored) may be revealed. Within the reasoning phase the meta-agent tries to maintain truthfulness of the model.
3. **community revision** – a mechanism for influencing operation of the object agents' community. This process is inevitable if the meta-agent reasoning phase results in such a goal hypothesis, that is not true in the community,

while it ought to be (such as efficiency improvements or agents' awareness of the intruder operating in the system). In this phase, the meta-agent may also affect the operation of the community in order to improve the meta-reasoning process.

The pieces of belief that are formed by the agent's A monitoring process are denoted as ground beliefs g-bel(A) and those constructed by the reasoning process are denoted as assumed beliefs a-bel(A). By replacing the term bel(A) in the equations (3) and (4) with g-bel(A) or a-bel(A), we can define truthfulness and perfectness of the monitoring and the reasoning processes separately.

In the following sections we will discuss each of the reasoning processes in more details.

4   Monitoring

Previously, people investigated ways of monitoring teams and communities of either competing or collaborative agents [6]. In principle, we distinguish between the query-based and subscription-based monitoring [3]:

- **query-based monitoring**, when the meta-reasoning agent itself is trying to detect new information or inspect truthfulness of the already stored knowledge. The query-based (active) monitoring can be implemented by *communication* where the meta-agent periodically checks with the object agents whether the monitored information has been changed. This has been done previously by *periodical revisions* [1], [17]. Similar option is implicit monitoring via *environment* where the agents act and interact. Huber and Kaminka [4], [6] suggest active monitoring via *plan-recognition.*
- **subscription-based monitoring**, when the meta-reasoning agent gets notified when truthfulness of the monitored proposition changes [5]. This type of monitoring is usually implemented by the *subscribe-inform* conversation protocol. The subscriber queries/subscribes an object agent for information that describes its computational state, beliefs, or goals. The object agent replies and keeps informing the subscriber each time this information becomes invalid. In [6] there was introduced the *monitoring selectivity problem* i.e. the challenging problem of deciding how much of monitoring is relevant and necessary for performing the required reflective task.

Naturally, the most appropriate monitoring/meta-reasoning component of a multi-agent system would be its central communication element (agent). Here the information can be collected and analyzed. From many important reasons such as robustness and fault tolerance of the system, autonomy of agents, assuring information privacy, dynamics and flexibility of the system, we wanted to avoid such a centralized approach.

If agents act autonomously and communicate peer-to-peer, a meta-reasoning agent may monitor the communication traffic by observing the communication exchange among the object agents. It subscribes the object agent for copies of communicated messages. This philosophy distinguishes the central communication agent from the meta-agent. Had the former one failed to operate, the entire community is paralyzed and can not continue to operate, while the operation of the latter one is independent from functioning of the community of object agents.

A more complicated problem, which has not been studied thoroughly yet, is monitoring of the object agents that do not want to be monitored (in the case of non-collaborative meta-reasoning). Another challenging problem is monitoring a community of agents in distributed manner. Several monitoring agents may be in charge of monitoring different parts of the community, in different times or monitoring different aspects of object agents' operation.

The monitoring process has been investigated in the past. The object agent's state reconstruction is performed in [7]. The domain is characterized by the huge amount of the communication acts, which are replaced by probability propagation over the possible states and restricted by the team oriented program. The socially attentive monitoring for failures identification in inter-agent communication has been reported in [6]. We will exploit a similar approach in non-collaborative environment, where we will identify the object agent's behavior patterns from the commitments between the object agents. The main difference between our domain and the socially attentive monitoring domain is in the amount of the communication acts. Our domain is characterized by a limited amount of communication acts with the information-rich content of the messages.

5   Reasoning

On top of the monitoring process, there is an independent reasoning and knowledge analysis, that distinguishes the meta-agent from a simple monitoring agent. While the monitoring agent only collects the information, the meta-agent uses this information for further analysis, deduction, prediction, or any other instance of reasoning.

The meta-reasoning agent's reasoning operation can be carried out in two different phases of the object agents' community life-cycle:

- *e*-time: the instance of the time when an event in the community happens and the community model is automatically revised or
- *q*-time: when the user (or other agent possibly) queries the model in order to find out about truthfulness of the goal hypotheses.

Balancing the amount of computational processes in the *e*-time and the *q*-time is really crucial. The proper design depends on the required meta-reasoning functionality. While for visualization and intrusion detection the most of computation is required in the *e*-time, for explanation, simulation and prediction an important part of computational processes will be carried out in the q-time.

5.1   Community Model Revision

Now, we will talk about the reasoning process more formally. Let us introduce the **community model revision** operation - $\uplus$, that is expected to happen in the e-time exclusively. The community model revision represents the change of the model $\mathsf{model}_t(m)$ in the time t with respect to the new formula (event_t) that describes an event in the community. We can also use a prefix notation of the community revision operator – **update**, where $\mathsf{model}_t(m) \uplus \mathsf{event}_t$ is the same as $\mathsf{update}(\mathsf{event}_t)|_{\mathsf{model}_t(m)}$.

When designing the $\uplus$ operator, one needs to take into account the background knowledge – **bk** (mentioned in 3). We may distinguish between two marginal effects of the meta-reasoning operation – $\uplus^{max}$ and $\uplus^{min}$ as follows:

$$\mathsf{model}_t(m) \uplus^{\mathrm{max}} \mathsf{event}_t = \{\varphi : \mathsf{bk} \cup \mathsf{model}_t(m) \cup \{\mathsf{event}_t\} \vdash \varphi\}, \qquad (5)$$

$$\mathsf{model}_t(m) \uplus^{\mathrm{min}} \mathsf{event}_t = \mathsf{model}_t(m) \cup \{\mathsf{event}_t\}. \qquad (6)$$

The $\uplus^{\mathrm{max}}$ operation revises the model so that it contains all possible true facts that logically follow from the background knowledge – **bk**, original model – $\mathsf{model}_t(m)$ in conjunction with the new observation – event_t. The $\uplus^{\mathrm{min}}$ operation only appends the new formula to the model. In many cases, the $\uplus^{\mathrm{max}}$ operation is hard to achieve as the resulting model may be infinite - we introduce such a model as an abstract marginal concept. The model that results from the $\uplus^{min}$ model revision shall be always a subset of the model constructed by $\uplus^{\mathrm{max}}$ operation.

When designing the community-model-revision process, we seek such an operation $\uplus$ that

$$\mathsf{model}_t(m) \uplus^{\mathrm{max}} \mathsf{event}_t \supseteq \mathsf{model}_t(m) \uplus \mathsf{event}_t \supseteq \mathsf{model}_t(m) \uplus^{\mathrm{min}} \mathsf{event}_t. \qquad (7)$$

The closer our operation gets to $\uplus^{min}$, the faster is the model revision process and the more complex will be the computational process in the q-time. The closer we are to $\uplus^{\mathrm{max}}$, the easier will be the query process while the revision process is getting really complex.

There are different types of events that initiate the community-model-revision process in the e-time. We talk primarily about initiating a contract-net-protocol, an offer for collaboration, accepting or rejection of the collaboration proposal, etc.

Example: Let us give an example of the following inference. Given the

$$\mathsf{model}_t = \{\mathtt{accept}(A, C_1, T), \mathtt{accept}(A, C_3, T), \mathtt{coalitions}(C_1, C_2, C_3)\},$$

which asserts two acceptance of collaboration and knowledge of structuring the community into 3 coalitions – and the event $\mathtt{accept}(A, C_2, T)$ – agent's A

acceptance to collaborate on a task T within a coalition C_2, we may model the following reasoning :

$$\mathsf{model}_{t+1}(m) = \mathsf{model}_t(m) \uplus \mathsf{happens}\{\mathsf{accept}(A, C_2, T)\}|_{\mathsf{model}_t(m)}. \qquad (8)$$

Provided that the meta-reasoning has been implemented by the $\uplus^{\min}$ operator, the model $\mathsf{model}_{t+1}(m)$ will look as follows:

$$\mathsf{model}_{t+1} = \mathsf{model}_t \cup \{\mathsf{accept}(A, C_2, T)\}, \qquad (9)$$

while in the case of the $\uplus^{\max}$ operator the model $\mathsf{model}_{t+1}(m)$ will look as follows:

$$\mathsf{model}_{t+1} \supseteq \mathsf{model}_t \cup \{(\mathsf{accept\text{-}task}(A, T), \mathsf{accept}(A, C_2, T))\}. \qquad (10)$$

As mentioned previously, the $\uplus^{\max}$ algorithm is hard to be implemented in complex multi-agent systems. One possible way how to relax the computational requirements for the automated reasoner (which implements meta-reasoning) is to apply the meta-reasoning operator only on selected event formulae (filtered according to the predicate or occurrence of constants). The concept of model revision is closely related to the concept of weak and strong update in the knowledge engineering area[12].

5.2   Community Model Inspection

Now, let us talk about the reasoning process at the q-time. The computational process of **community model inspection** provides the user (or any other agent) with a formula describing the properties of the community – the goal formula (**goal-h**). We introduce a special operation for model inspection – *query* with its infix symbol ↬ (the operation $\mathsf{query}\{\mathsf{goal\text{-}h}\}|_{\mathsf{model}(m)}$ can be expressed by $\mathsf{model}(m) ↬ \mathsf{goal\text{-}h}$). The **minimal** version of the community model inspection process corresponds directly to *instantiation* of the goal formula with the model. The relevant formula can be retrieved from the model with no further reasoning.[1]

$$\mathsf{model}(m) ↬ \mathsf{goal\text{-}h} = \begin{cases} yes & \text{if } \mathsf{goal\text{-}h} \in \mathsf{model}(m), \\ no & \text{if } \mathsf{goal\text{-}h} \notin \mathsf{model}(m). \end{cases} \qquad (11)$$

In the example in 5.1 we would get 'yes' when inspecting the model with the querry ↬ $\mathsf{accept}(A, T)$ (see 10) due to the fact that $\mathsf{accept}(A, T) \in \mathsf{model}_{t+1}(m)$, with no further computation.

---

[1] The goal formula can contain free variables that get bound to constants during the instantiation process.

In order to use the minimal version of the model inspection in the q-time, we need the maximal (or close to maximal) model revision ($\uplus^{\max}$) in the e-time of the meta-reasoning life-cycle.

If the reasoning triggered by the event has been **minimal** – $\uplus^{\min}$ (or simply did not produce the queried formula), the query process will be a more complex operation than simply parsing the existing model. The **maximal** version of the model inspection shall be, in principle, implemented by *theorem proving*. The meta-agent is expected to employ reasoning in order to find out the requested goal formula that logically follows from the model.

$$\mathsf{model}(m) \looparrowright \mathbf{goal\text{-}h} = \begin{cases} yes & \text{if } {}_{\mathsf{model}(m)} \vdash \mathbf{goal\text{-}h}, \\ \\ no & \text{if } {}_{\mathsf{model}(m)} \nvdash \mathbf{goal\text{-}h}. \end{cases} \tag{12}$$

The respective formula can also contain free variables.

5.3   Improving Meta-reasoning Efficiency

The maximal community model revision process is expected to produce all formulas that logically follow from the conjunction of the current model and the latest event. The space of all deducible formulae may be really enormous (or infinite). In order to reduce this space and thus decrease the complexity of the meta-reasoning process, the set of all considered goal hypotheses – G may be specified beforehand.

Provided that the goal formulae are not available, two extreme cases may be considered: (i) either the set $G = \emptyset$ which implies $\uplus = \uplus^{\min}$, or (ii) the set $G = \Im$, which implies $\uplus = \uplus^{\max}$. If the former case is true we may say that the set G gives the complexity of the $\uplus$ operation. There are two factors that are interesting about the set G: (i) the number of elements, and (ii) the length of an inference chain, each element may initiate. While the former is easy to compute, the latter parameter is rather more abstract.

The hypotheses with the unit length of the inference chain are **atomic observable formulas** that directly represent a possible event in the community of the object-level agents.

Another way how the community model revision can be made more efficient, is to use problem solving shortcuts – **partial reasoning plans**, specified ex ante, that link directly the goal formula with the atomic observable formulas. Therefore, the partial reasoning plans may structure the reasoning process in order to optimize the reasoning process complexity in complex meta-reasoning domains.

6   Community Revision

Community revision (CR) process is an important, inseparable part of the active meta-reasoning and reflection in multi-agent systems [10]. In principle, we distinguish between

- **direct community revision** process, which is based on sending revision (simple inform/request) messages directly to the object agents, and
- **indirect community revision**, when the meta-agent can indirectly influence the object agents' behavior through the environment in which the agents operate.

The CR phase has been primarily designed for improving the operation and efficiency of the operation of the object-level agents. However, there is an important potential of the community revision processes for improving the efficiency of meta-reasoning. Finding out about truthfulness of the atomic observable formulae, which define applicability of the partial reasoning plans, has the capability to accelerate the meta-reasoning process.

A meta-agent may interact with the community by sending messages that initiate specific operations. As a result of these operations, specific atomic observable formulae will get instantiated.

Example: In order to find out whether the agent A refutes to participate in the coalition C, we need to prove the goal formula [2]

$$\neg\texttt{accept-coalition}(A, C), \tag{13}$$

while knowing

$$\texttt{accept}(a, c, t) \Leftrightarrow \texttt{accept-coalition}(a, c) \wedge \texttt{accept-task}(a, t). \tag{14}$$

For proving the goal formula (13), we can design a simple reasoning plan as a consequence of (14):

$$(\exists c, t \neg\texttt{accept}(A, C, t) \wedge \texttt{accept}(A, c, t)), \tag{15}$$
$$\Rightarrow \neg\texttt{accept-coalition}(A, C).$$

This partial reasoning plan specifies two atomic formulas ($\neg\texttt{accept}(A, C, t)$ and $\texttt{accept}(A, c, t)$) that need to be satisfied for the goal formula to be assumed to be true. Instead of waiting for the particular event to happen, the meta-agent may try to invoke these events by sending messages with the content:

$$\texttt{propose}(A, C, t) \text{ and } \texttt{propose}(A, c, t). \tag{16}$$

Provided that the agent A either accepts the collaboration within the coalition C or refuses all other coalitions for the same task, the goal formula is refuted. If it rejects the coalition C and accepts another coalition for the same task, the goal formula is proved. We will refer to these messages as **stimulation events**. The "art" of finding out such a stimulation event, that will result in an event that will contribute the most to the meta-reasoning process, is not a trivial task. Methods of abductive reasoning [8] can be applied for this purpose.

---

[2] We will denote the constants with the capital letters and variables with the small letters.

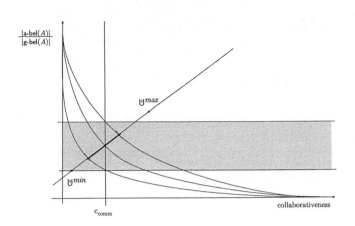

Fig. 2. Possible influence of collaborativeness of the object agent's community in meta-reasoning aimed at detection of agents intentional states. On the horizontal axis, there is the abstract quantity of *collaborativeness* (the sum of all atomic facts the object agents make accessible to the meta-agent). On the vertical axis there is the ratio between the number of hypotheses that were constructed by reasoning and monitoring, respectively. Different curves represent different complexities of the meta-reasoning processes. C_{comm} represents a degree of collaborativeness for which the meta-agent just observers all the communication traffic. For the given collaborativeness, the extent of $\frac{|a\text{-bel}(A)|}{|g\text{-bel}(A)|}$ is determined

7 Conclusion and Discussions

In this article, we have presented a theoretical and an abstract view on the reasoning and knowledge structure architecture of a meta-reasoning agent. We have suggested a formal model of a meta-reasoning agent and outlined the basic requirements for the meta-reasoning agent's functionality. Besides the suggested knowledge structures we have commented primarily the meta-reasoning process. Apart from the **community revision** process, by which the meta-agent affects the community operation, the meta-reasoning process is split between the **monitoring** and **reasoning** processes. The agent's meta-reasoning medium is the **community model** that describes the community. The community model may be either **revised** or **inspected**. The meta-reasoning can be carried out either in the **query-time**, when a user (or another agent) wants to inspect the object-agent community or in the **event-time**, when the community changes. Let us discuss the requirements for the different meta-reasoning processes in more details now.

Firstly, the community model can be constructed partially by monitoring and partially by the reasoning process. In an ideal situation, it is advantageous to

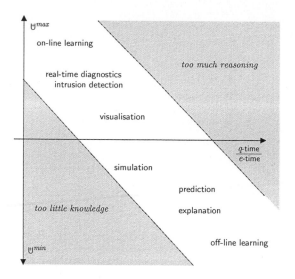

Fig. 3. Requirements for the ⊎ model revision function (vertical axis) and $\frac{q-time}{e-time}$ computational resources allocation (horizontal axis) in different meta-reasoning tasks (the shaded regions are irrelevant – powerfull model revision and powerfull meta-reasoning in the q-time is not unnecessary and $⊎^{min}$ with no computation in the q-time will result in really weak meta-reasoning)

monitor as much as it is possible and not to overload the meta-reasoning agent with unnecessary computation burden. However, not everything, that happens in the community, is relevant to the goals of the meta-reasoning process. With too much of irrelevant data being collected, we also increase the complexity of the reasoning process and have to face the classical situation of "*information-overload-knowledge-starvation*". Problem of suggesting the right scope of agent's monitoring is referred to as *monitoring selectivity problem* [7].

However, it may also happen, that there is a vital and relevant piece of information that is not available for monitoring. This information needs to be reconstructed by the reasoning process instead. The reason for this monitoring information unavailability is in lack of collaborativeness between the meta-agent and the object agents (see Figure 2). In principle, we may say that with an increased collaborativeness of the environment, monitoring may play more important role in the overall meta-reasoning processes.

As mentioned in the article, the reasoning process is critical and may cause that the whole meta-reasoning process fails to comply with calculative rationality requirements. For that reason we try to balance the computational resources that are devoted to the reasoning process in both the query-time and the event-time.

It would seem that doing the most computation in the query-time (even though the user response would be very slow) and designing the reasoning algorithms so that $\uplus = \uplus^{min}$, would comply with the calculative rationality requirement. However, there are several classes of meta-reasoning tasks where this is not possible (see Figure 3).

In the domain areas where we require the multi-agent system to be **self-adaptive** and to use meta-reasoning for on-line learning, the whole process of reasoning is carried out in the event-time. The function $\uplus$ is expected to be very powerful in this case (the closer to $\uplus^{max}$, the better). In order to make the reasoning algorithm efficient, the developers need to rely on the goal hypotheses specified ex ante and a complex set of partial reasoning plans. Meta-reasoning in this marginal case will be very case-specific. A powerful model update function is also required for **diagnostic** type of tasks, e.g. fault detection, intrusion detection. When implementing **visualisation** of the object-agents community, the most of computation has to be carried out in the event-time while some interaction with the user in the q-time is also required (e.g. switching views, etc.). Operation of the other type of meta-reasoning tasks is carried out primarily in the query-time. **Simulation** and **prediction** of the future/hypothetical courses of object-agent actions shall be implemented mainly as the community model inspection with some required '*preprocessing*' in the community model revision phase (e.g. identifying the agents' mental and intentional states, available resources, commitments, etc.). Off-line learning, knowledge and data discovery (KDD), and related tasks do not need any complicated community model revision in the event-time. The community model revison function should get very close to $\uplus^{min}$.

In the current phase of the project, we have been implementing a meta-agent that (i) complies with the above defined architectural specification and (ii) that will be open to encapsulation of different reasoning models. We have been studying applicability and experimenting primarily with automated reasoners, the version space algorithm (machine learning), inductive logic programming and truth maintenance. While the truth maintenance system, that will take care about the consistency of the model $model(A)$, shall be closely connected to the meta-agent reasoning core, the other algorithms can be loosely coupled with the core. The integration of the reasoning methods can be carried out either via standard integration channels, e.g. dll libraries, ActiveX components or directly through the socket integration. An alternative way is is to encapsulate the methods in agent wrappers, so they would become fully fledged members of the multi-agent system. The latter method is particulary suitable in the cases when different methods will run in parallel and their results should be put together in an intelligent way.

Acknowledgement

The project work has been jointly co-funded by European Office for Aerospace Research and Development (EORD) Air Force Research Laboratory (AFRL) -

contract number: FA8655-02-M-4056 and Office of Naval Research (ONR) -
award number: N00014-03-1-0292 and the Czech Ministry for Eduction, Youth
and Sports – project number LN00B096.

References

[1] Cao, W., Bian, C.-G., and Hartvigsen, G.: Achieving Efficient Cooperation in
a Multi-Agent System: The Twin-Base Modelling. In: *Co-operative Information
Agents (Kandzia, P., Klusch, M. eds.)*, LNAI No. 1202, Springer Verlag, Heidelberg, 210-221, 1995.

[2] Decker, K., Sycara, K., and Williamson, M.: Middle Agents for Internet. In: *Proceedings of International Joint Conference on Artificial Intelligence 97*, Japan,
1997.

[3] Grosz, B.J., and Kraus, S.: The Evolution of SharePlans. In: Wooldridge, M.
and Rao, A. (eds.), *Foundations of Theories of Rational Agency*, pp. 227-262,
1999.

[4] Huber, M.J., and Durfee, E.H.: On Acting Together: Without Communication. In: *Working Notes of the AAAI Spring Symposium on Representing Mental
States and Mechanisms*, pp. 60-71, 1995.

[5] Jennings, N.R.: Controlling Cooperative Problem Solving in Industrial Multi-
Agent Systems using Joint Intentions. *Artificial Intelligence*, 75(2), 195-240,
1995.

[6] Kaminka, G.A., and Tambe, M.: Robust Multi-Agent Teams via Socially-
Attentive Monitoring. *Journal of Artificial Intelligence Research (JAIR)*, Volume 12. pp, 105-147, 2000.

[7] Kaminka, G.A., Pynadath, D., and Tambe, M.: Monitoring Deployed Agent
Teams. In: *Proceedings of the fifth international conference on Autonomous
agents*, Montreal, Quebec, Canada, 2001.

[8] Konolige, K. Abduction Versus Closure in Causal Theories. *Artificial Intelligence*, 52:255-72, 1991.

[9] Maes, P.: Computational Reflection, Technical Report 87-2, Free University of
Brussels, AI Lab,1987.

[10] Mařík, V., Pěchouček , M., and Štěpánková, O.: Social Knowledge in Multi-
agent Systems. In: *Multi-Agent Systems and Applications*, Berlin: Springer, vol.
1, LNAI 2086, pp. 211 – 246, 2001.

[11] McGuire, J., Kuokka, D., Weber, J., Tenebaum, J., Gruber, T., and Olsen G.:
SHADE: Technology for Knowledge-Based Collaborative Engineering. *Concurrent Engineering: Research and Applications*, 1(3), 1993.

[12] Pěchouček M., Štěpánková, O. Mikšovský P.: Maintenance of Discovery Knowledge, In Rauch J. Zitkow, editor(s), *Priciples of Data Mining and Knowledge
Discovery*, pages 476-483, Berlin, Springer-Verlag, September 1999.

[13] Pěchouček, M., Mařík, V, and Bárta , J.: A Knowledge-Based Approach to
Coalition Formation. In: *IEEE Intelligent Systems*, vol, 17, no. 3, p. 17-25, 2002.

[14] Pěchouček , M. and Norrie, D.: Knowledge Structures for Reflective Multi-Agent
Systems: On Reasoning about other Agents. Research Report, Calgary: University of Calgary, 538, 47 p, 2000.

[15] Shen W., Norrie, D.H., and Barthes, J.A.: *Multi-Agent Systems for Concurrent
Intelligent Design and Manufacturing*, Taylor and Francis, London, 2001.

[16] Smith, B. C.: Reflection and Semantics in Lisp. In: *Proc. 11th ACM Symposium on Principles of Logic Programming*, Salt Like City, Utah, Also Xerox PARC Intelligent Systems Laboratory Technical Report ISL-5, 1984.

[17] Štěpánková O., Mařík V., and Lažanský J.: Improving Cooperative Behaviour in Multiagent Systems. In: *Advanced IT Tools*, Chapman and Hall, London, pp. 293-302, 1996.

[18] Sycara, K., Lu, J., Klusch, M., and Widoff, S.: Dynamic Service Matchmaking among Agents in Open Information Environments. *ACM SIGMOID Record*, vol. 28, No.1, 1999. 211-246, 2001.

[19] Wooldridge, M.: Reasoning about Rational Agents. *The MIT Press* Cambridge, Massachusetts, 2000.

Theory such that if the agent adopts the roles preferable by the society, it will be awarded to have higher motivation to be active in social network.

This paper is structured as follows. In section 2, we describe a model of the role adoption based on social network, where we include a number of definitions. In section 3, we describe our implementation and the experiments we conducted that show combinations of social influence and capability for role adoptions. Finally, section 4 offers concluding remarks and future works.

2   A Model of Role Adoption under Influence of Peer Network

A social network can represent relationships between agents. Agent social networks can be used to model peer influences and increase homogeneity among used agent's role adoption. It has been found that same-cluster members tend to be more similar in their opinions than different-cluster members [1]. A cluster can be viewed as an organization. Similarly, according to balance theory when agents adopt roles based on preference, they are likely to adopt the same type of roles that have been adopted by the agents with whom they have strong relationship and mutual influence in order to reduce tension among them. A dominant concept in social network analysis is *centrality* [10][11]. Actors are more *central* to the extent that they have more relationships with more members of the network, i.e., play a role that is more connected to other roles [24].

We focus on a dyadic relationship in a network with the properties of symmetry and transitivity [17]. Social networks are commonly represented by a graph. Each agent in the social network is a vertex, and the social relationship between two agents is an edge. Social relationships between agents have different potency among agents. If the relationship between agents is strong, the value will be large. We can use an n by n matrix whose elements are valued between 0.0 to 1.0 to represent relationships in agent social network graphs, where n is the number of agents. The relationship we are exploring is peer pressure for role adoption [2]. Agents with larger relationship values exert larger pressure on one another to adopt the same type of role. We realize peer pressure is only one of a myriad of influences individuals may have on one another. For example, a parent may influence a child about a role but this relationship is typically not symmetric. Henceforth, we will refer to a network of peer pressure values among agents as *peer network*. In this paper, handling of cycles in the network relationship is not covered.

Definition 1 *Social peer pressure value* (we abbreviate with *peer value* in the rest of this paper) is the strength of the peer pressure value between two agents.

The relationship can be direct relationship as well as indirect relationship, which means that the agents have strength of the peer value via intermediary agents. Two agents can be connected via different routes with the same length. We define the concept of *route set* to collect all the routes connecting two agents with the same length.

Definition 2 *Route set*, $R_i(a,b)$, is the aggregation of all routes connecting agents a and b with length i. I.e.,

$$R_i(a,b) = \{r \mid r \text{ is a path (a succession edges) of length } i \text{ between agent } a \text{ and } b\} \quad (1)$$

If two agents are not directly connected, the distance (i.e., the number of edges) between two agents will affect the strength of pressure. We define the influence value to represent the peer pressure between two agents via certain routes.

Definition 3 *Peer Influence value*, $Value_{e_1,e_2,\ldots,e_n}(a,b)$, is the peer pressure value between agents a and b via route $e_1,e_2,\ldots,e_n$, which connects agents a and b. I.e., $a,e_1,e_2,\ldots,e_n,b \in R_{n+1}(a,b)$, where e_i is an edge.

(1) if agents a and b are directly connected, the value is defined in social peer network matrix;

(2) If agents a and b are not directly connected, such that is connected via route $e_1,e_2,\ldots,e_n$,

$$Value_{e_1,e_2,\ldots,e_n}(a,b) = Value(a,e_1) \cdot (\prod_{i=1}^{n-1} Value(e_i,e_{i+1})) \cdot Value(e_n,b); \quad (2)$$

where $Value(a,e_1), Value(e_i,e_{i+1})$ and $Value(e_n,b)$ is defined in the social peer network matrix. For any agent a, $Value_\varnothing(a,a) = 1$.

Agents influence one another following certain routes. For any two agents a and b, they may influence with one another at levels of the different lengths of the route.

Definition 4 *Route Set Value* between agents a and b via $R_i(a,b)$, denoted by $RouteSetValue_i(a,b)$ is

$$RouteSetValue_i(a,b) = \max\left[\sum_{\text{for all } r_i \in R_i(a,b)} Value_{r_i}(a,b), \ 1 \right] \quad (3)$$

Route Set Value is reciprocal, i.e., agent a's capability to influence is the same as agent b's capability to influence. The influences between any two agents are the effects of the influences from all lengths of the routes.

Definition 5 *Total Value* between agents a and b, denoted by $TotalValue(a,b)$ is:

$$TotalValue(a,b) = \sum_{i=1}^{i=d} W_i \bullet RouteSetValue_i(a,b) \quad (4)$$

where d is the distance between agents and W_i is the relative weight for influence, which satisfies $W_1 + W_2 + \cdots + W_d = 1$, $W_1 \gg W_2 \gg \cdots \gg W_d$.

Intuitively, the nearer the distance, the more influence the agent has. The reason that we only calculate up to distance d instead of the largest distance between the agents is that we assume that if the connection distance is too long, the influence is negligible. For practical reasons, we suggest keeping d under 3.

Definition 6 The *Average Pressure* for an agent in a social network for agent a, denoted by $Average \Pr essure(a)$, is the average of influence value of agent a with its neighbors with whom it has direct connections.

$$Average \Pr essure(a) = \sum_{for\ All\ agent\ b} TotalValue(a,b) \Big/ num\_connection \qquad (5)$$

where $num\_connection$ is the number of direct connects that agent a has.

Agents consider peer network influence based on both average pressure from the connections and the number of connections.

Definition 7 Social *network peer value*, denoted by $NetworkPeerValue(a)$, is the weighted sum of number of connections and the average pressure of connections. I.e.,

$$NetworkPeerValue(a) = w_1 \cdot Average \Pr essure(a) + w_2 \cdot num\_connection \qquad (6)$$

where w_1 and w_2 are relative weights and $w_1 + w_2 = 1.0$.

If two agents have the same strength of connection, the agent who has more connections has more influence and vice versa. If we assume that we have a total of M agents and N roles, each agent has a role and each role requires m abilities. We expect each agent to adopt one and only one of the roles, and a role can be adopted by any number of agents. Besides, the agents have different pressure relationship in the peer network. They also have different capabilities, say agent A_i has m abilities, denoted by $C_{A_i}^1, ..., C_{A_i}^m$, where $0 \le C_{A_i}^j \le 1$, $1 \le j \le m$. Whereas roles require various capabilities, say role R_j requires m abilities, denoted by $C_{R_j}^1, ..., C_{R_j}^m$ for the agents to perform, where $0 \le C_{R_j}^k \le 1$, $1 \le k \le m$. When an agent adopts a role without considering social network, the agent will find the role that best matches its capabilities. Intuitively, the agent will take the roles that it fits best.

Definition 8 The *best match value*, denoted by BestMatchValue, for agent i is as follows:

$$BestMatchValue(i) = \max \left[\sum_{k=1}^{m} \left(\frac{C_{A_i}^k}{C_{R_1}^k} \right), ..., \sum_{k=1}^{m} \left(\frac{C_{A_i}^k}{C_{R_N}^k} \right) \right] \qquad (7)$$

where m is the total number of capabilities that the agents have and the role requires. N is the number of roles.

Each agent will compare its abilities with each role, and find the best role it fits. However, more realistically influences of peer network on agent's role adoption should also be considered. When an agent chooses the same role as the agents that have strong social connection with it, the agent can exchange more experience with others, gain more utility, and have higher motivation to perform the role. Therefore, the strategy of role adoption is based on both agent capability match and the social peer network influence.

Definition 9 The *role utility* for agent i is the weighted sum of capability match and social network influence:

$$RoleUtility(i) = W_1 \cdot BestMatchValue(i) + W_2 \cdot NetworkPeerValue(i) \qquad (8)$$

where $BestMatchValue(i)$ is the role adoption value that the agent i will adopt the role that best matches its capability; here, $. W_1 + W_2 = 1.0$.

Here we assume all agents have the same weights for best match versus influence. This will help us isolate the effects of these weights in a community of agents who share a similar weight. This is a simplifying assumption in our model. Generally, individuals will have different weights.

When performing a role long enough, the agent will exchange the experience with some other agents who perform the same type of role. So agents will get experience gain after performing the roles.

Definition 10 *Experience gain*, denoted by $ExperienceGain(a)$, for agent a is:

$$ExperienceGain(a) = W_1 \cdot t + W_2 \cdot \sum_{\text{for all agent i}} TotalValue(a,i) \qquad (9)$$

where t is the duration for performing the role, W_1 and W_2 are relative weights and $W_1 + W_2 = 1.0$.

Definition 11 *Intra Role Tension* between a pair of agents a_i and a_j, denoted by $IntraRoleTension(a_i, a_j)$, is defined as follows:

a) $IntraRoleTension(a_i, a_j) = 1 - Influence\_value(a_i, a_j)$, if a_i and a_j adopt same type of roles;

b) $IntraRoleTension(a_i, a_j) = 0$, otherwise, i.e., if a_i, a_j have different roles.

Whereas influence value is the amount of pressure and agreement two agents have about a role, intra role tension is the compliment of this value and reflects the disagreement between them. When influence is at maximum, this value is at 1.0 and there is no disagreement. Values below 1.0 leave some room for disagreement.

Definition 12 *Intra Role Tension for a group of agents* $A = \{a_i \mid a_i \in A\}$, denoted by $RoleConflict(A)$, with the same type of role is defined as follows:

$$RoleConflict(A) = \sum_{i=1}^{i=n} \sum_{j=1}^{j=n} IntraRoleTension(a_i, a_j), \tag{10}$$

where n is the size of group of agents A, $a_i, a_j \in A, i \neq j$

Definition 13 *Role Satisfaction* for an agent *a*, denoted by *RoleSatisfaction(a)*, is the difference between the sum of the influence value of the same type of relationship and the sum of the influence value of the different type of relationships, divided by the number of the relationships.

$$RoleSatisfaction(a) = (\sum_{b_i \in B} NetworkPeerValue(a, b_i) - \sum_{c_i \in C} NetworkPearValue(a, c_i))/n$$

$$\tag{11}$$

where B is the group of agents that adopt the same type of roles as agent a, C is the group of agent that adopt the different type of roles of agent a. "*n*" is the number of agent *a*'s relationships.

3   Experiments

We designed and implemented a system that simulated a town in an isolated island. We considered three roles of *Doctor, Rancher,* and *Farmer*, which we will refer to them as R1, R2, and R3. Let's assume three general capabilities C1, C2, and C3. We used a role capability table (not shown) to specify how much (a number between 0.0 and 1.0) capability is required for each of the three roles. Each agent is assumed to have a static capability. We used an agent capability table (not shown) to specify these static values. There may not be a perfect match between agents and roles. However, agents match roles to differing degrees. The simplest role adoption strategy for an agent is based on best match between its capability and needed roles. When considering social influences, agents will change roles they adopt based on both social pressures and their matching ability. The social network strength of influence between agents is randomly generated among agents. The following is the basic control loop for each agent:

```
1. Initialize Role-Capability, Agent-Capability tables
2. Loop
     a.  Sense global knowledge
     b.  adopt role
     c.  Perform role
     d.  Consider changing environmental factors
         that affect role adoption
```

Intra Role Tensions between agents is the first parameter we measured. As we defined earlier (see definition 11), intra role tension is a dissimilarity measure (i.e., disagreement) among a group of agents. When agents adopt the same type of roles, we consider them as a group. For each agent in this group, we measure the influence between this agent with all the other agents pair-wise in the group.   If there are influences between two agents, we measured the intra role tension as 1.0 minus the current influence. For example, if the agent shares no influence with other agents but adopts the same type of role, the pair-wise intra role tension is 1.0. If two agents have strong agreement such as 1.0, when they adopt the same type of role, the intra role tension between them is 0.0. We consider all pair-wise agents to calculate the intra role tensions, and sum them together to get group intra role tensions.

We assigned a weight for considering social network to balance role capability match and peer influence. The results shown as Figure 1 indicate that the intra role tension has been steadily decreased when considering the influence of social network. Without considering social network influence, the intra role tension remains unchanged. Within each simulation cycle, each agent considers role adoption with influences from its social peer network. Therefore, in each cycle the number of role considerations is the same as the number of agents. For example, in a simulation with 10 agents, each simulation cycle will have nine considerations for an agent, each for an individual agent.

In the above experiment, we assigned the weight for considering social network at 0.33, while we assigned the weight of considering ability matching is 0.67. We found out that when the number of agents increases in our experiment, the effect of peer influence network become stronger. If we maintain the same weights for considering social network influences, say 0.33 and 0.67, all of the agents are very likely to play the same type of roles, and the intra role tension for the agents will be high. When the number of agents increases (i.e., a larger population), the weight assignment for social network should be adjusted to lower tension. In our experiments, we explored the weights assignments in order to minimize the intra role tensions. We determined what weighting values in equation in definition 9 minimized intra role tension. There is an optimal set of weights that minimize the intra role tensions within the system. Figure 2 shows the relationship between the optimal weight for considering peer network in role adoption and the number of agents.

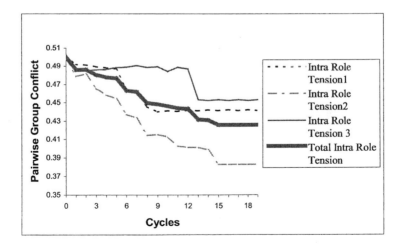

Fig. 1. Intra role tensions with considering Social Network "Cycles" are simulation cycles

[7]   Ch'ng, S., & Padgham, L. (1997). From Roles to Teamwork: a framework and architecture. *Journal of Applied Artificial Intelligence,* Vol. 12, special issue on Robocup, 211-231.

[8]   Contractor, N.S., and Eisenberg, E. M., Communication networks and new media organizations, Chapter 7 in *Organizations and Communications Technology*, Janet Fulk, Charles Steinfield (eds.), Sage Publications, Newbury Park, 1990, pp. 143-171.

[9]   Fasli., M. (2001). On Commitments, Roles, and Obligations. *2nd International workshop on Central and Eastern Europe on Multi-agent Systems* (CEEMAS 2001), 93-102.

[10]   Freeman, L.C., Centrality in Social Networks: Conceptual Clarification, *Social Networks*, No.1, 1979, pp. 215-239.

[11]   Freeman, L.C., Roeder, D., Mulholland, R. R., Centrality in Social Network: II Experimental Results, *Social Networks*, Vol.2, 1980, pp 119-141.

[12]   French, John R.P.Jr, A formal theory of social power. The Psychological Review 63, 1956.

[13]   Friedkin, Noah E., A formal theory of social power. In *Journal of Mathematical Sociology*, 1986, Vol. 12(2) pp. 103-126.

[14]   Heider, F. (1958). The Psychology of Interpersonal Relations. New York: Wiley.

[15]   Hubner, J.F., Sichman, J.S., Boissier, O., Towards a model which comprises the structural, functional, and deontic aspects of a MAS organization. In: Proc. 1st International Joint Conference on Autonomous Agents and Multi-Agent Systems (AAMAS'02), pages 501-502, Bologna, Italy, July 2002.

[16]   Osburn, J., An overview of social role valorization theory.   In *The International Social Role Valorization Journal*, 3(1), 7-12, 1998.

[17]   Kemper, Theodore D. Power, Status, and Emotions: A Sociological Contribution to A Psychophysiological Domain, In Approaches to Emotion, edited by Klaus R. Scherer, Paul Ekman. 375. Hillsdale, N.J.: Lawrence Erlbaum Associates, 1984.

[18]   Radcliffe-Brown, A.R., On Social Structure, In *Journal of the Royal Anthropological Society of Great Britain and Ireland*, Vol. 70, 1940, pp. 1-12.

[19]   Scott J., *Social Network Analysis: A Handbook.* Sage Publication, April 11, 1996.

[20]   Stokman F. N., Social Networks. *International Encyclopedia of the Social & Behavioral Science*, Editors-in-chief, NJ Smelser & PB Baltes, 2001.

[21]   Tambe, M., Scerri, P., & Pynadath, D. V. (2002). Adjustable Autonomy: from theory to implementation. *In Workshop on Autonomy Delegation and Control* (Hexmoor and Falcone Eds), AAAI-2002, Edmonton, CA, AAAI Press.

[22]   Trzebiatowski, G. L., The role concept for agents in multi-agent systems.

[23]   Wolfensberger, W., The principle of normalization in human services. Toronto: National Institutue on Mental Retardation, 1972.

[24]   Zack, Michael H., Researching Organizational Systems using Social Network Analysis. In *Proceedings of the 33rd Hawaii International Conference on System Sciences*, Maui, Hawaii, January, 2000.

From Social Agents to Multi-agent Systems: Preliminary Report

Maria Fasli

University of Essex, Department of Computer Science
Wivenhoe Park, Colchester CO4 3SQ, UK
mfasli@essex.ac.uk

Abstract. This paper presents a formal analysis of social interaction within a multi-agent system. The concept of a social agent is introduced as the elemental building block of multi-agent systems. Social agents can be individual (BDI) agents or aggregations of agents (groups). The structure of a multi-agent system and that of social agents is formally characterised in terms of roles and the relationships between them. Stability and regulation of activity in a multi-agent system and within social agents can be accounted for by means of a complex web of roles, commitments, obligations and rights.

1 Introduction

Agents rarely act in isolation; in contrast they are increasingly required to act as elements of large and complex systems and cooperate and coordinate with a number of other agents. As a consequence, theoretical and practical research in multi-agent systems needs to address issues such as stable group activity and regulation of behaviour that arise in cooperative problem solving and teamwork. To this end, a rich ontology of social and collective attitudes such as mutual intentions and commitments [1, 3, 6, 12, 15] as well as normative concepts such as obligations [4, 8] is required. Moreover, organisational concepts such as roles and relationships have been proven particularly useful in formal theories of multi-agent systems [2, 5] as well as in their analysis and design [11, 16, 17].

This paper presents a formal analysis of the dynamics of social interaction in a multi-agent system based on organisational concepts such as roles and other attitudes such as commitments and obligations. The underpinning idea is that the building blocks of multi-agent systems are *social agents* whose structure and that of a multi-agent system can be formally defined in terms of roles and relationships between them. Stability and regulation of activity in a multi-agent system and within social agents can be accounted for by means of a complex web of roles commitments and normative attitudes. The paper is structured as follows. In the following section formal definitions of a social agent and a multi-agent system are provided. The three subsequent sections present the logical preliminaries including the BDI axiomatisation and the basic group attitudes. Sections 6, 7 and 8 tackle obligations and rights, commitments and roles respectively. The paper ends with the conclusions and pointers to future work.

V. Mařík et al. (Eds): CEEMAS 2003, LNAI 2691, pp. 111–121, 2003.

2   The Core of Multi-agent Systems: Social Agents

Central to the approach advocated here is the idea that a multi-agent system is an aggregation of *social agents*. A social agent can be an individual agent (BDI) or an aggregation of agents (group). Social agents do not act in isolation; on the contrary, their decisions and actions affect other agents (even unintentionally) and they are themselves affected by those of others. There are different types of social agents: a football team is a social agent, but so is a department within a university and an individual agent such as a lecturer. Social agents can play a variety of roles in a multi-agent system and these roles and the relationships between them is what defines the structure of a multi-agent system. Moreover, agents within a social agent may play a variety of roles, but they will at least have one role, while a social agent itself will have at a least one role in relation to other social agents. The roles that can be played by agents within a social agent as well as their structure and their interactions, i.e. the relationships between roles, is what identifies and characterises a social agent.

Given a particular problem domain the sort *Roles* represents all the possible roles that can be played by social agents and the sort *RelTypes* includes all the valid generic relationship types that can exist between roles, $RelTypes \subseteq Roles \times Roles$. A *social agent structure* is a generic description of the roles and the relationships between them in a particular type of social agent. Formally, a social agent structure is a tuple $SAS_i = \langle R_i, RI_i \rangle$ where R_i is a finite set of roles $R_i \subseteq Roles$, i.e. R_i is the set of all possible roles that can be played by agents within a social agent of this type and RI_i is the relationship interaction graph that specifies all the valid generic relationship types between roles, $RI_i : R_i \times R_i \rightarrow RelTypes$. Each edge of the graph represents a relationship type (a, b) between roles $a, b \in R_i$. For the special case that a social agent is a singleton, the set of roles is the empty set $R_i = \{\emptyset\}$ and the interaction graph has no edges. The definition of a social agent structure is a flexible one. It only describes possible roles and relationships between them. The exact form of a social agent depends on how agents interact with one another as they come to form the social agent. Some of the roles and relationships may not be instantiated for example. Moreover, this definition does not place conditions on how a social agent is held together in terms of commitments (see section 7).

The sort *SATypes* is a set of constants representing the generic social agent structures within a domain. If *SAS* is the set of all generic social agent structures, then the function *ST* assigns a unique *SATypes* constant to every social agent structure $SAS_i \in SAS$, that is $ST : SAS \longrightarrow SATypes$. For instance, consider the generic social agent structure for a football team $SAS_{FT} = \langle R_{FT}, RI_{FT} \rangle$. The set of roles for such a type of social agent may include roles such as *coach, goalkeeper, defender*.... while the interaction graph describes the generic relationships between these roles. If *FT* is a constant that identifies this particular type of social agent structure and *Aces* is an instantiation of a football team structure, the predicate *TypeOf* is used in order to express that the social agent *Aces* is of type *FT* ($TypeOf(Aces, FT)$).

A multi-agent system is a tuple $MA = \langle SAgents, Roles, SG \rangle$ where $Roles$ is as above, $SAgents$ is the set of all social agents and SG is the structure interaction graph in which for each edge $S_a S_b$ we have $S_a, S_b \in SAgents$ and $a, b \in Roles$. For example, a multi-agent system representing a university is $MA_{UNI} = \langle SAgents_{UNI}, Roles_{UNI}, SG_{UNI} \rangle$ where $Roles_{UNI}$ is the set of roles that can be played by social agents within this multi-agent system. Among the possible roles may be $Finance$, $Accommodation$, $Library$, $Lecturer$, etc. $SAgents_{UNI}$ are all the social agents and SG_{UNI} is the interaction graph. Accordingly, there is an edge between the $Section_{Accommodation}$ and $Section_{Finance}$ since these two types of social agents clearly interact within an establishment such as a university.

3   Formal Language and Semantics

The work presented here is formulated within the BDI paradigm in which agents are considered to have beliefs, desires and intentions. The basic ideas and the extensions made to the original framework are briefly described here; the reader is referred to [13, 14] for the full details of the BDI paradigm.

The logical language $\mathcal{L}$ includes, apart from the usual connectives and quantifiers, three modal operators B, D, and I for expressing beliefs, desires and intentions respectively. The sorts $Roles$, $RelTypes$ and $SATypes$ are as described in the previous section. In addition to the $SAgents$ sort which is the set of social agents, there are two more: $Agents$ and $Other$. $Agents$ is the set of individual agents and in fact, each individual agent is considered to be a social agent and is included as such in $SAgents$ and $Other$ indicates all the other objects/individuals in the universe of discourse.

The framework includes a branching temporal component based on CTL* logic, in which the belief-, intention-, and desire-accessible worlds are themselves branching time structures. The operator $inevitable$ is said to be true of a path formula γ at a particular point in a time-tree if γ is true of all paths emanating from that point. O-formulas are wffs that contain no positive occurrences of $inevitable$ outside the scope of the modal operators B, D and I. The temporal operators $optional$, $\bigcirc$ (next), $\diamond$ (eventually), $\square$ (always), U (until) are also included. Furthermore the operators: $succeeds(e)$, $fails(e)$, $does(e)$, $succeeded(e)$, $failed(e)$ and $done(e)$, express the present and past success or failure of an event e. Finally, the operator $\in$ expresses membership in a social agent.

Semantics is given in terms of possible worlds relativised to time points. A model for $\mathcal{L}$ is a tuple $M = \langle W, E, T, \prec, S, U, \mathcal{B}, \mathcal{D}, \mathcal{I}, \pi, SAS, MA \rangle$ where W is a set of worlds, E is a set of primitive event types, T is a set of time points, $\prec$ is a binary relation on time points, S is the set of all situations $S \subseteq W \times T$, U is the universe of discourse which is a tuple itself $U = \langle U_{Agents}, U_{SAgents}, U_{Other}, U_{Roles}, U_{RelTypes}, U_{SATypes} \rangle$, $\mathcal{B}$ is the belief accessibility relation, $\mathcal{B} : U_{Agents} \to \wp(W \times T \times W)$, and $\mathcal{D}$ and $\mathcal{I}$ similarly for desires and intentions and finally π interprets the atomic formulas of the language. MA and SAS are as described in the previous section. Satisfaction of formulas is given in terms of a model M a mapping v of variables into elements of U, a world w and a time point t (i.e. a situation w_t):

$M_{v,w_t} \models P(\tau_1, ...\tau_k)$ iff $< v(\tau_1), ..., v(\tau_k) > \in \pi(P^k, w_t)$

$M_{v,w_t} \models \neg\phi$ iff $M_{v,w_t} \not\models \phi$

$M_{v,w_t} \models \phi \wedge \psi$ iff $M_{v,w_t} \models \phi$ and $M_{v,w_t} \models \psi$

$M_{v,w_t} \models \forall x\phi$ iff $\forall d \in U$, $M_{v[d/x],w_t} \models \phi$

$M_{v,w_t} \models B(i,\phi)$ iff $\forall w'_t$ such that $\mathcal{B}_i(w_t, w'_t)$, $M_{v,w'_t} \models \phi$

$M_{v,w_t} \models (\tau_1 = \tau_2)$ iff $\| \tau_1 \| = \| \tau_2 \|$

$M_{v,w_t} \models (i \in si)$ iff $\| i \| \in \| si \|$

$M_{v,w_t} \models optional(\phi)$ iff $\exists$ a fullpath $w_{t_0}, w_{t_1}, ..$ such that $M_{v,w_{t_0},w_{t_1},..} \models \phi$

$M_{v,w_t} \models succeeded(e)$ iff $\exists t_0$ such that $S_w(t_0, t_1) = e$

Similarly for the other connectives and operators.

4   The BDI Component Axiomatisation

In the BDI paradigm an agent's cognitive state is represented by beliefs, desires and intentions. For all three notions, the K axiom and the necessitation rule which hold in normal modal logics regardless of any restrictions imposed on the accessibility relation are adopted [7]. Illustrating with belief:

B-K. $B(i,\phi) \wedge B(i,\phi \Rightarrow \psi) \Rightarrow B(i,\psi)$

B-N. if $\vdash \phi$ then $\vdash B(i,\phi)$

No additional axioms are adopted for desires. For intention and belief the axiom of consistency (D) is also adopted:

B-D. $B(i,\phi) \Rightarrow \neg B(i,\neg\phi)$

Finally the positive and negative introspection axioms are included for belief:

B-S4. $B(i,\phi) \Rightarrow B(i, B(i,\phi))$

B-S5. $\neg B(i,\phi) \Rightarrow B(i, \neg B(i,\phi))$

Thus, $\mathcal{B}$ is restricted to be serial, transitive and euclidean, $\mathcal{I}$ is serial and no particular restrictions are imposed on $\mathcal{D}$. The interrelations between the three attitudes are described by a variation of the *strong realism* axioms [10]:

$I(i,\gamma) \Rightarrow B(i,\gamma)$

$D(i,\gamma) \Rightarrow \neg B(i,\neg\gamma)$

These correspond to the following semantic conditions:

C1. $\forall i \in U_{Agents}$, $\forall w_t, w'_t$ if $\mathcal{B}_i(w_t, w'_t)$ then $\exists w''_t$ s.t. $\mathcal{I}_i(w_t, w''_t)$ and $w''_t \sqsubseteq w'_t$

C2. $\forall i \in U_{Agents}$, $\forall w_t, \exists w'_t \mathcal{B}_i(w_t, w'_t)$ s.t. $\exists w''_t \mathcal{D}_i(w_t, w''_t)$ and $w''_t \sqsubseteq w'_t$

$w''_t \sqsubseteq w'_t$ means that the world w''_t is a sub-world of w'_t, that is the tree structure of w''_t is a subtree of w'_t and w''_t has the same truth assignment and accessibility relations as w'_t. By imposing this sub-world restriction between worlds the application of these axioms is restricted to O-formulas (γ) [13, 14].

5   Basic Group Attitudes

Social agents may be individuals or aggregations of agents. The fact that an agent i is a member of a social agent si is expressed simply as $(i \in si)$. The following set-theoretic relations are introduced:

$(sj \subseteq si) \equiv_{def} \forall i(i \in sj) \Rightarrow (i \in si)$

$(sj \subset si) \equiv_{def} (sj \subseteq si) \wedge \neg(sj = si)$

$singleton(si, i) \equiv_{def} \forall j(j \in si) \Rightarrow (j = i)$

$singleton(si) \equiv_{def} \exists i \; singleton(si, i)$

In order to be able to reason about a social agent's information state two modal operators $EB(si, \phi)$ and $MB(si, \phi)$ are introduced for "Every member of social agent si believes ϕ" and "ϕ is a mutual belief among the members of social agent si" respectively. Following [7] every member of a social agent believes ϕ if and only if every individual agent i in this social agent believes ϕ:

$EB(si, \phi) \equiv_{def} \forall i(i \in si) \Rightarrow B(i, \phi)$

Then ϕ is mutually believed by a social agent if every member believes it, and every member believes that every member believes it, and every member believes that every member believes that every member believes it..., and so on. Since infinite formulas cannot be expressed in the language, let $EB^1(si, \phi)$ be an abbreviation for $EB(si, \phi)$ and $EB^k(si, \phi)$ for $k \geq 1$ be an abbreviation for $EB(si, EB^{k-1}(si, \phi))$. If EB^k expresses the k-th level of nesting of belief of the agents in social agent si, then the social agent has mutual belief of ϕ:

$M_{v,w_t} \models MB(si, \phi)$ iff $M_{v,w_t} \models EB^k(si, \phi), k = 1, 2, ..$

Now define w'_t to be belief-si-reachable from w_t if there is a path in the Kripke model from w_t to w'_t along accessibility arrows $\mathcal{B}_i$ that are associated with members $i \in si$ [7]. Then the following property holds:

$M_{v,w_t} \models MB(si, \phi)$ iff $M_{v,w'_t} \models \phi$ for all w'_t that are belief-si-reachable from w_t

Using this property and the notion of reachability, the following axiom and rule can be soundly added to the KD45$_n$ system of belief:

$MB(si, \phi) \Leftrightarrow EB(si, \phi \wedge MB(si, \phi))$

From $\phi \Rightarrow EB(si, \psi \wedge \phi)$ infer $\phi \Rightarrow MB(si, \psi)$

Next two modal operators EI and MI to express what every member of a social agent intends and what is mutually intended by a social agent respectively, are introduced. In a similar way to EB, every member of si intends ϕ, if and only if every individual agent intends ϕ:

$EI(si, \phi) \equiv_{def} \forall i(i \in si) \Rightarrow I(i, \phi)$

Axioms similar to those for the EB and MB operators are then adopted accordingly. If the social agent is a singleton (individual agent) then the MB and MI operators reduce to their individual constituents. In other words, the mutual belief of a social agent which is an individual is simply its belief, and its mutual intention is simply an intention.

6   Obligations and Rights

General obligations are expressed via an obligation operator O that prefixes propositions $\phi, \psi, ...$ as in standard deontic logic (SDL). A formula $O(\phi)$ is read "It ought to be the case that ϕ". Relativised obligations are expressed via an operator $O(si, sj, \phi)$, read as "Social agent si is obligated to sj to bring about ϕ". An accessibility relation $\mathcal{O}$ for general obligations yields the deontically ideal worlds relative to a world w at time point t, while for relativised obligations an accessibility relation between pairs of social agents is used $\mathcal{O}^* = \{\mathcal{O}_{si,sj} | \forall si, sj \in U_{SAgents} \wedge si \neq sj\}$:

$M_{v,w_t} \models O(\phi)$ iff $\forall\ w'_t$ s.t. $\mathcal{O}(w_t, w'_t)$, $M_{v,w'_t} \models \phi$

$M_{v,w_t} \models O(si, sj, \phi)$ iff $\forall w'_t$ s.t.$\mathcal{O}_{si,sj}(w_t, w'_t)$, $M_{v,w'_t} \models \phi$

For general obligations, the D system is adopted. This ensures that deontic conflicts are not allowed, i.e. not both ϕ and $\neg\phi$ ought to be the case. The principle of veracity $(O(\phi) \Rightarrow \phi)$ is rejected since what ought to be the case may not be the case after all. For the relativised obligations operator the K_n system is adopted. As a consequence, deontic conflicts are allowed for relativised obligations. Finally, a permission operator P is defined as the dual of the general obligation operator as $P(\phi) \equiv_{def} \neg O(\neg\phi)$. It seems reasonable to suggest that if ϕ is a general obligation then each agent believes that this is the case (special constant s_0 denotes the set of all agents; the society of the domain):

$\forall i(i \in s_0) \Rightarrow (O(\phi) \Rightarrow B(i, O(\phi)))$ ~   (*)

In other words, if ϕ ought to be the case, then each agent i believes that it ought to be the case. This axiom requires the following semantic condition:

$\forall i \in U_{Agents}$, $\forall w_t, w'_t, w''_t$ if $\mathcal{B}_i(w_t, w'_t)$ and $\mathcal{O}(w'_t, w''_t)$ then $\mathcal{O}(w_t, w''_t)$

Since general obligations ought to be believed by all agents we also derive the following from (*) by the axiom defining EB and the induction rule for MB:

$O(\phi) \Rightarrow MB(s_0, O(\phi))$

This means that normative statements are mutually believed (ideally) by all agents. In addition, it seems reasonable to accept that if such an ought-to relation between a counterparty and a bearer agent is in place, then each one is aware of it and also they mutually believe that this is the case:

$O(si, sj, \phi) \Rightarrow \forall i(i \in si) \Rightarrow B(i, O(si, sj, \phi))$

$O(si, sj, \phi) \Rightarrow \forall j(j \in sj) \Rightarrow B(j, O(si, sj, \phi))$

$O(si, sj, \phi) \Rightarrow MB(\{si, sj\}, O(si, sj, \phi))$

Once a social agent si has managed to bring about the desired state of affairs for agent sj, or it has come to its attention that the state of affairs is no longer an option, it needs to take some further action in order to ensure that the counterparty agent is aware of the situation. The social agent successfully de-commits itself from a relativised obligation as follows (*communicate* is used in a generic way):

$succeeded(decommit(si, sj, inevitable\Diamond\phi)) \Rightarrow$

$(\neg O(si, sj, inevitable\Diamond\phi) \wedge done(communicate(si, sj, MB(si, \phi))))$

$\vee (\neg O(si, sj, inevitable\Diamond\phi) \wedge done(communicate(si, sj, \neg MB(si, optional\Diamond\phi)))$

$\wedge done(communicate(si, sj, \neg O(si, sj, inevitable\Diamond\phi))))$

If an obligation is not honoured, the counterparty agent may reserve the right to impose sanctions on the bearer agent. To this end, another relativised operator *Right* is introduced to describe that a social agent sj has the right ψ over another social agent si expressed as $Right(sj, si, \psi)$. No particular restrictions are imposed on the accessibility relation for this modality. The formula ψ may express the form of the sanction that sj has the right to impose on si. Obligations and rights as we will see in the subsequent sections are created pairwise. If an agent si drops a previously adopted relativised obligation towards sj, and sj

has a right over si, then sj may decide to exercise this right. Agents may have different policies on exercising rights which they may reveal or not to the other agents. An agent has a lenient strategy if it keeps its options open as to whether or not it will exercise its right over another agent:

$Right(sj, si, \psi) \wedge MB(sj, \neg O(si, sj, inevitable \diamond \phi)) \wedge$
$\neg MB(sj, \phi) \Rightarrow optional(MI(sj, optional \diamond \psi))$

On the other hand, a harsh/stringent policy means that an agent will always exercise its rights on the deviating agent:

$Right(sj, si, \psi) \wedge MB(sj, \neg O(si, sj, inevitable \diamond \phi)) \wedge$
$\neg MB(sj, \phi) \Rightarrow inevitable(MI(sj, inevitable \diamond \psi))U MB(sj, \psi)$

The agent will keep trying to bring about ψ until it actually comes to believe that it has managed to do so.

7   Commitments

Following the work of Castelfranchi [1], the view that commitments hold a group of agents together is endorsed here. However, the exact mechanism that enables this is not entirely clear since there are different types of social agents. Basically, two broad categories of social agents can be identified:

Tightly-Coupled Social Agents. Such agents have a common collective commitment or objective. This is known by every constituent agent. This collective commitment is supported by social commitments between the constituent agents and the social agent as a whole. Additional social commitments bound to roles that the agents adopt, contribute to the overall collective commitment.

Loosely-Coupled Social Agents. There may be a commitment that expresses the social agent's objective or goal which may not necessarily be known by all member agents. It is known at least by one who plays a pivotal role in the social agent, perhaps that of the manager/delegator and who coordinates the efforts of the other agents. The social agent's activity as a whole is supported by the social commitments that its members undertake towards each other.

This distinction extends to social agents of the same generic type. Consider the example of a research team consisting of a Professor and two Ph.D. students. The research team may be loosely-coupled or tightly-coupled. In the first case the Professor may have a clear idea of what needs to be accomplished and how. But he may only delegate parts of the original goal to his students who can then work independently, without having knowledge of the overall objective or even knowing about the existence and the work of one another. In the second case, the Professor may make the objective known to the entire team. In the former case, the overall objective of the team is supported by the social commitments that the students will take towards the Professor, while in the latter, the research team will actually have a collective commitment towards the objective which will be supported by the social commitments that each of the constituent members will then take towards each other. Thus social agents are flexible entities that can adapt according to the needs of their constituent agents and the tasks set before them. The formal definition of a social agent structure supports such flexibility.

Here social commitments will be expressed via an operator $SCom(si, sj, \phi)$ which is read "social agent si is committed to social agent sj to bring about ϕ". Adopting such a commitment is a rights and obligations producing act [1]:

$SCom(si, sj, \phi) \Leftrightarrow O(si, sj, \phi) \wedge Right(sj, si, \psi) \wedge MI(si, \phi) \wedge$
$MB(\{si, sj\}, (O(si, sj, \phi) \wedge MI(si, \phi) \wedge Right(sj, si, \psi)))$

Intuitively, there should be conditions under which an agent is allowed to drop its social commitments as discussed in [6]. In [9] two commitment strategies for social commitments were described, namely *blind* and *reliable*. A social agent has a *blind* social commitment strategy if it maintains its commitment until actually it believes that it has been achieved:

$SCom(si, sj, inevitable\Diamond\phi) \Rightarrow$
$inevitable(SCom(si, sj, inevitable\Diamond\phi) \ U \ MB(si, \phi))$

A social agent follows a *reliable* strategy if it keeps its commitment towards another agent as long as it believes that it is still an option:

$SCom(si, sj, inevitable\Diamond\phi) \Rightarrow inevitable(SCom(si, sj, inevitable\Diamond\phi) \ U$
$(MB(si, \phi) \vee \neg MB(si, optional\Diamond\phi)))$

A collective commitment is the internal commitment undertaken by all constituent agents of a social agent. Such a commitment seems to involve first of all social commitments on behalf of the individual members of the group towards the group, a mutual intention of the group to achieve ϕ, and finally a mutual belief that the social agent has the mutual intention ϕ:

$CCom(si, \phi) \Leftrightarrow \forall i(i \in si) \Rightarrow SCom(i, si, \phi) \wedge MI(si, \phi) \wedge MB(si, MI(si, \phi))$

8   Roles

In addition to *RelTypes* and *Roles*, the sort *Reln* is introduced. *Reln* constants represent relationship instances. E.g. if *Ray* is in a supervisor-student relationship with two different students, then these relationships will be represented by different *Reln* constant symbols. All student-supervisor relationships will be of the same *RelTypes* constant. This approach is very similar to [2].

Roles are related to relationship types via a predicate $RoleOf(a, R)$ which describes that a is one of the roles in relationship of type R. A three place predicate $In(si, a, r)$ asserts that social agent si is in role a of relationship r. Only one agent can fill a role in a given relationship at any given time:

$\forall i, j, a, r \ In(si, a, r) \wedge In(sj, a, r) \Rightarrow (si = sj)$

The roles of a relationship type are filled when any role of that type is filled (note: given a relationship r, $\hat{r}$ denotes its corresponding type):

$\forall r, \forall si, a \ In(si, a, r) \Rightarrow \forall b(RoleOf(b, \hat{r}) \Rightarrow \exists sj \ In(sj, b, r))$

To express that a role a involves the adoption of a social commitment ϕ, a new modality $RoleSCom(a, \phi)$ is introduced. No particular restrictions are imposed on the accessibility relation for this modality. If role a involves the social commitment ϕ and social agent si has the role a in relationship r, then there exists another social agent sj (different to si) that has the role b in relationship r towards whom agent si has the social commitment ϕ:

$RoleSCom(a, \phi) \wedge In(si, a, r) \Rightarrow \exists sj, b\ In(sj, b, r) \wedge SCom(si, sj, \phi) \wedge \neg(si = sj)$

An agent may decide to drop a role if it comes to believe that it has fulfilled its social commitments (e.g. a supervisor may drop its role once its Ph.D. student has succeeded in his examination), or when it believes it can no longer fulfil the commitments of its role. This may happen for a variety of reasons, for instance the agent may decide that it is not to its benefit to adhere to the role any longer, or another role is in conflict with the first one. However, the agent that decides to drop a role, needs to communicate this to the other agent:

$succeeded(droprole(si, sj, a)) \Rightarrow$
$(\neg In(si, a, r) \wedge \neg SCom(si, sj, \phi) \wedge done(communicate(si, sj, (\neg In(si, a, r) \wedge$
$\neg SCom(si, sj, inevitable \diamond \phi))))) \vee (\neg In(si, a, r) \wedge \neg SCom(si, sj, \phi) \wedge$
$done(communicate(si, sj, (\neg In(si, a, r) \wedge MB(si, \phi)))))$
$\vee(\neg In(si, a, r) \wedge \neg SCom(si, sj, \phi) \wedge done(communicate(si, sj, (\neg In(si, a, r) \wedge$
$\neg MB(si, optional \diamond \phi))))$

An agent may also decide to drop a commitment which is part of its role without dropping the role itself and perhaps accepting that a form of sanction will have to be imposed.

9   Conclusions and Future Work

This paper presented the beginnings of a formal analysis of social interaction within a multi-agent system. The approach followed here is different from current work in the literature in two essential ways. Firstly, multi-agent systems and their constituent social agents are formally defined in terms of roles and relationships between them. In particular, the definition of a social agent structure is a generic one as it allows for social agents of the same type to vary; i.e. some of the roles and relationships may not be instantiated. Secondly, roles are associated with social commitments which in turn give rise to obligations and rights. Commitments are considered to be the attitudes that hold social agents together. The type of commitment that holds an agent together depends upon the particular instantiation of a social agent structure and its conditions of creation. In this way, multi-agent systems and social agents are tied together with roles, commitments, obligations down to individual intentions and beliefs. In [11, 16, 17] roles and other organisational concepts have been used to describe the structure of multi-agent systems. Here such concepts are used to relate the macro level of interaction (societal) to the micro level (individual) in terms of the agents' cognitive state.

The issues tackled in this paper are hard theoretical issues for which there are no easy answers. As a consequence the formalism described is by no means a complete characterisation of social dynamics. There are several directions in which it needs to be extended. Firstly, this work does not account for how social agents are created in the first place. This is an essential extension which will ultimately shed some light into issues such as how different social agents are bound by different types of commitment and what happens when a social agent (aggregation) si is socially committed towards another social agent sj: who performs the action on behalf of si and who bears the responsibility if such a commitment or obligation fails. Secondly, roles within a multi-agent system and between social agents are closely related to authority relations. Thirdly, when agents adopt roles and commitments they may end up with conflicting obligations and they need to be able to express preferences over these. Finally, soundness and completeness need to be addressed.

References

[1] C. Castelfranchi. Commitments: From individual intentions to groups and organisations. In *Proceedings of the First ICMAS Conference*, pages 41–48, 1995.

[2] L. Cavedon and L. Sonenberg. On social commitments, roles and preferred goals. In *Proceedings of the Third ICMAS Conference*, pages 80–87, 1998.

[3] P. R. Cohen and H. J. Levesque. Teamwork. *Nous*, 25:485–512, 1991.

[4] F. Dignum, D. Kinny, and L. Sonenberg. Motivational attitudes of agents: On desires, obligations and norms. In *From Theory to Practice in Multi-Agent Systems, Proceedings of the Second International CEEMAS Workshop*, pages 83–92, 2002.

[5] V. Dignum, J.-J. Ch. Meyer, and H. Weigand. Towards an organizational model for agent societies using contracts. In *Proceedings of the First AAMAS Conference*, pages 694–695, 2002.

[6] B. Dunin-Keplicz and R. Verbrugge. Collective motivational attitudes in co-operative problem solving. In *Proceedings of the First International Workshop of Central and Eastern Europe on Multi-Agent Systems (CEEMAS-99)*, pages 22–41, 1999.

[7] R. Fagin, J. Y. Halpern, Y. Moses, and M. Y. Vardi. *Reasoning about Knowledge*. MIT Press, Cambridge, MA., 1995.

[8] M. Fasli. On obligations, relativised obligations and bilateral commitments. In *Proceedings of the Canadian Artificial Intelligence Conference*, pages 287–296, 2001.

[9] M. Fasli. On commitments, roles and obligations. In *From Theory to Practice in Multi-Agent Systems, Second International Workshop of Central and Eastern Europe on Multi-Agent Systems (CEEMAS-01), Revised Papers*, pages 93–102, 2002.

[10] M. Fasli. Heterogeneous BDI agents. *Cognitive Systems Research*, 4(1):1–22, 2003.

[11] J. Ferber and O. Gutknecht. A meta-model for the analysis and design of organizations in multi-agent systems. In *Proceedings of the Third ICMAS Conference*, pages 128–135, 1998.

[12] B. J. Grosz and S. Kraus. Collaborative plans for complex group action. *Artificial Intelligence*, 86(2):269–357, 1996.

[13] A. Rao and M. Georgeff. Modeling rational agents within a BDI-architecture. In *Proceedings of the Second Int. Conf. on Principles of Knowledge Representation and Reasoning*, pages 473–484, 1991.

[14] A. Rao and M. Georgeff. Decision procedures for BDI logics. *Journal of Logic and Computation*, 8(3):293–343, 1998.

[15] M. Wooldridge and N. R. Jennings. The cooperative problem-solving process. *Journal of Logic and Computation*, 9:563–592, 1999.

[16] M. Wooldridge, N. R. Jennings, and D. Kinny. The Gaia methodology for agent-oriented analysis and design. *Autonomous Agents and Multi-Agent Systems*, 3:285–312, 2000.

[17] F. Zambonelli, N. R. Jennings, and M. Wooldridge. Organisational abstractions for the analysis and design of multi-agent systems. In P. Cinacarini and M. Wooldridge, editors, *Agent-Oriented Software Engineering*, pages 127–141, 2001.

DAML-Based Policy Enforcement for Semantic Data Transformation and Filtering in Multi-agent Systems

Niranjan Suri[1,2], Jeffrey M. Bradshaw[1], Mark Burstein[3], Andrzej Uszok[1], Brett Benyo[3], Maggie Breedy[1], Marco Carvalho[1], David Diller[3], Renia Jeffers[1], Matt Johnson[1], Shri Kulkarni[1], and James Lott[1]

[1] Institute for Human and Machine Cognition, University of West Florida
{nsuri,jbradshaw,auszok,mbreedy,mcarvalho}@ai.uwf.edu
{rjeffers,mjohnson,skulkarni,jlott}@ai.uwf.edu
[2] Lancaster University
[3] BBN Technologies
{burstein,bbenyo,ddiller}@bbn.com

Abstract. This paper describes an approach to runtime policy-based control over information exchange that allows a far more fine-grained control of these dynamically discovered agent interactions. The DARPA Agent Markup Language (DAML) is used to represent policies that may either filter messages based on their semantic content or transform the messages to make them suitable to be released. Policy definition, management, and enforcement are realized as part of the KAoS architecture. The solutions presented have been tested in the Coalition Agents Experiment (CoAX) - an experiment involving coalition military operations.

1 Introduction

Software agents have been proposed as a solution to integrate existing heterogeneous and stovepiped information systems. Agent and service description mechanisms, discovery and matchmaking services, and agent communication languages all contribute to agents achieving ad-hoc and dynamic interoperability at runtime as opposed to at design time. Mechanisms such as DAML services and the CoABS Grid make it possible for agents to dynamically interoperate thereby increasing their effectiveness. These capabilities extend agent autonomy to encompass communication and information exchange. However, in sensitive or critical application areas such as the military or competitive business environments involving proprietary information this kind of transparent interoperability raises concerns about the nature of the information being exchanged. The dynamic and autonomous nature of this process complicates the task of system designers who wish to maintain control over the flow of information to and from their agents.

This paper describes an approach to provide runtime policy-based control over information exchange. Two different control mechanisms are discussed: semantic (content-based) filtering of messages as well as in-stream transformation

V. Mařík et al. (Eds): CEEMAS 2003, LNAI 2691, pp. 122–135, 2003.

of messages. Both of these control mechanisms are driven by policies at runtime. These mechanisms allow a far more fine-grained control over dynamic and autonomous agent interactions than a suite of policies created at design time, before all possible interactions are known. With such an approach, we hope to increase the confidence with which system designers will adopt agent-based approaches to building dynamic, heterogeneous systems.

Central to our approach is the KAoS architecture which provides a set of services for policy-based control over agent behavior. KAoS provides a framework for policy definition, management, distribution, and enforcement. The capabilities described in this paper have been realized as extensions within the KAoS framework which uses the DARPA Agent Markup Language (DAML) to represent policies. Our current implementation operates on top of the DARPA Control of Agent-based Systems (CoABS) Grid, which provides agent registration, lookup, and messaging services. However, the solution is portable to other platforms that provide the same basic services. Finally, the Nomads mobile agent system and the Flexible Data Feeds Framework (FlexFeed) are used to realize the enforcement mechanisms.

The rest of the paper is organized as follows. Section two provides an overview of the CoABS Grid, DAML, KAoS, Nomads, and FlexFeed components. Section three describes the Coalition Agents Experiment (CoAX) scenario that motivated the development of these capabilities. Section four describes the implementation of the semantic filtering capability. Section five describes the implementation of the dynamic transformation capability. Finally, section six concludes with a summary and discusses future work.

2   Components Overview

2.1   CoABS Grid

The DARPA CoABS Grid is an integration platform designed to support runtime interoperability of software agent systems[8][10]. The CoABS Grid was developed under the auspices of the DARPA Control of Agent-based Systems program. It is designed to be an agent-friendly layer on top of the Jini framework[12]. The CoABS Grid provides, among other capabilities, agent registration, lookup, and messaging.

Agent registration is handled by placing a descriptor for an agent along with a proxy for that agent into the Jini Lookup Service (LUS). Agent lookup is achieved by passing a partial descriptor to the Grid which then returns a set of proxies for the matching agents. Once a proxy to an agent has been retrieved, a message may be sent to the agent by invoking a method on the target agent's proxy.

The Grid also provides a logging service to keep track of the message traffic and a GUI administration tool to help configure and startup the Grid services, visualize registered agents, and perform other kinds of monitoring operations.

2.2 DAML

The DARPA Agent Markup Language (DAML)[9] is a semantic representation language jointly developed by the DARPA DAML program and the World Wide Web Consortium (W3C)[3]. Built on top of RDF, a description language developed by W3C and its contributing members, DAML provides a capability to describe classes, properties, and descriptions built using those in a syntax based on XML and SGML. A key notion in RDF and DAML is that there is a universal namespace built on URI's, so that ontologies developed at different locations and published at different locations on the web can refer to each other. DAML enhances RDF by providing a formal semantics, and includes additional constructs for indicating such things as the equivalence or disjointness of different classes, key concepts required to do useful classification inferences. Within the DAML program, a group of researchers has developed DAML-S[1][2], an ontology for describing web and agent services. This ontology, consisting of separate parts for service profiles (advertising services), service process models (including semantic descriptions of what are essentially messaging APIs), and service groundings, that describe how atomic processes are to be mapped into various messaging formats such as provided by SOAP, HTML, the CoABS Grid, and so forth. We make extensive use of both DAML and DAML-S in the examples described in this paper.

2.3 KAoS

KAoS is a collection of componentized agent services compatible with several popular agent frameworks, including the:

- DARPA CoABS Grid[8][10]
- DARPA ALP/Ultra*Log Cougaar framework (http://www.cougaar.net)
- CORBA (http://www.omg.org)
- Voyager (http://www.recursionsw.com/osi.asp)
- Nomads [13][14].

The adaptability of KAoS is due in large part to its pluggable infrastructure based on Sun's Java Agent Services (JAS) (http://www.java-agent.org). For a full description of KAoS, the reader is referred to[4][5][6][15].

There are two key KAoS services relevant to the effort described here: *policy services* and *domain services*.

Policy services are used to define, manage, and enforce constraints assuring coherent, safe, effective, and natural interaction among teams of humans and agents. Knowledge is represented declaratively in DAML ontologies. The current version of the KAoS Policy Ontologies (KPO) defines basic ontologies for groups, actors, actions, places, messages, various entities related to actions (e.g., computing resources), and policies. We have extended these ontologies to represent simple atomic Java permissions, as well as more complex Nomads, and KAoS policy constructs. New extensions to the ontologies are continually being developed to represent domain- and application-specific information.

Domain services are used to facilitate the structuring of agents into complex organizational structures, administrative groups, and dynamic task-oriented teams that may span many hosts, platforms, and locations. Domains also provide a common point of administration and policy enforcement. Through various DAML property restrictions, a given policy can be variously scoped, for example, either to individual agents, to agents of a given class, to agents belonging to intensionally- or extensionally-defined domains or teams, or to agents running in a given physical place or computational environment (e.g., host, VM).

2.4   Nomads

Nomads is a mobile agent system for Java-based agents. Nomads provides two implementations: Oasis and Spring. Oasis incorporates a custom Java-compatible Virtual Machine (named Aroma) whereas Spring is a pure Java implementation. The Aroma VM is a clean-room VM designed to provide the enhanced capabilities of execution state capture and resource control[13][14]. Building on top of the capabilities of Aroma, Oasis provides three capabilities:

1. Strong mobility where agents can move while preserving their execution state
2. Forced mobility where, completely transparent to them, agents may be moved from one system to another by an external asynchronous request
3. Secure execution of untrusted agents while protecting the host from denial of service and other forms of attack

The Spring implementation is fully interoperable with Oasis but does not provide the above features. Spring is well-suited for lightweight applications or environments that do not support Aroma (e.g., mobile telephones or PocketPC).

In the context of this paper, the Nomads system is used to provide policy enforcement mechanisms and in particular the enforcement of the dynamic data transformation policies. The FlexFeed architecture (described below) builds on top of Nomads and uses Nomads to deploy mobile agents to act as relay and transformation nodes within a data path.

2.5   FlexFeed

The FlexFeed framework[7] is a middleware communications service for multi-agent systems. FlexFeed provides bandwidth-efficient communication while at the same time addressing the limitations of processing capabilities on nodes in the communications framework. In particular, FlexFeed is designed to support low-powered sources and sinks while processing, relaying, and transforming data in-stream on intermediate nodes. FlexFeed is opportunistic in taking advantage of available resources and can adapt to a changing environment through mobility.

At the core of FlexFeed are a set of services and interfaces that facilitate the process by which agents can request and provide data streams. Data streams are transferred between agents as a sequence of individual messages. In general, data can be generated by one or more agents (sources agents) and possibly

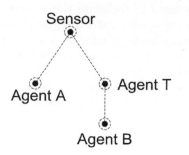

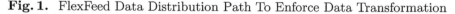

Fig. 1. FlexFeed Data Distribution Path To Enforce Data Transformation

aggregated and distributed to one or more sink agents. The role of the FlexFeed framework in this case is to continually evaluate data stream requests against communication and information release policies to establish and maintain logical distribution channels for the data streams.

The framework provides a simple API for service registration and request. The main difference is that the provisioning of the request will be checked and potentially modified, transparently to the agents, to enforce information release policies between two (or more) agents.

When an agent requests a data feed from some specific source, the framework calculates and establishes the data distribution path between the two agents. This can be a direct path between the two or, if required by policies, it can also involve relay agents through which the data will be filtered or modifed to comply with information release restrictions.

If data must be transformed between the source and destination agents to satisfy policies, the framework will deploy the necessary processing capabilities (usually in the form of a policy enforcement agent) to account for that. If the more than one agent is receiving the data, appropriate transformation agents are deployed along the path to ensure both policy enforcement and efficient bandwidth consumption with load distribution.

Figure 1 illustrates a simple example where two sink agents are receiving a data stream from the same source agent (a sensor). To satisfy local policies between the sensor and sink agent B, a transformation agent T has been deployed to participate in the data distribution path.

One important aspect to note here is that the deployment of the transformation agent T is transparent to the agent B. After requesting the feed, the agent B simply starts to receive the data stream but, for example, in lower resolution due to the policy restrictions.

There are currently two main implementations of the FlexFeed framework, one that ensures that every data packet is sent through the KAoS framework so each message is explicitly checked and evaluated against policies. A second implementation of the framework allows direct communication between the agents but only through the pre-defined data distribution path established by the framework, in compliance with the communication and information release policies provided by KAoS.

3   CoAX Binni Scenario

The Coalition Agents Experiment (CoAX) relies upon an unclassified fictitious military scenario named Binni[11] that was created to experiment with coalition military operations. Binni is set in the year 2012 and involves three imaginary countries in Africa - Binni, Gao, and Agadez. Due to a conflict in the region between these three countries, a multinational UN peacekeeping force is brought in stop the conflict. The multinational force includes the United States, the United Kingdom, Canada, and Australia. During the course of the scenario, a fourth imaginary country - Arabello - is called upon to join the coalition. The Binni scenario provides a rich and militarily-relevant setting for experimenting with agent-based systems for coalition operations.

One of the critical concerns in any coalition operation (military or civilian) involves protection of sensitive or proprietary information. The Binni scenario models the complexities and nuances of the relationships between different countries that make up the coalition peacekeeping force. For example, the US, UK, and Australia have a high degree of mutual trust whereas Gao, which is also a member of the coalition, is trusted to a lesser extent. Therefore, from the perspective of one country (such as the US), there are three different scopes for information sharing: agents that are part of the US, agents that are part of the UK and Australia, and agents that are part of Gao.

Moreover, Gao starts out as a member of the coalition force but is then found to be providing misinformation to the rest of the coalition in order to advance its own private agenda. When this deception is discovered, the trust relationships are altered and the degree of information sharing between agents has to be adapted accordingly.

Finally, during the scenario Arabello joins the coalition and new trust relationships must be established between the existing coalition members and Arabello. The coalition needs to be able to effectively manage their concerns about information released by its agents to Arabello's agents and vice versa.

4   Semantic Filtering Based on Message Types

In some situations, restricting agent communication based solely on attributes of the sending or receiving agent may be a too coarse grained form of control. Often, the content of the communication contains the critical features for determining if and how to filter the communication. For example, one might wish to restrict the sharing of sensitive personal data or proprietary business information. Just as we have used DAML-S as the language to express the capabilities and services of agents, we use DAML to express the semantic content of the information exchanged through services. Using DAML, we present a system for specifying and enforcing a semantic content filter. This system requires no modification of source code, allowing content filters to be dynamically defined during run-time.

We have demonstrated this system as part of the CoAX technology integration experiment. In the CoAX scenario, the country of Arabello joins the coalition. Consequently, a number of new agents and agent services need to be dynamically made available to coalition agents. These agents and services are dynamically discovered, resulting in a number of new agent interactions. For example, one interaction involves a coalition agent tasked to locate a hostile submarine and an Arabello agent capable of providing sensor reports from an underwater sensor grid. As new coalition partners, Arabello system administrators dynamically allow sensor contact reports to be sent to the coalition agent, but for security reasons, restrict the range of messages that could be sent outside of the Arabello domain. The limitation, described as part of a policy represented in DAML, limits these outgoing messages to those whose content are reports about a specific class of submarine, belonging to the enemy forces, but disallowing reports on other ships, such as those of Arabello itself.

4.1   Filter Specification

In order to enable domain administrators to specify a message content filter, it first becomes necessary to access the DAML ontology describing the possible outgoing message contents. This information is available as part of the DAML-S service description for each agent: specifically, the output message property in the agent's service process model. A DAML-S process model describes, among other things, the DAML classes representing the types of each service's inputs and outputs. The approach to specification of message filters we adopted enables a KAoS domain system administrator to specify or define a subclass of the most general allowed class of input or output messages that will be permitted to be sent or received by some class of agents.

For each content filter, a GUI is dynamically generated that lets the system administrator build up a specialized class definition that will be used as a filter by comparing it to each message being sent between the classes of agents covered by the policy. If the message is subsumed by this class, then the message is permitted to be sent or received in the case of a *positive authorization* policy, or blocked in the case of a *negative authorization* policy. The specialized DAML class is created by placing additional property range restrictions on the properties of the DAML class describing the message content specified in general by the agent's service process model. For each property to be restricted, we can create two types of DAML restrictions. The first, called a *toClass* restriction, requires that the value of the property be a member of a certain DAML class, the second, called a *hasValue* restriction, requires the property to have a specific value.

KPAT, our policy administration tool, provides an interface by which a system administrator can specify policies for interactions based on the properties of services and agents discovered dynamically at run-time. For the content filtering policies, the properties of the DAML class representing the output of each service are shown to the administrator in a dynamically generated GUI, along

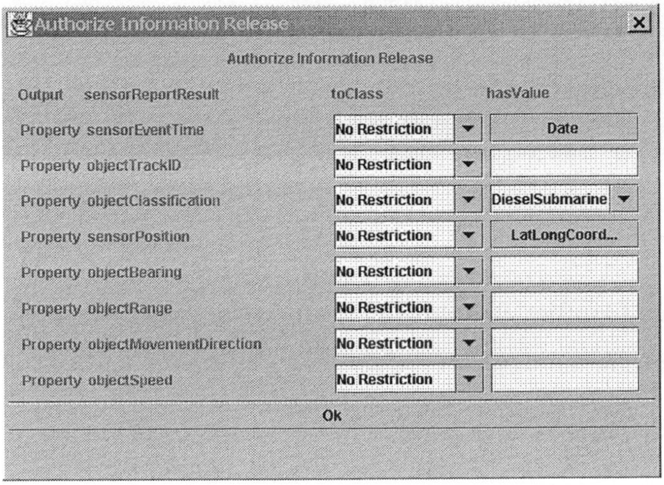

Fig. 2. The Semantic Content Filter Specification Dialog

with a *toClass* restriction editor, and a *hasValue* restriction editor. The *toClass* editor contains a list of previously-defined classes that could be selected in order to further restrict the property's range. This list is developed by expanding and linearizing the subclass tree of the DAML class defining the original *daml:range* of the property for the message class specified for the service. The *hasValue* editor allows the entry of freeform text representing the value of the property, or selecting from known instances of the range class, if it consists of a pre-defined closed list. Special graphical editors for certain DAML classes (e.g., dates and latitude/longitude coordinates) are also provided. In addition, if the *daml:range* is a *daml:Class*, meaning that the range of values of the property is a set of DAML class URIs, the possible values are automatically generated, just as for the emphtoClass restriction.

The interface generated for our CoAX example is shown in Figure 2. By selecting *DieselSubmarine* in the *hasValue* editor for the property *objectClassification*, the system administrator is restricting outgoing *sensorReportResult* messages from the Arabello agent that is the subject of the policy to those with property *objectClassification* having the value *DieselSubmarine*.

4.2   Filter Generation

Once the classes describing the message properties that indicate which messages are to be filtered is specified through this GUI, a persistent DAML class is created, representing the full set of these restrictions. This new DAML class is defined as an intersection of the original output message class and a *class expression* (specified using *daml:Restriction*) for each property that is further restricted by a toClass or hasValue expression. In our example, the resulting DAML class is given below:

```
<daml:Class rdf:ID="RestrictedASWSensorReport">
  <daml:intersectionOf rdf:parseType="daml:collection">
    <daml:Class rdf:about="\&asw;\#ASWContactReport"/>
    <daml:Restriction rdf:ID>
      <daml:onProperty rdf:resource="\&asw;\#objectClassification"/>
      <daml:toClass rdf:resource="\&vehicles;\#DieselSubmarine"/>
    </daml:Restriction>
  </daml:intersectionOf>
</daml:Class>
```

4.3   Policy Conflict Resolution

Changes or additions to policies in force, or a change in status of an actor (e.g., an agent joining a new domain or moving to a new host) or some other entity require logical inference to determine first of all which policies are in conflict and second how to resolve these conflicts. We have implemented a general-purpose algorithm within KAoS for policy conflict detection and harmonization whose initial results promise a high degree of efficiency and scalability. More details may be found in [15].

4.4   Policy Enforcement

The newly constructed harmonized policies inherit the precedence and the time of last update from the removed policy, and a pointer to the original policy is maintained so that it can be recovered if necessary as policies continue to be added or deleted in the future.

In CoAX, a message content *policy enforcer* used a message content *policy guard*, to test whether the policy applies to each message. This guard takes advantage of the Java Theorem Prover (JTP) developed at Stanford KSL. The enforcer provides to the guard the class describing the filter for which the policy is defined along with the URIs of the DAML ontologies referenced by this filtering class. Subsequently, whenever messages being transmitted between the classes of agents covered by the policy are detected, the content of those messages (also represented in DAML) is given to guard for comparison to the message filter class. This test succeeds if the message content is inferred to be an instance of the filter class. If it is, and the policy is a positive authorization policy, then the message passes the filter, and the enforcer permits it to be sent to its destination. If the policy is a negative authorization policy and the test succeeds, then the message is blocked. The reasoning provided by JTP in conjunction with a set of axioms defining the semantics of the DAML language and the sets of ontologies referenced by the message filter class and the message being tested enables the necessary reasoning about toClass and hasValue restrictions of the policy.

In order for our semantic content filters to be tested against agent messages, the message content must be a DAML instance. For the CoAX demonstration, all agent messages were specified directly in DAML, by using DAML-S in conjunction with a *grounding* mechanism that wrapped the DAML message content (a string in RDF syntax) in a CoABS Grid message. If, however, the content of the message was in some other form, a mapping would need to be defined between the raw content of the message and a semantic encoding as a DAML description in order to use this approach to message filtering.

5   Dynamic Transformation of Data Flow between Agents

Control of information release between agents may involve more than just the acceptance or rejection of messages based on policies and constraints. It is important, in some cases, to provide a mechanism to transparently modify the messages so they can satisfy the different policies for delivery in a secure and efficient way. Such a capability is especially important in critical scenarios such as military coalition operations or specialized sensor networks.

The FlexFeed framework relies on the automatic deployment of mobile agents with specialized data transformation capabilities to filter data streams so that they can satisfy policy constraints. These transformation agents act as policy enforcers that relay the data stream to the client agents. The framework is responsible for automatically customizing and deploying the agents that will constitute the distribution data path (or paths) between one or more source and sink agents.

The use of mobile agents as processing elements is an important feature of the FlexFeed framework, providing several additional capabilities such as: a) enabling the easy deployment of customized transformation code into intermediary nodes, and b) supporting the movement of transformation agents between nodes while retaining its state and redirecting resources (such as TCP connections) as needed.

Within the CoAX scenario, the need for data transformation arises when Arabello joins the coalition. As the scenario progresses, Arabello needs to obtain data from a Magnetic Anomaly Detection (MAD) sensor onboard an Australian ship. By default, policies do not allow any communication between agents in Arabello and agents in a particular country.

Direct communication between the to domains is not allowed but given the circumstances, the domain managers decide to allow a specific data feed to be provided as long as the full capabilities of the Australian sensor are not revealed to Arabello.

At this point, a new policy must be added to allow restricted communication between the nodes. KPAT is used by the Australian system administrator to create a new customized policy for data transfer. In this example, the policy refers to restrictions on video resolution given that the MAD data is transmitted as a series of images from the Australian sensor. To make this data available to Arabello, the resolution and the frame rate must be dropped, since the actual capabilities of the Australian sensor are classified.

The new policy is specialized to the type of data be transmitted. Because it is specific in terms of image resolution and frame rate, the policy can be added using a custom editor made available through a special pop-up menu in KPAT.

134   Niranjan Suri et al.

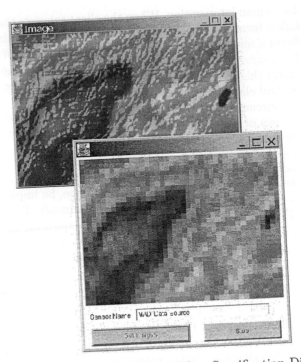

Fig. 5. The Semantic Content Filter Specification Dialog

entity, administrative domain, organization, or country. Incorporation of mechanisms such as those described in this paper are essential to providing (human) system administrators the control and the confidence to use agent-based architectures in real-world scenarios.

We are investigating extending our semantic content filters in order to handle more complex restrictions than was possible using constraints on individual message properties. In many cases this pushes the limits of DAML expressiveness as well as requiring extensions to the set of axioms used by JTP in order to test for other types of restrictions. For example, in the CoAX domain, it would be useful to allow only contact reports where the object position is inside a certain region, specified by a set of latitude/longitude points. The mathematical relationship between a point and a polygonal region cannot be expressed directly in DAML. Furthermore, the computation required is best done by functional attachment to an axiom, rather than using logical inference. We are currently working on ways to bring this kind of filtering within the range of the overall policy enforcement mechanism.

We are also working on additional types of transformation agents and the corresponding policy editors for KPAT.

References

[1] A. Ankolenkar, M. Burstein, J.R. Hobbs, O. Lassila, D. Martin, S. McIlraith, S. Narayanan, M. Paolucci, T.R. Payne, K. Sycara, and H. Zeng. DAML-S: Semantic markup for web services. In *Proceedings of the International Semantic Web Working Symposium (SWWS)*, July 2001.

[2] A. Ankolenkar, M. Burstein, J.R. Hobbs, O. Lassila, D. Martin, S. McIlraith, S. Narayanan, M. Paolucci, T.R. Payne, K. Sycara, and H. Zeng. DAML-S: Web service description for the semantic web. In *Proceedings of the First International Semantic Web Conference (ISWC)*, 2002.

[3] T. Berners-Lee, J. Hendler, and O. Lassila. The semantic web. In *Scientific American*, 2001.

[4] J.M. Bradshaw, S. Dutfield, P. Benoit, and J.D. Woolley. KAoS: Toward an industrial-strength open agent architecture. In J. Bradshaw, editor, *Software Agents*, pages 375–418. AAAI/MIT Press, 1997.

[5] J.M. Bradshaw, M. Greaves, H. Holmback, W. Jansen, T. Karygiannis, B. Silverman, N. Suri, and A. Wong. Agents for the masses: Is it possible to make development of sophisticated agents simple enough to be practical? In *IEEE Intelligent Systems*, pages 53–63, 1999.

[6] J.M. Bradshaw, N. Suri, M. Breedy, A. Canas, R. Davis, K.M. Ford, R. Hoffman, R. Jeffers, S. Kulkarni, J. Lott, T. Reichherzer, and A. Uszok. Terraforming cyberspace. In D.C. Marinescue, editor, *Process Coordination and Ubiquitous Computing*, pages 165–185. CRC Press, 2002.

[7] M. Carvalho and M. Breedy. Supporting flexible data feeds in dynamic sensor grids through mobile agents. In N. Suri, editor, *Proceedings of the 6th International Conference on Mobile Agents (MA 2002)*, 2002.

[8] I. Global InfoTek. Darpa coabs grid. http://coabs.globalinfotek.com.

[9] J. Hendler and D.L. McGuinness. The darpa agent markup language. In *IEEE Intelligent Systems*, pages 67–73, November 2000.

[10] C.C. Martha Kahn. Coabs grid scalability experiments. In O.F. Rana, editor, *Proceedings of the Second International Workshop on Infrastructure for Scalable Multi-Agnet Systems at the Fifth International Conference on Autonomous Agents*, 2001.

[11] R.A. Rathmell. A coalition force scenario 'binni - gateway to the golden bowl of africa'. In A. Tate, editor, *Proceedings of the International Workshop on Knowledge-based Planning for Coalition Forces*, pages 115–125, May 1999.

[12] I. Sun Microsystems. Jini network technology. http://www.sun.com/software/jini.

[13] N. Suri, J.M. Bradshaw, M. Breedy, P.T. Groth, G.A. Hill, and R. Jeffers. Strong mobility and fine-grained resource control in nomads. In *Proceedings of the 2nd International Symposium on Agent Systems and Applications and the 4th International Symposium on Mobile Agents (ASA/MA 2000)*, 2000.

[14] N. Suri, J.M. Bradshaw, M. Breedy, P.T. Groth, G.A. Hill, R. Jeffers, T.R. Mitrovich, B.R. Pouliot, and D.S. Smith. Nomads: Toward an environment for strong and safe agent mobility. In *Proceedings of the Autonomous Agents Conference (AA 2000)*, 2000.

[15] A. Uszok, J.M. Bradshaw, R. Jeffers, N. Suri, P. Hayes, M. Breedy, L. Bunch, M. Johnson, S. Kulkarni, and J. Lott. Kaos policy and domain services: Toward a description-logic approach to policy representation, deconfliction, and enforcement. In *Proceedings of the 4th IEEE International Workshop on Policies for Distributed Systems and Networks*, June 2003.

Architectures for Negotiating Agents

Ronald Ashri[1], Iyad Rahwan[2], and Michael Luck[1]

[1] Dept of Electronics and Computer Science
Southampton University, Southampton, UK
ra00r@ecs.soton.ac.uk
[2] Department of Information Systems
University of Melbourne, Melbourne, Australia
i.rahwan@pgrad.unimelb.edu.au

Abstract. Automated negotiation is gaining interest, but issues relating to the *construction* of negotiating agent architectures have not been addressed sufficiently. Towards this end, we present a novel agent construction model that enables the development of a range of agent architectures based on a common set of building blocks. In this paper we identify the fundamental components needed for two generic classes of negotiating agents: *simple negotiators* and *argumentative negotiators*, and use our model to describe them. We demonstrate how the model allows us to reuse fundamental components across these negotiation architectures.

1 Introduction

In multi-agent environments, agents often need to interact in order to achieve their objectives or improve their performance. One type of interaction that is gaining increasing interest is *negotiation*. We adopt the following definition of negotiation that reconciles views proposed by [6] and [13], which we believe is a reasonable generalisation of both the explicit and implicit definitions in the literature.

> *Negotiation is a form of interaction in which a group of agents, with conflicting interests and a desire to cooperate, try to come to a mutually acceptable agreement on the division of scarce resources.*

Agents typically have conflicting interests when they have competing claims on scarce resources, which means their claims cannot be simultaneously satisfied. Resources here are taken to be very general. They can be commodities, services, time, etc. which are needed to achieve something.

To address this problem, a number of interaction and decision mechanisms have been presented[1]. There has been extensive work on implementing frameworks of negotiation based on auction mechanisms (as evident, for example,

---

[1] For a more comprehensive comparison between different approaches to negotiation, the reader can refer to [6].

V. Mařík et al. (Eds): CEEMAS 2003, LNAI 2691, pp. 136–146, 2003.

in the Trading Agent Competition [12]) and frameworks that adopt heuristic-based bilateral offer exchange (e.g. [4, 5]). Recently, argumentation-based approaches [7, 8, 10] have been gaining interest. However, there are very few implemented systems that cater for more sophisticated forms of interaction such as argumentation. One of the reasons for this is that many of these frameworks involve complex systems of reasoning based on logical theories of argumentation, for which there are still many open research questions [9]. Another reason is that there are no software engineering methodologies that structure the process of designing and implementing such systems. This is why in most cases, these systems are implemented in an *ad hoc* fashion.

The aim of this paper is to address the software engineering issues related to the development of architectures for negotiating agents, ranging from simple *classical* agents to more complex *argumentative* negotiators. More specifically, this paper advances the state of the art in automated negotiation in the following ways. First, it presents a novel agent construction model that enables the description of a range of agent architectures through a common set of concepts and building blocks. Secondly, it uses this agent construction model in conjunction with a general negotiation framework to design and describe the architectures of two generic classes of negotiating agents: *simple negotiators* and *argumentative negotiators*. The paper demonstrates how a generic architecture for argumentative negotiators can be achieved by extending the simple negotiator architecture and reusing its components, and shows how this modularity is facilitated by the construction model.

We begin by presenting the agent construction model in Section 2, supported by a brief analysis of the engineering requirements the model seeks to fulfill. In Section 3, we discuss the negotiation framework before presenting a generic architecture for a basic negotiating agent. We then explain how the construction model allow us to *re-use* this basic negotiation architecture in developing a more complex architecture for an agent performing argumentation-based negotiation.

2   Engineering Agent Architectures

In this section, we present the design approach that we have applied to the specification of architectures for negotiating agents. In essence, we require an agent construction model that allows the description and development of a range of architectures. In order to achieve this we have two possible avenues to explore. One option is to define a generic agent architecture and describe other architectures in terms of this generic architecture. The drawback of this approach is that there may be features of other architectures that cannot be directly *translated* to the generic one. The second option, which we follow, is to provide an architecturally neutral model, so as to avoid this translation problem. The challenge is to provide a model that is specific enough so that it actually aids in the construction of agents. Through such a model we can view a range of architectures based on a common view of agents without any loss in expressive capability. Furthermore, any resulting model must also allow for the modular construction of agents in

order to meet general software engineering concerns and to delineate clearly the
different aspects of an architecture, as we discuss below. Such a fine-grained approach leads to a better understanding of the overall functioning of the agent
as well as how it can be altered. Finally, we need to be able to re-configure
the resulting architectures easily if possible, even at run-time, in order to deal
with dynamic, complex dependencies that develop in heterogeneous computing
environments.

SMART. The agent construction model is based on SMART [3] (Structured,
Modular Agent Relationships and Types), which provides us with the foundational agent concepts that allow us to reason about different types of agents, and
the relationships between them, through a single point of view. We chose SMART
because it provides us with appropriate agent concepts without restricting us to
a specific agent architecture. Furthermore, SMART has already been successfully
used to describe several existing agent architectures and systems (e.g. [2]).

We avoid a more complete presentation of SMART and focus on just those
concepts that are used for the agent construction model. In essence, SMART
provides a compositional approach to the description of agents that is based
on two primitive concepts, *attributes* and *actions*. Attributes refer to describable
features of the environment, while actions can change the environment by adding
or removing attributes. Now, an agent is described by a set of *attributes* and a set
of *capabilities*, where capabilities are actions an agent can perform. An agent
has *goals*, where goals are sets of attributes that represent desirable states of
the environment for the agent. On top of this basic concept of an agent, SMART
adds the concept of an *autonomous agent* as an agent that generates its own
goals through *motivations*, which drive the generation of goals. Motivations can
be preferences, desires, etc., of an autonomous agent that cause it to generate
goals and execute actions in an attempt to achieve those goals.

This approach to agent description fits well with our requirement for architecture neutrality but does not sufficiently address our requirements for modularity and run-time reconfiguration. We address these issues via a decoupling
of the different aspects of an agent and a component-based approach to agent
construction. Both these aspects of the construction model are described below.

Decoupling Description, Structure and Behaviour. In this subsection, we
describe how we extend SMART to provide a more flexible decoupling of agent
aspects. SMART allows systems to be specified based on an observer's point of
view, in terms of their attributes and goals, as well as the actions they can
perform. However, this description does not show how agents are built or how
they behave. In other words, the focus is on the *what* and not the *why* or *how*.
We call this a *descriptive specification*, since it essentially describes the agent
without analysing the underlying structures that sustain this description. Along
with the descriptive specification we need to have the ability to specify systems
based on their structure, i.e. the individual components that make up agents, as

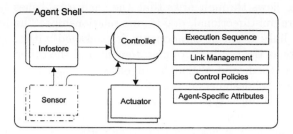

Fig. 1. Agent shell

well as their behaviour. Thus we extend SMART by the addition of a *structural specification* and a *behavioural specification.*

The structural specification enables the identification of relevant building blocks and how different sets of building blocks enable the instantiation of different agent types. The behavioural specification of an agent addresses the process through which the agent arrives at such decisions as what actions to perform. These views, along with the descriptive specification, can provide a more complete picture of the system. The agent construction model, described next, reflects these concepts by allowing direct access to these different aspects of agents, based on a clear decoupling at the architectural level.

2.1   Agent Construction Model

The basic principles of the model are illustrated in Figure 1. A *shell* acts as the container in which *components* are placed. It manages the sequence in which components execute and the flow of information between components. Control policies relating to the permissions an agent has in a specific environment are defined within the shell in order to make them independent of the agent architecture. Finally, attributes describing the agent as a whole are defined as part of the shell.

Components encapsulate specific types of actions that an agent can perform and are grouped into four categories. *Sensors* (dashed rectangles) receive information from the environment, *infostores* (rounded corner rectangles) store information, *actuators* (continuous line rectangles) perform actions that affect the environment and *controllers* (accented rounded corner rectangles) are the main decision-making components. Controllers analyse information and delegate actions to other components. By dividing components into these categories we can abstract between high level design, providing an understanding of an architecture early, and low level design, where specific mechanisms for controllers, sensors or actuators need to be defined. Each component is described using two types of attributes: *stateless attributes* refer to persistent characteristics, such as the kind of communication language the agent uses, while *situation attributes* refer to attributes describing the component's current state (e.g. the parties with whom the agent is currently negotiating).

Information flows through *links* that the shell establishes between components. Links are uni-directional, one-to-one relationships. The information that flows through links between components is packaged within *statements*. One component acts as the producer of a statement and the other as the consumer. Statements are typed, and although currently just two types are defined, IN-FORM and EXECUTE, designers may choose to define different ones depending on application needs. Inform-type statements are used when one component simply notifies another component about something, while execute-type statements are used when a component wants an action to be performed by another component. All statements are divided into a *body* and *predicates*. The body carries the main information (e.g. an update from a sensor), while the predicates carry additional information (e.g. the source of information or specific conditions associated with the execution of the action).

The sequence in which components execute is defined as the *execution sequence* of the architecture. Execution of a component includes the processing of statements received, the dispatch of statements and the performance of any other needed actions. The execution sequence is an essential aspect of most agent architectures and, by placing the responsibility of managing the sequence within the shell, we can easily reconfigure it at any point during the agent's operation.

Agent design begins with an empty shell. It is then specialised by defining control policies in order for it to meet application requirements or the demands of the environment within which it will operate. Then, shell-specific attributes can be defined to form part of the description of the agent to the outside world. The components can then be loaded into the shell, and links, as well as an execution sequence, can be defined. With the execution sequence in place, the operational cycle of the agent can begin. The agent lifecycle can be suspended or stopped by stopping the execution sequence and can be modified by altering the execution sequence, modifying relationships between components, or by applying alternative control policies.

One of the main benefits of this approach is that it is possible at any moment to have access to the three views of agents as described previously. The *descriptive specification* can be obtained by aggregating the situation attributes and stateless attributes from each component as well as the attributes contained in the shell; the *structural specification* is given by the components themselves; and the *behavioural specification* is given by the execution sequence and the links between components.

3   Negotiating Agent Architectures

With the agent construction model in place we can investigate the suitability of our model for specifying flexible negotiating agent architectures. Before we start describing negotiating agents, however, we discuss the main components of a *negotiation framework*. In addition to the negotiating agents, a negotiation framework usually includes a communication language and an interaction protocol. For example, a negotiation framework based on a simple English Auction protocol would need a communication language locution (or performative), say *propose*(.), that can express bids. The protocol is the set of rules that specify, at each stage of the interaction, what locutions can be made, and by whom. In addition, the framework needs a language for representing information about the world, such as agents, agreements, arguments, and so on. This information is used within the communication language locutions to form utterances. For example, a bid might be presented as *propose*($a, b, \{toyota, \$10K\}$), where a and b are the sending and receiving agents, and $\{toyota, \$10K\}$ is the specification of the proposal. Finally, a negotiation framework usually includes various information stores needed to keep track of various information during the interaction. This information may include proposals made by different agents, concessions they have committed to [13], and so on. Finally, the framework also needs a set of additional non-protocol rules. These may include rules that identify the winner in a particular negotiation, or rules that specify that agents cannot retract their previous proposals, and so on.

In this paper, we focus our attention on the construction of the agents within the framework. So we do not address, for example, how protocols can be specified in a modular fashion (this has been investigated in [1] for example), or how the locutions can be verified. We assume that developers have at their disposal definitions of the appropriate negotiating protocols, domain ontologies and communication languages, and instead deal with the problem of framing such mechanisms within an appropriate agent architecture. Note that we do not claim to have specified the *only* way of describing negotiating agents. Instead, we attempt to provide *a* construction model that is generic enough to capture a variety of negotiators.

3.1   Basic Negotiating Agent

Basic negotiating agents include those participating in auctions or those engaged in bilateral offer exchanges. The common aspect of these agents is that they engage in interactions in which the primary type of information exchanged between agents are proposals (i.e., potential agreements). We call the agents *basic* in order to distinguish them from agents that can engage in more sophisticated forms of negotiation which allow the exchange of meta-information (or arguments). The proposed architecture for basic negotiation agents is illustrated in Figure 2 and is described through the three different views below. We follow the conventions described earlier for illustrating the different types of components and the connecting arrows illustrate the flow of statements.

Descriptive Specification. The description of the negotiating agent is based on its attributes, capabilities, goals and motivations. The goals of the agent, i.e. the desired negotiation outcomes, can be represented in the *Mental Attitudes* infostore, and these refer to specific application domains. However, the architecture does not require explicit representation of agent goals. We could have as an overarching goal the achievement of the environmental state that represents the desired negotiation outcome for the agent. This desired state would

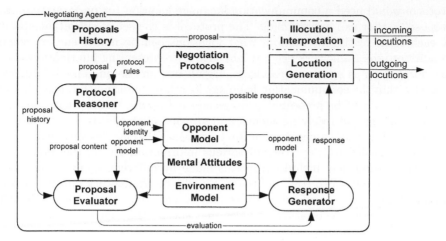

Fig. 2. Negotiating Agent Architecture

be determined by the mechanisms used by the *Proposal Evaluator* and *Response Generator* components, which ultimately decide when this environmental state has been reached. Here we see how access to an overarching, architecturally neutral, agent model allows us to reason about such things as goals even though they find no explicit representation in the architecture. Attributes of the agent are given by the information that is stored and interpreted inside components, and flows between them through statements. These attributes include representations of beliefs about the opponents, the environment, mental attitudes, negotiation protocols, and so on. Because all this information is explicitly represented within components, and stateless and state-dependent information is separated, we can easily extract it. The capabilities of the agent are given by the aggregation of capabilities of each component and can be understood, in our case, by referring to individual components in the architecture diagram. This is possible because our architecture attempts to represent the main capabilities with separate components so as to make clear the various functionalities required. However, alternative designs could (as in many implementations in the literature) combine a number of components (e.g. the representation of opponents, mental attitudes and environment) within a single component. In such cases, the descriptive specification remains unaltered, since the capabilities exist, but the structural specification refers to different components that combine those capabilities. Finally, the motivations of the agent, if the agent were autonomous, form part of the agent's mental attitudes, and ultimately guide the agent's decisions. Exactly how these are defined depends on the application. In many auction-based mechanisms, for example, the motivations are represented in the form of a utility function.

Structural Specification. The structure of the agent refers to the components that make up the architecture. Messages are received, checked and parsed through the *Illocution Interpreter*. The *Proposals History* infostore keeps track of the various proposals received, while the *Negotiation Protocols* infostore contains the rules relating to the negotiation protocols. By separating the rules dictating the protocol from the reasoning about the protocol we can more easily extend the agent to handle different protocols. The *Opponent Model* infostore keeps track of opponent models, while the *Environment Model* maintains information about the environment in which the agent is situated. Information such as the agent's preferences is stored in the *Mental Attitudes* infostore. Decisions are taken by three controllers that, abstractly, support the different negotiation stages. The *Protocol Reasoner* checks whether the proposal received by the opponent is a valid response based on the negotiation protocol. The *Proposal Evaluator* evaluates the proposal and the *Response Generator* generates an appropriate response based on this evaluation. Finally, the *Locution Generator* packages responses in the appropriate message format and handles outgoing communication.

Behavioural Specification. The behaviour of the agent is largely dictated by the flow of information through the architecture. It begins by message interpretation and storage in the *Proposals History*. The current proposal and information of the history of proposals is sent to the *Protocol Reasoner*, which uses rules in the *Negotiation Protocols* infostore to check the validity of the proposal. If it is valid it is forwarded to the *Proposal Evaluator*, which retrieves information about the opponent from the *Opponent Model* infostore. This controller uses this information along with information from the *Mental Attitudes*, *Environment Model* and *Proposal History* to evaluate the proposal. The result of the evaluation is sent to the *Response Generator*, and the opponent model may be updated. This controller also uses information from the now updated opponent model, the mental attitudes and environment model in order to generate a response. It also takes into account the negotiation protocol rules in order to generate the appropriate response. The response is packaged in the appropriate format by the *Locution Generator* before it is sent to the opponent.

3.2   Argumentative Negotiating Agent

Here, we instantiate the architecture of the basic negotiating agent in order to provide a generic description of agents capable of conducting argumentation-based negotiation (ABN). An argumentative negotiator shares many components with the basic negotiator. For example, it also needs to be able to evaluate proposals, generate proposals and so on. What makes argumentative agents different is that they can exchange meta-information (or arguments) in addition to the simple proposal, acceptance, and rejection utterances. These arguments can potentially allow agent to (i) justify their negotiation stance; or (ii) influence the counterparty's negotiation stance [7]. This may lead to a better chance of reaching agreement; and/or higher-quality agreements. In ABN, influencing the counterparty's negotiation stance takes place as a result of providing it with new information, which may influence its mental attitudes (e.g., its beliefs, desires, intentions, goals, and so on). This might entice (or force) the agent to accept a particular proposal, or concede on a difficult issue. Arguments can range from threats and promises (e.g. [11]) to logical discussion of the agent's beliefs (e.g. [8]) or underlying interests [10].

In order to facilitate ABN, the logical and communication language usually needs to be capable of expressing a wider range of concepts. For example, the proposal might instead be represented as $propose(a, b, P, A)$ where a and b are agents, P is a proposal, and A is a supporting argument denoting why the recipient should accept that proposal. ABN frameworks may also allow agents to explicitly request information from one another. This may be done, for example, by posing direct questions about agent's preferences or beliefs, or by challenging certain assumptions the agent adopts. Since in this paper we are more interested in the abstract structures within the agents, we shall not discuss these issues in more detail. In order to be capable of engaging in ABN, an agent needs the following additional capabilities:

1. **Argument Evaluation:** This component encompasses the ability of the agent to assess an argument presented by another, which may cause updates to its mental state. This is the fundamental component that allows negotiators' positions to change.
2. **Argument Generation:** This component allows the agent to generate possible arguments, either to support a proposal, or as an individual piece of meta-information. The locution generated may also be a question to present to the opponent.
3. **Argument Selection:** Sometimes, there might be a number of possible arguments to present. For example, an agent might be able either to make a promise or a threat to its opponent. A separate component is needed to allow the agent to choose the more preferred argument. Selection might be based on some analysis of the expected influence of the argument, or on the commitments it ties the utterer to.

Figure 3 shows the specification of an argumentative agent using our construction model. All components from the basic negotiating agent have been used, complemented by the additional capabilities needed for ABN. Note that the diagram has been simplified for clarity (e.g. a bidirectional link stands for a pair of unidirectional links). Furthermore, the link from *Negotiation Protocol* to *Response Generator* and *Argument Generator* has been omitted although it is, of course, necessary. Below we show how the descriptive and behavioural specification are changed. The structural specification changes by adding the three new components that deal with ABN.

Descriptive Specification. A crucial difference between the simple negotiation agent and the ABN agent is that arguments from opponents can change the agent's mental attitudes so the agent's goals or motivations may change based

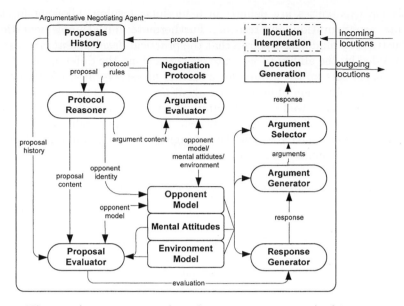

Fig. 3. Argumentation-based negotiation agent Architecture

on the new information obtained. As a result, even this aspect of the descriptive specification is dynamic and the ability to refer to this changing descriptive specification directly, at run-time, by extracting the relevant attributes is crucial. The descriptive specification must also include the new decision-making capabilities of the agent.

Behavioural Specification. Here the flexibility provided by the agent construction model is particularly evident. The agent essentially has the same links and information flows, and is simply *extended* with links to the new controllers and refined through changes to the execution sequence. The opponent model, mental attitudes and environment model are now updated by the evaluation of the argument received before the proposal is evaluated. The response is not sent directly to the opponent but arguments may be attached to the proposal by the *Argument Generator* and *Argument Selector* components. Finally, both the *Response Generator* and *Argument Generator* use the negotiation rules in order to determine what type of responses are possible.

4   Conclusions and Future Work

Automated negotiation is gaining increasing interest, but this growth is not matched by appropriate agent-oriented software engineering methodologies that cater for a variety of negotiating agent architectures. In this paper, we have taken a step towards enabling more effective design of negotiating agents, in which negotiation capabilities are defined in a modular fashion, allowing for reuse, dynamic reconfiguration, and recovery. Furthermore, initial implementations of the construction model have shown that the practical *development process* is also greatly aided by the ability to separate concerns along the different agent views.

This paper sets up the ground for a further investigation of the formal specification and verification of negotiating agent architectures through appropriate conceptual models as well as their empirical analysis through the direct implementation of such models. As such, it brings closer the possibility of negotiating-agent *construction toolkits*, which allow designers to easily configure their negotiators based on application requirements.

References

[1] C. Bartolini, C. Preist, and N.R. Jennings. Architecting for reuse: A software framework for automated negotiation. In *Proc. of AOSE-02*, pages 87–98, 2002.

[2] M. d'Inverno and M. Luck. Engineering AgentSpeak(L): A Formal Computational Model. *Journal of Logic and Computation*, 8(3):233–260, 1998.

[3] M. d'Inverno and M. Luck. *Understanding Agent Systems*. Springer-Verlag, 2001.

[4] P. Faratin. *Automated Service Negotiation Between Autonomous Computational Agents*. PhD thesis, UCL, Queen Mary and Westfield, Dept. of Electronic Engineering, 2000.

[5] S. Fatima, M. Wooldridge, and N.R. Jennings. Multi-issue negotiation under time constraints. In C. Castelfranchi and L. Johnson, editors, *Proc. of AAMAS-02*, pages 143–150. ACM Press, 2002.

[6] N.R. Jennings, P. Faratin, A.R. Lomuscio, S. Parsons, C. Sierra, and M. Wooldridge. Automated negotiation: prospects, methods and challenges. *Int. Journal of Group Decision and Negotiation*, 10(2):199–215, 2001.

[7] N.R. Jennings, S. Parsons, P. Noriega, and C. Sierra. On argumentation-based negotiation. In *Proc. of the Int. Workshop on Multi-Agent Systems*, pages 1–7, Boston, USA, 1998.

[8] S. Parsons, C. Sierra, and N. Jennings. Agents that reason and negotiate by arguing. *Journal of Logic and Computation*, 8(3):261–292, 1998.

[9] H. Prakken and G. Vreeswijk. Logics for defeasible argumentation. In D. Gabbay and F. Guenthner, editors, *Handbook of Philosophical Logic*, volume 4, pages 219–318. Kluwer, 2nd edition, 2002.

[10] I. Rahwan, L. Sonenberg, and F. Dignum. Towards interest-based negotiation. In *Proc. of AAMAS-03 (to appear)*, Melbourne, Australia, 2003.

[11] C. Sierra, N.R. Jennings, P. Noriega, and S. Parsons. A framework for argumentation-based negotiation. In M. Singh, A. Rao, and M. Wooldridge, editors, *Intelligent Agent IV: Proc. of ATAL 1997*, volume 1365 of *LNCS*, pages 177–192. Springer, 1998.

[12] TAC. *The Trading Agent Competition*. World Wide Web, http://www.sics.se/tac/, 2003.

[13] D.N. Walton and E.C.W. Krabbe. *Commitment in Dialogue: Basic Concepts of Interpersonal Reasoning*. SUNY Press, Albany, NY, USA, 1995.

RIO : Roles, Interactions and Organizations

P. Mathieu, J.C. Routier, and Y. Secq

Laboratoire d'Informatique Fondamentale de Lille – CNRS upresa 8022
Université des Sciences et Technologies de Lille, 59657 Villeneuve d'Ascq Cedex
{mathieu,routier,secq}@lifl.fr

Abstract. The notions of role and organization have often been emphasized in several agent oriented methodologies. Sadly, the notion of interaction has seldom been reified in these methodologies. We define here a model of runnable specification of interaction protocols. Then, we propose a methodology for the design of open multi-agent systems based on an engineering of interaction protocols. These interaction protocols are described in term of conversation between micro-roles characterized by their skills, then micro-roles are gathered in composite roles. Then, composite roles are used to build abstract agents. Lastly, these latter can be distributed on running agents of a multi-agent system.

1   Introduction

The idea of an agent based software engineering has appeared roughly ten years ago, with the paper from Shoham entitled *Agent Oriented Programming*[13]. Since these days, several methodologies have been proposed to help developers in their analysis and design[6, 2]. For that, the concepts of role, interaction and organization are often proposed to facilitate the decomposition and the description of distributed systems. However, we think that suggested methodologies do not clearly identify the various levels of abstraction making it possible to break up a system and especially they generally do not propose pragmatic concepts or principles facilitating the realization of such systems. Thus, our proposal relies on a model of minimal generic agent and a model of executable specification of interactions. The agent model is the infrastructure allowing the deployment and the management of interactions, while the specification of the interactions describes a global sight of the conversations between the agents of the system. In the first part of this article, we briefly present two methodologies which were proposed for the use of multi-agent systems for the design of complex distributed systems, then we put them in relation with interaction oriented approaches. In the second part, we propose a model of minimal generic agent and a formalism for the specification of interaction protocols between micro-roles. The latter are assembled in composite roles which are then atributed to the agents of the system. This specification is made executable by the generation of Colored Petri Nets for each micro-role. This executable specification and the use of a generic model of agent enable us to propose the RIO methodology facilitating the design, the realization and the effective deployment of multi-agent systems.

V. Mařík et al. (Eds): CEEMAS 2003, LNAI 2691, pp. 147–157, 2003.

2   Agent Methodologies and Interaction Languages

Several agent oriented methodologies have been proposed like AALAADIN[3] or
GAIA [16]. It is significant to notice that these two methodologies do not make
any assumption on agent models and concentrate mainly on the decomposition
in term of roles of a complex system. This point is fundamental, in particular because of the multiplicity of available agent and multi-agent systems models. This
multiplicity makes the task of the developer difficult: which agent model should
be used? Which organizational model should be chosen? Indeed, each platform
imposes too often both its own agent model and its organizational model. These
methodologies are interesting on many points, but remains too general to ease
the transition from the design stage to its concrete realization. Moreover, the
various levels of communication are not clarified in the description of interaction protocols. Indeed, works on agent communication languages (ACL)identify
three levels that constitutes a conversation: the semantic, the intention (these
two are expressed through languages like KIF or SL, and KQML or FIPA-ACL),
and the interaction level. However, even by considering heterogeneous platforms
sharing the same ontology, it remains difficult to have guarantees on the respect
of interaction protocols. This is the reason why works have been undertaken
to formalize this aspect with several objectives: to describe the sequence of the
messages, to have certain guarantees on the course of a conversation and to ease
interoperability between heterogeneous platforms.

Interaction Languages. To illustrate these approaches based on a formalization of the interactions, we studied three of them: APRIL[9], AGENTTALK[5]
and COOL[1]. APRIL is a symbolic language designed to handle concurrent
processes, that eases the creation of interaction protocols. In APRIL, the developer must design a set of *handlers* which treats each message matghing a given
pattern. According to the same principles, AGENTTALK adds the possibility to
create easily new protocols by specialization of existing protocols, by relying
on a subclassing mechanism. Another fundamental contribution of AGENTTALK
is the explicit description of the protocol: the conversation is represented by
a set of states and a set of transition rules. This same principle was employed in
COOL, which proposes to model a conversation using an finite state automata.
In COOL, the need for the introduction of *conventions* between agents to support coordination is proposed. This concept of *convention* must be brought closer
to the works of Shoham on *social rules* [14] and their contributions on the global
performance of the system. Thus, the introduction of this level of interaction
management while rigidifying in a certain way the possible interactions between
agents, brings guarantees on coordination and allows the reification of these interactions. The table below, inspired by work of Singh[15], illustrates the various
levels of abstractions within a multi-agent system:

Applicative skills	Business knowledge
Agent models and system skills	Agent oriented design
Conversation management	Interaction oriented design
Message transport	Agent platform (i.e. agents container)

To conclude, we would like to cite a definition suggested by Singh[15] of the interaction oriented approach, which characterizes our approach: *We introduce interaction-oriented programming (IOP) as an approach to orchestrate the interactions among agents. IOP is more tractable and practical than general agent programming, especially in settings such as open information environments, where the internal details of autonomously developed agents are not available.* It is the point of view that we adopt, by proposing a pragmatic method for the design and realization of multi-agent systems, relying on the concept of *executable* specification of interaction protocols.

3   Interaction Oriented Design

The heart of our proposal is a formal model to describe interaction protocols, and a transformation mechanism to generate the code that is necessary to the management of these protocols. In order for running agents to be able to exploit these new interactions, we rely on a minimal generic agent model, which authorizes the incremental construction of agent per skills addition. Thus, we will initially present this generic agent model, then we will study the model of specification of interaction protocols and the associated transformation mechanism.

A Minimal Generic Agent Model. The basis of our model is on the one hand the interactive creation of agent, and on the other hand a search on the fundamental functionalities of agenthood. We are not interested in the description of the individual behavior of agents, but rather in the identification of functions that are sufficient and necessary to an agent. Indeed, the management of interactions, the knowledge management or the management of organizations, are not related to the agent model, but are intrinsic characteristics with the concept of agent. In our model, an agent is a container which can host skills. A skill is a coherent set of functionalities accessible through a neutral interface. This concept of skill is to be brought closer to the concept of software component in object oriented technologies. Thus, an agent consists of a set of skills which carries out various parts of its behavior. We identified four layers which are characterized by the various levels of abstraction of functionalities that are proposed (table 1).

Table 1. The four layer of our abstract agent model

4	Applicative skills	Database access, graphical user interface ...
3	Agent model related skills	inference engine, behavioral engine, ...
2	Agenthood skills	Knowledge base, conversation management, organizations management
1	Minimal system skills	Communication and skill management

The first level corresponds to "system" skills, i.e. the minimal functionalities allowing to bootstrap an agent: the communication (emission/reception of messages) and the management of skills (dynamic acquisition/withdrawal of skills) [12]. The second level identifies *agent* skills: the knowledge base, media of interaction between skills and the place of knowledge representation, the management of interaction protocols (cf. following section) and the management of organizations (cf. last section). The third level is related to skills that define the agent model (reactive, BDI...), while the last level represents purely applicatives skills. Thus, the first and the second level characterize our generic minimal agent model. This model is generic with respect to the agent models that can be used, and minimal in the sense that it is not possible to withdraw one of the functionalities without losing a fundamental aspect of agenthood.

A skill is made of two parts: its *interface* and its *implementation*. The interface specifies the incoming and outgoing messages, while the implementation carries out the processing of these messages. This separation uncouples the specification from its realization, and thus makes it possible to have several implementations for a given interface. The interface of a skill is defined by a set of message patterns which it accepts and produces. These messages must be discriminated, it is thus necessary to type them.

$$\texttt{interface} := ((\texttt{m}_{in})+, (\texttt{m}_{out})*)* \text{ where } \texttt{m}_x = \texttt{message pattern}$$

The typing of message patterns can take several forms: a strong typing, which has the advantage of totally specifying the interfaces, while a weak typing offers more flexibility with regard to the interface evolution. Thus, if the content of messages are expressed in KIF or DAML+OIL, a strong typing will consist of an entire message checking, while a weak typing will only check it partially.

A Model of Executable Specification of Interaction Protocol. Many works have been done to specify interaction protocols. Recently, AgentUML[10] was defined like an extension of UML, to specify the conversations between agents, in particular by specializing sequence diagrams in UML. However, these specifications require the interpretation of developers, which must then translate them in their own system. Works of Labrou and Finin[11] explore the use of Colored Petri Nets[4] (CPN) to model conversations between agents. In [8], the same approach is used, but the concept of Recursive Colored Petri Nets is introduced to support conversations composition. Our work follows the same principles: to represent interactions in a global way, and to use a recognized and established formalism. However, contrary to preceding works, our goal is to produce an executable *specification*. i.e., a description of the interaction protocol which can be then directly integrated in a running system. Moreover, CPN are unquestionably adapted to the modeling of concurrent processes, and provide an interesting graphic formalism, but they are unfortunately not really user friendly. This is why it appears preferable to us to define a language adapted to the modeling of interaction protocols, and to use a projection mechanism that translates this language into CPN.

The Interaction Protocol Specification Model. The purpose of this model is to ease the specification, the checking and the deployment of interaction protocols within multi-agent systems. On all these stages, the designer has to define the specification, the other stages being automated. For that, we define a formalism representing the global view of an interaction protocol, and a projection mechanism which transforms this global view into a set of local views dedicated to each role. We will initially describe the specification of the global view, before presenting the projection mechanism which generate local views that agents use while a protocol is running. The interaction protocols are regarded here as social laws within the meaning of Shoham[14], that means that agents lose part of their autonomy (conversational rules are static), but the system gains in determinism and in reliability. Our model relies on the concept of skill, micro-role and a graph that represents the state of the conversation. An interaction protocol formally specifies the course of a conversation (regarded as a social law) between various entities, i.e. the nature of exchanged messages, the flow of these messages and skills that entities must implement for each stage of the conversation. These entities correspond to micro-roles, and are characterized by their name and their skills. One uses a graph to represent the course of the conversation: the nodes represent micro-roles which can be associated to a skill interface, and the arcs with a sending of message between two micro-roles (typed by a message pattern). An interaction protocol is thus defined by the following elements (figure 1): the name of the interaction protocol, a textual description of the goal of this pro-

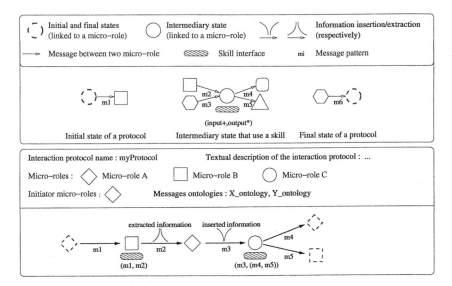

Fig. 1. Definition of the syntactic elements that constitute interaction protocols

tocol, the list of the micro-roles involved in the interaction and the geometrical symbol which is associated to them, ontologies of exchanged messages, a list of information necessary in input and produced at output, an interaction graph gathering information like the temporal course of the conversation, the synchronization and the nature of the exchanged messages, and the skills that are used by micro-roles. What it is significant to understand is that the designer has a global view of the interaction: the flow of the messages, their nature (the type of these messages corresponds to the annotations attached to the arcs), needed skills and information used or produced. In addition, all information necessary to the management of the interaction protocol is centralized here and can be used to carry out the generation of the code required to manage this interaction for each micro-role. The designer has thus only to define the interaction protocol by using a graphical tool, the projection mechanism takes care of the generation of descriptions for each micro-role, and the generic agent model can then use these descriptions.

The Projection Mechanism. The preceding section described the formalism representing interaction protocols, we will now explain the transformation making it possible to obtain a *runnable* specification. The specification of interaction protocols gives to the designer a global view of the interaction. Our objective is to generate for each micro-role a local view starting from this global view, this one could then be distributed dynamically to the agents of the system. The projection mechanism transforms the specification into a set of automata. More precisely, an automata is created for each micro-role. This automata manages the course of the protocol: coherence of the protocol (messages scheduling), messages types, side effects (skill invocation). The implementation of this mechanism is carried out by the generation of Colored Petri Nets. Indeed, we use the color of tokens to represent messages patterns, in addition we have a library facilitating the interactions between generated networks and the agent skills. On the basis of the interaction graph, we create a description of Colored Petri Net for each micro-role, and we transform this textual description to a Java class. This class is then integrated within a skill, which is used by conversation manager skill (level 2 in table 1). The interest of this approach is that the designer graphically specifies the global view of the interaction, the projection mechanism generates the skill needed to the management of this interaction. Moreover, thanks to the dynamic skill acquisition, it is possible to add new interaction protocols to running agents of the system.

Knowledge and Organization Management. The knowledge management and the management of organizations are also mandatory functionnalities of agent, and they should not be enclosed within the agent model. The knowledge management gathers at the same time their representation, the information storage, the means of reaching and of handling them. The implementation of these functionalities is strongly dependent on the used agent model (third level of table 1). The concept of organization is necessary to structure interactions that intervene between entities of the system. This concept brings some significant benefits: a means to logically organize the agents, a communication network per defect and a media to locate agents, roles or skills. Moreover, its reification provides a door in the system, making it possible to visualize and to improve interactions between agents[7].

4   RIO: Towards an Interaction Based Methodology

In this section, we will present the methodology that we are developing, and which relies on the previously presented concept of *runnable* specification . This methodology falls under the line of GAIA[16], and thus aims the same applicability. However, GAIA remains too general to easily be able to go from the system design stage to its realization. The purpose of our proposal is to facilitate this transition. The RIO methodology relies on four stages, the two first represent reusable specifications, while the two last are singular with the application (figure 2). Moreover, we will not speak about *application*, but about an agent society. Indeed, the RIO methodology proposes an incremental and interactive construction of multi-agent systems. By analogy with our minimal generic agent model, where an agent is a container which can receive skills, we see a multi-agent system like a container that has to be enriched by interactions. We will detail this approach by studying the four stages of our methodology.

Interaction Protocols Specification. The first stage consists in identifying the involved interactions and roles. Then, it is necessary to determine the granularity of these interactions. Indeed, for reasons of re-use of existing protocols, it is significant to find a balance between protocols using too many roles, these protocols becoming thus too specific, and protocols where there are only two roles, in this case the view of the interaction is no more global. The specification of the interaction protocols can then be done in three ways : either *ex-nihilo*, by specialization, or by composition. Creation *ex-nihilo* consists in specifying the interaction protocol by detailing its cartouche (figure 1). Specialization makes it possible to annotate an existing cartouche. Thus, it is possible to specify the

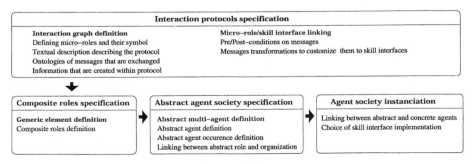

Fig. 2. The stages of the RIO methodology

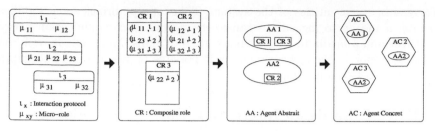

Fig. 3. Synthetic illustration of RIO stages

cartouche of an interaction protocol such as FIPA CONTRACTNET, its specialization will consist in changing micro-roles names to adapt them to the application, to refine message patterns, and if required to modify insertions/extractions
of information. Finally, the composition consists in assembling existing protocols
by specifying associations of micro-roles and information transfers. At the end of
this stage, the designer has a set of interaction protocols. He can then pass to the
description of composite roles, which will allow the aggregation of micro-roles
that are involved in complementary interactions.

Composite Roles Specification. This second stage specifies role models.
These models are abstract reusable descriptions. The composite roles correspond to a logical gathering of micro-roles. These patterns define *abstract* roles,
which gather a set of consistent interaction protocols. For example, a composite role SUPPLIES MANAGEMENT will gather the micro-role BUYER within the
PROVIDERS SEEKING interaction protocol and the micro-role STOREKEEPER of
the interaction SUPPLIES DELIVERY. Indeed, a role is generally composed of a set
of tasks which can be, or which must be carried out by the agent playing this
role. Each one of these tasks can be broken up and be designed as a set of interactions with other roles. The concept of composite role is thus used to give
a logical coherence between the micro-role representing the many facets of a role.

Agent Societies Specification. This third stage can be regarded as a specification of an abstract agent society, i.e. a description of abstract agents and their
occurrence, as well as the link between composite roles and organizations. Once
the set of composite roles is created, it is possible to define the abstract agents
(patterns of agent, or *agent template*), which are defined by a set of composite
roles. These abstract agents describe applicative agent models. These models are
specific, because they introduce strong dependencies between composite roles.
For example, the OFFICE STATIONERY DELIVERY composite role could be associated with the TRAVELLING EXPENSES MANAGEMENT composite role to characterize a LABORATORY SECRETARY abstract agent (fig 4). Once abstract agents
are defined, it is necessary to specify their occurrence in the system. It means
that each abstract agent has an associated cardinality constraint that specifies
the number of *instances* that could be created in the system (exactly N agents,

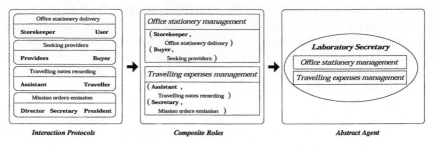

Fig. 4. The Secretary example

1 or more, *, or [m..n]). The second part of this stage consists in specifying for each abstract agent, and even for the composite roles of these agents, which organization should be used to find their acquaintances. Indeed, when agents are running, they have to initiate interaction protocols, but in order to do that they initially have to find their interlocutors. The organization is used as a media for this search. This association makes it possible to use various organizations for each interaction protocol.

Instantiating an Agent Society in a Multi-agent System. This last stage specifies deployment rules of the abstract roles on the running agents of a system. We have a complete specification of the agent society, that can be mapped on the concrete agents of the multi-agent system. For that, it is necessary to indicate the assignments from abstract agents to concrete ones. Then, the connection between a skill interface and its implementation is carried out. The designer indeed must, according to criteria that are specific to the hosting platform or applicative, bind the implementation with skill interfaces. It is during deployment that the generic agent model is justified as a support to dynamic acquisition of new skills related with the interaction. Indeed, the interaction, once transformed by the projection mechanism, is represented for each micro-role by a Colored Petri Net and its associated skills. All these information are sent to the agent, which adds applicative skills and delegates the CPN to the conversation manager. When an agent receives a message, the conversation manager checks if this message is part of a conversation in progress (thanks to the conversation identifier included in the message), if it is the case, it delegates the message processing to the concerned CPN, if not he seeks the message pattern matching the received message and instantiates the associated CPN. If it does not find any, the message will have to be treated by the agent model.

5   Conclusion

We have presented in this article a methodology falling under the line of GAIA, but relying on the concepts of the interaction oriented programming. The basis of the RIO methodology is the engineering of interaction protocols, and more precisely the engineering of *runnable* specifications. For that purpose, we use a tool facilitating the graphical design of interaction protocols, and a projection mechanism that generates the code corresponding to the vision that each participant has of the interaction. By using these specifications, it is possible to create abstractions characterizing the various roles and agents of a multi-agent system: the composite roles, which gather a set of micro-roles, and abstract agents, which gather a set of composite roles. An implementation of this approach is under development, and we use the following technologies: Coloured Petri Nets, DAML+OIL for messages ontologies and knowledge representation, OSGi as component model, and the Java language for the multi-agent platform.

References

[1] M. Barbuceanu and M. S. Fox. Cool: A language for describing coordination in multiagent systems. In *Proceedings of the First International Conference oil Multi-Agent Systems (ICMAS-95)*, pages 17–24, San Francisco, CA, 1995.

[2] F. M. T. Brazier, B. M. Dunin-Keplicz, N. R. Jennings, and J. Treur. DESIRE: Modelling multi-agent systems in a compositional formal framework. *Int Journal of Cooperative Information Systems*, 6(1):67–94, 1997.

[3] J. Ferber and O. Gutknecht. Operational semantics of a role-based agent architecture. In *Proceedings of ATAL'99*, jan 1999.

[4] Kurt Jensen. Coloured petri nets - basic concepts, analysis methods and practical use, vol. 1: Basic concepts. In *EATCS Monographs on Theoretical Computer Science*, pages 1–234. Springer-Verlag: Berlin, Germany, 1992.

[5] Nobuyashu Osato Kazuhiro Kuwabara, Toru Ishida. Agentalk : Describing multiagent coordination protocols with inheritance.

[6] E. A. Kendall, M. T. Malkoun, and C. H. Jiang. A methodology for developing agent based systems. In Chengqi Zhang and Dickson Lukose, editors, *First Australian Workshop on Distributed Artificial Intelligence*, Canberra, Australia, 1995.

[7] P. Mathieu, J. C. Routier, and Y. Secq. Principles for dynamic multi-agent organisations. In *Proceedings of Fifth Pacific Rim International Workshop on Multi-Agents (PRIMA2002)*, August 2002.

[8] Hamza Mazouzi, Amal El Fallah Seghrouchni, and Serge Haddad. Open protocol design for complex interactions in multi-agent systems. In *Proceedings of the first international joint conference on Autonomous agents and multiagent systems*, pages 517–526. ACM Press, 2002.

[9] Frank G. McCabe and Keith L. Clark. April – agent process interaction language. In M. Wooldridge and N. R. Jennings, editors, *Intelligent Agents: Theories, Architectures, and Languages (LNAI volume 890)*, pages 324–340. Springer-Verlag: Heidelberg, Germany, 1995.

[10] J. Odell, H. Parunak, and B. Bauer. Extending uml for agents, 2000.

[11] Tim Finin Yannis Labrou R. Scott Cost, Ye Chen and Yun Peng. Modeling agent conversations with colored petri nets. In *Third Conference on Autonomous Agents (Agents-99), Workshop on Agent Conversation Policies*, Seattle, May 1999. ACM Press.

[12] JC. Routier, P. Mathieu, and Y. Secq. Dynamic skill learning: A support to agent evolution. In *Proceedings of the AISB'01 Symposium on Adaptive Agents and Multi-Agent Systems*, pages 25–32, 2001.

[13] Y. Shoham. Agent-oriented programming. *Artificial Intelligence*, 60:51–92, 1993.

[14] Yoav Shoham and Moshe Tennenholtz. On social laws for artificial agent societies: Off-line design. *Artificial Intelligence*, 73(1-2):231–252, 1995.

[15] Munindar P. Singh. Toward interaction-oriented programming. Technical Report TR-96-15, 16, 1996.

[16] M. Wooldridge, NR. Jennings, and D. Kinny. The GAIA methodology for agent-oriented analysis and design. *Journal of Autonomous Agents and Multi-Agent Systems*, 2000.

Conversation Mining in Multi-agent Systems

Arnaud Mounier[1], Olivier Boissier[1], and François Jacquenet[2]

[1] SMA/SIMMO, ENS Mines Saint-Etienne
158, cours Fauriel, F-42023 Saint Etienne Cedex 2, France
{olivier.boissier,arnaud.mounier}@emse.fr
[2] EURISE, Université Jean Monnet
23, rue Paul Michelon, F-42023 Saint Etienne Cedex 2, France
francois.jacquenet@univ-st-etienne.fr

Abstract. The complexity of Multi-Agent Systems is constantly increasing. With the growth of the number of agents, interactions between them draw complex and huge conversations, i.e. sequences of messages exchanged inside the system. In this paper, we present a knowledge discovery process, mining those conversations to infer their underlying models, using stochastic grammatical inference techniques. We present some experiments that show the process we design is a good candidate to observe the interactions between the agents and infer the conversation models they build together.

1 Introduction

Multi-Agent Systems (MAS) are complex systems, made up of several autonomous agents that cooperate with each other to solve different goals. Applications of MAS are becoming more and more complex, e.g. the AgentCities project[14]. It is obvious that such a change of scale will emphasize the autonomy of the agents and raise problems of openness, robustness and quality of services. It will also increase the number and complexity of interactions between the agents. Interactions are the result of a subtle fusion of global interaction models imposing *conversation policies* on agents and local interaction models expressed in interaction strategies and agent autonomy. Thus, we need to be able to observe and to infer what is going on between the agents while interacting. In this paper, we propose a Knowledge Discovery (KD) Process for *Conversation Mining* in a MAS. This process, based on stochastic grammatical inference techniques, is used to learn the underlying conversation model that led to the different interactions, from the messages that were exchanged between the agents.

Observing the behavior of a system is a complex task. Thus, in a first section we will form a raw picture of what can be observed from interaction and which techniques are available. Starting with this survey, we will position more precisely our approach with respect to existing works dealing with knowledge discovery from interactions. After a global description of the KD Process for Conversation Mining, that we defined, we will go into the details of the stochastic grammatical

V. Mařík et al. (Eds): CEEMAS 2003, LNAI 2691, pp. 158–167, 2003.

inference technique that we used. Before concluding and giving some perspectives on our work, we will discuss the results that we obtained.

2   Knowledge Discovery from Interaction

In this paper, we are interested in KD from observation of interactions that take place in a MAS. These observations deal mainly with the messages that are exchanged between agents but also with their ordering. Various works in the community have based their KD on such observations. Systems described in [1] and [3] are examples of systems using KD to optimize and enrich individual agent reasoning. Based on Game Theory, both aim at improving the agents playing strategies. In [1], Bui and Venkatesh consider a *player* agent that tries to optimize its gain against several opposing agents. For this goal, a *Utility Engine* using neural networks, decides which are the next best plays *for the player*. A *Strategy Engine* tries to anticipate each opponents future action. It uses a genetic algorithm to maintain a population of action couples. Each couple consists of the past actions of the player and the past actions of its opponents. A classification technique is used to decide each opponents future action, taking into account the action chosen by the *Utility Engine*. In [3], Carmel and Markovitch use reinforcement learning in order to increase the capability of an agent to interact with other agents. A player agent maintains several weigthed game strategies, that are represented by finite state automata. When the agent has to choose an action, it explores the tree built with the possible plays expressed in the different weighted automata and choose the highest weighted branch. If the chosen strategy leads to success, the weight of the corresponding automaton is increased (decreased in the other case). In both systems, agents use interactions with other agents to improve their interaction strategies. They both consider that the conversation model is already given.

Another work learn from interactions of agents, in [9], the authors wants to infer the future action of a teammate using a stochastic tree. The messages exchanged are used to reestimate the value of the probabilities and so, to decide the most probable future action. In this work, the original structure of the tree is already given. In our work, we don't have a structure and are mainly interested in learning it.

Let's consider now systems that answer to this problem, that is to say systems that discover some knowledge about interaction from observing interaction. In [11], Mazouzi et al. propose a pattern matching process for recognition of interaction protocols from the observation of interaction. From the messages that are exchanged in the MAS, the system builds a causal graph. This latter is matched against different interaction protocols stored in a Data Base. When a match is found, the causal graph is forgotten and only the matched interaction protocol is considered. Besides the assumption that a set of interaction protocols exists, this work doesn't discover knowledge from interaction in the sense that it forgets the real interactions driven by the protocols. In our case, we are interested in learning the model which led to the causal graph.

4   Stochastic Grammatical Inference

Given I_+ a set of positive sentences, stochastic grammatical inference aims at infering a Stochastic Deterministic Finite Automaton (SDFA) that is able to recognize a probabilistic language that contains I_+. A Stochastic Deterministic Finite Automata is a 5-tuple $(Q, \Sigma, \delta, q_0, \gamma)$ in which Q is a finite set of states, Σ is a finite alphabet, δ is a transition function, i.e. a mapping from $Q \times \Sigma$ to Q, q_0 is the initial state, γ is the next symbol probability function, i.e. a mapping from $Q \times \Sigma \cup \{\#\}$ to $[0, 1]$. A special symbol $\#$, not belonging to the alphabet Σ, is the end of sentence symbol. Hence $\gamma(q, \#)$ represents the probability of ending the generation process in state q.

4.1   State Merging Algorithms

The general approach introduced by Carrasco and Oncina in [4] and used by most grammatical inference algorithms, consists in building what is called a prefix tree acceptor $PTA(I_+)$. It is an automaton that only accepts the sentences of I_+ and in which common prefixes are merged together resulting in a tree shaped automaton. A Stochastic Prefix Tree Automaton $SPTA(I_+)$ is an extension of $PTA(I_+)$ in which each transition has a probability proportional to the number of times it is used while generating, or equivalently parsing, the positive sentences of I_+.

In figure 2 we present the SPTA built from the training set $I_+ = \{abcab, abcbc, aacb, abcab, aacb, aacb\}$. A generalization step then aims at merging some states of the $SPTA(I_+)$ in order to infer a more general SDFA that recognizes sentences that could not have been recognized by $SPTA(I_+)$, that is sentences not belonging to the training set I_+. The choice of states to be merged is done using a breadth first strategy. A compatibility test, depending on a parameter α, is applied to successors of the chosen state. If two states are compatible, then they are merged.

For example, starting with the SPTA shown figure 2 step 0, a state merging algorithm tries to merge state 4 and state 6, giving the automaton shown figure 2 step 1. The merging of these two states does not preserve the determinism of the automaton, indeed, state 4 is not deterministic anymore[1]. Thus the algorithm tries to merge other states in order to make the automaton deterministic again. Step 2 of the figure 2 shows that the algorithm merges states 7 and 9 to maintain determinism.

The value of parameter α of the compatibility test may lead to infer various automata. For example, with a high value of α, states 7 and 10 are merged and we get the automaton shown figure 2 step 3. For a lower value of α, the algorithm would allow a greater difference between the probabilities in the compatibility test and states 2 and 4 would be merged.

A last merging between states 7 and 8 leads to the automaton shown on step 4 on figure 2 and the generalization stops. We can see that the infered SDFA is

---

[1] Starting in state 4, we acces two different states (7 and 9) with the same symbol b.

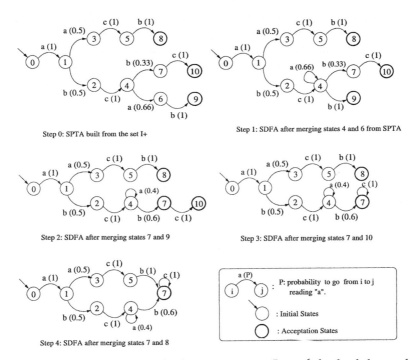

Step 0: SPTA built from the set I+

Step 1: SDFA after merging states 4 and 6 from SPTA

Step 2: SDFA after merging states 7 and 9

Step 3: SDFA after merging states 7 and 10

Step 4: SDFA after merging states 7 and 8

Fig. 2. Running example with the training set $I_+ = \{abcab, abcbc, aacb, abcab,$ $aacb, aacb\}$

more general than the initial SPTA . For example, sentences such as abcaaabcc, aacbcc or abcb are accepted by this automaton but not by the SPTA.

In the experiments we present in section 5, we use a particular instance of this state merging algorithm called the Minimal Divergence Inference algorithm (MDI) [13]. The criterion used to evaluate the compatibility between two states takes into account divergence and automaton size change. Let us call A_0 the SPTA, A_1 a temporary solution of a SDFA inference algorithm and A_2 a hypothetic new solution infered from A_1. Let A and A' be two automata, $D(A||A')$ will represent the divergence between A and A'. The divergence may be calculated using formulas given in [13]. Let $\Delta(A_1, A_2)$ be the divergence increment while going from A_1 to A_2 and assume that $\Delta(A_1, A_2) = D(A_0||A_2) - D(A_0||A_1)$. The new solution A_2 is considered to be compatible with the training set if the divergence increment relative to the size reduction, that is, the reduction of the number of states, is small enough. Formally, let α denote a compatibility threshold and $||A||$ denote the size of an automaton A. The compatiblity between two automata A_1 and A_2 is satisfied if:

$$\frac{\Delta(A_1, A_2)}{|A_1| - |A_2|} < \alpha \qquad (1)$$

the community may provide information needed by another member because of a sense of community. There may be an inherent expectation that since the relationships within the community are typically long lasting, sooner or later the favor is likely to be returned. However in distributed groups, although the common goal binding the members remains long-term, contacts and relationships may be relatively fluid with members entering and exiting as their task needs evolve. In this scenario, exchange of favors is likely to be based on reciprocity in a relatively short time-span. That is, collaboration will need to be based on concrete, explicit commitments making clear what each partner is supposed to contribute and expects from the others.

2.1   A Scenario for Collaboration and Knowledge Sharing

KennisNet is a project taking place at Achmea whose objectives are to structure, initiate and organize the sharing of knowledge between non-life insurance experts across Achmea by setting up a framework that assures the continuous availability of consistent and up-to-date knowledge [4]. Members of KennisNet are active across business units and are not part of any existing organizational structure.

In order to facilitate the creation of trust across the group, a dual approach for the development of KennisNet was chosen, which combines direct contacts between members of the group with an intranet-based knowledge sharing server. Direct contacts between participants were formalized as quarterly workshops attended by all members. In one hand, these workshops assure the creation, maintenance and uniformity of domain knowledge (for example, through talks by invited experts and facilitation of structured discussions around a theme), and on the other hand, the workshops contribute to the development of community feeling among the group.

Parallel to the workshops, a knowledge sharing server was developed, whose architecture is depicted in figure 1. During the first phase the knowledge description and knowledge repository components were implemented based on the existing technical infrastructure, a Lotus Notes network. The functionality of Lotus Notes was used to support direct access to contents, as well as publishing and browsing of knowledge items. This infrastructure, inspired by work on knowledge repositories and organizational memories (e.g. [7,10]) allows for the implementation of facilities for discussion and broadcast of questions and requests. We have conducted a user satisfaction survey after the system was running for one year. The two main conclusions from this survey are that the workshop structure is greatly appreciated and found of great value but the added value and potential of the knowledge server is not clear to the users and the server is hardly used. The main reason for this lack of use, as pointed in the survey, is that users need a more personal means of interaction to make them comfortable exchanging knowledge. The survey also indicates that knowledge owners prefer to share their expertise within a controllable, trusted group under conditions negotiated for the specific situation and partners. That is, users wish to keep the decision about sharing knowledge in their own hands, and want to be able to decide on a case by case basis whether an exchange is interesting to them or not, which is also explained by the need for reciprocity in knowledge exchange [1].

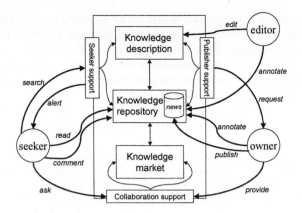

Fig. 1. The architecture of KennisNet

People will agree on sharing their knowledge with others if they feel that they will gain something from the exchange. For example, 'I will share the result of a market survey I've just done with you, if you will let me have a copy of the report you are making for which you want to have those results'. Therefore, a knowledge sharing system must be able to handle the negotiation and realization of this kind of agreements. We have chosen an agent-based approach for the Knowledge Market, the extension of KennisNet that will enable personalized knowledge sharing. In one hand agents ensure the preservation of individual needs and perspectives and on the other hand are employed to monitor and assist on the exchange. That is, the moment an agreement as in the example above is made, the personal assistants of the partners, will take care that deadlines are kept, that reports are effectively exchanged, that eventual changes are communicated, etc. Furthermore, agents are used to search the network for suitable partners, to publish and search results in the repository on behalf of their owners, and to monitor news and discussion groups.

The Knowledge Market that will be described in detail in section 4, was developed according to the Agent Society Model that is introduced in section 3. It adds the following functionality to KennisNet:

- Possibility to share knowledge that is not available in the knowledge repository
- Support for coalition formation (in order to develop new solutions when knowledge is not available)
- Support for direct exchange between parties where the negotiation of exchange conditions happens in a case to case basis.

3   The Agent Society Model

The **Agent Society** framework distinguishes between the mechanisms through which the structure and global behavior of the model is described and coordinated, and the aims and behavior of the service-providers (agents) that populate the model [3]. The framework emerges from the idea that in organizations interactions occur not just by accident but aim at achieving some desired global goals. That is, there are goals external to the individual participants that must be achieved through the interaction of those participants. In the framework, interaction between agents is represented in a way that (1) is independent of the internal design of the agents, and (2) integrates organizational characteristics and demands with the agent's own goals in a dynamic way that preserves the autonomy of the participating agents. Contracts are used to combine top-down specification of organizational structures with the autonomy of participating agents. Currently several related approaches, that take an organizational perspective on the development of multi-agents systems, are being developed, e.g. [8,9].

The framework consists of three interrelated models. The organizational structure of the society, as intended by the organizational stakeholders, is described in the **Organizational Model** (OM). The OM specifies an agent society in terms of four structures: social, interaction, normative and communicative. The **social structure** specifies objectives of the society, its roles and the model that governs coordination. The **interaction structure** gives a partial ordering of the scene scripts that specify the intended interactions between roles. Society norms and regulations are specified in the **normative structure**, expressed in terms of role and interaction norms. Finally the **communicative structure**, specifies the ontologies for description of domain concepts and communication illocutions. The way interaction occurs in a society depends on the aims and characteristics of the application, and determines the way roles are related with each other, and how role goals and norms are 'passed' between related roles. For example, in a hierarchical society, goals of a parent role are shared with its children by delegation, while in a market society, different participants bid to the realization of a goal of another role.

The agent population of an OM is specified in the **Social Model** (SM) in terms of social contracts that make explicit the commitments regulating the enactment of roles by individual agents. Social contracts describe the capabilities and responsibilities of an agent within the society, that is the desired way that an agent will fulfil its role(s). The use of contracts to describe the activity of the system allows in one hand for flexibility in the balance between organizational aims and agent desires and on the other hand for verification of the outcome of the system. Finally, given an agent population for a society, the **Interaction Model** (IM) describes possible interaction between agents. After all models have been specified, the characteristics and requirements of the society can be incorporated in the implemented software agents themselves. Agents will thus contain enough information and capabilities to interact with others according to the society specification.

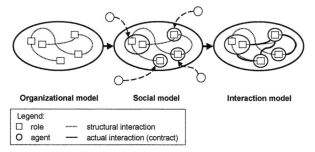

| Organizational model | Social model | Interaction model |

Legend:	
□ role	······· structural interaction
O agent	—— actual interaction (contract)

Fig. 2. Organizational framework for agent societies

Figure 2 depicts the relation between the different models. A generic methodology to analyze a given domain and determine the type and structure of the agent society that best models that domain is described in [6]. The methodology provides generic facilitation and interaction frameworks for agent societies that implement the functionality derived from the co-ordination model applicable to the problem domain. Standard society types as market, hierarchy and network, can be used as starting point for development and can be extended where needed and determine the basic norms and facilitation roles necessary for the society. These coordination models describe the different types of roles that can be identified in the society and issues such as communication forms, desired social order and co-operation possibilities between partners. In the next section we take the development of the Knowledge Market as an example for the specification of the different levels of the Agent Society Model.

4   Knowledge Market: An Agent Society for Knowledge Sharing

The Knowledge Market aims to support people exchanging knowledge with each other, in a way that preserves the knowledge, rewards the knowledge owner and reaches the knowledge seeker in a just-in-time, just-enough basis. In the remainder of this section the system, developed using the Agent Society Model, is described.

4.1   Organizational Model

Due to space limitations, and since the normative and communicative structures can be for the most part understood from the social and interactions structures, we will only describe the social and interaction structures in detail.

4.1.1 Social Structure

The global objective of the Knowledge Market is to support knowledge exchange. The requirements indicate the need for both *direct exchange*, directed at finding relevant partners, and *indirect exchange*, through the repository, in which case the task of the system is to support publishing the results of direct knowledge exchanges. The OM of an agent society consists of two layers: **operation** and **facilitation** and is dependent on the coordination model of the domain.

The Knowledge Market is characterized by informal relationships between independent partners, interested to collaborate in a win-win way. This, and other characteristics not discussed here, indicate that this community is coordinated according to the network type. This determines the following facilitation roles for the Knowledge Market [6]:

-    **Gatekeeper (GK):** is responsible for accepting agents and fixing their social contracts. It must check whether an applying agent represents a member of the KennisNet group.   The conditions and restrictions of agents concerning sharing of results related to their interaction with others are fixed in the social contract. Typically in the KennisNet, members do not have restrictions concerning sharing of knowledge they bring in. However, especially when new products are concerned it can happen that agents involved will require such knowledge to be shared only within a restricted group.

- **Matchmaker (MM):** keeps track of members, their needs and skills, and mediates the match of demand and supply[2]. In the present situation, matching is done using keywords. The matchmaker presents a list of potential partners to the requesting agent. In the case that no (good) matches are available for a knowledge request, the matchmaker can decide to send a call to knowledge owners asking whether they are available and interested in that request.
- **Notary (N):** registers collaboration agreements (interaction contracts) between members. These contracts are necessary to monitor the activity of the society and the participation of members. Contracts also enable the proactive action of agents to support the interaction between the people involved. The notary is also responsible for imposing sanctions upon violators of contracts.
- **Monitor (M):** keeps track of the realization of contracts (deadlines and results) and takes care of delivering its results to the agreed recipients and publishes results for further use by other members of the community[3]. Monitors must also tell the notary about eventual violations.
- Furthermore, the Knowledge Market OM must specify user roles, to be enacted by agents acting as avatars for KennisNet users. The sharing activities that characterize Knowledge Market require the presence of two roles:
- **Knowledge Seeker (KS):** represents needs of a user seeking collaboration. In the current approach, a knowledge seeker agent is created for each knowledge request. In principle, there can be several
- **Knowledge Owner (KO):** represents capabilities and interests of a user.

As described in [4], roles are specified in terms of goals and norms. For example, the role of knowledge seeker can be described as follows:

Role: Knowledge Seeker
Goals
acquire-knowledge(*description-of-request, resulting-item*)
Norms
1. Before placing a request, the seeker is required to first consult the KennisNet repository (in order not to ask unnecessary work from others)
2. Seekers will offer a retribution service within its means and according to the interests of the knowledge owner as 'payment' for received services
3. Seekers will make the knowledge received as result of an exchange available to others through the repository (within its sharing and privacy constraints)

For the sake of readability, norms, goals and landmarks are described throughout this paper in an informal and intuitive way. In the OM, this is formalized and made operational using the formal language LCR [5].

---

[2] The actual matching of supply and demand of knowledge is a very complex process that, due to space restrictions, will not be further discussed here.

[3] Publication of interaction results is done according to the publication rules (basically, who can access it, who cannot, etc.) specified in the social contract of the agents.

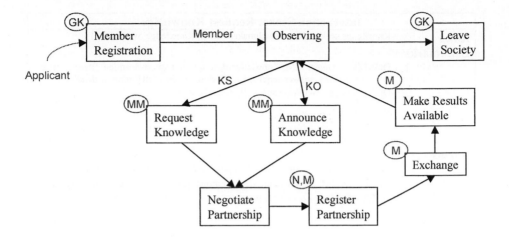

Fig. 3. Interaction structure of Knowledge Market

4.1.2 Interaction Structure

An interaction structure describes the transitions between interaction scenes. An interaction **scene script** describes a scenario of activity, that is, how roles interact and evolve in the context of a scene. Interaction structures are depicted as directed graphs where the boxes represent scenes and the arcs possible transitions between scenes. Facilitation roles active in a scene are represented by an oval linked to the scene box.

The interaction structure displayed in figure 3 describes the activity of the user roles (knowledge owner and seeker) in the Knowledge Market. Knowledge seekers and knowledge owners apply to enter the society through the 'Member registration' scene. If the application is successful, the agent proceeds to the 'observing' scene. In this scene the agent is not active in a knowledge exchange but can access the repository, follow newsgroups, etc. Both seeker or owner agents can initiate an exchange by respectively announcing a need or a skill. In the 'negotiate partnership' scene, seeker and owner discuss the conditions of an exchange. The result is a interaction contract that describes an instance of the 'exchange' scene.

Interaction scripts serve as a blueprint for the actual interactions between agents enacting roles. Landmarks are logical expressions that describe the characteristics (for instance, goals and action plans) of the scene. Landmarks are a very flexible mechanism to specify interaction. Landmarks specify families of protocols, which do not need to be fixed in the OM. The level of specification of landmarks determines the degree of freedom the actors have about their performance. In the Interaction Model, concrete interactions will be specified in interaction contracts that describe the actual protocols. Due to space limitations, it is not possible to describe each interaction scene script. We use the 'Request Knowledge' scene as an example. The informal specification of this scene script is as follows:

Interaction Scene: Request Knowledge

Roles   Knowledge seeker (KS), Matchmaker (MM), Knowledge owner (KO)

Landmarks

1. DONE(KS, request(MM, Knowledge-description, request-deadline, [Partners])) ≡
   DONE(MM, answer-request(KS, [Partners]) BEFORE request-deadline).
2. DONE(MM, answer-request(KS, [Partners])) ≡
   DONE
   (MM, find-partners(Knowledge-description, [Possible-Partners])
        AND (*forall* KO *in* [Possible-Partners], ask(KO, interested?, Partner))
).

Norms

1. PERMITTED(KS, request(KS, MM, Knowledge-description, [Partners]).
2. OBLIGED(MM, answer-request(KS, [Partners]) BEFORE request-deadline).
3. OBLIGED (KO, answer(YN) BEFORE answer-deadline | asks(MM, interested?))).

4.2   Social Model

In the Social Model, the action of independent agents in the society is specified. Such agents seek to enact one of the operational roles in the society. In the Knowledge Market, agents enacting a facilitation role are fixed in number and capabilities and are controlled by the society. Therefore, external agents cannot apply to a facilitation role. This is not the case in a generic Agent Society, which allows for independence of facilitation roles. However, in most cases, society design will specify a number of institutional roles in order to keep control over the society in some way or another.

People seeking collaboration through the Knowledge Market initiate a personal agent that acts as their avatar in the system. This agent uses the preferences and conditions specified by the user to find appropriate partners and negotiate exchange terms. Depending on the specific task, the personal agent will take either the role of **knowledge seeker** or **knowledge owner**. Requirements concerning privacy, secrecy and competitiveness between brands and departments that influence the channels and possibilities of sharing are also described in the specification of the personal assistants. Social contracts describe the agreements between participating agents and the Knowledge Market society. Negotiation of social contracts is done between the applicant agent and the Gatekeeper agent, which will watch over the interests of the society itself. For example, Anne is a member of the KennisNet group that is seeking knowledge on price policies from the competition. Anne will initiate an agent enacting the knowledge seeker role in the Knowledge Market. During the Member admittance scene, the conditions for Anne's agent will be negotiated and fixed in a social contract that specifies, for instance, which parts of the repository Anne is allowed to access, which are the obligations of Anne concerning the publication of knowledge items received as result of an interaction, and whether Anne allows for items that she provides to be published or not. This negotiation process can be very simple, in which case, Anne is offered a specification of the Knowledge Seeker role and either she accepts it as it is to be admitted or she refuses and admittance is denied. More sophisticated versions will require that agents are able to reason about goals, norms and objectives.

Social Contract: 'Anne-*ID* '
Clauses
1. PERMITTED(Anne, access-kb([KB1, KB3, KB7])
2. OBLIGED(Anne, publish-received-knowledge(item, KB3) |allows(KO, publish))
3. allows(Anne, publish(item-provided-by-Anne, kb-of-receiver's-group))

4.3   Interaction Model

The IM specifies the interaction agreements between role-enacting agents currently holding in the system. These agreements are specified using the contract language LCR, described in [5]. LCR allows the verification of society goals from the agreements specified in the contracts holding in the society.

The following example describes a contract between two members. In this example, fictive but typically possible in the domain of non-life insurance, Anne will provide Bob with a report about competition prices, on the condition that Bob will give her comments on the report (that she will have to present to her Unit directors) and eventually share with her his new pricing concept for car insurance. This contract is generated during the 'Negotiate partnership' scene and registered in the 'Register partnership' scene. In this scene, the notary agent will assign a monitor agent to check the fulfillment of the contract between Anne and Bob. Monitoring can be a very simple activity, where status is checked when a deadline is reached. However, we have chosen to use an agent as monitor because monitors can take a more active role, reminding parties of approaching deadlines or by suggesting possible actions when sanctions occur. The clauses of this contract are informally specified as follows:

Interaction Contract: '*ID* '
Parties   Anne (A), Bob (B)
Clauses
1. OBLIGED A TO receive(B, report-concurrent-prices) BEFORE *next-week*

2. IF received(B, report-concurrent-prices) THEN
        OBLIGED B TO
        (receive(A, comment-report-concurrent-prices) BEFORE *3-days*
             AND receive(A, concept-pricing) BEFORE *1-month*
)

3. IF delayed(B, concept-pricing) THEN   OBLIGED B TO inform(A, delayed(concept-pricing))

In the case that either one of the agents will not fulfil its commitments, sanctions will be applied. When sanctions are not explicitly specified in the contract, the norms of the society will be used. For instance, the Knowledge Market follows the norm that agents that do not fulfil their commitments are given less priority in exchanges. Also it is possible to consider the publication of a list of best and worse members.

5   Conclusions and Future Work

Agent concepts hold great promise for responding to the new realities of knowledge and collaboration management. In this paper, we have presented an agent-based model for organizations (ASM) that fulfills the specification requirements of collaboration management systems. The model is being applied to the development of the Knowledge Market system at Achmea. Although ASM has a formal semantics, which is described in [5], there is not of yet an implementation of ASM. This will greatly facilitate the evaluation of the model and is the subject of our upcoming research efforts.

Agent concepts can fundamentally alter the nature of KM both in the way KM systems are build as well as the way organizations are analyzed and modeled. On the one hand, the technical embodiment of these concepts can lead to advanced functionality of KM systems, e.g. personalization of knowledge presentation and matching supply and demand of knowledge. On the other hand, the rich representational capabilities of agents as modeling entities allow faithful and effective treatment of complex organizational processes. In our opinion, one of the main contributions of agent-based modeling of KM environments is that it provides a basis for the incorporation of individual initiative and collaboration into formal organizational processes.

References

[1]   Ahuja, M., Carley, K.: Network Structure in Virtual Organizations. Journal of Computer Mediated Communication, 3(4), June 1998.

[2]   Ali, I., Pascoe, C., Warne, L.: Interactions of organizational culture and collaboration in working and learning. IEEE Journal Educational Technology & Society. 5(2), April 2002.

[3]   Dignum, V., Meyer, J-J., Weigand, H., Dignum, F.: An Organizational-oriented Model for Agent Societies. In: Proc. Int. Workshop on Regulated Agent-Based Social Systems: Theories and Applications (RASTA'02), at AAMAS, Bologna, Italy, July, 2002.

[4]   Dignum, V.: A Knowledge Sharing Model for Peer Collaboration in the Non-Life Insurance Domain. In: Proc. German Workshop on Experience Management, Lecture Notes in Informatics, German Society for Informatics, Berlin, 2002.

[5]   Dignum, V., Meyer, J.-J., Dignum, F., Weigand, H.: Formal Specification of Interaction in Agent Societies. 2nd Goddard Workshop on Formal Approaches to Agent-Based Systems (FAABS), Maryland, October 2002.

[6]   Dignum, V., Weigand, H.: Towards an Organization-Oriented Design Methodology for Agent Societies. In: V. Plekhanova (Ed.), Intelligent Agent Software Engineering. Idea Group Publishing, 2003.

[7]   Domingue, J. B. and Motta, E.: A Knowledge-Based News Server Supporting Ontology-Driven Story Enrichment and Knowledge Retrieval. Proc. EKAW'99, 1999.

[8]   Esteva, M., Rodriguez, J., Sierra, C., Garcia, P., Arcos J.: On the formal specifications of electronic institutions, In Dignum F., Sierra C. (Eds.): Agent-mediated Electronic Commerce, LNAI 1991, pp. 126-147, Springer, 2001.

[9]   Ferber, J., Gutknecht, O.: A meta-model for the analysis and design of organizations in multi-agent systems. Proc. of ICMAS'98, IEEE Press, 1998.

[10]   Gandon, F., Dieng, R., Corby, O. & Giboin, A.: A Multi-Agent System to Support Exploiting an XML-based Corporate Memory. Proceedings PAKM'00, Basel, 2000.

[11]   Wooldridge, M., Jennings, N., Kinny, D.: The Gaia Methodology for Agent-Orient Analysis and Design. Autonomous Agents and Multi-Agent Systems, **3**(3) (2000).

Ontology of Cooperating Agents
by Means of Knowledge Components*

Edward Nawarecki, Grzegorz Dobrowolski,
Stanisław Ciszewski, and Marek Kisiel-Dorohinicki

Department of Computer Science
University of Mining and Metallurgy, Kraków, Poland
nawar@agh.edu.pl

Abstract. A special way of structuralisation of knowledge and functionality of multi-agent systems is proposed that allows (self-) organisation and realisation of their global goal. Formally based structuralisation
can also aid a process of designing (assembling) and documenting such
a system. The approach is illustrated by the case of knowledge structuralisation of the decentralised information decision system oriented to
diagnosis of casting defects.

1   Introduction

Multi-agent systems are ideally suited to represent problems that have multiple solving methods, multiple perspectives, or multiple problem solving entities. Such systems have all traditional advantages of distributed and concurrent
problem solving, but also have the additional advantages that come from decentralisation of decision and sophisticated patterns of interactions. Examples
of common types of interactions include: operation (working together towards
a common aim), coordination organizing problem solving activity so that harmful
interactions are avoided or beneficial interactions are exploited), and negotiation
(coming to the agreement, which is acceptable to all the parties involved).

Notion *agent* also provides useful abstraction in just the same way that procedures, abstract data types, and, most recently, objects do. They allow a software
developer to conceptualise a complex software system as a society of cooperating autonomous problem solvers. Agents of the system, having some elements
of knowledge represented somehow and communicating to each other, are able
to follow a common thread and synthesise an idea about solution to a problem faced by the system. The only problem here is to assure that agents base
in their activity on the coherent knowledge or that they share and sustain the
same common ontology.

Until recently full responsibility for a solution to the problem has lain in
hands of a designer that prepared an internally coherent system with an appropriate bunch of documentation to assure its proper utilisation. Now the problem

* This work was partially sponsored by State Committee for Scientific Research (KBN)
grant no. 7 T11C 033 21.

V. Mařík et al. (Eds): CEEMAS 2003, LNAI 2691, pp. 180–190, 2003.

gains a new dimension. Very often, a designer faces a number of elements (agents) that must be put together to constitute his system. The elements are of different origin and nature (a human being is often regarded as an agent) so that their mutual suitability must be checked. Moreover, they ought to be suspected of some inconsistencies — differences in ontologies they base on.

Among several possible definitions of term *ontology*, the closest to our consideration is as follows. Ontology is data that constitute a base for common understanding of some knowledge domain that can be interchanged between human beings and computer systems (or their elements [agents] when a system is distributed and decentralised). The postulate is hidden in the above definition that ontology can have a form that allows its storing and processing and, in consequence, that ontologies of the elements are accessible. Such systems can be called — of explicit knowledge representation contrary to traditional ones where at least a part of *wisdom* is hidden in structures and algorithms. Explicitly written knowledge creates a base for designing (organisation) and even self-organisation of such systems.

Although there are several technologies that automatically work with formally described ontologies, the problem — how to conform the agents' partial ontologies in the running system — is still open.

The paper presents an idea of how ontology of a multi-agent system can be structuralised and, in its explicit form, installed in the agents. The key notion here is *knowledge component*. There is a coherent fragment of knowledge of the system that also may formally describe one of its elementary functions. A component realises an aspect or stage of reasoning, allows resolution of some partial task of the system.

The paper is organised as follows. In section 2 the formal base of the structuralisation is proposed with a definition of *component* — that encompasses some concepts and their relations (ontology) and some computation defined that creates its functionality. Section 3 describes what types of knowledge (ontologies) structuralised as components can be and what are their possible roles in the process of design (assembling) of system of that kind. Section 4 contains illustration of consideration of the paper. It is an abbreviated description of the decentralised information decision system oriented to diagnosis of casting defects built using agent technology. Its main functionality is to integrate different sources of knowledge and information (relational databases, knowledge bases [expert systems] human experts) so that the complex technical evaluation could be produced. It is shown how structuralisation of knowledge of the diagnostic system can be done accordingly to the approach proposed.

2   Formal Introduction of Knowledge Component

The idea of *knowledge component* is proposed here to encompass a coherent fragment of knowledge of the system that may also formally describe one of its elementary functions called here *a computation*.

2.1   A Model of Computation

Let Ω be a finite non-empty set of names. A system of productions of the form is considered:

$$A \rightarrow B \tag{1}$$

where A and B are non-empty subsets of Ω and $A \cap B = \emptyset$. A production is interpreted as follows: assigning values to the names of set A is sufficient to obtain the values of names from set B.

Definition 1 *Let A_i and B_i for $i = 1, 2, ..., n$ be non-empty subsets of Ω. Description of a computational system S is a set of productions of the form $\{A_i \rightarrow B_i\}_{i=1,2,...,n}$ and each production — a computational axiom in the system. Ω is called a domain of S.*

Three rules of production are introduced into S that allow deriving some computational axioms $\{A_i \rightarrow B_i\}_{i=1,2,...,n}$ from a subset of others. The first one is a rule of **selection**:

$$\frac{A \rightarrow B, C \subset B}{A \rightarrow C} \tag{2}$$

for $A, B, C \neq \emptyset$. Its interpretation is following: if assigning values to the names of set A is sufficient to obtain the values of names from set B then is sufficient also in order to assign values to elements of each non-empty subset of B.

A rule of **cumulating** is inverse to the selection one:

$$\frac{A \rightarrow B, A \rightarrow C}{A \rightarrow B \cup C} \tag{3}$$

for $A, B, C \neq \emptyset$. It says that if assigning values to the names of some set is sufficient to obtain the values of names from other two sets then is sufficient also in order to assign values to the union of them.

Possibility to **combine** computation is done by the third rule:

$$\frac{A \rightarrow B, B \cup C \rightarrow D}{A \cup C \rightarrow D \backslash A} \tag{4}$$

for $A, B, D, D \backslash A \neq \emptyset$ and $B \cap C = \emptyset$. The rule indicates possibility to replace some or all of the assigned values by the values obtained from another computational axiom (it is assumed that C can be an empty set).

Definition 2 *Complete description of a computational system $C(S)$ is a closure of S under the rules of selection, cumulating, and combining.*

2.2   Computational Taxonomy

Introduced in the previous subsection the notion of the computational system is enriched with a partial order relation in Ω denoted by $\sqsubseteq$. The relation is to represent subsumption. The following formula:

$$a \sqsubseteq b \tag{5}$$

is interpreted that concept a is more detailed than b. Additionally, $\sqsubseteq^0$ depicts the direct subsumption what means that $a \sqsubseteq^0 b$ iff $a \sqsubseteq b$ and does not exist c such that $a \sqsubseteq c \sqsubseteq b$.

Definition 3 *Let $(\Omega, \sqsubseteq)$ be a partially ordered set and simultaneously a domain of computational system S. Direct subsumption $a \sqsubseteq^0 b$ for $a, b \in \Omega$ is computable if there exists computational axiom $a \to b$ in S.*

Due to the above idea and rule of combining (eq. (4)) the model of computation becomes more expressive. As an example, let us considered the status of integer and real numbers in the model. They are joined with the direct subsumption:

$$\text{an integer number} \sqsubseteq^0 \text{a real number}$$

that is computable. Then for a computational axiom that uses assigning a value to the real number is possible on the above base also assigning to the integer.

Definition 4 *Let $(\Omega, \sqsubseteq)$ be a partially ordered set and simultaneously a domain of computational system S. A concept is computable if it is an argument of the relation of direct subsumption that is computable in S. Ω_o stands for a set of all computable concepts in S. Complement $\Omega_s = \Omega / \Omega_o$ is called a set of structural concepts.*

As continuation of the example, let us add to the former two the new concept — *parameter* situating as follows:

$$\text{an integer number} \sqsubseteq^0 \text{a real number} \sqsubseteq^0 \text{a parameter}$$

Integer and real numbers are computable concepts of the system while parameter is a category and thus falls into set Ω_s — structural ones.

In the set of computable concepts the rule of combining is followed by a rule of **substitution**:

$$\frac{A \to B}{(A \backslash \{a\}) \cup \{b\} \to B} \tag{6}$$

for $B \neq \emptyset, a \in A, b \notin B, a, b \in \Omega_o, a \sqsubseteq b$. Applicability of the rule is restricted to the situation when the computable concepts follow (in the sense of $\sqsubseteq$) structural ones so let us reject the opposite situation from the consideration. It can be done also because of interpretation reasons: this is a computational system and something that is computable can be regarded as the most specific.

Definition 5 *A non-empty subset of the partially ordered set — $X \subset \Omega$ is called left-hand spanned one if for each $a \in \Omega$ from $a \sqsubseteq b \in X$ implies $a \in X$.*

Definition 6 *Tuple $T = (\Omega, S, \sqsubseteq)$ is called computational taxonomy where Ω is a domain of computational system S and $\sqsubseteq$ is a partial order relation in Ω when the two following conditions hold:*

1. *Subset Ω_o of S is left-hand spanned.*

2. *For each computation axiom $A \to B$ in $\mathcal{S}$, $A \cup B \subset \Omega_o$.*

Intention of the first condition is to prohibit subsumption within computable concepts that leads to structural ones. The taxonomy has a defined structure — the structural concepts only generate possible subsumptions. The second condition decides that a computational axiom can be defined for computable concepts only.

2.3   Components

Let us consider a family of computational taxonomies $\{\mathcal{T}_m\}_{m \in \mathcal{M}} = \{(\Omega_m, \mathcal{S}_m, \sqsubseteq_m)\}_{m \in \mathcal{M}}$ indexed by $\mathcal{M}$ — non-empty set of symbols (interpreted further as names of components). *Externalisation* of taxonomy $\mathcal{T}_m$ is a 3-tuple of the form $\mathcal{T}_m^e = (\Omega_m^e, \mathcal{S}_m^e, \sqsubseteq_m^e)$, where:

- each symbol $a \in \Omega_m$ corresponds to one and only one symbol $m.a \in \Omega_m^e$,
- each computational axiom $\{a_0, \ldots, a_n\} \to \{b_0, \ldots, b_m\}$ corresponds to one and only one axiom $\{m.a_0, \ldots, m.a_n\} \to \{m.b_0, \ldots, m.b_m\}$ in $\mathcal{S}_m^e$,
- each subsumption $a \sqsubseteq b$ — one and only one subsumption $m.a \sqsubseteq m.b$ with respect to relation $\sqsubseteq_m^e$.

Conclusion 1 *Externalisation of a computational taxonomy is a computational taxonomy.*

Let $m, n \in \mathcal{M}$, $a \in \Omega_m$, and $b \in \Omega_n$. Formulas:

$$a \sqsubseteq n.b \tag{7}$$

$$a \doteq n.b \tag{8}$$

describe import of the concepts from taxonomy n to taxonomy m. The first one is interpreted as subsumption between two concepts from different taxonomies. The second — identity of concepts.

Externalisation of an import formula $a \sqsubseteq (\doteq) n.b$ in taxonomy m is $m.a \sqsubseteq (\doteq) n.b$. If a and b are computable concepts both in taxonomies n and m it is necessary to produce additionally a computational axiom $\{a\} \to \{n.b\}$, which externalisation is $\{m.a\} \to \{n.b\}$.

Definition 7 *Let $\{\mathcal{T}_m\}_{m \in \mathcal{M}}$ be a family of computational taxonomies. A component is a 5-tuple $(\Omega_m, \mathcal{S}_m, AI_m, \sqsubseteq_m, I_m)$ consists of: $(\Omega_m, \mathcal{S}_m, \sqsubseteq_m)$, $m \in \mathcal{M}$ — an axiom, I_m — a set of import formulas, and AI_m — respective computational axioms.*

Definition 8 *Let $\{M_m\}_{m \in \mathcal{M}}$ be a family of components. 3-tuple of the form:*

$$(\cup_{m \in \mathcal{M}} \Omega_m^e, \cup_{m \in \mathcal{M}} \mathcal{S}_m^e \cup AI_m^e, \cup_{m \in \mathcal{M}} \sqsubseteq_m^e \cup \cup_{m \in \mathcal{M}} I_m^e) \tag{9}$$

is called an assembling of the components of the family. An assembling is correct if it is a computational taxonomy.

2.4 Reference to $\mathcal{ALC}$

The presented model of computation is independent on logical *apparatus* that defines subsumption. It seems that $\mathcal{ALC}$ logic and especially $\mathcal{SHIQ}$ are appropriate for our purposes due to their expressiveness [1, 2]. Such choice is additionally justified by availability of computer tools that support dealing with that logic, like: inference engine FaCT [3] distributed under GNU license or programs dedicate to language OIL [4] that is a *de facto* standard for semantic integration of the web [5] and other information sources [6].

3 Structuralisation of Ontology of MAS

Having the formal model of computation presented in the previous section, we can turn back to the consideration over multi-agent systems. Now it is possible to say what is ontology of such systems, what is its representation, and how it can be stored and available.

Ontology in this case is the representation of its computational taxonomy in the language of the particular logic. As it has been said, it can be $\mathcal{ALC}$-$\mathcal{SHIQ}$. The following conditions must be fulfil then:

- domain of a computational system Ω is included in the set of concepts of that ontology,
- subsumption $\sqsubseteq$ can be fully inferred from assertions included in the ontology,
- set of the computational axioms $\mathcal{S}$ can be represented by assertions of the ontology.

Three sets of assertion may be distinguished in the ontology. The first one defines concepts that are basic and indispensable for proper functionality of an information system. It is called a core of computational ontology (CCO) and encompasses:

- definitions of concepts used in order to describe (the model of) computation,
- definitions of types of variables used for calculation (e.g. real number, range, etc.),
- representation (knowledge about) computational axioms directly bound to the computational concepts.

The second part of the system ontology (SO) is a domain ontology — DO (or a number of them). Here the assertions describe the application field of a system providing a set of specific concepts (a part of them falls into set Ω_m [structural concepts]) and relations (of subsumption type) among them. The domain ontology contains also specification of computational axioms that deals with its computational concepts.

Extension of the core of computational ontology (CO) (the third part) contains assertions that define computational axioms and necessary concepts allowing putting together the former two elements. The following relations hold:

$$\text{System ontology} = \text{Computational ontology} \cup \text{Domain ontologies}$$
$$\text{Core of computational ontology} \subset \text{Computational ontology}$$
$$\text{Core of computational ontology} \cap \text{Domain ontologies} = \emptyset$$

It is worthwhile to mention yet another ontology that stays outside the system but must be taken into account by a designer. It can be called *user's* ontology (UO) and is, in fact, a superstructure of the system ontology

$$\text{System ontology} \subset \text{User's ontology}$$

Due to application profile of the system the user ontology is not (and it would be useless) explicitly described in it. Instead, the designer is obliged to ensure conformity of both ontologies and prepare the adequate documentation. Having the system ontology formally represented, this task seems to be easier. Relations between discussed part of the system ontology are shown in figure 1.

All differentiated above parts of the system ontology can be, in turn, partitioned and distributed for the sake of architecture of an agent system. It is done by introduction of term *knowledge component* (CC). Considerations of section 2.3 constitute a base for representation of a knowledge component (here CC_m) in the form of table 1.

A component has, in general, two parts — its knowledge and computation. The second part can be absent when only the system ontology is represented by a component. Contrary, components that embrace computational axioms are put together to give functionality of the system. A means for that is the externalisation poining at terms of other compoments (here CC_n) which are the same as or subsume the terms of the given one.

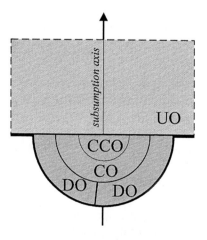

Fig. 1. Strucuturalisation of the system ontology

Table 1. Knowledge component m

CC_m
$\{\Omega_m, \sqsubseteq\}$
$\Omega_m \ni a \ \sqsubseteq n.b$
$\Omega_m \ni a \ \dot{=} n.b$
$\Omega_{om} \subset \Omega_m$
$A_i \rightarrow B_i \ ; \ A_i, B_i \subset \Omega_{om}$

What can be a benefit from it for multi-agent systems? A knowledge component (or a group of them) is encapsulated in an agent which offers its functionality to the community of other agents and their users. Finding opportunity, it undertakes decision to join the common work. At least two conditions must be fulfilled here. There must be possibility to communicate that is the main feature of and a means that constitutes a multi-agent system. The shared part of ontology must be specified that allows putting together knowledge components. The case of incoherent terminologies is to be solved by a human expert that can create a new agent — a carrier of *glue* terminology.

4 Design of Ontology of the System for Casting Defects

Discussion of the paper may be illustrated with some elements of the decentralised information system for diagnosis of casting defects [7, 8].

The system is to serve as a multi-purpose tool of technical assistance, aiding the skill of designing new technologies and quality assurance for foundry products. As typical tasks solved by the system, the following issues can be mentioned:

1. Assistance in reference literature from the field of foundry practices.
2. Analyses in the field of manufacturing technologies.
3. Expertises in the field of casting defects diagnosis.
4. Analyses for casting products — a module of knowledge to be designed in future.

Although the system is under development according to the ideas presented in the paper, it has been proving its applicability in former version of classical architecture — a team of relational databases accessible via the net.

The ontology of the considered information system has been designed and is partially reproduced beneath in order to illustrate the idea of the paper. The example show main elements of the ontology (basic concepts and relations) and how it can be extended to cover the field of application. The *core ontology* of the computational platform defines general concepts and relations (such as: computation, parameter, number etc.). The *domain (framework) ontology* defines basic concepts of casting and casting defects (see fig. 1). The ontologies are described using $\mathcal{ALC} - \mathcal{SHIQ}$ logic (as the main notation) together with the Unified Modelling Language (UML) class diagrams [9]. Introduction of the UML improves legibility of the example.

Here we present a skeleton of the domain ontology designed for the area of casting industry and, especially, for the casting defects diagnosis. The $\mathcal{SHIQ}$ formulas and the appropriate UML diagram are shown below.

$$\text{property} \sqsubseteq \text{parameter} \sqcap \forall \text{ describes.material}$$
$$\text{ingredient} \sqsubseteq \text{material} \sqcap \geq 1 \text{ is-part-of.mix}$$
$$\text{mix} \sqsubseteq \text{material}$$
$$\text{metal} \sqsubseteq \text{mix} \sqcap \forall \text{ is-part-of.casting-product}$$
$$\text{moulding-sand} \sqsubseteq \text{mix} \sqcap \forall \text{ is-part-of.casting-product}$$
$$\text{core-sand} \sqsubseteq \text{mix} \sqcap \forall \text{ is-part-of.casting-product}$$
$$\text{defect} \sqsubseteq \text{boolean} \sqcap \forall \text{ defect-of.casting-product}$$
$$\text{misrun} \sqsubseteq \text{defect}$$
$$\text{shrinkage-cavity} \sqsubseteq \text{defect}$$

The presented ontology defines the concept of casting-product and describes the relation between casting, parameters of its production (parameters of the production process), and the possible defects. For the presentation purpose we consider the castings with two possible kinds of defects: misrun and shrinkage-cavity, each of a computational type boolean (there is a defect or not). From the point of view of the defect diagnosis a casting consists of metal, moulding-sand and core-sand (generalized has-part role). Each of these elements is defined as a mix of ingredients. The ingredients are materials described by a set of properties, which are specializations of concept of parameter.

It is worthwhile to mention that, as a side effect of the proposed approach, a designer obtains easy way for introducing new functionality to the system (e.g., new type of casting defects).

5   Summary

The paper presents a way of structuralisation of knowledge of specialised multi-agent systems. It is foreseen that the approach proves its usefulness in designing, assembling, and documenting such computer systems marked by complexity, dispersal of elements, and decentralised way of organisation.

The point of departure is formal description of the whole knowledge of such a system and recording it in the form that allows its automatic processing. As formal base for the structuralisation, a knowledge component is proposed that encompasses some concepts together with their inter-relations (ontology) and some computation that defines its functionality. It is shown what types of knowledge (ontologies) can be structuralised as components and what are their

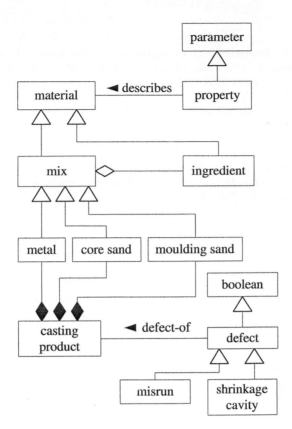

Fig. 2. Skeleton of the domain ontology of casting defects

possible roles in the process of design (assembling), organising or self-organising of system of that kind.

Discussion of the paper is illustrated based on the decentralised information system for diagnosis of casting defects.

Further research in the subject will be developed in the following directions:

- Elaboration of procedures that help to design a system or allow it to organise itself,
- Extending knowledge representation techniques and pointing at the way of their implementation,
- Defining appropriate communication protocols among agents of not-yet-agreed ontologies.

The proposed approach may also be considered as a step towards an open framework supporting cooperation of computer systems produced by different vendors, but providing information and services in the agent-oriented manner.

References

[1] Horrocks, I.: Reasoning with expressive description logics: Theory and practice. In Voronkov, A., ed.: Proc. of the 18th Int. Conf. on Automated Deduction (CADE-18). Number 2392 in Lecture Notes in Artificial Intelligence, Springer-Verlag (2002) 1–15

[2] Sattler, U.: Description logics for the representation of aggregated objects. In W.Horn, ed.: Proceedings of the 14th European Conference on Artificial Intelligence, IOS Press, Amsterdam (2000)

[3] Horrocks, I.: Using an expressive description logic: FaCT or fiction? In Cohn, A. G., Schubert, L., Shapiro, S. C., eds.: Principles of Knowledge Representation and Reasoning: Proceedings of the Sixth International Conference (KR'98), Morgan Kaufmann Publishers, San Francisco, California (1998) 636–647

[4] Fensel, D., Horrocks, I., Harmelen, F. V., Decker, S., Erdmann4, M., Klein, M.: Oil in a nutshell. In et al, R. D., ed.: Knowledge Acquisition, Modeling, and Management, Proceedings of the European Knowledge Acquisition Conference (EKAW-2000), Lecture Notes in Artificial Intelligence, LNAI, Springer-Verlag, October 2000 (2000)

[5] Dean, M., Connolly, D., van Harmelen, F., Hendler, J., Horrocks, I., McGuinness, D. L., Patel-Schneider, P. F., Stein, L. A.: OWL Web Ontology Language 1.0 Reference (2002) http://www.w3.org/TR/2002/WD-owl-ref-20020729

[6] Stuckenschmidt, H.: Using OIL for Intelligent Information Integration. (In: Proceedings of the Workshop on Applications of Ontologies and Problem-Solving Methods at ECAI 2000)

[7] Kluska-Nawarecka, S., Dobrowolski, G., Marcjan, R.: INFOCAST - a system for quality control procedures and diagnosis of casting defects. Acta Metallurgica Slovaca **7** (2001) 441–446

[8] Marcjan, R., Kisiel-Dorohinicki, M., Sniezynski, B., Dobrowolski, G., Nawarecki, E.: Knowledge components of a ddecentralized expert platform. In Hamza, M., ed.: Proc. of the Second IASTED Intl. Conf. on Artificial Intelligence and Applications (AIA 2002). IASTED/ACTA Press (2002)

[9] Cranefield, S., Purvis, M.: UML as an ontology modelling language. In: Proc. of the IJCAI'99 Workshop on Intelligent Information Integration, Sveden (1999)

Mapping between Ontologies
in Agent Communication

Marek Obitko and Vladimír Mařík

Gerstner Laboratory, Department of Cybernetics, Faculty of Electrical Engineering
Czech Technical University, Prague, Czech Republic
{obitko,marik}@labe.felk.cvut.cz

Abstract. One of the most important issues in the area of agent communication is the understanding of message content meaning. The meaning is captured in message ontology. In the "open" multi-agent systems we cannot guarantee that all agents share the used ontologies completely. To enable communication, messages must be translated from one ontology to the other one. We propose an algorithm for establishing a mapping between ontologies and describe how the mapping is used for translation of messages between different ontologies. The approach relies on a possibility to point to objects in the world that agents share. The process of refining the mapping is iterative and knowledge gained at any step can be used for translation. The proposed algorithm permits a certain information loss (e.g. when the source ontology is more detailed than the target one) but always provides a consistent translation.

1 Introduction

One of the most important issues in agent communication is the understanding of meaning of messages. Several layers can be distinguished in the process of understanding — agents must be able to parse messages as well as to understand their meaning. We focus on the understanding of meaning, i.e. on the semantic compatibility among agents. When agents want to exchange information, they have to *understand* the meaning of the message content. The meaning of a message is captured in a message ontology. The ontology provides interpretation of the message, e.g. it says what the words used in the message mean.

There is no problem with the semantic compatibility in the case when all the agents share one common ontology. This is the case of a "closed" multi-agent system where all agents are designed to work together and the meaning of ontology elements is usually hardcoded implicitly. However, the problem of semantic compatibility becomes an issue in open multi-agent systems, where agents have to communicate across various communities using different ontologies. Similar problem occurs when a newly created agent joins some already existing community and it is not aware of the ontology used. An example is a supply chain where new agents may enter an existing community at any time [6].

The paper is organized as follows: First we describe the problem in general and propose principles of communication between agents using different ontologies. Then we describe an abstract ontology model common to many current

V. Mařík et al. (Eds): CEEMAS 2003, LNAI 2691, pp. 191–203, 2003.

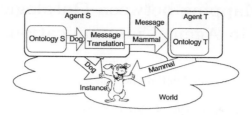

Fig. 1. Agents sharing world but using different ontologies. A concept in the message is translated from the source ontology to the target ontology (the concept "dog" from the source ontology can be mapped into the concept "mammal" in the target ontology)

ontology modelling languages. After that we explain — using the abstract ontology model — how the mapping between ontologies can be developed, maintained and refined and how the knowledge of mapping is used for message translation.

2　Communication between Different Ontologies

Ontology can be defined as an explicit specification of conceptualization. This means that ontology is a description of the concepts and relationships that can exist for an agent [3]. Only what can be represented using ontologies can be represented in agent's knowledge base, and only that can be described in messages exchanged among agents since the ontology forms the basic vocabulary of the content of messages.

The problem that we focus on in this paper can be stated as follows. There are two agents that want to communicate. They, however, do not share the ontology of the problem domain that the communication concerns. How could they proceed with communication? We expect that agents use their ontologies because their internal knowledge representation is in line with these ontologies. Therefore they are not willing to change their own ontology. A possible way to enable communication is to translate messages from one ontology to the other one. Note that a very similar problem is solved for example in the area of database integration [8], where it is necessary to translate between database schemas, and generally in system integration, where a translation between system interfaces is needed.

For translating messages it is important to know which elements of the source ontology can be mapped to what elements of the target ontology. This knowledge is currently provided and coded mostly by humans. They are able to understand the differences and similarities between ontologies so that they can establish the appropriate mapping and code the translation. Clearly, this approach is not scalable — agents should be able to establish the mapping by themselves and use the knowledge needed for message translation autonomously. Every agent may be able to translate a message or there can be a dedicated ontology agent to do this job as proposed e.g. in [2]. The overall architecture is an important issue that is however beyond the scope of this paper. The methods presented here can be used for both of the approaches.

We propose an algorithm for establishing a mapping between ontologies that is based on instances in a shared world (see Figure 1) as well as on the knowledge of the structure of the ontologies. We suppose that agents are able to recognize and point to instances in a shared world and describe them. The world can be either real or virtual, such as WWW (where instances are web pages and pointers are URLs). Our approach builds on the theory of language games [10] that are used to form common vocabulary for description of a shared world. Here we want neither to create new ontology nor to change existing ontologies. We use pointing to discover instances that are classified under certain concepts in both ontologies. Note that we do not require agents to share their worlds completely. Only a part of the world is needed to establish at least partial mapping between certain concepts.

Also, we do not require all the elements of ontologies to be mapped completely. In many cases we may be even unable to map in a satisfactory way all the ontology elements since the ontologies overlap only in their parts. The algorithm is incremental and at any time it is possible to use the knowledge gained so far. The knowledge of possible mapping is improved over time, so that the loss of information caused by mapping is being reduced.

The knowledge of mapping is then used for translation of messages. The translation is based on replacing elements of the source ontology by combinations of elements of the target ontology [11]. In our approach, a consistent mapping is always provided (see below for details). On the other hand, a loss of information is permitted. This loss is sometimes inevitable, for example in cases that the source ontology is very detailed and can be mapped to only several elements of the target ontology. In our approach, the loss of information also occurs when the knowledge of mapping is incomplete (due to the incremental character of the algorithm).

Let us recall all the assumptions for the approach presented in this paper: agents must be able to point to instances in a shared world, to recognize what the other agent is pointing to, to exchange instance descriptions as well as exchange ontology descriptions. Clearly, for this purpose at least the starting ontology for pointing and describing instances must be shared. Moreover we suppose that ontologies are consistent, which means that the subsumption of concepts (is-a relation) is preserved in a mapping. Without these conditions we will not be able to provide always a consistent translation.

3   Abstract Ontology Model

The most important languages that are used for the modelling of ontologies include RDFS [5], DAML+OIL [4], OWL [1], OKBC [2] and Conceptual Graphs (CGs) [9]. They vary in various detailed features, but they have much in common. The core of an ontology expressed in these languages is formed by concepts

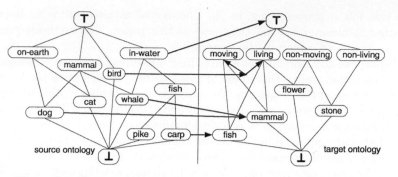

Fig. 2. Example of two concept lattices and example of (a part of) mapping of selected concepts from the source ontology O_S to the target ontology O_T. Mapping from "dog" to "mammal" is an example of a mapping from a more specific to less specific concept (the concept "dog" cannot be expressed more accurately in O_T). Note that the source concept "bird" is mapped to the subset of the target concepts "moving" and "living" (a concept that does not exist but can be expressed in O_T)

(or classes, types, frames, or other similar primitives that have various names in various ontology languages) and by relations (or roles, properties, attributes) among these concepts. In most of the ontology modelling languages, both the concepts and relations are primarily organized by the subsumption (is-a) relation.

For the purposes of describing ontology in this paper, we choose a subset of modelling primitives that is common to the majority of ontology modelling languages used today. We will refer to this model as to the abstract ontology model. This model is capable to express basic (the most used and often also the only used) constructs from the mentioned ontology languages. However, we are aware that additional modelling features may make the reasoning for establishing the ontology mapping more effective. The problem of relating various ontology modelling languages with different expressivity is further discussed in [6].

An ontology in the abstract ontology model is

$$O = (\mathcal{C}, \mathcal{R}) \qquad \mathcal{C} = (C, \sqsubseteq_C, \top_C, \bot_C) \qquad \mathcal{R} = (R, \sqsubseteq_R, \top_R, \bot_R, domain, range)$$

where $\mathcal{C}$ are concepts and $\mathcal{R}$ are relations among the concepts. C is the set of all concepts (concept names). The set C contains two special elements — the universal concept (everything) $\top_C$ and the absurd concept (nothing) $\bot_C$. The relation $\sqsubseteq_C$ forms a complete lattice[1] [9] on C, i.e. $\sqsubseteq_C$ is a partial ordering and

---

[1] A lattice can be informally described as a "tree with multiple inheritance" (see Figure 2). It is a a partially ordered set (i.e. a set with a reflexive, anti-symmetric and transitive relation $\sqsubseteq$) where there exists a unique least upper bound and a unique greatest lower bound for every two set elements and the ordering relation $\sqsubseteq$.

there exist both the least upper bound (supremum) and the greatest lower bound (infimum) for every subset of C. See Figure 2 for an example of concept lattices. The relations $\mathcal{R}$ are defined in a similar way. Moreover, there are additional relations *domain* and *range* over $R \times C$. If $(c_1 r_1 c_2)$ then $range(r_1) \sqsubseteq c_1$ and $domain(r_1) \sqsubseteq c_2$. We only focus on concept lattices in this paper.

The ontology is used to describe instances that exist in a domain agents operate on and to describe relations among these instances. Each instance can be classified into a set of concepts — to its most specific concept and superconcepts of this concept (including $\top_C$). The relation between two instances can be described by a relation from $\mathcal{R}$. The intensional definition of a concept is its position in the concept lattice and its occurrence in the *domain* and *range* of relations. A relation is described intensionally in a similar way. The meaning of concepts and relations is grounded in the instances and their relations. The extensional definition of concepts and relations is provided by the instances (of concepts and also of relations). Every concept can be (extensionally) defined by instances that can be classified under that concept. The subsumption of sets of instances classified under the concepts reflects the $\sqsubseteq_C$ relation. The extension of the universal concept (everything) $\top_C$ is the set of all instances while the extension of the absurd concept (nothing) $\bot_C$ is the empty set.

4   Mapping between Ontologies

In this section, we describe a mapping between ontologies that is then used to translate the content of messages between ontologies. Our goal is to get the best possible *consistent* translation. We prefer the consistency to precision, i.e. we are satisfied even with an approximate translation, but we do not want to introduce any inconsistency in the translation. In many cases, a loss of information is inevitable. An example is a very detailed source ontology that should be translated to a target ontology that describes all the concepts from the source ontology by just one concept. In this case the translation to that one concept introduces a vast information loss, but does not introduce any inconsistency.

By the *best possible* translation we mean that we would like to translate terms from the ontology as accurately as possible. For example, we could translate any concept as $\top_C$, but it will not be very useful. The lower we are in the lattice, the better the description is. The accuracy can be limited not only by the possibility to transfer all the information as described in the previous paragraph, but also by the information about the possible mapping that we have so far (in the process of learning translation). See Figure 2 for an example of mapping between ontologies.

4.1   Mapping Matrix

For translation, we need to know, which concepts of the target ontology can be and which cannot be used for translation from the source ontology. The knowledge for translation can be stored in a mapping matrix M, where rows correspond to concepts from O_S and columns correspond to concepts from O_T. Each matrix element $m_{i,j}$ corresponding to concepts $c_{S,i}$ and $c_{T,j}$ holds information whether it is possible to map from $c_{S,i}$ to $c_{T,j}$. There are three possible values that may be assigned to each element — *Yes*, *No*, and *Unknown*. The value *Yes* tells us that it is possible to map from $c_{S,i}$ to $c_{T,j}$, while the value *No* tells us that either it is not possible to map between these concepts or that the translation would not be accurate. The value *Unknown* tells us that we do not know anything about whether we can map between these concepts.

These values are filled in incrementally during the process of communication. In each step, it is possible to determine the best known mapping from the mapping matrix. At the beginning (when nothing is known) the matrix is filled with the *Unknown* values.

We will now discuss how the knowledge is maintained in the mapping matrix and how it is used for translation of messages. The main idea is that a concept is translated to the most general combination of concepts that is permissible and not forbidden by the current state in the mapping matrix. In this way, we may lose information, but we do not introduce inconsistency.

5   Maintaining Mapping between Ontologies

In this section, we discuss how to initialize and maintain the mapping matrix when two strange agents meet and want to communicate. Let us suppose that the agent A_S that uses the ontology O_S wants to communicate to the agent A_T that uses the ontology O_T. For the communication, A_S wants to be able to translate its messages from O_S to O_T before sending. Thus the agent A_S has to maintain the mapping matrix from O_S to O_T.

Because nothing is known at the start of the communication process, the matrix is initialized with the *Unknown* values. Then, as the communication continues, the matrix elements are filled in, so that the translation becomes possible and more accurate. Note that we suppose that before starting to learn the mapping, the agent A_S knows the structure of the target ontology O_T.

5.1   Establishing Mapping from Extension

There are several possibilities how to improve the mapping matrix by communication between agents. We can use the extensional or intensional properties of ontologies. An extension of every concept is the set of instances that can be classified under that concept. If we have descriptions of instances in both ontologies then we can use these descriptions to relate the concepts used for descriptions.

For establishing a possible mapping, we propose a pointing game that helps to see a classification of instances in different ontologies. Language games [10] are proposed to develop a common ontology for agents in a shared world. Here, the idea of pointing to instances to establish a mapping between existing ontologies is used. The necessary assumptions are that agents share a part of a world (a real physical world or a virtual world such as WWW), that they are able to point to objects in the world and that they are able to identify what the other agent is pointing to. The pointing game is simple — in one step of the game, an instance is chosen and described. This step is repeated until a satisfactory mapping is established. In the case of translation from O_S to O_T, we are interested in descriptions provided by the agent A_T. Both the agents can provide the description to each other if the mapping in both directions is required.

Two kinds of descriptions can be distinguished — positive and negative. By a positive description, a classification of the instance in a given ontology is meant. The most useful is the classification that is the closest to the bottom $\perp_T$, since we do not want to have all instances classified by $\top_T$ — we want to have instances classified as accurately as possible. The agent O_S knows what the agent O_T describes. Let us suppose that the instance is described by c_{S1} in O_S and by c_{T1} in O_T. From this information, the source concept c_{S1} can be approximated in at least one situation (for this instance) by the target concept c_{T1}. Therefore the mapping matrix can be modified so that $M[c_{S1}, c_{T1}] = Yes$.

By a negative description we understand any example of a concept under which the instance should not be classified, i.e. a description in a form $\neg c$. Obviously, if the instance can be described by $\neg c$, it is not possible to translate the source concept to that concept c. Similarly as in the positive description, the mapping matrix can be modified to $M[c_{S1}, c_{T1}] = No$. The value No is important for determining the upper bound for as accurate translation as possible, i.e. it helps to get better translation then to c_T. For all the concepts that are above the ideal translation concept, we can expect the values Yes as well, since they are also a consistent translation (for example in Figure 2 the concept "carp" can be translated to the concept "fish", and to the concept "living" as well). Because of the importance of No values over Yes values, No value is preferred wherever possible. This is particularly important for extending the mapping as described in the next section (see also the algorithm in Figure 3).

5.2   Extending Mapping from Intension

Let us recall that the intensional definition of a concept in our abstract ontology model consists of its relation to other concepts in C in terms of the $\sqsubseteq_C$ relation. Let us discuss how this knowledge can help us to extend the knowledge that we get from the extensional definition to other concepts.

Let us take an example of an instance that can be classified under c_S and c_T — in addition to updating the matrix field $M[c_S, c_T]$ it is also possible to extend this information to other concepts. When a concept c_S can be translated to c_T, then the same is true for all c_S superconcepts $c'_S \sqsupseteq c_S$. Similarly, if a concept can be translated to c_T, then it can be translated to all c_T subconcepts $c'_T \sqsubseteq c_T$. The information on a possible translation can be propagated in the mapping matrix based on these two properties of mapping.

In the case of instance classification under c_S and $\neg c_T$, the information can be extended to other concepts as well. The direction of extension is in the opposite direction here since the concept is negated in the description. If c_S is described by $\neg c_T$ then the same holds for all c_S subconcepts $c'_S \sqsubseteq c_S$. Also, if

---

Algorithm Update–Mapping–Matrix
Input: source ontology O_S, target ontology O_T, instance a, classification $c_{S,a}$
              of a in O_S, classification $c_{T,a}$ (positive) or $\neg c_{T,a}$ (negative) of a
              in O_T, mapping matrix M
Output: updated mapping matrix M

begin
    if classification is in positive form $c_{T,a}$ **then**
        for each $c_S \in C_S : c_S \sqsupseteq c_{S,a}$
            for each $c_T \in C_T : c_T \sqsubseteq c_{T,a}$
                if not $M[c_S, c_T] = No$ **then** $M[c_S, c_T] := Yes$
    else
        for each $c_S \in C_S : c_S \sqsubseteq c_{S,a}$
            for each $c_T \in C_T : c_T \sqsupseteq c_{T,a}$
            $M[c_S, c_T] := No$
    return M
end

Fig. 3. Mapping matrix update algorithm

the concept c_S should not be translated to c_T, then it should not be translated to c_T superconcepts $c_T' \sqsupseteq c_T$ as well.

For efficient filling of the matrix, it is also possible to use the knowledge gained so far and use that to request a description of a particular instance or to request an example of an instance for a given description. The strategy of selecting of instances is important for the speed of mapping learning. It is important for example in the case when it is desired to learn quickly a mapping only for a subset of concepts. The construction of strategies is based on the fact, that it is possible to update only the mapping of the concepts for which examples are available or for which the mapping knowledge can be derived from the example and from the knowledge of the $\sqsupseteq$ relation. An agent can request description of instances that are classified under the concepts from which it needs to learn the mapping. Note that this only requires adding a strategy for communication (instead of more or less random language game based communication) and no modification to the algorithms described in this paper is required. However, the discussion of these strategies in depth is beyond the scope of the paper.

5.3   Mapping Matrix Updating Algorithm

Let us summarize the algorithm for filling in the matrix from both the extensional and intensional knowledge about both the ontologies. The algorithm is schematically described in Figure 3. At the beginning, the matrix M is filled by *Unknown* values. Then, as new information is coming from the pointing game, the algorithm Update-mapping-matrix is executed for each instance and

Algorithm Translate-Message
Input: source ontology O_S, target ontology O_T, mapping matrix M,
            message G to be translated from O_S to O_T
Output: translated message G

begin
    for each occurrence of concept c_S **in** G
        if not $(\exists c_T : M[c_S, c_T] = Yes$ **and** $\exists c_T : M[c_S, c_T] = No)$ **then**
            return "cannot translate"
        $SetC_T := \{c_T \in C_T : M[c_S, c_T] = Yes\}$
        if occurrence of c_S is negative **then**
            $Uncertain := \{c_T \in SetC_T : c_T \sqsupseteq c'_T \in SetC_T \wedge M[c_S, c'_T] = Unknown\}$
            $SetC_T := SetC_T \setminus Uncertain$
        $Covered := \{c_T \in SetC_T : c_T \sqsubseteq c'_T \in SetC_T\}$
        $SetC_T := SetC_T \setminus Covered$
        replace this occurrence of c_S in G by $\bigvee SetC_T$
    return translated G
end

Fig. 4. Message translation algorithm

the mapping matrix gets updated so that the information for translation is becoming more accurate.

6   Translating Messages

In this section, it is described how the knowledge expressed in the mapping matrix is used for translating messages between two ontologies. The task is to translate the message from the source ontology O_S to the target ontology O_T. Replacing each occurrence of the source ontology concept by a consistent translation into the target ontology concept does this task. We have a consistent estimation how each concept from the source ontology O_S can be translated into the target ontology O_T.

Let us recall that a consistent translation is required — this means that a loss of information is permitted, but no inconsistency is permitted. In other words, we can consistently translate c_S to c_T only if the extension of c_T includes at least the extension of c_S, i.e. $Ext(c_T) \supset Ext(c_S)$. If the set $Ext(c_T) \setminus Ext(c_S)$ (i.e. the set of instances that are in c_T but are not in c_S) is not empty then the information loss is introduced. For example, the concept "carp" can be translated to the concept "fish" (see Figure 2), which introduces information loss (because the target ontology does not distinguish between "carp" and "pike"). But it is not possible to translate the concept "carp" to the concept "non-living", as this would introduce inconsistency (c_T does not cover c_S).

A concept c can occur in two forms in a message [11] — in the positive form c or in the negative form $\neg c$. In the case of positive occurrence, the concept can be translated by the most general combination of concepts that form a permissible translation of that concept. It is necessary to cover all concepts that are above the known possible translations (as it is uncertain whether they can be excluded from the best translation), but we cannot break any known upper restriction (formed by No values in the mapping matrix). If there is no known restriction, the only permissible consistent translation is the most general concept $\top_C$. On the other hand, in the case of negated occurrence $\neg c$, it is necessary to translate the source concept c to the combination of target concepts that cover all the known possible target concepts, but do not cover any uncertain concepts. For translation of negated occurrence, the subsumption $Ext(\neg c_T) \supset Ext(\neg c_S)$ must hold, and therefore $Ext(c_T) \subset Ext(c_S)$ must hold as well. The whole translation algorithm for translating a message is described in the Figure 4. Note that we are able to compute the translation from Yes values only because the No values overwrite them as explained previously (see the algorithm in the Figure 3).

7 Properties of Mapping and Translation

The result of translation is determined by the acquired mapping matrix, i.e. it is always clear to what target concept any source concept can be translated. Certainly, a source concept c_S can be mapped to more target concepts $\{c_T\}$ — see the example of translating the concept "carp" above. However, there is always only one most accurate consistent translation as described in the algorithm in the Figure 4. It is possible that the agent A_S does not have enough knowledge yet, so it can translate c_S into some c_T that is not the most accurate from the global view, but is the most accurate one from all the possible consistent translations that are based on the current knowledge. For example, if A_S knows (in a certain moment during the mapping learning) that "carp" can be translated to "living", but does not know yet, that it can be translated also to "fish", it uses the translation to "living", since it is the most accurate consistent translation possible. The translation to "fish" (or to "mammal" — see Figure 2) with this limited knowledge could turn out inconsistent later, so it is not used.

If the concept c_S can be mapped to some concept that does not exist in O_T and still it is possible to express it using existing concepts, the algorithm uses it. An example is shown in the Figure 2, where a "bird" is mapped into a subset of "moving" and "living". Of course, when the target ontology is more specific, the algorithm is not able to find a proper translation for particular instances. The knowledge that is gained from the described pointing game does not allow us to derive such a mapping — note that only names of concepts (not instances) are being translated with the goal of having always consistent translation.

Agents maintain their mapping themselves, i.e. for translation in both ways the agent A_S maintains the mapping from O_S to O_T and the agent A_T maintains the mapping from O_T to O_S. The described algorithm expects that both the agents have an access to both of the ontologies (see also the discussion below). Thus, the replication of ontologies is needed — so e.g. A_S needs to know O_T (in addition to O_S) as well. No replication of the mapping knowledge is needed.

8   Other Possibilities

For clarity purposes, we have illustrated the approach using a mapping matrix. The knowledge for translation can be expressed more economically in translation rules that express to what a target expression a concept can be or cannot be mapped. The process of maintaining these rules is in fact a combination of the two presented algorithms — when any rule is updated from an example instance, the bounds can be immediately computed as presented in the algorithm for translating messages. This can be done very quickly using the $\sqsubseteq_C$ relation. Rules can be then applied straightforwardly in the translation process.

We also expected that the agent A_S had obtained the definition of the target ontology O_T. This helped in refining the mapping from the beginning. However, it is also possible to proceed even without knowing the target ontology in advance. This might be useful when the replication of an ontology is not needed or wanted (e.g. when the ontology is proprietary). The terms used in ontology, i.e. concept and relation names, can be identified from instance descriptions in the target ontology. The subsumption relation $\sqsubseteq$ of both the concepts and relations can be determined from the subsumption that is observed on example instances. In this way, the target ontology can be constructed incrementally and it is not required to know the whole target ontology in advance. To handle this situation, another algorithm propagating any newly acquired subsumption knowledge in the existing mapping matrix would be needed. The translation algorithm will remain unchanged.

9   Related Work

Our approach is based on the idea of language games [10] that were used to develop a new common, shared ontology. During this process, the ontologies are changed to converge to one shared ontology. An approach that uses this for alignment of existing simple ontologies is presented in [12]. Common instances can be also used to infer operations for translation between schemas [13]. We presented an approach how a process similar to language games can be used to infer knowledge for mapping between existing ontologies for translating between them. A common approach to translation is the assumption of knowing all the relations between concepts in different ontologies explicitly in advance and then using a logic reasoner to compute the best approximation [11]. Our approach, in addition, is able to find a consistent translation even with partial knowledge about mapping and we do not require prior knowledge about the concept mapping. Moreover, our approach is of incremental nature in opposite to batch algorithms that are used for off-line human assisted ontology mapping [8].

10   Conclusion and Future Work

We have presented a way how agents can establish a mapping between their ontologies and use that mapping for translation between messages. The mapping can be established by a pointing game derived from the language games approach [10] when both the agents share a possibility to point to objects in a world that they share. The process is incremental and at any step the knowledge gained so far can be used to provide a translation.

Future work includes more precise specification of translation of relations $\mathcal{R}$ that form an integral part of an ontology. The lattice of relations can be translated in a similar way as concept lattices, however the fact that relations are attached to certain concepts (expressed by their range and domain [5, 4, 1]) can add a considerable piece of new information to the mapping matrix update algorithm. Another issue that we did not discuss in detail is the strategy in the pointing game. The presented approach relies more or less on a random language games approach [10] based pointing. A strategy for providing or requesting specific instances or concepts can speed up the process of refining the mapping considerably. The strategy can also help to focus only at a part of the ontology that is going to be used in further communication.

The presented approach helps the agents that do not share an ontology needed for communication to start establishing a mapping incrementally and to use the mapping for translation of messages. We see the autonomous establishing of ontology mapping for message translation as one of the key challenges for the success of open multi-agent systems.

Acknowledgements

This work is supported by the Ministry of Education of the Czech Republic within the project No. 212300013. We would like to thank anonymous reviewers for their comments that helped us to improve the explanation of approaches and algorithms described in this paper.

References

[1] Mike Dean, Dan Connolly, Frank van Harmelen, James Hendler, Ian Horrocks, Deborah L. McGuinness, Peter F. Patel-Schneider, Lynn Andrea Stein (eds.): OWL Web Ontology Language 1.0 Reference. 2002. http://www.w3.org/TR/owl-ref/.

[2] FIPA. Ontology Service Specification. 1998. http://www.fipa.org/specs/fipa00006/.

[3] Thomas R. Gruber: A Translation Approach to Portable Ontology Specifications. *Knowledge Acquisition.* **5.** 1993.

[4] Ian Horrocks, Frank van Harmelen, Peter Patel-Schneider (eds.): DAML+OIL (March 2001). http://www.daml.org/2001/03/daml+oil-index.html.

[5] Ora Lassila, Ralph R. Swick (eds): Resource Description Framework (RDF) Model and Syntax Specification. 1999. http://www.w3.org/TR/REC-rdf-syntax.

[6] Marek Obitko, Vladimír Mařík: Ontologies for Multi-Agent Systems in Manufacturing Domain. In *HoloMAS — Thirteenth International Workshop on Database and Expert Systems Applications.* IEEE Computer Society Press. pp. 597-602. 2002.

[7] *OAS2002 Workshop Proceedings.* Workshop on Ontologies in Agent Systems
     within 1st International Joint Conference on Autonomous Agents and Multi-
     Agent Systems. Bologna, Italy. 2002. `http://cis.otago.ac.nz/OAS2002/`.

[8] Erhard Rahm, Philip A. Bernstein: On Matching Schemas Automatically. *VLDB
     Journal.* Vol. **10**, 4, pp 334-350. 2001.

[9] John Sowa: *Knowledge Representation - Logical, Philosophical and Computa-
     tional Foundations.* Brooks/Cole. 2000.

[10] Luc Steels: Language Games for Autonomous Robots. *IEEE Intelligent Systems.*
     Vol. **16**, 5, pp 16-22. 2001.

[11] Heiner Stuckenschmidt, Ingo J. Timm: Adapting Communication Vocabularies
     using Shared Ontologies. In [7]. 2002.

[12] Jun Wang, Les Gasser: Mutual Online Ontology Alignment. In [7]. 2002.

[13] F. Wiesman, N. Roos and P. Vogt: Automatic Ontology Mapping for Agent
     Communication. *BNAIC01.* 2001.

A Social ACL Semantics by Deontic Constraints

Marco Alberti[1], Anna Ciampolini[2], Marco Gavanelli[1], Evelina Lamma[1],
Paola Mello[2], and Paolo Torroni[2]

[1] Dipartimento di Ingegneria
Università degli Studi di Ferrara, Via Saragat, 1 - 44100 Ferrara, Italy
{malberti,mgavanelli,elamma}@ing.unife.it
[2] Dipartimento di Elettronica, Informatica e Sistemistica
Università degli Studi di Bologna, Viale Risorgimento, 2 - 40136 Bologna, Italy
{aciampolini,pmello,ptorroni}@deis.unibo.it

Abstract. In most proposals for multi-agent systems, an Agent Communication Language (ACL) is the formalism designed to express knowledge exchange among agents. However, a universally accepted standard for ACLs is still missing. Among the different approaches to the definition of ACL semantics, the *social* approach seems the most appropriate to express semantics of communication in open societies of autonomous and heterogeneous agents.
In this paper we propose a formalism (*deontic constraints*) to express social ACL semantics, which can be grounded on a computational logic framework, thus allowing automatic verification of compliance by means of appropriate proof procedures. We also show how several common communication performatives can be defined by means of deontic constraints.

1 Introduction

Agent communication is one of the key issues in multi-agent systems. Traditional interprocess communication mechanisms are usually viewed as too low-level to effectively represent knowledge exchange among agents: thus, most proposals of standards for multi-agent systems propose an Agent Communication Language (ACL for brevity hereafter) as a formalism that abstracts away from implementation issues and provides sufficient expressive power for knowledge exchange at a high level.

However, there is still no agreed upon standard for ACLs, and many different approaches can be found in literature.

Mentalistic approaches [1, 2] define ACL semantics in terms of agents' mental states. For instance, FIPA ACL [2] assumes a BDI (Belief, Desire, Intention) model for the agents, and relies upon it for defining the semantics of communicative acts in terms of Feasibility Preconditions (i.e., the conditions that have to be satisfied for the communicative act to be planned) and Rational Effects (i.e., the expected effect of the communicative act).

While the mentalistic approach is adequate to account for *motivation* of communicative acts from an internal viewpoint, it is not safe to rely on it in

V. Mařík et al. (Eds): CEEMAS 2003, LNAI 2691, pp. 204–213, 2003.

open environments, when it is impossible to verify the effect of communication on the internal state of agents, as explained by Singh [3].

The social approach [4] moves from criticism to the mentalistic approach, and defines ACL semantics in terms of the effects of the communicative acts on a society of agents. Following this approach, even if agents' mental state cannot be accessed, it is possible to verify whether communicating agents in a society comply to the social laws that regulate the interactions. Thus, the social approach appears more appropriate to define the semantics of communication in open societies of agents.

Significant social proposals are based on the concept of *commitments* [5, 6], computational objects which keep track of agents' obligations and can evolve depending on agents' (observable) communicative and non-communicative acts, and eventually be resolved to fulfillments or violations.

In this paper, we present a logic-based approach to the definition of an ACL semantics which follows the principles of the social approach. It defines the meaning of communicative acts not as their effect on the mental state of single agents (upon which no *a priori* assumptions are made) but as their (verifiable) social effect. Our semantics is based on the concept of *expectation* (which, as explained in Sect. 4, is broader than that of commitment as adopted in [5]), linked to *socially significant events* by *deontic integrity constraints*, which provide a declarative specification of the proper interaction behavior in a society of agents. This specification can be grounded on a computational logic framework [7], thus obtaining the advantage of automatic verification by an appropriate proof procedure.

With respect to previous work [7], in this paper we introduce the concept of *alternative* expectations, which allow for different sequences of events to be compliant with protocols and semantics of communication.

The paper is structured as follows. In Sect. 2 we introduce the concept of deontic constraint, and in Sect. 3 we show how it can be exploited to specify the social semantics of communicative acts; discussion and directions for future work follow.

2   Interaction among Agents and Deontic Constraints

In this section, we briefly introduce our model of agent society, and focus on *deontic integrity constraints* (also *deontic constraints* or ic_Ds for brevity in the following) as a formalism to specify the desired behavior of interaction in a society of agents.

We consider interaction in an open society of autonomous and heterogeneous agents, and do not make any assumptions about the internal structure of individual agents. Deontic constraint are intended to constrain only the behavior of agents as required to ensure the desired operation of the society; thus, they regard *observable* and *socially significant* (i.e., effective over other agents or the environment[1]) events. We do not deal with modifications of the internal state of an agent that are not socially significant.

In the following, we assume that agents interact through a *social infrastructure*. This should be understood as a functional abstraction of a set of computational entities that provides a platform for agents' interactions. In particular, the social infrastructure is supposed to be aware of agents' socially significant actions and changes in the environment, and to be able to detect fulfillment or violations of expectations (explained later) by means of appropriate proof procedures.

A more detailed discussion of our model of society and of the functionalities of the social infrastructure can be found in [7].

Events can be produced by agents' actions or by modifications in the environment. We describe the content of events by atoms in a first order language. For instance, the atom

$$request(a_1, a_2, give(nail), a\_dialog, 10)$$

would represent a request issued at time 10, in the context of the dialog a_dialog, from agent a_1 to a_2 to *give* a *nail*.

We express the fact that an event has happened by the functor **H**. For instance, the event whose content is described above is represented as

$$\mathbf{H}(request(a_1, a_2, give(nail), a\_dialog, 10))$$

The desired behavior of a society of agents is expressed by *expectations*: events that should happen (*obligations*) and events that should not happen (*prohibitions*). Obligations and prohibitions are respectively expressed by the functors **O** and **ON**.

Deontic constraints relate events and expectations: intuitively, a deontic constraint expresses that, if some events have happened, then some other events are expected to (or not to) happen. Variables in an expectation can be constrained. We give here the syntax of deontic constraints, in BNF.

$$
\begin{aligned}
ic_D &::= \chi \to \phi \\
\chi &::= ExtendedLiteral\ [\ \wedge\ ExtendedLiteral\ ]^* \\
\phi &::= OughtList[: ConstraintList][\vee OughtList[: ConstraintList]]^* \\
ExtendedLiteral &::= EventAtom \mid Literal \\
DeonticAtom &::= \mathbf{O}(Atom) \mid \mathbf{ON}(Atom) \\
EventAtom &::= \mathbf{H}(Atom) \\
Literal &::= Atom \mid \neg Atom \\
OughtList &::= DeonticAtom\ [\ \wedge\ DeonticAtom\ ]^*
\end{aligned}
$$

$$(1)$$

---

[1] By environment, we mean the setting in which the agent operate. In this work, we do not formalize the concept; however, we suppose that significant properties of the environment can be described by a first order language.

Atom represents an atom as intended in logic programming, and *ConstraintList* is a conjunction of constraints on the variables in *OughtList*. For instance,

$$\mathbf{O}(do(a_1, a_2, give(nail), a\_dialog, T)) : T \leq 10$$

means that, in the context of dialog *a_dialog*, agent a_1 is expected to *give* a *nail* to agent a_2 by time 10.

Expectations may be fulfilled or violated by events. For instance, the following event:

$$\mathbf{H}(do(a_1, a_2, give(nail), a\_dialog, 7))$$

would fulfill the above expectation. In case of violations, appropriate recovery procedures should be triggered so to bring the society back to a proper behavior.

A formal declarative semantics of deontic constraints is described in [7].

Compliance of events to deontic constraints can be achieved by means of appropriate proof procedures in a computational logic setting (as done, for a restricted version of deontic constraints, in [7]). Intuitively, deontic constraints can be used as production rules to generate the expectations in the head when the events in the body happen; these expectations can be fulfilled or violated by the history of events. Obviously, in order to operate in real world applications, such a proof procedure should operate incrementally, i.e., generate expectations and detect fulfillment and violation of them while new events happen.

3   Constraint-Based ACL Semantics

In this section, we show how social semantics of an ACL can be defined by means of deontic constraints. We consider communicative acts from a social perspective, i.e., we do not constrain the internal communicative model of agents (by which communicative acts are *motivated*), but instead link communicative acts to the expectations they generate. Social semantics of communicative acts is thus verifiable regardless of the internal structure of agents.

Throughout this section, we refer to the classification of primitives described in [5] (see Sect. 4), and define some primitives for each of the classes considered in [5], namely *assertives, commissives, directives* and *proposals*.

In the remainder, we describe a communicative act by an atom of this structure:

$$primitive\_name(Sender, Receiver, Content, Dialog, Time) \tag{2}$$

Assertive primitives: inform. Assertive primitives are used to exchange pieces of knowledge between agents, e.g. to communicate the truth of a proposition.

Intuitively, an *inform* is used by an agent to assert the truth of the content to another agent. In a commitment-based setting like that of [5], this equates to the speaker agent to *commit* to the truth of the content to the hearer agent.

In our framework, a possible definition of *inform* is as follows:

$$\begin{aligned} &\mathbf{H}(inform(A, B, P, D, T)) \\ &\rightarrow \mathbf{O}(truthful(A, B, P)) \end{aligned} \tag{3}$$

where P is a predicate[2], and with $\mathbf{O}(truthful(A, B, P))$, we mean that the falsity of P would be considered the violation of a commitment of A towards B.

We are aware that verifiability is a problem here: who is supposed to verify the truth of P? According to our approach, built on the principle that it is not acceptable to make assumptions about agents (and, therefore, about their truthfulness) the social infrastructure should be equipped with a knowledge base allowing it to decide the truth value of P. If this is not the case, the only way is probably to associate no obligation to an *inform* act, and let the hearer agent decide about the trustworthiness of the speaker.

Commissive primitives: promise and conditionalPromise. Commissive primitives are used by an agent that wants to commit itself to the execution of some action, possibly specifying a deadline.

A *promise*, like an *inform*, commits the speaker to the truth of the content, but for the former the speaker is responsible for fulfilling it by a physical action.

$$\mathbf{H}(promise(A, B, P, D, T_p))$$
$$\rightarrow \mathbf{O}(do(A, B, P, D, T_d)) : T_d \leq T_p + \tau \tag{4}$$

The obligation in constraint (4) is *forward*, in that it regards an event that should happen in the future. *do* is a physical action, which fulfills the obligation of deontic constraint (4), provided that it is performed before a certain amount of time τ has passed since the promise, as expressed by the $T_2 \leq T_1 + \tau$ constraint. If no proper *do* action has been performed at the deadline, a violation should be detected.

The obligation in a *conditionalPromise* becomes effective only when an external condition (indicated by Q in the following deontic constraint) becomes true:

$$\mathbf{H}(conditionalPromise(A, B, P|Q, D, T_{cp}))$$
$$\wedge \mathbf{H}(true(Q, T_Q)) \tag{5}$$
$$\rightarrow \mathbf{O}(do(A, B, P, D, T_d)) : T_d \leq T_Q + \tau$$

where $true(Q, T_Q)$ represents the fact that, in the instant T_Q, the condition Q becomes true, and this is recognized by the social infrastructure as a significant event.

Directive primitives: request and conditionalRequest. The goal of directive primitives is to invite the hearer agent to perform some action. It is up to the hearer whether to *accept* or to *reject* the content of a directive communicative act.

A *request* does not, by itself, commit the hearer agent to its content, which becomes an obligation only when the request is *accepted*, as the following deontic

---

[2] Intuitively, the content should represent a condition that does not depend on the future behavior of agents, as, for instance, $sunnyDay(today)$.

constraint states:

$$\mathbf{H}(request(B, A, P, D, T_r))$$
$$\wedge \mathbf{H}(accept(A, B, P, D, T_a))$$
$$\wedge T_r < T_a \tag{6}$$
$$\rightarrow \mathbf{O}(do(A, B, P, D, T_d)) : T_d \leq T_a + \tau$$

However, if so desired, it is possible to commit the hearer to answer positively or negatively by a fixed amount of time, by means of following deontic constraint:

$$\mathbf{H}(request(A, B, P, D, T_{rq}))$$
$$\rightarrow \mathbf{O}(accept(A, B, P, D, T_a)) : T_a \leq T_{rq} + \tau) \tag{7}$$
$$\vee \mathbf{O}(reject(A, B, P, D, T_{rj})) : T_{rj} \leq T_{rq} + \tau)$$

The expectations in constraint (7) are *alternative*, i.e., they are fulfilled if at least one of them is.

A *conditionalRequest* is different from a *request* in that its content becomes an obligation only once (the hearer has *accept*ed it and) an external condition has become true:

$$\mathbf{H}(conditionalRequest(B, A, P|Q, D, T_{cr}))$$
$$\wedge \mathbf{H}(accept(A, B, P|Q, D, T_a))$$
$$\wedge T_{cr} < T_a \tag{8}$$
$$\wedge \mathbf{H}(true(Q, T_Q))$$
$$\rightarrow \mathbf{O}(do(A, B, P, D, T_d)) : T_d \leq T_Q + \tau$$

Proposal primitives: propose. A proposal is a conjunction of a conditional directive and a conditional commissive.

A *propose* is similar to a *conditionalRequest*, with the intuitive difference that for the former the speaker is able to fulfill the condition by a *do* action.

$$\mathbf{H}(propose(B, A, (P_A, P_B), D, T_p))$$
$$\wedge \mathbf{H}(accept(A, B, (P_A, P_B), D, T_a))$$
$$\wedge T_p < T_a \tag{9}$$
$$\rightarrow \mathbf{O}(do(A, B, P_A, D, T_{d_A})) \wedge \mathbf{O}(do(B, A, P_B, D, T_{d_B})) :$$
$$T_{d_A} \leq T_a + \tau_A \wedge T_{d_B} \leq T_a + \tau_B$$

As for *request* and *conditionalRequest*, however, *propose* does not, per se, generate any obligation (unless it is desired to force an answer as in constraint (7)). It is with *accept* that both the speaker and the hearer become committed to their respective obligations (see constraint (9)).

accept and reject. After receiving a *request*, a *conditionalRequest* or a *propose*, an agent can make the related obligations effective with an *accept* communicative act. This is expressed by constraints (6), (8) and (9).

It should be noticed that obligations are generated only by proper sequences of communicative acts.

It may be desirable to forbid a communicative act unless a certain condition holds. For instance, an *accept* only makes sense in reply to a *request, conditionalRequest* or *propose*. For this purpose, *backward* expectations can be used, i.e., expectations about events that *should* (or *should not*) *have happened* when the expectation is generated.

For instance, constraint (10) expresses that, if an *accept* has happened, a corresponding *request, conditionalRequest* or *propose* should have happened before. If none of the three holds, a violation should be detected.

$$\mathbf{H}(accept(A, B, P, D, T_a))$$
$$\rightarrow \mathbf{O}(request(B, A, P, D, T_r)) : T_r < T_a$$
$$\vee \mathbf{O}(conditionalRequest(B, A, P, D, T_{cr})) : T_{cr} < T_a \qquad (10)$$
$$\vee \mathbf{O}(propose(B, A, P, D, T_p)) : T_p < T_a$$

An agent that *rejects* a *request, conditionalRequest* or *propose* is obviously not committed to its content. Thus, the only obligation associated with a *reject* is backward, and it is needed to ensure (if so wanted) that a *reject* is only performed in reply to a corresponding *request, conditionalRequest* or *propose*.

$$\mathbf{H}(reject(A, B, P, D, T_{rj}))$$
$$\rightarrow \mathbf{O}(request(B, A, P, D, T_{rq})) : T_{rq} < T_{rj}$$
$$\vee \mathbf{O}(conditionalRequest(B, A, P, D, T_{cr})) : T_{cr} < T_{rj} \qquad (11)$$
$$\vee \mathbf{O}(propose(B, A, P, D, T_p)) : T_p < T_{rj}$$

With this semantics of *accept* and *reject*, it is not necessary to impose one more constraint to make the disjunction in constraint (7) exclusive: if an agent both *accepts* and *rejects* a *request, conditionalRequest* or *propose*, it is committed to the content anyway. However, if so desired this can be achieved by:

$$\mathbf{H}(accept(A, B, P, D, T_a))$$
$$\rightarrow \mathbf{ON}(reject(A, B, P, D, T_r)) \qquad (12)$$

Since there are no constraints on T_a and T_r, it is not necessary to impose the inverse constraint, because if both an *accept* and a *reject* were issued a violation would be detected, regardless of the order of the communicative acts.

4   Discussion and Related Work

In defining ACL semantics, we have followed a social approach which, better than the mentalistic, seems to fulfill the requirements of communication in open societies of autonomous and heterogeneous agents.

The syntax of deontic constraints here presented is an extension of that presented in [7], where the model of agent society here assumed is described in more detail, deontic constraints are given a formal declarative semantics and a prototypical implementation of deontic constraints exploiting the *CHR* language is sketched.

The additional syntactical elements here introduced allow us to express *alternative* expectations in the head of a deontic constraint, i.e., expectations which can be fulfilled by different sequences of events, as in constraints (7), (10) and (11).

The implementation of the computational framework described in [7] is currently being expanded in order to manage the syntactical (and semantical) extension.

In part, we draw inspiration from work on commitment-based ACL semantics, notably Fornara and Colombetti's [5], where an operational specification of an ACL is given in an object-oriented framework by means of the *commitment* class.

A commitment is described by a finite state automaton, whose state transitions can occur by application of methods of the commitment class, or of rules triggered by external conditions. Semantics of communicative acts is specified in terms of methods to be applied to a commitment when a communicative act is issued.

The approach there presented is similar to ours in that it is *social-based*: it makes no assumptions on the nature of agents, specifies semantics of actions as their social effects and assumes the existence of a social framework (which is called *institution* in [8]) for assigning agents with roles, verifying agents' social behavior and, possibly, recovering from violation conditions.

There are, however, some significant differences, originating, in part, from the different paradigms of the two frameworks (object-oriented and logic-based). For instance, a commitment can have several states, while expectations do not have states. Although some of the possible states of a commitment do not have a direct mapping to our framework, which could make our framework seem less expressive, as explained in [7] we can express an equivalent semantics (in terms of fulfillments and violations with respect to a sequence of communicative and physical acts) to one expressed in the framework of [5]. In general, it is sufficient to specify the sequences of communicative actions that should raise an expectation.

Furthermore, social semantics of communicative acts in Fornara and Colombetti's framework has a unique definition as a method application on a commitment: for instance, an *accept* will always turn a *pre-commitment* into a *conditional commitment*. In our framework, instead, it is possible to specify that a communicative act generates an expectation only in a given combination of events, thus allowing to give "context-sensitive" semantics to communicative acts.

Our notion of *expectation* is also more general than that of *commitment*: it represents the deontic necessity of a (past or future) event, and is not bound to have a debtor or a creditor, or to be brought about by an agent. For instance, if we want to express the constraint that an agent is only *allowed* to perform an act when a previous event has occurred (not necessarily for an agent's action), we can simply impose it as a backward obligation (as, for instance, constraint (10)), whereas it is not obvious how to express this in Fornara and Colombetti's framework [5]. In other words, the formalism of deontic constraint can express both social semantics of communicative acts and interaction protocols. In [9], for instance, we exploit deontic constraints for expressing protocols for an agent society, rather than the semantics of communication.

The deontic framework can, in part, be integrated with dialogue theory [10], where different types of dialogues which can occur between agents are modeled in terms of *initial situation*, *private aims* of the interlocutors and *joint aims* implicitly subscribed by the interlocutors. Deontic constraints can express the allowed sequences of utterances to compose a dialogue framework [11]. Moreover, the result of dialogues can raise expectations about the subsequent behavior of agents: for instance, once a collective intention [12] is established, the agents can be expected to fulfill it. However, since we make no assumptions about the mental structure of individual agents, the results of dialogues regarding beliefs (namely *persuasion*, *inquiry* and *information seeking*) are not verifiable in our framework.

Future work will regard both the declarative specification of a society of agents and its operational counterpart.

Declaratively, current work is devoted to the problem of deciding which agent is responsible for a violation of an expectation, which is not obvious in the general case. This is related to the definition of the recovery procedures mentioned in Sect. 2, which is, too, subject of current work.

Operationally, we plan to extend the prototypical implementation of deontic constraints [7] in order to handle alternative expectations, and to improve and refine it as needed to operate in a real world open environment.

In addition, we intend to investigate more deeply the formal properties of the proof procedures involved in the framework, such as soundness and completeness with respect to the declarative specification as done, for instance, in [13].

We are also considering the possibility of integrating deontic constraints as integrity constraint in a more general abductive framework.

Acknowledgments

This work is partially funded by the Information Society Technologies programme of the European Commission under the IST-2001-32530 project (SOCS). The information provided is the sole responsibility of the authors and does not reflect the Commission's opinion. The Commission is not responsible for any use that might be made of the data appearing in this publication.

References

[1] Finin, T., Labrou, Y., Mayfield, J.: KQML as an agent communication language. In: Software Agents. MIT Press, Cambridge (1997)

[2] FIPA: FIPA Communicative Act Library Specification (2001) Published on August 10th, 2001, available for download from the FIPA website: http://www.fipa.org

[3] Singh, M.: Agent communication language: rethinking the principles. IEEE Computer (1998) 40–47

[4] Singh, M. P.: A social semantics for agent communication languages. In Dignum, F., Greaves, M., eds.: Issues in Agent Communication. Springer-Verlag, Heidelberg, Germany (2000) 31–45

[5] Fornara, N., Colombetti, M.: Operational specification of a commitment-based agent communication language. In Castelfranchi, C., Lewis Johnson, W., eds.: Proceedings of the First International Joint Conference on Autonomous Agents and Multiagent Systems (AAMAS-2002). Part II, Bologna, Italy, ACM (2002) 535–542

[6] Yolum, P., Singh, M.: Commitment machines. In: Intelligent Agents VIII, 8th International Workshop, ATAL 2001 Seattle, WA, USA, August 1-3, 2001 Revised Papers. Volume 2333 of LNAI., Springer Verlag (2002) 235–247

[7] Alberti, M., Ciampolini, A., Gavanelli, M., Lamma, E., Mello, P., Torroni, P.: Logic based semantics for agent communication languages. In Dunin-Keplicz, B., Werbrugge, R., eds.: Proceedings of the Workshop of Formal Approaches to Multiagent Systems (FAMAS03), Warsaw, Poland. (2003)

[8] Colombetti, M., Fornara, N., Verdicchio, M.: The role of institutions in multiagent systems. In: Proceedings of the Workshop on Knowledge based and reasoning agents, VIII Convegno AI*IA 2002, Siena, Italy. (2002)

[9] Torroni, P., Mello, P., Maudet, N., Alberti, M., Ciampolini, A., Lamma, E., Sadri, F., Toni, F.: A logic-based approach to modeling interaction among computees (preliminary report). In: UK Multi-Agent Systems (UKMAS) Annual Conference, Liverpool, UK. (2002)

[10] Walton, D., Krabbe, E.: Commitment in Dialogue. SUNY, New York (1995)

[11] Reed, C. A.: Dialogue frames in agent communication. In: Proceedings of the 3rd International Conference on Multi Agent Systems (ICMAS98), Paris, IEEE Press (1998) 246–253

[12] Dignum, F., Dunin-Keplicz, B., Verbrugge, R.: Creating collective intention through dialogue. Logic J. of the IGPL **9** (2001) 145–158

[13] Ciampolini, A., Lamma, E., Mello, P., Torroni, P.: An operational semantic for the safe execution of tasks in a constrained multi-agent setting. In Greco, S., Leone, N., eds.: Proceedings of the 8th European Conference on Logics in Artificial Intelligence (JELIA). Volume 2424 of LNCS., Springer Verlag (2002) 14–26

A Formal Specification Language for Agent Conversations

Javier Soriano, Fernando Alonso, and Genoveva López

Technical University of Madrid, Campus de Montegancedo S/N
28660 Boadilla del Monte, Madrid, Spain
{jsoriano,falonso,glopez}@fi.upm.es

Abstract. Agents interact in the context of a society to exchange knowledge, to cooperate and to coordinate their activities. A standard approach is to describe these interactions as conversations specified by means of interaction protocols (IPs). The set of conversations in which an agent can participate defines its communication interface. Therefore, the standardised sets of IPs that specify these conversations can be viewed as Agent Interface Definitions (AID), just as procedure and function definitions make up programming interfaces (API) in other programming paradigms. This paper presents the abstract syntax and semantics of ACSL[1]: a new formal specification language that can clearly and precisely describe these interfaces so that they can be consumed both by designers and programmers (generally using CASE tools) and automatically by actual agents during interaction. This language fills a gap in the development of agent interface definition languages (AIDL). The paper focuses particularly on the newest features of the language, like (1) protocol composition, (2) protocol exceptions related to the reception of out-of-sequence messages or timeout expirations, (3) compensation protocols that adapt the classical concept of transaction to the autonomy and rationality of agents and, finally, (4) specification of message correlation and causality.

1 Introduction

The interaction model used in the agent paradigm is based on agents performing communicative acts in an attempt to suitably influence the state and behaviour of other agents. This attempt at dealing with communication as an action derives from speech act theory [1] and is based on the assumption that agents carry out speech acts in the same way as other actions, i.e. to further their intentions. These are the premises for the development of agent communication languages (ACL) that model speech acts as typed messages that make up the building blocks of communication. ARPA-KSI's KQML [2] and FIPA-ACL [3] are the two major examples of ACLs. However, agents do not participate in isolated message exchanges, they enter into conversations, i.e. coherent message

---

[1] This work is being supported by the Spanish Ministry of Science and Technology, Project TIC2001-3451.

V. Mařík et al. (Eds): CEEMAS 2003, LNAI 2691, pp. 214–225, 2003.

sequences, to carry out specific tasks that require coordination, such as negotiations or auctions. This exchange sequence may emerge spontaneously or have been agreed upon beforehand and specified by means of an interaction protocol. The a priori specification of interaction protocols and agreement upon the particular protocol to be followed in a given conversation eases the design of agents capable of entering into coherent conversations with other agents.

Interaction protocol specification is not a new idea in the agent paradigm. There are a host of approaches that have considered, adopted and syntactically and semantically enhanced a range of techniques traditionally used in communication protocol design associated with distributed systems. Some of these approaches have attached more importance to producing models that are easy to interpret and implement. This is the case of approaches based on state transition diagrams [4] and finite state machines [5]. At the cost of obscuring their interpretation, others have included more complex mathematical and/or logical formulas, enabling them to express concurrency or validate and simulate the specified protocol. These include proposals based on Petri Nets [6]. Other proposals are based on syntactic specification languages like LOTOS, Estelle or SDL [7]. Most of these techniques lack a graphic representation close to the designer's view of the protocol. This is all the more true, the more complex the interaction to be modelled is. The Protocol Diagrams proposed by Agent-UML [9] provide a view much closer to the designer's. However, these diagrams are no more than a notation for the analysis and design phases of a method, providing neither support for the formal specification of interaction protocols in a standard language to enable protocol validation and simulation, nor for protocol exchange, discovery and dynamic learning by the agents who intend to converse. FIPA has made an overall contribution to this effort by providing specifications in Agent-UML notation of many interesting protocols [10]. Neither should other formal logic-based description techniques, such as those presented in [11] and [12] be overlooked, although they are more oriented to automatically inferring message exchange patterns than to a priori specification.

We find that there is a huge void between the existing formal techniques, whose design is highly complex, and the graphic notations, which are devoid of precise semantics, complicate automatic protocol property proving and cannot be automatically interpreted by agents. This article proposes to narrow this gap, providing a new formal specification language, ACSL (Agent Conversation Specification Language), whose syntactic expressiveness is very close to the protocol view offered by the interaction diagrams in Agent-UML notation and whose semantic accuracy will make it possible to automate the interpretation of the specified protocols and examine some of their formal properties.

The remainder of the article is structured as follows. Section 2 presents the concept of agent interface definition language (AIDL) as an evolution of ACLs, which can be used to specify the set of conversations in which an agent can participate. Section 3 introduces the key interagent conversation modelling requirements. On the basis of an example of its use, section 4 introduces the key elements of the ACSL specification language, focusing on its newest features, like owing to the occurrence of the associated event and the behaviour associated with the branch in question has terminated.

- *All:* Executes a set of behaviours concurrently. This execution is not subject to any time order. Expresses the semantics of the AND connector in Agent-UML notation.
- *While:* Repeats the exchange pattern given by a *threadOfInteraction* an undefined number of times. The specified behaviour is executed until the *condition* in question is no longer true. The condition is opaque, as discussed earlier.
- *Repeat:* Repeats an exchange pattern given by a *threadOfInteraction* a pre-established number of times. The number of times it is repeated is opaque.

4.4   Exception Handling in the Sequencing Pattern

An out-of-sequence message may arrive at any point in an interaction protocol. Likewise, a timeout may be reached or, even, an internal error may occur that has a direct impact on the exchange protocol. The handling of all these eventualities can be provided for at protocol level. As they are not directly linked to the normal interaction flow, these cases will be termed *protocol exceptions* to distinguish them from the exceptions that can occur in the state and/or autonomous behaviour of agents and whose management is part of the internal processes of these agents and not closely related to interaction protocol specification. To make protocol exception handling more flexible, exceptions are declared at *context* level so that their scope is constrained to the exchange pattern subset specified in the context in question.

Exception handling is associated with an exception block element declared after defining the flow pattern (*orchestration* block) of the *context* with which the exception is to be associated. The *exception* block will contain a process control *pick* whose alternatives reference the different events that fire any protocol exceptions that occur during the flow defined in the context orchestration and which are to be handled. The *pick* process declared in an exception block of a context will be available as soon as the flow defined in the *orchestration* block of the above context starts. If any of the events declared in any of the alternatives of the above *pick* occur, the normal context flow will be stopped and control will be passed on to the process defined in the body of the alternative. If the normal flow of the context ends without any exceptional events occurring, the *pick* process of the exception block will end without executing any of its alternatives. A standard element in the alternatives definition of an exception block is *compensate*. This element, as we will see in the next section, references (i.e. invokes) *compensation* blocks of the embedded contexts in reverse order to their completion. Fig. 1 shows the invocation of an exception protocol from the exception block of the basic pattern.

4.5   Compensation Protocols

In the event of an error during a complex interaction that involves one or more protocols, the agent involved should be given the chance to start up a conversation characterised by one or more appropriate interaction protocols that compensate, as far as possible, for this error, taking the system back to a state to similar to what it was at the start of the interaction. This conversation is called *compensation protocol.* This approach is not equivalent to the concept of ACID transaction [16] as it is understood in the operating systems and databases context, as interaction between autonomous agents has two unique characteristics that rule out ACID transaction handling: (1) the interactions can take a long time, which means that the resources (locks, copies, etc.) required to assure the state of a global transaction at interaction level cannot be handled, and (2) the intrinsic autonomy of agents makes it impossible to assure transaction *rollback* from a centralised perspective, even though they behave rationally.

For a better understanding of the concept, suppose we have a conversation between a client agent that aims to negotiate the provision of a service that involves engaging an intermediary agent to contract the services offered by other agents. If the negotiation between the intermediary agent and service provider agents is carried out in several successive steps and an error occurs in any of the intermediate steps, the intermediary agent will be obliged to cancel the operations committed in earlier steps, for which purpose it would want to have a set of interaction protocols, previously agreed with each of the agents concerned, that would allow it to return, if not to the original state, at least to a state of compromise. For this purpose, it can initiate cancellation protocols, such as those presented in [13], for example.

The compensation behaviour is part of the interaction protocol and should, therefore, be explicitly specified. Contexts are used for this purpose. Contexts determine which part of the interaction flow could require a given compensation protocol (i.e. its scope). A compensation protocol is defined in a context by means of a named *compensation* block. A compensation block is explicitly invoked by means of the *compensate* process, which references the block name. A compensation process will only be able to be invoked from an *exception* block at the same level (i.e. same context) or from an exception block or compensation block at a higher level of the hierarchy.

The messages sent as a result of executing a compensation protocol usually identify an alternative from an *exception* block in the protocol followed by the receiving agent, which can then start to execute its part of the overall compensation protocol. Fig. 1 shows the invocation of a compensation protocol from the *exception* block of the basic pattern.

5   Related Work

Other work has been completed along the lines presented in this paper. Thus, [13] presents a coordination language called COOL, which is founded on speech act-based communication and a structured conversational framework that captures the coordination mechanisms used by agents. COOL has been used to design and validate coordination protocols for multiagent systems. The coordination activity is modelled as a conversation between two or more agents and is spe-

- coordinates of customer location,
- weight of load,
- service time window indicating the admissible real time interval for delivery and unloading,
- duration of unloading ("service time").

Load delivery is carried out by vehicles (trucks) with constrained capacity that is upper threshold for total weight of loads that is admitted for it.

Each customer has to be serviced within the given service-time window. If a vehicle reaches a customer before the service-time determined by time window, a waiting time occurs. The distance between a pair of customers is considered as equal to the travel time between them. The total time spent by a vehicle for all allocated services provision is determined as the sum of the total travel time, total waiting time and total service time[1].This time is one of the components of the quality of service vector mapped to the solution produced by multi-agent planning and scheduling system. Informally speaking, the main goal of MAS in question is to search a schedule that provide all customers with the requested services while minimizing the total time spent and meeting vehicles' capacity constraints and customers' time-service windows. In an alternative variant of problem statement minimization of the number of vehicles used is considered as the main goal instead of total time spent.

The benchmark consists of data sets of different characteristics. Task statements differ in the time-service windows, scheduling horizon and customers' coordinates. Scheduling horizon determines the number of customers per route. Customers' locations in different data sets are randomly generated, clustered and mixed. It is worthy to note that time-service windows noticeably affect the admissible routes. More details can be found in ([8]).

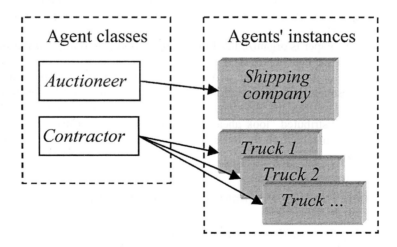

Fig. 1. Agent classes and agents' instances

---

[1] It is assumed in the benchmark that the time in measured in distance units ([8]).

3   Agent Classes, Roles and Software Agent Instances

Development and deployment of VRPTW MAS was carried out with use of a multi-agent platform called Multi-agent System Development Kit, MASDK ([6]). In this tool kit, functionalities and data structures that practically independent from application to application are implemented as a unified (reusable) components united within so-called *Generic Agent*. The latter comprises a hierarchy of invariant software classes and generic data structures. Generic agent is considered as a nucleus that is "boot-strapped" by the developer through specialization of the software classes and data structures and through replication of software agent classes in their instances composing MAS. Thus, design and implementation of the software agents of an applied MAS is reduced to the specification their application-oriented attributes and properties which are performed in three steps. At the first step, the shared application ontology and also agents' interaction protocols are specified by designers. The protocols are represented in terms of roles assigned to particular agents. At the second step, the functionalities of agents' classes and respective private components of the application ontology are specified. At the third step, the instances of agents' classes that are software agents are generated and also software agents' particular attributes and properties are specified. The above steps are supported by user-friendly editors provided with clear interfaces. In addition to Generic Agent, these editors together constitute the second component of MASDK tool kit.

The correlation between mentioned above notions "agent class" and "software agent's instance" is similar to the correlation between the notions "software class" and its instance in object-oriented programming. For example, specifications of application-oriented behavior scenarios defined for an agents' class are inherited by all software agent's instances of agents' class. Fig 1 graphically demonstrates the above property of the respective agents of the VRPTW MAS. In the application under consideration, two agents' classes are introduced, *Auctioneer* and *Contractor*. The former agents' class has single software agent instance, *Shipping company*, which performs the respective role and behaviors. The latter agents' class has many software agent's instances, that are *Truck 1, Truck 2, Truck ....*

The agents' classes determine the agents' roles and, respectively, their roles in interaction protocols. In VRPTW MAS several interaction protocols intended for solving different tasks are used. For example, these tasks are allocation and reallocation of resources and scheduling. Each protocol supposes that two classes of agents (roles) are involved in the interactions, *Auctioneer* and *Contractor,* at that the former has the single instance whereas the last one has multiple instances. In general case agents' classes can be assigned several roles within the same or different protocols. The functions performed by agents of different roles in VRPTW MAS are as follows:

Auctioneer
1. Meta-level management of the VRPTW task solving. This functionality manages the meta-level processes in MAS. In particular, it determines what of the processes must at the moment be executed, i.e. what of resource allocation and scheduling, preparation to execution of the process of resource reallocation or

re-scheduling, and what interaction protocol correspond to this or that chosen process.

2. Sequencing of orders in both allocation and reallocation auctions.
3. Analysis of quality of services offered by "contractors", winner selection.
4. Management of resource reallocation preparatory phase which aims at forming of a subset of orders considered as the subjects for reallocation.
5. Selection of the subset of potential contractors for the next auction.

Auctioneer also solves a number of auxiliary tasks.

All above functionalities can be executed in both automatic and interactive modes. The latter supposes that user can intervene into the solution procedure. In particular the approval of the final decision is here the user's responsibility. In interactive mode, user can agree with the allocation proposed by MAS (auctioneer) or disagree and select it manually.

Contractor
1. Any-time algorithm for search of the shortest route through-passing nodes cor- responding to the customer locations, i.e. loads destinations.
2. Calculation of bid proposals. The "cost" of a bid ("cost" of the order execution) is calculated as increase of total distance along the new rout in comparison with the total distance along the previous one.
3. Participation in computing of the subset of orders for reallocation.

4   Resource Allocation

Resource allocation is realized as a sequence of auctions, at that each of them aims at allocation of a particular order to a contractor. Every auction consists of the following sequence of steps (tasks):

1. Selection of an order "to be sold" during forthcomong auction.
2. Selection of a multitude of the potential contractors to participate in the forthcoming auction.
Auctioneer solves both above tasks.
3. Auction realization. In it, contractors ftom the selected subset receive from the auctioneer specification of the order to be allocated in current auction, calculate certain offers and send them to auctioneer.
4. Analysis of offers and decision making. The decision can be one of the following:

    - Auctioneer refuses from the current order allocation due to lack of satisfactory offers if no contractor has proposed an admissible variant.
    - Auctioneer selects a winner and allocates to it the order to execute.
    - Auctioneer cannot select a predominant winner between offers although admissible variants exist and decides to postpone the allocation of the current order.

- Auctioneer extends the multitude of contractors via adding a new one. This outcome takes place in case if the decision is not made in the current auction.
5. Auctioneer decides whether it is necessary to continue order allocation procedure. In general case resource allocation procedure is interrupted if all orders were proposed for bargaining at least one time independently of the results, i.e. even if some orders were not allocated due to lack of admissible proposals. Otherwise the allocation procedure continues.

As a rule, several iterations for order allocation are needed to find the final one. It is also possible to generate several such decisions between which the user is authorized to select the final one.

The most significant influence on the quality of the obtained decisions the tasks 1 and 4 affect. In the automatic mode, auctioneer makes decisions on the basis of knowledge base rules. As a matter of fact, the rules used in the VRPTW MAS are of heuristic kind and practically several sets of rules are used at that different sets of rules leads to different solutions obtained. For example, in procedure implementing the task 1 aiming at selection of order allocation sequencing, a number of rules are used. Between them, the simplest one is "first received first allocated". Other rule is sequencing of order allocation according to the increase of time service beginning. Both these rules are very simple and their truth values can be computed on the basis of the VRPTW database. The third rule is more sophisticated and requires additional computations. This rule supposes that firstly the most remote orders are allocated. Its usage leads to better results, i.e. to finding of shorter routes. There are also used several other rules of heuristic nature.

To select auction winner (Task 4), the proposed bids are compared and several rules are user to sequencing them according to "better-worth" order relation. The contractors' offers include attribute specifying "cost" of the order execution (increase of route distance), and also a number of other attributes that specify certain integral evaluations of spatial configuration of the location of the customer of current order and locations of customers of orders that have already been assigned to the contractors in the previous auctions. The simplest rule of winner selection is allocation the order to the contractor proposed the smallest "cost". The second variant is firstly to take into account the "cost" of offers, then, if there are several proposals with the close "costs", to take into account the second preferable attribute and so on.

Interactive mode of the VRPTW MAS performance permits to take several advantages. A characteristic feature of the VRPTW task as well as of several other planning and scheduling tasks is that experience accumulated during VRPTW MAS use can prompt to user new potentially very useful heuristics (rules) and this is an argument to use the interactive mode of the VRPTW MAS performance. Additional argument is that sometimes the user can select better decision than MAS. An example is if auctioneer receives offers with close qualities of services, the interactive mode of winner selection can be more profitable since user can take into account information concerning configuration of the customers' locations that cannot be processed automatically.

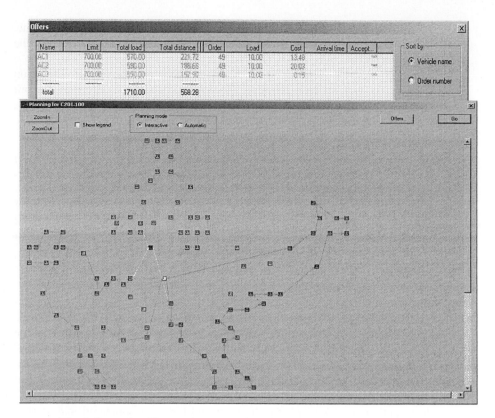

Fig. 2. Example of interactive mode of auction management for VRPTW task

In particular, Fig. 2 presents an example of user interface window which definitely can help to user to make or correct decisions at the current step of the VRPTW task solving procedure. The lower area of the window in Fig. 2 depicts the truck routes corresponding to the order allocations that have already been done previously and proposals for current order received from contractors. The orders that have not yet been allocated are also depicted in this window. The upper window presents the table specifying the contractors' attributes of the states of contractors and their offers. The presented graphics and table provide user for the important information needed for winner selection. Additionally, in the window in Fig. 2 the decision made by auctioneer on the basis of its heuristic knowledge base is also depicted. The user can either agree with the auctioneer or select its own decision. It is worthy to note that while selection a winner, the user additionally takes into account the visually presented information concerning the orders that were not yet allocated.

The same is true with regard to solving of other tasks, for example, with regard to tasks 1, 2 and 5. While solving the task 1, the user can select the following order to allocate at the forthcoming auction. While solving the task 2, the user can correct the list of participating contractors. While solving the task 5, the user can interrupt the process of resource allocation and initiate reallocation procedure.

It should be noted that interactive mode makes it possible to use heuristic rules that are more intuitive and cannot be specified formally in a simple way, for example, rules reflecting the topology of truck routes selected, locations of the order to be allocated and locations of unallocated orders.

5   Resource Reallocation

Resource reallocation procedure aims to improve the quality of the current decision (resource allocation) via reallocation of a subset of the orders that were allocated at the previous auctions. The major motivation of using resource reallocation procedure is that it can lead to changes of the routes of trucks leading to a less total cost. It is shown in ([5]) that in VRPTW application, such kind of allocation modifications can result in noticeable improvement of the resource allocation quality. Practice proved that this improvement takes place typically for each particular VRPTW task. Indeed, each auction takes into account the attributes of the current order and previously made decisions but cannot anticipate new constraints raised as a result of the currently made decision. Reallocation procedure allows to take into account the consequences of all the decisions made during allocation and thus to improve scheduling on the whole.

Let us consider the peculiarities of the reallocation procedure used in VRPTW MAS in question and firstly consider the reallocation protocol. The protocol of agent interaction proposed for the same task in ([5]) and called "*simulated trading protocol*" supposes to use both vertical agents' interactions (between auctioneer and contractors) and horizontal ones (between contractors). The protocol used in the developed and implemented *VRPTW* MAS differs in certain features from the simulated trading protocol. Particularly, the developed protocol doesn't use horizontal interactions between contractors because the latter leads to the significant increase of the agent communication traffic overhead and also requires significant increase of the computation cost.

The proposed protocol is executed in two stages. *First*, the subset of orders to be reallocated is chosen. This subset is chosen according to a criterion that helps to determine the orders which reallocation can potentially lead to increase of the allocation plan quality. *Second*, the reallocation procedure itself is performed. This procedure uses rules of heuristic kind. Let us specify the reallocation algorithm in more detail.

1.   Each contractor analyzes its own route and refuses from executions of the orders that it would like to pass to someone else. A criterion determining such kind of orders uses analysis of each order "cost" and its location within the contractor's route.

2.   Each contractor analyses orders from the batch of its offers during allocation phase but assigned to other contractors to select from them a subset of those that can be executed by it for the less total "cost".

3.   Join of the sets of orders offered by contractors for reallocation is sent to auctioneer. The latter forwards these orders to the contractors that were awarded by the respective contracts in allocation auctions. These contractors compare the received costs with those own costs and refuse from the offers of less "cost" (step 1).

4. Auctioneer selects the contractors that are potential executors for the orders to be reallocated and sends to each such contractor the list of respective orders.

5. Each contractor analyzes the auctioneer's offers and for every offered order calculates whether it is capable to execute the latter without violation of the constraints.

6. The list of such orders is returned to the auctioneer.

The steps 1-6 together can be interpreted as a preparatory phase. The reallocation procedure itself is realized at the subsequent steps.

Reallocation procedure is close to the basic allocation one. It is modified according to the ideas of the "*look ahead*" approach that was proposed for the task "pure scheduling without resource allocation" ([2]). Particularly, auctioneer acts according to the following steps.

7. Auctioneer determines the sequencing of orders reallocation taking into account the information returned by contractors at the step 6. To determine the above sequencing, auctioneer for each order returned computes the total number of contractors that are "ready" to execute it. The first order to be presented to auction is the order assigned the least number.

8. The selected order (with the least number of pretenders for its execution) is allocated through auction in which the winner is determined in a more sophisticated way than in the auction used in the allocation algorithm (see section 4). The potential contractors send to auctioneer two attributes: 1) the "cost" of the contract execution and 2) the list of the orders that it would be not capable to execute if it was the winner. Auctioneer uses several heuristics (rules) to determine the winner. The aim of the aforementioned heuristics is to select the winner between those contractors that propose the best "close" costs and, at that preserve for each remaining (unallocated) order as many potential executors as possible. Formally this condition means that the second aim is to maximize the number of potential contractors for the order having the least number of pretenders. The subset of unallocated orders which the winner became incapable to execute after its win is deleted from the respective list formed on the step 6.

9. If the set of unallocated orders is to this step not empty then the algorithm goes to the step 7 in which auctioneer sequences the rest of orders to determine the first one to be allocated (see step 8). If the set of unallocated orders is empty, then the algorithm stops.

Reallocation procedure is repeated iteratively and stops in cases if either allocation is not improved or if time resource assigned for allocation procedure is exhausted.

6   Conclusion: Experimental Results and Future Work

Testing of the developed approach and implemented MAS was carried out on the basis of the VRPTW benchmark data sets, generated by Solomon ([8]). The results of simulation can be concluded as follows. *First*, reallocation procedure improves the results of allocation procedure approximately from 10 till 15%. For instance, allocation of orders corresponding to data set RC107 ([8]) results in the total distance equal to 1358 whereas reallocation procedure leads to the total distance equal to 1168. *Second*, one can compare results of the developed approach with the other ones implemented in not multi agent manner. For instance, one of such approaches, implemented by use of the branch-and-bound method, is described in ([3]). This algorithm allows to search about optimal solutions and time of solving depends on data set. Experiments used this algorithm were performed on 300MHz Pentium II computer and parallel experiments were performed on a cluster of 32 of such workstations. Particularly for data set RC111 the algorithm was capable to search the result with about optimal total distance equal to 1048 but consumes for this computation 41879 seconds. For the same data set the developed multi agent system generates result with total distance equal to 1244 but consumes for it only 1800 seconds. At that experiment was performed for the case in which all agents were deployed on one 1400 MHz Pentium IV computer.

The further research will concern the followings:

- User-based extraction of new heuristics.
- Development of the reusable components peculiar to shipping logistics problem aiming at development of the problem-oriented MAS software tool.
- Enrichment of the MAS functionalities aiming at getting ready to development and implementation of practically interesting MAS applications in the shipping logistic scope.

Acknowledgement

This research is supported by grant of European Office of Aerospace R&D (Project #1992P)

References

[1]   Becker, M. and S.F. Smith, "Mixed-Initiative Resource Management: The AMC Barrel Allocator", In *Proceedings 5th International Conference on Artificial Intelligence Planning and Scheduling (AIPS-2000)*, Breckenridge, CO, April, 2000.

[2]   A. Cesta, A. Oddi, and S. Smith. A Constraint-Based Method for Project Scheduling with Time Windows. Tech. Report CMU-RI-TR-00-34, Robotics Institute, Carnegie Mellon University, February, 2000.

[3]   W. Cook and J.L. Rich. A Parallel Cutting-Plane Algorithm for the Vehicle Routing Problem with Time Windows. Technical Report TR99-04 Department of Computational & Applied Mathematics, Rice University, USA, http://www.isye.gatech.edu/~wcook/papers/vrptw.ps.

[4]   R. Davis and R.G. Smith. Negotiation as a metaphor for distributed problem solving, *Artif. Intell.*, vol.20, pp. 63-109, 1983.

[5]   K. Fisher, B. Chaib-draa. A Simulation Approach Based on Negotiation and Cooperation Between Agents: A Case Study. In IEEE Transactions On Systems, Man, And Cybernetics – Part C: Applications And Reviews, Vol. 29, No.4, November 1999.

[6]   V. Gorodetski, O. Karsaev, I. Kotenko, A. Khabalov. Software Development Kit for Multi-agent Systems Design and Implementation. In B. Dunin-Keplicz, E. Navareski (Eds.), From Theory to Practice in Multi-agent Systems. Lecture Notes in Artificial Intelligence, Vol. # 2296, pp. 121-130, 2002.

[7]   Multiagent systems: a modern approach to distributed artificial intelligence / edited by Gerhard Weiss, The MIT Press, London, 1999.

[8]   Solomon. http://web.cba.neu.edu/~msolomon/problems.htm.

[9]   W. Vickrey. Counter-speculation, auctions, and competitive sealed tenders, Journal of Finance, Vol. 16, No. 1, pp. 9-37, March 1961.

Towards Autonomous Decision Making in Multi-agent Environments Using Fuzzy Logic*

Hamid Haidarian Shahri

Faculty of Computer Engineering and Information Technology
Amirkabir University of Technology (Tehran Polytechnic), Tehran, Iran
hhaidarian@aut.ac.ir

Abstract. In this paper, a step-by-step procedure for designing a fuzzy decision making system for RoboCup agents is introduced and implemented. By using this mechanism agents can determine, which direction to look at. The development process and debugging of this approach are much less time consuming and very simple to follow, in comparison to other analytical hand coded implementations with complex conditions and many parameters in the code. The results show that, the methodology can be employed in many decision-making problems like the soccer agent's case and other potential fields, to decrease the development time and improve the efficiency of a decision making system. Up until now, fuzzy systems have been used rarely by any of the participating teams in the annual RoboCup competitions. This paper could serve as the first inception for the design of a RoboCup agent, which uses internal fuzzy systems for many of its decision-making tasks.

1   Introduction

Creating an *intelligent agent*, which acts in dynamic and noisy environments, in real-time fashion is a difficult and time-consuming task [6]. An intelligent agent is a computer system that is capable of *flexible* autonomous action in order to meet its design objectives. Here *flexible* means that the system must be *responsive, proactive, and social* [21]. One contributing factor to this difficulty is, coming up with a generalized solution for a system to do the decision making in any scenario. The only option available is to follow a trial and error approach and trying to simulate natural behavior by utilizing complex conditions and many parameters. This work mainly concentrates on providing a step-by-step method for developing a fuzzy decision making system (DMS) for making visual decisions in such a situation; i.e. to tell an agent in which direction he must look. Rational decision making is choosing among alternatives in a way that "properly" accords with the preferences and beliefs of an individual decision maker or those of a group making a joint decision [10], [15].

---

* This research was sponsored in part by the Ministry of Petroleum.

V. Mařík et al. (Eds): CEEMAS 2003, LNAI 2691, pp. 247-257, 2003.
© Springer-Verlag Berlin Heidelberg 2003

The testbed used for this problem is the RoboCup soccer server. It provides an excellent platform for the development of multi-agent systems without getting researchers involved in the intricacies of hardware in physical robots [14].

Given the set of feasible actions A, the set of relevant states S, the set of resulting events E, and a (rational) utility function u (which orders the space of events with respect to their desirability), the *optimal decision* under certainty is the choice of that action which leads to the event with the highest utility. Such a decision can be described properly by the quadruple {A, S, E, u}. There are two sorts of decision making systems: individual and multi person. Contrary to the former, in the latter case the agent is not alone against the world; he interacts with other agents [24]. According to the type of interaction, three situations arise, which includes gaming [10], team decision [11], and group decision. In designing a DMS for a player in a multi-agent environment such as the RoboCup Simulation League, we are obviously making *team decisions* and that will be our prime concern here.

The remainder of this paper is organized as follows. Related works is provided in the next section. In section three a straightforward and general method for designing any fuzzy inference system is explained. Section four exemplifies this method by showing the implementation of the fuzzy visual system for a soccer agent. Also a tool for this design procedure is introduced. Section five contains the evaluation of our experimentation and debugging. Section six is the conclusions and future work.

2   Related Works

FCPortugal team has designed a technique called Strategic Looking Mechanism, in which a utility function is used to calculate the usefulness of all directions by employing different weights for different objects depending on the situation, position of the ball and self-position [16]. This technique is somehow used in other successful teams such as Tsinghuaeolus. Since the neck movement model has been introduced to the soccer server from RoboCup 2000, there is not much work done in this field. Up to now, fuzzy systems have not been popular in the RoboCup domain, but it is the opposite case, about reinforcement learning [20], [17] and neural networks. Fuzzy rules have been employed to provide group formation and robust navigation capabilities for autonomous mobile robots, and implemented on two physical robots [4]. In this way cooperation among soccer playing robots has been achieved. Hierarchical Fuzzy Intelligent Control [7] system has been adapted to soccer agents by Zeng99 team from Japan, for experimenting with the design of cooperative behavior in the HFIC system [8], but no actual results have been reported.

3   Fuzzy Design Method

The following steps should be used for the design of any fuzzy DMS [1]. *Definition* of *linguistic variables* is the first step. Each linguistic variable contains terms, which are interpretation of technical figures. The number of these terms is usually three, five, or seven; odd numbers balancing out symmetrically over a pivot. A suitable membership function, which maps each value of a technical figure to a membership degree in the linguistic term, is chosen. Membership functions with sharp edges are sufficient for most control applications. However for more complex data analysis and decision support problems like this case spline membership functions provide better performance because of their smooth curves. This step should be applied to all input and output variables.

The second step is the creation of a fuzzy logic *rule base*. The rules supply the knowledge of the system, enabling us to make control rules from human knowledge. These rules should be normalized to reduce the computational effort and also for the sake of readability. The antecedent part of a normalized rule should be a conjunction of atomic sentences and the consequent must be an atomic sentence as well. While this would work fine for small systems, as the number of input variables increase filling in all the possible rules becomes a cumbersome task. Therefore rules that only include a few of the input variables and cover greater subspaces in the control space, are used. Fuzzy systems are not sensitive to the completeness of the rule base, and even sometimes by removing half of the rules from a working system the performance does not degrade, as long as the boundary rules are preserved in the fuzzy associative memory [9].

Any rule based system needs an inference mechanism, which consists of, evaluating the antecedent of a rule, applying that result to the consequent of that rule (implication), and producing the overall consequent from the individual consequents contributed by each rule in the rule base (aggregation). The reasoning mechanism used for our implementation (section 4) was Mamdani implication (minimum) with a disjunctive system of rules; i.e. at least one rule must be satisfied and the rules were connected by "OR" connectives. Based on the Mamdani method of inference, the aggregated output (y) is found by fuzzy union of all individual rule contributions (y^i), where i =1, 2,..., r and r is the number of rules. Although different methods of inference yield different shapes for the aggregated fuzzy consequents, after the next step (defuzzification), the (defuzzified) output value is fairly consistent. No chaining [3] is used in our fuzzy system and the rules are one shot, because the output variable (priority) is not included in the antecedent part of any rule, as explained in section 4.

The third step for the design of a fuzzy system is, choosing an apt *defuzzification method* [24], [18]. The objective of a defuzzification method is to derive the non-fuzzy (crisp) value that best represents the fuzzy value of the linguistic output variable. To select the proper defuzzification method, you need to understand the linguistic meaning that underlies the defuzzification process. Experience shows that two different linguistic meanings of defuzzification are of importance: determining the "best compromise" and determining the "most plausible result".

Some of the defuzzification methods available are center of area (CoA), center of maximum (CoM) and mean of maximum (MoM). For more explanation about the characteristics of each method and its usage, refer to [1]. Table 1 shows a comparison of different defuzzification methods. The continuity property is important for most closed-loop control applications, to avoid instability and oscillation in the output variable. Hence CoM is a good choice. In pattern recognition applications, MoM is usually used, since as shown in the table, it produces the most plausible result. In decision support systems, for quantitative decisions like project prioritization or as in this case study for making visual decisions, CoM is employed. For qualitative decisions such as credit card fraud detection MoM is utilized. CoA and CoG are computationally intensive and not widely used in practical applications.

Table 1. Comparison of different defuzzification methods

	Center of Area (CoA, CoG)	Center of Maximum (CoM)	Mean of Maximum (MoM)
Linguistic Characteristic	"Best compromise"	"Best compromise"	"Most plausible result"
Continuity	Yes	Yes	No
Computational Efficiency	Very low	High	Very high
Applications	Control, decision support, data analysis	Control, decision support, data analysis	Pattern recognition, decision support, data analysis

4   Case Study: Design and Implementation of a Soccer Agent with a Fuzzy Visual DMS

The source code of Tsinghuaeolus, the champion of the RoboCup Soccer Simulation League competitions in 2001 and 2002 from China, has been used for implementing the fuzzy visual DMS [19]. The architecture of a player in this team consists of two main parts. One handles the basic skills and the other is concerned with strategy control and mediation of actions [23]. The principles mentioned in the previous section were applied, to design and implement a fully functional DMS to decide which direction each player must look at, in the appropriate time intervals. The fuzzy system was expected to fit in well in the RoboCup environment, considering the *noise* introduced by the soccer server, which affects all the perceptions and actions of the agents. Also, the *uncertainties* in the agent's actions, make fuzzy decision-making very suitable.

In the design process of the system, it was observed that the priority (output variable of the fuzzy DMS) of an object (direction) is related to three factors, namely: *confidence* about the current position of the object, *strategical interest* of the object, *and urgency*. For the first factor, since objects like the ball and the players are moving, and the estimation about the location of stationary objects like the flags around the field and the goal posts deteriorate, the confidence of all objects decrease by time. Hence the agent needs to re-look at those objects that he is forgetting. The last two factors are very much dependent on the type of action that the agent has decided to undertake, in the mediation part of the code. Hence the value of these factors must be partitioned into different categories by all the possible actions available to the agent.

For strategical interest and urgency, the actions available to the agent are divided into three types: 1) Pass, in which players on my side are more important. 2) Dribble, hold ball, interception, avoid enemy, positioning for defense, block and mark in which players on the opposite side are more important. 3) Shoot, clear, pass wait, positioning for offense, and no action in which players of both sides are of equal importance.

Although the ball is the most critical object in the field for most actions, the urgency of looking at any object is determined by the action that the agent plans to undertake. For example if the agent is going to pass the ball, the urgency of a player in his own team is more than the urgency of the opponent team's player. Also looking at the player who is going to receive the passed ball is more urgent than looking at other teammates. Considering the above mentioned points, the three factors for each object (direction) were set between 0 and 1.

Subsequently, according to the *first step*, the following five terms: {very-low, low, medium, high, very-high} were used for strategical interest, which is the input variable and similarly for priority, which is the output variable. The following three terms: {low, medium, high} were used for urgency (input) and confidence (input), which was due to their lower significance in the code. Choosing three terms for these linguistic variables reduced the total number of rules required for filling in the rule bank of the fuzzy system as well. Figure 1 shows the membership functions for all the variables.

It should be obvious (our knowledge about the problem) that, confidence has an inverse relation with priority, while, strategical interest and urgency have direct relations with priority. By knowing these relations the bank of fuzzy if-then rules is completed easily, and *step two* is also finished. The rules were structured as a combination of 2 out of the 3 input variables (confidence, strategical interest, and urgency). 15 rules contained strategical interest and urgency in the antecedent, 15 rules for the strategical interest and confidence combination, and 9 rules for the urgency and confidence combination. This produces a total of 39 rules for the bank. For all of these rules, priority is always the consequent (output variable). The rules are simply a verbal description of the relations mentioned above, and a linguistic interpretation of how we think rationally. For example: IF (*Urgency* is high) AND (*Strategical interest* is very-high) THEN (*Priority* is very-high). The decision surface produced by these rules (step two), is demonstrated in Figure 2a.

Figure 2b, shows the architecture of the agent. As illustrated in the diagram, the fuzzy visual decision making system (DMS) is completely isolated from the rest of the agent's mediation mechanisms; i.e. there is one module for deciding which direction to look at, and another independent module for deciding which action to undertake (the two actions can be done concurrently as permitted by the simulator). In the case of real world robots with different physical abilities, if the physical architecture does not allow the neck (visual system navigator) to work in parallel with another effector, only a mediation module is needed to decide, whether to move the neck or do another action (for example shoot). This mediator can be implemented as another layer, on top of the two mediators in our architecture. Therefore the proposed DMS can be integrated into other constrained physical domains, with a trivial effort.

For *step three*, center of maximum defuzzification method was employed which is continuous and computationally efficient. As demonstrated by this case, following the above methodology enables us to develop a fuzzy system naturally and effortlessly without any ambiguity and in a very short time, compared to any other hand-coded method. Some software packages on the market such as the Matlab Fuzzy Logic Toolbox [12] and FuzzyTECH [13] can be deployed for implementing a fuzzy system. The implementation for this case study was done with the aid of the Matlab Fuzzy Logic Toolbox very quickly. The result is a text file, which is used by inline procedures of the fuzzy system, to do the required calculations in real-time. These procedures are invoked from inside the code.

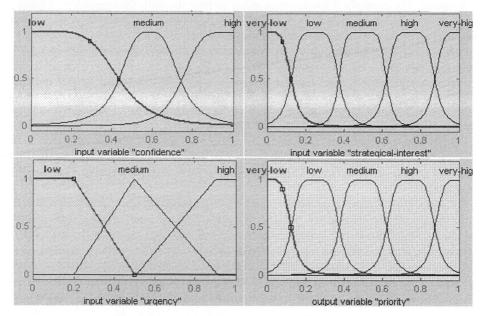

Fig. 1. The membership functions for all the variables

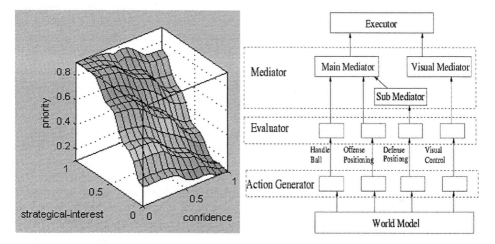

Fig. 2a. The decision surface produced by the rules (left)

2b. Architecture of the agent (right)

5   Evaluation

After replacing the fuzzy visual DMS with the hand-coded version that was previously used by Tsinghuaeolus, the players functioned correctly, but the quality of the play for the whole of the team showed some deficiencies. The code was observed carefully and some fine-tuning was done. For example, the code was changed so that the values of the factors like the strategical interest of an object would match its proper value more closely. At the same time, all effort was put in to make the rate of change, for these factors more gradual from one object to another. This helped the decision-making process to become more realistic, and rationally better results were achieved. The final score of the team improved with these changes and in the final version the performance became very close to the hand coded performance; tied or close matches.

Table 2 below, summarizes the results of the experiments. The team with the fuzzy system was run against the hand coded system, before and after the fine-tuning, 10 times, and the average results were calculated. The RoboCup environment allows noise to be introduced into the system, both for actions (movement noise) and visual sensors, but in our experiments, only the noise for visual sensors was used. For the details of the noise model see [2]. The quantize-step parameter has a default value of 0.1 (some noise). This was increased to 0.2 and 0.3 to make the environment noisier. It can be seen that the fuzzy DMS responds very well to noise and the efficiency of the system is increased, which makes the system very practical for real world robot domains. Additionally, the average ball holding time of the hand coded system in the second table is lower than that of the first table. That is due to the general situation in the games. After fine tuning, the fuzzy system acts better, takes opportunities from the opponent, and gains a greater share of possession of the ball.

Table 2. Experimental results of the system

		Hand Coded System		Fuzzy System Before Fine Tuning	
		Average ball holding time (cycles of 6000)	Average score	Average ball holding time (cycles of 6000)	Average score
Noise	Default	3698	3	2302	2.0
	High	3592	3	2408	2.1
	Very High	3379	3	2621	2.3

		Hand Coded System		Fuzzy System After Fine Tuning	
		Average ball holding time (cycles of 6000)	Average score	Average ball holding time (cycles of 6000)	Average score
Noise	Default	2962	3	3038	3.0
	High	2654	3	3346	3.2
	Very High	2406	3	3594	3.4

An important point to mention is that, when it comes down to *evaluating* the performance of a system like this case, the final score of the match is not always a good measuring stick. Many things other than the visual system could affect the score. However, for the case of visual decisions it is quite difficult to come up with a rational and appropriate utility function. Average ball holding time was also measured in cycles. A complete game consists of 6000 cycles. The results also showed that, when the visual system works better, ball holding time for the team also increases. In fact it matches with the score and performance of the visual system closely.

One of the most challenging tasks in developing a program for the soccer agent is the *debugging* and manipulation of the code [6]. That is due to the real-time nature of the system, which makes it difficult to re-evaluate the same case twice. The server provides the required perceptual information for the agents and must be running at the same time as the agents. In this case, the playing of the team and in which direction a player is looking, were carefully observed with the aid of the soccer monitor developed by the WrightEagle team [22]. This monitor provides more flexibility than the standard version. One can see and monitor the viewing area of any player highlighted in green as shown in Figure 3. The viewing cone is divided into three zones showing the view quality, which in turn, reflects the amount of noise introduced into the system by the soccer server. Many other facilities like play back and other information about a player are available as well (illustrated in the right pane of Figure 3). This was used to fine-tune the code and improve the performance of the team. It was actually the only part of the development, which took some time, thinking, and intuition.

The results also show that, CPU-time of making a decision has a sharp decrease, particularly if simpler triangular membership functions are used. This could degrade the system's performance, but is a crucial improvement in *real time* and time-critical environments.

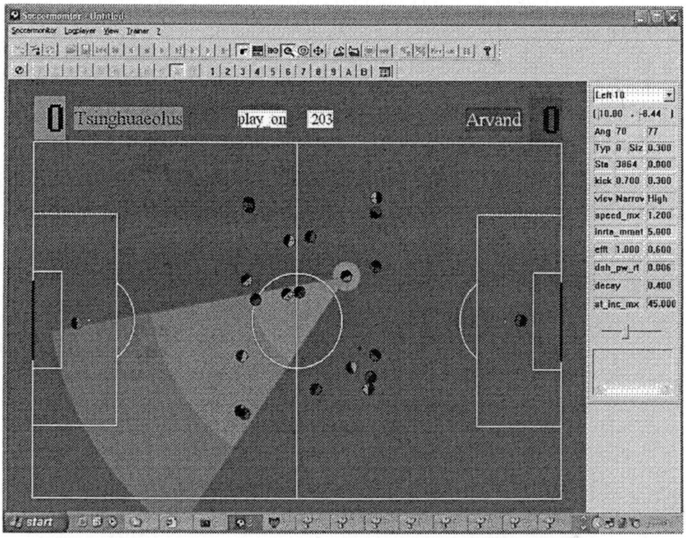

Fig. 3. WrightEagle soccer monitor, which highlights the viewing area of any player

6   Conclusions and Future Work

The development of an agent for playing soccer in the RoboCup Soccer Simulation environment is a very *long* process. In this case study, a *step-by-step* procedure has been used to produce a visual decision making module to tell the agent which direction he must look at. This method is many times *faster* in terms of development time.

After optimizing (fine-tuning) the code, similar results were achieved compared to the previous hand coded version, which was developed, with a lot of effort and included very complex conditions and many parameters. The system's performance increased by introducing more noise into the system, since the average ball holding time was improved as well. The final score was used for the evaluation of the system. However it might be worthwhile to look for a more suitable utility function.

Finding a *procedural* method for handling the tedious task of developing a decision making system in a multi agent environment is not something to be taken for granted. This paper could serve as the inception for the designing of a RoboCup agent, which uses internal fuzzy systems for many of its decision-making tasks. Considering the proposed architecture, this visual system can be integrated into other noisy agent-based domains successfully and with a trivial effort.

Fuzzy decision making has been used rarely by any of the participating teams in the annual RoboCup competitions. In this work, it has been shown that fuzzy systems provide a very simple and step by step means of producing a decision making system in comparison with the cumbersome and tedious job of hand coding and poking different conditions in a code for achieving the required results.

Fuzzy systems alone, unlike neural networks, do not have the power to learn from examples. Neural networks are not descriptive and are like black boxes, which make them hard for manipulation. But the membership functions of a fuzzy system can be molded into shape, more easily. By using ANFIS (adaptive network-based fuzzy inference system), both of the above characteristics can be harvested. ANFIS [5] is a fuzzy system, which can learn from examples. Working on ANFIS and its training possibilities could be pursued, for further research. However a way of producing a complete training set, that covers all the state space must be devised first, because without proper training, deploying ANFIS or a neural network is inherently inappropriate.

Acknowledgements

I would like to thank Dr. Kahani, Saied Haidarian Shahri, whose experience in RoboCup and coding is very valuable, A. Tavalayi, National Iranian Oil Company, J. Yao, M. Shirazi for their assistance in different aspects of the project.

References

[1] Altrock, C.V.: Fuzzy Logic & Neurofuzzy Applications Explained. Prentice Hall PTR (1995)
[2] Chen, M., et al.: Users Manual RoboCup Soccer Server. July 26 (2002) Available at http://sserver.sourceforge.net/docs/manual.pdf
[3] Driankov, D., Hellendoorn, H.: Chaining of Fuzzy IF-THEN Rules in Mamdani-Controllers. Proc. IEEE Int. Conf. on Fuzzy Systems (1995)
[4] Duman, H., Hu, H.: Fuzzy Logic for Behaviour Coordination and Multi-agent Formation in RoboCup. Int. Conf. on Recent Advances in Soft Computing (2000)
[5] Jang, J.S.R.: ANFIS: Adaptive-Network-Based Fuzzy Inference Systems. IEEE Trans. on Systems, Man and Cybernetics, Vol. 23, No. 3, June (1993) 665-685
[6] Jennings, N.R., Wooldridge, M.J.: Applications of Intelligent Agents. In: Agent Technologies: Foundations, Applications and Markets (1998)
[7] Junji, N., et al.: Hierarchical Fuzzy Intelligent Controller for Gymnastic Bar Actions. J. of Advanced Computational Intelligence (1999)
[8] Kawarabayashi, T., et al.: Zeng99 in RoboCup99. In: RoboCup99 Team Description: Simulation League (1999) Available at http://www.ep.liu.se/ea/cis/1999/007
[9] Kosko, B.: Neural Networks and Fuzzy Systems: A Dynamical Systems Approach to Machine Intelligence. Prentice Hall (1992)
[10] Luce, R.D., Raiffa, H.: Games and Decisions. John Wiley & Sons Inc., New York (1957)
[11] Marschak, J., Radner, R.: Economic Theory of Teams. Yale University Press (1972)
[12] Matlab Help for the Fuzzy Logic Toolbox, Version 6, Release 12
[13] N.N.: FuzzyTECH 4.0 online Edition Manual. INFORM GmbH Aachn/Inform Software Corp., Chicago (1995)
[14] Noda, I., Matsubara, H., Hiraki, K., Frank, I.: Soccer Server: a Tool for Research on Multi-agent Systems. In: Applied Artificial Intelligence (1997)
[15] Raiffa, H.: Decision Analysis: Introductory Lectures on Choices Under Uncertainty. Reading, MA: Addison-Wesley (1968)
[16] 16. Reis, L.P., Lau, N.: FC Portugal Team Description: RoboCup 2000 Simulation League   Champion. RoboCup 2000: Robot Soccer World Cup IV. Springer Verlag, Berlin (2001)
[17] Riedmiller, M., et al.: Karlsruhe Brainstormers -a Reinforcement Learning Approach to Robotic Soccer. In: Stone, P., Balch, T., Kraetszchmar, G. (eds.): RoboCup 2000: Robot Soccer World Cup IV. Springer Verlag, Berlin (2001)
[18] Tong, R.M., Bonissone, P.P.: Linguistic Solutions to Fuzzy Decision Problem. In: Zimmermann, H.J., Zadeh, L.A., Gines (eds.): Fuzzy Sets and Decision Analysis (1984)
[19] Tsinghuaeolus (2001) Available at http://www.lits.tsinghua.edu.cn/robocup/download.htm
[20] Uchibe, E., Asada, M., et al.: Vision Based Reinforcement Learning for RoboCup: Towards Real Robot Competition. Proc. IROS `96 Workshop on RoboCup (1996)

[21] Wooldridge, M., Jennings, N.R.: Intelligent Agents: Theory and Practice. The Knowledge Engineering Review, Vol. 10, No. 2 (1995) 115-152

[22] WrightEagle team source code and Soccer Monitor (2001) Available at http://wrighteagle.org/legged-robot/eindex.html

[23] Yao, J., et al.: Architecture of Tsinghuaeolus. RoboCup 2001: Robot Soccer World Cup V. Springer Verlag, Berlin (2002)

[24] Zimmermann, H.J.: Fuzzy Sets, Decision Making, and Expert Systems. Kluwer Academic Publishers (1987)

Towards an Object Oriented Implementation of Belief-Goal-Role Multi-agent Systems

Walid Chainbi

ENIS
Departement d'Informatique
B. P. W - 3038 - SFAX - TUNISIA
{wchainbi@lycos.com}

Abstract. One of the most driving forces behind multi-agent systems research and development is the Internet. Agents are populating the Internet at an increasingly rapid pace. Unfortunately, they are almost universally asocial. Accordingly, adequate agent concepts will be essential for agents in such open environment. To address this issue, we show in the first part of this paper that agents need to have communication concepts and organization concepts. We argue that instead of the usual approach of starting from a set of intentional states, the intentional structure should be deduced in terms of interaction. To this end, we come up with conceptualizations related to communication and organization. The second part of this paper deals with a study which compares the agent paradigm to the object paradigm. We also show the capabilities as well as the limits of the object paradigm to deal with the agent paradigm. We illustrate our work with the well known prey/predator game.

1 Introduction

Over the past three decades, software engineers have derived a progressively better understanding of the characteristics of complexity in software. It is now widely recognised that interaction is probably the most important single characteristic of complex software. Software architectures that contain many dynamically interacting components, each with their own thread of control, and engaging in complex coordination protocols, are typically orders of magnitude more complex to correctly and efficiently engineer than those that simply compute a function of some input through a single thread of control. Unfortunately, it turns out that many (if not most) real-world applications have precisely these characteristics. As a consequence, a major research topic in computer science over at least the past two decades has been the development of tools and techniques to model, understand, and implement systems in which interaction is the norm. Indeed, many researchers now believe that in future, computation itself will be understood chiefly as a process of interaction.

Modern information systems, exemplified by Internet and corporate intranets, are typically large and complex. The software applications and other components composing them are also complex. It is now widely recognised that in

V. Mařík et al. (Eds): CEEMAS 2003, LNAI 2691, pp. 258–267, 2003.

the months and years ahead, agents will become an essential part of most web-based applications. This recognition is due to the fact that agents mitigate the complexity.

The study presented in the first part of this paper stresses the study of cooperation to deduce a model of agents that can take part in a cooperative activity. Ferber used the term *mass conception* to qualify this way of starting with interaction[1][1]. Indeed, starting with the hypothesis that communication and organization constitute , at least in a pragmatic point of view, two complementary ways to implement cooperation, we come up with a conceptualization of communication as well as a conceptualization of organization. We subsequently, identify the underlying concepts of an agent. These concepts consist of beliefs and goals as communication concepts, and roles as concepts related to organization.

The second part of this paper deals with the practical aspects related to multi-agent systems implementation. The agent technology community has made substantial progress in recent years in providing a theoretical and practical understanding of many aspects of agents and multi-agent systems. Most of the time, the agent theory is expressed by modal logic which is a good specification tool since it eases the description of intentional agents. However, this formalism is not computational tractable: it cannot be refined easily into implementation even if some counter-examples exist (see[2]for example). Actually, a large and ugly chasm still separates the world of formal theory and infrastructure from the world of practical nuts-and-bolts agent system development[3]. In part this is due to the absence of mature languages and software tools.

The object paradigm has become popular in the past few years due to the appearance of new programming languages that enforce the applicability of some good properties such as reusability and maintainability. The object oriented design and development environment is well supported by diagram editors and visualization tools. There is even a convergence of viewpoints amongst the major proponents of different variations on the object oriented theme: the Unified Modelling Language (UML) fuses the concepts of Booch, OMT, and OOSE; the result is a single, common, and widely usable language for users of these and other methods. Over the past few years, there has been an increasing trend in the object-oriented community towards the development of "agent-like" features. Examples include distributed objects (CORBA), applets, mobile object systems. The second part of this paper addresses the following questions: What are the capablities and the limits of the object paradigm to deal with the agent paradigm? What are the key attributes of an agent-oriented paradigm that make it distinctive ? This paper is organized as follows. The next section deals with an ontology for cooperation. Section 3 identifies the agent concepts. Section 4 describes informally the object paradigm by neglecting the aspects which are out of the scope of the subject of this paper.

---

[1] He opposed it to the *individual conception* which consists in adopting the intentional stance (which is the point of view adopted by most researchers in agent technology).

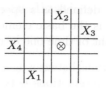

Fig. 1. A configuration of the prey $(\otimes)$/predators $(X_i)_{i:1..4}$ game

Cooperation Mode The concept of cooperation mode has been previously stated in [8]. A cooperation mode specifies the responsibilities attributed to the partners taking part in a collective activity. A cooperation mode is defined by an n-uplet representing the respective roles of the agents.

Example 5. The cooperation mode regarding the configuration given by figure 1 can be: $<<$ *move_right, move_right, move_up* $>$, $<$ *move_down* $>$, $<$ *move_down, move_left* $>$, $<$ *move_right, move_right* $>>$[3] where *move_direction* is a physical action. The relevance of a cooperation mode is measured by the cooperation strategy which will be described in the following paragraph.

Cooperation Strategy In distributed problem solving, each agent member of the system is able to process a set of tasks by applying some resolution methods within his competences. Agent competences can be complementary or redundant. For the same tasks, an agent may be more competent than another (he puts into practice a resolution method more efficaciously). For other tasks, the agents can have different methods but there is no way to determine a priori which method is the most efficient. Accordingly, to select an agent to achieve a task, the resolution context should be taken into account. Hence, a dynamic distribution of tasks seems to be more appropriate than a static distribution. If the abilities of the agents are redundant, then they can play the same role. In this case, an agent should be selected to accomplish each role. According to the context, we can specify different indications concerning the way the choice is done: for example, in the case of system-human cooperation, we can indicate that the user must play all the decision roles even if the system is competent to accomplish such roles.

We call a cooperation strategy, a process which determines the appropriate cooperation mode to a given situation. In this case, we talk about *dynamic organization*. A cooperation strategy can be implemented by using a refereeing function. In the prey/predator problem, this function can take the current players' positions and their goals as input and return the new players' goals. Accordingly, new roles have to be achieved to reach the new goals.

Example 6. In the prey/predator game, a cooperation mode where an agent role is "*getting closer to a prey from the north*" can be substituted for a cooperation

---
[3] No optional task is mentioned in this example.

mode where the same agent play the following role: *"getting closer to a prey from the east"*. It is because of the respective positions of the predators on the grid, that the cooperation strategy administer this transition in cooperation mode.

In order to guarantee the coherence of an organizational model, some properties should be verified. We don't address those properties in this paper, but we think they are closely related to the application domain.

3   Agent Concepts

A conceptualization of cooperation has been presented so far. Indeed, two aspects have been mentioned as mainstays of cooperation: communication and organization. Concerning communication, the terminology includes the concepts of beliefs, goals, actions and a message. Organization is dynamic because of the concept of cooperation strategy. Obviously, an organizational structure in which roles distribution is dynamic increases communication cost, but can give better results for some complex problems. A static structure doesn't cope with the environment hazards and limits the possible configurations that can occur in the resolution process[4].

Multi-agent systems put into practice a set of techniques and concepts allowing some concrete (e.g., robots) or abstract (e.g., software) entities called "agents" to cooperate according to some cooperation modes. By focusing on interaction and individual satisfaction, multi-agent systems ban thinking in a centralized or global way[5]. Hence, we keep from our previous study the following concepts for an agent: *beliefs* and *goals* as communication concepts and *roles* as concepts related to organization.

We think that our beliefs correspond to the notion of knowledge in more traditional artificial intelligence terms. The concept of role is very similar to "plan". The concept of role as stated here (an organisational concept) denotes the importance of the organization dimension whenever we talk about agent systems (which has not been stated for plans in the literature). We think that the term "role" is better (more expressive) whenever we talk about organization. Besides, plans and roles represent both the deliberative state of an agent but they come from different approaches: the former was the fruit of the adoption of the intentional stance, whether the latter is the result of what is adopted in this paper as a mass conception approach. The same thing could be said about the relation Role-Intention.

The types of activity an agent can perform may be classified as either external (in which case the domain of the activity is the environment outside the agent i.e. the other agents and the spatial environment) or internal (in which

---

[4] In certain kinds of problems, a static structure may be more appropriate than a dynamic one. Such discussion is beyond the scope of this paper; it can be addressed apart in another study with more details. Generally, and according to the essence of multi-agent systems, a dynamic structure can respond better to complexity.

[5] Accordingly, it is forbidden to talk about cooperation mode (see §2.2) whenever we talk about agent systems.

case the domain of the activity is the agent itself). An agent interacts with the other agents by executing communicative actions (emission actions and reception actions). Generally an emission action does not modify the set of beliefs of an agent, whereas a reception action may have an impact on its beliefs. An agent can also execute physical actions on its spatial environment (e.g., moving on the grid in the prey/predator game). Each action from the spatial environment (a stimulus) on an agent will be interpreted. The results of the interpretation activity, agent's beliefs and goals, resolution methods, and the communication protocols form the parameters of the decision activity. The latter can update an agent's beliefs. It can also modify the agent's role by generating any action (physical, private or communicative) which will be integrated into an interaction paradigm (for example an agenda). The internal activity of an agent includes also its private actions which act on its beliefs.

4   The Object Paradigm

Each object is an instance of its class which defines completely its structure, and constitutes a common pattern to its instances. An object behavior is described via its well defined interface. It is strucured in terms of responsabilities. An object system is seen as a collection of such objects interacting with each other. The system composition is dynamic i.e., during its evolution, a system can create new objects and disappear others. The following reflections aim to situate the expression power of the object paradigm with respect to autonomy and interaction.

4.1   An Object Activity

An object activity depends on its internal state and the received requests. At the same time, its state is the result of its proper activity (see the diagram of figure 2). An object state holds the trace of its previous activity. It also includes the knowledge about its environment on which it depends by the transmitted information via the sent and received requests.

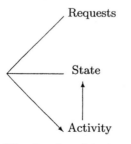

Fig. 2. An object activity

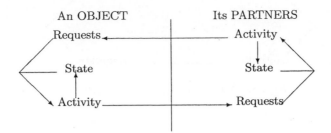

Fig. 3. An object interaction

4.2 Activity and Interaction

It is due to its activity that an object sends requests and interacts with its servers, and the received requests are the consequence of its clients' activity.

The object cooperation with its partners is defined by its position sometimes as a client sending requests and other times as a server via its interface. Each object can be a client and a server (see figure 3). According to the symmetrical diagram of figure 3, we have two kinds of loop: an internal loop and an external loop. The internal loop which is illustrated by the diagram of figure 4, is available in each object. This loop corresponds to the autonomy of an object, its capacity to determine itself and adapt its behavior. Recall that the defining charachteristic of object-oriented programming is the pinciple of encapsulation–the idea that objects can have control over their own internal state[9]. An object can be thought of as being autonomous over its state. Nevertheless, an object does not exhibit control over its behavior: if a method is made available for other objects to invoke, then they can do so whenever they wish; the object has no contol over whether or not that method is executed. The external loop illustrated by the diagram of figure 5, describes a mutual dependance situation in which the objects are situated in their interactions.

4.3 An Object versus an Agent

If the agent concept as a distributed object is very close to that of the object, it is not the case of the agent as intentional entity[1]. Indeed, the objects have neither goals nor personal satisfaction, and the message passing mechanism amounts to a simple procedure call. There is not a proper communication language. The interaction mechanisms are among the programmer's prerogatives. The main

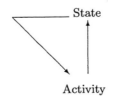

Fig. 4. An object autonomy

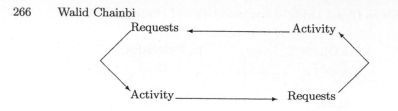

Fig. 5. A mutual dependance situation

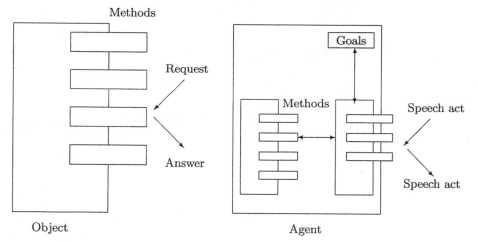

Fig. 6. An object versus an agent

difference which exists between objects and agents is illustrated by figure 6. Like an object, an agent provides a message-based interface independant of its internal data structures and algorithms. The primary difference between the two approaches lies in the language of the interface. In general object-oriented programming, the meaning of a message can vary from one object to another. In agent-oriented software engineering, agents use a common language with an agent-independant semantics.

An object is defined by a set of offered services (its methods) and which can't refuse to carry out when another object requires it to do. By contrast, agents have goals which allow them a decision autonomy to the received messages. Thus, an agent can be considered as an object with further capacities: personal satisfaction (intentions), and higher-level-language based communications (speech acts), which are intrinsically related. Inversely, an object can be considered as a "degenerated" agent (this term has been used by Ferber in[1]) which has become a simple executant: each received message is considered as a request.

5   Conclusion

This paper has presented in its first part a conceptualization for cooperation, which has ended in Belief-Goal-Role agents. Actually, conceptualizations are used in this paper as natural arguments to Belief-Goal-Role agents. Unlike most previous work, our model stresses the study of interaction as a preliminary to deduce the cognitive structure of agents. The second part of this paper studies the possibility of joining the object paradigm and the agent paradigm. An object is able to adapt its behavior according to the received interactions (and conversaly, to determine its proper interactions). However, it can't evolve (it can't either acquire new attributes to memorize new kinds of information, or provide new services if the rendered ones become obsolete). Such structural transformations come under mutation. We think that they are not difficult to consider if we deal with an artificial system whose designer changes some elements or replace them by others. In opposition to the previous option, another language is required if we have to deal with living objects which transform themseleves their structure through their activities. We share the idea that it is not envisaged that agent-based approaches will supplant techniques such as object-orientation. Rather, agent-based computing should be seen as providing a higher level of computational abstraction and this may, in turn, be realised through object-based systems [6]. In future, the work presented in this paper may be extended to build up an agent methodology easily understood by those who are familiar with the object paradigm.

References

[1] J. Ferber, *Les systémes multi-agents: un aperçu général*, [T. S.I, Volume 16, 1997].
[2] M. Wooldridge, *This is MYWORLD: The Logic of An Agent-Oriented DAI Testbed*, [LNAI 890, Springer-Verlag, 1994].
[3] J. M. Bradshaw, M. Greaves, H. Homback *Agents for the masses* [IEEE intelligent systems, March/April, 1999].
[4] C. Hewitt & J. Inman, *DAI Betwixt and Between: from "Intelligent agents" to Open Systems Science*, [IEEE Transactions on SMC,Vol.21, No 6, November 1991].
[5] D. Anzieu & J. Y. Martin, *La dynamique des groupes restreints*, [ed. puf, 1968].
[6] J. L. Austin, *How to do things with words*, [Oxford University Press, 1962].
[7] S. Bandinelli & E. Di Nitto & A. Fuggetta, *Supporting cooperation in the SPADE-1 environment*, [IEEE Transactions on Software Engineering, Vol.22, No 12, December 1996].
[8] J. L. Soubie & A. H. Kacem, *Modèles de cooperation homme/système intelligent*, [Systèmes coopératifs: de la modélisation à la conception, ed. Octares, 1994].
[9] N. R. Jennings & K. Sycara & M. Wooldridge, *A Roadmap of Agent Research and Development*, [Autonomous Agents and Multi-Agent Systems, 1, 7-38, 1998].

---

[6] Actually, an implementation of the prey/predator game in its initial release (one prey/four predators) as well as an extended release (two preys/four predators) was done using the C++ language.

Fuzzy Coalition Formation
among Rational Cooperative Agents

Leonid B. Sheremetov[1,2,3] and José C. Romero Cortés[3,4]

[1] Mexican Petroleum Institute (IMP), Mexico
[2] St. Petersburg Institute for Informatics
and Automation of the Russian Academy of Sciences (SPIIRAS), Russia
[3] Center for Computing Research, National Polytechnic Institute, Mexico
[4] Autonomous Metropolitan University, Mexico
sher@imp.mx, rcjc@correo.azc.uam.mx

Abstract. Formation of coalitions in multi-agent systems (MAS) enables the development of efficient organizations. In the article, a model of fuzzy cooperative game with coalitions is described. It extends the model of the fuzzy coalition game with associated core, introduced by M. Mareš by including in the fuzzy core (i) the fuzzy individual payments, and (ii) the binary values to form the structure of effective coalitions. The properties of the model are defined. The solution of the game is obtained using genetic algorithms. Experimental results for the MAS prototype from the domain of supply chains applying the proposed model with non-linear membership functions are discussed.

1 Introduction

Cooperation among agents in MAS enables the development of efficient organizations, since agents acting in a team fashion can considerably increase their capacities producing a synergetic effect, being able to offer more services and to achieve more benefits than acting individually [7-10]. Rational agents decide to cooperate with others (forming coalitions) and thus to coordinate their actions to achieve better results [3, 12]. To participate in the coalition, each agent determines the utility of its actions by an individual utility function. The value of a coalition among agents is computed by a characteristic function which determines the guaranteed utility the coalition is able to obtain. The distribution of the coalition's profit between its members is supposed to ensure individual rational payoffs and to provide an incentive of the agents to collaborate. Coalition formation is a rapidly developing area within the MAS research looking for methods enabling to form temporary coalitions on demand, on the fly, and at any time to inherently enable and even advance the development of effective e-commerce and collaborative work applications [17, 19, 23].

V. Mařík et al. (Eds): CEEMAS 2003, LNAI 2691, pp. 268–280, 2003.

The theory of games with coalitions offers results showing the general form of possible cooperation and conditions under which this is achieved. In many cases, a broad class of attainable patterns of cooperation and of distributions of the final payments exists, and it is important to select the best one or the most unbiased. Negotiations and bargaining generally take place before the application of coordinated strategies when agents have only a vague idea about the expected gains of the coalitions, so distribution of the gains can be vague, imprecise, and uncertain [1, 14, 16]. Using the theory of the fuzzy cooperative games (FCG) with coalitions it is possible to study the vagueness and to follow the way from the input of the vague idea about the gains via the bargaining process to the output corresponding to the possibilities of the vagueness of the distributions of the individual benefits.

In [15], an approach to the problem of coalition forming in MAS based on FCG with associated core, first introduced by M. Mareš [13], was described. In the present paper, an extended definition of the core is proposed. In this definition, (i) fuzzy individual payments are introduced, and (ii) the binary values y_{ij} are included in the fuzzy core to form the structure of effective coalitions. Finally, an application is presented in the context of Supply Chain Networks (SCN). A prototype that consists of 16 agents generating a structure of 4 overlapping coalitions is considered. The complexity issues, advantages and limitations of the proposed approach are also discussed.

2   Fuzzy Coalition Games Model

Different models to form fuzzy coalitions are described in the literature [1, 4, 14, 16, 22]. First, we briefly introduce the basic concepts and notions of co-operative game theory, which are necessary to introduce our model of coalition formation. More details can be found in [11, 14].

2.1   Basic Concepts

A co-operative game (I, v) is determined by a set I of agents wherein each subset of I is called a coalition, and a real-valued characteristic function $v : 2^I \rightarrow R$, assigning each coalition its maximum gain, the expected total income of the coalition (the so-called coalition value). The solution of a co-operative game with side payments is a coalition configuration (S, x) which consists of (i) a partition S of I, the so-called coalition structure, and (ii) an efficient payoff distribution x which assigns each agent in I its utility out of the value of the coalition it is member of in a given coalition structure S.

It is commonly assumed that every coalition may form, including singletons or the grand coalition I. However, the number or size of coalitions to be formed using a coalition formation method is often restricted to ensure, for example, polynomial complexity of the formation process.

Individually rational distributions are assigning each agent at least the gain it may get without collaborating within any coalition. In coalition configurations with so-called Pareto-optimal payoff distributions, no agent is better off in any other valid payoff distribution for the given game and coalition structure. A coalition configuration (S, x) is called stable if no agent has an incentive to leave its coalition in S due to its assigned payoff x_i.

The core of a game with respect to a given coalition structure is the set of coalition configurations with not necessarily unique payoff distributions such that no subgroup of agents is motivated to depart from the given structure. Only coalition structures that maximize the social welfare, i.e., the sum of all coalition values of coalitions in the considered structure, are core-stable or effective.

2.2   Motivation for the Research

The approach developed in this article is based on FCG of players with full involvement [13, 14]. As shown in [15], that model has the following advantages while being applied to coalition forming in MAS:

-   Permits to consider cooperation in MAS as utility function.
-   Presents a formal approach to coalition formation.
-   The approach of fuzzy core considers games with full involvement of the players. A fuzzy coalition generates a fuzzy membership function of the players' payments, while in the coalition games introduced by Aubin [1], their fuzzy nature is based mainly on the partial participation of the players in the game.
-   Permits at least partially, to avoid the well-known problem with core-stable configurations that the core may be empty for certain co-operative games. The property of a convex game guarantees a non-empty core.
-   Permits to avoid high communication costs typical for the conventional negotiation processes.

Nevertheless, our experiments showed that that model also has a number of serious limitations that prevent its use in real-life MAS applications, just to mention few of them:

-   Generating the imputations or elements of the fuzzy core (that is in turn a fuzzy set) among the exponential number of possible coalition structures is computationally hard since one has to try at least 2^I-1 coalition structures. The optimum imputation can be obtained analytically, for example using the method of the fuzzy Pareto optimum, for limited number of players and types of membership functions. Combinatorial algorithms, those from graph or optimisation theory can be used only for small agent populations (about 20 players).
-   To deal with the stability of the solution, the notion of effectivity is introduced. Nevertheless, the definition of the core is not related with the condition of the effective coalition. To consider only effective coalitions, all the coalitions must be considered first to select those satisfying the effictivity criterion.
-   Individual payments are real variables and only characteristic functions are fuzzy. As a consequence, fuzzy coalition payment has to be distributed among the unique players' payments. It is a serious limitation of the possibility for agents to "negotiate" their payments. On the other hand, the only way to define these

characteristic functions (for each coalition and for the grand coalition) is to do it externally, which seems to be very difficult if not impossible in real applications.

- The complexity of the model is the main reason to consider only linear membership functions and super-additive games.

- The use of Shapley values [18] for solution computation obviously is also exponentially hard. Moreover, it requires a universal (trapezoidal) membership function to be adopted by all agents, which seems to be very restrictive and unreal requirement and limits the type of the game to the game with side-off payments.

2.3   An Extended Model of a Game with Fuzzy Coalitions

In order to handle the limitations mentioned above, an extended model of a game is proposed. Let I be the set of players such that: $I = \{1,2,...,n\}$, n, finite or infinite, where the set of possible coalitions is the power set:

$$2^I = \{\phi, \{1\}, \{2\}, ... \{n\}, \{1,2\}, ..., \{n-1,n\}, \{1,2,3\}, ..., \{n-2,n-1,n\}, ..., \{1,2,...n\}\} \quad (1)$$

A structure of n coalitions $K_1, ..., K_m$ is: $\kappa = \{K_1, ..., K_m\}$. The fuzzy coalition game is defined as a pair (I, w), where I is nonempty and finite set of players, subsets of I are called coalitions, and w is called a characteristic function of the game, being $w : 2^I \rightarrow R^+$ a mapping connecting every coalition $K \subset I$ with a fuzzy quantity $w(K) \in R^+$, called characteristic function of the game, with membership function $\lambda_k : R \rightarrow [0,1]$, where $v(K)$ is the modal value of $w(K)$ with $w(\phi) = 0$. The fuzzy core for the game (I, w) with the imputation $X = (x_{ij})_{i \in I, j \in \kappa} \in R^I$ is defined as a fuzzy subset C_F of R^I:

$$C_F = \left\{ X \in R^I : v \succ= (w(I), \left\langle \sum_{\substack{i \in I, \\ j \in \kappa}} x_{ij} y_{ij} \right\rangle), \min_{K_i \subset \kappa} (v \succ= (\left\langle \sum_{\substack{i \in I \\ j \in K_i}} x_{ii} y_{ij} \right\rangle, w(K_i))) \right\} \quad (2)$$

with x_{ij} = Fuzzy payment of the agent i participating in the coalition j, $i = 1,2,...,n$ $j = 1,2,...,K_i$

$$y_{ij} = \begin{cases} 1, \text{if the agent i is involved in the coalition j} \\ 0, \text{if the agent i is not involved in the coalition j} \end{cases}$$

The core C_F is the set of possible distributions of the total payment achievable by the coalition of all players, and none of coalitions can offer to its members more than they can obtain accepting some imputation from the core. The first argument of the core C_F, unlike the definition of the core in the case of cooperative game with transferable utilities, or TU-game [2], indicates that the payments for the great coalition are less than the characteristic of I. This restriction is added by the nature of the problem domain. The second argument is the set of imputations relative to each coalition.

The membership function $\mu_{C_F} : R^I \rightarrow [0,1]$, is defined as:

$$\mu_{C_f}(x) = \min_{\substack{i \in K_i \\ j \in K}} \left\{ X \in R^I : v \succ= (w(I), \left\langle \sum_{\substack{i \in I, \\ j \in K}} x_{ij} y_{ij} \right\rangle), \min_{K_l \subset K} (v \succ= (\left\langle \sum_{\substack{i \in I \\ j \in K_l}} x_{ii} y_{ij} \right\rangle, w(K_i)) \right\} \qquad (3)$$

In the following statements, usually only coalitions K, L are mentioned and only in the last ones, the core is involved. This doesn't represent any problem, because the binary variables are multiplying by the fuzzy quantities, and their product is the same fuzzy quantity or the zero. With that, the extended model diminishes the number of summed variables in all the arguments of the core, but the form continues to be the same. The membership functions corresponding to the terms $x_{ij} y_{ij}$ are:

$$\mu_{x_{ij} \bullet y_{ij}}(z) = \mu_{x_{ij}}(z), \text{ for } y_{ij} = 1 \text{ and } \mu_{x_{ij} \bullet y_{ij}}(z) = \mu_0(z), \text{ for } y_{ij} = 0 \qquad (4)$$

The game (I, w) can be super-, sub- or additive, with $K, L \subset I$, $K \cap L = \phi$, according to the following:

is superadditive $\Leftrightarrow w(K \cup L) \succ= w(K) \oplus w(L)$

is subadditive $\Leftrightarrow w^*(K \cup L) \prec w^*(K) \oplus w^*(L)$ $\qquad (5)$

is additive $\Leftrightarrow$ the game is superadditive and subadditive

The asterisks which appear in the definition of the sub-additive and additive cases refer to the super-optimum of the corresponding coalition.

It can be proved that the game (I, w) with the core defined according to (1), has the following properties.

Definition 1. The game with fuzzy coalitions, is convex [13] if and only if for some couple of coalitions $K, L \subset I$, there is the following relationship of weak order:

$$w(K \cup L) \oplus w(K \cap L) \succ= w(K) \oplus w(L), \qquad (6)$$

which happens with the possibility:

$$v^*(K, L) = v \succ= (w(K \cup L) \oplus w(K \cap L) \succ= w(K) \oplus w(L)) \qquad (7)$$

According to the definition of preferences among fuzzy quantities, the possibility that (I, w) is fuzzy convex is:

$$\delta(I, w) = \min(v *(K, L) : K, L \subset I) \qquad (8)$$

Let us define some Lemmas for the main properties of the game. As shown in [5], the product of a real variable is distributed with fuzzy numbers, then the core of the extended model is of the same form as the standard core, so all the statements and demonstrations are valid for the standard case as corollary. Due to the space limits, only two proofs are provided below.

Lemma 1. The possibility that a non-empty core C_F for the extended game (I, w) exist, is given by:

$$\gamma_{C_F}(I,w) = \sup\left(\mu_{C_F}(x) : x \in \mathfrak{R}^I\right) \tag{9}$$

Lemma 2. Let (I,w) be a fuzzy extension of the convex crisp game (I,v), then the possibility that (I,w) is convex is 1.

Lemma 3. Let (I,w) be a fuzzy extension of the crisp game (I,v) with the core C supposed to be non-empty, then for some imputation $x \in C_F \subset \mathfrak{R}^I$, $\mu_{C_F}(x) = 1$.

Proof.-From the definitions of the crisp [13] and fuzzy cores (1) we have:

$$\sum_{i,j} x_{ij} y_{ij} \leq v(I) \Rightarrow v \succ = (w(I), \sum_{i,j} x_{ij} y_{ij}) = 1$$

In the same way, for the second argument of the cores, we have that:

$$\sum_{i,j} x_{ij} y_{ij} \leq v(K_j) \Rightarrow v \succ = (w(K_j), \sum_{i,j} x_{ij} y_{ij}) = 1$$

Then, from (3) $\mu_{C_F}(x) = 1$.

Proposition.- Let (I,w) be a fuzzy extension of the crisp coalition game (I,v), with its fuzzy characteristics defined within the trapezoidal family (trapezoidal, triangular, ramp, step, etc), then for the parts where the characteristic is strictly positive, we have that: $\gamma_{C_F}(I,w) \geq \delta(I,w)$.

Proof.- Given that $\delta(I,w)$ is the possibility that a fuzzy coalition game (I,w) is convex, then $\exists v^*(K) \ni \mu_K(v(K^*)) \in [0,1]$, $\forall K \subset I$ with $\min(v^*(K) : K \subset I) = \delta(I,w)$ and a crisp game (I,v^*) is convex. From the theorem that for a convex crisp game (I,v) with side-off payments, its core is not empty, as proved in [14], we have that the core C^* is not empty. Considering that the fuzzy game (I,w) obtains its values from the crisp game (I,v^*) with the possibility $\delta(I,w)$, then $C^* \subset C_F$ at least with the same possibility and: $\gamma_{C_F}(I,w) \geq \delta(I,w)$.

It is necessary to mention that the above statements only consider the characteristics of the game (I,w), so any crisp like argument can be included in the fuzzy core. For example, constraints on the number of agent players for each coalition can be fixed, any other constraints defining coalitions as overlapping or not or defining the sequence in the development of tasks can be established.

3   Experimental Results

3.1   Description of the Case Study

In this paper, an automotive SCN example has been utilized for experimentation in order to demonstrate how the proposed model works [20]. For simplicity, the product (a *car*) consisted of four major parts (fig. 1): Body (consisted of 14 Pre-formed Tubes, 5 Exterior Sheets), Interior (consisted of Dashboard, 2 Front Seats, Rear Seat), Under Carriage (consisted of Wheels, Front and Rear Axles, 2 Front and 2 Rear Shock Absorbers) and Power Train (consisted of Engine, Transmission, Cardan Shaft). This simplification of product structure, however, does not impact on the generality of the described approach.

Coalitions are formed based on the product structure, i.e. a group of suppliers for each major part with the associated assembler unit form a coalition. This way, three coalitions are formed with corresponding assembly. External manufactures (car body) form the fourth coalition of two enterprises (fig. 1). This domain ontology is used to define the coalition structures through the y_{ij} variables. The main parameters of the experiments can be found in [16]. To consider the case of overlapping coalitions, initially, the game was arranged with five enterprises capable of producing different components and assembling with a total of 16 players (Table 1).

Table 1. Distribution of the enterprises, coalitions and membership functions

Function (Enterprise)	Type of the membership function	Parameters	Coalition	Associated variable
Shaft, axes and wheel manufacturing (1, 4)	Triangular	(3, 6, 9) (4, 6, 8)	1	$x_{11}, y_{11}, x_{41}, y_{41}$
Shock absorber manufacturing (2)	Ramp (+)	(10, 15)	1	x_{21}, y_{21}
Under Carriage Assembly (3)	Ramp (+)	(8, 12)	1	x_{31}, y_{31}
Engine manufacturing (3, 4)	Triangular	(3, 6, 9) (3, 5, 7)	2	$x_{32}, y_{32}, x_{42}, y_{42}$
Transmission manufacturing (2)	Triangular	(6, 8, 10)	2	x_{22}, y_{22}
Power Train Assembly (1, 5)	Triangular	(8, 10, 12) (9, 10, 11)	2	$x_{12}, y_{12}, x_{52}, y_{52}$
Dashboard and seat manufacturing (5)	Step	(4, 6)	3	x_{53}, y_{53}
Interior Assembly (4)	Step	(10, 15)	3	x_{43}, y_{43}
Exterior Sheet manufacturing (4, 3)	Ramp (+)	(3, 5) (4, 6, 8)	4	$x_{44}, y_{44}, x_{34}, y_{34}$
Exterior Tubes manufacturing (1)	Ramp (+)	(10, 20)	4	x_{14}, y_{14}
Wheel manufacturing (5)	Triangular	(2,3,5)	1	x_{51}, y_{51}
Seat manufacturing (2)	Ramp (+)	(1, 6)	3	x_{23}, y_{23}
Grand coalition	Ramp (+)	(80, 120)	I	$\sum_{i,j} x_{ij} y_{ij}$

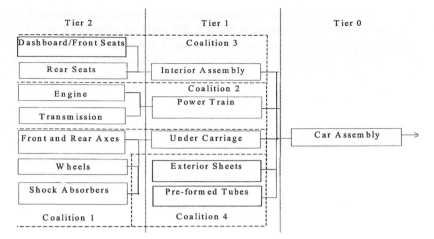

Fig. 1. Structure of the Production Process

3.2   Results of Coalition Formation

To conduct the experiments, the test-bed described in [15] was used. The MAS resides on the Component Agent Platform (CAP) and has an access to the standardized problem solving techniques (Evolver package for genetic programming [6] and Excel solver) implemented as modules of legacy software through the Wrapper Agents (WA).

The core is non-empty according to (6), because individual and coalition payoffs are convex fuzzy sets. For the case study, fuzzy core looks like follows:

$$C_F = \left\{ X \in \mathfrak{R}^I, with\, I = \{1,2,3,4\} : v \succ = (w(I), \left(\sum_{\substack{i \in I, \\ j \in \kappa = \{K_1, K_2, K_3, K_4\}}} x_{ij} y_{ij} \right)), \min_{K_i \subset \kappa} (v \succ = ((\sum_{\substack{i \in I \\ j \in K_i}} x_{ii} y_{ij}), w(K_i))) \right\},$$

where:

- $w(K_1)$, is a fuzzy payment to the first coalition with a triangular membership function (27, 42, 48),
- $w(K_2)$, is a fuzzy payment to the second coalition with a triangular membership function (29, 39, 49),
- $w(K_3)$, is a fuzzy payment to the third coalition with a positive ramp membership function (15, 27),
- $w(K_4)$, is a fuzzy payment to the forth coalition with a triangular membership function (15, 35, 45),
- $w(I)$, is a fuzzy payment to the grand coalition with a positive ramp membership function (80, 40).

The imputation vector x^* satisfying (3), is obtained using Evolver package with the following parameters of the genetic algorithm: mutation rate - 6%, crossover rate - 50% with the population of 50 organisms with adjustment function referring to (3)

The proposed model has the following advantages:

- The definition of the fuzzy core involves the effectivity component by including the binary variables y_{ij} in the fuzzy core. When an effective solution is found, not only the individual utilities for the game players are increased (the effectivity of the agreement), but also the ability of the coalition to find an effective and stable agreement is increased.
- This model defines a game without side payments because it can be assumed that fuzzy payments $\{(w(I), x_{ij}, w(K_i))\}$ have any associated membership function (lineal or non-linear, universal or not). Additive, sub-additive and super-additive games can also be considered.
- Using genetic algorithms we obtain an approximate solution for games with large number of players with any type of membership function. Being any-time algorithm, it permits to find the best solution given time constraints.
- Using the ontology corresponding to the application domain a number of viable coalitions is reduced significantly decreasing the complexity of the problem.
- Avoids the problem of synchronization critical for distributed algorithms with large agent population.
- The proposed approach also has some disadvantages:
- Solution method is centralized.
- Solution can correspond to the local optimum. For the game without side-payments there are no algorithms permitting to obtain optimum solution.
- Each solution is a trade-off between the solution quality and computational cost. For considerable number of agents computational cost is high. Nevertheless, as it was shown in our experiments, for the examples with linear membership functions conventional Excel's solver can be used where solutions were obtained in a couple of seconds.
- Membership functions are difficult to generate in an automatic fashion, though the algorithm based on the non-linear fuzzy regression method for the case when historical data are available, is under development.

Some remarks concerning the application of the developed FCG model to the development of dynamic coalition formation (DCF) schemes can be found in [12]. Reasonable solutions for such types of games lead to co-operation schemes which enable the agents to cope with issues of uncertainty, including, for example, vagueness of expected coalition values and corresponding payoffs. As in the described example, such uncertainties are induced mostly by the vague idea of agents about the possible payoffs. Actually, the dynamic nature of coalition formation is implicitly captured by the core-based approaches (as developed in this article) during the search of sub-optimal imputations, formation of the coalition structure and the search for effective coalitions when agents enter and leave coalitions. We can also consider that the uncertainties in agents payoffs are induced by dynamic events such as network faults, changes of trust or reputation ratings of possible coalition partners, and receiving vague or even incomplete information and data during task execution or negotiation. The development of algorithms for dynamic fuzzy coalition forming appears to be most promising and challenging at the same time.

The fields of FCG and DCF are still in their very infancies and require further basic research efforts. Concepts of super-additive FCG and "stable" fuzzy payoff distribution according to the fuzzy extension of the core and the Shapley-value were investigated in detail in [14]. However, fuzzy sub-additive games, concepts of "vague" stability and appropriate coalition algorithms for FCG are the topics of current research.

Acknowledgements

Partial support for this research work has been provided by the CONACyT, Mexico within the project 31851-A "Models and Tools for Agent Interaction in Cooperative MAS" and by the IMP within the project D.00006 "Distributed Intelligent Computing".

References

[1]   Aubin, J.P.: Cooperative fuzzy games. Mathematics of Oper. Research, 6(1):1-13, (1981).

[2]   Aumann, R. J. and Maschler M.: The bargaining set for cooperative games, in M. Dresher, L. S. Shapley, and A. W. Tucker, eds., Advances in Game Theory, Princeton University Press, Princeton, NJ, (1964) 443 – 476.

[3]   Axelrod, R.: The complexity of cooperation: agent based models of competition and collaboration. Princeton University Press (1997).

[4]   Butnariu, D. and Klement, E. P.: Triangular norm-based measures and games with fuzzy coalitions. Kluwer Academic Publishers (1993).

[5]   Dubois, D., and Prade, H.: Mathematics in science and engineering. Volume 144. Academic Press Inc. (1980).

[6]   Evolver Release 4.01. Palisade. 2001

[7]   Ferber, J.: Multi-Agent Systems, Addison-Wesley, Reading, MA, (1999).

[8]   Gasser, L.: Social conceptions of knowledge and action: DAI foundations and open system semantics, Artificial Intelligence 47(1--3): 107--138, (1991).

[9]   Jennings, NR.: On agent-based software engineering. Artificial Intelligence, 117:277-296, (2000).

[10]   Jennings, N.R., Faratin, P., Lomuscio, A.R., Parsons, S., Sierra, C. and Wooldridge, M.: Automated negotiation: prospects, methods and challenges. Int. J. of Group Decision and Negotiation 10(2) 199-215 (2001).

[11]   Kahan, J.P., and Rapoport, A.: Theories of coalition formation. Lawrence Erlbaum Associates, New Jersey (1984).

[12]   M. Klusch and A. Gerber.: Dynamic Coalition Formation among Rational Agents. IEEE Journal of Intelligent Systems, Vol. 3, (2002).

[13]   Mareš, M.: Fuzzy coalition forming. In Proc. of the Seventh IFSA World Congress, Prague, (1997) 1-18.

[14]   Mares, M.: Fuzzy Cooperative Games – Cooperation with Vague Expectations, Physica Verlag, (2001).

[15] Romero Cortés, J. and Sheremetov L.: Model of Cooperation in Multi Agent Systems with Fuzzy Coalitions. B. Dunin-Keplicz, E. Nawarecki (Eds.): From Theory to Practice in Multi-Agent Systems. LNAI, Springer Verlag, 2296: 263-272, (2002).

[16] Roth, A., Game-theoretic models of bargaining. Cambridge, (1995).

[17] Sandholm, T., Larson, K., Andersson, M., Shehory, O., and Tohmé, F.: Coalition Structure Generation with Worst Case Guarantees, Artificial Intelligence, 111(1-2): 209-238, (1999).

[18] Shapley, L. S.: A value for n-person games. In Kuhn, H. W. and Tucker, A. W., eds., Contributions to the Theory of Games II, Princeton University Press, Princeton. (1953) 307–317.

[19] Shehory, O.: Optimality and Risk in Purchase at Multiple Auctions, Proceedings of 5th International Workshop on Cooperative Information Agents (CIA 2001), M Klusch, F Zambonelli (eds.), Lecture Notes in Artificial Intelligence, Vol. 2182, Springer, (2001).

[20] Smirnov, A.,V., Sheremetov, L.B., Chilov, N., and J. Romero Cortes, Configuring of Supply Chain Networks Based on Constraint Satisfaction, Genetic and Fuzzy Game Theoretic Approaches. In: Information Technology for Balanced Automation Systems in Manufacturing and Services. Selected papers of the IFIP, IEEE International Conference BASYS'02 Conference, Kluwer Academic Publishers, (2002) 183-192.

[21] Tanaka,H. and Haekwan,L., Fuzzy aproximation with non- symetric fuzzy parameters in fuzzy regression analysis. Vol.42 No.1, 98-112. 1999.

[22] Wang, J.: The theory of games. Oxford Science Publications. (1988).

[23] Yamamoto, J. and Sycara, K.: A stable and efficient buyer coalition formation scheme for e-marketplaces. Proceedings 5th International Conference on Autonomous Agents, Montreal, Canada, ACM Press, (2001).

Multi-agent Simulation of Work Teams

Antonio Moreno, Aïda Valls, and Marta Marín

Computer Science & Mathematics Department, Universitat Rovira i Virgili
ETSE. Campus Sescelades. Av. dels Països Catalans, 26, 43007-Tarragona, Spain
{amoreno,avalls}@etse.urv.es

Abstract. When a new project starts, one of the most difficult tasks is to choose the most suitable members of the work team. It is necessary to take into account many factors in the selection process, such as the professional qualification of each candidate, his previous experience, or his willingness to work in a team. In this paper we propose the use of a multi-agent system to simulate the behaviour of different work teams engaged in the development of a complex project. The project manager may use the information provided by this multi-agent system to find the most appropriate set of candidates.

1   Introduction

In any complex project, in which a group of people has to work together, it is very important to have a work team that can tackle successfully all the tasks composing the project. Finding a good team is not easy, because a large number of factors have to be taken into account. The most relevant factors may be grouped into three categories:

- *Individual characteristics:* Among the characteristics of each person it is necessary to know his *professional level* and his *degree of expertise*. These features define the *types of tasks* that the person can undertake (e.g. a high-degree engineer can solve more complex problems than a low-degree one), the *time* that will be spent to solve a task (an experienced worker will do the tasks more quickly than a novice one) and the *economic cost* (which depends on the professional level).
- *Social characteristics:* When a person has to be a member of a team, his *willingness to work with other people* is a very important factor in order to decide if that person is a good choice for the work team.
- *Temporal and economic costs:* The manager of a project wants to find a team of people that can develop the project in the minimum amount of time and with an optimum economic cost (or, at least, satisfying certain constraints on time and budget). In general, these two requirements are difficult to meet simultaneously: for instance, if the work team is composed of very qualified and experienced people the project will finish quickly, but the economic cost will be high.

V. Mařík et al. (Eds): CEEMAS 2003, LNAI 2691, pp. 281–291, 2003.

All these factors make it very hard to select the most appropriate set of people to develop a project efficiently. In this paper we present a tool that can help the project manager to make this selection process. We have developed a *multi-agent system* (MAS, [1,2]) that simulates the behaviour of different work teams and provides statistical results that help to find out which are the teams that can potentially sort out the project with minimal temporal and financial costs.

The rest of the paper is structured as follows. In the next section it is argued why multi-agent systems are an appropriate tool to tackle this problem. After that, we show the architecture of the MAS that has been implemented and we explain the process of simulation of work teams, detailing the results provided by the system. The paper concludes with a brief discussion and a sketch of some lines of future work.

2   Adequacy of Agent Technology

Recently different proposals of using agents for modelling work teams have appeared ([3,4,5]). The multi-agent systems technology seems to be adequate to simulate the behaviour of groups of people working together because it allows:

- *Individual modelling:* Each candidate to join the work team can be represented by a specific agent that will interact with other agents in a way that will depend on the characteristics of that person (e.g. his degree of sociability). It seems a very natural idea to have an autonomous agent encapsulating the behaviour of each person, and to simulate the interactions between the people with messages between the agents that represent them.
- *Modularity:* The simulation process will have different phases. We can distribute the simulation procedure between different agents; in that way, the development of the simulator will be simpler than the construction of a single system (e.g. a traditional monolithic decision aid expert system).
- *Task distribution, reliability:* We can distribute the agents in different computers, so that several agents may be executing concurrently (e.g. each personal agent may be running in a different machine). If a machine goes down, the rest of the system can adapt dynamically to the new situation and continue the simulation process.
- *Flexibility:* With the agents approach we can add or remove new entities during the simulation in a dynamic way. We can also modify the characteristics of a person in order to see how the global behaviour of the team is modified.

3   Multi-agent System Architecture

Different types of agents have been developed in order to make possible this team simulator. Taking into account the different steps of the simulation process, we have identified the following agents (Fig.1):

- Personal Agents:
  Each of the members of the team will be represented by its personal agent. This agent will know the individual and social characteristics of its owner and will use this information to simulate the behaviour of this person when doing a job. Candidates may have different levels of studies. In particular, we have considered *skilled workers* (with different degrees of engineering studies) and *unskilled workers* (without engineering studies).
- Manager Agent:
  This agent is in charge of selecting the best personnel for the project. It will configure different possible work teams, and will send them to the *Simulator Agent* to find out their expected performance.
- Simulator Agent:
  The simulation agent is in charge of simulating the solution of the task using the teams provided by the manager agent. This agent must control the correct execution of all the tasks in the project, respecting the precedence constraints of each task.
- Statistical Agent:
  The purpose of this study is to see if multi-agent systems can be used as simulators of teams of people working together to solve a complex task. For this reason, we have included an agent that will keep track of all the simulations done to allow the user to make a statistical analysis.

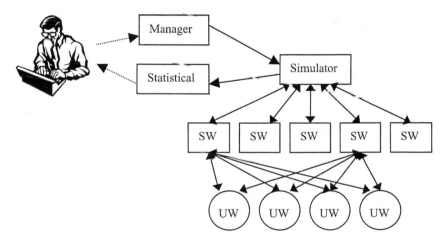

Fig. 1. Multi-Agent System Architecture

4   The Simulation Process

All the different types of agents must cooperate to perform a simulation. For each project simulation we are interested in knowing the time spent in solving the problem and the cost for the company (which is related to the salary of the people that has done the work).

This system is intended to work with complex projects that can be decomposed into basic tasks. Each task is assigned to a single engineer, who can be helped by an unskilled worker. Depending on the level of difficulty of the task, the minimum level of knowledge of the engineer is different. For example, a simple producing task will normally be assigned to a low-degree engineer although it could also be assigned to a high-degree engineer or a project leader; however, a design task should only be assigned to a project leader. The professional levels are specified in section 4.1.

In addition to the level of difficulty, each task, T_i, has an estimated time for completion and a set of pre-requisites (i.e. other tasks that must be finished before T_i can be started). These precedence relations can be represented in an acyclic directed graph (see Fig.2). Each node of the graph represents a single task that cannot be decomposed. A directed arc between two nodes, a and b, indicates that task a must be completed before b starts. For example, in Fig.3 we can see that tasks 2 and 3 cannot begin until task 1 is finished. Nevertheless, when task 2 ends, tasks 4 and 5 can be done in parallel. In this case, tasks 4 and 5 could be assigned to different people.

The precedence graph is given by the user to the Manager Agent (codified in a text file). For each graph, different simulations are done. In each simulation there is a skilled work assigned to each task (more details will be given in section 4.2). During the simulation the agents will act as if they were doing the task assigned to them, and the Simulator Agent will guarantee that the precedence relations indicated by the graph are correctly followed. Due to the fact that the result of a simulation depends on some probabilistic values, several executions of the same assignment are done. The number of tests of the same simulation is indicated by the user of the system. With the introduction of a random factor we imitate the behaviour of the worker, because the same person doing the same task can sort it out in different times according to unpredictable factors (f.i. state of mind). Once all the executions of the same team and task scheduling have been done, the average results are given to the Statistical Agent. Then, another simulation can start. The user also establishes the number of simulations (different assignments of workers to tasks) as well as the number of people to be changed between a simulation and the next one. In the following sections, we explain in detail the steps of the simulation process.

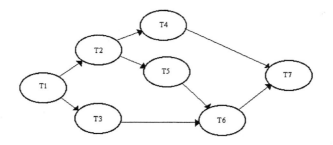

Fig. 2. Graph of tasks

4.1   Personal Agents

Each candidate to participate in the project must configure a personal agent that will act on his behalf during the simulation. In this initial prototype of the system, we have considered 4 characteristics to describe the person:

- *Name*: personal identifier.
- *Professional level*: (this property is only applied to skilled workers) three different categories are distinguished according to the degree of studies of the person : *Project Leader* (PL), *High-degree engineer* (HE) and *Low-degree engineer* (LE)[1].
- *Degree of Expertise*: according to the experience of each person we distinguish 3 degrees: *good, medium* and *poor*. This factor will be used to determine the probability of correctly solving a task and the time spent to do it.
- *Team willingness*: this is a social characteristic that is applied to skilled workers. Two possible values have been considered: *open* and *closed.* If the person prefers to work in a group, the agent can decide to collaborate with an unskilled worker to complete a task in less time.

Once this information has been obtained, the agent sends a registration message to the Directory Facilitator[2] (DF), which is an agent that provides a yellow-pages service. Then, the personal agent waits for requests or queries of the agents responsible for the simulation.

4.2   Assignment of Tasks to Agents

The Manager Agent generates a set of task allocations that assign each task to a different skilled worker according to these constraints: (i) any personal agent assigned to a particular task must have a professional level at least equal to the minimum level required for this task, and (ii) a personal agent will not be assigned to a set of tasks that can be done in parallel (for example, tasks 2 and 3 of Fig.2 must be assigned to different agents, while tasks 2 and 4 may be assigned to the same agent).

In this problem, the number of possible combinations of workers and tasks is exponential. Therefore, we cannot simulate the behaviour of all the possible teams and schedules. The user must indicate how many different combinations to try (i.e. the number of simulations or different teams). The user also establishes the amount of changes from one simulation to the next one. That is, we can change all the workers or only a percentage of them. Depending on these parameters, the system will explore different areas of the solution space.

To start, the Manager Agent selects form the set of available agents - the ones that still have not been assigned to any task - a worker that fulfils the minimum conditions of the task; that is, he has the professional level indicated as minimum. If this is not possible, another person with a higher professional level is selected. With this heuristic algorithm we find a set of workers that is cheap (because the price is related

---

[1] This multi-agent system will be used to find teams for engineering projects, for this reason the categories indicated are related to engineers.

[2] The Directory Facilitator is an agent of any multi-agent system that follows the FIPA specifications [6].

to the professional level), which is one of the usual requirements of the user due to limited budgets.

When a feasible allocation has been found, the information is sent to the Simulator Agent, which will start the process of execution of several simulations. In the meantime, the Manager Agent can build another work team. The next team is obtained by introducing some modifications to the previous one. The parameter given by the user - the number of changes - indicates how many tasks must be reassigned. These tasks are randomly selected. Then, from among the personal agents that have not participated in the previous simulation, the system selects the ones that are capable to do the tasks that are unassigned.

4.3   The Simulation of a Work Team

The agent responsible of simulating the result obtained by a team of workers is the Simulator Agent. This agent receives a request from the Manager Agent with the following information: the graph of tasks, the assignment of a skilled worker to each task, the maximum time for completing the simulation with success and the number of executions to be done.

As it has been said above, we perform different executions for each team because we have introduced some probabilistic components to imitate the possible changes in the behaviour of the persons (more details will be given in section 4.4). The result of a simulation consists of two elements: (1) the amount of time spent to finish all the tasks of the project and (2) the cost of the project. The cost is calculated with the salaries of the workers (which depend on their professional level).

To optimise the process, the Simulator Agent uses different threads to make the executions in parallel. Once all of them have finished, the average time and average cost are passed to the Statistical Agent.

When an execution starts, the Simulator Agent behaves like the project manager, because it indicates to each personal agent when it must start to work in a particular task. Therefore, it must control all the tasks that are currently being done in order not to start any task before their preceding ones have not finished. To do this, it maintains a data structure where the following information of each task is kept: preceding tasks not yet completed, skilled agent assigned to the task (by the Manager Agent), time spent in performing the task and unskilled worker that has helped in the task (if any). The two initial values are needed before starting the simulation of this task, and the two last ones are the result of the simulation, as it will be explained below.

When all the preceding tasks of a task T have been done, the Simulator Agent sends a message to the personal agent associated to the skilled worker assigned to task T. Then the personal agent will try to do the task, using some help if appropriate. Once the task has been completed, the Simulator Agent will receive a notification of the corresponding agent with the amount of time spent in sorting the task out and indicating if the task has been done in collaboration with any other agent (this is needed to calculate the total cost of the salaries).

Each time that a task is completed, the Simulator Agent saves all the information related to it, and checks if any other task can be started. This process is repeated until all the tasks of the project have been completed or until one of the following situations occurs:

- A task has not been completed. It may happen if the person has not been able to solve the task. In real life, sometimes we are not able to sort a problem out due to different factors. For instance, the person gets sick or the worker finds a better job elsewhere. Details about these unexpected situations are given in the next section.

- The deadline of the project is reached. This may happen with the tasks of the end of the project when we have spent too much time to solve the previous tasks.

- The Simulator Agent detects these two abnormal situations, and immediately reacts aborting the simulation and informing the Statistical Agent about the failure. In fact, the user is specially interested in knowing these cases because if the proportion of failures is high, it should revise the parameters given (f.i. the deadline or the minimum level of expertise of the tasks).

4.4   Simulation of the Execution of a Task

Any agent representing a skilled worker can receive a request from the Simulator Agent with the details of a particular task to be solved. Due to the fact that the Manager Agent has controlled that an agent is not assigned more than one task simultaneously, the personal agent will always accept to do the task for which it is required.

To simulate the execution of the task, different probabilistic components have been considered. The degree of expertise and the professional level are related to the probability of finishing the task successfully and to the time employed for it, whereas the social characteristics of the agent are related to the probability of preferring to work alone over to collaborate with an unskilled worker.

The first thing that the personal agent does is the calculation of the probability of not finishing the task. This corresponds to the first failure case explained in section 4.3. For each different professional level and degree of expertise a maximum percentage of failure, p_{fail}, has been set up (f.i. an experienced project leader will only fail, at most, 2% of the times it solves a task). Then, a uniformly random integer value is taken from $0..100$; if this value falls in $0..p_{fail}$ the worker fails to sort out the task (which is immediately communicated to the Simulator Agent). Otherwise the task can be successfully done by the worker.

To simulate the execution of the task, the agent can decide to work alone or with the help of an unskilled worker. Depending on the social character of the person in charge of the task, the agent calculates the probability of working as a group. Different maximum threshold values, t_{group}, have been established for open and closed characters. For example, 30 % for a closed character, which means that he prefers to work alone in the majority of situations. In the next section we describe with more detail how a skilled worker requests help from unskilled ones.

The last thing to simulate is the duration of the task. In a similar way to the previous ones, we have fixed two thresholds in $0..100$: the maximum level for the probability of delay, t_{delay}, and for the probability of finishing before the estimated time, t_{fast}. In this case, these thresholds not only depend on the characteristics of the person but also on the fact of working alone or as a group. If the agent has decided to work with the help of other workers, the threshold t_{delay} will be decreased and t_{fast} increased.

Finally, a randomly picked value, *time*, from 0 to 100 says the duration of the solution of the task. For example, if the task was expected to be done in 5 days, then the effective duration is calculated as follows:

if $t_{fast} < time < t_{delay}$ then the task is finished in the estimated time, 5 days

if $time < t_{fast}$ then the task has been done in: $5 * \dfrac{100 - (t_{fast} - time)}{100}$ days

if $time > t_{delay}$ then we have spent: $5 * \dfrac{100 + (time - t_{delay})}{100}$ days

The Simulator Agent will use the duration of the task to know at what time the successive tasks can be started. Although we have simplified the problem considering that the task can only be done successfully or with a failure, an interesting extension will be to take into account different degrees of fulfilment of the task.

4.5   Requesting Help from Unskilled Workers

There are some tasks in which the main part of the work must be done by a qualified engineer (f.i. the analysis of the data); however, part of the task is a simple and routine process that can be delegated to another person (f.i. the introduction of the data to the computer). Working in parallel, the task can be finished earlier.

If Bob decided to collaborate with another worker, it should find an available unskilled agent that would like to do the job. The first step consists of searching for the unskilled agents in the system, which can be done using the services provided by the DF agent. Then, the agent can use a negotiation protocol to select one of them. We have implemented the well-known Contract-Net Protocol ([7]). That is, Bob sends a Call for Proposals to all the unskilled workers and waits until some proposals are received or a deadline is reached. If no proposal is obtained, Bob will have to perform the task alone. Otherwise, it has to select one of the proposals received. Different criteria can be used to make this selection. The more information provided in the proposals, the better the selection will be. In this initial prototype the agents propose an estimated time to solve the task.

When the unskilled agents receive a Call for Proposals for doing some work, they can be working for other agent at the same time. In this case, they will not do any proposal because they are not able to do two jobs simultaneously. However, if an unskilled agent (e.g. Sue) is free, she will try to estimate the time for accomplishing that goal of the task. This will be the proposal sent to Bob. This estimation is done in a similar way to the ones explained in the previous section. We consider a maximum time according to the skills of the person. For example, being Sue a person with good experience, she may propose to be able to reduce the total duration in 30% in case Bob decides to work with her. Imagine that Bob accepts her proposal and rejects the rest. Then, Sue will simulate the execution of her part of the task during the period of time proposed. In all this period, she will not be able to make any other proposal.

With the consideration of these additional agents, we are able to simulate a more complex team-working model. So, in each simulation, there is a dynamic component in the team composition that may influence the result, since there is some probability associated to the fact of deciding to work alone or as a group. We are also interested in studying the behaviour of the team in relation to the number of unskilled agents available in the system. At the moment, we do not penalize the fact of desiring to work as a group and not being able to do it; however, following the results of [4], it could be interesting to do so because it seems to decrease the effectiveness of the worker.

5   Statistical Results

The Statistical Agent receives the average result of a group of executions for each assignment of workers to the tasks. This agent gathers all this information, which is provided to the user with the graphical interface[3] in Fig.3.

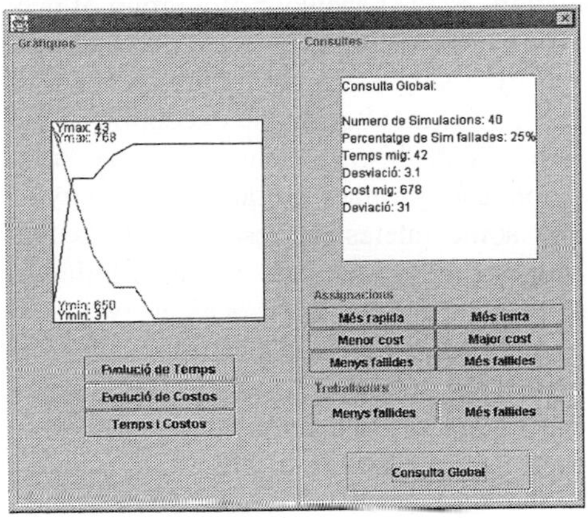

Fig. 3. Statistical Agent Interface

The interface window has two different areas. In the left-hand side, the user can obtain graphical representations of the evolution of the average times and costs of diiferent work teams. For example, in Fig.3 we can see that when time decreases, cost increases. This result is due to the fact that we can only reduce the time by means of: (i) contracting more qualified and experienced workers (with a high salary), and (ii) having open-minded personnel which works together with unskilled workers to sort out the problem in less time but increasing the salaries because we also have to pay these additional workers.

The right-hand side of the interface shows details about the groups that have solved all the tasks in less time, have spent more time, require the minimum/maximum amount of money or have the minimum/maximum number of failed tasks.

For each case, the user can know the composition of the team (skilled and unskilled agents) and the average time, cost and percentage of failure of the team.

The rest of the options allow the user to see which are the workers with the minimum and maximum failure rate. This result is particularly interesting because the

---

[3] The system displays the information in Catalan.

user can know who are the most successful candidates and also the ones that are not recommended to be included in our team because their results have been very bad. In addition, the user can also know the characteristics of the simulation done: number of executions, failure rate, average number of days and cost (with their respective standard deviations).

6   Conclusions and Future Work

Agents constitute an appropriate paradigm to build models of individuals. Each agent can act on behalf of a particular person, taking into account some of his/her personal characteristics. In the system presented in this paper we have made a first attempt to model the behaviour of a group of people that must work in the same project.

In this paper we have presented an architecture of a multi-agent system that allows the user to make simulations of the behaviour of a group of people that must complete an industrial project. We have considered projects that can be decomposed in a graph of tasks that are solved by a single engineer. Our approach is a centralised one, in which there is one agent that is monitoring the execution of the tasks and indicates to each agent when to start. With this, we achieve a very simple way to control the simulations and obtain interesting values that are analysed by an statistical agent.

The system provides some interesting results such as the expected cost of the project, the expected number of days and the expected failure rate. Moreover, we can know who are the best workers and the worst ones, as well as the configuration of the most successful team, or the cheapest one. Therefore, this can be a useful decision support tool for the head of the project in order to make a good selection according to his/her priorities (i.e. the budget or the deadline).

This system has been implemented in JADE [8,9], which is a collection of Java libraries that facilitate the deployment of multi-agent systems that follow the FIPA specifications [6]. To do the tests outlined in this paper, we have used a single personal computer, with all the agents executed in the same platform. However, JADE supports the possibility of executing agents in different machines, which is interesting to have a more reliable and scalable system.

We are now studying the possibility having interactions among the personal characteristics, following the ideas outlined in [5]. Finally, a sensitivity analysis should be performed in order to set up the most appropriate thresholds for the parameters considered.

References

[1]   Weiss, G.: Multiagent systems. A modern approach to Distributed Artificial Intelligence, M.I.T. Press (1999).

[2]   Wooldridge, M. An introduction to MultiAgent Systems. Wiley Ed. (2002).

[3]   Conte, R., Gilbert, N., Sichman, J.S.: MAS and Social Simulation: a suitable commitment, Lecture Notes in Computer Science, 1534 (1998) 1-9.

[4]   Martínez, J., Aldea, A., Bañares-Alcántara, R.: Simulation of work teams using a multi-agent system. To be presented at the Second International Joint Conference on Autonomous Agents and Multi-Agent Systems, AAMAS-2003. Melbourne, Australia.

[5]   Martínez, J., Aldea, A., Bañares-Alcántara, R.,: A social agent model to simulate human behaviour in teamwork. Pr.3rd ws. on agent-based simulation, Germany (2002) 18-23.

[6]   FIPA: Foundation for Intelligent Physical Agents: http://www.fipa.org.

[7]   Reid G. Smith, The Contract Net Protocol: High Load Communication and Control in a Distributed Problem Solver, IEEE Transactions on Computers, 29:12 (1980) 1104-1113.

[8]   Bellifemine, F., Poggi, A., Rimassa, G.: JADE- A FIPA compliant agent framework, Proc. of Practical Applications of Intelligent Agents and Multi-Agents, PAAM (1999) 97-108.

[9]   JADE: Java Agent Development Environment: http://sharon.cselt.it/projects/jade/

Some members of agent community are located on the same host (server) and use a shared directory for information exchange. They write auxiliary information to temporary files, read and modify them. Using developed mechanisms of file naming each agent knows which file it has to use for its work. Wrappers are distributed on different computers to provide access to KSs. Facilitator stores information about each agent location.

Most multi-agent systems require using agent negotiation models to operate. The negotiation models are based on the negotiation protocols defining basic rules so that when agents follow them, the system behaves as it supposed to. The main protocols including voting, bargaining, auctions, general equilibrium market mechanisms, coalition games, and constraint networks [[8], [9]].

In the system "KSNet" the negotiation is required in two scenarios: (i) negotiation between *configuration agent* and *wrappers* during KS network configuration and (ii) negotiation for expert knowledge conformation during distributed direct knowledge entry [[3], [10]].

The main specifics of the KSNet-approach related to making a choice of the agent negotiation model were formulated as follows:

1. *Contribution*: the agents have to cooperate with each other to make the best contribution into the overall system's benefit – not into the agents' benefits;
2. *Task performance*: the main goal is to complete the task performance – not to get profit out of it;
3. *Mediating*: the agents operate in a decentralized community, however in all the negotiation processes there is an agent managing the negotiation process and making a final decision;
4. *Trust*: since the agents work in the same system they completely trust each other;
5. *Common terms*: since the agents work in the same system they share a common vocabulary and use common terms for communication.

Based on the analysis of the agents negotiation protocols and the above requirements to them, a the contract network protocol (CNP) [[11]] was chosen as a basis for the negotiation model in the KSNet-approach. As it can be seen from Table 1 this protocol meets most of the requirements. In CNP the agent initiating negotiation process is called *manager*. Agents involved in the negotiation process by manager are called *contractors*. In the first scenario the configuration agent is a manager and the wrappers are contractors.

Performed experimentation with CNP has showed that for the system "KSNet" to operate efficiently utilizing the conventional CNP is not enough. It was necessary to provide mechanisms of agents' knowledge representation, deals analysis and negotiation which would ensure task performance. Since the system "KSNet" uses object-oriented constraint networks for the knowledge representation this formalism has been also chosen for the representation of agents' knowledge and for communications between agents. Two types of constraints were defined for agents: "local" and "global". Each contractor agent deals with the local constraints describing its limitations, e.g. time of the task execution cannot be less than some value. The manager also deals with the local constraints, e.g. the task execution cannot last longer than some time, and with the global constraints defined by an agents' community, e.g. resource limitations. The constraints can concern such parameters as time, costs, reliability, agents/resources availability, network traffic, etc. The manager can also have objectives such as minimization of the task execution costs.

Contractors' proposals besides a content part contain constraints corresponding to manager's objective and own constraints. If contractors cannot meet the requirements of the manager they still can propose the closest possible parameters and it is up to the manager to decide whether to accept the proposal or not.

The negotiation process terminates when an acceptable solution is found or no improvement is achieved at the current iteration.

Modification of the CNP-based negotiation model includes introduction of additional messages and features required for KL related tasks, some of which are presented in Table 2.

Experiments have proved that proposed constraint-based CNP allows achieving better solutions than the conventional CNP. In other words, given U_C, U_M – solution's utility for conventional and modified constraint-based CNP respectively, $U_M \geq U_C$ holds. On the other hand, it is obviously, that negotiation time for the proposed protocol increases. It can be seen that, given $T_{i=1...n}$ – response time of contractors (n – is the number of participating contractors), T_{man} – manager's response time, and T_C, T_M – negotiation time for conventional and modified constraint-based CNP respectively, $T_C \leq T_M \leq T_C + T_{max} + T_{man}$ holds, where $T_{max} = \max_{i=1}^{n} T_i$. This difference does not directly depend on the number of participating agents but it depends on T_{man} that in turn may depend on the task complexity and thereby on the number of participating agents. This dependency should be estimated for any particular case of the protocol usage.

3   Implementation of Multi-agent Community

The research prototype of the system "KSNet" has a client-server architecture (Fig. 1). This architecture was chosen in accordance with the following reasons: (i) minimization of requirements to user computers (web-based application allows user to have only HTML-compatible web-browser and an access to the Internet because the procedures are executed on the server – not on the user's computer), (ii) requirement of processing large amounts of information received from distributed KSs on the central (server) computer, and (iii) specifics of the agent community implementation.

Table 1. Comparison of negotiation protocols for KSNet approach

Protocols Criteria	Voting	Bargaining	Auctions	General Equilibrium Market Mechanisms	Coalition Games	Contract Nets
Contribution	☑	☑	☐	☐	☐ / ☑	☑
Task performance	☐ / ☑	☑	☐	☐	☐	☐ / ☑
Mediating	☐	☐	☑	☐	☐	☑
Trust	☑	☑	☑	☑	☐	☑
Common terms	☑	☑	☑	☑	☑	☑

Table 2. Changes in features of the conventional CNP required for the system "KSNet"

Protocols Feature	Convention al CNP	Constraint-based CNP for the system "KSNet"
Iterative negotiation	-	the negotiation process can be repeated several times until given constraint are satisfied
Conformation	-	concurrent conformation between manager and contractors
Available messages	fixed set of 8 messages	flexible set: new messages specific for KF process and corresponding to FIPA *Request* and *Confirm* communicative acts, and message *Clone* not corresponding to any FIPA communicative act are included
Participants roles	manager and contractors	manager and two types of contractors: (i) "classic" contractors negotiating proposals, and (ii) auxiliary service providers not negotiating but performing operations required for KL (e.g., ontology modification, user interfacing, etc.)
Role changing	-	agents can change their roles during a scenario

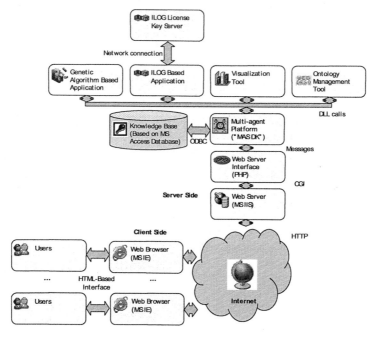

Fig. 1. Prototype architecture

For agent community implementation it was necessary to choose a tool for prototype development. Based on the analysis of the multi-agent systems development toolkits [[12] - [14]] the following requirements to them for implementation of KL technology were formulated:

- availability of the source code;
- possibility of standard agent functions and features extension (introduction of new functions specific for KL technology);
- possibility of external functions calls (e.g., methods of registered COM/DCOM-objects, DLLs, etc.);
- possibility of configuration recovering after system faults;
- availability of a name server storing information about registered agents;
- availability of message exchange mechanisms;
- availability of agent's knowledge repository creation and modification for storage of agent's knowledge, operation scenarios, and behaviour rules;
- availability of agent's "pro-activity" functions.

As a result of the carried out analysis of the development toolkits for multi-agent systems the MAS DK environment [[5]] developed in SPIIRAS has been chosen as a toolkit for agents interaction modelling. Agents' scenarios use finite state automata starting when one or more predefined conditions are met (an agent receives a message from another agent or from the system). Each finite state automaton is implemented using the internal MAS DK language. It is represented by a set of conditional statements, messages to other agents, and agent's functions. Conditional statements are used to check error codes of problem-oriented functions, to compare values of different variables stored in the agents' repository, etc.

Agents' functions were extended using Microsoft Visual C++, Microsoft Access XP, Microsoft Access ODBC drivers, constraint satisfaction/propagation technology ILOG (Configurator 2.0, Solver 5.0, Concert Technology 1.0) [[15]], lexical reference system WordNet [[16]] etc. It was motivated by the following reasons: (i) ILOG is a world leader in constraint satisfaction/propagation technologies and optimization algorithms that would enable a very efficient processing of large amounts of constraints, (ii) ODBC allows utilizing unified functions for accessing relational databases of different database management systems and allows easy modification of the DBMS used in the prototype, (iii) Microsoft Visual Studio 6.0 (Visual C++) allows accessing ILOG features, databases, writing efficient programs, and (iv) Microsoft Access XP allows rapid database design and creating simple database applications. Some intermediate and auxiliary forms for data preparation and results visualization were designed using Microsoft Access. For representation and interchange of agent's messages XML was used. Due to a large number of tools working with this format and specifications describing it the application of XML was useful and convenient.

During the system "KSNet" architecture development main system scenarios were designed using UML-based conceptual projects. Particularly, these projects include the agents' architecture, a list of actions performed by agents in the different system scenarios, a list of messages for agent interactions. One of the developed projects is presented in Fig. 2.

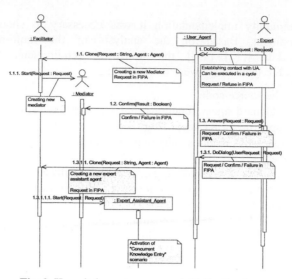

Fig. 2. Knowledge entry process initialization by expert

To start multi-agent community operations the following works have been done. First, templates of all the agents were defined. A template includes agent's type, structure of knowledge repository, set of agent's messages for communication with other agents and a set of agent's work scenarios describing its behaviour. After that instances of agents were created. Each instance contains a unique agent's name and an address of its host. When the system starts only two agents are active: the facilitator and the monitoring agent. They wait for new tasks and activate other agents in accordance with the prepared scenarios. One of the possible scenarios of the user template-based request processing is presented in the following section.

4   Case Study

The Binni scenario was chosen as a case study for the prototype of the KSNet-approach. It is a hypothetical scenario based on the Sudanese Plain [[17]]. The aim of the Binni scenario is to provide a multi-agent environment, focusing on new aspects of coalition problems and new technologies demonstrating the ability of coalition-oriented agent services to function in an increasingly dynamic environment [[18], [19]]. The experimentation with Binni scenario is intended for demonstration of how the developed KSNet-approach can be used for the supply chain management, logistics and other coalition operations problems. As an example, a task of the portable hospital configuration for a given location in the Binni region is considered. An analysis of the task showed a necessity of finding and utilizing KSs containing the following information/knowledge: (i) hospital related information (constraints on its structure, required quantities of components, required times of delivery), (ii) available UN and friendly suppliers (constraints on suppliers' capabilities, capacities, locations), (iii) available UN and friendly providers of transportation services (constraints on available types, routes, and time of delivery), (iv) the geography and weather of the Binni region (constraints on types, routes, and time of delivery, e.g. by air, by trucks, by off-road vehicles), and (v) the political situation, e.g. who occupies used for transportation territory, existence of military actions on the routes, etc. (additional constraints on routes of delivery).

In the presented small example the following request is considered: "Define suppliers, transportation routes and schedules for building a hospital of given capacity at given location by given time".

Input data for a template was prepared by an expert team using specially developed screen forms. Experts' tasks included definition of a list of possible hospital locations and a list of suppliers, a specification of dependencies between the weather and delivery types (routes), and analysis of hospital supplies delivery costs. Parts of ontologies corresponding to the described task were found in Internet's ontology libraries [[20] - [23]]. The application ontology of this humanitarian task was built and a connection of the found sources was performed. Three wrappers were developed to process information about: (i) suppliers, (ii) transportation service, and (iii) weather conditions and prepared HTML forms for user request input (Fig. 3).

One of the scenarios of agent community interaction during the user request processing is given in Fig. 4.

In the framework of the case study there were modelled agents' interactions for user request processing entered in an arbitrary form and based on other templates. Analysis of time distribution between members of the agent community during different scenarios processing has shown that a re-distribution of the tasks and adding new functions to the most unloaded agents can increase a rapidity of the system.

5   Conclusion

Agent-based technology is a good basis for knowledge logistics since agents can operate in a distributed environment, independently from the user and use ontologies for knowledge representation and interchange. For coalition based operations it is possible to describe management systems as organizational combination of people, technologies, procedures and information (knowledge & data). People in an organization share knowledge of their relationships through the delegation of tasks, transferring of information, obligation, synchronization of tasks, etc. An applicability of the KSNet-approach to the area of e-health (portable hospital configuration for a given location taking into account a current situation in the locations' region) demonstrates possibility of its usage for coalition-based operations support.

Acknowledgements

Some parts of the research were carried out under the ISCT partner project # 1993P funded by EOARD, the project # 2.44 of the research program "Mathematical Modelling, Intelligent Systems and Nonlinear Mechanical Systems Control" of the Presidium of the Russian Academy of Sciences, the grant # 02-01-00284 of the Russian Foundation for Basic Research, and the project of the research program "Fundamental Basics of Information Technologies and Computer Systems" of the Russian Academy of Sciences.

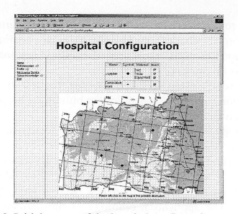

Fig. 3. Initial screen of the hospital configuration scenario

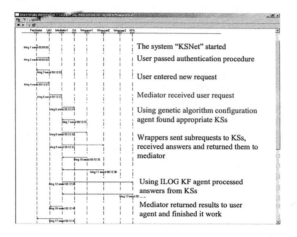

Fig. 4. An example of agents' interaction

References

[1]   Smirnov, A., Pashkin, M., Chilov, N., Levashova, T.: Multi-agent Architecture for Knowledge Fusion from Distributed Sources. In: Lecture Notes in Artificial Intelligence, Vol. 2296. Springer-Verlag (2002) 293—302

[2]   Smirnov, A., Pashkin, M., Chilov, N., Levashova, T.: Business Knowledge Logistics: an Approach and Technology Framework. In: Proceedings of the Sixth International Research Conference on Quality, Innovation & Knowledge Management (QIK'2002). Kuala Lumpur, Malaysia, February 17-20 (2002) 936—945

[3]   Smirnov, A., Pashkin, M., Chilov, N., Levashova, T.: Knowledge Source Network Configuration in e-Business Environment. In: Proceedings of the 15th IFAC World Congress (IFAC'2002). Barcelona, Spain, July 21-26 (2002) (electronic proceedings)

[4]   FIPA Documentation. Geneva, Switzerland, Foundation for Intelligent Physical
        Agents (FIPA) (2003) URL: http://www.fipa.org
[5]   Gorodetski, V.,   Karsayev, O.,   Kotenko, I.,   Khabalov, A.:   Software
        Development Kit for Multi-agent Systems Design and Implementation. In:
        Proceedings of the Second International Workshop of Central and Eastern
        Europe   on   Multi-agent   Systems   (CEEMAS'01).   (B.Dunin-Keplicz,
        E.Nawarecki (eds.)). Krakow, Poland, September 26-29 (2001) 99—108
[6]   Marik, V., Pechoucek, M., Bárta, J.: Reduction of Task Complexity in
        Coalition Planning. In: Proceedings of the International Symposium "From
        Agent Theory to Agent Implementation" (AT2AI-3). Vienna, Austria (EU),
        April 3—5, (2002) URL: http://www.ai.univie.ac.at/~paolo/conf/at2ai3/
[7]   Brustoloni, J.C.: Autonomous Agents: Characterization and Requirements. In:
        Technical Report CMU-CS-91-204, School of Computer Science, Carnegie
        Mellon University, November (1991)
[8]   Sandholm, T.: An Implementation of the Contract Net Protocol Based on
        Marginal Cost Calculations. In: Proceedings of the National Conference on
        Artificial Intelligence, Washington, D.C., July (1993) 256—262
[9]   Sandholm, T.: Distributed Rational Decision Making. In: Multiagent Systems:
        A Modern Introduction to Distributed Artificial Intelligence (G.Weiss, ed.).
        MIT Press, (1999) 201—258 URL: http://www-2.cs.cmu.edu/~sandholm/
        rational.ps
[10]   Smirnov, A., Pashkin, M., Chilov, N., Levashova, T.: Distributed Knowledge
        Entry Based on Intelligent Agents and Virtual Reality Technologies. In:
        Proceedings of the 9th International Conference on Neural Information
        Processing; 4th Asia-Pacific Conference on Simulated Evolution and Learning;
        2002 International Conference on Fuzzy Systems and Knowledge Discovery
        (ICONIP'02-SEAL'02-FSKD'02). Orchid Country Club, Singapore, November
        18-22 (2002) Vol. 2 437 441
[11]   Smith, R.: The Contract Net Protocol: High-level Communication and Control
        in a Distributed Problem Solver. In: IEEE Transactions on Computers,
        No 29(12) (1980) 1104—1113
[12]   Java Agent DEvelopment Framework JADE (2002) URL:
        http://sharon.cselt.it/projects/jade/
[13]   FIPA-OS toolkit (2002) URL: http://fipa-os.sourceforge.net/
[14]   Intelligent Agents. ISR Agent Research (2002) URL:
        http://193.113.209.147/projects/agents.htm
[15]   ILOG Corporate Web-site (2002) URL: http://www.ilog.com
[16]   WordNet (2002) URL: http://www.cogsci.princeton.edu/~wn/, 2002
[17]   Rathmell, R.A.: A Coalition Force Scenario "Binni – Gateway to the Golden
        Bowl of Africa. In: Proceedings on the International Workshop on Knowledge-
        Based Planning for Coalition Forces (ed. by A/ Tate). Edinburgh, Scotland,
        (1999) 115—125
[18]   CoAX - Coalition Agents eXperiment. Coalition Research Home Page (2002)
        URL: http://www.aiai.ed.ac.uk/project/coax/

[19] Clement, B.J., Cox, J.S., Durfee, E.H.: Infrastructure for Coordinating Hierarchical Planning Agents. In: Proceedings of the 10th Annual IPoCSE Research Symposium, (1999) URL: http://www.umcs.maine.edu/~wagner/-workshop/15_clement_et_al.pdf.

[20] Clin-Act (Clinical Activity). The ON9.3 Library of Ontologies: Ontology Group of IP-CNR (a part of the Institute of Psychology of the Italian National Research Council (CNR)), December (2000) URL: http://saussure.irmkant.rm.cnr.it/onto/

[21] Hpkb-Upper-Level-Kernel-Latest: Upper Cyc/HPKB IKB Ontology with links to SENSUS, Version 1.4, February, 1998. Ontolingua Ontology Server. (1998) URL: http://www-ksl-svc.stanford.edu:5915

[22] North American Industry Classification System code, DAML Ontology Library, Stanford University, July (2001) URL: http://opencyc.sourceforge.net/daml/naics.daml

[23] The UNSPSC Code (Universal Standard Products and Services Classification Code), DAML Ontology Library, Stanford University, January (2001) URL: http://www.ksl.stanford.edu/projects/DAML/UNSPSC.daml

Learning User Preferences
for Multi-attribute Negotiation:
An Evolutionary Approach

Yutao Guo[1], Jörg P. Müller[1], and Christof Weinhardt[2]

[1] Intelligent Autonomous Systems, Siemens AG, Corporate Technology
Otto-Hahn-Ring 6, 81730 Munich, Germany
{yutao.guo.external,joerg.mueller}@mchp.siemens.de
[2] Department of Economics and Business Engineering, University of Karlsruhe
Englerstrasse 14, 76131 Karlsruhe, Germany
weinhardt@iw.uni-karlsruhe.de

Abstract. This paper investigates how agents that act on behalf of users in electronic negotiations can elicit the required information about their users' preference structures. Based on a multi-attribute utility theoretic model of user preferences, we propose an algorithm that enables an agent to learn the utility function over time, taking knowledge gathered about the user into account. The method combines an evolutionary learning with the application of external knowledge and local search. The algorithm learns a complete multi-attribute utility function, consisting of the attribute weights and the individual attribute utility functions. Empirical tests show that the algorithm provides a good learning performance.

1 Introduction

Negotiation is a fundamental mechanism to automate business processes and to increase their flexibility. In many situations, decision processes in negotiations require consideration of multiple attributes such as quality, delivery time, or terms of payment. The challenge that we are facing is to automate negotiation processes by using software agents [7], i.e., proactive software components that act on behalf of humans or organizations in negotiations [11, 15, 10], and are endowed with an economic model (which can be modelled by a utility function) that guides their behavior in these negotiations. A crucial question in the context of automated negotiation is how the human users in a negotiation can instruct their agents to act in an appropriate manner. This question essentially can be rephrased as follows: How can agents elicit their user's utility function(s) relevant to negotiation-related decision making? While this question can be considered for agents representing buyers and sellers alike in marketplace situations, in this paper, we focus on the buyer's side.

In this paper, we propose an algorithm that enables a user agent to learn a user utility function. Our approach overcomes limitations of traditional methods for acquiring user preference information which requires users to explicitly

V. Mařík et al. (Eds): CEEMAS 2003, LNAI 2691, pp. 303–313, 2003.
© Springer-Verlag Berlin Heidelberg 2003

specify their utility function. The learning method is based on an evolutionary framework with three-step learning in each generation. It combines population-based evolution with the possibility to apply external knowledge, and with individual learning through simulated annealing for further refinement of the solution. The learning method reveals good performance in our simulated experiments. In particular, we can show that a substantial improvement of basic learning can be achieved by adding the steps of knowledge integration and local search. This preference elicitation component is also implemented in the INTELLIMARKET agent marketplace infrastructure developed at Siemens Corporate Technology.

The rest of this paper is structured as follows: Section 2 summarizes related research. Section 3 describes the utility elicitation framework. Section 4 gives the formulation of the learning algorithm. Section 5 outlines the implementation of the model within the INTELLIMARKET negotiation platform. Section 6 gives the empirical results. Finally, in Section 7, we present conclusions and perspectives of future research.

2   Related Work

While the design of mechanisms, protocols and strategies for autonomous agents has been the subject of research in multi-agent systems for more than a decade [9, 10, 15], there have been some initial research efforts to tackle the problem of user preference elicitation in negotiations.

The Software Agents Group at MIT Media Lab conducted a research project MARI [12]. MARI allows users to specify weights and function types for individual attributes and then applies the resulting utility function on behalf of the user. This explicit approach to instructing agents is complicated and time-consuming. In addition, it is an accepted phenomenon that humans often find it difficult to specify their preferences adequately and correctly, even if asked explicitly.

A few efforts have been made to learn the user's utility function or part of its components. IBM Research developed the WORA [1] method to derive attribute weights from a user's ordinal ranking over subsets of the bids. The method is based on linear programming by applying the bid rankings as constraints, and not specifying the optimization goal. There are usually multiple feasible solutions and the learning performance is evaluated by ranking prediction of the bids. So this method can not ensure that the real user preference of attribute weights are elicited.

3   Negotiation and Preference Elicitation

The two basic ingredients of a multiagent negotiation process are the negotiation protocol and the individual agents' negotiation strategies. An agent's negotiation strategy determines how it will act within the protocol trying to achieve a good outcome. It is based on a model of its user's economic preferences and possibly on other parties' behavior / strategies. In many situations, the decision

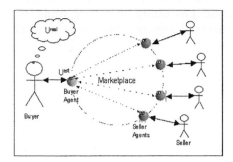

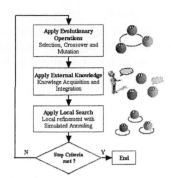

Fig. 1.   User preference elicitation
scenario

Fig. 2. Utility elicitation algorithm

making is based on consideration of multiple attributes. For example, a buyer's valuation of a digital camera will depend on multiple attributes like resolution, weight, zoom, memory, and price. In this work, Multi-Attribute Utility Theory (MAUT) is adopted to model the preferences of a user. MAUT is widely used in decision making of multi-attribute negotiation and has been applied in the commercial sourcing software packages like those from Perfect [8] and Frictionless Commerce [4]. A user's utility function U applied to a product $\mathbf{p}$ with n attributes is defined as $U(\mathbf{p}) = \sum_{i=1}^{n} w_i f_i(a_i)$. Here $w_i \in I\!R$ denotes the weight of attribute a_i, i.e., the importance of the attribute; $f_i(a_i) : Dom(a_i) \mapsto I\!R$, with $Dom(a_i)$ being the domain for attribute a_i, denotes the attribute utility function of attribute i, i.e., the function applied to compute product $\mathbf{p}$'s score on attribute a_i. For instance, in the digital camera domain, we could have $f_{price}(x) = 1 \quad x$, $f_{zoom}(z) = z^{0.5}$, where attribute values x and z are normalized in $[0,1]$.

The basic usage scenario of the preference elicitation is to allow a buyer-side agent to acquire the amount of knowledge about its user's preference structure to bid for a product in an automated marketplace, e.g., in an auction, as illustrated in Figure 1. A variant of this scenario could be to enable an automated sales representative to learn a potential buyer's preferences with the goal to provide him better service. Another variant would apply preference information of the agent issuing the request for bids in a reverse auction where this preference information would be made available to potential sellers to help them streamline their bids to meet the demand.

Existing methods of acquiring user's utility require users to specify the whole utility function explicitly or involve complex ranking procedures as described in Section 2. These approaches impose hard tasks on the users: even if we assume that the utility function actually applied by a user can be expressed by MAUT, it is not necessarily true that the user *knows* this function. Experiences from the Human Resources domain [13] seem to indicate that at least in some applications, most humans perform poorly in revealing their preferences in terms of MAUT.

So eliciting sufficiently accurate preference with limited user input and the information user easily to provide are required. The utility elicitation framework described in this paper is based on these practical requirements, overcoming the limitations of traditional methods:

1. Our utility eliciting algorithm is to be flexible in that it accepts different types of information for learning, e.g.: a) product rating, e.g., I rate product p_1 with 0.6, and product p_2 with 0.5; b) product ranking, e.g., product p_1 is better than product p_2; c) partial knowledge of the solution, e.g., *resolution is more important than price*. This knowledge can be provided as direct information from the user, or it can be learnt from information provided by or observed from the user.
2. Our algorithm shall not only provides utility values to be ascribed to product instances, but shall learn the complete utility function, i.e. both the attribute weight and attribute function.
3. The method needs be efficient in acquiring user utility information, requiring only a limited amount of user inputs and a short learning time.

4   Utility Elicitation Algorithm

4.1   Overview of the Algorithm

In this section, we describe a utility elicitation approach that satisfies the requirements stated in Section 3. To elicit the user utility function from a complex solution space with flexible user input, we use a hybrid evolutionary approach. During the evolutionary learning process, user or market knowledge is also applied to the solution population using a methodology similar to that of Artificial Immune Systems [2]. In addition, individual learning by local search is applied, which has been introduced in memetic algorithms [6]. In our approach, the individual learning will not only refine the solutions from evolution operation, but also help improve the effects of applying knowledge. The overall structure of the approach is illustrated in Figure 2. For each generation in the learning process, three operations are applied to the learning population:

- **Apply evolutionary operations:** Evolution operations (selection, crossover, and mutation) are applied to the solution population for improved solutions. This stage involves communication and exchange of knowledge inside the solution population.
- **Apply external knowledge:** The base solution is now modified by injecting external knowledge into the solution population; the knowledge will be accepted based on the correctness of the knowledge and a certain probability. At this stage, knowledge from sources outside the solution population is integrated.
- **Apply local search:** Each solution is rendered by a local search method. In our paper, the *Simulated Annealing* method is used.

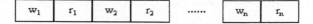

Fig. 3. Encoding utility function as chromosome

The user inputs of product rating and ranking are applied in the fitness function of both global and local search. The direct knowledge on the solution is applied in the knowledge integration stage. This hybrid learning method accepts multiple types of user input and enhances learning performance with this information. Details of the three steps of operations are described in the following sections.

4.2 Applying Evolutionary Operations

The learning approach is based on an evolutionary framework, so a solution needs to be encoded as a chromosome. As described above, the utility function contains two parts: attribute weights and attribute functions. The solution chromosome **s** carries information about the attribute weights **w** and the attribute functions. For the sake of this paper, we assume that attribute functions are of the form $f_i(a_i) = a_i^{r_i}$ (see Section 6). This allows us to encode the attribute functions by a single function parameter **r**. The solution chromosome encoding is illustrated as Figure 3. Using other function types requires corresponding modification of the chromosome scheme.

The fitness $g(\mathbf{s})$ of a solution **s** is composed of two aspects: $g(\mathbf{s}) = w_h h(\mathbf{s}) + w_q q(\mathbf{s})$, where w_h and w_q are weights of rating fitness $h(\mathbf{s})$ and ranking fitness $q(\mathbf{s})$, with $w_h + w_q = 1$. Usually the ranking information provide weak constrains [1]. In our experiments, we mainly consider the rating information to test the whole algorithm. The rating fitness can be calculated as $h(\mathbf{s}) = 1/\sum_{i=1}^{m} |u_i^{est} - u_i^{real}|$. Here m is the number of sample products; u_i^{est} and u_i^{real} are the estimated utility and the real user rating of the ith product.

In this step, three operations are applied to the solution population: selection, crossover, and mutation. In our experiments, we use Roulette wheel selection and two point crossover. The probability of crossover and mutation are: $P_c = 0.6$ and $P_m = 0.001$.

4.3 Applying External Knowledge

At this step, external knowledge is injected into the solution population. The knowledge can result directly from user input or derived from user observation. A suitable knowledge elicitation method need provide a certain level correctness of the knowledge, and will not consume a large amount of computing resources. In this paper, we use an information-theoretic approach to elicit attribute weights directly from a user-rated product set.

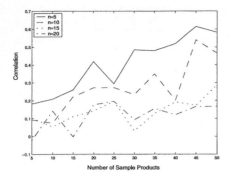

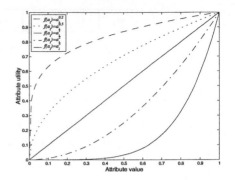

Fig. 4. Estimation of attribute weights with Mutual Information

Fig. 5. Attribute functions with different value of parameter r_i

Knowledge Acquisition In information theory, *Mutual Information* of two variables is defined as the reduction in uncertainty (*Entropy*) of the value of one variable given knowledge of the value taken by other variable. Mutual Information analysis has been successfully applied in feature-weighting in instance-based learning [14]. Based on this concept, we developed a method to estimate attribute weights based on the mutual information $H(a_i; v)$ between the user rating v of a product and an attribute a_i of the product. Here, $H(a_i; v)$ measures the amount of information the attribute conveys about the user valuation. In case attribute value or user valuation are continuous values, computing the mutual information between them requires to divide their ranges into k predefined intervals[14]. So the class set $\mathbf{c}_{a_i}$ and $\mathbf{c}_v$ both have k elements. In our experiments, both attribute value and user valuation are equally divided into $k = 3$ intervals in $[0,1]$. Then the weight of attribute a_i can be calculated as $w_i^{mi} = \frac{H(v;a_i)}{\sum_{j=1}^{n} H(v;a_j)}$.

As the correctness of the knowledge gathered through this method is crucial for the learning effect of knowledge integration, we carried out a number of experiments for different attribute and sample product number to analyze its suitability (see also Section 6). The analysis is based on the average value of 10 repeated tests, as shown in Figure 4. The estimation quality is measured by the Bravais Pearson correlation efficient between true and estimated weights. The experimental results reveal that this method is effective when the number of attribute is small, e.g. $n = 5$ or 10, whereas the estimation quality decreases with increasing number of attributes. Also, for a given number of attributes, the quality of estimation improves roughly at a linear scale as the number of rated products increase, which are given the algorithm as input information.

Knowledge Integration The knowledge integration method is designed to reflect the level of correctness of the knowledge and prevent assimilation of the solution populations. The major procedures are: First, the estimated attribute weights knowledge $\mathbf{w}^{mi}$ is applied to the solution population with probability of P_k. Then each selected solution replaces current attribute weights $\mathbf{w}^e$ with

$\mathbf{w}^{mi}$, and the fitness of the new solution is evaluated. If the fitness is better, accept the knowledge that $w_i^k = w_i^e + Random(\beta, 1) * (w_i^{mi} - w_i^e)$, where β is the *acceptance rate*. Otherwise, the knowledge will be rejected. In our experiments, we used $P_k = 0.1$, and $\beta = 0.8$.

4.4 Applying Local Search

After evolution and knowledge integration, each solution in the population performs additional local learning to render its current solution. In this paper, *Simulated Annealing* is used to achieve local learning. Each solution obtained from evolutionary and knowledge integration is used as the initial solution. A new solution is created by adding a random vector to the solution. The fitness of the new solution is evaluated and compared with current solution. If the new solution has a higher fitness, it is adopted. If the fitness of the new solution lower, then it is nevertheless accepted with probability P_a. The loop will continue until the stop criteria are met. The probability P_a is calculated as $P_a = \exp[(g(\mathbf{s}_{new}) - g(\mathbf{s}_{current}))/t]$. The temperature lowering function with each step is $t_{i+1} = \lambda t_i$. λ is the cooling rate, in our experiments $\lambda = 0.9$.

5   The INTELLIMARKET Platform

The preference elicitation approach is built into INTELLIMARKET an agent-based marketplace platform developed at Siemens Corporate Technology. In INTELLIMARKET agent-based negotiation is supported at three levels. First, market agents are provided to enable easy creation of marketplace application, including infrastructure services and protocol libraries for the most common auction types. Second, preference elicitation agents help acquiring user preference information, in the form of a utility function, for decision making in negotiation. Third, negotiation agents support mechanisms for negotiation-related decision making based on information observed during the negotiation process. The basic collaboration roles in INTELLIMARKET are: the *User Agents* interact with the user and logically represent the user in the marketplace. The *Preference Elicitation Agents* and *Negotiation Support Agents* help the *User Agents* acquire user preferences and decision making during the negotiation process. The *Market Agents* are responsible for market member management and negotiation administration.

The INTELLIMARKET system is implemented with JADE [5], a FIPA-compliant agent platform [3]. To ensure the basic requirements of persistence, security and transaction management required for a marketplace platform, we integrated JADE agents with server-side J2EE components; a web based user interface is provided, with Microsoft Agent COM components to provide customizable user avatar support. The flexible architecture can be easily extended supporting a single user with Web-based and mobile user interface at the same time.

6   Empirical Results

6.1   Test Methodology

In our experiments, a virtual user is generated with his preference model in the form of a utility function. After the user rating on a set of sample products according to his preference, the agents will learn his preference model based on the rated products and we measure how well the agents are able to approximate this user's utility function. The virtue user's utility function U is established with randomly generated attribute weights and attribute function parameters. Attribute weights are random values in the range of [0,1] and normalized to ensure $\sum_{i=1}^{n} w_i = 1$. In our experiments, the attribute functions are defined as instances of the function schema $f_i(a_i) = a_i^{r_i}$ with $r_i \in [0, 10]$. Figure 5 illustrates how varying the parameter r_i affects the user's preference distribution on attribute i. The sample products set are randomly generated and consist of m products, where each product has n attributes. Attribute j of product i is a randomly assigned value with $a_{j,i} \in [0, 1]$. All products' valuation and rank are computed with the real utility function U generated above.

The experiment vary certain parameters: The problem size (the number of product attributes) n=5, 10, 15, 20; The information available (the number of rated products) m ranging from five to 50; The experiments were performed with four learning algorithms: pure evolution algorithm (EA), EA combined with application of external knowledge (EA+KI), EA combined with local search (EA+SA), and EA, KI, combined with SA (EA+KI+SA). To make comparison, all algorithms operate on the same data set, with the same size of learning population and number of generations. The population size is set to 50 and the stop criteria is defined as when maximum number of generations (50) reached. In Simulated Annealing, both number of steps and iterations in each step are set to 10. As the tests operate on randomly generated products and utility function, the analysis of each scenario is based on average values of ten repeated experiments.

6.2   Analysis

To evaluate the quality of learning, we use different coefficients for attribute weights and attribute functions. The attribute weight result **w** is measured by the Bravais Pearson correlation coefficient between true and learned weights. The attribute function is evaluated by the mean absolute error of the function parameters **r**: $\sum_{i=1}^{n} |r_i^{est} - r_i^{real}|/n$. Figures 6 and Figures 7 are the learning results of attribute weights and attribute functions. The results show that all the learning algorithms converge to the real utility function as the number of rated products increases. It also reveals that the quality of the results is improved dramatically by applying external knowledge and by local search. This effect for attribute weights estimation becomes stronger as the number of attributes increases. In addition, applying external knowledge leads to an improvement of the accuracy and seems to make the learning more stable. However, the positive effect of applying external knowledge depends very critically on the quality and correctness of that knowledge.

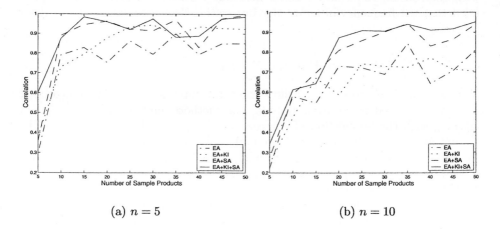

(a) $n = 5$ (b) $n = 10$

Fig. 6. Experiment results of attribute weights

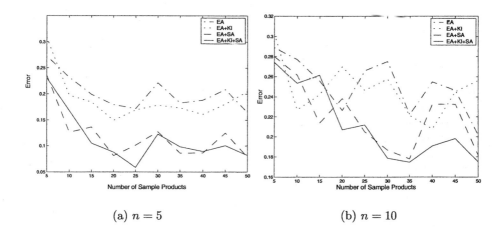

(a) $n = 5$ (b) $n = 10$

Fig. 7. Experiment results of attribute function parameters

The experimental results also show that external knowledge is accepted more often by our algorithm as the number of products increases. Compared to Figure 4, this coincides with the experiment result of the weight estimation quality with the Mutual Information based method. We also observed in the experiment that the frequency of knowledge integration decreases during the learning process.

7   Conclusions and Future Work

In this paper, we proposed a utility elicitation approach and implemented it in an agent based negotiation system. The method combines an evolutionary learning with the application of external knowledge and local refinement. The algorithm implicitly learns a complete multi-attribute utility function with flexibility to accept several types of information for learning. Hence it can be used in a wide variety of applications. Empirical tests showed that the algorithm provides a good learning performance.

A limitation of the work evaluated in the experiments is that only a single parameter has been used for modelling individual attribute functions. More flexible modelling will be studied either by using additional parameters or using genetic programming. In addition, symbolic attribute types will be considered by defining their domain ontologies to be accommodated in our current framework.

References

[1] Martin Bichler, Juhnyoung Lee, Chang Hyun Kim, and Ho Soo Lee. Design and implementation of an intelligent decision analysis system for e-sourcing. In *Proc. Int. Conf. on Artificial Intelligence*, pages 84–89. IBM, June 2001.

[2] P. D'haeseleer, S. Forrest, and P. Helman. An immunological approach to change detection: Algorithms, analysis, and implications. In *Proc. of the 1996 IEEE Symposium on Computer Security and Privacy*, 1996.

[3] FIPA. http://www.fipa.org.

[4] FrictionlessCommerce. http://www.frictionless.com/.

[5] JADE. http://sharon.cselt.it/projects/jade/.

[6] P. Moscato. On evolution, search, optimization, genetic algorithms and martial arts: Towards memetic algorithms. Technical Report Caltech Concurrent Computation Program, Report. 826, California Institute of Technology, Pasadena, CA, USA, 1989.

[7] J. P. Müller. *The Design of Intelligent Agents. Lecture Notes of Artificial Intelligence, Vol. 1077.* Springer-Verlag, 1997.

[8] Perfect. http://www.perfect.com/.

[9] J. S. Rosenschein and G. Zlotkin. *Rules of Encounter: Designing Conventions for Automated Negotiation among Computers.* MIT Press, Cambridge, 1994.

[10] T. Sandholm. emediator: A next generation electronic commerce server. In *Proc. 4th Int. Conf. on Autonomous Agents*, pages 341–348. ACM, 2000.

[11] R. G. Smith. The contract net protocol: High-level communication and control in a distributed problem solver. *IEEE Transactions on Computers*, 29, 12 1980.

[12] G. Tewari and P. Maes. Design and implementation of an agent-based intermediary infrastructure for electronic markets. In *Proc. 2nd ACM Conf. on Electronic commerce*. ACM, 2000.

[13] D. Veit, J. P. Müller, and C. Weinhardt. An empirical evaluation of multidimensional matchmaking. In *Proc. 4th Int. Workshop on Agent-Mediated E-Commerce (AMEC IV)*, Bologna, July 2002.

[14] D. Wettschereck, D. W. Aha, and T. Mohri. A review and empirical evaluation of feature weighting methods for a class of lazy learning algorithms. *Artificial Intelligence Review*, 11:273–314, July and Oct. 1997.

[15] P. R. Wurman, M. P. Wellman, and W. E. Walsh. The michigan internet auctionbot: A configurable auction server for human and software agents. In *Proc. 2nd Int. Conf. on Autonomous Agents*, pages 301–308. ACM, 1998.

A Model of Co-evolution in Multi-agent System

Rafał Dreżewski

Department of Computer Science
AGH University of Science and Technology, Kraków, Poland
drezew@agh.edu.pl

Abstract. Co-evolutionary techniques are aimed at overcoming limited adaptive capacity of evolutionary algorithms resulting from the loss of useful diversity of population. In this paper the idea of *co-evolutionary multi-agent system* (CoEMAS) is introduced. In such a system two or more species of agents co-evolve in order to solve given problem. Also, the formal model of CoEMAS and the results from runs of CoEMAS applied to multi-modal function optimization are presented.

1 Introduction

Evolutionary algorithms (EAs) have demonstrated in practice efficiency and robustness as global optimization techniques. However, they often suffer from premature loss of population diversity what results in premature convergence and may lead to locating local optima instead of a global one. What is more, both the experiments and analysis show that for multi-modal problem landscapes a simple EA will inevitably locate a single solution [10]. If we are interested in finding multiple solutions of comparable fitness then a multi-modal function optimization technique (*niching method*) should be used [10]. The loss of diversity also limits the adaptive capacities of EAs in dynamic environments. Co-evolutionary techniques are aimed at improving adaptive capacities and introducing open-ended evolution into EAs [11, 12].

This paper introduces the idea of *co-evolutionary multi-agent system (Co-EMAS)*, which opens new possibilities of modeling different ecological interactions between species such as competition for limited resources, predator-prey and host-parasite co-evolution, sexual preferences, and so on. Also the formal model of CoEMAS and preliminary results from runs of niching co-evolutionary multi-agent system (NCoEMAS) against commonly used test functions are presented.

2 Previous Research in Co-evolutionary Algorithms

In classical EAs each individual in the population is considered to be a potential solution of the problem being solved. The fitness of each individual depends only on how well it solves the problem. Selection pressure causes that better fit individuals have the greater chance to survive and/or reproduce and the less fit ones have the smaller chance.

V. Mařík et al. (Eds): CEEMAS 2003, LNAI 2691, pp. 314–323, 2003.

In co-evolutionary systems the fitness of each individual depends not only on the quality of solution to the given problem but also on other individuals' fitness. As the result of ongoing research many co-evolutionary techniques have been proposed. Generally, each of these techniques belongs to one of two classes: "Competitive Fitness Functions" (CFF) or multi-population [11]. Also some of the niching techniques may be considered as co-evolutionary.

In CFF based systems two (or more) individuals compete in a game and their "Competitive Fitness Functions" are calculated based on their relative performance in that game [1, 4]. Each time step given individual competes with different opponents, so its fitness value varies. Because in such systems an individual's fitness depends on other individuals' fitness, they are co-evolutionary in nature.

The second group consists of systems that use multiple populations. In such systems a problem is decomposed into sub-problems and each of them is then solved by different EA [14, 13]. Each individual is evaluated within a group of randomly chosen individuals coming from different sub-populations. Its fitness value depends on how well the group solved the problem and on how well the individual assisted in the solution.

Some of the niching techniques may also be considered as being co-evolutionary since fitness of each individual depends on other individuals in a population. In fitness sharing techniques [5] each individual is considered to be the member of a niche with radius σ_{sh}. Fitness of each individual is reduced for every other individual, which lives in its niche, in a proportion to their similarity. In *co-evolutionary shared niching (CSN)* technique [6] (inspired by the economic model of *monopolistic competition*) two co-evolving populations are used. The customer population is the usual population of candidate solutions. The businessman population evolve to obtain largest payoff (best cover the peaks in multi-modal domain).

Haynes and Sen [7, 8] used co-evolution and genetic programming (GP) to design behavioral strategies of agents acting in predator-prey domain. Yong and Miikkulainen [15] studied cooperative co-evolution of agents controlled by neural networks (NNs). Although all these works also deal with the co-evolution in multi-agent systems there are some differences with our model. First, all techniques mentioned above utilize classical centralized EAs to evolve strategies or NNs, which are then evaluated in multi-agent predator-prey domain, while we are focusing on modeling of co-evolution process in multi-agent system. Second, their goal is to evolutionary design control mechanisms of agents while our CoEMAS is used as computational technique.

In [11] Morrison and Oppacher presented a general model of co-evolution for genetic algorithms. Their model can express all types of co-evolutionary relations studied in the ecological literature. However, it can not be easily applied to co-evolutionary multi-agent systems. Our approach differs to their in two points. First, we will focus on co-evolutionary relations between species rather than between individuals. The second difference results from decentralized nature of

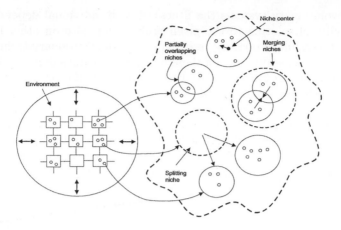

Fig. 1. Sample niching co-evolutionary multi-agent system

CoEMAS what implies different selection mechanisms and more complicated individuals that should be modeled.

In the following sections we will present the idea of co-evolution realized in multi-agent system and the formal model, which allows us to define many co-evolutionary interactions that exist in nature.

3   The Idea of Co-evolutionary Multi-agent Systems

The main idea of *evolutionary multi-agent system (EMAS)* is the modeling of evolution process in multi-agent system (MAS) [3]. *Co-evolutionary multi-agent system (CoEMAS)* allows co-evolution of several species of agents. CoEMAS can be applied, for example, to multi-objective optimization and multi-modal function optimization (*niching co-evolutionary multi-agent system — NCoEMAS*).

In CoEMAS several (usually two) different species co-evolve. One of them represents solutions. The goal of the second species is to cooperate (or compete) with the first one in order to force the population of solutions to locate Pareto frontier or proportionally populate and stably maintain niches in multi-modal domain.

In figure 1 sample system for multi-modal optimization with two co-evolving species: niches and solutions is presented. In such NCoEMAS we can model niches as individuals that are characterized by parameters like location, radius, etc. and evolve to best cover real niches in multi-modal domain. Two additional operators can be introduced for niches: splitting and merging. Each niche can make decision on splitting into two niches based on the current distribution of its subpopulation. Also, the decision of merging can be made by two niches that are close enough and that are located on the same peak in the multi-modal domain. In order to proportionally populate niches the mechanism of *explicit* resource sharing can be introduced. Agents' *life energy* can be treated as a resource for which individuals compete. This mechanism can be called *energy sharing*.

It seems that CoEMAS is especially suited for modeling different co-evolutionary interactions (resource competition, predator-prey and host-parasite coevolution, sexual preferences, etc.)

4 The Model of CoEMAS

In this section the formal model of CoEMAS is presented. The model is based on the idea of M-Agent [2] and on the model of EMAS [9].

4.1 CoEMAS

The CoEMAS may be described as 3-tuple

$$CoEMAS = \langle ENV, \mathcal{S}, \mathcal{R} \rangle, \tag{1}$$

where ENV is an environment of the $CoEMAS$, $\mathcal{S}$ is a set of species that coevolve in $CoEMAS$ ($S \in \mathcal{S}$), $\mathcal{R}$ is a set of relations between species.

$$\mathcal{R} = R^+ \cup R^-, \tag{2}$$

where:

$$R^+ = \left\{ \xrightarrow{r_i+} : r_i \in RES \right\}, \tag{3}$$

$$R^- = \left\{ \xrightarrow{r_i-} : r_i \in RES \right\} \tag{4}$$

RES is a set of resources that exist in $CoEMAS$, $RES = \langle r_1, r_2, \ldots, r_n \rangle$.
$\xrightarrow{r-}$ and $\xrightarrow{r+}$ are relations between species:

$$\xrightarrow{r-} = \{ \langle S_i, S_j \rangle \in \mathcal{S} \times \mathcal{S} : \text{agents from species } S_i \text{ decrease fitness of agents} \tag{5}$$
$$\text{from species } S_j \text{ via the influence on the amount of resource } r \}$$

$$\xrightarrow{r+} = \{ \langle S_i, S_j \rangle \in \mathcal{S} \times \mathcal{S} : \text{agents from species } S_i \text{ increase fitness of agents} \tag{6}$$
$$\text{from species } S_j \text{ via the influence on the amount of resource } r \}$$

Having such relations defined we can easily define different co-evolutionary interactions between species that can be modeled in CoEMAS.

Definition 1 *Mutualism between two species, A and B, occurs if and only if* $\exists r_i, r_j \in RES$ *such that* $A \xrightarrow{r_i+} B$ *and* $B \xrightarrow{r_j+} A$.

Definition 2 *Commensalism between two species, A and B, occurs if and only if* $\exists r_i \in RES$ *such that* $A \xrightarrow{r_i+} B$ *and* $\forall r_j \in RES \neg (B \xrightarrow{r_j+} A \vee B \xrightarrow{r_j-} A)$.

Definition 3 *Predator-prey interactions between two species, A (predators) and B (preys), occurs if and only if* $\exists r_i \in RES$ *such that* $A \xrightarrow{r_i-} B$ *and* $B \xrightarrow{r_i+} A$.

Definition 4 *Competition for limited resources between two species, A and B, occurs if and only if* $\exists r_i \in RES$ *such that* $A \xrightarrow{r_i-} B$ *and* $B \xrightarrow{r_i-} A$.

4.2   Environment

The environment of CoEMAS may be described as 3-tuple

$$ENV = \langle T_{ENV}, RES, INF \rangle \tag{7}$$

where T_{ENV} is the topography of environment ENV, $RES = \langle r_1, r_2, \dots, r_n \rangle$ is a set of resources that exist in $CoEMAS$, $INF = \langle i_1, i_2, \dots, i_m \rangle$ is a set of informations that exist in $CoEMAS$.

The topography of the environment ENV is usually a graph. The distance between two nodes is defined as the length of the shortest path between these nodes.

4.3   Species

Species S that exist in $CoEMAS$ ($S \in \mathcal{S}$) can be defined as

$$S = \langle AG^S, INT^S \rangle \tag{8}$$

AG^S is a set of agents that belong to species S ($ag^S \in AG^S$). INT^S is a set of interactions with another species

$$INT^S = \langle int_1, int_2, \dots, int_n \rangle \tag{9}$$

where

$$int_i = \langle S, S_j \rangle, \quad \text{such that } S \xrightarrow{r-} S_j \vee S \xrightarrow{r+} S_j, \quad r \in RES, \quad S, S_j \in \mathcal{S} \tag{10}$$

4.4   Agent

An agent ag^S ($ag^S \in AG^S$) can be defined as 4-tuple

$$ag^S = \langle GEN, RES^S, PRF, ACT \rangle \tag{11}$$

GEN is a genotype of a given agent, for example $GEN = (gen_1, gen_2, \dots, gen_k)$, $gen_i \in \mathbb{R}$, $GEN \in \mathbb{R}^k$. RES^S is a set of resources of agent ag^S that belongs to species S ($RES^S \subseteq RES$). PRF is a set of agent's profiles with the order relation $\succ$ defined.

$$PRF = \langle prf_1, prf_2, \dots, prf_n \rangle$$
$$prf_1 \succ prf_2 \succ \cdots \succ prf_n \tag{12}$$

Here, profile prf_1 is the most basic profile which means that goals within this profile have precedence of another profiles' goals. ACT is a set of actions that an agent can perform.

Profile k may be the resource profile

$$prf^k = \{ RES^{S,k}, ST^k, RST^k, GL^k \} \tag{13}$$

or the information profile

$$prf^k = \{ MDL, ST^k, RST^k, GL^k \} \tag{14}$$

where

$RES^{S,k}$ is a set of resources that are used in a profile k, $RES^{S,k} \subseteq RES^S$;

MDL is a set of informations that represents agent's knowledge about the environment and other agents.

ST^k is a set of strategies that an agent may apply in a given profile, $ST^k = \langle st_1, st_2, \ldots st_l \rangle$;

RST^k is a set of strategies that are realized within profile k, $RST^k \subseteq ST^k$;

GL^k is a set of goals that an agent should realize within given profile, $GL^k = \{gl_1, gl_2, \ldots gl_p\}$.

Single strategy consists of actions taken by an agent in order to realize a goal. If agent should apply strategy that is not realized within active profile then the appropriate profile is activated.

In the case of $CoEMAS$ the set of profiles should at least include the following profiles

$$PRF = \langle prf^{res}, prf^{rep}, prf^{int}, prf^{mig} \rangle \tag{15}$$

Resource profile prf^{res} is the most basic profile and it is responsible for maintaining agent's resources above the minimal levels. Reproductive profile prf^{rep} realizes all strategies connected with reproduction process. Interaction profile prf^{int} is responsible for interactions with other individuals. The migration profile prf^{mig} is responsible for migration of given agent within the environment of CoEMAS.

5   The Application of CoEMAS to Multi-modal Function Optimization

In this section the application of the idea of CoEMAS to multi-modal function optimization problem is presented. First simulation experiments were aimed at testing if CoEMAS is able to detect and stably maintain all peaks in multi-modal domain throughout the search process. In the following sections the system, test functions and the results of experiments are presented.

5.1   The System

The system presented in this paper is the first one, which construction is based on the idea of CoEMAS (see fig. 2). There exist two different species: niches and solutions. All agents live in 2D space, which has the structure of discrete torus. Every node of this graph-like structure has connections with its four neighbors.

All agents representing niches are located in nodes and can not change their location. Agents representing solutions are also located in nodes but they can change their location in environment migrating from node to node. Every agent-solution has some amount of resource called *life energy*. There is closed circulation of energy in the system, which means that the total energy possessed by agents and the environment is constant during the whole simulation. Agents need energy for almost every activity: migration, reproduction etc. An individual

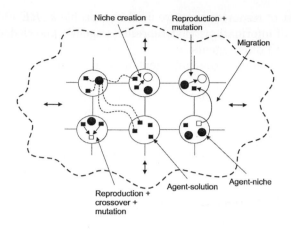

Fig. 2. NCoEMAS used in experiments

dies when its energy is equal to 0. An agent can migrate from one node to another guided by the total energy of agents living in that node. The reproduction process can take place when agent's energy is above the given level. Agent starts reproduction, searches in its neighborhood for partner and then new agent is created. Mutation and crossover (one point crossover is used) are applied with the given probability in order to produce child's chromosome. An agent created in reproduction process obtains energy from the environment.

The EA for niche population is very similar to that used for businessman population in co-evolutionary shared niching technique [6]. Each time step a single mutation site is selected randomly. The resulting individual replaces its parent if it is at least d_{min} from other niche and it is better fit than its parent. Otherwise another mutation site is selected (max. n_{limit} times).

In the time t every agent-solution searches for the closest niche (the weighted sum of Hamming distance in genotype space and Euclidean distance in environment is used). If there is no niche, such that its distance from the agent is less than given value, then the new niche is created with the copy of agent's chromosome (imprint mechanism).

In each time step less fit agents must give some amount of their energy to better fit agents (according to fitness function). Agents are compared within niches and also outside niches in the environment space. The latter comparisons are realized within nodes. Given agent is compared with agents that stay in its node and also with agents from the neighboring nodes.

5.2   Test Functions

There were four test functions used in experiments (see fig. 3 and 4): F_1, F_2, F_3, F_4 [5, 10]. These functions are commonly used as baseline tests in studies of niching methods. They are a starting place for testing new niching techniques and

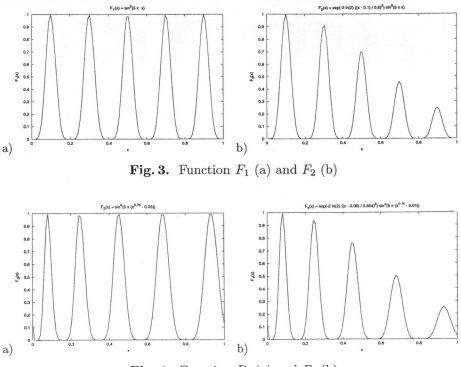

Fig. 3. Function F_1 (a) and F_2 (b)

Fig. 4. Function F_3 (a) and F_4 (b)

comparing them to earlier works. Although these are very simple functions many potential nichers have in the past had problems with detecting and maintaining all of their peaks.

5.3   Results

In this section the results from runs of NCoEMAS against test functions are presented.

Figure 5 shows the average numbers of agents representing solutions within each niche from ten runs of NCoEMAS against F_1 and F_2 functions. It can be seen that NCoEMAS properly detected and stably maintained peaks of these two test functions. What is more, peaks were populated proportionally to their relative fitness.

In case of F_3 function (see fig. 6a) NCoEMAS also properly detected and stably maintained all peaks in multi-modal domain. However peaks were not properly populated. All niches should be equally populated but it seems that agents preferred wider peaks. Peaks of F_4 function (fig. 6b) were also properly located and populated almost proportionally to their relative fitness. The problems mentioned above are connected with energy sharing mechanism, what is the subject of ongoing research.

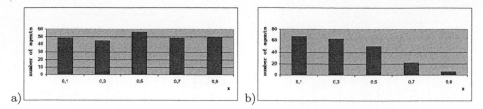

Fig. 5. The average number of agents-solutions within each niche from ten runs of NCoEMAS against function F_1 (a) and F_2 (b)

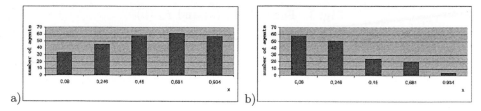

Fig. 6. The average number of agents-solutions within each niche from ten runs of NCoEMAS against function F_3 (a) and F_4 (b)

6   Concluding Remarks

The idea of *co-evolutionary multi-agent system (CoEMAS)* allows us to model many ecological co-evolutionary interactions between species such as resource competition, predator-prey and host-parasite co-evolution, sexual preferences, etc.

In this paper the formal model of co-evolution in multi-agent system was presented. Also, we applied this model to the construction of system for multimodal function optimization (*niching co-evolutionary multi-agent system*).

NCoEMAS presented in this paper was based on co-evolution of two species: niches and solutions. System properly detected and maintained all peaks of test functions and, as presented preliminary results show, has proved to be the valid and promising niching technique.

Future research will include: experiments with more complex test functions, the comparison to other co-evolutionary approaches (especially to Goldberg and Wang's CSN technique), CoEMAS based on the mechanisms of predator-prey (host-parasite) co-evolution and sexual preferences, the application of CoEMAS to engineering shape design problems, and parallel CoEMAS.

References

[1] P. J. Angeline and J. B. Pollack. Competitive environments evolve better solutions for complex tasks. In *Proc. of the 5th Int. Conf. on Genetic Algorithms (GA-93)*, 1993.

[2] E. Cetnarowicz, E. Nawarecki, and K. Cetnarowicz. Agent oriented technology of decentralized systems based on the m-agent architecture. In *Proceedings of the Management and Control of Production and Logistics Conference – MCPL'97*, Sao Paulo, Brazil, 1997. IFAC, PERGAMON.

[3] K. Cetnarowicz, M. Kisiel-Dorohinicki, and E. Nawarecki. The application of evolution process in multi-agent world to the prediction system. In *Proc. of the 2nd Int. Conf. on Multi-Agent Systems — ICMAS'96*, Osaka, Japan, 1996. AAAI Press.

[4] P. J. Darwen and X. Yao. On evolving robust strategies for iterated prisoner's dilemma. *Lecture Notes in Computer Science*, 956, 1995.

[5] D. E. Goldberg and J. Richardson. Genetic algorithms with sharing for multimodal function optimization. In J. J. Grefenstette, editor, *Proc. of the 2nd Int. Conf. on Genetic Algorithms*, Hillsdale, NJ, 1987. Lawrence Erlbaum Associates.

[6] D. E. Goldberg and L. Wang. Adaptive niching via coevolutionary sharing. Technical Report IlliGAL 97007, Illinois Genetic Algorithms Laboratory, University of Illinois at Urbana-Champaign, Urbana, IL, USA, 1997.

[7] T. Haynes and S. Sen. Evolving behavioral strategies in predators and prey. In S. Sen, editor, *IJCAI-95 Workshop on Adaptation and Learning in Multiagent Systems*, Montreal, Quebec, Canada, 1995. Morgan Kaufmann.

[8] T. Haynes and S. Sen. The evolution of multiagent coordination strategies. *Adaptive Behavior*, 1997.

[9] M. Kisiel-Dorohinicki. Agent-oriented model of simulated evolution. In W. I. Grosky and F. Plasil, editors, *SofSem 2002: Theory and Practice of Informatics*, volume 2296 of *Lecture Notes in Computer Science*. Springer-Verlag, 2002.

[10] S. W. Mahfoud. *Niching methods for genetic algorithms*. PhD thesis, University of Illinois at Urbana-Champaign, Urbana, IL, USA, 1995.

[11] J. Morrison and F. Oppacher. A general model of co-evolution for genetic algorithms. In *Int. Conf. on Artificial Neural Networks and Genetic Algorithms ICANNGA 99*, 1999.

[12] J. Paredis. Coevolutionary algorithms. In T. Bäck, D. Fogel, and Z. Michalewicz, editors, *Handbook of Evolutionary Computation, 1st supplement*. IOP Publishing and Oxford University Press, 1998.

[13] M. A. Potter and K. De Jong. A cooperative coevolutionary approach to function optimization. In Y. Davidor, H.-P. Schwefel, and R. Männer, editors, *Parallel Problem Solving from Nature – PPSN III*, Berlin, 1994. Springer.

[14] M. A. Potter and K. A. De Jong. Cooperative coevolution: An architecture for evolving coadapted subcomponents. *Evolutionary Computation*, 8(1), 2000.

[15] C. H. Yong and R. Miikkulainen. Cooperative coevolution of multi-agent systems. Technical Report AI01-287, Department of Computer Sciences, University of Texas at Austin, 2001.

Emergence of Specialized Behavior in a Pursuit–Evasion Game

Geoff Nitschke

Artificial Intelligence Laboratory
Department of Information Technology, University of Zurich
Andreasstrasse 15, CH-8050, Zurich, Switzerland
nitschke@ifi.unizh.ch

Abstract. This research concerns the comparison of three different artificial evolution approaches to the design of cooperative behavior in a group of simulated mobile robots. The first and second approaches, termed: *single pool* and *plasticity*, are characterized by robot controllers that share a single genotype, though the plasticity approach includes a learning mechanism. The third approach, termed: *multiple pools*, is characterized by robot controllers that use different genotypes. The application domain implements a pursuit-evasion game in which a team of robots, termed: *pursuers*, collectively work to capture one or more robots from a second team, termed: *evaders*. Results indicate that the multiple pools approach is superior comparative to the other two approaches in terms of measures defined for evader-capture strategy performance. Specifically, this approach facilitates behavioural specialization in the pursuer team allowing it to be effective for several different pursuer team sizes.

1   Introduction

Traditionally collective behaviour and multi-agent systems have been studied using a top down classical approach. Such approaches have achieved limited success given that it is extremely difficult to specify the mechanisms for cooperation or collective intelligence in all but the simplest problem domains. The study of emergent cooperative behavior remains a relatively unexplored area of research in the pursuit and evasion domain [1] and related predator-prey systems [9] using multiple predators and prey. Various approaches have been used to study the pursuit evasion domain, where the task is for multiple pursuers to capture an evader by surrounding it [5], [6], though few researchers have investigated emergent cooperation in these systems, with notable exceptions such as [3], [5] and [13].

This paper describes a comparison of three artificial evolution approaches for the synthesis of cooperative behaviour evaluated within a team of simulated *Khepera* robots [10]. For each approach, teams of various sizes, for both evaders and pursuers,

V. Mařík et al. (Eds): CEEMAS 2003, LNAI 2691, pp. 324–334, 2003.

are compared. The three approaches are evaluated in terms of pursuer fitness scored, and the time period for which an evader is immobilized. Experimental results support a hypothesis that the multiple pools approach, which encourages behavioural speciali-zation, would yield a superior performance in terms of the two measures defined to quantify evolved evader-capture strategy performance and this superior performance would prove consistent for all pursuer team sizes tested.

2   Artificial Evolution Approaches

Cooperative behaviour was only evolved for the pursuers. The behaviour of the evader team was not evolved, but instead used static obstacle avoidance behaviour. Also, each evader was able to move 20 percent faster than the pursuers. Functionally, each pursuer was the same in terms of movement and sensor capabilities. The pursuer team is rewarded fitness proportional to how much it was able to slow down an evader, where maximum fitness was rewarded for an immobilized evader. A control experi-ment using a single pursuer, demonstrated that at least two pursuers are needed to accomplish this task.

Comparison of Approaches

Four different group configurations of pursuers and evader were tested for each artifi-cial evolution approach. These groups were named and defined as follows. *Group type 1:* 6 pursuers and 1 evader; *Group type 2:* 6 pursuers and 2 evaders; *Group type 3:* 8 pursuers and 1 evader; *Group type 4:* 8 pursuers and 2 evaders.

Single Pool Approach: As illustrated in *figure 1* (left) this approach generates and tests *n* copies of a single genotype, meaning that the pursuer team is homogenous. In this approach there is no plasticity so the pursuers cannot adapt during their lifetime. The fitness assigned to each pursuer is the simply the fitness calculated for the single genotype that specifies the pursuer team. The main advantage of this approach is its simplicity in terms of behavioral encoding and calculation of team fitness.

Plasticity Approach: As illustrated in *figure 1* (center) this approach generates and tests *n* copies of a single genotype, so that as with the *single pool* approach, the pur-suer team is homogenous. The difference is that individual phenotypes are able to adapt during their lifetime as a result of a recurrent neural network learning process. The advantage of the plasticity approach is that it allows for specialization of behav-iour by individual pursuers without being affected by the problem of needing to esti-mate fitness contribution of different pursuers to the team as a whole. For both the single pool and plasticity approaches, every individual genotype in the population is tested against *20* randomly selected genotypes from the same population. This proc-ess is repeated for all 10 epochs of a pursuer's lifetime.

Multiple Pools Approach: As illustrated in *figure 1* (right) this approach takes a single genotype from every population of genotypes where the number of populations corre-sponds to the number of pursuers. Each genotype is then decoded into a separate phenotype, where this set of phenotypes then represent the team of pursuers. In each generation, every individual genotype in a population is tested against *20* other genotypes, randomly selected from one of the other populations of genotypes. This process is then repeated for every epoch. The advantage of the multiple pools approach is that it encourages behavioural specialization in the group of pursuers, in that the artificial evolution setup provides for more genetic diversity.

Evaluation of Approaches

For both the *single pool* and *plasticity* approaches a single genotype specifies the entire pursuer team. That is, pursuers are clones of each other, so evaluation of team performance in this case is not problematic. The performance of a pursuer team executed under either of these approaches is simply measured as the fitness value assigned to the genotype that specifies the team. In contrast to these approaches a pursuer team using the multiple pools approach is specified by *n* genotypes selected from *n* different populations. Hence, each genotype must be assigned an individual fitness score, and team performance evaluation needs to be computed by estimating the fitness contribution of each genotype to the team as a whole.

A method of evaluation widely known as: *fitness sharing* [2] was implemented for the multiple pools approach, where an equal fitness score is assigned to each individual genotype, thereby assuming that each individual contributed to team performance equally. The advantage of this method is that fitness for individual genotypes is easily calculated and there is no disparity between team fitness and the fitness of individual team members.

In order to quantify the effectiveness of emergent evader capture strategies, two different measures were used to evaluate performance. The first was pursuer team fitness, where fitness awarded to the team was proportional to how much an evader was slowed during the team's lifetime. The second was evader capture time, which was the time period for which an evader was immobilized by the collective efforts of at least two pursuers.

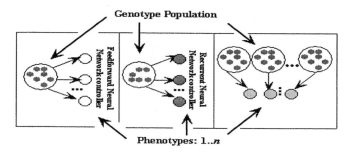

Fig. 1. Left: Single Pool - Each pursuer phenotype corresponds to a genotype selected from a population and copied *n* times. **Center:** Plasticity – As with Single Pool except phenotypes implement a recurrent neural network controller. **Right:** Multiple Pools - Pursuer phenotypes correspond to *n* different genotypes selected from *n* separate pools of genotypes

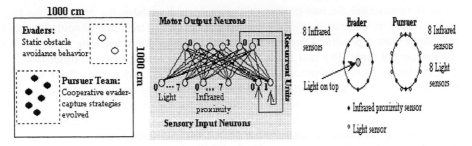

Fig. 2. Left: The pursuers and evaders are placed into a 1000cm x 1000cm arena. The number of pursuers and evaders depends upon the group type being tested. This figure illustrates an example of group type 2: 6 pursuers and 2 evaders. **Center:** A two-layered feed forward neural network controls all pursuer and evaders using the Single Pool and Multiple Pools approaches, and a recurrent neural network controls all pursuers and evaders using the Plasticity approach. **Right:** Each pursuer and evader is a simulated *Khepera* robot. Pursuers have 8 infrared proximity sensors, and 8 light sensors. Evaders have 8 infrared proximity sensors, and a light so that pursuers can distinguish them from fellow pursuers and obstacles

Agents, Environment and Artificial Evolution

For all experiments a generational evolutionary algorithm using linear rank-based selection was used [4]. Each population contained 100 genotypes, where initial populations consisted of randomly generated genotypes. Genotype length was set to 24 genes, where each gene consisted of several bits encoding each neuron type and connection weights. At the turn of each generation, the 20 genotypes that have accumulated the highest fitness were allowed to reproduce. The total fitness of an individual genotype was the sum of all its fitness for all epochs of its life.

Reproduction was done via generating five copies of each genotype in order to create the next generation. During this copying process 10 percent of the connection weights were mutated. Mutation added a random value between −1.0 and +1.0 to the weights current value. This process was repeated for the 500 generations that the simulation ran for.

As illustrated in *figure 2* (right), the body of each pursuer and evader was a Khepera mobile robot [10]. The pursuer robots were equipped with 8 infrared proximity sensors, and 8 light sensors positioned on the periphery of the Khepera. The evader robots were equipped with 8 infrared proximity sensors, as well as a light on its top. This light could be detected by pursuer light sensors and was used so as each pursuer robot could distinguish fellow pursuers from an evader.

All pursuers and evaders used a two-layer feed forward neural network. The network consisted of an input and output layer with no hidden units [8] controlled all robots. In the case of the pursuers, the input layer consisted of 16 units that encoded the activation level of the robots 16 sensors. These 16 input units were connected to 4 output units. *Figure 2* (center) also illustrates the recurrent neural network used for the plasticity experiments. For these experiments, the activation level of two additional output units was copied back into two additional input units. The first two output units represented the two motors of the robot and encoded the speed of the two wheels. These motor units controlled the robots behavior in the environment. The next two output units represented two teaching units that encoded a teaching input for the first two output units. The two motor units used this teaching input in order to learn using the back propagation procedure [12]. In the plasticity experiments there were an additional two output units that were the recurrent units and contained activation values for the motors from the previous cycle. For the robots that were the evader, a network connecting 8 sensory input units to 4 motor output units was trained for an obstacle avoidance behavior before being placed in the environment.

As illustrated in *figure 2* (left), the environment corresponded to a 1000cm x 1000cm arena with no obstacles. When a pursuer robot was placed in the environment, sensory input was received via the input units, and activation values were passed to the two motor units, and the teaching units. The activation value of the two motor units was used to move the robot, thus changing the sensor input for the next simulation cycle. The activation value of the two teaching units was used to change the weights that connected the input units to the motor units using back propagation. This cycle was then repeated.

3   Results

The three artificial evolution approaches were comparatively tested and evaluated for the task of having a pursuer team immobilize one or more evaders, where three sets of experiments were run to test each approach. Ten replications of each experiment were made and each replication ran for 500 generations. The pursuer team 'lived' for *10 epochs*, where each epoch consisted of *1000 cycles* of simulation time. Each epoch constituted a test scenario where all pursuers and evader were tested for different, randomly generated orientations and starting positions in the environment.

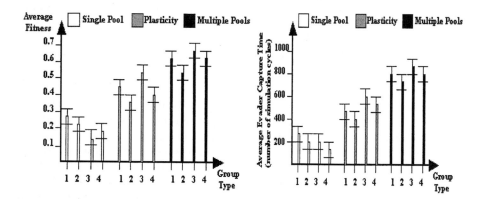

Fig. 3. Left: Average fitness, with standard error bars, presented for all group types tested under the three artificial evolution approaches. **Right:** Average evader-capture time, with standard error bars, presented for all group types tested under the three artificial approaches

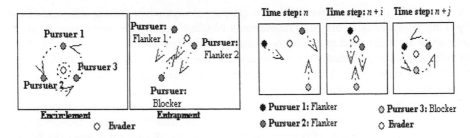

Fig. 4. Left: The cooperative encirclement and entrapment pursuit strategies; each used three pursuers, though neither strategy was successful at immobilizing an evader. **Right:** The role-switcher pursuit strategy, using three pursuers. The difference between the multiple pools and plasticity versions of this strategy are not depicted in this figure. Namely, this difference is the dynamic (plasticity approach) versus the set (multiple pools approach) adoption of behavioral roles in the formation of the strategy

Figure 4 illustrates the average fitness, with standard error bars, attained for all groups of pursuers using the single pool, plasticity and multiple pools approaches. *Figure 5* presents the average evader capture time, with standard error bars, attained for pursuer teams using each of the three evolutionary schemas. The term: *evader capture* refers to the instance when the evader is immobilized for a time interval $t_0 .. t_i$. For all results presented, the average is taken for 10 experimental replications, each running for 500 generations.

Evolved Behavior

Evolved behavior observed for each of the three artificial evolution approaches is described in this section. *Single Pool*: For all four group types tested only two cooperative evader-capture strategies consistently emerged.

These strategies, termed: *encirclement* and *entrapment* are illustrated in *figure 4* (left), and further detailed elsewhere [10], though briefly described in the following.

In the encirclement strategy at least three pursuers move to circle the evader, each moving in the same direction in close proximity to the evader, for some period of time. The strategy was rarely able to immobilize the evader and was only effective in slowing the evader for a short period of time, given that the pursuers were not able to coordinate their movements for an extended period. The entrapment strategy also used at least three pursuers, where either one or two pursuers moved to each side of the evader, while another pursuer, termed: a *blocker*, moved around the flanking pursuers, to approach the evader from the front, in order to trap the evader in a triangular formation. When the evader moved to escape, the flanking pursuers moved also, turning one way to force the evader in a specific direction. The blocker then moved around in order to affront the evader again. This system of entrapment, movement, and then entrapment continued for several times before the evader was able to evade the pursuers.

Plasticity: In these experiments only one emergent cooperative evader capture strategy was observed. This was a derivative of the entrapment strategy termed: *role switcher*. In this strategy a form of behavioural specialization emerged during the lifetime of the pursuers so that a *blocker* pursuer always moved along side one of the flanking pursuers and role of a flanker and blocker switched between two pursuers whenever a evader tried to evade the pursuers. This dynamic adoption and switching of roles served to coordinate the movements of the pursuers and thus effectively slow an evader's movement. Also, relative to the entrapment strategy, role switcher was able to more frequently immobilize an evader.

Multiple Pools: As with the plasticity experiments the *role switcher* strategy was the only cooperative evader-capture strategy that consistently emerged, though a specific difference was noted. Different pursuers adopted different roles from the beginning of their lifetimes. Specifically, particular pursuers always assumed the role of a flanker, while other pursuers always assumed the role of a blocker or that of an idle pursuer. This adoption of roles that was maintained throughout the lifetime of the pursuers served to increase the effectiveness of the role switcher strategy in terms of the three measures defined for evader capture strategy performance. Notably the strategy was consistently effective at immobilizing an evader, for all four-group types tested.

4   Analysis and Discussion

In this section the cooperative evader capture strategies that emerged under each of the three approaches tested are discussed. The discussion relates the relative success of emergent evader-capture strategies to the group types tested and the two performance measures defined.

Single Pool: Two cooperative evader-capture strategies, each using at least two pursuers, consistently emerged for all four group types tested. Though, relative to the plasticity and multiple pools approaches these emergent strategies performed poorly in terms of average *team fitness*, and *evader-capture time*. These results are presented in *figures 4*, and *5* respectively and as shown were consistent for all group types tested. The low fitness, and evader-capture time of the encirclement and entrapment strategies was found to be a result of interference that occurred as three or more pursuers collectively approached a evader. This result was found to be due to confused infrared sensor readings of pursuers in close proximity to each other, and the fact that individual pursuers did not possess any memory, explicit form of communication, or coordination to facilitate a successful cooperative evader capture strategy. As illustrated in *figures 4*, and *5* this result is especially prevalent for *group types 3* and *4*, where teams of eight pursuers were used.

Plasticity: In experiments using this approach the role switcher strategy frequently emerged for all group types tested. In the role-switcher strategy a form of dynamic behavioral specialization emerged in at least three pursuers. This behavioral specialization was in the form of dynamic role adoption that emerged during the lifetime of a pursuer and varied from pursuer to pursuer depending upon the group type being tested. This dynamic role adoption facilitated cooperation between the pursuers affording the pursuer team a high average *fitness*, and *evader-capture time* comparative to the single pool approach. This result is presented in *figures 4*, and *5* respectively. In experiments testing *group types 1* and *2*, at least three and at most six pursuers flanked the evader, where a maximum of three flanked either side, and the role of a flanking and blocking pursuer switched whenever the evader turned so as to escape. In experiments testing group *types* *3* and *4*, at least three and at most four pursuers flanked each evader, where a maximum of two flanked either side of each of the two evaders. As with the experiments testing *group types* *1* and *2*, the role of a pursuer closest to the evader and the blocking pursuer switched whenever the evader turned so as to escape, though the difference for experiments testing *group types* *3* and *4*, was that two sub-groups of pursuers emerged, so that the two evaders were simultaneously engaged by two pursuer sub-teams.

The dynamic assumption of roles during a pursuers lifetime allowed for the formation of sub-groups in the pursuer team, and thus served to yield a higher team fitness, and evader capture time. Though, as presented in *figures 4*, and *5* respectively, these three measures were relatively higher in experiments testing *group types* *3* and *4*, and low in experiments testing *group types* *1* and *2*. In experiments testing group *types* *1* and 2, this result was due to multiple pursuers attempting to assume the same behavioral role as they collectively approached the single evader. Where as, in experiments testing *group types* *3* and *4*, the use of two evaders served to reduce the number of pursuers that collectively approached a single evader at any given time, thus increasing the likelihood of an unhindered dynamic adoption of a behavioral role in the role-switcher strategy.

It is theorized that behavioral specialization for role switching emerged as an indirect result of physical interference that occurred when at least three pursuers collectively approached the evader. Such interference was observed in the single pool experiments and often caused emergent strategies to fail prematurely, thereby making it more difficult for such strategies using at least three pursuers to be selected for and propagated by the evolutionary process. Where as, the *role-switcher* strategy was able to achieve a high team fitness, and evader-capture time, it was at best only able to slow the evader, never completely immobilizing the evader in experiments testing *group types* *1* and *2*. This is reflected in *figure 6*, which presents an average evader capture time comparative to that resulting from strategies that emerged under the single pool approach. Where as, experiments testing *group types* *3* and *4* proved more effective in immobilizing the evader. This is reflected in the relatively higher evader capture time attained in experiments testing group *types* *3* and *4*. Note in *figures 4*, and *5*, that in experiments testing *group types* *3* and *4*, that all three measures are relatively higher. Thus, the dynamic adoption of behavioral roles that defined the role-switcher strategy only proved effective in an environment with two evaders. So, as with the single pool approach, the interference that occurred between pursuers as they collectively approached an evader prevented the role switcher from succeeding in all but a few instances. However, the plasticity approach was able to exploit an environment with two evaders, via the formation of two specialized pursuer sub-groups.

Multiple Pools: In experiments using the multiple pools approach only a single cooperative evader-capture strategy emerged. This strategy was classified as a derivative of the role-switcher strategy observed in the plasticity experiments. The multiple-pools version of role-switcher used a genetic based specialization. In the plasticity experiments the adoption of specialized behaviour was dependent upon the positions of the pursuers at a given time, where as in the multiple pools experiments, different pursuers initially behaved differently and assumed genetically pre-determined roles prior to engaging in the multiple pools version of the *role-switcher* evader-capture strategy. That is, one pursuer always assumed the role of the blocker while the others always assumed the role of a flanker, or that of an idle pursuer. Idle pursuers served the purpose of reducing any potential interference between pursuers as they collectively approach an evader, and also increased the chance of success of the role-switcher strategy via limiting the number of pursuers that constitute the strategy. The fact that the pursuers are genetically different is one explanation for the evolution of specialized behavioural roles that complemented each other in the emergence of the multiple pools role switcher strategy. In experiments testing *group types 1* and *3*, a single specialized group of pursuers emerged in the evolutionary process. This group consisted of at least three and at most four pursuers. In the experiments testing *group types 2* and *4*, two specialized sub-groups of pursuers, comprising either two groups of three pursuers in the case of *group type 2*, or two groups of three or four pursuers in the case of *group type 4*. The effectiveness of these two specialized sub-groups is illustrated in *figures 4*, and *5* which present a relatively high average fitness, and evader-capture time for these group types, comparative to the single pool and plasticity approaches. Note that as with the plasticity approach, the multiple pools approach is more effective at exploiting an environment containing two evaders via the formation of two specialized pursuer sub-groups. Thus, the multiple pools approach facilitated the evolution of specialized pursuer sub-groups to capture two evaders, where genetic based specialization proved to be more effective, in terms of measures for *fitness scored*, and *evader capture time*. This comparison was made with the dynamic assumption of behavioral roles as adopted by pursuers using the plasticity approach.

5   Conclusions

This paper presented a set of experiments testing three different artificial evolution approaches for the synthesis of cooperative behaviour within a team of pursuers, where the task was to cooperatively capture one or more evaders. Results compared the performance of these three approaches for four different group configurations.

Results presented indicated the multiple pools approach to be superior for all group types tested. The superiority of the multiple pools approach was found to be a result of a genetic form of behavioral specialization that assigned behavioral roles at the beginning of a pursuers lifetime. The multiple pools approach also facilitated the evolution of two specialized sub-groups of pursuers in scenarios using two evaders. Evolution of these sub-groups served to improve the effectiveness of these strategies in terms of higher *team fitness*, and *evader capture time*, comparative to the single pool and plasticity approaches. Specifically, the specialized sub-groups aided in reducing interference between pursuers as they collectively approached an evader. An analysis of emergent strategies revealed that behavioural specialization is a necessary aspect for the emergence of effective cooperative behaviour in the described task domain. This was especially evident in the single pool experiments, where a low fitness, and evader-capture time was observed as a result of emergent strategies only being able to slow, and not immobilize an evader.

A comparison with other evolution of cooperation approaches in the pursuit-evasion domain [5], [7] and [13] is difficult given the real world nature of the experiments described in this paper. Though the robots were simulated, the environment was a continuous domain and the simulation incorporated noise in sensory data, namely confused infrared sensor readings resulting from two or more Khepera's being in close proximity to each other. This noisy sensor data was a key reason for interference between multiple pursuers as they collectively approached an evader. Also, a continuous environment does not allow for the selection of distinct sets of situation/action values that are possible in grid world implementations [3] where a finite set of actions and resultant outcomes can be defined. While, the emergence of cooperation is simpler to analyze in these grid world domains, they are limited by their own implementations, so the study of mechanisms that facilitate emergent cooperation such as behavioral specialization is limited to trivial situations.

Finally, experimental results highlighted that artificial evolution is an effective method for deriving cooperative evader capture strategies using pursuer teams with no explicit communication, or coordination mechanisms.

References

[1]   Benda, M., Jagannanthan, V., and Dodhiawalla, R. An Optimal Cooperation of Knowledge Sources. Technical BCS-G2010-28, Boeing AI Center, Bellevue, WA (1985).

[2]   Bull, L., and Holland, O. Evolutionary Computing in Multi-Agent Environments: Eusociality. In: Koza, J. R. Deb, K., Dorigo, M., Fogel, D, B., Garzon, M., Iba, H., and Riolo, R. L.   (eds.) Proceedings of the Second Annual Conference on Genetic Programming, Morgan Kaufmann, Stanford (1997) 347-352.

[3]   Denzinger, J., and Fuchs, M. Experiments in Learning Prototypical Situations for Variants of the Pursuit Game. In: Durfee, E., and Tokoro, M (eds.) Proceedings of the Second ICMAS conference, AAAI Press, Kyoto, Japan, (1996) 48-55.

[4]   Goldberg, D. Genetic Algorithms. Addison Wesley, New York, USA. (1989).

[5]   Haynes, T., and Sen, S. Evolving behavioral strategies in pursuers and evader. In: Sen, S (ed.). Adaptation and Learning in Multi-Agent Systems, Morgan Kaufmann, Montreal, Quebec (1996) 32-37.

[6]   Korf, R. E. A simple solution to pursuit games. In: Weißand, G., and Sen, S. (eds.)   Working Papers of the Eleventh International Workshop on DAI, Springer Verlag, Berlin (1992) 195-213.

[7]   Levy, R., and Rosenschein, J. S. A Game Theoretic Approach to Distributed Artificial Intelligence and the Pursuit Problem. In: Rosenschein, J. S (ed.) Decentralized AI III, Springer-Verlag, Berlin (1992) 129-146.

[8]   Mondada, F., Franzi, E., and Ienne, P. Mobile Robot Miniaturization: A tool for Investigation in Control Algorithms. In: Yoshikawa, T. and Miyazaki, F. (eds.) Proceedings of Third International Symposium on Experimental Robotics, IEEE Press, Kyoto (1993) 501-513.

Several authors have already noticed that the RD can emerge from simple learning models, [1, 8, 9]. In this paper not only the dynamics of the Cross model and Learning Automata will be a topic of interest, but also the dynamics of Q-learning agents. These dynamics open a new perspective in understanding and fine tuning the learning process in games and more general in MAS. It will become clear that in the framework of games the Cross model is sufficient for learning equilibria. In other words, Occam's Razor can be applied.

The outline of the paper is as follows. In section 2 we elaborate on three RL models in order of their complexity. Section 3 describes the replicator dynamics from EGT. We continue with a section on the dynamics of these models. Section 5 describes the experiments. Finally, we end with a discussion.

2 Reinforcement Learning Models

In this section we introduce the three reinforcement learning models under consideration in order of complexity. We start with the Cross model and continue with Learning Automata and Q-learning. After considering these three learning models it will become clear that the Cross model is the most simple model of the three presented. More precisely, it is a less complex model then LA and Q-learning in the sense that you don't have to initialise and finetune as many parameters as with LA and Q-learning. Cross doesn't consider a learning rate, a discount factor and temperature as Q-learning does, nor needs a reward and penalty parameters as LA do.

2.1 The Cross Learning Model

The cross learning model is a special case of the standard reinforcement learning model [1]. The model considers several agents playing the same normal form game repeatedly in discrete time. At each point in time, each player is characterized by a probability distribution over her strategy set which indicates how likely she is to play any of her strategies. At each time step (indexed by n) , a player chooses one of its strategies based on the probabilities which are related to each isolated strategy. As a result a player can be represented by a probability vector:

$$p(n) = (p_1(n), ..., p_r(n))$$

In case of a 2-player game with payoff matrix U, player k gets payoff U_{ij}^k when player 1 chooses strategy i and player 2 chooses strategy j. Players don't observe each others strategies and payoffs. After each stage they update their probability vector, according to,

$$p_i(n + 1) = U_{ij} + (1 - U_{ij})p_i(n) \tag{1}$$

$$p_{i'}(n + 1) = (1 - U_{ij})P_{i'}(n) \tag{2}$$

Equation (1) expresses how the probability of the selected strategy (i) is updated and equation (2) expresses how all the other strategies $i' \neq i$ are corrected. The probability vector of $Q(n)$ is updated in an analogous manner. This entire system of equations defines a stochastic update process for the players $\{p^k(n)\}$. This process is called the "Cross learning process" in [1]. Börgers and Sarin showed that in an appropriately constructed continuous time limit, this model converges to the asymmetric, continuous time version of the replicator dynamics, see section 3.

2.2   Learning Automata

A LA formalizes a general stochastic system in terms of states, actions, probabilities (state or action) and environment responses [3]. In a variable structure stochastic automaton[1] action probabilities are updated at every stage using a reinforcement scheme. An automaton is defined by a quadruple $\{\alpha, \beta, \mathbf{p}, T\}$ for which α is the action or output set $\{\alpha_1, \alpha_2, \ldots \alpha_r\}$ of the automaton , β is a random variable in the interval $[0, 1]$, $\mathbf{p}$ is the action probability vector of the automaton or agent and T denotes an update scheme. The output α of the automaton is actually the input to the environment. The input β of the automaton is the output of the environment, which is modeled through penalty probabilities c_i with $c_i = P[\beta \mid \alpha_i], i \subset \{1 \ldots r\}$.

Important examples of update schemes are linear reward-penalty, linear reward-inaction and linear reward-ϵ-penalty. The philosophy of those schemes is essentially to increase the probability of an action when it results in a success and to decrease it when the response is a failure. The general algorithm consist of two update rules, one to update the probability of the selected action and one for all the other actions.

$$p_i(n + 1) = p_i(n) + a(1 - \beta(n))(1 - p_i(n)) - b\beta(n)p_i(n) \qquad (3)$$

when α_i is the action taken at time n.

$$p_j(n + 1) = p_j(n) - a(1 - \beta(n))p_j(n) + b\beta(n)[(r - 1)^{-1} - p_j(n)] \qquad (4)$$

when $\alpha_j \neq \alpha_i$.

The constants a and b are the reward and penalty parameters respectively. When $a = b$ the algorithm is referred to as linear reward-penalty (L_{R-P}), when $b = 0$ it is referred to as linear reward-inaction (L_{R-I}) and when b is small compared to a it is called linear reward-ϵ-penalty $(L_{R-\epsilon P})$.

If the penalty probabilities c_i of the environment are constant, the probability vector $\mathbf{p}(n + 1)$ is completely determined by probability vector $\mathbf{p}(n)$ and hence $\mathbf{p}(n)_{n>0}$ is a discrete-time homogeneous Markov process. Convergence results for

---

[1] As opposed to fixed structure learning automata, where state transition probabilities are fixed and have to be chosen according to the response of the environment and to perform better than a pure-chance automaton in which every action is chosen with equal probability.

the different schemes are obtained under the assumptions of constant penalty probabilities [3].

A multi-agent system can be modeled as an automata game. A game $\alpha(t) = (\alpha^1(t) \ldots \alpha^n(t))$ of n automata is a set of strategies chosen by the automata at stage t. Correspondingly the outcome is now a vector $\beta(t) = (\beta^1(t) \ldots \beta^n(t))$. At every instance all automata update their probability distributions based on the responses of the environment. Each automaton participating in the game operates without information concerning payoff, the number of participants, their strategies or actions.

2.3   Q-Learning

Common reinforcement learning methods, which can be found in [7] are structured around estimating value functions. A value of a state or state-action pair, is the total amount of reward an agent can expect to accumulate over the future, starting from that state. One way to find the optimal policy is to find the optimal value function. If a perfect model of the environment as a Markov decision process is known, the optimal value function can be learned with an algorithm called value iteration. Q-learning is an adaptive value iteration method see [7], which bootstraps its estimate for the state-action value $Q_{t+1}(s, a)$ at time $t + 1$ upon its estimate for $Q_t(s', a')$ with s' the state where the learner arrives after taking action a in state s:

$$Q_{t+1}(s, a) \leftarrow (1 - \alpha)Q_t(s, a) + \alpha(r + \gamma \, max_{a'} Q_t(s', a')) \tag{5}$$

With α the usual step size parameter, γ a discount factor and r the immediate reinforcement.

The players could therefore use the algorithm of (5) where the state information s is removed. Solutions are formulated in terms of equilibrium situations for the players.

3   The Replicator Dynamics

In Biology, a simple abstraction of an evolutionary process combines two basic elements: a selection mechanism and a mutation mechanism. The mutation provides variety, while selection favors particular varieties over others. Replicator dynamics highlights the role of selection, it describes how systems consisting of different strategies change over time. They are formalized as a system of differential equations. One important assumption of this model is that each replicator represents one (pure) strategy. This strategy is inherited by all the offspring of the replicator.

The general form of a replicator dynamic is the following:

$$\dot{x}_i = [(A\mathbf{x})_i - \mathbf{x} \cdot A\mathbf{x}]x_i \tag{6}$$

In equation (6), x_i represents the density of strategy i in the population, A is the payoff matrix which describes the different payoff values each individual replicator receives when interacting with other replicators in the population. The state of the population ($\mathbf{x}$) can be described as a probability vector $\mathbf{x} = (x_1, x_2, ..., x_R)$ which expresses the different densities of all the different types of replicators in the population. Hence $(A\mathbf{x})_i$ is the payoff which replicator i receives in a population with state $\mathbf{x}$ and $\mathbf{x} \cdot A\mathbf{x}$ describes the average payoff in the population. The growth rate $\dot{x}_i/x_i$ of the population share using strategy i equals the difference between the strategy's current payoff and the average payoff in the population. For further information we refer the reader to [10, 2].

Now, if we assume there exists a relation between the state of the replicator population $\mathbf{x}$ and the probability distribution for a player $p(n)$, two populations will be required, one for each player. Hence, the game is played between the members of two different populations. As a result, we need two systems of differential equations: one for the first player (p) and one for the second player (q). This setup corresponds to a replicator dynamic for asymmetric games. If $A = B^t$, equation (6) would again emerge.

This translates into the following replicator equations for the two populations:

$$\dot{p}_i = [(A\mathbf{q})_i - \mathbf{p} \cdot A\mathbf{q}]p_i \tag{7}$$

$$\dot{q}_i = [(B\mathbf{p})_i - \mathbf{q} \cdot B\mathbf{p}]q_i \tag{8}$$

As can be seen in equation (7) and (8), the growth rate of the types in each population is now determined by the composition of the other population. Note that, when calculating the rate of change using these systems of differential equations, two different payoff matrices (A and B) are used for the two different players.

4   The Dynamics of Learning Models in Games

4.1   The Cross and LA Dynamics

The Cross and LA dynamics are considered in the same section because it will become clear that the Cross model is a special case of LA. In [1] it is proven that the RD emerge from the Cross model, and therefore will also emerge from the LA model.

If it is assumed that $b = 0$ and $a = 1$ in equations (3) and (4), the relation between (1) and (2) with (3) and (4) becomes apparent. In this association, when the reward penalty term $a = 1$, the feedback from the environment $(1 - \beta(n))$ equals the game reward U_{ij}^k. Hence the equations become equivalent. As a result the conditions and implications from the relation between the Cross Learning Model and RD also hold for LA games.

4.2   The Q-Learning Dynamics

In this section we briefly[2] describe the relation between Q-learning and the RD. More precisely we present the dynamical system of Q-learning. These equations

---

[2] The reader who is interested in the complete derivation, we refer to [9].

illustrates the direction field of the replicator dynamic and the figure on the right shows the learning process of LA. We plotted for both players the probability of choosing their first strategy (in this case defect). As starting points for the LA we chose a grid of 25 points. In every point a learning path starts and converges to the equilibrium at the point $(1,1)$. As you can see all the sample paths of the reinforcement learning process approximate the paths of the RD.

For games of the second subclass (battle of the sexes) we have

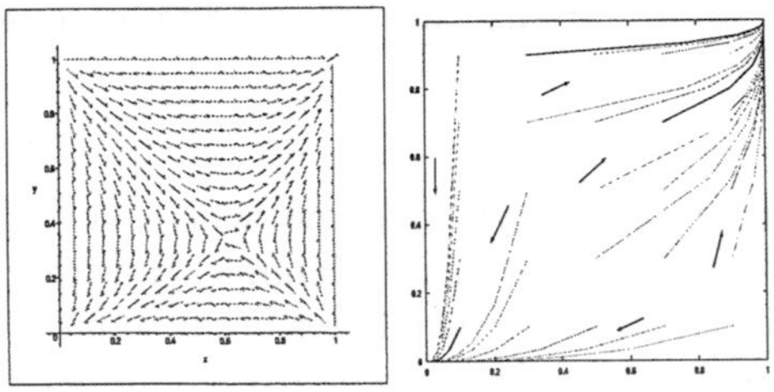

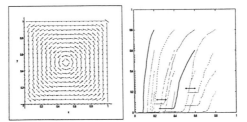

Fig. 3. *Left*: The direction field of the RD of the battle of the sexes game. *Right*: The paths induced by the learning process

Here you can see two pure equilibra at $(0,0)$ and at $(1,1)$, and one mixed at $(2/3, 1/3)$. Now we have convergence to the 2 strict equilibria. The third equilibrium is very unstable as you can see in the direction field plot. This instability is the reason why it will not emerge from the learning process on the long run. For games of the third subclass 3 we have,

Fig. 4. *Left*: The direction field of the RD. *Right*: The paths induced by the learning process

As can be seen the behavior is not completely the same for this type of game as that of the replicator dynamics. It is a known fact that the asymptotic behaviour of the learning process can differ from that of the replicator dynamics [1].

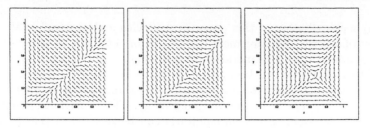

Fig. 5. The direction field plots of the battle of the sexes (subclass 2) game with $\tau = 1, 2, 10$

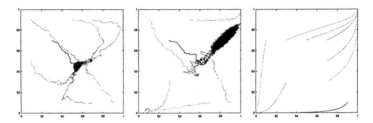

Fig. 6. The Q-learning plots of the battle of the sexes (subclass 2) game with $\tau = 1, 2, 10$

5.3 The Q-Learning Experiments

We only describe the experiments of subclass 2. All the experiments can be found in [9]. The important aspect is that obtaining convergence to a Nash equilibrium with Q-learning is more cumbersome than with Cross. In figure 5 the direction field plot of the differential equations of this game is plotted. Again the direction field of the equations are plotted for 3 values of τ, more precisely $1, 2, 10$. In the first 2 plots τ isn't big enough to reach for one of the three Nash equilibria. Only in the last one the dynamics attain the Nash equilibria (the 3 attractors in the last plot) for the game at the coordinates $(1, 1)$, $(0, 0)$ and $(\frac{2}{3}, \frac{1}{3})$. The mixed equilibrium though is very unstable. Any small perturbation away from this equilibrium will typically lead the dynamics to one of the 2 pure equilibria.

In figure 6 we also plotted the Q-learning process for the same game with the same settings as for the system of differential equations. In the chosen points a learning path starts and converges to a particular point. If you compare the plots with the direction field plots for the same value of τ you can see that the sample paths of the learning process approximates the paths of the differential equations. The instability of the mixed equilibrium is the reason why this equilibrium doesn't emerge from the learning process.

6 Discussion

The major contribution of this paper is that with a theoretical analysis of the dynamics of different reinforcement learning algorithms can be shown that in the context of games the Cross model suffices to attain the right equilibria. In other words, Occam's Razor can be applied to the field of reinforcement learning in games. It turns out that the Cross model keeps things most simple in the sense of setting parameters and computational effort. The experiments confirm that with the Cross model, the Nash equilibria can be reached in the most elegant way. As opposed to LA, where a lot of tuning is needed with setting the reward and penalty variables to the correct values. Also Q-learning demands a lot of finetuning as can be seen in the experiments 6. There is the temperature τ, the learning rate α and the discount factor γ. In the context of learning agents in games, there is no need to complicate the learning algorithm more then the Cross learning model.

Another interesting remark is that learning can be very time consuming, especially when you need to fine tune some parameters. As the experiments illustrate, plotting the direction field of the dynamical system of the learning model beforehand gives information on how to initialise the learning agents so that they end up in the most interesting attractors of the game.

References

[1] Börgers, T., Sarin, R., Learning Through Reinforcement and Replicator Dynamics. Journal of Economic Theory, Volume 77, Number 1, November 1997.

[2] Hofbauer, J., Sigmund, K., Evolutionary Games and Population Dynamics, Cambridge University Press, 1998.

[3] Narendra, K., Thathachar, M., Learning Automata: An Introduction. Prentice-Hall (1989).

[4] Redondo, F. V., Game Theory and Economics, Cambridge University Press, (2001).

[5] Schneider, T. D., Evolution of biological information. journal of NAR, volume 28, pages 2794 - 2799, 2000.

[6] Stauffer, D., Life, Love and Death: Models of Biological Reproduction and Aging. Institute for Theoretical physics, Köln, Euroland, 1999.

[7] Sutton, R. S., Barto, A. G. : Reinforcement Learning: An introduction. Cambridge, MA: MIT Press (1998).

[8] Tuyls, K., Lenaerts, T., Verbeeck, K., Maes, S. and Manderick, B, Towards a Relation Between Learning Agents and Evolutionary Dynamics. Proceedings of BNAIC 2002. KU Leuven, Belgium.

[9] Tuyls, K., Verbeeck, K. and Lenaerts, T., A Selection-Mutation model for Q-learning in MAS. Accepted at AAMAS 2003. Melbourne, Australia.

[10] Weibull, J. W., Evolutionary Game Theory, MIT Press, (1996).

Forgiveness in Strategies
in Noisy Multi-agent Environments

Colm O' Riordan[1], Josephine Griffith[1], and Humphrey Sorensen[2]

[1] Dept. of Information Technology
National University of Ireland
Galway, Ireland
[2] Dept. of Computer Science
University College Cork
Ireland

Abstract. Game theory has been widely used in modelling interactions among autonomous agents. One of the most oft-studies games is the iterated prisoner's dilemma. Prevalent assumptions in the majority of this work have been that no noise is present and that interactions and gestures by agents are interpreted correctly. In this paper, we discuss two classes of strategies that attempt to promote cooperation in noisy environments. The classes of strategies discussed include: forgiving strategies which attempt to re-establish mutual cooperation following a period of mutual defection; and memory-based strategies which respond to defections based on a longer memory of past behaviours. We study these classes of strategies by using techniques from evolutionary computation which provide a powerful means to search the large range of strategies' features.

1 Introduction

Cooperation and cooperative behaviour are central issues in the design and development of multi-agent systems. In many multi-agent systems, agents are assumed to be non-competitive and to have non-conflicting goals. These assumptions hold in many domains, but there also exist many domains where these assumptions are not valid. Often agents are in direct competition with one another.

In multi-agent systems, many forms and types of cooperation may exist ranging from joint agreements wherein a set of agents form a binding agreement to cooperate to achieve some shared goal, to looser notions of cooperation where agents partake in cooperative acts while pursuing individual goals. Agents may also cooperate to preserve or improve their reputation or to conform to laws or social norms. Many approaches have been adopted to reason about cooperative behaviour in such systems. These include game-theoretic approaches, decision theoretic approaches, norm based computing and techniques based on trust and reputation schemes.

Game-theoretic approaches have involved the study and analysis of games to capture, and to reason about, the abstract features of behaviour in biology[1, 2,

V. Mařík et al. (Eds): CEEMAS 2003, LNAI 2691, pp. 345–352, 2003.

3], political sciences[4], economics[5] and computer science[6, 7, 8]. The game-theoretic approach is typified by the abstraction of behaviour to a game, in which one attempts to capture the salient features of that behaviour. Analysis and exploration of ideas regarding behaviours can be achieved via studying these games (through formal analysis of these games and through the simulation of strategies playing these games).

An assumption often adopted in multi-agent systems is that the domain is noise-free. This again does not hold in all multi-agent systems. For example, an *intended* cooperative gesture by one participant may be interpreted as a non-cooperative gesture by the receiver due to a number of reasons (for example, ambiguity in the message; conflicting goals and differences in ontologies maintained by the participants). A gesture may be lost or damaged in transmission which may result in the receiver mis-interpreting the message. These potential problems may result in a cooperative gesture being recognised by the receiver as a non-cooperative gesture and vice versa.

The issue of noisy environments has not been widely tackled with only a handful of researchers considering noise and errors in games such as the iterated prisoner's dilemma[9, 10, 11, 12].

Recent work in the iterated prisoners dilemma has shown the usefulness of forgiveness to help overcome mutual defection on behalf of participants. This has been shown in static, clean environments with well known strategies[13] and also in evolutionary settings[14].

In this paper, we consider the effects of noise in a multi-agent system environment, and develop and analyse classes of strategies in these environments.

2   Related Research

2.1   Prisoner's Dilemma

In the prisoner's dilemma game, two players are both faced with a decision—to either cooperate(C) or defect(D). The decision is made by a player with no knowledge of the other player's choice. The game is often expressed in the canonical form in terms of pay-offs:

		Player 1	
		C	D
Player 2	C	(λ_1, λ_1)	(λ_2, λ_3)
	D	(λ_3, λ_2)	(λ_4, λ_4)

where the pairs of values represent the pay-offs (rewards) for players **Player 1** and **Player 2** respectively. In order to have a dilemma the following holds: $\lambda_3 < \lambda_1 < \lambda_4 < \lambda_2$, where λ_2 is the sucker's payoff, λ_4 is the punishment for mutual defection, λ_1 is the reward for mutual cooperation and λ_3 is the temptation to defect. The constraint $2\lambda_1 > \lambda_2 + \lambda_3$ also holds.

In the iterated version, two players will play numerous games (the exact number not known to either player). Each player adopts a strategy to determine whether to cooperate or defect on each of the moves in the iterated game.

A computer tournament[15] was organised to pit strategies against each other in a round-robin manner in an attempt to identify successful strategies and their properties. The winning strategy was *tit-for-tat*; this strategy involved cooperating on the first move and then mirroring opponents move on all subsequent moves. The initial results and analysis indicated that the following properties are necessary for success—niceness (cooperate first), retaliation, forgiveness and clarity.

No best strategy exists; the success of a strategy depends on the other strategies present. For example, in a collection of strategies who defect continually (*ALL-D*) the best strategy to adopt is *ALL-D*. In a collection of strategies adopting a *tit-for-tat* strategy, an *ALL-D* strategy would not perform well.

2.2   Noisy Environments

The majority of work in the iterated prisoner's dilemma has focused on the games in a noise-free environment, i.e., there is no danger of a signal being misinterpreted by the opponent or the signal being damaged in transit. However, this assumption of a noise-free environment is not necessarily valid if one is trying to model real-world scenarios where both mis-perception and mis-implementation are possible.

It can be shown that in an infinitely long game of the iterated prisoner's dilemma, with noise present, two *tit-for-tat* strategies playing together would spend an equal amount of time in states of mutual cooperation and mutual defection.

Research by Bendor[9], Kahn and Murnighan[10] and Hoffman[16] report that in noisy environments, cooperation is more difficult to maintain. In [17], it is argued that "if mistakes are possible evolution may tend to weed out strategies that impose drastic penalties for deviations". Miller's experiments in genetic algorithms applied to the prisoner's dilemma leads to the conclusion that cooperation is at its greatest when there is no noise in the system and that this cooperation decreases as the noise increases[11].

2.3   Forgiving Strategies

A shortcoming of many strategies, like the well-known *tit-for-tat* strategy, is that they may react too quickly to defections and find themselves in a spiral of mutual defection which will be detrimental to the overall fitness of the strategy.

For example, if we consider *tit-for-tat* playing against nasty-tit-for-tat (*tit-for-tat* but attempts to exploit non-retaliatory strategies by playing a DD with some probability. Note this can also happen with *tit-for-tat*s in noisy environments.)

```
tit-for-tat        C C C C C C C C C C C D D D...
nasty-tit-for-tat C C C C C C C C C C C D D D...
```

The *forgiving* strategy[13] attempts to overcome this shortcoming by trying to re-establish cooperation by forgiving previous defections by the opposing player. The idea is to punish defections initially to prevent exploitation, but to also, upon recognising a spiral of defection, attempt to forgive the other strategy by playing cooperatively for a period of time, irrespective of the opponent's behaviour[1].

The class of *forgiving* strategies can be defined by a number of parameters, namely, the length of a mutual defection before forgiving is invoked *(ld)*; the length of a forgiving gesture *(lf)*; and finally the number of times a strategy forgives *(#f)*. If *ld* mutual defections are encountered, then a *forgiving* strategy plays a cooperative gesture *lf* times provided that *#f* is greater than zero. Having completed *lf* number of cooperations, *#f* is decremented. In other cases, *forgiving* strategies behave like *tit-for-tat*.

This approach has been investigated in clean environments against a range of well-known strategies but moreover has been shown to be selected for in evolutionary settings where a range of behaviours were encoded in a genotype which was then subject to evolutionary pressures via a genetic algorithm wherein the scores achieved in the iterated prisoner's dilemma where taken as a measure of fitness[14].

2.4   Memory-Based Strategies

As identified in section 2.3, a shortcoming of strategies like *tit-for-tat* is their likelihood of entering a spiral of mutual defection. This is due to their immediate reactions to defections by opponents. A means to avoid these spirals is to not act quite so reactively and instead base reactions on a longer history or memory of the game. We can define a class of *memory-based strategies* using a *tolerance* parameter where *tolerance* is defined as the ratio of the number of defections to cooperations that the strategy will tolerate before responding with a defection.

3   Experimental Setup and Results

Prior to beginning experiments, we investigated the effect of introducing noise to some sets of well-know strategies (initially reported in the context of a noise-free environment). These results showed, unsurprisingly, that strategies that do not incorporate any form of forgiveness, are not likely to do well. Strategies like *tit-for-tat*, perished relatively quickly. The class of *forgiving* strategies described in the previous section faired better by attempting to maintain and re-establish mutual cooperation. However, we discovered that those strategies that performed

---

[1] It is important to note, to avoid confusion, that Axelrod's notion of contrition is fundamentally different to this notion of *forgiveness* discussed here. Axelrod's notion of contrition effectively amounts to modifying *tit-for-tat* such that it "avoids responding to the other player's defection after its own unintended defection".

best were the ones which employed a form of forgiving based on a longer memory than other strategies and were less reactive than other strategies.

Given the initial results, we wished to further investigate these classes of strategies in an evolutionary setting to ascertain which of the two features would be selected: the ability to attempt to re-establish cooperation following mutual defection, or the ability to utilise a longer memory in deciding more accurately to retaliate and therefore possibly avoid entering a costly spiral of mutual defection.

In current experiments, we co-evolve populations of strategies playing the iterated prisoner's dilemma in noisy environments. A genetic algorithm is used to evolve successful strategies. In each genotype, features of strategies are represented. We employ a simple genetic algorithm with standard one-point crossover at 80% and mutation at 0.01%. Roulette wheel selection is used with fitness calculated by playing each represented strategy against all other represented strategies. A population size of 50 is employed.

Noise is implemented via a mis-implementation, i.e., a strategy when playing a cooperative move, will instead play a non-cooperative move with probability equal to the noise in the system.

4 Co-evolution of *Forgiving* Strategies

The genotype used in these experiments encodes a number of features of the strategies. These are:

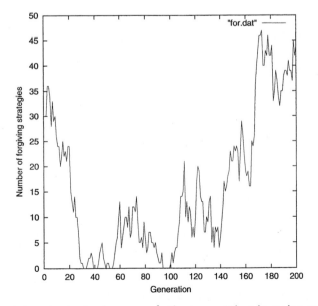

Fig. 1. *Forgiving* strategies in an evolutionary setting in noisy environments

- the first move,
- the move following a cooperation,
- the move following a defection,
- whether or not to forgive,
- the length of time to wait during a spiral of mutual defection before invoking cooperative moves to play as a cooperative gesture (forgiving) (ld),
- the number of cooperative moves to play as this cooperative gesture (lf),
- how often to forgive ($\#f$).

The results, over simulations, with 1% noise are plotted in Figure 1. The figure plots the number of *forgiving* strategies in the population against time (number of generations). We find *forgiveness* is not being selected consistently and, in some cases, where it does become a dominant feature in the population, it is not stable. For higher levels of noise, this becomes even more pronounced—forgiving (re-establishing cooperation after a defection) is not selected for consistently.

5   Co-evolution of Memory-Based Strategies

In these simulations, we report on strategies that ignore defections by invoking the use of a *memory-based* strategy. In these experiments we encode the following:

- whether or not to use a memory-based decision rather than *forgiving*,
- a *tolerance* threshold, indicating the tolerance the strategy has to defections (effectively a measure of the ratio of the number of cooperations to the number of defections played).

In these simulations, we find that these memory-based features are selected in most cases. Figure 2 plots the number of *memory-based* strategies in the population against time (number of generations).

6   Conclusion

The iterated prisoner's dilemma is an oft-studied game in many domains. This paper examined some features of strategies playing the game in a noisy environment. The introduction of a low level of noise into the system has an immediate effect on well-known strategies and we see that their willingness to react to defections causes a decrease in their fitness.

In previous work, we have identified the usefulness of *forgiving* type strategies in maintaining high degrees of cooperation in clean environments.

In the evolutionary experiments we see that *forgiveness* based on attempting to re-establish mutual cooperation is not consistently selected. We also see that the use of a longer memory is selected more readily but in most runs is not stable.

These results lead us to conclude that these approaches are superior to existing reactive strategies. However, they are not necessarily stable. Future work will involve further investigation into features that may promote stable cooperation in noisy environments.

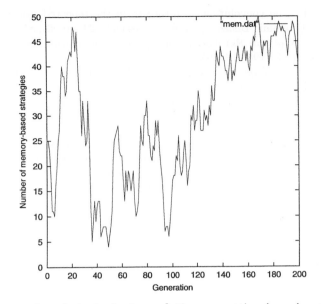

Fig. 2. Memory-based strategies in evolutionary setting in noisy environments

Ab
aut
of a
Inte
tems
MAS
tive c
cate v
over se
primiti
the ma
SyMPA
pletenes

1   Introdu

During the last
tended to propo
engineering. Mos
the specifications
(AUML). Neverth
ming languages a
1) Propose an age
signer to reduce t
(i.e. the designer s
through agents). 2)
putation which beco
code paradigm. In fa
computation over the
aging latency and ba
entities.

Many existing agen
endowed with cognitiv
lack clear standards to

V. Mařík et al. (Eds): CEEM
© Springer-Verlag Berlin Hei

References

[1] Dugatkin, L. A.: Do Guppies Play TIT FOR TAT during Predator Inspection Visits? Behavioral Ecology and Sociobiology 2 (3), (1987) 395-399

[2] Dugatkin, L. A.: N-person Games and the Evolution of Co-operation: A Model Based on Predator Inspection in Fish. Journal of Theoretical Biology 142, (1990) 123-135

[3] Lombardo, M.: Tree Swallows and TIT FOR TAT : Response to Koenig. Ethology and Sociobiology 11, (1990) 521-528

[4] Bendor, J., Mookherjee, D.: Institutional Structure and the Logic of Ongoing Collective Action. American Political Science Review 81, (1987) 129-154

[5] Sober, E.: Stable Cooperation in Iterated Prisoner's Dilemmas. Economics and Philosophy 8, (1992) 127-139

[6] Sen S.: Reciprocity: A foundational principle for promoting cooperative behavior among self-interested agents. Proceedings of the First International Conference on Multi–Agent Systems", (1995) MIT Press, (ed. Victor Lesser)

[7] Bazzan A., Bordini R.: Evolving Agents with Moral Sentiments in an Iterated Prisoner's Dilemma Exercise. 2nd Workshop on Game Theoretic and Decision Theoretic Agents (2000)

[8] Gmytrasiewicz P., Lisetti, C.: Using Decision Theory to Formalize Emotions in Multi-Agent Systems. Proceedings of the 4th International Conference on Multi-Agent Systems 2000, 391-392, Boston, MA

[9] Bendor, J., Kramer, R. M., Stout, S.: When in Doubt Cooperation in a Noisy Prisoner's Dilemma. Journal of Conflict Resolution 35, (4), (1991) 691-719

[10] Kahn, L. M., Murnighan, J.K Conjecture, uncertainty, and cooperation in prisoner's dilemma games: Some experimental evidence. Journal of Economic Behaviour & Organisation 22, (1993), 91-117

[11] M...
Jo...
[12] Mu...
Res...
[13] O'R...
of A...
[14] O'Ri...
in M...
and M...
[15] Axelr...
[16] Hoffm...
of Arti...
[17] Fundu...
The An...

to the rapid evolution of mobile computation which is poorly supported with formal languages and technologies. This work attempts to combine, in an unified language, the advantages of intelligent agent paradigm (e.g. autonomy and cognitive skills) with those of the concurrent languages such as the ambient calculus which has been recently proposed [2,3] as a theoretical framework for distributed and mobile objects/agents. This paper is organized as follows: the second section presents the related work concerning the AOP languages and the framework of ambient calculus. The third section provides the specifications of our language-CLAIM. It presents the agent definition and details its components. An example is also given to illustrate CLAIM specifications. The fourth section resumes the caracteristics of SyMPA, the platform that supports the CLAIM agents. The fifth section discusses the expressiveness of our language and studies the completeness property for our mobility implementation. The sixth section concludes our paper and outlines our perspectives towards an operational semantics of CLAIM.

2 Related Work

The language we propose - CLAIM - combines elements from the AOP languages (e.g. agents' internal state, reasoning and communication) with elements from the concurrent languages (e.g. agents' mobility).

2.1 Agent Oriented Programming Languages

In the literature there are several AOP languages that allow to represent agents' intelligence, autonomy and interactions.We'll briefly present the main characteristics of some of these languages.

AGENT-0 [9] agents have a mental state composed of **beliefs**, that represent the state of the world, the mental states and the capabilities of the agent and of the other agents, from agent's point of view, at certain times, **capabilities**, that represent what the agent can do at certain times and **decisions(choices) and commitments**, that determine the agent's actions, in accordance with his beliefs and with his anterior decisions. A decision is a commitment to oneself to perform an action. The agent's behavior in **AGENT-0** consists in reading the current messages, updating the mental state and executing the commitments for the current time. Although **AGENT-0** presents many useful elements, especially for agents' mental state and reasoning, important features such as planning, parallelism, and mobility are not taken into account. **Agent-K** has been proposed in [5] as an extension of **AGENT-0** that uses KQML for agents' communication. Nevertheless, still no parallelism and no mobility can be used.

AgentSpeak [11] agents are autonomous, distributed and have the following characteristics: **mental state** that includes beliefs, desires (goals), plans and intentions; reactive and proactive (goal-directed) **behavior**; **communication** through messages; **concurrent execution** of plans; **reasoning**

capabilities. Although in **AgentSpeak** the agents have a complex mental state, powerful reasoning capabilities, plans that are concurrently performed, the language doesn't allow the agents' mobility.

3APL [6] is a programming language for intelligent agents that combines the imperative and logic programming. An agent has a **mental state** composed of *beliefs, desires, plans* and *intentions*, a **goal directed** behavior and **reasoning capabilities** realized by the *practical reasoning rules*. In **3APL** the agents can execute several plans in parallel, but there are no mobility primitives.

Other significant specification languages such as **dMARS** [7], **APRIL** [4] and **VIVA** [10] have been proposed. In general, the main AOP languages allow to represent agents' intelligence and reasoning, several have plans executed in parallel and communication primitives, but the agents' mobility is not considered. In our language, we utilize cognitive elements for representing agents' mental state and reasoning, but for representing agents' migration, we defined mobility primitives inspired from the **ambient calculus** [2,3].

2.2   Mobility Formalism: The Ambient Calculus

An ambient is a bounded place where computation happens. An ambient has a name used to control the access to the ambient, a set of local processes and a set of sub-ambients. The ambients form a tree structure, being hierarchically organized. The ambients can move in and out of other ambients. An ambient moves as a whole, with all his components. For the migration, the ambients use the main mobility capabilities: *in, out* and *open*. There are also some additional mobility capabilities, such as *acid, mv in* or *mv out*.

In CLAIM, the agents are delimited places that have names, a set of local processes and a set of local sub-agents. Our mobility primitives are inspired from the **ambient calculus**'s mobility capabilities. But, in our language, it is possible to parameterize the mobility's granularity: we can have the migration of an agent as a whole, of an agent's clone or of a process enclosed in an ambient. In the **ambient calculus**, to execute a mobility operation, a structure condition must be verified (e.g. for *in*, the agents involved in the operation must be at the same level in the hierarchy). In our language, we maintain this condition, but in order to guarantee the security and yhe agents'autonomy, we added protocols for asking *enter* or *exit* permissions.

3   CLAIM - Language Specification

A CLAIM agent is an autonomous, intelligent and mobile entity that can be seen as a bounded place where the computation happens (similar to ambients) and has a list of local processes and a list of sub-agents. An agent has also some mental components such as knowledge, capabilities, goals, that allow a forward and backward reasoning and a goal driven behavior.

over several platforms and to move from one to another with respect to MASIF specifications. Our current work focuses on the operational semantics of CLAIM and the introduction of the security primitives as intrinsic elements of our language.

Acknowledgements

A part of this work was done in the context of a LAFMI[2] project. Authors would like to thank Christophe Fouquere and Patrick Baillot.

References

1. Luca Cardelli - Mobile Ambients Synchronisation, *SRC Technical Note*, Digital Equipment Corporation System Research Center, 1997.
2. Luca Cardelli, A. D. Gordon - Mobile Ambients, in *Foundations of Software Science and Computational Structures*, Maurice Nivat (Ed.), Lecture Notes in Computer Science, Vol. 1378, Springer, pages 140-155, 1998.
3. Luca Cardelli - Abstractions for Mobile Computation, in *Secure Internet Programming: Security Issues for Mobile and Distributed Objects*. Lecture Notes in Computer Science, Vol. 1603, Springer, pages 51-94, 1999.
4. K. L. Clark, N. Skarmeas and F. McCabe - Agents as Clonable Objects with Knowledge Base State. *in Proc. of ICMAS96*, AAAI Press, 1996.
5. Winton H. E. Davies, Peter Edwards - Agent-K: An Integration of AOP and KQLM, *Proceedings of the CIKM'94 Workshop on Intelligent Agents*, 1994.
6. K. V.Hindriks, F. S.deBoer, W.van der Hoek, J. J.Ch.Meyer - Agent Programming in 3APL, *Intelligent Agents and Multi-Agent Systems*, Vol. 2, pages 357-401, 1999.
7. M. d'Inverno, D. Kinny, M. Luck, M. Wooldridge - A Formal Specification of dMARS, *In Intelligent Agents IV:Procedings of the Fourth International Workshop on Agent Theories, Architectures and Languages*, Singh, Rao and Wooldridge(eds.), Lecture Notes in AI, 1365, pages 155-176, Springer-Verlag, 1998.
8. D. Milojicic, M. Breugst, I. Busse, J. Campbell, S. Covaci, B. Friedman, K. Kosaka, D. Lange, K. Ono, M. Oshima, C. Tham, S. Virdhagriswaran, J. White - MASIF, The OMG Mobile Agent System Interoperability Facility, 1998.
9. Yoav Shoham - Agent Oriented Programming, *Artifficial Intelligence (60)*, pages 51-92, 1993.
10. Gerd Wagner - VIVA Knowledge-Based Agent Programming, Preprint (on-line at: www.inf.fu-berlin.de/ wagner/VIVA.ps.gz), 1996.
11. D.Weerasooriya, Anand S. Rao, K. Ramamohanarao - Design of a Concurrent Agent-Oriented Language, *Intelligent Agents. Proceedings of First International Workshop on Agent THeories, Architectures and Languages (ATAL'94)*, number 890 in LNAI, Springer Verlag, 1994.

---

[2] http://lafmi.imag.fr

Tailoring an Agent Architecture to a Flexible Platform Suitable for Cooperative Robotics

Lars Kock Jensen[1], Yves Demazeau[1,2], and Bent Bruun Kristensen[1]

[1] The Maersk Mc-Kinney Moller Institute for Production Technology, University
of Southern Denmark
Campusvej 55, 5230 Odense M
{lkj,yves,bbk}@mip.sdu.dk
http://www.mip.sdu.dk/people/Staff/{lkj.html,yves.html,bbk.html}
[2]Laboratoire LEIBNIZ - Institut IMAG
46, avenue Felix Viallet 38031 Grenoble cx – France
Yves.Demazeau@imag.fr
http://www-leibniz.imag.fr/MAGMA/People/demazeau/demazeau.html

Abstract. Flexibility and adaptability are essential properties of intelligent manufacturing systems. However, it is a major challenge to realize these properties and the benefits of a flexible and adaptable system rarely make up for the expenses imposed by the process of designing and building such a system. The use of a cheap and flexible but yet realistic platform is a necessity if we want to overcome these challenges. In this paper we present a practical use of the hybrid agent architecture InteRRaP and introduce a flexible platform for prototyping multi-agent systems consisting of a heterogeneous set of cooperating robots. We address the transformation of the abstract agent model into a concrete model that obliges the demands of the technological platform and thus supports the implementation of the agent. We finally evaluate on the approach of tailoring an existing architecture to suit a specific application domain and discuss the resulting architecture for our prototype.

1   Introduction

This paper addresses the practical concerns in the development of a prototypical autonomous transportation system that has been based on an agent-oriented approach. We briefly address the topics present in the FLIP (FLexible Inter Processing) project [6] but focus on the tailoring of the InteRRaP [1] hybrid agent architecture and the design of the technological platform making up the prototype. We start out by introducing the problem domain of the transportation system.

V. Mařík et al. (Eds): CEEMAS 2003, LNAI 2691, pp. 363-372, 2003.

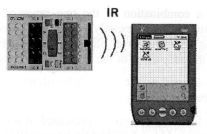

Fig. 2. The RCX on the left contains a 16 MHz H8/3292 Hitachi processor chip. It offers three input ports for sensory input and three output ports for actuator control. The PDA on the right contains a 33 MHz Motorola processor. The two devices communicate by infrared signals

We have deployed 2 mobile LEGOBots, 1 conveyer belt, 2 input stations, 1 output station, and 1 station with empty pallets. Each of the LEGOBots, both stationary and mobile, is constructed by an RCX brick and a Visor PDA that communicate with each other through their respective infrared (IR) ports. Each PDA has been equipped with a Wireless Ethernet Adapter and they are all configured for a peer-to-peer network.

2.1   Prototype Technology

The RCX shown in figure 2 is a small computer embedded in a LEGO brick. It provides input and output ports for sensors and actuators and in combination with additional LEGO components it can be transformed into a variety of robotics inventions. We have installed a Java Virtual Machine (VM) called leJOS on each RCX that enables us to develop the control system for the RCX in a high level language.

The Visor is a standard PDA running PalmOS 3.5. It has been equipped with a Xircom Wireless Ethernet Adapter that enables wireless communication between PDAs. On top of the PalmOS 3.5 operating system we have installed the IBM J9 VM that follows the Java 2 Micro Edition (J2ME) Connected Limited Device Configuration (CLDC) reference implementation. The IR sensors of the RCX and the PDA will be of particular interest in the design of our agent architecture, as reported in section 3.

2.2   Mobile LEGOBot

The design and construction of the mobile LEGOBot is out of the scope of this paper and can be found in [9], however, we briefly describe its basic principles. The RCX controls three motors, two for driving and one for the forklift. It receives input from a light sensor pointing downwards in order to read the color of the surface thus being able to identify landmarks in the environment. Touch sensors are used to detect the position of the fork as well as pallets and obstacles. A rotational sensor detects the rotation of the right wheel. If we apply the same speed, but not necessarily the same direction, to the two motors controlling the wheels, we can determine the position as well as orientation of the LEGOBot relative to some initial position. The Visor serves as the communicating device as well as the high level planner of the LEGOBot. The responsibility of motion planning, task scheduling, and social issues such as cooperation is hence put on the Visor and low level behaviors such as obstacle avoidance and simple movements are left for the RCX.

3   An Architecture for the Prototype Technology

3.1   InteRRaP Agent Architecture

The InteRRaP (Integration of Reactive behavior and Rational Planning) agent architecture shown in figure 3 is an architecture that integrates the qualities from the deliberative architectures, which rely on the BDI theory, as well as the qualities from the layered architectures such as Brooks' subsumption architecture.

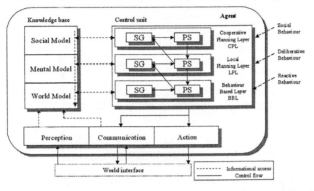

Fig. 3. The InteRRaP architecture contains a knowledge base and a control unit that have been split into three layers

The integration of reactivity and cognitive capabilities such as reasoning and planning combined with the ability to communicate makes this architecture suitable for designing autonomous interacting agents in dynamic multi-agent environments such as the FLIP system and the FORKS application presented in [1]. An InteRRaP agent consists of a world interface, a knowledge base, and a control unit. The world interface enables the agent to perceive and manipulate the environment as well as communicate with other agents. The world model is updated based on perceptual input and incoming messages. Changes to the world model are reflected upwards in the knowledge base in order to represent knowledge at different levels of abstraction. The three layers of the knowledge base correspond to the three layers of the control unit, that is, the behavior-based layer (BBL), the local planning layer (LPL), and the cooperative planning layer (CPL) respectively.

The BBL enables the agent to react to critical changes in the world model. For instance a mobile LEGOBot in the prototype should be able to avoid obstacles and thus be able to activate a so-called reactor pattern of behavior (PoB) without thinking too much. Routine situations such as moving from one point to another should also be performed in the BBL by so-called procedure PoBs. PoBs are triggered by changes in the world model (reactor PoBs) or they can be requested by the LPL (procedure PoBs). The LPL has access to the world model as well as the mental model that maintains the current goals as well as local beliefs and intentions of the agent. The

CPL enables the agent to cooperate with other agents by having joint plans. It can access the social model and retrieve beliefs about goals and commitments of other agents.

3.2   InteRRaP for the Prototype Technology

In this section we tailor the InteRRaP architecture in order to make it more suitable for the FLIP system and more realistic to the technological platform as shown in figure 4. We have decided to break up the InteRRaP model into two pieces, the Visor and the RCX, glued together by the IR interface. Conceptually this distinction seems reasonable and thus enhances the comprehensibility of the model. It also allows us to develop the control for the RCX independently of the Visor and the IR interface.

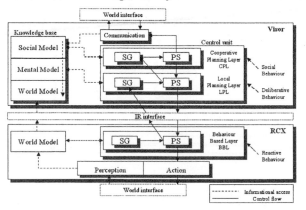

Fig. 4. The tailored InteRRaP architecture is split into an RCX component and a Visor component that are glued together by the IR interface

This modification has the following consequences:

- The communication module is moved to the Visor component.
- Both the Visor and the RCX components maintain a world model in order to minimize the amount of IR communication.

We regard communication as a social property of the agent and it therefore makes sense to move the communication module to the top layer of the InteRRaP model. However, communication may affect the lower layers and hence it should also be possible to revise beliefs in a top-down fashion.

3.3   Communication and Task Delegation

The communication module in the tailored InteRRaP architecture is located in the Visor component and has direct access to the world interface. Agents in general have to obey certain protocols if they want to communicate and our agents adopt the modified FIPA contract net protocol [7,8] pictured in figure 5.

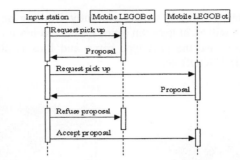

Fig. 5. The input station issues a *call for proposals* (cfp) to the participants (Mobile LEGOBots). The participants then return a proposal. The initiator only accepts one proposal

We adopt the protocol for two different scenarios. In the event of a full pallet that has to be collected a stationary LEGOBot will request a number of mobile LEGOBots to reply with a proposal on that task. The best proposal will be accepted and the mobile LEGOBot will be responsible for that task. When the full pallet has been collected the mobile LEGOBot has the possibility to delegate the remaining part of the task, i.e. replacing the full pallet with an empty one, to another mobile LEGOBot. This is also done by the contract net protocol. The protocol itself is encapsulated by the communication module and does not affect the remaining part of the architecture shown in figure 4. Only if a proposal has been accepted the knowledge base will be updated i.e. the exchange of proposals, preconditions, rejections, and so on is not reflected in the knowledge base.

4   Experiments and Evaluation

4.1   Prototype

The technological platform i.e. the Visor/RCX configuration allows us to build almost any robot that one could imagine and even at a very reasonable price. Unfortunately the flexibility of the LEGO bricks also results in rather inaccurate robots. The limited amount of input and output ports on the RCX restricts the use of sensors. In our case we can only afford to use one input port for measuring wheel rotations on the mobile LEGOBot (figure 6). This means that the LEGOBot is only capable of driving straight or turning on the spot if it has to maintain its location in the environment. If we tell the LEGOBot to move along a smooth curve it simply looses the orientation. Even if we do apply the same speed to the two motors a small error will inevitably occur and as time goes by the position will become more and more inaccurate. Therefore the LEGOBots frequently have to adjust their position. This is done when known landmarks are encountered in the environment. Another shortcoming is the speed. Currently the speed is only about 5 mm per second. Even though speed has never been a key requirement it makes testing much more difficult.

Experiments have shown that with the current speed we can only perform two pick up and replace tasks within the battery lifetime. This is not enough to conduct any serious experiments with respect to multi-robot collaboration in intelligent manufacturing systems. However, we are currently working on a new design for a mobile LEGOBot that will be at least ten times faster. It relies on input from a camera that has been placed above the prototype setup and thus is able to determine the positions of the mobile LEGOBots.

Fig. 6. The mobile LEGOBot is on the left. The conveyer belt and input station are on the right

4.2   Architecture

The prototype consists of 2 mobile and 5 stationary LEGOBots the latter being of different types. Each LEGOBot is based on the Visor/RCX configuration. The main focus with respect to the prototype has been on the design and development of the mobile LEGOBots. The decision of tailoring the InteRRaP architecture instead of another architecture has been biased by this focus i.e. the chosen architecture should at least accommodate the design of a mobile robot. Another major bias was the technological platform that forced us to search for an architecture that we could dissect and map to the RCX and the Visor without violating the conceptual model. The InteRRaP agent architecture seemed to be one of the only rare hybrid architectures that could meet these requirements.

The experiences with respect to the tailoring process have been really positive. We know that the InteRRaP architecture is well tested and hence the foundation for our work is rock solid. We merely had to be careful about not corrupting the architecture.

5   Conclusion

5.1   FLIP Characteristics

The technological platform presented in this paper consists of physical autonomous agents (LEGOBots) represented by hardware and software. Below we summarize some of the characteristics of the FLIP prototype and address its strengths and weaknesses.

An advanced, understandable, and working platform that relies on standard technologies such as Java and general wireless communication.

A flexible platform that both supports development of heterogeneous robotic prototypes and accommodates extensions with respect to functionality and further addition of agents.

It is still only a prototype. Even though we are getting much closer, the full deployment to the real world application is still missing.

Our work includes a specific realization of the InteRRaP architecture with a distinct separation of low and high level behavior. It is straightforward to adopt this architecture for other applications based on this particular technological platform.

5.2   MAS Results

In this paper we have tailored the InteRRaP agent architecture for a specific technological platform and applied it in the design of a set of mobile cooperating robots. Below we characterize the tailored architecture and address some of the strengths and weaknesses of this architecture with respect to general MAS issues.

The tailored architecture encapsulates the inter-agent communication in the cooperative part of the agent. This is due to the technological platform but it also emphasizes that there should be a distinction between communication and simple sensory input.

The local and the cooperative planning layer of the InteRRaP architecture accommodates the integration of a state-of-the-art local or cooperative planner respectively.

The agent interaction protocols can easily be replaced or extended because of the encapsulation of communication.

The approach of tailoring an existing architecture to suit a specific application domain has proven to offer a low risk and time efficient way of designing MAS applications that inherently benefit from the features of the general architecture.

5.3   Perspectives

Currently we have only adopted the InteRRaP agent architecture for the mobile LEGOBots but we intend to adopt the architecture for the stationary agents as well.

In addition, since the prototype only consists of very few agents and since they only provide one kind of service, we have only employed a simple organizational model that associates a role to each agent. There is no need for different groups or communities of agents at the moment but we should investigate this area if we decide to extend the prototype to include other scenarios of the LEGO manufacturing system.

Finally, from a MAS point of view, it is our strong belief that too many agent architectures have been proposed in the past, discussing their respective merits solely on their theoretical properties. It is our belief that the range of agent architectures is large enough so that for every problem in every domain, one would find a sufficient basis and tailor it for one's purpose.

Acknowledgements

This research was supported in part by the Danish National Center for IT Research, Center for Pervasive Computing Project No. 212, Flexible Inter Processing (FLIP) and the A. P. Møller and Chastine Mc-Kinney Møller Foundation. We thank the LEGO Company and the SWEAT group at the Maersk Mc-Kinney Moller Institute for collaboration and contributions to this article.

References

[1]   K. Fischer, J.P. Muller and M. Pischel: Readings in Agents, A Pragmatic BDI Architecture, Morgan Kaufmann Publishers, San Francisco, California, 2001.

[2]   Gerhard Weiss (edit.): Multiagent Systems: A Modern Approach to Distributed Artificial Intelligence, The MIT press, 1999, pp. 27-77.

[3]   H. Baumgärtel, S. Bussmann, and M. Klosterberg: Combining Multi-Agent Systems and Constraint Techniques in Production Logistics, in: *Proc. of the 6th Annual Conf. on AI, Simulation and Planning in High Autonomy Systems*, La Jolla, Ca, USA, 1996, pp. 361-367.

[4]   S. Bussmann, N.R. Jennings, M. Wooldridge: On the Identification of Agents in the Design of Production Control Systems, in: P. Ciancarini, M.J. Wooldridge (eds.), *Agent-Oriented Software Engineering*, LNCS 1957, Springer-Verlag: Berlin, Germany, 2001, pp.141-162.

[5]   R.A. Brooks: A Robust Layered Control System For a Mobile Robot, *IEEE Journal of Robotics and Automation*, 1986.

[6]   L.K. Jensen: A Multiagent System Methodology for Simulations, Prototypes, and Real Life Applications in Production System Domains. *Master thesis*. The Maersk Mc-Kinney Moller Institute for Production Technology, University of Southern Denmark, September 2002.

[7]   K. Cetnarowicz and J. Kozlak: Multi-agent System for Flexible Manufacturing Systems Management, Insitute of Computer Science, AGH – University of Mining and Metallurgy, Al. Mickiewicza 30, 30-059 Krakow, Poland, *Proceedings of the Second International Workshop of Central and Eastern Europe on Multi-Agent Systems CEEMAS'01*. Springer Verlag.

[8]   Foundation for Intelligent Physical Agents: http://www.fipa.org/, *FIPA Interaction Protocol Library Specification*, 2001.

[9]   B. Jensen: Konstruktion og eksperimentering med LegoBots til simulering af et industrielt system, *Bachelor project*, The Maersk Mc-Kinney Moller Institute for Production Technology, University of Southern Denmark, 2002.

Airports for Agents:
An Open MAS Infrastructure for Mobile Agents

Jan Tožička

Gerstner Laboratory, Agent Technology Group, Department of Cybernetics
Faculty of Electrical Engineering, Czech Technical University in Prague,
Technická 2, 166 27, Prague 6, Czech Republic
jan.tozicka@matfyz.cz

Abstract. *Airports for Agents*[1] (AA) is an implemented distributed multi-agent infrastructure designed for dynamic and unstable Internet environment. The infrastructure consists of platforms called *Airports* that enable agents to communicate together and to be persistent. Furthermore, the Airports allow agents to migrate trough the system and to use local resources. Any Airport can host any agent from the network, therefore we considered high requirements for the security. Network of Airports can dynamically change in the time as new Airports connect to the system, or disconnect. We designed distributed stochastic algorithm keeping the system connected, because AA has no central element. The agent migration brings a communication problem known in the field of distributed systems: where to find the agent I have been communicated with, previously, while he changed his location (platfrom)? We present *Kept Connection* as a transparent solution of this problem. System is designed to be distributed over large amount of computers.

1   Introduction

Using distributed MAS with mobility can reduce network traffic and the waste of the time caused by the network slack. A stable, widely accessible and extensible infrastructure seems to be necessary to get maximum of the potentials of multi-agent systems.

We will use the following terminology. A *MAS platform* is an empty system without any agent. A *MAS* can be either a platform with implemented agents, or only several agents communicating together (in this case the MAS platform is the operating system). *Distributed MAS infrastructure* consist of several MAS platforms running on several host computers. If agents can migrate form one host platform to another in the distributed MAS infrastructure we say, that it

---

[1] Project team was led by Mgr. Roman Neruda, CSc., and included also these members: Jaroslav Kameník, Tomáš Kasl, Eva Poučková, Pavel Socha and Roman Vaculín. Project was developed at Charles University, Faculty of Mathematics and Physics, Prague, Czech Republic. The implementation in Java language has been demonstrated with several demo-agents. More information can be found at web site http://letiste.zde.cz.

V. Mařík et al. (Eds): CEEMAS 2003, LNAI 2691, pp. 373–382, 2003.

is an infrastructure supporting the agent *mobility*. An platform supporting the mobility is *open* if unknown agents can come over the network. All components of open platform defending the host computer and other agents against misbehavior and cheating of hostile agents compile platform *security*. Distributed MAS with the elements, which can shutdown and start anytime or are connected to the network only temporarily, is called *dynamic*.

In this paper, we present open dynamic distributed MAS infrastructure supporting the agent mobility called *Airports for Agents*.

The rest of the paper is organized as follows: in section 2 we define main features of the distributed MAS; in section 3 we discuss our implementation of the *Airports for Agent* infrastructure; in section 4 we compare AA infrastructure with the most known MAS; in section 5 we present several main points of our further work and finally we conclude in section 6.

2   Distributed Multi-agent System

We consider these requirements for MAS:

- **Agent communication.** Two potentially the most used types of agent communication are message-based communication and communication using the function calling.
- **Agent persistency.** Agent does not have to carry about his data and his existence as whole.

Additionally, we consider these requirements for the distributed MAS, that has the potential to be widely used:

- **Agent mobility.** Agents can easily move trough the system with their data.
- **Openness.** Unknown agents can come to the host connected to the system.
- **Security.** In open MAS platform, security against agents misbehavior or cheating is very important. Generally, there are four types of security [6, 7]:
  - security for the host against the agents,
  - security for other agents,
  - security for the agents against the host, and
  - security for the underlying network.
  Researchers have found serious solution only for first two types. Our security model also focuses on these two issues. The enlargement of current security model to include remaining issues is one of the points of our future work.
- **Dynamics.** The set of elements of distributed MAS changes in the time.
- **Complete distribution.** Distributed system has no central element. This requirement is necessary when we design system distributed over unstable network, e.g. Internet, and consider its dynamics.
- **Accessibility.** All on-line platforms are findable for all agents in the system.

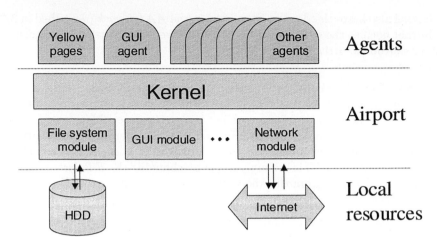

Fig. 1. High-level Airport architecture. Two main components of an airport are kernel and modules. Kernel provides necessary services for the agents, and facilitates them access to modules to access additional services

3   Airports for Agents

AA platform provides all the infrastructure allowing the MAS designers to concentrate on agent's functional core implementation.

AA infrastructure consists of the elements called Airports. Every Airport is denoted by an unique identifier. Airports are distributed and connected over a network. The topology of the Airports' connection is dynamic. Airports can connect to the network or disconnect anytime. Dynamics of AA topology is described in subsection 3.2.

The *Airports for Agents* infrastructure was implemented in Java language.

Let us describe main features of AA infrastructure in the following subsections.

3.1   System Architecture

The high-level architecture of an Airport is illustrated in figure 1. Airport composes of kernel and several modules. Agents can be understood as the top level of the architecture.

Kernel. Airport's kernel provides necessary services for the agents' life-cycle:

- agents creation,
- agents migration between Airports (see 3.4),
- inter-agent message-based communication (see 3.6),
- agent persistency, etc.

Kernel also keeps the Airport connected in the *AA network* (described in 3.2).

Kernel notifies the agents about important events via bit-based signals, e.g. system shutdown, arrive of new message, etc.

Modules. Kernel functionality is extended by plug-in modules. They are used for accessing local resources, such as filesystem, network communication, user interface, etc. These resources either do not have to be accessible in every Airport or can be accessible in different way. For example, consider a disk less station. It is necessary to fulfil agents necessity to backup data in another way, e.g. storing them on a remote disk. This is simply made by changing the *FileSystem* module. And agent is shielding from the knowledge of these unsubstantial details.

Agents. Agent's access to kernel and module functionality is controlled by access policy.

From the Airport view, all the agents are treated the same way based on individual access rights. There are no privileged system-agents. The only one exception is *Yellow Pages Agent* (described in 3.7), which is known also under his alias name in the Airport.

A module can offer agents several interfaces. One of them is often used for managing the resource and the access policy. Only agents responsible for the resource can access this interface. In our system, we call them *System agents*, although, from the Airport view, they are only ordinary agents. E.g. The *FileSystem* module offers two interfaces. First one is used for agent's direct access to the files on the HDD. This access is controlled by agent's access rules. These rules can be changed only using the second interface. It is accessible only by the *FileSystem System Agent*.

3.2   AA Dynamics

AA infrastructure is designed to be widely used, also by users, which has dial-up or another type of *not-still-online* internet connection.

Every Airport platform connected to the Internet should be findable, to be useable by other agents. Because we assume not to operate any central element, we decided to create a network connecting all Airports. This network is called *AA network*. So, agent can find the Airport with desired services, if it exists and is on-line. We prefer this approach to store the list of all other Airports because the *AA network* consists only of the Airports currently on-line. The communication traffic is smaller when a new Airport is connecting to the *AA network* and when an agent is looking for an accessible Airport. Of course, some traffic is necessary for *AA network* updating.

Note that, *AA network* is only logical network and its topology has no relation to the physical network connecting the host computers.

When a newly installed Airport wants to connect to the *AA network*, it needs to know at least one address of any Airport already connected. It is used for searching other Airports and connect into the *AA network*. It is important to create a network which will satisfy requirements for attainability of all other Airports even if several Airports will shutdown. Therefore, we specify these two main requirements on created network: maximize the number of Airports which can shutdown at one moment and minimize the network traffic during creating and updating the network.

This problem can be converted to the graph theory problem of creating and maintaining connected directed graph. In the graph, the nodes represent Airport platforms and the set of edges is defined by the relation 'is connected with'. In the best case, the created graph is k-connected, where k is number of Airports which is every Airport connected with. It ensures that the graph remains connected even as any $(k-1)$ Airports will shutdown at one moment. There has not been found an algorithm for creating and maintaining such a graph in distributed (*AA network* has no central element) and dynamic (Airports are continually connecting and disconnecting) environment. Therefore, we designed distributed stochastic algorithm keeping the *AA network* connected.

Our algorithm keeps with the list of neighborhoods also information about all their neighborhoods. When an adjacent Airport disconnects, some of his neighborhoods are chosen for his replacement. From time to time, the list of adjacent Airports is consolidated not to contain needless platforms (e.g. that ones, which are neighborhoods of other adjacent Airport).

3.3   Security Features

In AA infrastructure, strong security for the host [6, 7] is implemented.

The security model is based on the information fortress model [3] where the host is protected by maintaining a closed system accessed through well defined and controlled interfaces. In *AA platform*, all local resources are maintained by modules. The modules know the *access rules* for the restrictions of agent access to the resources. User can define specific rules for every known agent (agent, whose classes has been already installed) and default rules for other agents.

When newly coming agent needs to access other services, he has three main possibilities how to achieve it. Firstly, he can try to negotiate direct access with the system agent administering this service. Further, he can request another agent for facilitation of undirect access. Or finally, he can request the user to permit the access to desired services; but it is possible only if agent has access to the user interface.

Protection of other agents uses basic Java feature, that programs have no direct access to the memory. Therefore agent can not affect other agent even though there are implemented as threads of one application.

As a protection of CPU overloading by hostile agent runs in a single thread created by the kernel during agent creation. Agents can not create other threads.

3.4   Agent's Mobility

Mobility is the agent's ability to autonomously migrate from one MAS platform to another and to use their distributed resources locally. This approach reduces network traffic and agent's response can be faster then usage of far access to the data.

Mobility is almost necessary in dynamic environment. Consider, for example, an agent which needs to be still on-line. In our platform, an agent receives a system signal when the system is going to shutdown. Therefore, the agent can save his work and safely move to another Airport.

AA infrastructure offers agents an easy way to be transported.

The process of agent's migration consists of two phases. In the first phase, the agent asks his current Airport for moving him to the target Airport. Current Airport ask target Airport whether it will accept this agent, or not. If the target Airport accepts him, the transport of agent's data begins. It is necessary to transport agent's *Kept Connections* (see 3.6), private data, sometimes also agent's classes, etc. During this process, agent is still running and finishes his work, e.g. processes unread messages in mailbox, stores uncompleted work. If something happens agent can still decide to not move. Otherwise, agent confirms his decision to move. After his ending, his private files and identity are moved.

AA infrastructure warrants that agent will be at exactly one Airport after the moving. Even if communication error occurs at any time, or any Airport will shutdown.

There is not implemented any security for the agent against the host because agent decides where he want to move and moreover, only migration within AA infrastructure is currently implemented.

3.5   Agent Life-Cycle

An Agent's life begins by his creation. New unique (in the whole system) ID is generated and assigned to the agent during the creation. We use proprietary ID semantics different then the FIPA name. The ID does not change during whole agent's life.

The agent can freely migrate trough the system or fall asleep waiting any system signal. Weak persistency is warranted during these actions.

When agent finishes his work and decides to die, his identity and all his private files are removed from the system.

3.6   Agent Communication

Only message based communication between the agents is implemented in AA infrastructure. It is implemented in two ways.

Firstly, it is common agent communication protocol compliant with FIPA ACL standard [5]. Agent can simply send a message specifying receiver's unique ID and receiver's current Airport (only ID is necessary if the sender and the receiver are on the same Airport).

Second type of communication solves a problem known from distributed systems with migration of components. Problem is how to find the agent I have been communicated with, a while ago, if he is not at his previous position (he moved away)? One possible solution is the *tracking*. The *signs* with new location are put when any agent leaves local platform. Following these *sings*, starting in the last known position, allows to find the desired agent. This solution does not work in dynamic environment, because any host in the agent's track can be currently off-line. Therefore we designed and implemented another solution of this problem called *Kept Connection*. It enables two agents to create a communication channel between them. This connection is kept between them even as they migrate trough the *AA network*.

Kept Connection allows agent also to address his partner only by his ID. No additional information about his (current or previous) location is necessary. It also ensures that the message will be delivered if the receiver is accessible.

In the Airport kernel, there is an *address book* associated with every currently presented agent. It contains all agents, which agent has *Kept Connection* established with.

Agent advices to the platform, that he would like to establish new *Kept Connection* with an agent, by adding his current address to the address book. The connection does not become active unless the second agent also adds the address of the first one to his address book. Once the connection is created, the platform itself updates addresses of agents in the address book.

When the agent wants to move to other platform, all address books of agents in his address book are notified about it. They tag appropriate connection to be temporarily unavailable. Messages sent through this connection are blocked until the migration is over or the specified time is out. End of moving is notified from old platform, if the moving has not succeed, or from the new platform if the moving has succeed.

Additional network communication load during moving can be a disadvantage of this solution mainly if it is used within a group of agent which moves a lot (e.g. group of search agent looking for a resource). In this case, it is better to use an immobile agent, which agents can communicate with using common messages, because *Kept Connection* is not obligated.

Any agent can cancel his *Kept Connection* with other agent. This way, he can estop the harassment and tracking (see [7]) by the other agent.

Both types of communication ensure that the agent named as message sender has really sent this message, because agent cannot change this information. Therefore, agent cannot send a message and make target agent believe, that the message has been sent by another agent.

Messages are stored in the agent message-box queue and the agent is responsible for managing this queue, e.g. in the cases of moving or shutting down. The message-box allows to rigidly separate the kernel and the agent's body. It seems to be important because of the security.

3.7   Facilitators

In [5], there are presented two facilitator agents, which are also often used in MAS: Directory Facilitator (DF) and Agent Management System (AMS).

In our system, DF is presented by *Yellow Pages Agent* which should be at every Airport and allows each agent to register to his database of locally running agents. Every agent can also make public some of his services which he want to offer other agents. *Yellow Pages Agent* has always the alias 'YellowPages' associated with him. Therefore, newly created agent can send him a message without any other a priori knowledge about the system, e.g. ID of any agent. He simply fill in the 'YellowPages' string as the receiver ID.

In Airports terminology, AMS is *White Pages Agent*. He manages list of agents which could be possibly created on local Airport. In Java terminology, he knows which agent classes are installed and can be used for agent creation.

We recognize another type of facilitator agent. *Black Pages Agent* manages a list of agents, which has been present on the local Airport and moved away, with information where they have moved to. It enables tracking of agents. But only in the case that every Airport in the track is currently on-line. Better and transparent solution to this problem is offered by the *Kept Connection* (see 3.6).

All of these facilitators are ordinary agents with a small exception of *Yellow Pages Agent*, which has its alias in the Airport and this alias is the same everywhere. All three services provided by these agents are currently implemented in one agent.

Facilitator agents know only registered agents and types. These registrations are voluntary, therefore agent can make himself invisible to other agents. He can use it as defense against harassment (see [7]).

4   Comparison to the Related Work

In this section we will try to point the main differences between our infrastructure and some other MAS.

4.1   JADE

JADE [8] is often used as undistributed MAS, even if it enables to be distributed. JADE does not offers any possibility how to find another JADE platform. Therefore, if we need to keep the system connected, agent or user has to carry about it. AA keeps the hosts connected in the *AA network* and the user has to provide only one address of on-line Airport after the installation.

Agents in JADE system can define behaviors, which are evoked when appropriate message arrives. AA infrastructure uses simpler and possibly faster way to handle messages. Every agent has his queue, where all his messages are stored. This simple solution can be expanded to implement JADE's behaviors or other more sophisticated solution.

JADE Agents can run their own threads. AA platform does not allow it because of the security against hostile agents, which wants to overload the system (no other solution in Java has been found).

4.2   Aglets

The agents in Aglets platform [2, 10] are programmed using event-driven scheme, as in windows system programming. They implement only handlers which are evoked when appropriate event occurs. It enables to simply create a reactive agent which responds to incoming messages. But the creation of more sophisticated algorithm using some communication protocol can be more difficult. In comparison, in AA platform, every agent has the message-box where all incoming messages are stored. Agent can pick out a message anytime. It enables to simply create agent implementing some communication protocol, although the creation of a simple reactive agent can be more difficult then in Aglets platform.

Aglets platform solves security problems similar to the problems solved in AA platform. Authors of Aglets platform defined several supported local resources and solved the security policy for them [9]. The Airport kernel does not contain any security for the local resources access. It allows agents only to access several main services. The modules are responsible for the access policy for all local resources, e.g. filesystem, network, etc. This solution seems to be more flexible, because everybody can write the module with specific security policy or the module accessing specific resource (possibly currently unknown), and no changes to the Airport kernel has to be made.

5   Future Work

In present time, implementation of the next version of CPlanT project [4] is created using AA infrastructure.

Our further work will be focused to several main direction: cooperation with other MAS, *Enhanced Kept Connection* and enhanced security model.

Cooperation with other FIPA compliant MAS infrastructures (e.g. JADE [8] or Agentcities [1]) is considered at two layers. Firstly, communication with the agents residing there. It is already designed in current architecture, only implementation of some support functionality is necessary. Secondary, migration between both infrastructures. Only logical migration of agents is considered (migration without agent code).

Enhanced Kept Connection, which implements contact transmission (one agent gives the second one the contact to the third one) and other services, could be fully functional replacement of addressing using receiver address.

Enhancing the security to include the protection of agents against the host and the protection of underlying network. Better security against CPU overloading should not be possible without also changing the Java virtual machine.

Also improving of algorithm keeping the *AA network* connected is a permanent challenge for us.

6   Conclusion

Open dynamic distributed MAS infrastructure with high security level has been presented. It supports agent mobility and weak form of persistency.

To the best of our knowledge, *Airports for Agents* infrastructure contains two features which have not been presented ever before in MAS context: *Kept Connection* and *AA network* (ensuring infrastructure connectivity).

The *Kept Connection* has been presented as an arbitrary replacement of agent tracking. It is transparent, simple to use and cannot be abused for harassment or tracking by a hostile agent.

Connectivity of dynamic *AA network* is ensured using distributed stochastic algorithm. It allows agents to find any Airport with desired services if any is currently on-line.

References

[1]   Agentcities: http://www.agentcities.org.
[2]   Aglets: http://www.trl.ibm.com/aglets/.
[3]   Blakley B. (1996): The Emperor's Old Armor. *Proceedings of New Security Paradigms Workshop.*
[4]   CPlanT: Multi-Agent System for Planning Humanitarian Relief Operations. http://agents.felk.cvut.cz/cplant.
[5]   FIPA: Foundation for Intelligent Physical Agents. http://www.fipa.org.
[6]   Gray R. S. (1996): Agent Tcl: A Flexible and Secure Mobile-Agent System. *Proceedings of Fourth Annual Tcl/Tk Workshop (TCL 96).*
[7]   Greenberg M. S., Byington J. C., Harper D. G. (1998): Mobile Agents and Security. *IEEE Communicitaions.*
[8]   JADE: Programmer's Guide. http://sharon.cselt.it/projects/jade/.
[9]   Karjoth G., Lange D. B., Oshima M. (1998): A Security Model for Aglets. *Mobile Agents and Security*, pp. 188–205
[10] Lange D. B., Oshima M. (1997): Java Agent API: Programming and Deploying Aglets with Java, *Addison-Wesley.*

Beyond Prototyping in the Factory of Agents

Rem Collier, Gregory O'Hare, Terry Lowen, and Colm Rooney

University College Dublin
Belfield, Dublin 4, Ireland
{Rem.collier,gregory.ohare,terry.lowen,colm.rooney}@ucd.ie

Abstract. This paper introduces Agent Factory, a cohesive framework supporting a structured approach to the development and deployment of agent-oriented applications. We describe Agent Factory together with an accompanying agent development methodology. We detail the key attributes of Agent Factory, namely: visual design, design reuse, behaviour enactment, migration, and ubiquity. Agent Factory functionality is exercised by way of a case study. We offer cross comparison of our system with exemplar agent prototyping environments.

1 Introduction

The provision of cohesive support for the construction of multi-agent systems is essential if agent technologies are to be employed within industry. To this end, it is vital that software engineering frameworks be devised that promote structured approaches to the development and deployment of agent-oriented applications. This paper introduces one such framework, the *Agent Factory System* [5] [14].

2 The Agent Fabrication Process

Agent Factory provides a cohesive framework for the development and deployment of agent-oriented applications. Specifically, it delivers extensive support for the creation of Belief-Desire-Intention (BDI) agents [5] which embrace the Intentional Stance. As is illustrated in this fig 1, Agent Factory is organised into two core environments: the Agent Factory Development Environment, and the Agent Factory Run-Time Environment. The former environment delivers a set of Computer-Aided Software Engineering (CASE) tools that support the Agent Fabrication Process, whilst the latter delivers support for the deployment of agent-oriented applications over a wide range of network-enabled Java-compliant devices.

The Agent Factory system constitutes a membrane within which several distinct layers exist. The innermost layers provide the necessary deductive apparatus to execute BDI agents and an Agent Communication Language (ACL) to facilitate inter-agent communication. Enveloping this is *the Agent Factory Development*

V. Mařík et al. (Eds): CEEMAS 2003, LNAI 2691, pp. 383–393, 2003.

Environment a cohesive toolset that assists in the various stages of design, implementation and deployment. The outermost layer provides an associated methodology, the *Agent Fabrication Process (AFP),* which imposes a partial ordering upon the invocation of such tools and consequently oversees a logical and disciplined sequence of steps that should be followed when implementing an agent-oriented application with Agent Factory.

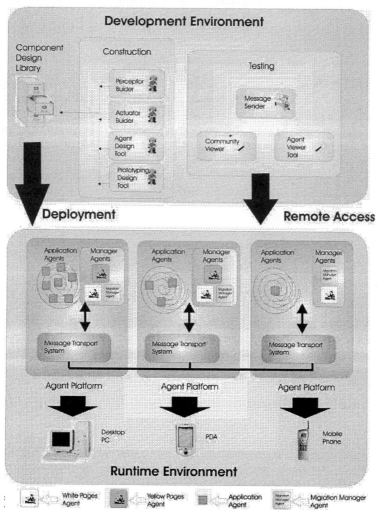

Fig 1. The Agent Factory Framework

Much recent work has been undertaken in the area of agent methodologies including: Agent UML [1], GAIA [22] Prometheus [16], ROADMAP [11] and MaSE [8]. The Agent Fabrication Process is complete in the sense that it offers end-to-end support for the development process and in this respect is similar to Prometheus. However the Agent Fabrication Process is closely coupled with the Agent Factory Development Environment and unlike many agent methodologies that are largely paper based we offer software tool support for all development stages but analysis. For this we use Behaviour diagrams that are currently without tool support.

The AFP is comprised of 5 broad steps namely: *Ontology Definition; Actuator and Perceptor Building; Agent Coding ; Agent Testing; Application Deployment.* Figure 2 depicts these stages and specifically the tool support provided for each stage. This paper merely focuses upon the support for agent coding, testing and deployment.

3   Development Environment

Tool-based support for all steps of the Agent Fabrication Process (AFP) is delivered through an integrated toolset, the Agent Factory (AF) Development Environment which focuses upon the development of various components and their composition into coherent *agent designs*.

BDI agent types are realised through some mental state and an associated agent interpreter that manipulates the mental state, allowing the agent to reason about how best to act. The mental state itself is modelled using multi-modal temporal logic. Within AF, this logic is realised as a set of programming constructs within a purpose-built agent programming language. Details of this programming language can be found in [5]. From an agent construction perspective, agents are viewed as instances of agent designs. These designs are a combination of an *agent program,* written in the above agent programming language, and a set of actuators and perceptors. Actuators represent the primitive actions that are directly executable by an agent. Perceptors deliver the mechanism by which raw sensory data is transformed and encoded in the agent's mental state.

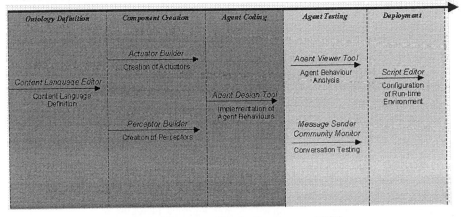

Fig 2: The Agent Fabrication Process (AFP)

Currently Agent Factory provides tools that support: the definition of ontology's, the development of actuator and preceptor units, the coding of agent programs, and the testing and deployment of published agent designs. The components that underpin an agent design (namely, the actuators, and perceptors), and the designs themselves are stored within a specific module of the Development Environment known as the

Component Design Library (CDL). Agent designs that are published to a CDL may, at some later point in time, be deployed into the Run-Time Environment using the *Deployment Tool*. Currently, the CDL is realised as a set of folders that are stored within an instance of the Concurrent Versions System (CVS) [7], a client-server version-control system.

3.1   Reuse in Agent Factory

An agent is realised as an instance of an *agent design*. Many agent designs have common functionality, for example, support for agent communication is delivered through a set of actuators (one for each communicative act), and through a perceptor that monitors the agents message queue. Consequently, any agent design that requires inter-agent communication must include these components.

This motivates the inclusion, of support for the reuse of agent designs through *inheritance*. To this end, an agent design is decomposed into a set of *agent classes* that are organised into a *class hierarchy*. Each agent class specifies a set of components and a partial agent program. This class is basically a templated solution that may be extended as required in the subclasses. An example class hierarchy can be found on the left-hand side of figure 3. The right-hand side of the tool presents the developer with a structured set of views for editing the agent design. To instantiate an agent from a design, the developer must first publish the design. This involves the compilation of the agent design from its constituent agent classes. Thus, the compiled agent design is a union of all the partial agent programs and components specified within the relevant agent classes. Each agent class specifies a set of components and a partial agent program. From this perspective, an agent design is viewed as a *path* within the class hierarchy. The construction of agent classes from prefabricated components is central to the Agent Fabrication Process presented in section 2. This forces an ordering on the use of the tools provided within the Development Environment where a component must be built before it may be associated with an agent class. A drawback of inheritance arises from cases where two agent designs use the same code, but do not share the same parent class in the class hierarchy. Similar issues have commonly arisen in Object-Oriented Programming [17]. One accepted solution is not to use inheritance, but instead to use *composition*. An agent design can be viewed as an aggregation of pre-existing modules and protocols that are joined through *integration code*.

3.2   Visualising Behaviour Enactment

A second key feature of Agent Factory is tool support for the visualisation of agents, offering support for the testing phase. Agent Factory provides tools that allow the developer to explore and monitor how the agents will react to various potential scenarios. Currently, three tools have been developed to monitor the enactment of agent behaviours, namely: the Agent Viewer Tool, the Community Monitor, and the Message Sender. Agent Factory also provides visual agent programming tools that assist the user in creating agent designs that may be published and deployed.

3.3   Visual Tools for Agent Design

Agent interactions play a crucial role in many Multi-agent Systems. As a result, a range of graphical formalisms have been adopted that allow agent developers to abstract away from implementation details and focus on the core aspects of such interactions, e.g. Petri Nets, Timed Petri Nets [6], Agent UML (AUML) [1]. In order to facilitate the fabrication and deployment of collaborative agent communities, Agent Factory provides a tool that assists agent developers in the creation of agent interaction protocols through the application of such graphical formalisms.

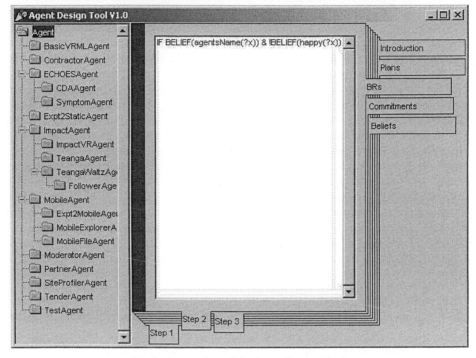

Fig 3: Screenshot of the Agent Design Tool

The *AF Protocol Tool* is a graphical tool that allows users to diagrammatically construct agent interaction protocols, which are then compiled into usable agent designs. Three components provide the core of the protocol editing functionality: The *Interface Component* is the medium by which the user views and edits the protocol.

The *Model Component* stores the elements that make up a protocol diagram (e.g. messages, threads) and the associations between them. The *Semantic Checker* maintains the *model* and its consistency, in the sense that it enforces the implementation of the protocol meta-model (i.e. the rules that constrain elements and associations within a protocol diagram, e.g. the AUML interaction protocol specification). The flow of control is as follows: Any non-cosmetic user updates to the protocol (i.e. those that affect the *model*) are forwarded from the Interface to the Semantic Checker. The Semantic Checker then queries the current state of the *model* and evaluates the user's request in light of this information and the constraints set down in the meta-model. If the request is successful the *model* is updated and communicated to the Interface component, which displays the result to the user. If rejection occurs the Interface is also notified and can inform the user of such.

The Protocol Tool uses a modular event-based architecture written in Java. The loose coupling between the system components facilitates a *plug-and-play* approach. This entails that we are not constrained to a single implementation of the Interface, *model*, or the Semantic Checker. We could, for example, alter how the user interacts with the protocol without changing the underlying protocol representation, or change the underlying protocol representation without changing how the user interacts with the protocol. This permits flexibility in the types of graphical formalism applied.

Within this architecture, the components themselves have been implemented in such a fashion as to provide as much flexibility as possible, so that different graphical formalisms may be applied without needing to alter or replace the components. The current Interface utilises an XML initialisation file that defines what protocol elements to include and their associated details, e.g. display classes, events generated, menu icons. This initialisation file has a corresponding Constraints Definition File (CDF) that defines the meta-model. The Model component accepts any {Component, Component, Association} 3-tuple and stores their details in key-value pairs. The Semantic Checker is implemented as an AF agent. This agent evaluates user requests based on the constraints in the CDF, the current state of the *model* and the rules set down in the agent design. Changing the agent rules can alter the tool functionality without the need for recoding and without degrading the *model*, e.g. the commitment rules could determine which error message to send back to the Interface, or could apply additional application specific constraints to the protocol that are not sufficiently generic to include in the basic meta-model. Other facilities provided include a parser component for the input and output of protocol diagrams, image rendering and agent management (see fig. 4).

Currently, the Protocol Tool allows users to define agent interaction protocols as per the AUML specification. The flexible design of the system was inspired in part by the nascent state of this specification, so that new updates could be readily incorporated. In fig 6, we can see the Interface Component of the AF Protocol Tool together with the mental state of the Semantic Checker at a given instance. While such a graphical tool is useful as a visual aid, what the developer really needs in the end is agent code. The Protocol Tool thus provides a second service. When a protocol has been published (i.e. a version is ready to be applied) this can be compiled into an *agent skeleton*. This skeleton defines the external agent behaviour in terms of rules but leaves the (application specific) internal behaviour for the developer to implement. The Protocol Tool has a Rule Editor that allows users to associate code with diagram elements that represent blocks of agent deliberation. This code consists of user-defined modules linked together by pre- and post-conditions in order to maintain the coherence of the protocol. Currently, the Protocol Tool provides a mapping between AUML diagram elements and AF rule blocks. However, the Rule Editor interface and the model used to represent agent rule blocks are independent of this mapping. Thus protocols developed using a different graphical formalism may be compiled into agent designs once a suitable mapping is specified.

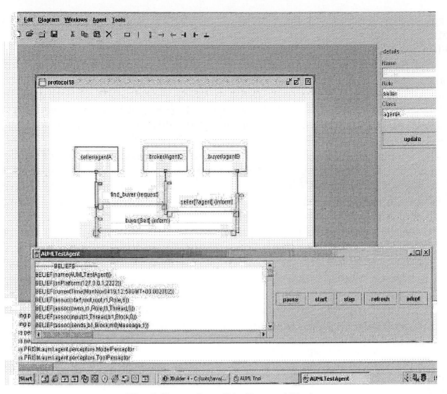

Fig. 4. Screenshot of the Protocol Tool

4   Run-Time Environment

The term Run-Time Environment encompasses the architecture that delivers support for the deployment of agent-oriented applications over a wide range of Java compliant desktop, PDA and mobile telephone devices.

The Agent Platform (AP) provides the physical infrastructure in which agents can be deployed. Each Agent Factory AP contains a Message Transport System, and three components implemented as Agent Factory agents, namely, a White Pages Agent, a Migration Manager Agent and may contain a Yellow Pages Agent. The Message Transport Service is responsible for the delivery of messages between agents within the platform and to agents resident on other APs. The White Pages Agent (WPA) [2] [10] exerts supervisory control over access to and use of the Agent Platform. It is responsible for the creation and deletion of agents on the AP. It also maintains a directory of Agent Identifiers, which contain transport addresses for agents registered with the Agent Platform. The Migration Manager Agent (MMA) is responsible for overseeing the migration of agents to and from the AP. Together the WPA and the MMA fulfill the role of the Agent Management System in the Foundation for Intelligent Physical Agents (FIPA) specification [9]. The Yellow Pages Agent (YPA) as the name suggests provides a yellow pages directory service to agents. Agents may register their services with the YPA or query the YPA to find out what services are offered by other agents. The YPA fulfils the role of a Directory Facilitator in the FIPA specification.

The functionality of an Agent Factory AP takes cognisance of the computational power and memory restrictions of the device it is operating upon. A PDA can host the full AP functionality but for fewer agents. A mobile phone cannot offer the same level of functionality, and offers no YPA and typically can merely support two agents. If the mobile needs a YPA it can register to a YPA resident on a desktop AP. Where device agent accommodation is limited migration is crucial.

AF supports weak migration in that only the mental state and design of the agent should have to migrate. Agent migration from one AF Agent Platform to another is achieved through cloning. When an agent commits to migrate it informs the Migration Manager Agent (MMA) on the destination platform that it wishes to do so. The agent then sends its agent design to the destination MMA. Along with the mental state, the agent design contains the names of the actuators and perceptors, which the agent utilises during its execution. The destination MMA on receipt of the agent design checks to see if all the necessary actuators and perceptors for the agent are present on the destination Agent Platform. Omissions can be downloaded from the source of the migration. Once the destination platform has all the required functionality a new agent is then created using the downloaded design and mental state. The MMA then informs the source Agent Platform to dispose of the old agent and the new agent begins execution.

5   Case Study

To exercise the Agent Factory System a mobile computing demonstration was designed and trailed. The Where Are You (WAY) system [15][12] is a simple, yet effective application for assisting mobile users in the location, tracking and rendezvousing with a variety of moving entities. In particular one of the most common and costly usage of mobile devices is the synchronisation

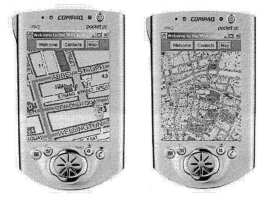

Fig. 5. A Screenshot of the WAY System and rendezvous of people

The WAY system seeks to provide an alternate solution to this problem by deploying mobile agent based technologies, namely Agent Factory. The WAY system enables location postings and updates to be passed between users via map updates (see figure 5). User trials have been conducted using a Compaq Ipaq 3760 equipped with a dual PCMCIA sleeve in order to accommodate a PCMCIA GPS and a Nokia card phone 2.0. The former provides the localisation data and the later the wireless communication infrastructure. Development on this device utilised the Jeode EVM. At present detailed field trials are underway and the results thus far are favourable. This application has verified the robustness and scalability of Agent Factory, demonstrating it constitutes a viable platform for PDA devices.

6   Related Work

Agent Prototyping Environments (APEs) have proved a rich vein of research over the last decade with the AgentLink website currently listing some 107 available for download. In this paper, we compare Agent Factory (AF) with some of the more pre-eminent offerings, namely LEAP [3], JACK [4], ZEUS [13], JADE [2] and the FIPA OS [10]. This has been realised through the selection of various evaluation criteria. From a deployment perspective, we were concerned with: BDI support, mobility, white and yellow page support, and FIPA compliance. From a development perspective, we were concerned with: the mode of fabrication, use of inheritance, construction and visualization and methodological support. The results of this comparison are summarised in table 1.

Table 1. A Comparison of Agent Prototyping Environments

	AF	LEAP	JACK	ZEUS	JADE	FIPA-OS
BDI	√		√			
Mobility	√	√			√	√
White Pages	√	√		√	√	√
Yellow Pages	√	√		√	√	√
FIPA Compliance		√		√	√	√
Fabrication Mode	Design	Instance	Design	Instance	Design	Design
Inheritance	√		√		√	√
Construction	Graphical	Graphical	Graphical	Graphical	None	None
Visualisation	Graphical	Graphical	None	Graphical	None	None
Integrated Methodology	√	√		√		

7   Conclusion

In this paper, we have introduced AF, a cohesive framework for the development and deployment of agent-oriented applications. This framework has been designed to support the deployment of agent-oriented applications on Java-compliant devices. In particular, it includes a visually intuitive development environment that promotes design reuse, has strong links with Agent UML, and which delivers a rich set of tools to support the development and debugging of agent designs.

The system provides a rich coupling between an Agent Development Methodology, the *Agent Fabrication Process (AFP)*, and the cohesive AF Toolset. The AFP oversees the controlled and appropriate temporal invocation of the component tools providing a structure and frame for the agent design and development process. We show how the Run-Time Environment delivers support for mobile agents. We illustrate the system usage, robustness, and scalability via the WAY Case Study and finally situate our work within the broader research landscape.

References

[1]   Bauer, B., Muller, J., Odell, J., Agent UML: A Formalism for Specifying Multiagent Interaction. Agent-Oriented Software Engineering (Paolo Ciancarini and Michael Wooldridge eds), Springer, Berlin, pp 91-103, 2001.

[2]   Bellifemine, F., Poggi, A., Rimassa, G., JADE – A FIPA-compliant agent framework, in Proceedings of the 4th International Conference and Exhibition on The Practical Application of Intelligent Agents and Multi-Agents (PAAM), London, UK, 1999.

[3]   Berger, M., Bauer, B., Watzke, M., A Scalable Agent Infrastructure, 2nd Workshop on Infrastructure for Agents, MAS and Scalable MAS. Autonomous Agents'01, Montreal, 2001.

[4]   Busetta, P., Ronnquist, R., Hodgson, A., and Lucas, A., JACK Intelligent Agents –Components for Intelligent Agents in Java, in AgentLink Newsletter 1, Jan 1999.

[5]   Collier, R.W., Agent Factory: A Framework for the Engineering of Agent-Oriented Applications, Ph. D. Thesis, University College Dublin, Ireland, 2001.

[6]   Colom, J.M., Koutny, M. (eds), Applications and Theory of Petri Nets, Proceedings of the 22nd International Conference ICATPN 2001 Newcastle upon Tyne, UK, June 25-29, LNCS 2075, Springer-Verlag Publishers, 2001.

[7]   CVS Home Page, http://www.cvshome.org/

[8]   DeLoach, S.A., Wood, M.F., Sparkman, C.H., Multiagent Systems Engineering, International Journal of Software Engineering and Knowledge Engineering, Volume 11, No. 3, pp 231-258, 2001.

[9]   The FIPA Website, http://www.fipa.org/.

[10]   The FIPA-OS Website, http://fipaos.sourceforge.net/.

[11]   Juan, T., Pearce, A., Sterling, L., Extending the GAIA methodology for complex open systems, Proceedings of Autonomous Agents and Multi-Agent Systems (AAMAS-2002), Bologna, July 15-19, 2002

[12]   Lowen, T.D., O` Hare, P.T., O` Hare G.M.P, Mobile Agents point the WAY: Context Sensitive Service Delivery through Mobile Lightweight Agents. Proc of Autonomous Agents and Multi-Agent Systems (AAMAS-2002), Bologna, July 15-19, 2002

[13] Nwana, H., Ndumu, D., Lee, L., Collis, J., ZEUS: A Tool-Kit for Building Distributed Multi-Agent Systems, in Applied Artificial Intelligence Journal, Vol. 13 (1), p129-186, 1999.

[14] O'Hare, G.M.P., Agent Factory: An Environment for the Fabrication of Distributed Artificial Systems, in O'Hare, G.M.P. and Jennings, N.R.(Eds.), Foundations of Distributed Artificial Intelligence, Sixth Generation Computer Series, Wiley Interscience Pubs, New York, 1996.

[15] O'Hare, P., O'Hare G.M.P., and Lowen, T., Far and a Way: Context sensitive service delivery through mobile lightweight PDA hosted agents. In Proc. FLAIRS 02, 2002.

[16] Padgham, L., Winikoff, M., Prometheus: A Methodology for Developing Intelligent Agents, Proceedings of Autonomous Agents and Multi-Agent Systems (AAMAS-2002), Bologna, July 15-19, 2002

[17] Venners, B., Inheritance versus Composition: Which one should you choose? Javaworld, http://www.javaworld.com/javaworld/jw-11-1998/jw-11-techniques.html

[18] Wooldridge, M., Jennings, N.R., Kinny, D., The Gaia Methodology for Agent-Oriented Analysis and Design, in Journal of Autonomous Agents and Multi-Agent Systems, Kluwer Academic Publishers, Volume 3, pp 285-312, 2000

Agent Oriented Software Engineering with INGENIAS*

Juan Pavón and Jorge Gómez-Sanz

Universidad Complutense Madrid, Dep. Sistemas Informáticos y Programación
28040 Madrid, Spain
{jpavon,jjgomez}@sip.ucm.es
http://grasia.fdi.ucm.es

Abstract. INGENIAS is both a methodology and a set of tools for development of multi-agent systems (MAS). As a methodology, it tries to integrate results from other proposals and considers the MAS from five complementary viewpoints: organization, agent, tasks/goals, interactions, and environment. It is supported by a set of tools for modelling (graphical editor), documentation and code generation (for different agent platforms). INGENIAS is the result of the experience developing MAS in different areas, such as workflow management systems, recommender systems, Robocode teams, and PC assistants.

1   Introduction

As software agent technology has matured, several methodologies for building agent-based systems have appeared. We are now in a similar situation to what happened with object-oriented methodologies a decade ago, with different approaches that finally integrated into a common notation (the Unified Modelling Language, UML) and development process (the Unified Process, UP). There are many valid approaches to MAS development based on different ideas of what a Multi-Agent System should be. One attempt towards an integration of agent-oriented methodologies was MESSAGE [1]. The main contribution of MESSAGE was the definition of meta-models for specification of the elements that can be used to describe each of the aspects that constitute a multi-agent system (MAS) from five viewpoints: organization, agents, goals/tasks, interactions, and domain. MESSAGE adopted the Unified Process and centred on analysis and design phases of development. INGENIAS starts from the results of MESSAGE and provides more complete and consistent meta-models, based on more experience building agent-based applications, and a set of tools that support analysis, design and code generation activities.

This paper provides an overview of INGENIAS methodology and tools. It starts by a discussion of common features that can be found in current agent-oriented methodologies, and identifies open issues that INGENIAS tries to address in a unifying

---

* This work has been funded by Spanish Ministry of Science and Technology under grant TIC2002-04516-C03-03

V. Mařík et al. (Eds): CEEMAS 2003, LNAI 2691, pp. 394-403, 2003.

framework. This is followed by an account of the main entities that are required to model MAS, as specified by INGENIAS. Then, there is a presentation of available tools (which can be downloaded from http://ingenias.sourceforge.net) and their use in the development life-cycle. Finally, the conclusions highlight main contributions of the methodology, discuss the experience from using INGENIAS, and its expected evolution.

2   Agent-Oriented Methodologies

Although there are multiple agent-based applications around, most of them are built from scratch without the support of a sound agent-oriented methodology. In the same way as it happened with object-oriented software, there are different proposals and we can consider that there will be also an unification process, integrating the most relevant aspects of all the methodologies.

In several points seems to be an agreement and they should be adopted by such unified methodology for MAS development:

- The agent paradigm extends the object paradigm, and an agent-oriented methodology should take advantage of the experience of the object-oriented approach. Object-oriented methodologies have already acquired a high degree of maturity and their advantages are widely recognized. A great part of software developers are familiarized with them and a wide game of tools is available. An iterative and incremental development life-cycle, use cases and architecture-based approach are quite appropriate for dynamic systems such as MAS. Methodological extensions should take care of social issues (organizations, interactions, coordination), dynamic behaviour (autonomy, mental state, goals, tasks), concurrency and distribution.

- MAS modelling can be considered from different complementary viewpoints to manage the complexity of a MAS: Vowel Engineering (Agent, Environment, Interactions, Organization) [8], AAII (external, agents and interactions, and internal, Believes, Desires, and Intentions) [5], MAS-CommonKADS (agent, task, experience, organization, coordination, user interaction, and design) [4], and MESSAGE (organization, agent, goals/tasks, domain, and interactions) [1].

- Most of the proposals concentrate on the analysis phase (e.g., Gaia [9]). The agent concept is quite flexible and is near to some anthropomorphic modelling, which is convenient for understanding the problem to analyse. Roles and services help to organize the functionality associated to an agent or a group of agents, contributing to the understanding and manageability of complex systems. On the other side, design is not always fully considered, unless there is an underlying framework or well established semantics that allow designers to think in a feasible implementation architecture. A key element in the design is the presence of an agent architecture (for instance, Zeus provides agent templates [7], AAII defines BDI agents [5], and MaSE agents are Java classes implemented as automata [2]).

- Several concepts are specific to agent technology and they should be clearly defined for their use in the MAS development process [10]. In this sense, the use of meta-models in MESSAGE and INGENIAS [3] follows the activity in OMG for the MOF and UML (http://www.omg.org/technology/uml/), and has revealed as a powerful instrument for its expressiveness and as a basis for building development tools.

• Experience from Zeus, MaSE and MESSAGE shows the relevance of tool availability to control the development process in all phases and help developers to produce and measure the quality of results according to the methodology. One issue that has not yet been undertaken is the management and coordination of activities of members in a development team.

INGENIAS, as an evolution of MESSAGE, starts from the consideration of these elements. INGENIAS integrates results from existing agent research by applying techniques and concepts to determine the elements that should be used to specify a MAS and what should be present in the agent architecture. Graphical editors and documentation generation tools support analysis and design. Automatic code generation tools for different implementation languages and agent platforms cover implementation.

INGENIAS structures its proposal in three aspects:

1. Specification and notation for the elements that constitute a MAS, structured in five viewpoints: organization, agent, goals/tasks, interactions, and environment. They are described as meta-models, by refining those developed in MESSAGE and identifying consistency rules among the models. The control of the agents is based on a BDI model.

2. Development life-cycle process, initially adopting the Unified Process, defining those activities that should be carried out in different stages of the development life-cycle.

3. Supporting tools for the activities of the development life-cycle. Currently there are model editors, documentation and code generation tools.

The next section provides an overview of the elements for modelling MAS in INGENIAS (the development life-cycle process is described with examples in [3]). This is followed by a brief presentation of the way tools are generated from meta-model specifications. The basic idea is to show that the methodology can evolve, together with the supporting tools. In this way we can incorporate new agent technology concepts in the same way as the experience requires them.

3   Modelling with INGENIAS

A MAS in INGENIAS is considered from five viewpoints (see Figure 1): organization, agent, goals/tasks, interactions, and environment. For each viewpoint, a set of concepts and relationships among them are provided to the developer to describe the MAS. As far as the object-oriented software developer has to deal with classes, interfaces, objects, inheritance, etc., the agent-oriented software developer can use those concepts and others such as agent, organization, goal, task, mental state, resource, etc. These concepts may appear in the specification of one or several viewpoints, therefore the need to identify consistency rules among the these.

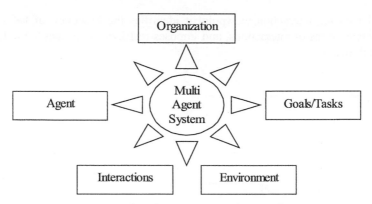

Fig. 1. Five viewpoints to model a MAS

The organization describes a structure for agents, resources, goals and tasks. It is defined by:

- Purpose and tasks of the organization. An organization has one or several purposes, a goal, and is capable of performing certain tasks to achieve them
- An structure of groups and workflows (Figure 2). From a structural viewpoint, the organization is a set of entities with relationships of aggregation and inheritance. This structure defines a framework where agents, resources, goals, and tasks are placed. And on this structure there are relationships that induce the formation of workflows and social rules.
- Workflows define associations among tasks and general information about their execution (e.g., for each task, the agent or role responsible of its execution and which resources requires).
- Groups may contain agents, roles, resources, or applications. Assignment of such elements to a group obeys to some organizational purpose, i.e., because the grouping facilitates the definition of workflows. Groups are useful when the number of elements in a MAS (agents, roles and resources) increases.
- Social relationships. They can be established at different levels: between organizations, groups, agents, or roles. There are service relationships (for instance, client-server relationship), conditional or unconditional subordination, etc. They state restrictions on the interactions between entities.

The organization viewpoint is central to the definition of a MAS and has to be checked against the other viewpoints. Examples of relationships that exist between the organization viewpoint and others are:

- With the agent viewpoint, it identifies roles and agents, and states the relationships between agents in the context of the workflows.
- With the goals/tasks viewpoint, it shows which goals are relevant for the system, and the relationships among tasks in workflows.
- With the environment viewpoint, it involves agents, resources and applications from the environment and integrates them with the rest of the entities in the system.

- And with the interaction viewpoint it identifies the execution of tasks in other agents in terms of interactions, and imposes restrictions through the definition of social rules.

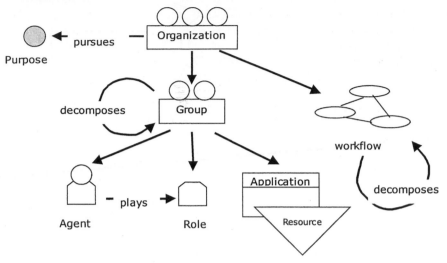

Fig. 2. Structural description of a MAS organization

The agent viewpoint is concerned with the functionality of each agent: responsibilities (what goals an agent is compromised to pursue) and capabilities (what tasks is able to perform). The behaviour of the agent is defined through three components:

- Mental state, an aggregation of mental entities such as goals, believes, facts, compromises.
- Mental state manager, which provides for operations to create, destroy and modify mental entities.
- Mental state processor, which determines how the mental state evolves, and it can be described in terms of rules, planning, etc.

Mental state can be seen as all the information that allows the agent to take decisions. This information is managed and processed in order to produce agent decisions and actions, by the mental state manager and processor. The advantage of separating management and processing of mental state is the decoupling of the mechanisms that implement the autonomy and intelligence of the agent from the conceptualisation of the agent.

The tasks/goals viewpoint considers the decomposition of goals and tasks, and describes the consequences of performing a task, and why it should be performed (i.e., it justifies the execution of tasks as a way to satisfy goals, and these change as tasks execute). The mental state processor takes the decision of which task to execute, and the mental state manager provides the operations to create, destroy and modify the elements of the mental state and their relationships. In fact, a goal may have associated a life-cycle, as shown in Figure 3.

The interaction viewpoint addresses the exchange of information or requests between agents, or between agents and human users. The definition of an interaction requires the identification of:

- Actors in the interaction: who plays the role of initiator and who are the collaborators. Which is the reason (goal) that motivates each actor to participate in the interaction.
- Definition of interaction units: messages, speech acts.
- Definition of the possible orders of interactions units: protocols.
- Which actions are performed in the interaction.
- Context of the interaction: which goal pursues the interaction and which are the mental states of its participants.
- Control model: coordination mechanisms.

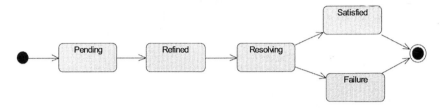

Fig. 3. Goal life-cycle

INGENIAS does not uses a single formalism for interaction specification. It admits different notations for specifying interactions, such as Agent UML (http://www.auml.org), FIPA protocol diagrams (http://www.fipa.org), or our own, Grasia diagrams (see http://grasia.fdi.ucm.cs/ingenias for some examples).

Finally, the environment viewpoint defines the entities with which the MAS interacts, which can be:

- *Resources*. Elements required by tasks that do not provide a concrete API. Examples of resources are the CPU, File descriptors, or memory. Resources are assigned to agents or groups in the current system.
- *Applications*. Normally they offer some (local or remote) API. In some cases, applications are wrapped by agents to facilitate their integration in the MAS. Their main use is to express the perception of the agents: applications produce events that can be observed. Agents define their perception indicating which events they listen to.
- Other agents (from other organizations), which satisfy the *rationality* principle [6]. The agents in the MAS interact with these agents to satisfy system functionality.

The environment viewpoint is important to describe how the MAS fits in the target system. Elements identified here appear in other viewpoints as extra actors or system applications that can be used. Also helps in determining what components compound our agents or are shared among different agents or groups.

4   INGENIAS-IDE Generation from Meta-models

INGENIAS methodology is supported by a visual modelling language tool, the INGENIAS IDE, complemented with a set of tools for code generation, validation, and documentation. The INGENIAS IDE is generated from a XML file that describes the meta-models of each viewpoint, as shown in figure 4. This file can be modified at any time, and the editor regenerated again. The advantage for developers is the possibility to adapt the visual language to their needs. This tool requires as input basic description of the capabilities and look and feel of the editor (editor template), which could be generic. What is particular is the description of each meta-model, and some specific information concerning each element of the meta-model, for instance, the icons that are used for their graphical representation. They are associated with another XML description (Relationship Editor Attributes). This way, it is easy to make changes in the meta-models and generate updated editors.

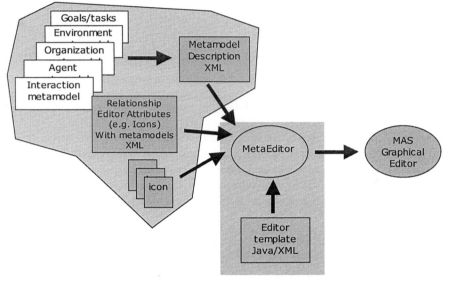

Fig. 4. Meta-tools for INGENIAS

Current INGENIAS IDE is available at http://sourceforge.net/projects/ingenias/. It has been developed under GNU General Public License (GPL). Code and documentation generation tools are still under testing.

Code generation bases on rewriting templates of code with information from the diagrams. These templates represent parts of the system that have to be instantiated with concrete domain information. INGENIAS IDE works in this case as a front end for a framework instantiation.

The MAS developer uses INGENIAS IDE to build diagrams that describe the MAS. Fig. 5 shows how the editor looks like. Agent developer can start depicting an organization for the MAS (such as in Fig. 6) to identify main goal of the MAS and basic entities. This goal can be decomposed in a goals/tasks diagram. Interactions between entities can be described in several interaction diagrams. At the end the developer has created several diagrams, which are stored as XML files and can be used, later on, by the code generation tools to produce the code for a target agent platform.

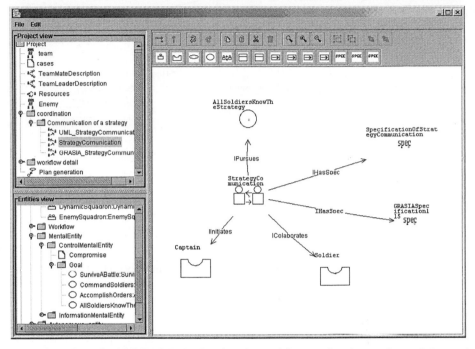

Fig. 5. Snapshot of INGENIAS IDE, showing the participants of an interaction and the goal that is pursued with the interaction. More specific information of the way interaction proceeds is specified with other diagrams, referenced at right side

For instance, if the MAS model Robocode teams (as in Fig. 6) and the agents will be implemented as Robocode robots (http://robocode.alphaworks.ibm.com), the code generation tool integrate tasks and goals in a customized BDI architecture, and translate organization concepts to how they are understood in Robocode. Therefore, the developer focuses in the strategy of each of the robots instead of the internals of each one (the translation is provided by the code generation tool). This has the advantage of allowing the developer to concentrate in agent-related concepts and the independence from a specific agent programming language or platform.

5   Conclusions and Further Steps

The INGENIAS methodology is the result of experience in developing agent-based applications during the last five years, and in particular the work developed in the MESSAGE project. According to our practice, the use of a methodology is the key to control and manage the development process of MAS, and helps to identify the elements and relationships that make the MAS.

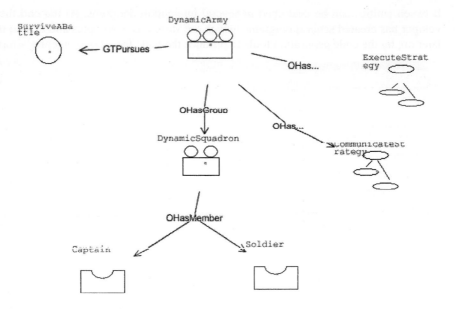

Fig. 6. Organization viewpoint of agents in an army of tanks for Robocode. The army pursues the goal of *surviving the battle*. The organization consists of a set of *squadrons* commanded each one by a *Captain*. Main workflows in the organization are *CommunicateStrategy* and *ExecuteStrategy*

INGENIAS extends MESSAGE with a more complete definition of the meta-models that describe each viewpoint of a MAS, and considering the consistency among the different viewpoints. The methodology is supported by a set of tools and has been validated with several projects. For some of them, analysis and design documentation, as generated by the tools and describing the way to apply the methodology, can be found at http://grasia.fdi.ucm.es/ingenias/ejemplos.

References

[1]   Caire, G., Coulier, W., Garijo, F. Gomez, J., Pavon, J., Leal, F., Chainho, P., Kearney, P., Stark, J., Evans, R., and Massonet, P.: Agent Oriented Analysis using MESSAGE/UML. In: Wooldridge, M., Weiss, G., and Ciancarini. P. (Eds.): The Second International Workshop on Agent-Oriented Software Engineering (AOSE 2001). Lecture Notes in Computer Science, Vol. 2222. Springer-Verlag, Berlin Heidelberg New York (2002) 119-135

[2]   DeLoach, S.: Analysis and Design using MaSE and agentTool. In: Proceedings of the 12th Midwest Artificial Intelligence and Cognitive Science Conference (MAICS 2001). Miami University, Oxford, Ohio (2001)

[3]   Gomez-Sanz, J. J., and Pavón, J.: Meta-modelling in Agent-Oriented Software Engineering. In: Garijo, F., Riquelme Santos, J., and Toro, M. (Eds.): Advances in Artificial Intelligence - IBERAMIA 2002. Lecture Notes in Artificial Intelligence, Vol. 2527. Springer-Verlag, Berlin Heidelberg New York (2002) 606-615

[4]   Iglesias, C., Garijo, M., Gonzalez, J.C., and Velasco, J.R.: Analysis and design of multiagent systems using MAS-CommonKADS. In: Singh, M. P., Rao, A., and Wooldridge, M. J. (Eds.): Intelligent Agents IV. Lecture Notes in Computer Science, Vol. 1365. Springer-Verlag, Berlin Heidelberg New York (1998) 313-327

[5]   Kinny, K., Georgeff, M.P., and Rao, A.S.: A Methodology and Modelling Technique for Systems of BDI Agents. In: Van de Velde, W. and Perram, J. (Eds.): Agents Breaking Away, 7th European Workshop on Modelling Autonomous Agents in a Multi-Agent World. Lecture Notes in Computer Science, Vol. 1038. Springer-Verlag, Berlin Heidelberg New York (1996) 56-71

[6]   Newell, A.: The knowledge level, Artificial Intelligence 18 (1982) 87-127

[7]   Nwana, H. S., Ndumu, D. T., Lee, L. C., and Collis, J. C.: ZEUS: A Toolkit for Building Distributed Multi-Agent Systems. Applied Artificial Intelligence Journal, Vol. 1, no. 13 (1999) 129-185

[8]   Ricordel, P. M. and Demazeau, Y.: Volcano, a Vowels-Oriented Multi-agent Platform. In: Dunin-Keplicz, B. and Nawarecki, E. (Eds.): From Theory to Practice in Multi-Agent Systems, Second International Workshop of Central and Eastern Europe on Multi-Agent Systems, CEEMAS 2001. Lecture Notes in Artificial Intelligence, Vol. 2296. Springer-Verlag, Berlin Heidelberg New York (2002) 253-262

[9]   Wooldridge, M., Jennings, N. R., and Kinny, D.: The Gaia Methodology for Agent-Oriented Analysis and Design. Journal of Autonomous Agents and Multi-Agent Systems 3 (2000) 285-312

[10]   Zambonelli, F., Bergenti, F., and Di Marzo, G. 2002. Methodologies and Software Engineering for Agent Systems. AgentLink News 9 (2002) 23-25

Requirement Analysis for Interaction Protocols

Marc-Philippe Huget[1] and Jean-Luc Koning[2]

[1] Agent ART Group, University of Liverpool
Liverpool L69 7ZF, United Kingdom
`M.P.Huget@csc.liv.ac.uk`
[2] INPG-CoSy
50, rue Laffemas, BP 54, 26902 Valence cedex 9, France
`Jean-Luc.Koning@esisar.inpg.fr`

Abstract. Designing agent interaction protocols need first to consider what the requirements are. This is done in the requirement analysis phase. The output of this phase is an informal document written in natural language. To our best knowledge, this phase is barely considered in the literature neither in communication protocol engineering nor in interaction protocol engineering. As a consequence, it is difficult for designers to do it easily. Experience seems to be the key. In order to help designers, we propose to structure the requirement analysis document into fields. These fields gather protocol's features. This paper presents such document and applies the structuration to the electronic commerce protocol NetBill.

1 Introduction

Communication is recognized as a first class citizen in multiagent systems since it allows agents to exchange information, to cooperate and to coordinate so as to complete their tasks. As a consequence, communication between agents should be considered cautiously when designing multiagent systems. The usual way to represent communication in multiagent systems is to use protocols. An agent interaction protocol is a set of rules that guide the interaction among several agents. For a given state of the protocol, only a finite set of messages may be sent or received. If one agent uses a given protocol, it must conform to such a protocol and obey the various rules. Moreover, it must comply with its semantics. Such protocols are similar to the ones found in distributed systems [3] except that agents' autonomy is increased and these agents employ richer messages following Speech Act theory [9]. Recently, we made the proposal of an interaction protocol engineering to help designers [6, 5]. This interaction protocol engineering is based on the communication protocol engineering [3] and covers protocol design cycle from the requirements to the test of the runnable protocol.

The first phase in design cycle is to gather requirements for the product to design —in our case, a protocol. This phase is done in cooperation with end users. End users describe the protocol function, its goals, what it is possible to do with it and what is not. In our proposal of interaction protocol engineering,

V. Mařík et al. (Eds): CEEMAS 2003, LNAI 2691, pp. 404–412, 2003.

we call *requirement analysis* this phase. There is a difference in comparison with communication protocol engineering since the latter considers two distinct phases *Analysis* and *Design* whereas we gather these two phases in our proposal. The reason is that we think it is better for designers to address both the messages and their meaning at the same time and not at two different moments. The output of this requirement analysis phase is an informal document used in the remaining of the design cycle. This phase is different from others in interaction protocol engineering since there is no clear method to help designers. Experience seems to be the key to manage this phase. As a consequence, requirement analysis is scarcely present in literature and to our best knowledge, it seems that this proposal is the only one available. Throughout this paper, we try to help a little designers when designing interaction protocols. We propose for that to structure the informal document into fields. Each field corresponds to a protocol's feature such as pre-conditions, post-conditions, execution, agents involved, etc.

The remainder of this paper is as follows. Section 2 defines what the requirement analysis phase is. Section 3 describes the structured document and presents the place of the requirement analysis phase in the interaction protocol engineering. Section 4 applies the requirement analysis phase to the NetBill example. The NetBill protocol is an electronic commerce protocol to sell small amount value electronic goods. Section 5 concludes the paper and presents future directions.

2   Requirement Analysis Definition

Whatever the product is, the first phase in design cycle is to gather requirements for such product. The set of requirements is obtained through meetings between end users and designers or through a questionnaire to end users. End users express what they want to find in the product. This phase is difficult since end users do not know how to describe their needs or end users and designers do not understand each other. We do not address this point which is far beyond the scope of this paper. We consider that end users and designers understand each other.

An informal document is defined from the meetings between end users and designers. It is easy to understand that this document is informal since end users are not necessarily aware of formal description techniques. The document is written in natural language.

In the case of protocols, several information have to be included in the document:

- agents involved in the protocol
- the definition of the protocol, i.e. the message combination
- the good properties to be present (liveness properties)
- the bad properties to avoid (safety properties)
- the type of the messages and the data
- the conditions

In [5], we proposed to merge the *Analysis* and the *Design* phases in an unique phase. We think it is better for designers to address at the same time, the messages and their meaning. In the communication protocol engineering [3], designers first describe the combination of messages then the message meaning and the related data.

3   Requirement Analysis Document

As stated above, the output of the requirement analysis phase is an informal document written in natural language. In order to help designers, we propose to structure the document into fields. These fields correspond to specific features in the protocol such as conditions, function, agents involved, etc. This section describes the structure of the document and the place of this document in the design cycle: the use of each field in the following phases of the protocol engineering.

3.1   Document Structure

Our proposal of document is composed of several fields:

- protocol's name
- keywords
- agents' roles
- initiator
- prerequisite
- function
- behavior
- constraints
- termination

The remaining of this section describes these different fields.

The field **Protocol's name** gives the name of the protocol. This information is used by designers in a context of reuse. The protocol's name should be unique in order to help reuse. Actually, if two protocols have the same name, it requests more work from designers to distinguish them. They particularly have to read the *function* and *behavior* fields. For instance, examples of protocol's name are *Contract Net* or *English Auction.*

The field **Keywords** gives a list of keywords to characterize the protocol. The choice of keywords is free but it seems to be more interesting to provide accurate and meaningful keywords. Keywords could refer to:

- the number of agents involved in the protocols,
- the kind of message sending: broadcast, multicast,
- the class of protocols: information request, negotiation, synchronization,
- the agent communication language used: ACL, KQML,
- the ontology used,
- the specific features: security, anonymity, fault-tolerance, electronic commerce

Obviously, this list of keywords' domain is not exhaustive and it depends on the purpose of the protocol.

The field **Agents' roles** refers to the agents involved in the protocol. Agents in protocols play at least one role. A role denotes a particular behavior in the interaction. For instance, in the context of auction protocols, two specific roles are defined: auctioneer and participant. This piece of information is for instance used when designing agent interaction protocols with Agent UML sequence diagrams [7]. A second piece of information is supplied by this field: the number of agents per role. The number of agents is used in a context of open multiagent systems in order to constrain the size of the system.

The field **Initiator** is related to the previous one. The initiator of an interaction is an agent playing a specific role. For instance, for auction protocols, the initiator is the auctioneer. The initiator's role must be a role defined in the field *Agents' roles*.

The field **Prerequisite** defines the conditions that must be satisfied before executing protocols. These conditions can be written as a free-format text or as a formal description. A possible formal description language is OCL [8] also employed for UML. Such prerequisite can deal with the agents' mental states, the agents' acquaintances or the environment state. For instance, an agent must be authenticated to a server prior requesting information.

The field **Function** is a summary of the protocol execution. It allows designers to have a bird's eye view of the protocol. Usually, protocol's description is a long text, it is better for designers, in a context of reuse, to read an excerpt of the protocol rather than this long description.

The field **Behavior** is the main field in the requirement analysis document. It gives the complete definition of the protocol, the different combination of messages as well as the message type and the data used. Unlike communication protocol engineering where the execution paths are separated from message and data types, we put together these two pieces of information. We think it is better for designers if they can refer to message type when they consider a path of the interaction. The natural-language description can be associated with chronograms to ease understanding. We also add the agents' mental states and actions to the execution. It means that it is important to describe as well under what conditions, a message is sent. For instance, if agents use the communicative act *inform* from FIPA ACL [2], it is written in FIPA specifications that the sender must believe what is sent. Moreover, some actions may arise after sending or receiving a message. For instance, agents which receive a *cfp* message have to check if they are able to do the task and under what conditions.

The field **Constraints** allows designers to write the good properties to be present in protocols and the bad properties to avoid. Good properties and bad properties refer to properties that designers want to check during the validation stage [3]. It might be deadlock freeness, termination, absence of acceptance cycles, absence of non-progressing states, mutual exclusion, etc. Constraints can be defined as a temporal logic formula. Thus, it is easier to check the properties with model checker such as SPIN [4]. Constraints can also be defined as a free-format text or an OCL formula [8]. This field can also contain the standards that protocols have to conform to. For instance, standards could be: using ACL for communicative acts or XML for message format.

The field **Termination** defines the valid termination of protocols. This field is related to the purpose of protocols. For instance, for a secure auction protocol, the seller has the money and no longer the good; and the buyer has the good and no longer the money. This field can be described through a free-format text or temporal logic formulae. Then, these formulae can be used in model checker for the validation.

3.2 Document Use

The aim of a requirement analysis document is to gather the requirements. This document is interesting if it is used during the design cycle. This section presents the use of this proposal of requirements analysis document in the design cycle.

As stated in the introduction, we made a proposal of interaction protocol engineering [6]. This interaction protocol engineering is composed of several phases:

1. Requirement Analysis where the requirements for the protocol to design is gathered.
2. Formal Description where the protocol is described formally to remove all ambiguities and misunderstandings. Moreover, this formal description can be checked more easily.
3. Validation where designers test if the protocol exhibit some properties.
4. Protocol Synthesis where a runnable version of the protocol is generated.
5. Conformance Testing where designers test if the runnable version conforms to the informal specification.

Table 1 summarizes the use of the different fields of the analysis document in the design cycle.

Table 1. Use of Analysis Document Fields in Interaction Protocol Engineering

	description	validation	protocol synthesis	conformance testing	reuse
name					✓
keywords					✓
agents' roles	✓				
initiator	✓		✓		
prerequisite		✓	✓	✓	
function					✓
behavior	✓	✓	✓	✓	
constraints	✓	✓	✓	✓	
termination	✓	✓	✓	✓	

The last column refers to reuse. Designers should have the ability to reuse past protocols trough projects. As a consequence, it is important that it is easily possible to know the purpose of a specific requirement analysis document.

The remaining of this section explains the table.

Three fields *Name, Keywords, Function* are only used in a context of reuse. Designers who want to reuse protocols read first these three fields in order to know if the current requirement analysis document is the correct one. If the information in these three fields is incomplete, designers could read the field *Behavior*.

The field *Agents' roles* is used in the formal description stage. It is particularly interesting if designers use Agent UML sequence diagrams for representing interaction protocols [7]. Sequence diagrams describe agents involved in the protocol by their roles.

The field *Initiator* is used mainly in the protocol synthesis stage and could be used in the formal description stage. The name of the initiator is required when designers have to generate code for protocols. This information can be used in formal description stage if designers use a formal description technique which describes agents by their roles such as Agent UML sequence diagrams.

The field *Prerequisite* is used during validation stage and protocol synthesis stage. Prerequisite presents the properties to check during validation stage. Prerequisite is used during protocol synthesis stage in order to define what are the properties to be satisfied before executing protocols. Prerequisite is also used for the conformance testing stage in order to check if the implementation conforms to the protocol requirements.

The field *Behavior* is used from formal description stage to conformance testing stage. This field is important. It is the blueprint for designers tp describe formally the protocol. Then, during validation stage, it helps designers to define the properties to check. This field could be removed for protocol synthesis stage since designers mainly use the protocol formal description. However, this field is used as a support for the code generation. It is the same for conformance testing stage: this field is used as a support.

The field *Constraints* is also used from formal description stage to conformance testing stage. During formal description stage, good properties, bad properties and standards are used to design the protocol formal description. During validation stage, constraints give properties to check on protocols. During protocol synthesis stage, constraints are inserted into the code. Finally, constraints are employed during conformance testing stage for checking properties on the protocol implementation.

The field *Termination* is mainly used during validation stage and conformance testing stage to check if protocols end properly. Termination is used during formal description stage and protocol synthesis stage to guide the design.

4   NetBill Example

In order to exemplify such analysis document, let us introduce the agent-based NetBill purchase protocol [1]. The aim of the NetBill protocol is to sell small amount electronic goods. It involves three agent roles: customer, merchant and bank. The transaction between customers and merchants are secured. We do not present more in detail the protocol since it is done in the analysis document defined below.

The corresponding analysis document could be the following.

Name: NetBill
Keywords: electronic commerce, secured transaction, purchase, low value electronic goods, atomicity
Agents' role: customer, merchant, bank (NetBill server)
Initiator: customer
Prerequisite: both the client and merchant must have an account at the bank
Function: Let us quote Cox et al.'s definition [1]: *"We are building a system called NetBill which is optimized for the selling and delivery of low-priced network goods. A customer, represented by a client computer, wishes to buy information from a merchant's server. An account server (the NetBill server), maintains accounts for both customers and merchants, linked to conventional financial institutions. A NetBill transaction transfers information goods from merchant to customer, debiting the customer's NetBill account and crediting the merchant's account for the value of the goods."*
Behavior: The NetBill protocol may be decomposed into three steps:
1. The **Price Request Phase** happens between the customer and the merchant agents. The former requires the price of a good and the latter sends it in return.
2. The **Goods Delivery Phase** happens again between the customer and the merchant agents. The former requests the electronic good which the latter sends back in an encrypted form.
3. The **Payment Phase** takes place between the three agents role. The customer sends the merchant its signed electronic payment order. The merchant endorses it by including the key to decrypt the good and sends it to the bank in order for the financial transfer to take place. Once completed, the bank gives back a payment slip to the merchant who in turn gives it (along with the encrypting key) to the customer.

We now describe in detail the protocol.

The first message in the protocol is sent from the customer to the merchant. The customer asks the price of an electronic good. The customer uses for that the message *PriceRequest*. The content of the message is the reference of the electronic good. The merchant answers to this message by the message *PriceQuote* sent to the customer. The content of the message is the price of the electronic good. After this message, the customer can leave the interaction or it can enter in the second phase called *Goods Delivery Phase*. The customer does not have to inform the merchant if it leaves the interaction.

The first message of the *Goods Delivery Phase* is sent by the customer to the merchant. The message is *GoodsRequest*. It contains the reference of the electronic good it wants to purchase. The merchant sends an encrypted version of the electronic good with the message *Electronic Good*. The content of the message is the encrypted electronic good. This second message ends the second phase of the NetBill protocol. At this point of the interaction, the customer has the electronic good but this one is encrypted and the customer does not have the key to decrypt it. The merchant has the key for the electronic good. No financial transaction has been performed.

The last phase is the main one. The first message is sent from the customer to the merchant. The message is *ElectronicPaymentOrder*. It contains the order of debiting the customer's bank account of the specified amount. The merchant sends this electronic payment order to the bank with the message *EndorsedElectronicPaymentOrder*. It adds the key to the message. There are two situations after this message: if the financial transactions are completed, the bank sends the message *SignedResult* to the merchant else it sends the message *NoPayment* to the merchant. The merchant forwards the message to the customer: either the *SignedResult* message or the *NoPayment*. If the message is *SignedResult*, it contains the key to decrypt the electronic good. A particular message can be sent at any time as soon as the customer has sent the *ElectronicPaymentOrder* message: this is the *TransactionEnquiry* message. This message can be sent between different parties: from the customer to the merchant, from the customer to the bank or from the merchant to the bank. It requests the current status of the transaction. The merchant or the bank can answer either with the message *PaymentSlip* meaning that financial transaction is done or with the message *NoPayment* meaning that no financial transaction is done.

Constraints: It is impossible that the customer has both the electronic good and the key without previously paying for this good.

It is impossible that the merchant has the electronic good, the key and money coming from customer's bank account.

Termination: the customer has the electronic good and the key to decrypt it. Its bank account has been debited with the value of the good. The merchant has no longer the electronic good and its bank account has been credited with the value of the good. If the customer does not have both the electronic good and the key, the financial transactions are withdrawn and no bank account has been charged.

5   Conclusion

Requirement analysis is a crucial stage in design cycle since it determines the quality of the final product. If the analysis is not accurate or complete, the designed product does not conform to the users' expectations. Interaction protocol engineering is also concerned with requirement analysis but, unfortunately, few work has been done on this subject. Gaia presents how to describe protocols' analysis but is unclear on the content of the analysis [10]. This situation seems to be the same in communication protocol engineering [3]. Designers need some guidelines to help them to design interaction protocols.

The aim of this paper is to present our proposal of requirement analysis phase through a structured document called requirement analysis document. This document is organized into fields dealing with agents involved, properties and the paths of the protocol. Then, we apply this requirement analysis stage to the example of NetBill protocol.

The fields defined in the document are not enough satisfying to help designers. They need more guidelines. Future work will focus on extracting relevant information from interaction protocols and defining some guidelines for designers.

References

[1] B. Cox, J. Tygar, and M. Sirbu. Netbill security and transaction protocol. In *Proceedings of the First USENIX Workshop in Electronic Commerce*, July 1995.

[2] FIPA. Specification. Foundation for Intelligent Physical Agents, http://www.fipa.org/repository/fipa2000.html, 2000.

[3] G. J. Holzmann. *Design and Validation of Computer Protocols*. Prentice-Hall, 1991.

[4] G. J. Holzmann. The model checker SPIN. *IEEE Transactions on Software Engineering*, 23(5), May 1997.

[5] M.-P. Huget. *Une ingénierie des protocoles d'interaction pour les systèmes multi-agents*. PhD thesis, Université Paris 9 Dauphine, June 2001.

[6] M.-P. Huget and J.-L. Koning. *Engineering Interaction Protocols for Multiagent Systems*, volume Communication in Multiagen Systems" Bacground, Current Trends and Future. Springer-Verlag, marc-philippe huget edition, 2002. to appear.

[7] J. Odell, H. V. D. Parunak, and B. Bauer. Representing agent interaction protocols in UML. In P. Ciancarini and M. Wooldridge, editors, *Proceedings of First International Workshop on Agent-Oriented Software Engineering*, Limerick, Ireland, June, 10 2000. Springer-Verlag.

[8] OMG. UML 1.4. Technical report, OMG, 2001.

[9] J. Searle. *Speech Acts: An Essay in the Philosophy of Language*. Cambridge University Press, 1969.

[10] M. Wooldridge, N. R. Jennings, and D. Kinny. The Gaia methodology for agentoriented analysis and design. *Journal of Autonomous Agents and Multi-Agent Systems*, 3(3):285-312, 2000.

Engineering a Protocol Server Using Strategy-Agents

Cosmin Carabelea[1,2] and Philippe Beaune[2]

[1] „Politehnica" University of Bucharest, Romania
[2] Ecole Nationale Supèrieure des Mines de Saint-Etienne, France
`{cosmin.carabelea,philippe.beaune}@emse.fr`

Abstract. This paper addresses the idea of using a server of negotiation protocols to facilitate negotiations in an open multi-agent system. The agents that do not know the negotiation protocols of the system can query the server for a description of the protocol and use it in negotiations. After pointing out some of the major problems encountered by the existing approaches, we propose a special type of agent (called strategy-agent) that knows how to negotiate using a fixed protocol and negotiation strategy. Such an agent will then negotiate for the benefit of other agents that do not know the required protocol.

1 Introduction

In a multi-agent system, an agent exists and performs its activity in a society in which other agents exist and act. Therefore, coordination among agents is essential for achieving their goals and acting in a coherent manner, for both self-interested and collectively motivated agents. However, the coordination is difficult to achieve in open multi-agent systems, where designers can introduce, eliminate and modify their agents at any time. Due to the emergence of standards for agent communication languages like FIPA-ACL or KQML, we can assume that, even in open systems, the agents will all speak the same language, but problems may arise from the use of interaction protocols, i.e., the rules that guide the conversations between agents.

Although we are describing the use of negotiation protocols, the ideas presented in this paper can easily be adapted to any interaction protocol in general. New agents arriving in the system cannot be assumed to know a priori the protocols used by the other existing agents, so a mechanism, which allows them to use these protocols, is necessary. The solution that we propose in this paper is to endow the system with a server that contains all the negotiation protocols used there and that can be queried by the agents for these protocols. The idea has been initially proposed in [11] and it has been reformulated later, in [14], but without providing a practical implementation solution in a multi-agent system.

The remainder of the paper is structured as follows. Section 2 presents related work and several solutions for the implementation of a protocol server, while the solution we propose is described in Section 3. The experiments using this solution and their results are described in Section 4, while in the next section we are drawing some conclusions and tracing directions for future work.

V. Mařík et al. (Eds): CEEMAS 2003, LNAI 2691, pp. 413–422, 2003.

2   Engineering a Protocol Server

Although the idea of using a server that contains protocols and can be queried by agents seems simple and attractive, it is difficult to put it into practice. The two main questions one has to answer when defining a protocol server are: how are the agents interacting with the server (i.e., what queries is the agent able to make and how is the server responding to these queries), and what is the form of the protocols stored on the server that allows the agents to choose and use them? In what follows, we will describe the approaches we have investigated to answer the later and in the next section we will propose an answer for the former.

2.1   A Server Containing Protocol Descriptions

Most of the work done in the multi-agent community to create agents able to automatically understand and use negotiation protocols is aimed at creating a language to describe the protocol and equipping the agent with an interpreter for this language, thus enabling it to understand the protocol description (see Fig.2.a). A lot of work has been done in this domain and it seems a good idea to use such a language for our protocol server. However, we will show that it is very difficult to create a language able to describe all the characteristics of a protocol and hence to enable the agent to fully negotiate using the protocol, not just understand it.

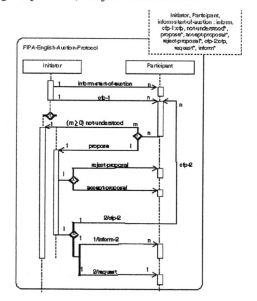

Fig.1. FIPA English auction interaction protocol

One of the languages used for protocol description, that is also adopted by FIPA [3] for its specifications concerning interaction protocols, is AUML [10]. Although it is a semi-formal (graphical) language, formal representations of it have been proposed, such as the one based on XML from [5] or the one from [7]. Unfortunately, as the authors of [1] have remarked, there is a huge difference between what is usually called a negotiation protocol (in FIPA terminology and as presented in Fig.1), which contains some rules to be followed during a negotiation, and a negotiation mechanism, which should include all the rules that guide a negotiation, from start to end. For example, using the FIPA English auction interaction protocol shown in Fig.1, one can create two agents that are not able to participate in the same auction, even if their negotiation is conforming to this protocol. There are many "details" of the negotiation that are missing from the description of the protocol, like how long the initiator should wait until declaring the end of the auction or what are the valid bids.

But AUML is not the only language used to represent the protocol. An exhaustive survey of all the proposed formalisms is difficult to make and it is out of the scope of this paper, but the most used are the states machines and the Petri nets [6]. Other languages have been proposed as well, like the one in [4], but none of the above-mentioned formalisms allows one to express all the rules that govern the interactions between agents. We do not intend to disqualify this research, but rather advocate the need of more complete negotiation mechanism descriptions to allow the agents to automatically negotiate.

Moreover, another problem rises from the separation that is done between the negotiation protocol and the objects that are negotiated. If we want to allow an agent to automatically understand and use a protocol, we have to specify what are the objects that it is supposed (allowed) to use in each step of the negotiation, but, to our knowledge, very few languages deal with this characteristic of the negotiation mechanism, one exception being the one in [11].

Another category of languages for protocol description is represented by symbolic logics, specifically modal logics, as in [12]. The high representation power of these languages has the drawback of computational complex interpreters that have to be created for them. However, a possible solution using this approach is given in [13], where the authors are using multi-context systems to reduce the complexity of logic-based agents. Starting from this, one can envisage the description of protocols in terms of a chosen logic and the dynamic integration of such protocol in a multi-context based agent, enabling it to negotiate.

2.2   A Server Containing Protocol-Components

As presented in the preceding sub-section, it is difficult to find a suitable description of a negotiation protocol that will allow one to completely specify all the aspects of the negotiation mechanism and permit the agent equipped with an associated interpreter to negotiate using that protocol. This is probably the reason why all the existing negotiation mechanisms are hard-coded in the agents and not external. Hard-coding the protocols solves all the problems raised by the use of an external description and associated interpreter, but agent's negotiation following multiple protocols is extremely heavy-weighted.

To overcome these difficulties, we propose the introduction of special components, called protocol-components, which know how to negotiate using only one protocol, hard-coded inside. Creating such components for every needed protocol and placing them on the protocol server will then allow an agent that doesn't know how to negotiate to participate in negotiations using a protocol-component. When the agent willing to negotiate will ask the server how to negotiate using a specific protocol, the server will create a dedicated component that will be used to negotiate by the first agent.

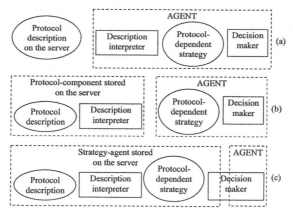

Fig. 2. Possible solutions to architect a protocol server

As Fig. 2.b shows, our view is based on the clear distinction between the negotiation protocol and the decision-making module in a negotiation proposed in [9]. The agent makes decisions based on its desires, beliefs or, generally speaking, its mental state, but the execution of the negotiation protocol is done by the protocol-component. Thus, the need of defining an interaction between an agent and the component negotiating in its place, allowing communication of agent's decisions and protocol-component's replies.

Regardless of the complexity of such an interaction (we don't even know if it is possible), there is another problem with the separation of protocols and decision-making modules on different components: there are decisions during a negotiation that are protocol-dependent. For example, very often during a negotiation, an agent has to make the choice between making an offer or not. But the effect of the choice is strongly dependent on the protocol used: in a Dutch auction, making an offer will end the auction, while in an English one, neither making nor not making an offer will not end the auction. It is thus impossible to make "intelligent" decisions without knowing the effects of the decision on the negotiation process (i.e. without knowing the protocol).

2.3   A Server Containing Strategy-Agents

To solve the above-mentioned problem, we have endowed the protocol-components with some decision-making capabilities (i.e., those that are protocol-dependent), thus transforming them into strategy-agents, as presented in Fig.2.c. These agents are able to negotiate following a given protocol and a given strategy for that protocol. We call these new components 'agents' because they are now able to make some decisions and thus to show some forms of autonomy.

An agent wanting to negotiate will query the server about the protocols it knows and the negotiation strategies for each protocol, and will choose one of them. The server will create a strategy-agent (or will extract one from an agent-pool) and will recommend it to the first agent who will ask it to negotiate in its place. The strategy-agent will negotiate following the protocol it knows and making the needed decisions according to the negotiation strategy it represents. Because some of the decisions require information from the first agent, the interaction between the strategy-agent and the initial agent still exists, but it is now less complex, because the decisions the agent has to make now do not concern anymore the interactions, but the delegations it wants to make. More than this, this approach allows one to build protocol-independent decision-making modules on the agents.

An interesting question is how can an agent be sure it is using an honest strategy-agent, which is negotiating for its best interest and it's not trying to make another agents gain more, i.e. how can an agent trust its strategy-agent. More than this, during the negotiation, the strategy-agent may need information about the mental state of the first agent, information classified by the later as confidential. Even if we don't provide solutions to these problems in this paper, we would like to mention that the same trust issues appear when the agents are using protocol descriptions taken from an external source (as depicted in section 2.1). The developers have to choose between coding all the protocols in their agents or trusting an external source that provides negotiation knowledge to their agents. We can say that this external source is a service provider (e.g. the protocol server) that offers some services (e.g. protocol descriptions, strategy-agents) and then the agents have to trust these services.

3   A Strategy-Agent Server

The solution we have chosen to engineer the protocol server in our system is to use what we have called strategy-agents. These agents know how to negotiate using a given strategy for a given protocol and nothing more. An agent willing to negotiate will query the server to obtain the reference of a strategy-agent and will communicate with it to allow negotiation in its place. Fig.3 is describing what is happening in the system when an agent wants to negotiate with another using a strategy-agent. Note that if we mask the interactions between the agents and their strategy-agents, all that one can see is two agents negotiating, which means that the overall behaviour of the system doesn't change.

One can see that are three types of interactions here: the interaction between the agent and the server, the interaction between the agent and its strategy-agent, and the interaction between the strategy-agents (i.e. the negotiation). The next sub-sections will detail the first two interactions, the third being out of the scope of this paper, as it represents the different negotiations that may exist in the system.

3.1   Interactions between an Agent and the Server

An agent wanting to start a negotiation and not knowing what protocol to use, will query the server to obtain the list of existing protocols and strategies and will chose one of them. This server-query protocol is a very simple one and it is similar with the ones used by FIPA or in KQML for the yellow pages service; for space considerations it will not be detailed here.

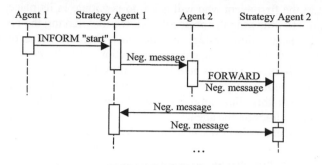

Fig. 3. Negotiation using strategy-agents

The available protocols and strategies must have a description of their characteristics on the server, description that will be communicated to the agents to allow them to choose between different protocols and strategies. Thus, a language for the meta-description of protocols and strategies must be used, but such a language is far from being easy to identify. Even for humans, it is difficult to express in natural language what are the differences between two negotiation strategies, for example, without describing how the decision-making process is taking place. However, it should be easier to describe what are the properties of a protocol than to describe the protocol itself, like the languages described in section 2.1 are trying to do.

Such a language is subject of future work. Towards this aim, one of the research directions we are currently investigating is the protocol description criteria proposed in [2]. A step forward towards creating languages for the description of protocol characteristics is presented in [15], where the authors describe the use of a negotiation ontology that describes protocols and that can be understood by the agents willing to negotiate.

For the moment, each agent is keeping statistics of the used protocols and strategies and is associating a probability to each protocol/strategy according to the previous experiences it has had using it (e.g. the percentage of successful negotiations ended using that protocol/strategy). After each negotiation an agent updates these probabilities and when it has to choose a protocol/strategy, it will make a random choice between the available options but taking into account the associated probability.

3.2   Interactions between an Agent and Its Strategy-Agent

After obtaining the id of a strategy agent from the server, an agent will ask the strategy agent to start negotiating in its place and will wait to be informed of the negotiation result. However, as seen in Fig. 4, the strategy-agent may ask the agent to provide information needed in the decision-making process several times, for example its related beliefs or desires, if the agents are built using the BDI model. The strategy coded in the strategy-agent is a general strategy that needs to be customized by every agent and this is done using the *request-inform* pairs of messages displayed in Fig. 4. Although it may seem that the information passed between the two agents is complex, our practical tests (see Section 4) have shown that the strategy-agent needs to know very few things.

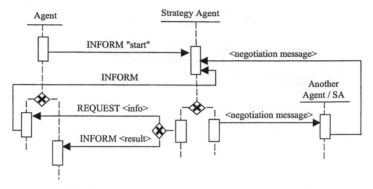

Fig. 4. Agent – strategy-agent interaction protocol

One may argue that we haven't treated at all the problems raised by the use of different negotiation objects. After all, if we want to create open multi-agent systems where all agents can negotiate, we have to allow them to use different negotiation objects. But nothing stops us of having domain-dependent strategy-agents and the agents will have to choose a strategy not only based on its characteristics, but also based on the negotiation objects it handles.

4   Practical Tests

In order to test if our approach using strategy-agents is practicable and to identify what are the practical problems raised by this approach, we have created a multi-agent system in which the agents do not know any negotiation protocol *a priori*. The system was implemented in JADE [8] and it consists of a seller agent and three buyer agents. The seller has a list of objects that it tries to sell and each agent associates a private value to each existing object.

We have also created a special agent in the system, called *Strategy Server*, which contains a list (in XML format) with four auction protocols: the English auction, the Dutch auction, the First Price Sealed Bid auction, and the Vickerey auction. This special agent represents nothing else but an infrastructure service, like a facilitator agent. The major difference between a classical facilitator and our *StrategyServer* is that the later is creating the agents before recommending them.

From the implementation point of view, a negotiation protocol is viewed as a JADE behaviour with several abstract methods that are used to make the decisions. These methods are implemented in subclasses that represent the strategies for that protocol. This implementation allows one to solve the problems raised by a protocol description language by hard coding the negotiation mechanism.

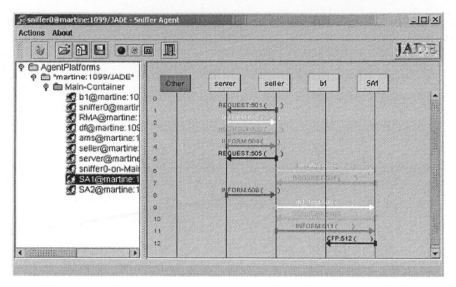

Fig. 5. Interactions in our system as viewed by the *Sniffer* agent from JADE

A snapshot of the interactions between the agents as viewed by the Sniffer agent is presented in Fig.5. When a strategy agent is requested, the server will create this agent and will introduce it in the system. It will also create an object of the class representing the requested strategy and will add it as the behaviour of the strategy agent just created.

As we mentioned before, each agent is keeping statistics of the used protocols and strategies and is associating a probability to each protocol/strategy according to the previous experiences it has had using it (e.g. the percentage of successful negotiations ended using that protocol/strategy). Because the description of the protocol characteristics (using a negotiation ontology, for example) is still subject of future work, the agent is using these statistics to choose between several protocols or strategies.

One of our concerns was the amount of information the strategy-agent needs from the agent in order to make decisions during the negotiation. Our practical tests have shown that it needs to know only few things: with whom to negotiate, what to negotiate (i.e., the negotiation object) or what is the agent's desire regarding this negotiation object. This simplicity is due to two factors. One is the agent's architecture we used for this test: they are simple BDI-based agents that have beliefs concerning the value of the existing objects and that may have desires to acquire them or not. The second is the simplicity of the negotiation protocols we used (auction protocols) and of the decision-making modules with which we embedded the strategy-agents. For further tests and to identify other types of information exchanged between agents and their strategy-agents, we want to extend the negotiations in our system using more complex protocols and more developed decision-making modules.

5   Conclusions and Future Work

In this paper, we have addressed the task of engineering a protocol server, a tool that will allow negotiation in open MAS. We have shown that current trends proposing the description of a negotiation protocol in a formal language are facing significant difficulties, firstly because it is difficult to encapsulate all the aspects of a negotiation in such a language and secondly, even if this will be done, it is impossible to create agents able to make negotiation decisions using a protocol not known a priori.

To avoid these problems we came back to the idea of hard-coding the negotiation protocol inside the agents, like in most of the existing multi-agent systems, but instead of coding in our agents all the virtually needed protocols (task that, if possible, will lead to extremely heavy agents), we have decided to create small strategy-agents that know how to negotiate using only one strategy for one protocol. Then one can populate the protocol server with these strategy-agents and remove from the system agents all the negotiation-related knowledge, allowing them to request the strategy-agents to negotiate on their behalf.

A needed extension to our work is to propose a language for the meta-description of protocols and strategies to allow the agents to better choose the protocol/strategy in a particular negotiation. Towards this aim, the work presented in [2] will be further investigated, but our practical tests have shown that the agents need to know at least what negotiation objects are handled by the protocol and what are the roles they can play. As for choosing the protocol/strategy to use, our approach using statistics based on the results obtained in previous negotiations seems to give good results. Another approach will be to let the agents use a form of learning (e.g. reinforcement learning).

As we mentioned before, an interesting question is what trust the agents may have in the server and the services it provides. Once this trust problem has been solved, one can imagine the creation of strategy-agent libraries on the Internet, available for all, where developers can upload their own strategy-agents that will be then available to other agent developers, hence reducing the time spent with the development of agents able to negotiate and allowing heterogeneous agents not only to understand each other, but to be able to interact with each other too.

Acknowledgements

The authors would like to thank dr. Olivier Boissier from Ecole Nationale Supèrieure des Mines de Saint Etienne and prof. dr. Adina Florea from "Politehnica" University of Bucharest for their contribution to this article.

References

[1]   Bartolini, C., Preist, C., Jennings, N.: Architecting for reuse: A software framework for automated negotiation. In Proc. of the 3rd International Workshop on Agent-Oriented Software Engineering, Bologna, Italy (2002) 87-98

[2]   Bussman, S., Jennings, N., Wooldridge, M.: Re-use of interaction protocols for agent-based control applications. In Proc. of the 3rd International Workshop on Agent-Oriented Software Engineering, Bologna, Italy (2002) 51-62

[3]   FIPA – Specification, Interaction Protocol Library. Foundation for Intelligent Physical Agents, http://www.fipa.org (2001)

[4]   Freire, J., Botelho, L.: Executing explicitly represented protocols. In Proc. of the Workshop Challenges in Open Agent Systems, Bologna, Italy (2002)

[5]   Huget, M-Ph.: A language for exchanging Agent UML Protocol Diagrams. Technical Report ULCS-02-009, University of Liverpool (2002)

[6]   Koning, J-L.: Designing and Testing Negotiation Protocols for Electronic Commerce Applications. AgentLink (2001) 34-60

[7]   Koning, J-L., Romero-Hernandez, I.: Generating machine processable representations of textual representations of AUML. In Proc. of the 3rd International Workshop on Agent-Oriented Software Engineering, Bologna, Italy (2002) 39-50

[8]   JADE (Java Agent DEvelopment Framework), http://jade.cselt.it/

[9]   Jennings, N., Faratin, P., Lomuscio, A., Parsons, S., Sierra, C., Wooldridge, M.: Automated Negotiations: Prospects, Methods and Challeges. Int. Journal of Group Decision and Negotiation, 10(2) (2002) 199-215

[10]   Odell, J., van Dyke Parunak, H., Bauer, B.: Representing Agent Interaction Protocols in UML. In P.Ciancarini, M.Wooldridge (eds.) Proc. of first Interantional Workshop on Agent-Oriented Software Enginnering, Limerick, Ireland, Springer-Verlag (2000)

[11]   Populaire, P., Demazeau, Y., Boissier, O., Sichman, J. : Description et Implémentation de Protocoles de Communication en Univers Multi-Agents. Actes des premières journées francophones sur les Systèmes Multi-Agents organisées par l'AFCET, Toulouse (1993)

[12]   Quintero, A, Ucros, M, Takahashi, S.: Multi-agent System Protocol Language Specification. In Proc. of the CIKM Workshop on Intelligent Information Agents (1995)

[13]   Sabater, J., Sierra, C., Parsons, S., Jennings, N.: Engineering executable agents using multi-context systems. Journal of Logic and Computation 12 (3) 413-442

[14]   Sycara, K.: Agents transacting in Open Environments. Course presented at the Advanced Course on Artificial Intelligence (ACAI'01), Prague (2001) 181-221

[15]   Tamma, V., Wooldridge, M., Dickinson, I.: An ontology based approach to automated negotiation. In Proc. of the 4th International Workshop on Agent-Mediated Electronic Commerce (AMEC-2002), Bologna, Italy (2002)

Refinement of Open Protocols for Modelling and Analysis of Complex Interactions in Multi-agent Systems[*]

Nabil Hameurlain

LIUPPA Laboratory
Avenue de l'Université, BP 1155, 64013 Pau France.
nabil.hameurlain@univ-pau.fr

Abstract. This paper proposes to study a refinement of open and concurrent interaction protocols, allowing hierarchical construction of complex interactions in multi-agent systems. The generic approach presented in this paper integrates Petri nets formalism and component based approach. The study of the refinement of the protocols by the principle of component-substitutability has been used to address one of the key issues of component-based software development, *consistency*: will a *component protocol* fit or not? This paper provides new results to deal with some protocol engineering issues through the specification and the verification of such protocols.

1 Motivation

Interaction is a fundamental component of the dynamic of open multi-agent systems. It is the fondation for cooperative or competitive behaviour among several autonomous agents. An *interaction protocol* is a means to structure and organise the different interactions that take place in a course of agent's conversation (communication, cooperation, coordination) [3]. In the last years, many efforts and frameworks (such KQML [13], ACL [4], …) have been made in order to support the organisation of interactions in MAS. These frameworks intend to develop interaction language by specifying messages and protocols for inter-agent conversation. Nevertheless, engineering issues raised related to the use of protocols, such as: design of complex protocols, especially the specification and the verification of open and concurrent one, implementation and reuse of protocols, and performance analysis and testing of protocols.

The main contribution of this paper is to propose a formal design for modelling and analysis of complex interactions and open protocols. We are interested in open proto-

---

[*] This research is funded by the STIC-CNRS Department, under the grant SUB/2002/0097/DR16, in the context of C2ECL (Coordination et Contrôle de l'Exécution de Composants Logiciels) Project.

V. Mařík et al. (Eds): CEEMAS 2003, LNAI 2691, pp. 423-434, 2003.
© Springer-Verlag Berlin Heidelberg 2003

cols based on abstraction/ refinement concept, and propose a formal semantics for the refinement of protocol taking into account behavioural property preservation, together with some verification and validation aspects.

Protocol engineering is one of the emerging problems of agent-based software computing, becoming actually one of the challenging problems. Up to now, few works tackle the above issues of protocols engineering. [7] propose *Agentis*, a framework for building interactive multi-agent applications, providing the specification of protocols based on services, together with the formal specification in Z. The authors also provide some general guidelines which may be applied to the specification of protocols for agent interaction. In [12], the authors propose an extension of AUML for the modular design of interaction protocols by composing micro-protocols; the main contribution of this approach is to reduce the gap between informal specification of interaction and semi-formal one by using protocol diagrams (AUML sequence diagrams). In [2] the authors study the problem of re-use of protocols for agent-based control applications; they give a classification scheme enables a designer to select a suitable interaction protocol for his interaction problem without going through all the interaction protocols available. All these approaches focus on the structure for complex interactions: elements required in the specification of interaction and different levels (hierarchy) of protocols [7], graphical language for designing protocols by the composition of sub-protocols [12], number of agents (and roles) involved in the conversation, compatibility of constraints and preferences [2]. Nevertheless, specification and verification of open interaction protocols remains non trivial process [7, 9, 14], and protocol engineering issues raised an open problem for MAS. Recently [9], a generic and global approach for protocol engineering through the analysis, the specification, and the verification of interaction was proposed. The approach is independent from any ACL, and covers the relevant protocol engineering issues. The authors first, give guidelines for AUML protocol diagrams (semi-formal specification) translation to (formal specification by means of) coloured Petri nets. Then they define the main properties and their validation to be satisfied in order to build reliable protocols, and finally propose a model for open protocols based on abstraction/ refinement using recursive coloured Petri nets. Nevertheless, no semantics are associated to the refinement. In addition, the property preservation by refinement is not addressed.

This paper aims to provide formal semantics for the refinement of interaction protocols. We are interested in open and concurrent interaction protocols. In our approach, protocols are designed by means of *Components Protocol* Petri nets formalism (CP-nets): Petri nets are used for specification, verification of protocols, and component-based approach [15] is used as a high-level concept for the abstraction of the specification.

The paper is organised as follows: the second section presents the basic definitions of Labelled Petri nets together with Components Protocol formalism and their main properties. In the third section, we present actions-refinement, and show how to model complex and open interaction protocols in an elegant and easier way, together with the study of the property preservation by refinement. Then, we give semantics for refinement of protocols by substitutability principle followed by the main result of this paper: the refinement of protocols by substitutability guarantees the consistency property from component-based approach point of view [16]: " will the component protocol operate as specified if the specification is replaced by the actual component proto-col?".

2   Formal Specification of Open Interaction Protocols

In this section we define *Components Protocol* formalism, based on Petri nets [10] and component-based approach [15]: Petri nets are used as a formalism for protocol engineering [1, 9]. They allow concurrency, analysis, validation, and refinement of the modelled protocols. Component-based approach is used as a high level concept of abstraction which consider a protocol as a collection of sub-protocols, dealing with modelling complex interactions (conversations) between agents (integration, compo-sition of sub-protocols, and so on). Components Protocol nets (CP-nets) consider communicative acts and internal processing of the underlying contents as actions. These actions can be processed in some specific order, sequentially or concurrently. The way in which the protocol processes these contents (storing and extracting of the information) is not taken into account by the specification of the component.

For the simplicity, and in order to make our approach more general, we will specify protocols by Labelled classical Petri nets instead of high level (e.g., Coloured) Petri nets since from theoretical point of view, any Coloured Petri nets may be translated to classical Labelled Petri nets [10] [1].

2.1   Backgrounds on Labelled Petri Nets

A Petri net is represented by directed bipartie graph with two node types: places and transitions. Graphically, we represent places by circles and transitions by rectangles. An arc can only connect a place to a transition or a transition to a place. In the first case, the place is called an input place, and in the second case, an output place.

Most of the time, the resources of a system are described by places, and the opera-tions by transitions. The number n of available resources in a place is represented by n tokens (black dots) in p. At a given time, the state (*marking*) of the system is defined by its distribution of tokens over places. The dynamic (*behaviour*) of the system is described by the execution of transitions which moves tokens from input places to output places according to the two following rules: (1) A transition t is said to be en-abled under a marking M, noted M (t >, if each input places p of t has at least one token. An enabled transition may fire. In this case t may occur, and its *occurrence* yields the follower marking M', noted M(t > M'. (2) If a transition t fires, then t re-moves one token from each input place p of t and deposes one token on each output place. The enabling and the firing of a sequence of transition are defined inductively.

Formally, a marked Petri net $N = (P, T, W, M_N)$ consists of a finite set P of places, a finite set T of transitions where $P \cap T = \varnothing$, a weighting function $W : P \times T \cup T \times P \rightarrow \mathbb{N}$, and $M_N : P \longrightarrow \mathbb{N}$ is an initial marking. The preset of a node $x \in P \cup T$ is defined as $^\bullet x = \{y \in P \cup T, (y, x) \in W\}$, and the postset of $x \in P \cup T$ is defined as

---

[1] This result is valid if and only if the coloured Petri nets does not contain inhibitor arcs.

$x^{\bullet} = \{y \in P \cup T, (x, y) \in W\}$. We denote as $LN = (P, T, W, M_N, l)$ the (marked, labelled) Petri net (see [10] for further information) in which the events represent actions, which can be observable. It consists of a marked Petri net $N = (P, T, W, M_N)$ with a labelling function $l : T \longrightarrow A \cup \{\lambda, v\}$, where A is the set of services, that is the alphabet of observable actions, and *{λ}* denotes the special unobservable action, which plays the usual role of an internal action, whose execution is under the control of the net alone, and the symbol *{v}* stands for action which is unobservable to a particular client of a server net, but is not under the control of the net alone; it may have to be executed together with another client of the net. A sequence of actions $w \in A^* \cup \{\lambda\}$ is enabled under the marking M and its occurrence yields a marking M', noted $M(w \gg M'$, iff either $M = M'$ and $w = \lambda$ or there exists some sequence $\sigma \in T^*$ such that $l(\sigma) = w$ and $M(\sigma > M'$. (The first condition accounts for the fact that λ is the label image of the empty sequence of transitions). Reach $(N) = \{M; \exists \sigma \in T^*; M_N(\sigma > M\}$ is the set of reachable markings of the net N.

A labelled Petri net makes some services available to the nets and is capable of rendering these services. Each offered service is associated to one or several transitions, which may be requested by nets, and the service is available when one of these transitions is enabled. On the other hand it can request services from other net and needs these requests to be fulfilled. Thus, a net may be a server (and/ or client) if and only if it accepts (and/ or requests) at least one service.

Definition 2.1 (Trace and Language)
Let $N = (P, T, W, M_N, l)$ be a labelled Petri net. Tr $(N) = \{\sigma \in T^*; M_N(\sigma >\}$ is the trace of N, i.e. the set of enabled transition sequences of N. The label image of the trace of N is its language $L(N) = l(Tr(N)) = \{w \in A^*; \exists \sigma \in Tr(N), l(\sigma) = w\}$.

Definition 2.2 (Failure)
The failure of the net N, noted by $F(N) = \{(\sigma, S); \sigma \in T^*, S \subseteq T$, and there exists some marking M such that $M_N(\sigma > M$, and $\forall t \in S$, not $(M(t >)\}$, are the pairs (σ, S) where σ is a sequence of transitions processed by a net, and S is a set of transitions that the net may refuse to perform after undergoing σ and reaching a stable marking[2].

The label image of the failure of N is $F(N, l) = \{(w, X); w \in A^* \cup \{\lambda\}, X \subseteq A$, and there exists some marking M such that $M_N(\sigma > M$, $l(\sigma) = w$, M stable, and $\forall a \in X$, not $(M(a \gg))\}$.

Operations on Labelled Petri Nets. To give a semantics to the refinement of protocols, we will need two basic operations on the nets, abstraction and cancellation:

- *Abstraction* of an action "*a*" renames all "*a*"s transitions into λ transitions. An abstraction introduces new non-stable states, from which the refusal sets are not taken into account for the failure semantics. The *abstraction operator* λ labels as not observable and internal actions, some transitions of a Labelled net. Formally, given a net $N = (P, T, W, M_N, l)$, for each $I \subseteq A$, $\lambda_I(N) = N' = (P, T, W, M_N, l')$ such that $l'(t) = l(t) = s$, if $t \in T$ and $s \in A \setminus I$, $l'(t) = \lambda$ else.

---

[2] A marking is *stable* if no unobservable action λ is enabled.

- Cancellation is another kind of abstraction, which does look at the new non-stable states when computing failures. The *cancellation operator* δ labels as not observable, but not internal actions, some transitions of a Labelled net. It renames transitions into v transitions. Formally, given a net $N = (P, T, W, M_N, l)$, for each $H \subseteq A$, $\delta_H(N) = N' = (P, T, W, M_N, l')$ such that $l'(t) = l(t) = s$, if $t \in T$ and $s \in A \setminus H$, $l'(t) = v$ else.

2.2   Components Protocol Nets

For the specification of protocols, we use labelled Petri nets with specific structure. We will name these nets *Components Protocol* nets (CP-nets). Components Protocol formalism are closed to the Recursive Coloured Petri Nets (RCPN) [9], with a subtle difference concerning the operational semantics: CP formalism uses (preserves) the classical operational semantics of the labelled Petri nets, including observable and unobservable actions (both internal actions controlled locally, and those controlled by another component). In addition, within CP formalism, the specification of protocols should be structured according to the component-based approach.

Semantically, a Component Protocol involves actions, which are observable or not observable together with two special places: the first one is the input place for instance creation of the component; and the second one is the output place for instance completion of the component. The observable actions involve both atomic actions (send/ receive performatives) and complex actions, called *abstract-actions*. These last are considered as complex operations or composite communicative acts and their execution requires a substitution (refinement for example) by a new sub-component protocol. This distinction allows the use of the refinement concept providing concise modelling of complex and open interactions between agents. We will see (section 3) that components protocol formalism provides abstraction and dynamics in the structure of agents' conversation.

Definition 2.3 (CP-net)
Let $N = (P \cup \{I, O\}, T, W, M_N, l)$ be a labelled Petri net. N is a *Component Protocol* net (CP-net) if and only if the following conditions are satisfied:

1. *Instance creation*: the set of places contains a specific *Input* (source) place I, such that $^\bullet I = \varnothing$,
2. *Instance completion*: the set of places contains a specific *Output* place O, such that $O^\bullet = \varnothing$.
3. *Visibility*: for any $t \in T$ such that $t \in \{I^\bullet \cup ^\bullet O\}$: $l(t) \in A$.

The last requirement states that all the transitions related to the Input place I, and to the Output place O, are necessarily observable actions. They give input (parameters) and output (results) of the performed protocol.

Notation. In the rest of this paper, we denote by [I] and [O], which are considered as bags, the markings of the Input and the Output place of CP, together with its initial marking M_N, and by Reach (CP, [I]), the set of reachable markings of the component net CP obtained from its initial marking M_N within one token in its Input place I.

Definition 2.4 (Soundness)

Let CP = (P ∪ {I, O}, T, W, M_N, l) be a *Component Protocol* net (CP-net). CP is said to be *sound* if and only if the following conditions are satisfied:

1. *Completion option*: for any reachable marking M ∈ Reach (CP, [I]), [O] ∈ Reach(CP, M).
2. *Reliability option*: for any reachable marking M ∈ Reach (CP, [I]), [O] ∈ M implies M = [O].

A *Sound* Component Protocol has a life-cycle which satisfies the completion and the reliability options. *Completion* option states that, if starting from the initial state, i.e. activation of the protocol, it is always possible to reach the marking with one token in the output place O. *Reliability* option states that the moment a token is put in the output place O corresponds to the termination of a protocol without leaving dangling references.

2.3   Property of Interaction Protocols

Since Components Protocol nets model the behaviour of protocols by means of Petri nets, two kinds of properties should be verified [10]: structural property which are related to Petri nets topology. These kinds of properties help designer to build correct specification of the protocol, independent of the number of agents, resources; and behavioural properties, depend of the fixed initial state of the protocol, and concerns qualitative behaviour of the protocol. In this paper we are interested in behavioural properties of protocols and their interpretation in the context of multi-agent systems. Some of them have been discussed in [9].

*   *Quasi-liveness*. This property guarantees that there are no dead actions in the protocol. This means that for each action of the protocol, there is a firing sequence activating it.
*   *Boundedness*. This property ensures that any message received by the Component Protocol during the conversation will be treated in the future. It will not be accumulated in the component.
*   *Deadlock/ Successful termination*. We want to distinguish successful termination of the protocol from deadlock. When a protocol is in a state in which it cannot perform any action or terminate successfully, then it said to be in deadlock. The state with one token in Output place corresponds to successful termination.
*   *Deadlock-free*. This property ensures the absence of deadlock, i.e., from an initial state, at least an operation can be carried out whatever the state reached during a conversation.
*   *Liveness*. It ensures that all the operations (actions) can always be processed whatever the state reached during the conversation. The liveness property is stronger than deadlock-free one.
*   *Accessibility*. It makes possible to lead a conversation to a desired state starting from the initial marking.

3   Refinement and Substitutability of Protocols

Abstraction and refinement are often used together in specification, and validation of large, complex, and open MAS. The abstraction concept is derived from its ability to hide irrelevant details reducing the complexity of interactions in MAS. Refinement is a crucial component in the production of provably reliable software. In the context of open interaction protocols, the designer tends to start with abstract view of the protocol, and progressively refines that specification by adding more detail. In this section we use the concept of abstraction/ refinement to design open interaction protocols. We are interested in action-refinement; our proposals differ from those found in the context of (high level) Petri nets where substitution transitions, for example, are like macros or textual substitution. They maintain structural compatibility but there is no concept of abstract behaviour. Therefore our proposals are more constrained than textual substitution, since they require behavioural consistency between a refinement and its corresponding abstraction.

3.1   Semantics for the Refinement and Property Preservation

It consists in replacing an abstract-action of the Component Protocol by another sub-component Protocol. Then, the output (respectively input) transition of the *Input* (respectively *Output*) place may have more than one arc from (respectively to) the abstract component. This (canonical) refinement ensures that the output transitions of the *Input* place fire before the input transitions of the *Output* place in the refined component.

Definition 3.1 (Refinement)
Let $CP = (P \cup \{I, O\}, T, W, M_N, l)$, $a \in A$, be an abstract-action of CP, $CP' = (P' \cup \{I', O'\}, T', W', M'_N, l')$. Let $\underline{CP'} = (P', T', W', M'_N, l')$ be the component CP' without its Input and Output place.
The substitution of an action a by CP' in CP, noted [a/ CP'] CP, is the Component Protocol-nets [a/ CP'] CP obtained by the substitution of all the transitions t such l(t) = a, by $\underline{CP'}$ in the component CP. We say that [a/ CP'] CP is an action-refinement of CP.

Property 3.1 (Property Preservation by Completion)
Let CP and CP' be two components protocol. Let $a \in A$, be an abstract-action of CP, and $M \in$ Reach (CP, [I]).
  If CP' satisfy the *completion* option then,
  CP is quasi-live (respectively, $M \in$ Reach (CP, [I]))

  $\Rightarrow$ [a/ CP'] CP is quasi-live (respectively, $M \in$ Reach ([a/ CP'] CP, [I])).

Property 3.2 (Property Preservation by Soundness)
Let CP and CP' be two components protocol. Let $a \in A$, be an abstract-action of CP, and $M \in$ Reach (CP, [I]).
  If CP' is a *sound* CP-net then,
  CP is bounded (respectively, deadlock /termination, deadlock-free, live)

$\Rightarrow$ [a/ CP'] CP is bounded (respectively, deadlock/termination, deadlock-free, live).

The completion option ensures that the quasi-liveness and the accessibility properties are preserved by action-refinement, whereas the soundness ensures in addition the preservation of the boundedness, and the liveness properties (deadlock/termination, deadlock-free and liveness).

Example. The example consists to apply the FIPA-Request protocol (fig. 1) to an information gathering Protocol: an agent sends his request to a Cooperative Information Gathering System (CIGS). Note that the handling of the request depends on the CIGS, since each CIGS has a proper context (search engines), and a proper protocol. Let us suppose for instance the following CIG Protocol, managed by an Agent-Manager, which builds several (N) mobile agents for gathering information exploring the world Wide Web. The protocol is as follow: once the Agent-Manager receives the request *(Request-Handling)*, it decomposes the agent task in sub-tasks (action *Decomposing Task*). Then, run each agent that will make its trip, performing the sub-task *(Performing sub-task)* and will return the expected results. Finally, the agent-Manager merges *(merging results)* these results to build the final response. The formalisation of this protocol by means of Components protocol nets is given in fig. 2. This protocol is sound, and then the refinement of the FIPA-Request Protocol preserves its liveness, deadlock/ termination, and the boundedness property.

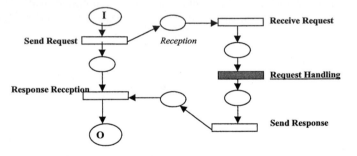

Fig. 1. FIPA-Request Protocol (Component Protocol modelling Request for gathering information)

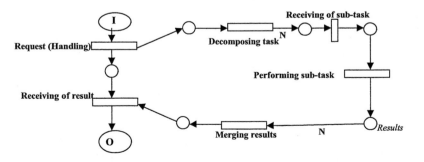

Fig. 2. A Cooperative Information Gathering Component Protocol, CIGCP

3.2   Refinement and Compositionality

Our main interest is in capturing *substitution* that is the ability to replace composite communicative acts in the component with another Component Protocol without losing behaviours (properties of the protocol). In this section we address this *consistency* property from component-based software development point of view, that is: "a component is consistent if, its component implementation (its internal architecture referring to other components) provides the functionality specified in its component specification" [15, 16].

Consistency can be characterised by the term *substitutability*: will the Component Protocol operate as specified if the specification is replaced by the actual Component Protocol? In earlier works [5, 6], we have proved that there are clear links between substitutability of components and behavioural inheritance. This paper uses the notion of weak and optimal behavioural inheritance, to check whether a component actually provides the external behaviour required.

Substitutability of Components. In [5], we have defined substitutability relations in the context of agent component-based approach. The (behaviour) protocol of an agent is constructed in a way similar to a regular expression, using the *Request Substitutability* (RS) relation [11] according to the Wegner and Zdonik's substitutability principle [8]. Substitutability allows extension of functionality, that is the subtype may have new services in addition to the one of the supertype. Basically there are two possibilities to treat the new services: we hide them (abstraction), and we cancel them (cancellation). In this paper , we use substitutability principle to give a characterisation to the concept of interaction protocols' refinement. First, we start to define Request Substitutability, then using the abstraction operator, we define the Weak Substitutability relation, and finally using the cancellation operator, we define the Optimal substitutability relation. Weak Substitutability is less restrictive than Optimal Substitutability.

Definition 3.2 (Request Substitutability (RS))
Let CP_1 and CP_2 be two CP-nets such that $A_1 \subseteq A_2$.
CP_2 is less or equal to CP_1 w.r.t *Request Substitutability (RS)* denoted $CP_2 \leq_{RS} CP_1$ iff $l_1(L(CP_1)) \subseteq l_2(L(CP_2))$ and $\forall (w, X') \in F(CP_2, l_2)$, $w \in l_1(L(CP_1))$, there exists $(w, X) \in F(CP_1, l_1)$ such that $X' \subseteq X$.

If CP_2 is less or equal to CP_1 w.r.t *Request Substitutability*, then the language of CP_2 must include the language of CP_1, and if the language of CP_1 is performed by CP_2, then its possible failures must be a subset of the corresponding failures of CP_1.

Definition 3.3 (Weak Substitutability)
Let CP_1 and CP_2 be two CP-net such that $A_1 \subseteq A_2$.
CP_2 is less or equal to CP_1 w.r.t *Weak Substitutability*, denoted $CP_2 \leq_{WS} CP_1$, iff there exists a set $I \subseteq A_2 \setminus A_1$ such that $\lambda_I(CP_2) \leq_{RS} CP_1$.

If CP_2 is less or equal to CP_1 w.r.t *Weak Substitutability*, then the component CP_1 can be substituted by the component CP_2 and any agent interacting with CP_1 will not be able to notice the difference since the new services added in the component CP_2 are considered unobservable, through the abstraction operator λ_I.

Definition 3.4 (Optimal Substitutability)

Let CP_1 and CP_2 be two CP-nets such that $A_1 \subseteq A_2$.

CP_2 is less or equal to CP_1 w.r.t *Optimal Substitutability*, denoted $CP_2 \leq_{OS} CP_1$ iff $\delta_H(CP_2) \leq_{RS} CP_1$ for $H = A_2 \setminus A_1$.

If CP_2 is less or equal to CP_1 w.r.t *Optimal Substitutability,* then the component CP_1 can be substituted by a component CP_2 and the client-agent will not be able to notice the difference even there exists another client-agent using the new services added in the component CP_2. In fact, these new services are considered unobservable, through the cancellation operator δ_H and can be executed *concurrently* with the old one.

Property Preservation by Substitutability. In [6], we show that Weak substitutability is the right relation if we would like to preserve, by substitutability, safety properties (quai-liveness, accessibility, deadlock-free). Optimal substitutability is the strongest relation. It guarantees the preservation of safety and liveness properties (deadlock/ termination, liveness). In addition, the weak substitutability is only suitable for components with single access (new performatives added must be operated in the sequential way with the old ones), whereas optimal substitutability is useful for shared components protocol (new performatives added could be performed concurrently with the old one). Finally, these two substitutability relations are compositional for component-agents interacting in asynchronous way by sending and receiving performatives, ensuring their compatibility with the incremental design of MAS according to bottom-up approach.

Theorem 3.1 (Consistency)

Let CP be a Component Protocol, and CP_1, CP_2 be two Components Protocol. Let a $\in$ A, be an abstract action of CP. Then:

$$CP_2 \leq_{WS} CP_1 \implies [a/\ CP_2]\ CP \leq_{WS} [a/\ CP_1]\ CP,$$

$$CP_2 \leq_{OS} CP_1 \implies [a/\ CP_2]\ CP \leq_{OS} [a/\ CP_1]\ CP.$$

This theorem ensures the consistency property: the weak and optimal substitutability relations are compositional for the refinement operation. It ensures the compatibility of the substitutability's principle with the refinement operation for the Components Protocol nets. This result is fundamental and necessary for designing complex and open interaction protocols in an incremental way by abstraction/ refinement, without loosing the behaviours of the protocol (properties of the protocol).

4   Conclusion

This paper proposes a formal semantics for the abstraction/refinement of open and concurrent interaction protocols. Refinement is characterised by the substitutability principle, taken into account the properties preservation of the protocol. The approach presented in this paper uses Components Protocol nets, a formalism integrating Petri nets and component-based approach. Petri nets are used to tackle the protocol engineering issues providing good properties to specify, validate and execute concurrent protocols. Component-based approach is used as a high level mechanism for the abstraction allowing hierarchical construction of complex protocols: a protocol could be considered as a collection of sub protocols, which can be executed sequentially or concurrently.

The study of the semantics of the refinement of protocols presented in this paper has been used to address one of the key issues of component-based software development, *consistency*: will a Component Protocol fit or not? To give an answer to this question, we use results about behavioural substitutability to check whether a Component Protocol actually provides the external behavioural required.

It is clear that the results presented in this paper could be fruitfully applied to other formalisms supporting behavioural specification of interaction protocols such as recursive coloured Petri nets formalism, since our approach (Component Protocol formalism) is independent of any ACL. The next future works intend to tackle the problem of the composition of protocols (in the context of bottom-up approach): how and when we could compose/refine two protocols? What are the semantics of the composition of protocols? What are the properties preserved by the composition? Our intention is to use both semantics and criteria taken from the specification of an interaction protocol such as compatibility of constraints and preferences, learning and number of agents and role [2], ontological aspects of (interaction protocol) components.

References

[1]   R. S. Cost, Y. Chen, T. Finin, Y. Labrou, Y. Peng. Using Colored Petri Nets for Conversation Modeling, Dignum and M. Greaves (Eds): Agent Communication, LNAI 1916, pp 178-192, Springer-Verlag, 2000.

[2]   N. Bussmann, N.Jennings, M. Wooldridge. Re-use of Interaction Protocols for Agent-based Control Applications. AOSE'02, Springer-Verlag, 2002.

[3]   J. Ferber. Les Systèmes Multi-agents : vers une intelligence collective, InterEditions, 1995.

[4]   FIPA. Specification Part 2: Agent Communication Language, November 1997.

[5]   N. Hameurlain. Formal Semantics for Behavioural Substitutability of Agent Components: Application to Interaction Protocols, CEEMAS 2001, LNAI 2296, Springer-Verlag, pp 131-140, 2002.

[6]   N. Hameurlain. Behavioural Subtyping and Property Preservation for Active Objects; Fifth IFIP International Conference on Formal Methods for Open Object-Based Distributed Systems, FMOODS'02, pp 95-110, Kluwer 2002.

[7]   M. d'Inverno, D. Kinny, M. Luck. Interaction Protocols in Agentis. In Proceedings of the Third International conference on Multi-agent systems, pp 112-119, IEEE Press, 1998.

[8]   B. H. Liskov, J. M. Wing. A Behavioral Notion of Subtyping; in ACM Trans. on Programming Languages and Systems, Vol 16, n° 6, Nov. 1994.

[9]   H. Mazouzi, A.El Fallah seghrouchni, S. Haddad. Open Protocol Design for complex Interactions in Multi-agent Systems. AAMAS 2002, ACM.

[10]   T. Murata. Petri Nets: Properties, Analysis and Applications; Proc. of the IEEE, vol. 77, N° 4, pp. 541-580.

[11]   O. Nierstrasz. Regular Types for Active Objects. In O. Nierstrasz and D. Tsi-chritzis eds, Object Oriented Software Composition, pages 99-121. Prentice-Hall, 1995.

[12]   J.-L. Koning, M-P. Huget, J. Wei, X. Wang. Extended Modeling Languages for interaction Protocol Design. In the proc. of AOSE'2001, Springer-Verlag, pages 93-100, 2001.

[13]   KQML. Specification of he KQML. Agent-communication Language. Techni-cal report, DARPA Knowledge Sharing Initiative External Interfaces Working Group, 1993.

[14]   S. Paurobally, J. Cunningham. Verification of Protocols for Automated Nego-tiation. ECAI 2002, pp 43-47, IOS Press.

[15]   C. Szyperski. Component Software: Beyond Object-Oriented Programming. ACM Press, Addison-Wesley, Reading, MA, USA, 1999.

[16]   W.M.P. Van der Aalst, K.M. van Hee, R.A. van der Toorn. Component-Based Software Architectures: A framework Based on inheritance of Behaviour. Sci-ence of computer Programming, 2002.

Biological Approach to System Information Security (BASIS): A Multi-agent Approach to Information Security

Victor Skormin[1], James Moronski[1], Dennis McGee[2], and Douglas Summerville[1]

[1] State University of New York at Binghamton
Electrical Engineering Dept.
Vestal, NY 13851 United States of America
{vskormin,james.moronski,dsummer}@binghamton.edu
[2] State University of New York at Binghamton
Biology Dept.
Vestal, NY 13851 United States of America
dmcgee@binghamton.edu

Abstract. Biological systems employ an inherently multi-agent approach for protection from external biological assault. If properly modeled and expanded to computer networking systems, new systems for information security can be designed and adopted. These approaches would be efficient and effective at not only preventing systems failure and damage from known forms of attack, they would be able to detect and limit the damage from an unknown form of attack. In this paper, the biological system is studied and compare to a computer networking system. A simple model is also developed to aid in the study of response to an attack.

1   Introduction

As computer networks become increasingly vulnerable to cyber terrorism, an attempt to develop a proactive defense mechanism inevitably steers designers towards already existing, naturally evolved, biological defense mechanisms. Biological immune systems are adaptable, self-regulating, automatic natural defense mechanisms that work to protect vertebrates from disease. Using the immune system, an inherent multi-agent system, as a model, a system to protect computers and computer networking systems from information attacks can be created.

1.1   The Components of a Biological Immune System

The immune system's function can be broken up into two functional units, innate immunity and acquired immunity. Innate immunity, also referred to as non-specific immunity, forms the basic resistance to infection that is possessed by any given species. It is comprised of many different types of barriers that are the first line of

V. Mařík et al. (Eds): CEEMAS 2003, LNAI 2691, pp. 435-444, 2003.

defense which protect the body from infection. These are the anatomic barrier, physiologic barrier, endocytic and phagocytic barriers, and the inflammatory response. Acquired immunity, additionally known as specific immunity, is the active portion of the immune system that is capable of recognizing and eliminating antigens. Acquired immunity is a much more complex system than innate immunity and is composed of specialized cells responsible for the detection and destruction of pathogens [1][2].

The anatomic barrier is comprised of the skin and other epithelial surfaces (stomach, intestine, respiratory, urinary tracts and others). These are the interfaces between the body and the outside world and work to effectively stop antigens before they are able to enter the body and start infection or cause damage. Problems such as damage to the tissues are detected and initiate the inflammatory response, which subsequently activates phagocytic cells.

The inflammatory response is characterized by an increase in the diameter of the blood vessels (vasodilatation), increased capillary dilation and an increase of the presence of phagocytic cells. Vasodilatation and increased capillary dilation allow for white blood cells, which are composed mostly of phagocytic cells, to migrate to the affected area. Also, inflammation serves to contain any potential infection to a localized area.

Physiologic barriers, working with the anatomic barrier further decrease the risk of infection. Temperature and pH are examples of physiologic barriers. When a pathogen comes in contact with, or passes by, the skin or epithelial surface, the environment that is present can slow or potentially prevent its growth and spread. Physiologic barriers provide some explanation as to why different animals are naturally immune to certain diseases. For example, chickens are naturally immune to anthrax because their high body temperature prevents growth and infection.

A more complex innate immune behavior is found in the endocytic and phagocytic barrier. Here, extracellular materials are ingested through endocytosis or phagocytosis. Ingestion occurs as certain cells internalize, by folding their cell walls around, the extracellular material forming endocytic vesicles. Upon internalization, these vesicles are routed to endosomes where the process of dissociation of the extracellular material begins.

When antigens breech the innate defense systems, acquired immunity is the next system involved in elimination of specific foreign microorganisms and molecules. The acquired immune system displays specificity, memory, diversity, and self/non-self recognition. Acquired immunity however does not act independently from the innate system, but in concert with it. Innate responses trigger responses from the acquired immune system.

The acquired immune system is composed of two groups of cells called lymphocytes and antigen-presenting cells. These of agents form the foundation for the active part of the immune system. Lymphocytes are one of many types of white blood cells that are produced in the bone marrow and circulate in the blood and lymph system. Lymphocytes are responsible for the specificity, memory, diversity, and self/non-self recognition found in the immune system. B-lymphocytes and T-lymphocytes comprise the majority of the lymphocytes.

B-lymphocytes, upon maturity, leave the bone marrow with a unique antigen-bonding receptor, which is an antibody, on their membrane. When the B-lymphocyte first encounters an antigen that matches its receptor, it begins to divide rapidly. Both memory B cells and effector cells called plasma cells are created. The memory B cells that are created retain the antigen-bonding receptor on their membranes and function as B-lymphocytes. The plasma cells do not form an antigen-bonding receptor. Instead, the antibody is secreted and acts as an effector molecule.

T-lymphocytes, unlike B-lymphocytes, mature in the thymus gland. Like B cells, T cells have an antigen-binding receptor on their membrane. Unlike the B cells, the T cell receptor cannot bind with an antigen unless the antigen is also associated with cell membrane proteins known as major histocompatibility complex (MHC) molecules. When a T cell comes in contact with an antigen associated with an MHC molecule, it begins to divide forming other effector T cells.

The lymph nodes are the home of many of the immune cells of the body. T cells act as the directors of the immune system. B cells produce antibodies, which bind to foreign antigens, and cytotoxic T cells kill virus infected cells. Amongst the immune cells are the antigen presenting cells (macrophages and dendritic cells) which sample antigen throughout the body, process them, transport them to the lymph nodes and present the processed antigen to the T cells. The sampling of antigen is continuous, including the sampling of self, for which there are no T cells to bind with, thus preventing a self-attack.

1.2   The Components of Computer Networking Systems

Computer systems and networks of computer systems already posses many of the characteristics of the immune system. In computer systems, anatomic barriers exist in the form of simple username/password security, connection encryption and process/user privileges. Extended to computer networks, hubs, switches, gateways and routers in their basic form provide effective barriers against many types of potential attacks. Furthermore, these systems can provide added security when an attack is underway by blocking or shunting potentially harmful network traffic away from sensitive systems or networks. The diversity of computer systems and networks also form another barrier to attack. Security holes and exploits usually affect specific operating systems on specific hardware platforms.

Antivirus and intrusion detection packages are created to further protect systems from infection and damage. One could almost consider this the "active" part of the computer's or computer network's immune system, but, in reality, these are nothing more than "dumb" barriers that are sometimes updated, usually after infection, after damage has already been done. Furthermore, no one tool has been developed to solve the problems with computer systems infection as infections can occur across platform, with different operating systems and different network implementations.

2   Anatomy of a Biological Attack

Infectious agents can enter a body in many ways. The consumption of food, air, and water required for life also constitute sources of infectious agents. Tissue damage, such as scrapes and cuts, provides additional paths for possible infection. The anatomic barriers prevent most sources of infection by making the environment inhospitable for infectious agents or just preventing their entry into the body. However, when an antigen makes is past these anatomic barriers, the active parts of the immune system work in concert with the anatomic barriers to first detect, then fight off infection [3].

One of the first responses of the immune system is the inflammation response. Inflammation occurs as a result of a release of chemical moderators from damaged cells. The cellular damage can be from trauma, temperature, contact with foreign substances and a host of other reasons. With the presence of the chemical moderators the local blood vessels dilate (vasodilatation). When this occurs, liquid fills in the affected region and it swells. This works to prevent contaminants from spreading beyond the affected region, in effect, isolating the damage. Furthermore, cells from the active portion of the immune system are attracted to inflamed areas and flow outside of cellular walls into the affected areas.

Macrophages are constantly working by picking up extra cellular material, processing it and transporting it the lymph nodes. In the lymph nodes, the macrophages will present the material to the T cells. If a T cell is present that recognizes the material, it (with potentially several T cells) will activate. The activated T cell will then undergo cell division many times to increase the number of cells which can respond to the infection (amplification of the response) and then these cells will begin to differentiate into effector T cells which will actually do the response.

The effector T cell has a fixed lifetime of two to five days, after which it will automatically die. This allows for the proper regulation of the response to ensure that the response does not go on longer than needed. The selected effector T cell then goes to the epithelium and directs the execution of the protection.

Effector T cells can secrete soluble factors (cytokines) to tell the epithelium to do things like express new receptors, produce new cytokines, open or close passages between epithelial cells, etc. They also could tell the tissue macrophages to become better antigen presenting cells and become better phagocytic cells. Finally, the effector T cells may be of a killer type (cytotoxic T lymphocytes or CTLs), which seek out virus-infected cells and kill them.

The nature of the infection and the type of cells activated would then determine the effector response generated such that the response is fine tuned to the infection. The immune response continues as long as there are functional effector T cells and that there is a need for the response. As long as there is antigen present, more effector T cells will be generated to replace the ones that are dying because of their fixed lifetime. This ensures that the immune response is maintained as long as needed. Once the antigen level begins to fall, there are fewer stimuli to produce new effector T cells. The remaining effector T cells simply die off at their prescribed lifetime.

Immune system memory is also developed during this process. As effector T cells are created, memory B cells, specific to the attacking antigen are also created. As more effector cells are created, the larger the infection, more memory cells are created. The memory B cells accumulate and have a much longer lifetime of ten to twenty years. Therefore, any second encounter with the antigen or pathogen will trigger the immune response more quickly, unlike the first encounter with the antigen or pathogen where there were only a few B cells with could respond to the antigen. If the body is continuously exposed to the antigen throughout its life, memory agents are continuously are produced, therefore making the memory permanent in the body.

2.1   The Denial of Service (DoS) Attack

The Denial of Service (DoS) attack is one of the most common and threatening types of attacks that can be launched against a computer or network of computers. The DoS attack endangers all computers systems connected to the Internet, including servers, clients (workstations), routers, and firewalls. In a DoS attack scenario, the attacker sends malicious traffic to the target with the aim of crashing, crippling, or jamming communication between the target system and legitimate users, effectively "killing" the computer system or the services that it offers.

Fundamentally, there are three DoS attack scenarios, all of which effectively disable the target and prevent its legitimate use. In the first scenario, the attacker exploits bugs in network software implementations, crashing or disabling the target's communication processing capabilities. The second attack type is aimed at weaknesses in network protocols, aiming to overload the system's communication resources, which virtually disconnects the target from the outside world. The third type of attack exploits the limited network bandwidth to the target, inundating it with enormous volumes of traffic.

Clearly, all three forms of attack have the common result of preventing legitimate use of the target system. Although patchwork solutions have been developed for many of the DoS attacks currently identified, new attacks are continually being developed. The purpose of connecting computer systems to a network is to provide access for their legitimate use. Although network protocols can be made more secure, any mechanism that allows outside access to a system can be exploited and makes that system vulnerable to attack. Thus, protecting networked systems requires accepting the dynamic, uncontrollable, and potentially hostile environment in which they exist and developing protection mechanisms that can cope with this environment.

3   Comparison of Biological Systems and Network Systems

It could be seen that functions of both systems are similar. Both systems have a complex configuration, however, the biological immune system is more reliable and dependable. Partially, this could be explained by the fact that the "immune problem" is much simpler: the immune system has to differentiate only self from non-self. With this ability, potential attacks can be thwarted before any damage is done [4]. The equivalent in the computer systems world would be the ability to determine normal and abnormal network traffic and malicious software. Abnormal network traffic and malicious software, when discovered should be ignored or blocked.

Biological and computer systems exist in an environment where pathogen or antigens are plentiful, ready for attack. Since a connection to the "world" is required for either survival or providing services it is not possible to preempt or stop the assault. Furthermore, antigens hide within the volume of materials that must be taken in for survival. Computer network systems may be unable to spot specific patterns as they may be encrypted within a data stream.

The biological system also possesses a wide variety of agents that offer early warning that something is wrong. For example, the inflammation response occurs upon damage, without the presence of an infectious agent. This type of response works to limit the damage that could possibly be done if there are any infectious agents. In a DoS attack against a computer network, by default, all networking components work to "assist" the attack. All of the networking components pass along the malicious packets without any regard to source or content as long as the packets meet the minimum network protocol specifications. The target server even responds as though these packets are legitimate traffic.

In a computer security system, usually only one facility is available for the response to any specific type of attack. The immune system is composed of many components, some layered and some independent, any of which can be inactive, disabled, or defeated without preventing a successful immune response.

The immune system components also communicate with each other in an ad-hoc measure. Most communication is a simple interaction with chemical moderators that are often released to initiate a further response pending presence of other immune system components. Once the response is underway, the responders also release moderators that control the rate of both the number of responders and the size of the response. In computer networks, there is little or no coordination between the network safeguarding systems. Often, the system administrator intervention is the reacting mechanism. Unfortunately, this happens long after an attack begins and perhaps even after major damage has been sustained.

Since the immune system is composed of many different types of agents, many of which operate independently, the resources of the immune system are scalable with many functions working in parallel to fight off an attack and prevent further assaults. If there is an infection, once detected, many of the immune system components can increase their presence by multiplying, with many actively working to suppress the immediate attack and some remaining to fight off a recurrence. In the computer network, often each system is isolated, working independently, with a few pieces of software running to prevent or detect an attack. Each piece of software added adds processing load to the system, decreasing performance. Typically, the response to an attack on the computer network is either all or nothing. There is no scalability depending on the size or success of the attack.

Finally, the immune system is completely automatic. Little "user intervention" is required for it to successfully prevent or eliminate an attack against the host. The immune response scales to the size of the perceived attack and properly scales back when the assault ends. An attack against a computer network often involves direct intervention by the administrators of the network. Many man-hours are spent in the detection, prevention, and response to assaults against these networks. Often computer attacks are successful from complacency, poor training, lack of attention to software holes and patches, and plain incompetence.

4   Dynamics of the Immune Response

Once detected, the adequateness of the response should depend on the severity of the attack. In many attacks, early warning signs include packets that probe the target network looking for weaknesses or gathering intelligence. Ideally, the defense system should not overreact to such events but possibly use them to prepare for a full-scale attack. When a network is truly under attack, individual systems may be isolated and/or killed in order to prevent the damage from spreading.

A quantitative description of the autonomic immune response provides a means for understanding major interactions between the components of the immune system and the intruding antigen, and the dynamics of these interactions. Moreover, it allows for the establishment of the conditions for three possible outcomes of interaction, full recovery from infection, chronic infection, and death of the host. It should be clear that the proposed equations provide a simplified description of the actual biological phenomena. Moreover, these equations are only as accurate as their constants. In the case of the immune system these constants can be only roughly guessed. Therefore, the equations cannot be effectively used for the prediction of the outcome of a disease caused by the antigen or for the modification of the immune "control law". However, the importance of these equations for the computer network applications shall not be underestimated.

First, they describe the principle of operation of a system providing very successful defense against attacks. Second, since in the case of computer network parameters, the equations could be accurately estimated, making them accurate and dependable. Third, they could be instrumental for the analysis and design of defense mechanisms intended for computer networks.

The specific immune response is the main mechanism enabling the immune system to destroy intruding antigen. A variety of agents that are uniquely equipped for counteracting any particular antigen accomplish this. Each lymphocyte is keyed with a specific receptor for specific non-self proteins. The actual ability of the immune system to destroy the intruding antigen depends on the concentration of corresponding specialized fighter cells and antigen. If a specific antigen has not attacked the host, the concentration of fighter cells responsible for a respond to an attack from the particular antigen are minimal.

Since it is unlikely that a host will be attacked by antigen matching the total number of specific receptors, an immune memory is developed to increase the background concentrations of the receptors responsible for identifying the most common infections. During a response to a specific attack, two types of immune cells are created. To assist in the current assault, short-lived "fighter cells" are created. For potential future assaults, long term "memory cells" are created with a lifetime of ten to twenty years. These memory cells increase the natural background level of the specific antigen responsible for the assault thereby increasing the probability of the detection of an attack in any period of time [5].

Consider the immune response in the case when a specific antigen infects a biological organism. Introduce quantity C(t) representing the concentration of the immune cells carrying the genotype of the intruder and, therefore, uniquely specified in counteracting it. This concentration is time-dependent, and in the absence of the corresponding antigen is subject to a slow natural decrease that could be expressed as a slow decaying exponential process

$$C(t) = C_0 e^{-\alpha t}. \tag{1}$$

The current time is represented by t, C_0 represents the concentration of immune cells at $t = 0$ and α is a positive constant that could be chosen to reflect the following reality: during a 50-year period the concentration decreases to less than one percent of its initial value. Equation (1) should be considered the "natural motion" equation of the immune defense mechanism. It could be seen that the natural dynamics of the immune mechanism is stable.

Introduce quantity P(t) representing the concentration of the intruding antigen cells. This concentration is also time-dependent: the antigen utilize the available resources of the biological organism to multiply, and in the absence of the corresponding fighter cells this concentration is subject to a relatively fast increase that could be expressed as

$$P(t) = P(t_1)e^{\beta(t-t_1)} . \tag{2}$$

t_1 represents the moment of infection, $t_1 < t$, and β - is a positive number where $\beta \gg \alpha$. Equation (2) represents the antigen multiplication process within a biological organism in the absence of the immune response attempting to counteract this process. Therefore (2) should be considered the "natural motion" equation of the antigen multiplication process. It could be seen that the natural dynamics of this process is unstable. It should be realized that the antigen multiplication takes place at the expense of the invaded biological organism and therefore quantity β could be viewed as the "available share of resources" of the organism and it is time-dependent.

The immune response is preceded by the detection of the invading antigen. This is accomplished by the physical contact between the antigen and the specialized immune fighter cells that takes place some time after the moment of infection, t_1. Consider the moment of the detection of the antigen, $t_2 = t_1 + t$. While both the antigen and fighter cells are dispersed within the body, the time delay is a random variable and could be characterized by the its average value that is inversely proportioned to the concentrations of these cells, C(t) and P(t),

$$\tau = \frac{k}{C(t)P(t)} . \tag{3}$$

After the invaded antigen has been detected, the immune response could be visualized as a negative feedback control process that maintains the concentration of the fighter cells sufficient for the complete elimination of the antigen. It could be theorized that until the intruders are present, the concentration of the fighter cells exponentially increases following the equation

$$C(t) = C(t - t_1 - \tau)e^{\delta(t-t_1-\tau)} . \tag{4}$$

Note that during the time interval t concentration C(t) changes very little, and therefore (4) could be rewritten as

$$C(t) = C(t_1)e^{\delta(t-t_1-\tau)} \tag{5}$$

where δ is a non-negative number dependent on the current concentration of the antigen as follows

$$\delta(t) \begin{cases} > 0 & \text{if } P(t) > 0 \\ = -\alpha & \text{if } P(t) = 0 \end{cases} \tag{6}$$

It could be seen from (6) that in the absence of antigen C(t) reverts to the natural motion pattern.

The existence and multiplication of fighter cells also consumes limited resources of the biological organism, competing for these resources with the multiplying antigen cells. The quantity $\delta(t) > 0$ also could be viewed as the "available share of the resources" and therefore the following constraint should be expected:

$$K_1[\beta(t)+\delta(t)]+ K_2[C(t)+P(t)] \leq \text{const} \tag{7}$$

K1 and K2 are coefficients reflecting the "cost of multiplication" and the "cost of living" of the immune fighter cells and antigen cells.

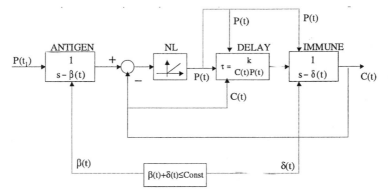

Fig. 1. Block diagram showing the logistics and dynamics of the immune response.

In figure (1), block ANTIGEN represents the dynamics of the multiplication of the antigen cells according to equation (2). IMMUNE describes both the "natural" and "forced" dynamics of the multiplication of the immune fighter cells in consistence with equations (1), (5) and (6). It could be seen that the multiplication rate of both types of counteracting cells is limited as they share the limited resources of the infected biological organism. DELAY is responsible for the implementation of the variable delay in the immune response channel, as per equation (4). NL prevents the simulation system from the appearance of negative concentrations of the immune and antigen cells.

The simulation of immune responses is initiated by applying a pulse-type signal. Depending on the initial choice of the simulation constants, the simulation will lead to one of the following outcomes. The antigen cells multiply faster than the fighter cells and consequently overwhelm the immune defenses (lethality). Or, an unstable balance between the concentration of fighter cells and the concentration of the specialized and meteorology [19][20][21][22][23]. The bigger the area under the ROC curve is (A_{ROC}) the bigger the IDS effectiveness is [17].

In this scope agents may play an important role: agents intend a complete automation of complex processes acting in behalf of human users [11]. Several definitions and approaches to agent term have led to some confusion. From the Artificial Intelligence point of view, agents are classified as reactive or deliberative according to the external or internal nature of the intelligent behavior. In this way, deliberative agents often accomplish the so called BDI paradigm [12] where knowledge is structured in three different levels of abstraction: beliefs, intentions and desires.

Intelligent agents presumably can adapt decision making through the cooperation with other agents [10]. Communication between agents is usually modeled through human-like typed messages including performatives inspired in Speech Act Theory (for instance, KQML [13]).

Particularly, agents have been applied to this dominion in the past [2]. For instance, a methodology [3], an architecture [1] were proposed, and also some IDS were implemented as agent systems using genetic algorithms [5], and neurofuzzy controllers [4].

2   The Analysis of Relative Operating Characteristic

In order to asses the skill of a probabilistic prediction (based on several IDS agents) we use the Receiver Operating Characteristic (ROC) in a slightly different way [23]. In our case study, *ROC* measures the success and false alarm rates of an ensemble; made by assuming an event E will occur if it is predicted with a probability exceeding some specified probability threshold p_t. The difference with usual ROC approximation in intrusion detection is that the threshold we vary is not the false alarm threshold, but the probability of occurrence the "event". Indirectly, this is like tuning the false alarm threshold of the probabilistic system.

This definition is based on the notion that a prediction of an event E is assumed if E is predicted by at least a fraction $p = p_t$ of ensemble members, where the threshold p_t is defined a priori.

Let us consider first a deterministic (single model) prediction of E (either that it will occur or that it will not occur). Over a sufficiently large sample of independent predictions, we can form the prediction contingency matrix (Table 1) giving the frequency that E occurred or not, and whether it was predicted or not.

Based on these values, the hit rate(H) and false alarm rate (F) for a deterministic prediction are given by

$$H = \delta/(\beta + \delta).$$
$$F = \gamma/(\alpha + \gamma). \tag{1}$$

Hit and false alarm rates for a probabilistic prediction can be redefined as follows [24]. Suppose it is assumed that E will happen if the probability of the

Table 1. Prediction contingency matrix

		Ocurrs	
		No	Yes
Prediction	No	α	β
	Yes	γ	δ

prediction p is greater than p_t (and will not if $p < p_t$). By varying p_t between 0 and 1 we can define $H = H(p_t)$, $F = F(p_t)$.

The ROC curve is a plot of $H(p_t)$ against $F(p_t)$. A measure of skill is given by the area under the ROC curve (A_{ROC}). A perfect deterministic forecast will have $A_{ROC} = 1$, while a no skill-forecast for which the hit and false alarm rates are equal, will have $A_{ROC} = 0.5$.

In our case study the event E is "an intrusion". We will have different models (different IDS) that try to detect intrusions. These models must deal with the same traffic and must not take any action on it.

3   The Role of Agents

The proposed system has three different types of agents: predictor, assessor and manager. In the scenario considered, there are several predictor agents and only one assessor agent and one manager agent. But it would make sense to use several assessor agents rather than just one, since not every predictor would be asked by each assessor agent, and they would also adopt different weighting criteria.

The main role of a predictor agent consists of suggesting if there is an intrusion or not when an assessor agent asks him for a prediction. On the other hand, major goal of assessor agents is giving proper weights to predictor agents according to the previous level of success, and afterwards, making a binary decision based on such weighted references. Finally the manager agent calculates H and F and, at last, it communicates the results to the assessor agent. The manager agent knows if there was an intrusion or not because the experiment is done under a training environment. The interactions between agents are typed as KQML messages. You can see an illustrative example of such interactions in figure Fig. 1.

All of this agents adopt a BDI-like architecture, where abstract desires became in concrete goals when external perceptions would be sensed. Each of these goals has an associated generic plan composed of a sequence of atomic intentions.

The intelligence of agents relies on how predictions are weighted according to the success of previous predictions in order to make a suggestion. Nevertheless plans of predictor and manager agents show a straightforward behavior rather than the adaptive reasoning of assessor agents.

Our proposal in this publication involves the use of the ratio H-F as a weight in the aggregated sum of predictor agents. Therefore, the reputation of certain predictor agent would increase if the number of hit rates became higher, and

Table 3. Ten days measures on the event E. Prediction (based on a threshold $p_t = 0.2$) and what really happened is binary represented

Day	1	2	3	4	5	6	7	8	9	10	11	12	13	14	15
$p_t = 0.2$	0	1	1	1	0	1	1	1	1	1	0	1	1	1	0
Occurs	1	0	0	0	0	0	0	0	0	1	0	1	1	1	0

Day	16	17	18	19	20	21	22	23	24	25	26	27	28	29	30
$p_t = 0.2$	1	1	1	1	0	1	1	1	1	1	0	1	1	1	0
Occurs	1	0	0	0	0	0	0	1	0	1	0	1	1	1	0

- For $p_t = 0.8$: $H = 0.273$ $F = 0.053$
- For $p_t = 1.0$: $H = 0.000$ $F = 0.000$

The suggestions from the assessor agent for $p_t = 0.6$ are:

- With a constant evaluation of predictor agents (average sum):
  $H = 0.545$ $F = 0.158$
- With an adaptive evaluation of predictor agents (dynamic weights):
  $H = 0.545$ $F = 0.107$

From these data we observe a similar number of hit rates and a slightly lower number of false alarms with an adaptive evaluation.

At last, the suggestions from the assessor agent for $p_t = 0.4$ are:

- With a constant evaluation of predictor agents (average sum):
  $H = 0.545$ $F = 0.263$
- With an adaptive evaluation of predictor agents (dynamic weights):
  $H = 0.909$ $F = 0.421$

From these data, we can observe more hit rates in the adaptive evaluation than in the constant evaluation, but it also appears to be more false alarms. So at first glance it does not show clearly which alternative is better. But Fig. 2 representing the A_{ROC} curves of both possible evaluations shows that an adaptive evaluation of agents include a greater area than the constant evaluation.

Mathematically, the area of both alternatives is:

- With a constant evaluation of predictor agents (average sum): 0.75
- With an adaptive evaluation of predictor agents (dynamic weights): 0.81

So an improvement of 7.25% is achieved with the adaptive behaviour of agents proposed in this paper.

5   Conclusions and Future Work

In this paper, we have proposed a system of different types of agents cooperating in order to detect intrusions. One of these types implements IDS models,

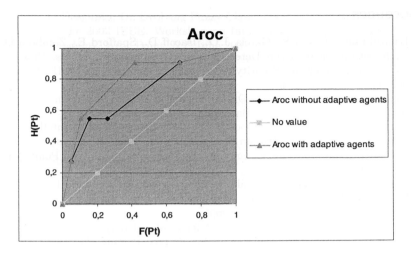

Fig. 2. A_{ROC} of adaptive agent approach vs. average one. Area corresponding to adaptive agent model is bigger, showing a better effectiveness of the model

other evaluates the predictions from them, and finally a third kind of agent considers the suggestions and emulates the results with which future evaluations will be more accurate. The dynamic weights involved in the adaptive evaluation performed to generate a final suggestion from several different Intrusion Detection models showed a better performance than classical approach based on the average sum of the predictions received.

Furthermore, the multiagent system applied to this dominion, allow us different future directions of research. For instance, the use of a fuzzy threshold applied over the average sum of predictions causes a relevant improvement in the overall performance of Intrusion Detection task [6]. Such fuzzy threshold may be used also as adapted dynamically in order to obtain even better results.

In the future, we intend to use the architecture of agents proposed to compute and represent the reputation of predictor agents as a fuzzy set in the same way that AFRAS [9]. In order to do such fuzzy evaluation we will use an analysis of the economical costs involved in the precautionary action taken by the manager agent. This reputation mechanism showed a fast convergence, while sensitivity to sudden changes avoids a high level of deception [8]. Finally, it could be interesting to try with real data, and also to test several assessor agents analyzing different traffic data.

Communication Security in Multi-agent Systems

Petr Novák, Milan Rollo, Jiří Hodík, Tomáš Vlček

Gerstner Laboratory, Agent Technology Group
Department of Cybernetics, Faculty of Electrical Engineering,
Czech Technical University in Prague,
Technická 2, 166 27, Prague 6, Czech Republic
{novakpe,rollo,hodik,vlcek}@labe.felk.cvut.cz

Abstract. Both, research and application development in the area of multi-agent systems currently undertakes rapid expansion. In order to use multi-agent technology in real applications, it is inevitable to ensure security, integrity and authenticity of inter-agent communication. Various securitysystems, developed for different applications have been used in multi-agent system (MAS). Alternatively, MAS are designed with respect to the specific communication security requirements. This paper describes the architecture and implementation of the security (X-Security) system, which implemets authentication and secure communication among agents. System uses certification authority (CA) and ensures full cooperation of secured agents and already existing (unsecured) agents. Principle of the system integration into already existing MAS is described here as well as possibility of its usage for mobile agents. Paper deals as well with security mechanism's activity during inaccessibility of CA and possibility of CA's recreation. Security system was designed according the FIPA standards.

1   Introduction

In order to use multi-agent technology in real applications (such as industrial applications or e-business), it is inevitable to implement security communication among agents. This can be reached either by the message encryption (security against monitoring by undesirable side) or signing (assuring of message content's integrity). In some cases it is not necessary to secure whole message but only its parts.

There are a number of systems and principles allowing secured communication in multi-agent systems (MAS). Using the existing security systems in MAS brings a couple of disadvantages (see later). The proposed approach attempts to avoid them and suggests a set of recommendations how to implement security in any programming language and any multi-agent platform.

These security instruments should increase trust and confidentiality within and among agent communities/technology and provide security mechanisms, such as encryption, authentication, message integrity services, etc., employing cryptography algorithms. The security mechanisms can utilize existing agent platform mediators such

V. Mařík et al. (Eds): CEEMAS 2003, LNAI 2691, pp. 454–463, 2003.

as the Agent Management System (AMS), Directory Facilitator (DF), or Agent Communication Channel (ACC), e.g. for authentication purposes, while these new tasks enforce the requirements for these mediators much more thoroughness [1].

Existing FIPA specifications are proposed as open standards for agents' behavior and interactions. This paper highlights selected notions of trust and security used in ExtraPlanT MAS. Although FIPA specifications pertaining to security and network communication were started in 1998, there is still no complex and coherent document at disposal. Architectures proposed, e.g. [2] offers on different level the security and trust services defending MAS against corrupted naming (mapping or matchmaking) services, insecure communication channels, insecure agents delegations, lack of accountability, etc. [3]. Essential security services presented in this paper constitute an important part of the overall architecture being developed.

Our approach provides principles for secure messages transfer and allows expansion of security into the area of mobile agents (agents migrating between platforms). It also defines a message extension for a new element that describes a form of the message security and tries to solve problems with inaccessibility of the central authority CA , which issues security certificates to particular agents. Agents use these certificates to prove their identity.

Proposed approach has been partially implemented as an extension of the multi-agent platform JADE [4] and tested within the AgentExchange project.

2   Security System Requirements

This paper describes design of security system prototype and implementation of its parts for multi-agent projects AgentExchange and ExPlanTech [5].

AgentExchange project aims at development of simple open trading environment. It is expected to operate as open MAS accessible to any agents. It is necessary to assure a certain degree of safety and trust within the community. ExPlanTech project (production planning and supply chain management) on the other hand presents closed MAS, but its agents can also run outside the agent platform (variety of databases) or special agent (for particular operating system) can be created. Platform integrates third-party information systems (e.g. ERP system) those company is running. In this case the security within the whole MAS is naturally required.

Security mechanisms, described in the only published FIPA security specification [6], are for mentioned systems unsuitable (possibility to secure only whole message not its part, ensures security for agents placed on agent platform only not for standalone agents, no support for mobile agents, etc.). Further on are described some additional requirements and dissimilarities from mentioned FIPA specification and outline of solution.

a) *Possibility to secure not only the whole ACL Message but only its part* is required as well. E.g. possibility to send a delegation (passed from one agent to another), sign certain part of text or data for storing in database along with its signature and guarantee its authentication for later use (record of transactions) or encrypt only password required for access to particular resource, to allow subsequent detection of kind of requested data (e.g. from log file). This can be reached using the structure (class) containing not only carried text (signed or encrypted) but also additional information concerning security (type of security action, created signature, identification of used key). On the receiving side, this structure (class) is processed and original text obtained.

b) *Preferably not to bind security support tightly into the agent platform* because agents can run on different platforms (without this type of security) or even without platform. For example agent collects data from appropriate company database server, running on different operating system, and provides data to MAS (in secure way). It is possible to ensure this including the security directly into the agent (its communication wrapper) or by library supplied with agent.

c) *Avoid agent's core necessity to choose, set type or negotiate about algorithms used in secure communication.* These actions have to be done by security module automatically. Negotiation about security algorithms can be very time-consuming on occasional connection. If agent sends over such connection message with security algorithm which recipient does not understand, recipient cannot inform the sender about it immediately. Every agent (its security module) has to register (with certain authority) some list of security algorithms (and public keys) [7], which it uses. Agent that wants to send a secured message has to ask for a list of receiver supported algorithms and use one of them for secure communication. This is suitable for mobile agents too [8, 9].

d) *All private keys and other security related data have to be available to their owner only.* Data have not to be accessible to anyone else (even the agent platform). Platform can be distributed across many computers and hence it is impossible to ensure security within the whole platform, if the private data are managed by platform. Every agent has to keep its private data secured, even during its migration on other platform.

3   X-Security Prototype

In our proposed approach dedicated central authority is required to organize security mechanisms. This authority issues appropriate licenses – certificates. Agents use issued certificates to prove their identities and execute security related actions within the system [10]. Function of the central authority is in the proposed system exerted by the Security Certification Authority (SCA). Each agent using a security has to register its certificate with this SCA.

3.1   Certificates and Their Importance

Certificate contains mandatory information requested by SCA and may contain additional information supplied by an agent. Information requested by SCA is agent's identification, public keys (and their description) and requested validity time and security level in MAS. SCA verifies these data and stores them into certificate. SCA can't guarantee validity of optional data, but can assure their constancy (originality) when providing other agents with the certificate. SCA signs whole certificate and thus allows receiver to verify the integrity of contained data.

Security level is set up by SCA according to username and password, which agent sent in its registration request.

If agent needs to send encrypted message to another agent, verify signature of received message or check the security level, it asks SCA for particular certificate. Here is an example of certificate issued for agent called testAgent:

```
certificate-ident                SCA_CERTIFICATE_1
        sca-ident                        (agent-identifier :name
                                 sca@platform.net)
    agent-ident          (agent-identifier :name testAgent@platform.net)
    time-from            Wed Jan 01 00:00:00 CET 2003
    time-to              Wed Dec 31 23:59:59 CET 2003
    security-level       VISITOR
    key-description
    ident                    SIGN_1
    time-from        Wed Jan 01 00:00:00 CET 2003
    time-to          Wed Dec 31 23:59:59 CET 2003
    type                     public-key
    key-param        SHAwithDSA/1024
    key-value        56A7ED89C2.........6AC54DF983
    key-description
    ident                    CRYPT_1
    time-from        Wed Jan 01 00:00:00 CET 2003
    time-to          Wed Dec 31 23:59:59 CET 2003
    type                     public-key
    key-param        RSA/1024
    key-value        5A234DC82B.........85329B76DC
```

3.2   Integration of Security into Massage

In proposed system agents communicate using ACL Messages according to the FIPA standard [11]. Message is extended to contain a new slot called X-Security. This slot specifies how the message content has been secured. Extended message may look as follows:

```
(inform
        :sender  (sender@platform.net)
        :receiver        (receiver@platform.net)
        :language        (FIPA-SL0)
        :content („Text to be signed")
        :X-Security  (    :type SIGN
    :signature 48A7.........20AD
        :certificate-ident SCA_CERTIFICATE_1
        :key-ident SIGN_1 ) )
```

Items of the X-Security slot inform that message content was signed (signature is included) and it can be verified by public key SIGN_1 stored in certificate SCA_CERTIFICATE_1.

Next example presents encrypted message:

```
(inform
        :sender   (sender@platform.net)
        :receiver         (receiver@platform.net)
        :language         (FIPA-SL0)
        :content („28AD.........7BA4")
        :X-Security  (    :type CRYPT
        :certificate-ident SCA_CERTIFICATE_1
        :key-ident CRYPT_1 ) )
```

X-Security slot items now inform that message content is encrypted by public key CRYPT_1 stored in certificate SCA_CERTIFICATE_1.

Analogously it is possible as well to secure only parts of the content.

3.3   Description of SCA's Activity

Common security system (completely) fails when SCA (or similar central authority) is inaccessible. System described here also uses SCA and certificates but in a different way. Registered certificates are not stored only in the SCA but after signing they are also sent back to the registering agents. If one agent requires certificate of another one, it should at first ask SCA for it. In cases of SCA inaccessibility agent is allowed to ask for it directly target agent. Certificate is signed by SCA and therefore its validity can be verified. Now the security can work, even if the SCA is (temporarily) inaccessible.

Described approach also allows using the security in the area of mobile agents. When two agents meet, they can exchange their certificates and prove their identities. Certificates contain full identification of their owners and are completed with SCA's signature. Using the public keys from the certificates allows verification when the particular agents own appropriate private keys. Thus when mobile agent registers its certificate with SCA, it can migrate and still use the certificate to prove its identity.

3.4   Session Keys and Their Use

In the case of encrypting a huge amount of data or in the case of frequent communication between two agents the usage of asymmetric keys is not apposite because of the time and computational consumption. Instead of asymmetric keys the symmetric session keys can be used. When this situation occurs security module generates session key and sends it directly (encrypted by asymmetric key) to the other agent. Transferred data are encrypted using the new symmetric temporary key now, as the symmentric key encryption algorithms are not so time/resources consuming. As soon as the communication is finished the session key is invalidated. Activities related with generating and using session keys are completely assured by security module.

3.5   Common Agent Key Replacement

After a certain period of time or when the suspicion on the key misusage occurs, an agent is allowed to generate new keys. Immediately after generating them the agent asks SCA for new certificate registration and at this moment the previous one becomes invalid. By this way it is possible to register new certificate before the validity time of the old one expires. Every certificate contains unique identification (ID). If an agent signs message using the new certificate the X-Security slot will contain ID of this certificate. Receiver agent does not have a new version of the sender's certificate and has to ask SCA for it. Similar situation occurs when the agent receives message encrypted by invalidated key. In that case receiver informs sender that used key has been invalidated and for future communication requires messages encrypted by the new one. Security module can be set up by agent's core to accept messages encrypted only according to the latest certificate or (for a certain period of time) accept messages encrypted according to older (but still time valid) certificates.

This approach can be used not only for key replacement but also for immediate decreasing of cooperator security level. This can happen when an agent with high security level asks SCA to do it.

3.6   SCA Key Replacement

Key replacement of SCA is much complicated than replacing keys of common agent. As the first step SCA generates new keys and creates new corresponding certificate. In the second step SCA sends this certificate signed by last valid publicly known key to all registered agents. All of them have to accept the change of the SCA's keys. When SCA has received the confirmations from the registered agents (except inaccessible ones) it sends them their original certificate signed by the new key. Now SCA can start to use the new certificate. Common agent's security module clears its certificate database and this causes requesting for all new necessary certificates from SCA.

Other problems are caused by inaccessibility of some agent. From this reason certificates' ID's are changed during the replacing of SCA's certificates too. Thus mobile agents also can detect this change and ask for their new certificates from SCA as soon as possible. It is only up to SCA how long time after change of its certificates SCA allows agents to update their certificates.

3.7   SCA Inaccessibility

As was already stated each of agents has its own certificate and these certificates are registered with SCA. During the temporary SCA inaccessibility agents are allowed to provide their certificates each other. In this time agents can't register new certificates but already existing security is not influenced. But permanent lost of SCA causes troubles for the communication security. This problem can be solved either by recovery SCA from backup or creating a brand new one.

There could be second SCA present in the agents' community. This SCA is only a backup and synchronizes its database with the main one for the case of losing the main SCA. In other case certain number of backup SCA is required. When the main SCA is lost the first backup becomes the main one and new backup SCA is created to complete number of backups. Another possible variant is that all of SCAs are active and can register common agents' certificates. All active SCAs synchronize their databases.

In a special situation of the MAS crash no SCA and only some of common agents could stay active. Then there is no backup of SCA that could be used for its recovery. In such a case agents must be able to create new SCA. At first agents create new instance of empty SCA and give it (during the start-up) the last known certificate of the original SCA (each of active agents has to know it). New SCA cannot use it for new certificate registration because of not having the private parts of keys but can use the public key from it to verify signatures of other agents' certificates. New SCA generates new keys and certificate for itself. Common agents send their certificates confirmed by old SCA to the new SCA. SCA sends them their new certificates and SCA's certificate signed by its new keys. These certificates are sent only to agents, which certificates new SCA verified by the key of the old SCA. The new certificates are sent encrypted because common agents do not know the public key of the new SCA for signature verification but SCA has the certificates of these agents.

This way can be also used for creating new SCA by group of mobile agents for example for creating other secured temporary agents. Mobile agents have to keep their older certificates that are relevant for their home platform.

4   Implementation

SCA is a standalone agent that does not influence common agents' communication. There is only requirement to start SCA as a first agent of the community. Distribution of agents on platform is on Figure 1.

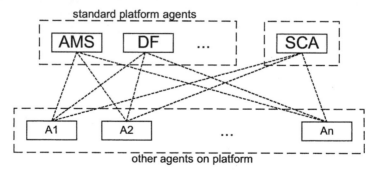

Fig. 1. Agent platform with Security Certification Authority

Security service is provided by security module that is placed between the agent's core and communication layer [12], as could be seen on Figure 2.

Messages are withdrawn from the input queue. These messages could serve for security management (e.g. required certificates); they could be secured (e.g. by encryption, signature, etc.), or unsecured that are passed directly to the agent's core.

The queue of outgoing messages contains messages created by security module (e.g. request for certificate) and messages created by the agent's core. The second ones are secured according to the requirements of the core. Agent core is allowed to restrictedly influence behavior of the security module. Inner structure of security module is shown on Figure 3.

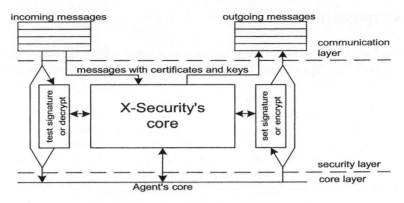

Fig. 2. Integration of security module to agent

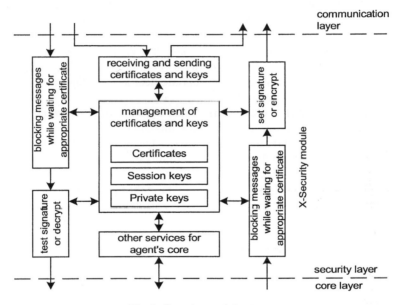

Fig. 3. Security module structure

Security module contains several individual units. One of them provides encrypting, decrypting, creating and checking the message signature [13]. Second one provides connection to SCA and exchanges certificates with other agents. Next unit maintains database of received certificates, private keys and session keys. This unit provides them to other units. It is also required to store data safely during agent's migration. Last unit provides interface between security module and agent's core, which is necessary e.g. to configure the security or when partial encryption is required.

5   Experiments

Described security system has been included and tested within the Agent Exchange (AX) project. This project aims at developing a model of trading environment and a test-bed for modeling various market situations, investigation of market trends in environment of specific groups of traders' behaviors.

AX agent business community consists of Trading-agents (buy and sell commodities), Bank-agents (maintain commodity accounts), Exchange-agents (find matching orders to buy and sell), User-agents (lead the team of Trading-agents) and the Scenario-agents (influence the market according the pre-prepared plan). Each of these agents has to register its certificate including agent's role and competences (agent gains them at the creation time). The certificates are registered with SCA trusted by all community members. During the registration agent sends its username and password to SCA. According this data SCA sets up a security level in the registered certificate. When agent asks other one to perform any action, the second one proves competence of the first one by its certificate. Two simple cases of certificate exploitation are described bellow.

If Bank-agent wants to establish a new bank, it asks Central Trading Authority (CTA) for permission. CTA checks up security level in Bank-agent's certificate and if it is correct, CTA issues to Bank-agent appropriate license. This license allows Bank-agent to create and carry on new bank.

If a Trading-agent wants to create a new bank account, Bank-agent creates it and links agent's certificate with this account. From this time every attempt to access this account must contain signature. Bank-agent verifies the signature, using the certificate linked with this account and in the case of authenticity executes requested action.

Another MAS, in which described security system will be tested, is ExPlanTech, a production planning and supply chain management multi-agent system. There may be agents running outside the agent platform (variety of databases) and sending data to MAS in a secure way. Agents may also run on PDAs and other mobile devices for remote access to the system to set and verify orders as well. Every access to orders will be verified by agent's certificate.

6   Conclusion

Selected functions of the described system appropriate for the application were implemented in Java [14] programming language as an extension of JADE multi-agent platform. Developed library includes SCA agent and security module to be integrated into the common agents.

This system tries to avoid some disadvantages of the current security systems such as failure of security functions during SCA inaccessibility, security uses other communication channels then MAS and security system is controlled from outside of the MAS. Proposed system has following advantages: security can be included into already existing MAS, only parts of the message can be secured, system is usable in the area of mobile agents.

This design represents a fundamental for universal security model which can be used for both research and application purposes.

References

[1]   Vlček T., Zach J.: Considerations on Secure FIPA Compliant Agent Architecture. In: Proc. of IEEE/IFIP International Conference on Information Technology for Balanced Automation Systems in Manufacturing and Services (BASYS 02). V.Marik, L.M.Camarinha-Matos, H.Afsarmanesh (Eds.). Kluwer Academic Publishers, Boston/Dordrecht/London (2002) 11-124

[2]   Foner, L.N.: A security architecture for multi-agent matchmaking. In: Proceedings of the Second International Conference on Multi-Agent Systems (ICMAS96) AAAI Press, (1996) 80-86

[3]   Wong, H. C., Sycara, K.: Adding Security and Trust to Multi-Agent Systems. In: Proceedings of Autonomous Agents '99 (Workshop on Deception, Fraud and Trust in Agent Societies). Seattle, Washington (1999) 149-161

[4]   JADE. http://jade.cselt.it, Java Agent DEvelopment Framework (2003)

[5]   Pěchouček, M., Říha, A., Vokřínek, J., Mařík, V., Pražma, V.: ExPlanTech - applying multi-agent systems in production planning. In: International Journal of Production Research, vol. 40, no. 15 (2002) 3681-3692

[6]   FIPA 98 http://www.fipa.org/repository/obsoletespecs.html Agent Security Management Specification (obsolete)

[7]   Burr, W., Dodson, D., Nazario, N., Polk, W.T.: Minimum Interoperability Specification for PKI Components, NIST Special Publication 800-15 (1998)

[8]   Jansen, W., Karygiannis, T.: Mobile Agent Security, NIST Special Publication 800-19 (1999)

[9]   Karnik, N.: Security in Mobile Agent Systems. Ph.D. Dissertation, Department of Computer Science, University of Minnesota (1998)

[10]   Lyons-Burke, K.: Federal Agency Use of Public Key Technology for Digital Signatures and Authentication, NIST Special Publication 800-25 (2000)

[11]   FIPA. http://www.fipa.org, Foundation for Intelligent Physical Agents (2003)

[12]   Bradshaw, J.M. (ed.): Software Agents, AAAI Press/MIT Press (2002)

[13]   Welschenbach, M.: *Cryptography in C and C++*. Springer-Verlag, Germany (2001)

[14]   Sun Microsystems. http://java.sun.com, Java Programming Language (2003)

Teamwork of Hackers-Agents: Modeling and Simulation of Coordinated Distributed Attacks on Computer Networks[*]

Igor Kotenko

St. Petersburg Institute for Informatics and Automation
ivkote@mail.iias.spb.su

Abstract. The paper considers an approach to the agents' teamwork implementation. It is described on an example of simulation of the co-ordinated distributed attacks on computer networks fulfilled by a group of hackers-agents. The approach is based on main positions of the "joint intentions" theory and the "common plans" theory. The offered technology of creation of the agents' team includes the following stages: (1) formation of the subject domain ontology; (2) determination of the agents' team structure and mechanisms of their interaction and coordination; (3) specifications of the agents' actions plans as a hierarchy of attribute stochastic formal grammars; (4) assignment of roles and allocation of plans between the agents; (5) state-machine based interpretation of the teamwork. The stages of ontology creation, agents' plans specification and state-machine based interpretation of attack generation are considered. The Attack Simulator software prototype and its evaluation results are described.

1   Introduction

Among various variants of agents' interaction the special place is occupied by so-called "*teamwork*". About agents who make joint efforts for achievement of the common long-term purpose, function in a dynamic environment at presence of "noise" and counteraction on the part of the adversary it is accepted to talk, that they form *the team of agents*. Thus, the behavior of agents' team is something that greater, than simply coordinated set of individual actions of separate agents. It is accepted to talk, that agents "*cooperate*" in teamwork, i.e. they solve together some task or carry out some activity for achievement of common goal. Therefore the main problem, which is necessary to solve at organization of agents' teamwork , consists in how it is possible to ensure the functioning of agents as the uniform team in a situation when each agent, generally speaking, realizes own intentions by individual actions executed in parallel or consistently with actions of other agents.

[*] This research is being supported by grant 01-01-108 of Russian Foundation of Basic Research and European Office of Aerospace R&D (Projects #1994 P)

V. Mařík et al. (Eds): CEEMAS 2003, LNAI 2691, pp. 464–474, 2003.
© Springer-Verlag Berlin Heidelberg 2003

Now the research on teamwork is an area of steadfast attention in multi-agent systems [2, 8, 9, 10, 11, etc.]. This problem has many practically important and interesting applications. The paper considers an approach to *teamwork of hackers-agents* for modeling and simulation the complex coordinated distributed attacks on computer networks. This task is extremely actual today. In competition between security officers and means of computer network defense, on the one hand, and the hackers inventing more complex exploits and smarter attacks, on the other hand, the significant advantage is on the side of malefactors [5-7]. This advantage becomes even more essential in case when attack is coordinated and distributed in space and in time. Now it is not possible to detect such attacks fulfilled by professional hackers automatically. It emphasizes a necessity of deeper studying an essence of modern attacks on computer networks. Thus the goals and strategies of attacks, and also methods of its realization should be the objects of modeling and simulation. Such results could appear very valuable for construction of modern computer network defense systems.

The rest of the paper is structured as follows. *Section 2* outlines suggested common approach for creation of hackers-agents teamwork. *Section 3* describes the "Computer network attacks" ontology used. *Section 4* describes specifications of the agents' actions plans. *Section 5* presents the Attack Simulator software prototype implemented and its evaluation results.

2   Common Approach for Creation of Hackers-Agents Teamwork

For the organization of teamwork of hackers-agents realizing coordinated distributed attacks, we have used the base ideas stated in the joint intention theory [2], the shared plans theory [8] and the combined theories of agents' teamwork [9, 10, 11, etc.].

As in the joint intention theory, the basic elements, allowing the agents' team to fulfill a common task, are common (group) intentions, but its structuring is carried out in the same way as the plans are structured in the shared plans theory [10, 11]. The common (group, individual) intention and commitment are associated with each node of a general hierarchical plan. These intention and commitment manage execution of a general plan, providing necessary flexibility. During functioning each agent should possess the group beliefs concerning other team-mates. For achievement of the common beliefs at formation and disbandment of the common intentions agents should communicate. All agents' communications are managed by means of common commitments built in the common intentions. For this purpose it is supposed to use the special mechanism for reasoning of agents on communications. Besides it is supposed, that agents communicate only when there can be an inconsistency of their actions. This property is called "selectivity of communications". It is important for reaction to unexpected changes of environment, maintenance of redistribution of roles of the agents failed or unable to execute some part of a general plan, and also at occurrence new, earlier not planned actions [10, 11].

For support of teamwork it is offered to use *three groups of procedures* [10]: (1) maintenance of a coordination of actions; (2) monitoring and restoration of agents' functionality; (3) maintenance of communication selectivity.

The procedures of first class are intended for realization of coordinated initialization and termination of actions on some general plan. The coordinated initialization means, that all members of the team (group) begin execution of the same plan at the defined time. It assumes an appointment for the fixed roles in concrete scenario of concrete agents, their notification about the appointed scenario and role, and also reception of confirmations on their readiness to play the defined role in the given scenario. The coordinated termination of a common action (refusal of the common intention) demands also mutual informing of agents of the team (group) about this action at presence of corresponding conditions. Such conditions can determined by achievement of the common goal, finding-out by even one member of the team of unattainability of the goal or its prevarication (the goal has ceased to be actual). For example, the attack goal "increase of authority up to a level of superuser" is achieved, if some hacker managed to penetrate into a target host and to increase the authority up to a level of superuser. Also the purpose is unattainable, if one of obligatory actions on penetration into a target host is not executed. And the purpose is irrelevant, if the target host is switched off from the network.

Procedures of monitoring and restoration of the team (group) functionality should provide supervision of some agents over others that it was possible to establish loss of capacity for work by the agent or a group of agents. It is directed on fast restoration of functionality of the team at the expense of reassignment of the "lost" roles to those team-mates which can perform corresponding additional job. For example, if one of the hackers-agents who are carrying out intention "Identification of operating system of a host" is blocked by firewall of a target network or other obstacle for realization of this intention takes place, this agent (or other hacker-agent who found out state of nonoperability of "colleague") should send this information to a "leader" of the scenario. If there will be other agent, capable to solve the task this role should be assigned to him. Check of rules and realization of reasoning results should entail corresponding communications of agents by means of some communication protocol.

Procedures of maintenance of communication selectivity order the communication act when the probability and cost of agents' coordination loss is great enough. They are based on calculation of the message importance in view of the "costs" and benefits of this message. It is necessary to guarantee that the benefit of the message exchange for maintenance of agents' coordination surpasses a "cost" of the communication act (for example, a network security system, having intercepted agents' messages, can detect and "suppress" an attack). Therefore it is very important to choose those communication acts which will bring the greatest benefit to the team.

The suggested *technology for creation of the hackers-agents' team* (that is fair for other subject domains) consists in realization of the following chain of stages: (1) formation of the subject domain ontology; (2) determination of the agents' team structure and mechanisms of their interaction and coordination (including roles and scenarios of an agents' roles exchange); (3) specifications of the agents' actions plans (generation of attacks) as a hierarchy of attribute stochastic formal grammars; (4) assignment of roles and allocation of plans between the agents; (5) state-machine based interpretation of the teamwork.

Formation of the subject domain ontology is an initial stage of the agents' team creation. Modeling in any subject domain assumes development of its conceptual model, i.e. set of basic concepts of a subject domain, relations between the concepts, and also data and algorithms interpreting these concepts and relations.

The agents' team structure is described in terms of a hierarchy of group and individual roles in the common scenario. Leaves of the hierarchy correspond to roles of individual agents, but intermediate nodes - to group roles.

The plan hierarchy specification is carried out for each role. For group plans it is necessary to express joint activity obviously. The following elements are described for each plan: (a) entry conditions when the plan is offered for execution; (b) conditions at which the plan stops to be executed (the plan is executed, impracticable or irrelevant on conditions); (c) actions which are carried out at a team level as a part of a common plan. It is offered to carry out the plan hierarchy specification as a hierarchy of attribute stochastic formal grammars, connected by substitution operation.

The assignment of roles and allocation of plans between the agents is carried out in two stages: at first the plan is distributed in terms of roles, and then the agent is put in correspondence to each role. One agent can execute a set of roles. Agents can exchange roles in dynamics of the plan execution. Requirements to each role are formulated as union of requirements to those parts of the plan which are put in correspondence to the role. There are group and individual roles. Leaves correspond to individual roles. Agents' functionalities are generated automatically according to the roles.

For setting the agents' team operation in real-time *a hierarchy of state machines* is used. These state machines are built as a result of interpretation of a hierarchy of attribute stochastic formal grammars which set the plan hierarchy specification. The state machines realize a choice of the plan which will be executed and a fulfillment of the established sub-plans in a cycle "agents' actions - responses of environment". At joint performance of the scenario agents' coordination is carried out by message exchange. As the agents' team function in antagonistic environment agents can fail. Restoration of lost functionalities is carried out by means of redistribution of roles of the failed agent between other agents and cloning of new agents.

3   "Computer Network Attacks" Ontology

The developed ontology comprises a hierarchy of notions specifying activities of team of malefactors directed to implementation of attacks of various classes in different layers of detail. In this ontology, the hierarchy of nodes representing notions splits into two subsets according to the *macro- and micro-layers* of the domain specifications. All nodes of the ontology of attacks on the macro- and micro-levels of specification are divided into the *intermediate* (detailable) and *terminal* (non-detailable) [7].

The notions of the ontology of an upper layer can be interconnected with the corresponding notions of the lower layer through one of three kinds of *relationships*: (1) "*Part of*" that is decomposition relationship; (2) "*Kind of*" that is specialization relationship; and (3) "*Seq of*" that is relationship specifying sequence of operation.

High-layer notions corresponding to the intentions (see above) form the upper layers of the ontology. They are interconnected by the "*Part of*" relationship. Attack actions realizing malefactor's intentions (they presented at the lower layers as compared with the intentions) are interconnected with the intentions by "*Kind of*" or "*Seq of*" relationship.

The developed ontology includes the detailed description of the network attack domain in which the notions of the bottom layer ("*terminals*") can be specified in terms of network packets, OS calls, and audit data.

Let us consider a high-layer fragment of the developed ontology.

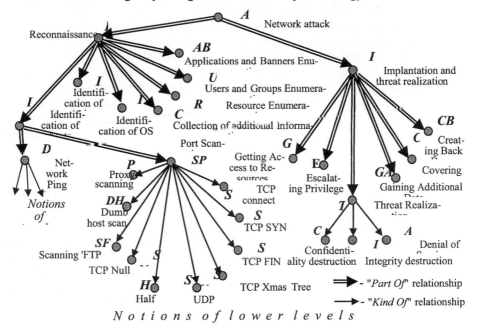

Fig. 1. Macro-level fragment of the "*Network attack*" domain ontology

At the upper-level of the *macro-specification of attacks*, the notion of "Network Attack" (designated by A) is in the "*Part of*" relationship to the "Reconnaissance" (R) and "Implantation and threat realization" (I). In turn, the notion R is in the "*Part of*" relationship to the notions IH, IS, IO, CI, RE, UE, and ABE. The notion I is in the "*Part of*" relationship to the notions GAR, EP, GAD, TR, CT, and CBD. In the next (lower) level of the hierarchy of the problem domain ontology, for example, the notion IH is in the "*Kind of*" relationship to the notions "Network Ping Sweeps" (DC) and "Port Scanning" ($SPIH$). At that, the notion "Network Ping Sweeps" (DC) is the lowest ("terminal") notion of the macro-level of attack specification, and the notion "Port Scanning" ($SPIH$) is detailed through the use of the "*Kind of*" relationship by a set of "terminal" notions of the macro-level of attack specification.

The "terminal" notions of the macro-level are further elaborated on the *micro-level of attack specification*, and on this level they belong to the set of top-level notions detailed through the use of the three relationships introduced above.

In micro specifications of the computer network attacks ontology, besides the three relations described ("*Part of*", "*Kind of*", "*Seq of*"), the relationship "*Example of*" is also used. It serves to establish the "type of object– specific sample of object" relationship. For example, this type of relationship is used to establish the connection between the echo-request of the protocol ICMP ("ICMP ECHO REQUEST") and its specific implementation specified, for example, as a message of the program *tcpdump*: `<time> <src_addr> > <dest_addr>: icmp: echo request,` where `<time>` − a time stamp, `<src_addr>` − source IP address, `<src_port>` − source port, `<dest_addr>` − destination IP address.

4   Specification of Hackers-Agents' Plans

Common formal plan of distributed attacks implemented by team of hacker-agents has three-level structure: (1) *Upper level* is a level of intention-based scenarios of malefactors' team specified in terms of time-ordered sequences of intentions and negotiation acts; (2) *Middle level* is a level of intention-based scenarios of each malefactor specified in terms of an ordered sequences of sub-goals; (3) *Lower level* is a level of malefactor's intention realization specified in terms of low-level actions.

Mathematical model of attacks is specified in terms of a set of *formal grammars* interconnected through "*substitution*" operations [1, 3, 4]: $M_A = <\{G_i\}, \{Su\}>$, where $\{G_i\}$ − the formal grammars, $\{Su\}$ − the "substitution" operations. The sequences of symbols ("strings", "words" − in formal grammar terminology) generated by *each* of such grammars correspond to the sequences of time ordered malefactor's intentions or actions. It is assumed that every sequence of a malefactor's actions viewed as a "word" in a formal language is specified through a family of enclosed context-free grammars recognizable by a corresponding family of state machines. At the scenario specification layer (it was earlier called *macro-layer*) such sequences correspond to the specification of scenarios in terms of the malefactor's intentions and actions.

The formal model of attack scenarios in terms of formal grammars are based on the attacks ontology described above. It is noteworthy to notice that each node of the ontology that is not "terminal" one is mapped to particular grammar, which is capable to generate only admissible sequences realizing this intention in terms of symbols, corresponding to the ontology nodes of the immediately lower layer. Depending on the required level of detail, these nodes may be represented by the terminal nodes of the macro or micro-level. In the former case, the grammar may be used to visualize the malefactor's actions, and in the latter case − for attack simulation in the lowest layer terms (if the "terminal" nodes of the micro-level are represented by network packets, OS commands and/or calling applications with specified parameters).

Every formal grammar is specified by quintuple [1, 3, 4]: $G = <V_N, V_T, S, P, A>$, where G is the grammar identifier (name), V_N is the set of non-terminal symbols (that are associated with the upper and the intermediate levels of representation of the steps of an attack scenario), V_T is the set of its terminal symbols (that designate the steps of a lower-level attack scenario), $S \in V_N$ is the grammar axiom (an initial symbol of an attack scenario), P is the set of productions (production rules) that specify the refinement operations for the attack scenario through the substitution of the symbols of an upper-level node by the symbols of the lower-level nodes, and A is the set of attributes and algorithms of their computation.

Attribute component of each grammar serves for several purposes. The first of them is to specify *randomized choice of a production* at the current inference step if several productions have the equal left part non-terminals coinciding with the active non-terminal in the current sequence under inference. These probabilities could be recalculated on-line subject to the pre-history of attack development and previous results of attack. So, in order to specify a stochastic grammar, each production is supplemented with a specification of the probability of the rule being chosen in case of an attack implementation. The length of the string of actions (intentions) that disclose the upper-level action (intention) depends primarily on the attack goal that has been set and on the degree of the target protection. The length of the string is determined by the specified probabilities of the selected productions. For the productions with the same left parts the sum of probabilities of choice is 1. The probability of a certain type attack is determined by the multiplication of probabilities of productions used.

Also the attribute component is used to check *conditions determining the admissibility of using a production* at the current step of inference. These conditions depend on task specification (general attack goal), configuration of computer network (host) and its resources and results of the malefactor's previous actions.

Algorithmic interpretation of the attack generation specified as a family of formal generalized grammars is implemented by a family of state machines. The basic elements of each state machine are states, transition arcs, and explanatory texts for each transition. States of each state machine are divided into three types: first (initial), intermediate, and final (marker of this state is *End*). The initial and intermediate states are as follows: non-terminal, those that initiate the work of the corresponding nested state machines; terminal, those that interact with the host model; abstract (auxiliary) states. Transition arcs are identified with the productions of grammars, and can be carried out only under certain conditions. Within the state, besides the transition choice depending on the intention and the current transition probability, the following types of action can be performed: *Entry action* (an action performed on entering the state); *Do action* (a set of basic actions, including actions of transition to the nested state machine or realizing the host response model); *Exit action* (an action performed on exiting). For the fragment of the attack domain elaborated, the family of finite state machines includes 50 state machines.

5   Attack Simulator Prototype and Its Evaluation Results

The software prototype for computer network attack simulation is built as a *multi-agent system* that uses two classes of agents: (1) Network Agent and (2) Hacker Agent. The *Network Agent* simulates the attacked computer network and its defensive system. The *Hacker Agent* simulates a malefactor performing attack against computer network. The developed technology makes it possible to model and simulate a team of hackers and a team of agents responsible for computer network security.

The aforementioned agents are implemented on the basis of the technology supported by Multi-Agent System Development Kit (MASDK) [5] that is a software tool aiming at support of the design and implementation of multi-agent systems of a broad range. The Attack Simulator comprises the multitude of reusable components generated by use of the MASDK standard functionalities and application-oriented software components developed in terms of programming language MS Visual C++ 6.0 SP 5.

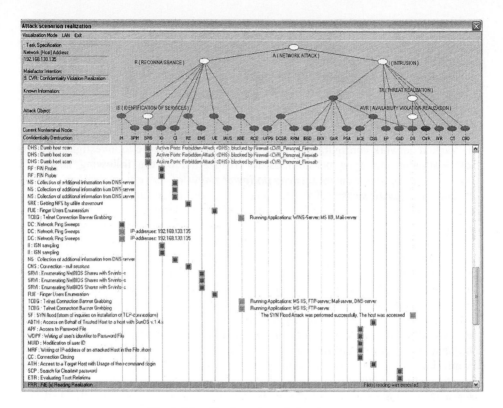

Fig. 2. Visualization of attack development

Each agent operates using the respective fragment of the application ontology that is designed by use of an editor of MASDK facilities. The interaction between agents in the process of attack simulation is supported by the communication environment, which design and implementation is also supported by MASDK. While simulating an attack in order either to obtain response providing it with the needed information from the Network Agent (on the reconnaissance stage) or to perform an attack action (on the threat realization stage) Hacker Agent sends a certain message to the Network Agent. The Network Agent, like this takes place in real-life interactions, analyzes the received message and forms a responsive message. This message is formed based on the Network Agent's knowledge base that models the network configuration and all its attributes needed to simulate the real-life response. This knowledge base also uses information about possible existing attacks and reaction of the network on them.

The key components of both agents correspond to so-called kernels that are the modules written in C++ and compiled into a dll. These components provide interface between the part of the software written in C++ and the components implemented through use of MASDK. The kernels provide interfaces to the respective fragments of the application ontology, and initialize the state machines executing scripts.

The Hacker Agent comprises the following main components: Kernel; fragment of the application domain ontology; state machines model; scripts; attack task specification component; probabilistic (stochastic) decision making model with regard to the further actions; network traffic generator; visualization component of the attack scenario development. The main components of the Network Agent are as follows: Kernel; fragment of the application domain ontology; state machines model component; scripts component; network configuration specification component; firewall model (implementation) component; generator of the network's response to attack action.

The main objective of the *experiments* with the Attack Simulator prototype has consisted in demonstration of its efficiency for various specifications of attacks and an attacked network configuration. The authors had the purpose to investigate the Attack Simulator prototype possibilities for realization of the following tasks: (1) *Checking a computer network security policy at stages of conceptual and logic design of network security system*. This task can be solved by simulation of attacks at a macro-level and researches of responding a being designed (analyzed) network model; (2) *Checking security policy (including vulnerabilities recognition) of a real-life computer network*. This task can be solved by means of simulation of attacks at a micro-level, i.e. by generating a network traffic corresponding to real activity of malefactors on realization of various security threats. The *simulation-based exploration* has demonstrated the Attack Simulator efficacy for accomplishing various attack scenarios against networks with different structures and security policies implemented.

In the experiments with simulation of attacks on macro-level, explorations of attacks for all malefactor's intentions implemented have been accomplished. These experiments were carried out for various parameters of the attack task specification and an attacked computer network configuration. Besides malefactor's intention, it was investigated the influence on attacks efficacy of the following *input parameters*: protection degree of network and personal firewall, protection degree of attacked host (for example, how strong is the password, does the host has sharing files, printers and other resources, does the host use trusted hosts, etc.), and degree of hacker's knowledge about a network. To investigate the Attack Simulator capabilities, the following *parameters of attack realization outcome* have been selected: number of terminal level attack actions (NS), percentage of the hacker's intentions realized successfully (PIR), percentage of "effective" network responses on attack actions (PAR), percentage of attack actions blockage by firewall (PFB), percentage of "ineffective" results of attack actions (when attack is not successful) (PRA). In all experiments the Attack Simulator allows to generate the clearly interpretable results.

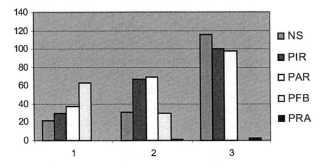

Fig. 3. Diagram of attack outcome parameters for intention *IS*

As an example of scenario, fulfilled by Attack Simulator, let us consider screen indicating generation of the attack CVR ("Confidentiality Violation Realization") (Fig.2). In the figure the information is divided on four groups: (1) the attack task specification units are mapped in the left top of the screen; (2) to the right of them the attack generation tree is visualized; (3) the strings of the malefactor's actions are placed in the left part of the screen below the attack task specification; (4) on the right of each malefactor's action a tag of success (failure) as green (black or red) quadrate and data obtained from an attacked host (a host response) are depicted.

Graphical representation of attack realization outcome parameters values at realization of intention *IS* (*Identification of the host Services*) depending on values of protection degree of network firewall (1 - "Strong"; 2 - "Medium"; 3 - "None") is displayed in Fig.3.

6   Conclusion

In the paper we described basic ideas of the *modeling and simulation of coordinated distributed attacks by teamwork approach*. Mathematical methods and techniques realizing attack agent-based modeling and simulation were developed.

Software prototype of Attack Simulator is presented. The attack simulator allows simulating a wide spectrum of real life attacks. Its software code is written in terms of Visual C++ 6.0, Java 2 version 1.3.1, KQML and XML languages. The developed technology makes it possible to simulate *adversary interactions* of a team of hackers and a team of network defense agents.

Two *types of experiments* have been fulfilled: (1) simulation of attacks on macro-level (generation and investigation of malicious actions against computer network model have been carried out); (2) simulation of attacks on micro-level (generation malicious network traffic against a real computer network has been fulfilled). The *simulation-based exploration of the Attack Simulator prototype* has demonstrated its efficacy for accomplishing various attack scenarios against networks with different structures and security policies implemented.

The *further research* can consist of more detailed developing teamwork support procedures, extending attack classes, supporting more complicated structures of the attacked networks, implementing more sophisticated attack scenarios using different attack objects and exploits, etc.

References

[1]   Aho, A.V., Ullman, J.D.: The Theory of Parsing, Translation, and Compiling, Vol. 1, 2, Prentice-Hall, Inc. (1972)

[2]   Cohen P.R., Levesque H.J.: Teamwork. Nous, 25(4) (1991)

[3]   Fu, K.S.: Syntactic Methods in Pattern Recognition, Academic Press, New York (1974)

[4]   Glushkov, V., Tseitlin, G., Yustchenko, E.: Algebra, Languages, Programming. Naukova Dumka Publishers, Kiev (1978) (In Russian)

[5]   Gorodetski, V., Karsayev, O., Kotenko, I., Khabalov, A.: Software Development Kit for Multi-agent Systems Design and Implementation. Lecture Notes in Artificial Intelligence, Vol. 2296, Springer Verlag (2002)

[6]   Gorodetski, V., Kotenko, I.: The Multi-agent Systems for Computer Network Security Assurance: frameworks and case studies. IEEE International Conference "Artificial Intelligence Systems". Proceedings. IEEE Computer Society (2002)

[7]   Gorodetski, V., Kotenko, I.: Attacks against Computer Network: Formal Grammar-based Framework and Simulation Tool. Lecture Notes in Computer Science, Vol.2516, Springer Verlag (2002)

[8]   Grosz B., Kraus S.: Collaborative plans for complex group actions. Artificial Intelligence, Vol.86 (1996)

[9]   Jennings N.: Controlling cooperative problem solving in industrial multi-agent systems using joint intentions. Artificial Intelligence. No.75 (1995)

[10] Tambe, M.: Towards Flexible Teamwork. Journal of Artificial Intelligence Research, No.7 (1997)

[11] Tambe M., Pynadath D.V.: Towards Heterogeneous Agent Teams. Lecture Notes in Artificial Intelligence, Vol.2086 (2001)

Formal Modeling of Dynamic Environments for Real-Time Agents

Miguel Rebollo, Vicente Botti, and Eva Onaindía

Dept. Sistemas Informáticos y Computación
Universidad Politécnica de Valencia (Spain)
{mrebollo,vbotti,onaindia}@dsic.upv.es

Abstract. Application of agent technology to dynamic environments makes developers to take into account some considerations that common agent-based systems need not meet.

ARTIS agent architecture is our proposal for agent-based systems that require bounded response times. This kind of systems are characterised by their sensitivity to the moment in which the response is obtained. If the answer does not arrive on time, the consequences for the systems are catastrophic. They are hard, real-time systems.

This paper proposes a formalisation, using an extension of RTCTL logic, to specify the ARTIS agent behaviour. It does not pretend to be a formal validation prove for the agent, but a way that allows the designer to check the fulfilment of the agent's design goals.

1 Introduction

The definition of a real-time agent stresses the *reactivity* concept of agent design. It is due to the fact that the correct response for environmental changes is critic for maintaining the system under control. Hence, an agent performs three processes. Firstly, the agent *perceives* the current state of its environment throughout a set of sensors. After that, it *reasons* using the available information to compute a response as good as possible. Finally, it *acts* over the environment.

These three phases—perception, cognition and action—form a cycle which constitutes the execution scheme for the agent. In the specific case of real-time agents, the quality of the response depends on the amount of time the agent needs to obtain the answer. In that way, a non-optimal, in-time response is preferred to the optimal, out-of-time answer. So, the reasoning process must be time-bounded and its 5 worst-case execution time must be known.

This paper proposes a formalisation which involves both, the agent model and the world model, for hard, real-time systems. In this kind of environment, the stability of the system depends on the time the response is available in. A formal model is a useful tool for the developers of real-time agents, because the correctness of time properties can be evaluated to ensure that the agent achieves its design goals.

The proposed model focuses in the representation of a dynamic environment, with critical, temporal restrictions. After the environment is characterised, a formal model for real-time agent is showed in order to guarantee that the agent

V. Mařík et al. (Eds): CEEMAS 2003, LNAI 2691, pp. 475–484, 2003.

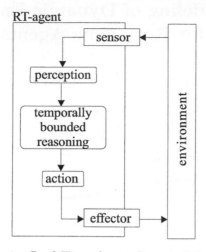

Fig. 1. Real-Time Agent Generic Scheme

satisfies its temporal constraints and it is able to maintain the environment under control.

ARTIS has been implemented taking into account these requirements. Its reasoning processes are based on anytime or interruptible behaviours: the quality of the response increases with the time and the process can be interrupted at any time and the system always has an available response.

Reasoning processes in ARTIS are divided into two levels: the *reflex* level, which calculates a first, low-level, time-bounded response; and the *deliberative* level, which spends all its available time on the improvement of the quality of the previous response. Thus, the global agent behaviour remains bounded, allowing even the use of elaborated reasoning processes including AI techniques.

Two of the most used formalisms for agent specification are based on *intentional logics*, which describe systems by means of believes, desires and intentions; and *temporal logics*, which proceed from reactive systems [10].

Many of reactive systems use propositional logics, based on time-points and including reasoning about future [5]. Continuous temporal structures and linear logics are commonly used for real-time systems. Branched logics, as CTL*, are more frequently used for intelligent agents modeling.

2 Temporal Logics for Real-Time Systems

Nowadays we can find several formalisms allowing to model, to specify and to test temporal properties of reactive systems. The nearest approach to formalisms used in intelligent agent specification is based on modal logics. The use of temporal logics to specify reactive systems is not new [9]. The main reason to choose modal logics is its application to the specification and verification of the two

ARTIS related areas: intelligent agents and real-time systems. Two examples of modal logics that extends CTL for each one of these areas are:

- CTL* [4] is the widely used logic in agents' formal definition. BDI architectures [8] are based on this logic.
- RTCTL [6] is an adaptation for RTS working with reasoning processes involving branched future.

The main drawback of using a modal logic in real-time systems is that it does not allow to express quantitative relationships. Then, it is not valid for representing periods and deadlines, which determines the behaviour of the reactive system. Emerson [4] revises different kinds of useful temporal logics for dynamic systems. Any of them can be extended in order to represent temporal constraints.

Three possibilities for adding temporal properties in w.f.f. are presented in [3]:

Temporally-bounded operators. It replaces temporal operators by their corresponding bounded versions. For instance, $\Diamond_{[2,4]}$ is interpreted as *sometimes between 2 and 4 time units*. The formula $\Box_t \phi$ (or $\Diamond_t \phi$) is true in $t \in \mathbb{R}$ of a sequence $(\bar{\sigma}, \bar{I})$ iff ϕ is true in every (some) time instant in the interval $t + I$. In that way, Equation 1 is interpreted as follows: *whenever p are observed, then q is occasionally true before 3 time units.*

$$\Box(p \rightarrow \Diamond_{\leq 3} q) \tag{1}$$

Freeze quantification. It associates to each state the time instant in which it is true throughout a freeze quantifier "x.". A formulae $x.\phi(t)$ is true in t iff $\phi(t)$ is true. For instance, in the formulae $\Diamond y.\phi$, the temporal variable y is bounded to those states in which ϕ is occasionally true. This alternative allows us to express facts like

$$\Box x.(p \rightarrow \Diamond y.(q \wedge y \leq x + 3)) \tag{2}$$

that is, *in every state in time instant x, if p is true then there is a later state in time y in which q is true. Futhermore, y occurs 3 time units after x.* This kind of formulae cannot be expressed directly using temporally-bounded operators.

Explicit clock variable. A dynamic state variable T, which represents the system clock, and quantification for temporal variables are defined. Equation 2 can be re-written as:

$$\forall x, \Box((p \wedge T = x) \rightarrow (q \wedge yT \leq x + 3)) \tag{3}$$

x takes as its values all time instants in which p is true.

There are some extensions to RTCTL logic that allow adequately represent relations between time intervals, like Parametrized Real-Time Computation Tree Logic (PRTCTL) [7]. So we can express the relation showed in Equations 2 and 3 using this logic:

$$\forall x, \Box(p \rightarrow \Diamond_{\leq x+3} q) \tag{4}$$

3   Real-Time Environments for Intelligent Agents

It is usual to use the term *environment* to denote all the external components of the system, excluding the agent. Sometimes, the environment can be represented just as another agent. Wooldridge and Lomuscio [11] define it as a tuple formed by four elements:

Definition 1 (Environment) *An environment is a tuple*

$$Env = \langle E, vis, \tau_e, e_0 \rangle$$

where

- $E = \{e_1, e_2, e_3, \ldots\}$ *is an instantaneous states set*
- $vis : E \to \wp(E)$ *is a visibility function. It divides E into subsets mutually excluded and $e \in vis(e) \forall e \in E$. The elements of E are called* visibility sets.
- $\tau_e : E \times Act \to E$ *is a transformation function for the environment, where $Act = \{a_0, a_1, a_2, \ldots\}$ defines the set of agent's actions.*
- $e_0 \in E$ *is the environment initial state.*

Usually, domains in which the agents are situated are non-deterministic: the result of the execution of agent's actions cannot be predicted/modeled. In such case, the function τ_e needs to be redefined.

The intersection of an agent over its environment defines an state sequence:

$$e_0 \xrightarrow{a_0} e_1 \xrightarrow{a_1} e_2 \xrightarrow{a_2} e_3 \xrightarrow{a_3} \cdots \xrightarrow{a_{u-1}} e_u \xrightarrow{a_u} \cdots \tag{5}$$

The *vis* function defines equivalence classes over the states set E, each one is formed by states indistinguishable each other. When the interaction with the environment has to be defined, any representant of the equivalence class can be chosen.

This situation is particularly interesting for multiagent systems. Let us consider a team of two robots who need to collaborate to realise some task. But each one has its own sensorisation. Let us assume that robot A has a sonar and robot B has infrared sensors.

Some environmental states will be indistinguishable for robot A, because there is no appreciable differences by using ultrasonic waves. But these states are not the same for robot B. So the total set of environmental states E is common for both robots, but should be several *vis* functions—external; they are a property of the environment— which generates different sets of states.

From real-time area, several formal definitions are been made. We consider the definition proposed in [3] due to its resemblance to the previous one:

Definition 2 (Real-time system) *A real-time system is a tuple*

$$RTS = \langle \mathcal{S}, \mathcal{P}, \mu, \mathcal{T} \rangle$$

where:

- $\mathcal{S} = \{s_1, s_2, \ldots\}$ *is the system states set,*
- $\mathcal{P} = \{p_1, p_2, \ldots\}$ *is the observable set, formed by external events and propositions,*
- $\mu : \mathcal{S} \to \wp(\mathcal{P})$ *associates an observations set to each state* $s_i \in \mathcal{S}$. $\mu(s)$ *represents both, the set of events produced in the current state* s, *and the propositions that are true in that state.*
- $\mathcal{T} : \mathbb{R}^* \to \mathcal{S}$ *determines a set of temporised state sequences. The sequence* $\tau \in \mathcal{T}$ *represents one behaviour of the system, where* $\tau(t) \in \mathcal{S}$ *identifies a unique state* $\forall t \in \mathbb{R}^+$.

A RTS verifies the following property:

Property 3 (Finite variability) *There exists a sequence of temporal intervals* $\bar{I} = I_0, I_1, I_2, \ldots$ *such that* $\forall t, t' \in I_i, \mu(\tau(t)) = \mu(\tau(t'))$.

That is, the observable component of the system does not change during a time interval. Furthermore, each system state contents all the needed information to determine its evolution.

Let $\bar{\sigma} = \sigma_0, \sigma_1, \sigma_2, \ldots$ be a *observation sequence*, finite or infinite, where $\sigma_i \in \wp(\mathcal{P})$. If we add to each observation the time interval in which it is true, then a *temporised observation sequence* $\rho = (\bar{\sigma}, \bar{I})$ is obtained. It can be rewritten as a sequence of pairs:

$$(\sigma_0, I_0) \to (\sigma_1, I_1) \to (\sigma_1, I_1) \to \cdots \tag{6}$$

As it can be seen, the two definitions of environment are quite similar. So we only need an small effort to get close both definitions.

4   ARTIS System

Now, we are in position to build our own definition of ARTIS *system*. The existence of a non-deterministic, real-time environment and and agent, which interacts with it, have to be taken into account.

4.1   ARTIS Agent Conceptual Model

ARTIS agent conceptual model describes two aspects: the components that constitute the mental state of the agent and the existing relation among them (see Fig. 2).

- Current agent *perception*. It is formed by all the information the agent receives through its sensors in a time instant t. A set Σ, which maintains these data, can be defined.
- A set of *believes* that represent the internal state of the agent and the environment model. Δ is the set of believes of the agent.

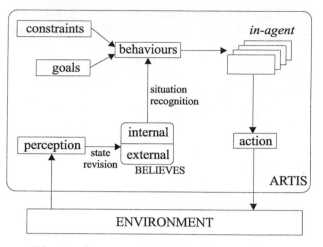

Fig. 2. Conceptual Model of ARTIS Agent

- A set of agent *goals* $\mathcal{G}$. We can distinguish two kinds of goals—*goals* in the strict sense and *constraints*—. We define a set $G^+ = \{g, g', \ldots\}$ which represents the current agent goals, and a set $G^- = \{r, r', \ldots\}$ with the agent constraints. The main difference between them is the same difference we can see between liveness and safety rules in concurrent systems, formally defined by Alpern y Schneider [2][1].
- A set of *situations* that describes the internal state of the agent. The response the agent provides facing the same event can be different in different situations, depending on the active behaviour in that moment.
- A set of so-called *in-agent*. Each one contains the problem-solving knowledge and defines how the agent acts under the current situation.

4.2   ARTIS Formal Definition

The entity which finally maintain real-time requirements in the ARTIS agent architecture is the *in-agent*. It contains the problem-solving knowledge and takes into account the temporal constraints that limite the available time to build a satisfactory response to a situation.

Definition 4 (in–agent) *An* in-agent *is an structure:*

$$a_i = \langle \Sigma_i, \mathcal{A}_i, \Delta_i, \rho_i, \delta_i, D_i, T_i \rangle$$

where:

- Σ_i *is the perceptions set;*
- $\mathcal{A}_i$ *is the actions set over the environment;*
- Δ_i *is the believes set;*
- ρ_i *is the reflex actions set;*

- δ_i is the deliberative actions sets;
- $D_i \in \mathbb{R}^+$ is the deadline;
- $T_i \in \mathbb{R}^+$ is the period.

A *believes revision function*, that updates *in-agent*'s believes from the information tuned through the sensors, is defined as follows:

$$brf : \Delta_i \times \Sigma_i \rightarrow \Delta_i \tag{7}$$

The problem-solving process is performed by the actions stored in ρ_i and δ_i. Two functions are defined. The first one represents the critic, real-time behaviour of the *in-agent*.

$$reflex : \Delta_i \times \rho_i \rightarrow \Delta_i \times \mathcal{A}_i \tag{8}$$

This function calculates a first, elemental answer. Its *worst-case execution time* is known and the agent can use it to schedule the reflex componentes of all active *in-agent* to guarantee the availability of a response.

The *reflex* function modifies the *in-agent* believes and proposes a first action to execute. This action will be the result of the *in-agent* if the next level does not conclude its reasoning process.

The second function improves the first response if it has enough available time. It implements the optional cognition process of the agent.

$$delib : \Delta_i \times \delta_i \rightarrow \Delta_i \times \mathcal{A}_i \tag{9}$$

We can distinguish three kinds of *in-agent*, depending on the actions they can perform:

- *reflex in-agent*: they are those in which $\delta_i = \varnothing$;
- *deliberative in-agent*: they are those in which $\rho_i = \varnothing$;
- *complete in-agent*: they are those in which $\rho_i \neq \varnothing$ y $\delta_i \neq \varnothing$;

$InAg = \{a_i | i \in \mathbb{N}\}$ denotes the set of all the *in-agent* of an ARTIS agent.

In-agent are grouped into behaviours, that response to concrete situations the agent can found in it.

Definition 5 *A* behaviour *is a set of* in-agent:

$$beh \in \wp(InAg)$$

Two behaviour *beh* and *beh'* are *different* if:

$$\forall beh, beh' \in \wp(InAg), \exists a_i \in InAg | a_i \in beh \wedge a_i \notin beh' \tag{10}$$

At last, we are in position to define a complete ARTIS agent.

Definition 6 (Agente ARTIS) *An* ARTIS *agent is an structure:*

$$AA = \langle \mathcal{B}, \mathcal{G}, \Delta \rangle$$

where:

- $\mathcal{B} \subseteq \wp(InAg)$ *is a finite behaviours set;*
- $\mathcal{G}$ *is the goals set*
- Δ *is the believes set*

$$\Delta = \bigcup_{\forall a_i \in InAg} \Delta_i$$

We define a function τ that determines the active behaviour of the agent, as follows:

$$\tau : \mathcal{B} \times \Delta \to \mathcal{B} \tag{11}$$

Property 7 *Let be $\mathcal{B}$ the behaviours set of an* ARTIS *agent. Then:*

$$\forall beh_i, beh_j \in \mathcal{B}, beh_i \neq beh_j$$

The fulfilment of the agent design goals can be guaranteed from the formal agent model.

Definition 8 *Let be Δ the agent believes set, g a goal and ρ_i, δ_i the deduction rules set. Then $\Delta \overset{\rho_i,\delta_i}{\vdash} g$ iff there is a prove of g from Δ using the rules of ρ_i or the rules of δ_i.*

A goal can be achieved if $\exists a_i \in InAg$ such that, by applying its deduction rules, the goal can be deduced from the current agent believes. This definition can be generalised in order to consider several *in-agent* to take part in the goal achievement.

Definition 9 *A integrity constraint is a goal g that verifies:*

$$g \in \mathcal{G}, \exists a_i, \Delta \overset{\rho_i}{\vdash} g$$

ARTIS agent goals must verify that:

1. there exists al least one *in-agent* to achive the goal, and
2. the *in-agent* period must allow to detect the environment situation on time.

This is guaranteed by the followinf property:

Property 10 *Goals defined for the* ARTIS *agent must verify*

$$\forall g^{[l,h]} \in \mathcal{G}, \exists a_i, (\Delta \overset{\rho_i}{\vdash} g \vee \Delta \overset{\delta_i}{\vdash} g) \wedge T_i \leq l$$

If g is a survival goal, only one *in-agent* $a_i \in InAg$ must be able to achieve it by applying rules of ρ_i. The remaining goals can be achieved using rules of ρ_j and δ_j from any *in-agent* $a_j \in InAg$.

An interval I is defined by two time points $a, b \in \mathbb{R}^+$ such that $a \leq b$. We define $\bar{I} = I_0, I_1, I_2, \ldots$ as an interval sequence that forms a partition over the timeline and that verifies:

- $\forall I_i \in \bar{I}, \exists I_{i+1} \in \bar{I}$ adjacent to I_i.
- $\forall t \in \mathbb{R}^+, \exists! I_i$ such that $t \in I_i$.

Definition 11 (Real-time environment) *A real-time environment is a tuple*

$$RTE = \langle E, vis, \tau_e, e_0 \rangle$$

where

- $E = \{e_1, e_2, e_3, \ldots\}$ *is a set of environment states.*
- $vis : E \to \wp(E)$ *is the visibility function.*
- $\tau_e : E \times Act \to \wp(E)$ *is the transformation function for the environment (we use $\wp(E)$ to express the non-determinism).*
- $e_0 \in E$ *is the initial environment state.*

The modifications realised to the model are:

1. the exigence of instantaneous states $e_i \in E$ is eliminated. Futhermore (see Definition 12), temporal intervals will be included to indicate the validity period of the systems states.
2. the co-dominium of the transformation function τ_e is changed into $\wp(E)$ to represent the environment non-determinism.

An ARTIS system is a system formed by a real-time environment and an AR-TIS agent, situated in the environment. Both are synchronised, so the interaction between them follows the classic cycle: perception–cognition–actuation.

Like in the previous case occurs, a global state sequence $e_0, e_1, e_2, \ldots$ represents the AA execution over a real-time environment. If temporal intervals are added to this sequence (see Equation 6), a *temporalised global sequence* are obtained, representing the AA execution.

Definition 12 (ARTIS system execution) *The execution of an AA over RTE is a pair $(\bar{g}, \bar{I})$ formed by a global state sequence and an interval sequence, both with the same length.*

The agent execution can be rewritten as a pair sequence:

$$(g_0, I_0) \xrightarrow{\alpha_0} (g_1, I_1) \xrightarrow{\alpha_1} (g_2, I_2) \xrightarrow{\alpha_2} (g_3, I_3) \xrightarrow{\alpha_3} \cdots \xrightarrow{\alpha_{u-1}} (g_u, I_u) \xrightarrow{\alpha_u} \cdots \quad (12)$$

We can see the resemblance between this sequence and the sequences described in Equations 6 and 5.

5   Conclusions

This paper describes a model for agents situated in real-time environments. The formalisation means a way to check some properties of the model. So the developer can test if the agent verifies its design goals.

At the moment, the only purpose of the formalisation is to provide a manual checking technique, and not to supply the designer with an automatic prove method.

A model for a real-time environment has been exposed, by getting close the definitions provided in real-time and intelligent agents areas.

In future works, we will concentrate our efforts on obtaining an efficient method to manage the cost of formal checking of the correctness of the system. Model checking techniques are under revision because they have been applied successfully to prove real-time system specifications and intelligent agent formalisations.

References

[1] Martín Abadi, B. Alpern, K.R. Apt, N. Francez, S. Katz, L. Lamport, and F.B. Scheider. Preserving liveness: Comments on "safety and liveness from a methodological point of view". *Information Processing Letters*, 40(3):141–142, 1991.

[2] Bowen Alpern and Fred B. Schneider. Defining liveness. *Information Processing Letters*, 21(4):181–185, 1985.

[3] R. Alur and T.A. Henzinger. Logics and Models of Real-Time: A Survey. In *Real Time: Theory in Practice*, volume 600, pages 74–106. Springer-Verlag, 1991.

[4] E. Emerson. *Temporal and Modal Logic*, volume B of *Handbook of Theoretical Computer Science*. Elsevier Science, 1990.

[5] E. Emerson. Automated temporal reasoning about reactive systems. In *Banff Higher Order Workshop*, pages 41–101, 1995.

[6] E. Emerson, A.K. Mok, A.P. Sistla, and J. Srinivasan. Quantitative temporal reasoning. *Real-Time Systems*, (4):331–352, 1992.

[7] E. Emerson and R.J. Treffler. Parametric quantitative temporal reasoning.

[8] M. Georgeff and Rao A. Modeling Rational Agents within a BDI-Architecture. In *Proceedings of the Second International Conference on Principles of Knowledge Representation and Reasoning*, San Mateo, CA, 1991. Morgan Kaufmann.

[9] A. Pnueli. The temporal logic of programs. In *Proc. of Eighteen Symposium on the Foundations of Computer Science*, 1977.

[10] M. Wooldridge. Temporal Belief Logics for Modelling Distributed Artificial Intelligence Systems. In G. M. P. O'Hare and N. R. Jennings, editors, *Foundations of Distributed Artificial Intelligence*. John Wiley & Sons, 1995.

[11] M. Wooldridge and A. Lomuscio. A Computationally Grounded Logic of Visibility, Perception and Knowledge. *Journal of the IGPL*, 9(2):273–288, 2001.

Deliberative Server for Real-Time Agents*

Carlos Carrascosa, Miguel Rebollo, Vicente Julián, and Vicente Botti

Dept. Sistemas Informáticos y Computación
Universidad Politécnica de Valencia
Camino de Vera s/n – 46022 – Valencia (Spain)
{carrasco,mrebollo,vinglada,vbotti}@dsic.upv.es

Abstract. Over the last few years more complex and flexible techniques
have been needed to develop hard real-time systems. The agent paradigm
seems to be an appropriate approach to be applied in this area. ARTIS
is an agent architecture suitable for hard real-time agents. This paper
is focused on an extension of the control module of ARTIS agents that
provides a soft real-time control architecture inside of a hard real-time
agent. This extension incorporates a deliberative component that allows
to change the control module policy depending on the data environment
and the reactivity degree of the agent.

1 Introduction

This paper takes the application of agents technology to hard real-time environments as a starting point. In order to situate the topics, different definitions
are presented. First, a *Real-Time Environment* is defined. This is an environment with temporal restrictions that may have different features which affect its
control. A Real-Time Environment is controlled by a *Real-Time System (RTS)*,
which is defined as a system in which the correctness of the system depends
not only on the logical result of computation, but also on the time at which
the results are produced [21]. In a RTS, some tasks have deadlines. A *deadline*
defines the greatest time interval in which the system can provide a response.
If the response is obtained after this time, it will probably not be useful. The
main feature of a RTS is not to always be interconnected or to be the fastest
system. A RTS should guarantee its temporal restrictions and, at the same time,
it should try to accomplish its goals. Researchers differentiate between two types
of RTS. First, a *Hard Real-Time System* is a RTS where the execution of a task
after its deadline is completely useless. Systems of this kind are critical systems,
and severe consequences will result if the timing requirements are not satisfied.
On the other hand, a *Soft Real-Time System* is characterized by the fact that
the execution of a task after its deadline only decreases the quality of the task
result [21]. Different techniques are needed for hard and soft RTS. In this paper,
only hard real-time systems are considered.

---

* Work funded by grant number TAP98-0333-C03-01 of the Spanish government.

V. Mařík et al. (Eds): CEEMAS 2003, LNAI 2691, pp. 485–496, 2003.

Once a RTS is defined, it is possible to define a *Real-Time Artificial Intelligence System (RTAIS)* as a system that must accomplish complex and critical processes under a probably dynamic environment with temporal restrictions by using AI techniques. Previous approaches to RTAIS can be found in the literature. Anytime algorithms [6] and approximate processing [8] are the most promising. One line of research in RTAIS has been to build large applications or architectures that embody real-time concerns in many components [8], such as Guardian [11] and Phoenix [12]. All these applications are soft RTS because they do not assure the fulfillment of their temporal restrictions.

Within RTAIS research area, a *Real-Time Agent (RTA)* can be defined as an agent with temporal restrictions. In the same way as RTS, it is possible to talk about "hard" or "soft" RTA. Almost all the existing approaches, like PRS [13], the CELLO agent model [17] and, more recently, DECAF [10], are designed as soft RTA (without critical temporal restrictions). On the other hand, CIRCA [15] [9] [16] manages hard real-time restrictions, but in this case, the AI and the RT subsystems are solving different problems: the AI subsystem builds RT systems, its knowledge is about RT system building, whereas the RT system knows about the domain problem. In this way, RT subsystem has a high reactivity degree, but AI subsystem has a low reactivity degree.

It is very important to take into account the different activities the agent can dedicate its time to. So, as it is commented in [18], they can be classified in:

- Domain activities: They are executable primitive actions which achieve the various high-level tasks.
- Control activities: They may be of two types:
  - Scheduling activities, which choose the high-level goals, set constraints on how to achieve them and sequence the domain level activities;
  - Coordination activities, which facilitate cooperation with other agents in order to achieve the high-level goals.
- Meta-level control activities: They optimize the agent's performance by allocating appropriate amount of processor and other resources at appropriate times to the domain and control activities.

One of the subjects that should be addressed more frequently is the one related with the *meta-reasoning*. This process tries that the agent does not waste its resources (mainly process time in real-time systems) calculating actions that are available too much late to be useful or their expected improvement do not outweighs the expected cost. This process only could be flawless in a deterministic environment, where the effect of an action can be known before its execution. The problem of how to approximate this ideal of sequencing domain and control activities without consuming too many resources in the process, is called [18] the *meta-level control problem* for a resource bounded rational agent.

ARTIS [3] [20] is an agent architecture suitable for hard real-time agents. This architecture incorporates a Control Module to manage the agent behaviour and to control the execution of the different agent components. From a functional point of view, it is in charge of the *cognitive behaviour* of the agent.

This paper is focused on an extension of the control module of ARTIS agents. This new control module provides a control architecture able to manage soft real-time restrictions into a hard real-time agent architecture. This extension incorporates a deliberative component that incorporates some meta-reasoning in the ARTIS agents allowing to change the control module policy depending on the data environment and the reactivity degree of the agent.

The paper is structured as follows: section 2 focuses on the problem of developing hard, real-time, intelligent agents. Section 3 presents an overview of the ARTIS agent architecture for hard real-time environments. Section 4 goes into a specific module of the architecture, the Deliberative Server, which is the control module part in charge of managing the intelligence of the agent. Finally, some conclusions are mentioned in section 5.

2 Is a Hard, Real-Time, Intelligent Agent Possible?

A real-time agent is situated at anytime in an environment, and it has to react to this environment. The basic architecture of a hard, real-time, intelligent agent should consist of three components: a set of sensors, a set of effectors, and a cognitive capability which computes what actions must be done on the environment to react to sensor perceptions of the environment in a bounded time. More specifically, there must be a module that senses the current state of the environment (perception) and updates the internal state of the agent, a module of cognition which is in charge of computing the set of actions allowing the agent to react to the environment and to reach its goals, and a module of action in charge of executing the set of actions on the environment (actions that could modify the environment). However, it is necessary for all of these modules in a hard real-time agent to have a bounded worst-case execution time (*wcet*), in order to determine whether the system reacts in any situation according to its temporal restrictions. That is, to determine the schedulability of the system. It is usually easy to obtain the *wcet* of the methods employed in perception and action modules. Using classical analysis techniques in RTS, such as *Rate Monotonic* [14], it is possible to analysis the schedulability of a set of RT tasks.

The main problem in this architecture in order to analysis the schedulability is related to the cognition module. This module uses AI techniques as problem-solving methods to compute more *intelligent* actions. In this case, it is difficult to extract the time required by this module because it can either be unbounded or if bounded, its variability is very high. When using AI methods, it is necessary to provide techniques that allow their response times to be bounded. These techniques are based on RTAIS techniques [8].

If the agent must operate in a hard real-time environment, the agent construction complexity is increased enormously. Evidently, different environments require different software structures. Therefore, in an agent context, it is necessary to define an appropriate structure in order to use agent features in hard real-time environments.

RTS tasks have temporal restrictions which must be previously guaranteed. This limitation in the system functionality mentioned above affects the features of an agent that tries to be modeled as a RTS. For example, the time-unbounded problem-solving methods are a serious problem because their execution cannot be temporally restricted. The real existence of a hard, real-time, intelligent agent depends on the ability to overcome this problem and to be able to incorporate the typical features of agency while maintaining the system's real-time behavior.

The hard real-time ARTIS agent architecture [3] incorporates all the necessary aspects that the agency features provide to a software system (autonomy, proactivity, reactivity, ...), but adapted to hard real-time environments. This architecture includes techniques of RTAIS, which overcomes the problem. This approach starts from the basic real-time architecture presented above, and it guarantees reacting on the environment in a dynamic and flexible way. The ARTIS agent architecture guarantees an agent response that satisfies all the critical temporal restrictions and it tries to always obtain the best answer for the current environment status. This is due to its capacities for problem-solving, adaptability and proactivity, which have been added to the architecture.

3   ARTIS Agent: A Hard, Real-Time, Intelligent Agent

This point provides a short description of the ARTIS Agent (AA) architecture, for hard real-time environments (a more detailed description can be found in [3] [20]). The AA architecture could be labelled as a vertical-layered, hybrid architecture with added extensions to work in a hard real-time environment [3].

One of the main features of the AA architecture is its hard real-time behavior. It guarantees the execution of the entire system's specification by means of an off-line analysis of the specification. This analysis is based on well-known predictability analysis techniques in the RTS community, and it is defined in [7].

The off-line analysis only ensures the schedulability of real-time tasks. However, it does not force the task sequence execution. The AA decides the next task to be executed at run-time, allowing it to adapt itself to environment changes, and to take advantage of the tasks using less time than their *wcet*.

The AA reasoning process can be divided into two stages. The first one is a mandatory time-bounded phase. It obtains an initial result of satisfactory quality. After that, if there is available time left (also called *slack time* in the RTS literature), the AA may use this time for the second reasoning stage. This is an optional stage and it does not guarantee a response. It usually produces a higher quality result through intelligent, utility-based, problem-solving methods. This split reasoning process is described in detail in [3].

3.1   ARTIS Agent Architecture

The architecture of an AA can be viewed from two different perspectives: the user model (high-level model) [3] and the system model (low-level model) [22].

The user model offers the developer's view of the architecture, while the system model is the execution framework used to construct the final version of the agent.

From the **user model** point of view, the AA architecture is an extension of the blackboard model which is adapted to work in hard real-time environments. It is formed from the following elements:

- A set of **sensors** and **effectors** to be able to interact with the environment. Due to the environment features, the perception and action processes are time-bounded.
- A set of **in-agents** that models the AA behavior. The main reason to split the whole problem-solving method is to provide an abstraction which organizes the problem-solving knowledge in a modular and gradual way.

  Each in-agent periodically performs an specific task. An in-agent is also an agent according to the Russell's agent definition [19]. Each in-agent has to solve a particular subproblem, but all the in-agents of a particular AA cooperate to control the entire problem, and an in-agent may use information provided by other in-agents.

  In-agents can be classified into critics and acritics. The first ones are in charge of solving essential problems of the AA, so its execution is assured at least for calculating a low-quality answer. The last ones are in charge of solving non-essential problems of the AA to improve its performance quality. A **critic** in-agent is characterized by a period and a deadline. The available time for the in-agent to obtain a valid response is bounded. It must guarantee a basic response to the current environment situation. From a functional point of view, an in-agent consists of two layers: the reflex layer and the real-time deliberative layer. The reflex layer assures a minimal quality response (an off-line schedulability analysis of the AA, considering all the in-agents in the AA, guarantees that this reflex layer will be fully executed). On the other hand, the real-time deliberative layer tries to improve this response (this level will be executed in slack time). The reflex layer of all the in-agents make up the AA mandatory phase. On the other hand, the real-time deliberative layers form the optional phase. An **acritic** in-agent only has the real-time deliberative layer.
- A set of **believes** comprising a world model (with all the domain knowledge which is relevant to the agent) and the internal state, that is the mental states of the agent. This set is stored in a frame-based blackboard [2].
- A **control module** that is responsible for the real-time execution of the in-agents that belong to the AA. The temporal requirements of the two in-agent layers (reflex and deliberative) are different. Thus, the control module must employ different execution criteria for each one.

The **system model** provides a software architecture for the AA that supports all the high level features expressed in the user model. The main features of this model are [7]:

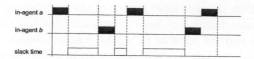

Fig. 1. AA execution timing diagram

- Off-line schedulability analysis.
- Task Model that guarantees the critical temporal restrictions of the environment.
- Slack extraction method to on-line calculate the available time for executing the real-time deliberative layer.
- Set of extensions to the Real-Time Operating System incorporating features for managing real-time capabilities.

To translate the user model' specification into the system model a toolkit, called InSiDE [20], is used. This toolkit allows to define the AA's user model and to convert this model to the corresponding system model automatically [7]. The result is an executable AA.

Figure 1 shows a possible chronogram of the execution phase of an AA by a timing diagram. In this example, the AA is comprised by two in-agents (a and b). Black boxes represent the processor time intervals assigned to the in-agent reflex layer execution. Between these executions there exists slack time (white boxes). This time is used by the AA in order to increase the execution time allocated to unbounded problem-solving methods. One of the tasks of the control module is the management of this slack time. It will allocate this time among the real-time deliberative layers of the in-agents in order to maximize the AA's quality.

The integration of intelligence in an AA lies in the effective management of the slack time by the control module as will be explained in the following sections. So, the rest of the paper explains this module in detail.

3.2   Control Module: Intelligence for RTA

The control module of an AA is the component in charge of controlling how and when the different components of the AA are executed.

The goal of the AA control module is to guarantee that the agent always reacts to the environment and that from the knowledge that the agent has available this response is the best possible result according to the slack time. Therefore, an AA is an agent with a reflex level which is always guaranteed by means of an off-line schedulability analysis [7]. This level provides a first time-bounded response with a minimum quality. Moreover, the AA has a second level, with a deliberative behavior using time-unbounded artificial intelligence techniques. The main goal of this second level is to provide a better response than the reflex one. The execution of this last level is conditioned by the available time that the agent has to run this level and for the real-time restrictions (period, deadline) of the in-agents in the AA. Another condition for executing the second level is that the agent considers it appropriate depending on the real situation (i.e. if the AA is in an emergency mode and decides to act as soon as it has an answer, not dedicating any time to improve it).

Therefore, the control module of an AA is divided in two submodules (that communicate through events): the reflex server and the deliberative server.

- **Reflex Server (RS)** This module is in charge of controlling the execution of reactive components, that is, the components with critical temporal restrictions. Due to these restrictions, it is part of a Real-Time Operating System (RTOS)[1] [22]. It includes the First Level Scheduler (FLS) that must schedule the execution of all the reactive components, in order to guarantee their temporal restrictions. This scheduler is implemented according to a common RTS scheduling policy, a Fixed-Priority, Pre-emptive Scheduling Policy [1].

  Once the execution of the critical parts is assured, there are slack time intervals between the execution of these critical parts. These slack times (calculated using an algorithm based on the Dynamic Slack Stealing algorithm [5]) can be employed by the second submodule of the control module in order to do different functions, the goal of which is to refine the reactive response and to improve its quality.

  This module carries out the following functions to accomplish its purpose:
  - To schedule the execution of all in-agents with critical temporal restrictions. This process must guarantee the fulfillment of these restrictions.
  - To cede the agent control to the DS during the system idle time.
  - To inform the deliberative server of the execution state of the in-agent reflex part and the time it has available to use. This slack time is calculated just before informing the DS to take into account the tasks using less time than their wcet.
- **Deliberative Server (DS)** This module is in charge of controlling the execution of the deliberative components. Therefore, this server is the intelligent element of the control module, but with soft real-time restrictions.

4 Deliberative Server

As it has been stated in the previous point, the Deliberative Server is the AA control module part in charge of managing the intelligence of this agent by means of the slack time management. That is, it provides the soft real-time control in the hard real-time agent.

Its main purposes are: to improve the quality of the agent responses, to adapt the agent to important environment changes and to pursue its own objectives taking into account the real-time restrictions of in-agents in the AA. In order to achieve its goals, some functionalities, that are described in section 4.2, have been implemented.

---

[1] The current version of the AA architecture uses RT-Linux as its RTOS.

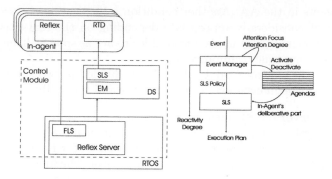

Fig. 2. a) Two Schedulers Control Schema (left). b) DS Interactions (right)

4.1 Internal Structure

It can be said that the DS is implemented following a control blackboard architecture. This architecture is an event-driven module. More specifically, it implements a variation of the so-called "satisfacing cycle" [11]. This cycle has been adapted to be used with temporal restrictions and bounded execution time due to the DS is executed in slack time (figure 1).

Moreover, the DS control cycle has been implemented through two modules, the Event Manager (EM) and the Second Level Scheduler (SLS). The first one receives significant events and reacts to them. It comprises the trigger and condition testing phases of the "satisfacing cycle". The second one is in charge of scheduling the use of the slack time and comprises the rating, schedule and interpret phases.

In this way, when the DS begins to work, the Event Manager looks for new events and takes the appropriate measures to react to them (trigger phase). The events are sorted by their contribution to system quality to be able to respond to the most appropriate event at each moment.

Next, it checks what is available to be scheduled in its available time (condition testing phase). When the Event Manager ends, it is time for the SLS to work. First of all, it rates all the deliberative in-agent parts that it has available for scheduling (rating phase). After this, it makes an schedule for the slack time that it has available (schedule phase). Lastly, it makes the execution of this schedule possible (interpret phase).

At this point, an overview of the control schema can be made. It follows a schema with two schedulers (FLS and SLS) as can be seen in Figure 2. The FLS schedules the reflex parts of the in-agents assuring the fulfillment of hard temporal restrictions. In the slack time, it cedes the control to the DS, where the SLS schedules the Real-Time Deliberative (RTD) parts of the in-agents.

The main purpose of the SLS is to decide what to execute to improve the agent's response. The decision may be to execute the optional part of a critic in-agent, or to execute an acritic in-agent previously activated by the event manager. To make this decision, the SLS has a set of scheduling policies with different features which are appropriated for different situations. The available scheduling policies [4] can be classified into two types: **Greedy Policies** (they rate all the items in the agenda and choose the best one for execution, that is the one providing the most quality system response) and **Deliberative Policies** (they construct several plans with the sequence of items to execute and select the best one). Both types of scheduling policies has bounded planning time, that is controlled by the RTOS. In this way, both kinds of policies must take into account the slack time available to execute the agenda items and their own computing time.

The SLS fixes the maximum execution time available for each item it sends to execution. This time will be the minimum between the item's wcet and the slack time still available to the SLS. If the item doesn't end its execution before this time, it is suspended and inserted back at the agenda so that it may be resumed in the future if its computation is still useful (its relevant input data has not significatively changed).

4.2   Describing EM Functionalities

The two deliberative server modules and their interactions can be seen in Figure 2. The main functionalities which are implemented in the Event Manager to achieve the main goals of the DS are shown in this figure:

- To activate and to deactivate acritic in-agents: The EM may activate / deactivate deliberative processes that are independent of the in-agents whose reflex part has just been processed.
- To manage the Attention Degree: The DS divides its execution time between its two modules. This time assignment does not have to be equitable. In fact, one of the ways to make the agent adaptive is to control the percentage of execution time provided to event management. This percentage is the Attention Degree and may be modified by the event manager. The time assigned to the event manager allows it to receive all the events or only some of them. This variation is gradual, when the extreme situations are the following: all the events are attended (the deliberative server is totally focused on the environment) and no event is attended (the deliberative server is totally focused on its own objectives).
- To manage the Attention Focus: The Event Manager may change the agent attention focus. That is, the belief subset which updates will direct the deliberative process. Changes in this subset will produce the events that the EM is interested in. This feature has two extreme situations: the EM is interested in the whole belief set, controlling all the modifications, and the EM is interested in variations of only one belief (any other belief data modification will be transparent for the DS).
- To change the SLS Policy: The EM will control the SLS policy to be used by this scheduler. It will make a change when the environment state and / or schedule quality make it necessary. For instance, if the SLS policy is a deliberative one, and there is very little execution time available, then it seems appropriate to adopt a greedy SLS policy.

— To manage the Reactivity Degree: The Reactivity Degree is the percentage of slack time dedicated to cognition processes. This parameter allows the EM to control the slack time that it can use for its execution.
The usual working of an AA delays the execution of its actions on the environment as late as possible for trying to improve them as much as possible. This behavior leaves the maximum time for the cognition process. Nevertheless, sometimes it might be interesting to execute an action even if there is slack time left. This feature has two extreme situations: all the slack time may be used to deliberate (this is the default mode and the agent has the lowest Reactivity Degree), and there is no cognition process (the agent behaves as a reflex agent and it has the highest Reactivity Degree).

4.3 DS Goal Achievement

The DS is responsible for the fulfillment of almost all the AA agency features through the use of this set of functionalities:

— Improvement of the agent answer quality: The Reflex Server is in charge of obtaining a low-quality first response from the AA (which is implemented as the mandatory time-bounded phase). The DS is responsible for using the available time to improve the quality of this response. This process is carried out by controlling the AA reasoning capability at two levels:
  • It decides at each moment what subject to focus its attention on in the slack time. Thus, it decides what to run from the active items stored in the agenda (real-time deliberative layers of the critic in-agents and acritic in-agents). These items are what really solve the problem.
  • Meta-reasoning: it decides when to change the SLS scheduling algorithm, the reasoning process focus or the Attention Degree. This improves the reasoning process and, thus, the agent response quality obtained
— Adapting to important environment changes: The adaptability of the agent is expressed in its ability to change dynamically. Actually, any functionality change that the Event Manager triggers as a reaction to an event helps to adapt the AA to new situations. For instance, if the agent is very focused on the changes in the environment (the Attention Degree is very high) and the event rate is also very high, a greedy scheduling policy should work better than a deliberative one. If the SLS is working with a deliberative policy, the EM would change it.
— Pursuing its own objectives: The Attention Focus allows the AA to focus its reasoning process on different belief sets. Therefore, in some situations, the AA is able to focus its deliberation on its own initiatives and to "avoid" the environment changes. This effect can be augmented by tuning the attention degree to dedicate all the available time to the SLS.

5 Implementation

There exists a toolkit called *InSiDE* (Integrated Simulation and Development Environment) [20] that allows the especification of an ARTIS Agent, building its system model. This model works over Linux/RT-Linux. In fact, it uses an specific improvement of RT-Linux called *Flexible RT-Linux* [22] that offers all the services and the low-level model task needed by the AA system model.

So, all the tasks with hard real-time restrictions are executed in Flexible RT-Linux whereas the rest of tasks are executed as highest priority Linux tasks. Hence, the Reflex Server Control Module is executed in Flexible RT-Linux and the Deliberative Server is executed in Linux.

Though the base language in which all the different architecture modules are implemented is the C language, there is no restriction to the language the system designer must use to implement the different parts of an in-agent.

6 Conclusions

ARTIS is an agent architecture suitable for hard real-time agents. The work presented in this paper shows the control module of ARTIS agents and an extension of it that provides the soft real-time control of this hard real-time agent architecture. This extension incorporates a deliberative component that allows to change the control module behaviour depending on the data environment and the reactivity degree of the agent. In fact, it is able to adapt the agent features (such as the scheduling policy, the attention focus or the attention degree) to significative changes in the environment or in the agent's internal state.

This architecture has been successfully applied to mobile robot control [20], by means of a prototype running over Flexible RT-Linux. Further investigation is centered on social aspects of the AA architecture, by extending the architecture in order to develop real-time, multi-agent systems. This new feature will allow the AA to offer services and to make them available to other agents through the control module. New examples are considered in order to study this new behavior. More specifically, a train traffic control system is being developed, where each train is modelled as an AA. Moreover, it is planned to incorporate learning capacities in the DS module to improve the adaptation capability.

References

[1] N.C. Audsley, A. Burns, Davis R.I, Tindell K.W., and A.J. Wellings. Fixed priority pre-emptive scheduling: An historical perspective. *Real-Time Systems*, 8:173–198, 1995.

[2] F. Barber, V. Botti, E. Onainda, and A. Crespo. Temporal reasoning in reakt: An environment for real-time knowledge-based systems. *AICOMM*, 7(3):175–202, 1994.

[3] V. Botti, C. Carrascosa, V. Julian, and J. Soler. Modelling agents in hard real-time environments. *Proc. of the MAAMAW'99. LNCS, vol. 1647*, pages 63–76, 1999.

[4] V. Botti and L. Hernandez. Control in real-time multiagent systems. In *Proceedings of the Second Iberoamerican Workshop on DAI and MAS*, pages 137–148, Toledo, Spain, 1998. Garijo, F., Lemaitre, C. (Eds.).

[5] R.I. Davis, K.W. Tindell, and A. Burns. Scheduling slack time in fixed priority preemptive systems. In *Proc. R-T Systems Symposium, North Carolina*, pages 222–231. IEEE Comp. Society Press, 1993.

[6] T. Dean and M. Boddy. An analysis of time-dependent planning. *Proceedings of the seventh National Conference on Artificial Intelligence. St. Paul, Minessota,*, pages 49–54, 1988.

[7] A. Garcia-Fornes, A. Terrasa, V. Botti, and A. Crespo. Analyzing the schedulability of hard real-time artificial intelligence systems. *EAAI*, pages 369–377, 1997.

[8] A. Garvey and V. Lesser. A survey of research in deliberative real-time artificial intelligence. *The Journal of Real-Time Systems*, 6:317–347, 1994.

[9] R. P. Goldman, D. J. Musliner, and K. D. Krebsbach. Managing online self-adaptation in real-time environments. In *Proc. of Second International Workshop on Self Adaptive Software*, Balatonfured, Hungary, 2001.

[10] John R. Graham. *Real-Time Scheduling in Distributed Multi-agent Systems*. PhD thesis, Dept. of computer and Information Science. University of Delaware, 2001.

[11] B. Hayes-Roth, R. Washington, D. Ash, A. Collinot, A. Vina, and A. Seiver. Guardian: A prototype intensive-care monitoring agent. *AI in Medicine*, 4:165–185, 1992.

[12] A. E. Howe, D. M. Hart, , and P. R. Cohen. Addressing real-time constraints in the design of autonomous agents. *The Journal of Real-Time Systems*, 2:81–97, 1990.

[13] F. Ingrand, M. P. Georgeff, and A. Rao. An architecture for real-time reasoning and system control. *IEEE Expert*, pages 34–44, December 1992.

[14] C. L. Liu and James W. Layland. Scheduling algorithms for multiprogramming in a hard-real-time environment. *Journal of the ACM*, 20(1):46–61, 1973.

[15] D. Musliner, E. Durfee, and K. Shin. Circa: a cooperative intelligent real-time control architecture. *IEEE Transactions on Systems, Man and Cybernetics*, 23(6), 1993.

[16] D. J. Musliner. Safe learning in mission-critical domains: Time is of the essence. In *Working Notes of the AAAI Spring Symposium on Safe Learning Agents*, Stanford, California, 2002.

[17] M. Occello and Y. Demazeau. Modelling decision making systems using agents satisfying real time constraints. *IFAC Proceedings of 3rd IFAC Symposium on Intelligent Autonomous Vehicles*, 1:51–56, 1998.

[18] Anita Raja and Victor Lesser. Real-time meta-level control in multi agent systems. In *Proceedings of Multi-Agent Systems and Applications - ACAI 2001 and EASSS 2001 Student Sessions. Also Adaptability and Embodiment Using Multi-Agent Systems: AEMAS 2001 Workshop. Prague, Czech Republic*, 2001.

[19] S. Russell and P. Norvig. *Artificial Intelligence: A Modern Approach*. Prentice Hall International Editions, 1995.

[20] J. Soler, V. Julian, C. Carrascosa, and V. Botti. Applying the artis agent architecture to mobile robot control. In *Proceedings of IBERAMIA'2000. Atibaia, Sao Paulo, Brasil*, volume I, pages 359– 368. Springer Verlag, 2000.

[21] J.A. Stankovic. Misconceptions about real-time computing. *IEEE Computer*, 12(10):10–19, 1988.

[22] A. Terrasa, A. Garca-Fornes, and V. Botti. Flexible real-time linux. *Real-Time Systems Journal*, 2:149–170, 2002.

Regional Synchronization for Simultaneous Actions in Situated Multi-agent Systems

Danny Weyns and Tom Holvoet

AgentWise, DistriNet, Department of Computer Science
K.U.Leuven, B-3001 Heverlee, Belgium
{danny.weyns,tom.holvoet}@cs.kuleuven.ac.be

Abstract. Agents of a multi-agent system (MAS) must synchronize whenever they want to perform simultaneous actions. In situated MASs, typically, the control over such synchronization is centralized, i.e. one synchronizer has the supervision on all agents of the MAS. As a consequence, all agents are forced to act at a global pace and that does not fit with autonomy of agents. Besides, global synchronization implies centralized control, in general an undesirable property of MASs. In this paper we present an algorithm that allows agents to synchronize with other agents within their perceptual range. The result of the algorithm is the formation of independent groups of synchronized agents. The composition of these groups depends on the locality of the agents and dynamically changes when agents enter or leave each others perceptual range. Since in this approach agents are only synchronized with colleagues in their region, the pace on which they act only depends on the acting speed of potential collaborating agents. The price for decentralization of synchronization is the communication overhead to set up the groups. In the paper, we discuss experimental results and compare the benefits of regional synchronization with its costs.

1 Introduction

Whenever agents of a multi-agent system (MAS) interact by performing *simultaneous actions* they need to synchronize. With simultaneous actions, we mean a set of interfering actions that are executed together and that produce a compound result[1]. We distinguish between three kinds of simultaneous actions: *joint actions*, *influencing actions* and *concurrent actions*. Joint actions are actions that must be executed together in order to produce a successful result. An example of joint actions is two or more agents that pick up an object that none of them can pick up by itself; or agents that carry such object to a certain location together. Influencing actions are actions that positively or negatively affect each other. An example of influencing actions is two agents that push together the same object. When they push the object in the same direction it likely moves faster, however when they push it in opposite directions the object might not

---

[1] We do not take *independent actions* that happen together into account. Independent actions do not interfere with one another and as such do not affect each other.

V. Mařík et al. (Eds): CEEMAS 2003, LNAI 2691, pp. 497–510, 2003.

move at all. Finally, concurrent actions are simultaneously performed actions that conflict. An example of concurrent actions is two or more agents that try to pick up the same object at the same time. When only one of the involved agents can get the packet, synchronization resolves which of the agents this will be, i.e. typically a non-deterministic selection. Other researches make a similar distinction between different types of interacting actions. We give a number of examples. Allen and Ferguson [1] differentiate between 'actions that interfere with each other' and 'actions with additional synergistic effects'. Bornscheuer and Thielsher [3] define the notion of 'compound actions', i.e. 'a non empty, finite subset of a given set of unit actions'. The execution of a compound action is modeled as the manipulation of the composing subset of unit actions. Boutilier and Brafman [4] distinguish 'concurrent actions with a positive or negative interacting effect'. Griffiths, Luck and d'Iverno [6] introduce the notions of a 'joint action that a group of agents perform together' and 'concurrent actions, i.e. a set of actions performed at the same time'. These definitions are build upon the notions of 'strong and weak parallelism' described by Kinny [8].

Most of the work regarding simultaneous actions in MAS is done in the context of languages for action description and planning for agents. In this paper we focus on simultaneous actions for situated MASs, where agents execute *situated actions*. A situated action is an action selected by an agent on the basis of the position of the agent, the state of the world which he perceives and limited internal state[2]. For planning–agent systems, simultaneity of actions is realized through planning. In situated MASs however, agents do not coordinate through planning but select their actions according to the actual situation. In order to allow agents to coordinate their interactions, support for synchronization is required. Such synchronization guarantees, that simultaneous actions that conceptually must happen together, but that are executed separated in time[3], are treated as if they happened together.

The focus of this paper is on the *achievement* of synchronization. The formation of groups of synchronized agents determines the *granularity* of synchronized groups, i.e. the number of agents that belong to a group of synchronized agents. Typically, synchronization for simultaneous actions is organized for the entire group of agents of the MAS, examples are Ferber's synchronizer [5] or Look, Talk and Do Synchronization [12]. The major advantage of this approach is its simplicity: there is no overhead to setup synchronization, a single synchronizer controls the synchronization of all agents. However centralized synchronization has a number of disadvantages. A single synchronizer centralizes control and that conflicts with the distributed nature of MAS. Since all agents are synchronized with one another, the activity in the MAS evolves at the pace of the slowest agent. Agents that have concluded their action selection are blocked by

---

[2] Wavish and Connah [10] adopted the concept of situated action in MAS for the stimulus/response–like actions of an agent that are only related to the agent's external perception. In this paper we allow a situated action to be influenced also by limited internal state of the agent, e.g. a commitment in an ongoing collaboration.

[3] E.g. on a single/sequential processor system.

the synchronizer until all other agents of the MAS have concluded, even if their current state or situation does not require synchronization with the other agents. Besides, centralization of control makes the system more vulnerable to errors. When e.g., the synchronizer invokes the agents to select their next action, and for some reason one of the agents fails, without special provisions the synchronizer waits for the completion of the action selection of the failing agent for ever, leaving the system in a deadlock. In this paper we present an algorithm that allows agents to dynamically synchronize with other agents only if they are located within each others perceptual range. Agents organize themselves in synchronized groups, resulting in a much finer grained synchronization. The composition of the groups depends on the locality of the agents and dynamically changes when agents enter or leave each others perceptual range. Since in this approach agents are only synchronized with colleagues in their region, the pace on which they act only depends on the neighboring and thus potential collaborating agents.

The price for decentralization of synchronization is an overhead of communication to set up groups of regional synchronized agents. In the paper, we discuss experimental results and compare the gain stemming from decentralizing the synchronization with its costs.

The rest of the paper is structured as follows. In section 2 we discuss the algorithm for regional synchronization in detail. Section 3 reports simulation results and evaluates the algorithm. Finally, we conclude and look to future work in section 4.

2   Discussion of the Algorithm

In this section we discuss the algorithm for regional synchronization. First we give a high–level overview of the algorithm and zoom in on the goal of the algorithm. Then we discuss the main challenges we have to deal with. Next, we introduce a number of definitions for the major concepts used in the algorithm. Finally we present the algorithm and discuss each step in detail.

2.1   Goal of the Algorithm

Synchronization of simultaneous actions must ensure that conceptually simultaneous actions are treated as if they happened together. Typically, the synchronization of simultaneous actions follows two major phases: the phase of *synchronization setup* and the *acting phase*. During synchronization setup, an agent synchronizes with all agents within his perceptual range. When no other agent is visible at that moment, the agent can act asynchronously with respect to all other agents. Otherwise the agent starts synchronizing with the visible agents. During synchronization setup, the agent blocks his activity until all agents in his region are synchronized. Agents synchronize by exchanging synchronization messages. When all agents within their perceptual range have concluded synchronization, they act together during the acting phase. Fig. 1 illustrates some synchronization situations. The left part of the figure depicts a snapshot of the

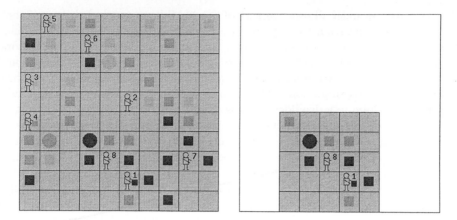

Fig. 1. Examples of synchronization situations in the Packet–World

Packet–World, i.e. a simple MAS we use as a case in our research[4]. In the Packet–World agents have to bring colored packets (rectangles) to their corresponding colored destination (circles). Agents are allowed to make one step at a time to a free neighboring field or pick up a packet from a neighboring field. An agent is able to carry one packet that he can deliver at any free field or at the destination of the packet. The job of the agents is to deliver all packets efficiently, i.e. with a minimum steps, packet manipulations and message exchanges. In the Packet–World each agent has only a limited view on the world. In the example, we suppose a view size of 2, illustrated for agent 8 in the right part of Fig. 1. To optimize the job execution agents can cooperate in different ways. They can for example, request each other for information or set up a chain to pass packets. For more information about the Packet–World we refer to [11].

Synchronization is necessary if we allow agents to interact by means of simultaneous actions, e.g. when we allow direct transfer of packets between agent 1 and agent 8 in Fig. 1. Synchronized agents are able to execute simultaneous actions since they act together, i.e. during the same acting phase. Applied to the example: the packet transfer only succeeds when agent 1 passes a packet and agent 8 accepts that packet during the same acting phase. With the synchronization algorithm we present in this paper, agents synchronize with colleagues within their perceptual range. With a view size of 2 we have, besides agents 1 and 8, two other groups of synchronized agents in Fig. 1: agents 5 and 6, and agents 3 and 4. Each group of synchronized agents act on its own pace. For the first group with agents 5 and 6, synchronization benefits as soon as agent 5 makes a step in the direction South–East (SE[5]), after which he can transfer

---

[4] The Packet–World is based on an exercise proposed by Huhns and Stephens in [7] as a research topic to investigate the principles of sociality in MASs.

[5] We denote a particular neighboring field of a field with the first capital letter(s) of the direction from the field to that neighboring field. E.g., agent 8 is positioned NW to agent 1.

a number of packets to agent 6 for direct delivering. For the third group with agents 3 and 4, the actual synchronization contributes little since both have no collaborating intentions (they carry a packet of different color). Anyway, as soon as agent 3 steps NE toward the delivering field of the packet he carries, he will no longer be synchronized with agent 4, but synchronizes with agent 5 and 6 enabling collaboration between these three agents. The other agents in Fig. 1, agents 2 and 7, are not synchronized with any agent (there is no other agent inside their perceptual range), so they act asynchronously.

Summarizing, the goal of the synchronization algorithm is to ensure that: (1) during the synchronization setup each agent synchronizes with the colleagues inside his perceptual range and hence also with all agents within the perceptual range of the latter, and so on; and (2) during the action phase, synchronized agents act together, allowing them to perform simultaneous actions.

2.2   Main Challenges of the Algorithm

The algorithm to set up regional synchronization is not trivial. To illustrate the complexity we briefly discuss the main challenges. Since agents have only a limited view on the environment it may be the case that two agents positioned inside each others perceptual range see different candidates to synchronize with. So at the end of synchronization setup an agent typically knows only a limited number of the agents of the synchronized group to which he belongs. This property hides a hard problem the algorithm has to tackle: avoiding deadlock when a sequence of overlapping perceptual regions of agents form a cycle. An example: in Fig. 1 agent 8 and agent 1 have overlapping perceptual regions and so they act synchronized. Suppose that in the given situation agent 2, (who act in the depicted situation asynchronously, remember the view size is 2) decides to make a step in the direction S and agent 7 (also acting asynchronously) makes a step in the direction NW. Now the perceptual regions of the agents 1, 8, 2 and 7 form a loop. The algorithm must ensure that, in whatever order the involved agents in such a loop enter synchronization setup, synchronization of the next action may not lead to deadlock. Note that since the synchronization between agents is reached by message exchange and the agents of a MAS run in separate processes there is no guarantee for the algorithm when these message are delivered.

Another problem the algorithm has to deal with, arises when an agent A requests two agents, X and Y, of a group of synchronizing agents of which one, e.g. X, has concluded synchronization, while the other, Y, is still busy with synchronization. If the conditions for synchronization between A and Y are satisfied, the two synchronizers establish synchronization. However, since synchronized agent X is unable to handle incoming messages, agent A will not receive an answer to his request from X and so he is unable to conclude synchronization. Since agents A, X and Y belong to the same group of synchronizing agents, this scenario leads to deadlock. Therefore the algorithm must offer requesting agents a mains to detect and handle such blockades.

2.3   Definitions for the Algorithm

In order to cope with the problems discussed in the previous section we developed
an algorithm that combines a distributed 2-phase commit protocol with a logical
clock. Before we discuss the different steps of the algorithm in detail, we first
give an overview of the definitions we use in the remainder of the paper and then
explain them in an intuitive description of the algorithm.

- S_i is the synchronizer of agent A_i of the MAS with view size VS
- $V_{S_i}^{t_i}$ is the view–set of S_i composed by the environment at logical clock time t_i:
  $V_{S_i}^{t_i} = \{S_j : dist(A_i, A_j) \leq VS \text{ at time } t_i\}$; we call t_i the synchronization–
  time of S_i during synchronization setup with the synchronizers of $V_{S_i}^{t_i}$
- $mset_i^{t_i}$ is the member–set of S_i: $mset_i^{t_i} \subseteq \{M_{j \prec i} : M_{j \prec i}.S_j \in V_{S_i}^{t_i}\}$
  where $M_{j \prec i} = (S, s, t)$ is a member j of S_i, i.e. the representation of S_j
  that is maintained by S_i with $S = S_j$, $s \in \{ini, req, ack, com, sync\}$ and
  $t \in \{t^0, t_j\}$ ($t^0 = 0$, and we denote S_j of $M_{j \prec i}$ as $M_{j \prec i}.S$ etc.)
- $sset_i^{t_i}$ is the synchronization–set of S_i: $sset_i^{t_i} = (S_i, mset_i^{t_i}, t_i)$
- $synchronizedWith$ is the equivalence relation over a set S of synchronizers:
  $\forall S_i, S_j \in S : ((\exists p \in N : S_0, \ldots S_p \in S)) :$
  $(\exists M_{i \prec 0} : M_{i \prec 0}.S = S_i \wedge M_{i \prec 0}.s = sync) \wedge (\exists M_{0 \prec 1} : M_{0 \prec 1}.S = S_0 \wedge M_{0 \prec 1}.s = sync) \wedge \ldots \wedge (\exists M_{p \prec j} : M_{p \prec j}.S = S_p \wedge M_{p \prec j}.s = sync))$
- $region_{S_i}^{t_i}$ is the region of S_i based on the view–set composed at time t_i, i.e.
  the equivalence class of synchronizers related with the equivalence relation
  $synchronizedWith$ whereof S_i is a representative.
- $msg_{from \rightarrow to} = (from, to, perform, time)$ is a synchronization message sent
  from S_{from} to S_{to} with $perform \in \{req, ack, nack, com, sync\}$ and $time \in \{t^0, t_{from}\}$

Each agent is equipped with a synchronizer who is responsible for handling synchronization. Synchronization setup starts when the synchronizer receives its
view–set, together with the synchronization–time from the environment. The
view–set is the initial set of candidates for synchronization, containing all synchronizers within the perceptual range of the associated agent. The synchronization–time is the value of the logical clock when the synchronizer's view-set was
composed. This logical clock is a counter maintained by the environment[6]. Each
time a group of synchronized agents has concluded the acting phase, the value
of the logical clock is incremented and new view–sets for the agents are composed. With the information the synchronizer receives from the environment
it composes a synchronization–set. Besides its own name and synchronization–
time, such synchronization–set contains a member–set. In the member–set each
synchronizer in the view–set of the synchronizer is represented by a member.
A member is a triplet, containing the name of the candidate for synchronization, a state and a time stamp. Initially each member of the member–set is in the
initial state denoted by ini, while the time stamps have the value t^0 that stands

---

[6] Notice that the value of the logical clock is not a global variable. In a distributed
setting, the local environment of the MAS on each host maintains its own local clock.

for the initial value, zero. During the execution of the algorithm, synchronizers progressively try to synchronize with the members[7] of their synchronization–set by means of sending messages back and forth. During this interaction, negotiating synchronizers pass two phases. During the first phase they decide whether they agree about synchronization and subsequently during the second phase they mutually commit to the agreement. During this process, synchronizers exchange the value of there synchronization–time and mutually register the received values for the member of that particular synchronizer. Throughout the algorithm, the state of each member evolves from *ini* to *ack* (synchronization accepted), *com* (committed) and finally *sync* (mutually synchronized). The decision whether a synchronizer continues synchronization with a particular synchronizer depends on (1) the membership of a requesting synchronizer; and (2) the comparison between the value of the synchronization–time of the member and the value of the synchronizers own synchronization–time; and finally (3) the combination of states of all members of the member–set. In case synchronization can not be achieved, the rejecting synchronizer informs its colleague. As far as they belong to each others member–set, both synchronizers then remove the corresponding member from their member–set. As soon as all members of the member–set of a synchronizer have reached the state *sync*, the synchronizer concludes synchronization setup and activates its associated agent to enter the acting phase.

2.4   The Algorithm in Detail

In this section, first we describe the algorithm in Java–liked code and elaborate on each step in the algorithm. Then we discuss an example scenario in the Packet–World, and show how the algorithm deals with the challenges described in section 2.2. We conclude with a brief discussion how our algorithm integrates existing mechanisms from distributed algorithms.

The Algorithm. Fig. 2 depicts the algorithm for regional synchronization in Java–liked code. When a synchronizer enters synchronization setup, he first executes *makeSynchronizationSet()*, composing a new synchronization–set with the last received view–set and synchronization–time. Next, the synchronizer checks his mailbox, verifying whether there are pending requests, i.e. requests received by the synchronizer during the previous acting phase. In *handleMail()* the synchronizer handles requests according to the following rule:

> **R1.** A request is accepted (i.e. an *ack* message is sent and the state as well as the synchronization–time of the corresponding member is updated with the received information in the message) if the requesting synchronizer belongs to the synchronizer's member–set; otherwise the request is rejected (a *nack* message is sent).

---

[7] In the remainder of the paper we use the term member for the concept we formally have defined as well as for the synchronizer of a member that belongs to a particular member–set. The interpretation follows from the context where we use the term.

```
private void setupSynchronization() {

  makeSynchronizationSet();
  if(not mailbox.isEmty())
     handleMail();

  if(not toActAsynchronously()) {
     sendRequests();
     while(not synchronized()) {
       handleMail();
       if(blockedToCommit())
          unBlock();
       sendCommits();
       if(readyToSendSyncs())
          sendSyncs();
     }
  }
}


private void handleMail() {

  while(not mailbox.isEmty()) {

    Message msg = mailbox.pickMessage();
    Performative perform = msg.getPerformative();
    Synchronizer from = msg.getFrom();
    int time = msg.getTime();

    if(isRequest(perform)) {
       if(belongsToSynchronizationSet(from)) {
          sendAck(from,synchronizationTime);
          updateMember(from,"ack",time);
       } else
          sendNack(from);
    }
    else if(isAcknowledge(perform))
            updateMember(from,"ack",time);
    else if(isNack(perform))
            removeMember(from);
    else if(isCommit(perform))
            updateMember(from,"com");
    else if(isSync(perform))
            updateMember(from,"sync");
  }
}
```

Fig. 2. The algorithm for regional synchronization in Java–liked code

R1 ensures that a pending request is rejected if a synchronizer detects that, since the time of the request, he has left the requesting synchronizer's perceptual range. Furthermore, R1 ensures that a synchronizer only synchronizes with known colleagues, i.e. the synchronizers belonging to its member–set.

After the pending requests are handled, the synchronizer verifies *toActAsynchronously()*. This method returns true if the member–set of the synchronizer is empty. In that case the remainder of the algorithm is skipped and the agent immediately enters the acting phase to act asynchronously. Otherwise the synchronizer sends requests to the members of his member–set according to the second rule:

> **R2.** To every member of the member–set in the state *ini*, the synchronizer sends a request to synchronize, i.e. a *req* message.

Subsequently, the synchronizer enters a while loop in which he stays until *synchronized()* returns true. This condition is determined by rule 3:

> **R3.** As soon as all members of member–set of a synchronizer have reached the state *sync*, the synchronizer concludes synchronization setup and activates its associated agent to enter the acting phase.

Inside the loop, the synchronizer starts checking his mail. Besides requests (R1), the synchronizer handles the other messages according the following rules:

> **R4.** For every received *ack* message the state as well as the synchronization–time of the corresponding member is updated with the received information in the message.

> **R5.** Every member from which the synchronizer receives a *nack* message is removed from the member–set.

> **R6.** For every received *com* or a *sync* message, the state of the member is updated according to the information of the received message.

After handling mail, the synchronizer verifies whether he is *blockedToCommit()*. This state is described by rule 7:

> **R7.** A synchronizer is *blockedToCommit* if (1) there is at least one synchronizer in his member–set in the state *com*; and (2) there is at least one synchronizer in his member–set in the state *req*; and (3) all other members are in the state *sync*.

In this state the synchronizer is allowed to remove blocking members of his member–set, described in rule 8:

> **R8.** If a synchronizer is *blockedToCommit*, he is allowed to eliminate the blocking synchronizers of his member–set; blocking synchronizers are in the state *req*; during unblocking a synchronizer removes subsequently these blocking members from his member–set and informs them with a *nack* message.

This rule is necessary to deal with the blocking situation we briefly discussed in section 2.2. We discuss a concrete example of R8 below.

An interesting side effect of R8 is that it gives the algorithm some degree of robustness. Since synchronizers, due to R8, reject colleagues that do not react to a request in time, they also reject synchronizers that have failed and no longer are able to react to requests.

Subsequently, the synchronizer sends commits, according to rule 9:

> **R9.** To every member in the state *ack* with a synchronization–time younger or equal to the synchronizer's own synchronization–time, the synchronizer is allowed to send a commit, i.e. a *com* message.

In the last step of the loop, the synchronizer verifies whether he is able to conclude synchronization with the members of his member–set. The conditions are described in rule 10:

> **R10.** A synchronizer is allowed to confirm a commitment with the members of his member–set (by means of sending them a *sync* message and updating their state) if all the members of his member–set are *synchronizable*, i.e. their state is (1) *com* or *sync*; or (2) the state is *ack* and the synchronizer's synchronization–time is younger or equal to the member's synchronization–time.

Subsequently, the synchronizer verifies whether he has concluded synchronization setup (R3). If this is the case, he activates its associated agent to enter the acting phase, otherwise he starts a new cycle in the loop.

Discussion. We now apply the algorithm to an example situation in the Packet–World that deals with the challenges described in section 2.2. Suppose in Fig. 1, agents 8, 1, 7 and 2 all are executing the acting phase. Now agent 7 makes a step NW, entering the perceptual range of agents 1 and 2. S_7 starts synchronization setup by requesting S_1 and S_2 for synchronization. Subsequently, agent 1 and 8 conclude their action (suppose they transferred a packet) and enter synchronization setup. Now things can evolve in different ways. We look to three scenarios:

- Agent 2 steps W and enters synchronization setup before S_7, S_1 and S_8 have concluded synchronization setup.
- Agent 2 steps S and enters synchronization setup when S_8 already has concluded synchronization setup, while S_7 and S_1 are still busy synchronizing.
- Agent 2 steps S and enters synchronization setup while S_7, S_1 and S_8 are still busy synchronizing.

First scenario. This scenario is rather simple. When S_2 enters synchronization setup, he detects that S_7 do not belongs to his member–set and according to R1, he rejects the pending request of S_7, sending him a *nack* message. Since S_2's member–set is empty, no further synchronization is required and A_2 immediately can enter the acting phase. When S_7 receives the rejection, he removes S_2 from his member–set (R5) and subsequently concludes synchronization setup with S_1.

Second scenario. In this scenario, S_2 confirms the pending request of S_7. Subsequently, S_2 synchronizes with S_8 and S_7 (R9, R10). In the end S_8, S_1 and S_7 have concluded synchronization setup, while S_2 still waits for a response of S_8. Fortunately, in this blocked situation (R7), S_2 can apply R8, liberating himself from the non-responding S_8 and subsequently conclude synchronization setup.
Third scenario. If in this scenario S_8 receives S_2's request too late (i.e. S_2's request message is scheduled after S_8 concludes synchronization setup) we have the previous case. Otherwise S_8 rejects, according to R1 (S_2 does not belongs to S_8's member–set), the request. S_2 then removes S_8 from his member–set, after which the four synchronizers normally can conclude synchronization setup. Note that in this case, S_2 and S_8 not have synchronized directly, although in the end they are indirectly synchronized via the chain of synchronizers between them.

Integration of Existing Mechanisms from Distributed Algorithms. To conclude this section, we briefly discuss how our algorithm for distributed synchronization integrates the two building blocks we have used to design it: two-phase commit (2PC) and a logical clock (LC). The goal of standard 2PC is to reach a full agreement between a set of processes (participants) whether or not to perform some action. The result is all–or–nothing, i.e. if a commitment is reached the action should be executed by all participants, otherwise the operation as a whole is aborted. The protocol is normally initiated by one process, i.e. the coordinator. The coordinator collects votes from the participants and decides about the outcome of the interaction. For a detailed description of 2PC, see [2]. On the other hand we use a logical clock. Lamport [9] invented logical clocks to capture numerically causal ordering of events within process groups.

In our algorithm, synchronizers are peers and can play both the role of participant as well as coordinator during one ongoing synchronization setup. Which role one synchronizer plays with respect to the other depends on the comparison of the values of both their synchronization–time, i.e. the value of the logical clock they received when they entered synchronization setup. As for 2PC, the result of our algorithm is a set of synchronizers that have reached an agreement, i.e. execute their next action phase synchronized. However, during synchronization setup, some of the candidates for synchronization might be shut out from the synchronizing group.

3   Evaluation

Evaluation compares the gain from regional synchronization with its costs. The major advantage of the algorithm is that agents, after regional synchronization, only need to wait for agents of the region to which they belong. The algorithm tunes the granularity of synchronized groups to the number of agents that are candidates for simultaneous interaction. For centralized synchronization, agents act on the pace of the slowest agent of the entire MAS. Thus the size of the region in comparison with the total number of agents in the MAS is a measure for the gain of the algorithm. The cost of using the algorithm is an overhead

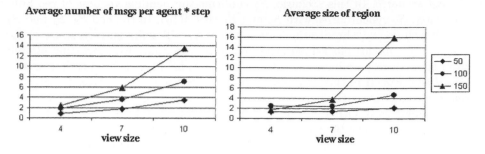

Fig. 3. Quantitative simulation results for populations of 50, 100 and 150 agents

to setup the groups of synchronized agents. This cost includes three parts: (1) the number of sent messages; (2) the cost for sending the messages; and (3) the computational overhead induced by handling the messages.

We did a great number of tests on a MAS with a 2D–grid environment, sized 100x100. First, we selected one number of agents of the set {50,100,150}, with one view size of the set {4,7,10}[8]. For each such combination, we did three separated tests. In the first test we used random moving agents, in the second test the agents attracted each other and in the third test we used agents that repulsed each other. Each test started with a random distribution of the agents, and subsequently the agents run for 1000 cycles through the algorithm. Each time a region was composed, the agents of that region acted simultaneously, i.e. each agent made a step according to its behavior. During the runs, agents are randomly scheduled. Fig. 3 depicts the results of our measurements. The left graph depicts the average number of sent messages per agent and per step, for different numbers of agents and different view sizes. The right graph shows the average size of regions for the same parameters. Both graphs combine the results for the three kinds of agents used in the tests. The results of the right graph confirm the intuitive expectation that regions grow with (1) increased density of agents in the MAS and (2) increased view size of the agents. The results of the left graph show that the number of exchanged synchronization messages for the algorithm is proportional to the size of the regions. Moreover, the results for our tests show that an agent sends as an average about one message for each agent of the region to which he belongs for each action he performs. Note that a higher average number of synchronization messages is not a disadvantage on itself, since more sent messages corresponds to higher sizes of regions and thus increased possibilities for simultaneous interaction.

Whether the gain of the algorithm, for a particular MAS, outweighs the costs, is application dependable. For example, for a MAS populated with 150 agents with a view size 7, the average number of sent messages is 6, while the average size of the region is about 4, see the upper points for view size 7 in Fig. 3.

---

[8] The view size is the number of squares and agent is able to perceive in each direction, similar to the view size in the Packet–World, see Fig. 1.

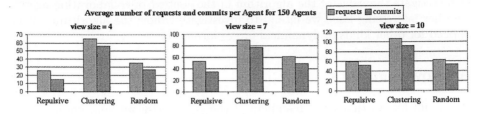

Fig. 4. Simulation results for success of synchronization

For this particular MAS, the pace on which agents are able to act depends on only 3 neighboring agents. In comparison with centralized synchronization, where the pace of each action for each agent depends on the entire population, in this case 150 agents, this gain appears to be very significantly. In practice however, the order of this gain will be influenced by the heterogeneity of agent activity in the MAS. If some of the agents act quickly while others are very slow, the first will be no longer concerned about the latter. Opposite to the gain, there is for each agent the cost associated with the handling of an average of 6 messages for every performed action. Since the communication between the synchronizers is defacto regional, the cost induced by synchronization will mainly be computational. Fig. 4 gives an idea about how successful the agents establish synchronization. The graphs depict for the three kinds of agents in the tests, in a MAS populated with 150 agents for view sizes 4, 7 and 10, how much requests lead to synchronization. The results show that most of the communication lead to synchronization. For the depicted results, an average of 80 % of the requests finally result in synchronization.

4   Conclusions and Future Work

In this paper we have presented an algorithm that allow agents to synchronize with the agents in their region, enable them to perform simultaneous actions. The algorithm combines a distributed two phase commit protocol with a logical clock. The gain of the algorithm is a much finer grained synchronization in comparison with centralized synchronization, increasing the efficiency of acting for the agents significantly. The cost for regional synchronization is an overhead of communication to setup regional groups of synchronized agents. Since synchronizing agents communicate regional, the overhead of sending messages are minor to the computational cost. Therefore, the gain appears to outweighs the costs, however in practice the balance must be made according to the characteristics of the application.

Future work includes formal verification of the algorithm and integration in a multi-agent application. Actually, we are finalizing a Colored Petri–net to prove formally our algorithm is free of deadlock. We also are integrating the algorithm in a full Java implementation of the Packet–World. This will allow us to investigate the value of the algorithm in the context of collaborating agents. Another interesting issue we intend to investigate is how the algorithm can be applied for other kinds of dynamical group formations.

Acknowledgments

We would like to thank the members of the AgentWise working group at the K.U.Leuven for the many valuable discussions that have contribute to the work presented in this paper. Also a word of appreciation goes to Wouter Joosen for his useful comments to improve this paper.

References

[1] J. F. ALLEN AND G. FERGUSON, *Actions and Events in Interval Temporal Logic*, in Journal of Logic and Computation, Special Issue on Actions and Processes, 1994.

[2] K. BIRMAN *Building Secure and Reliable Network Applications*, Cornell University, Ithaca NY, 14853, 1995.

[3] S. E. BORNSCHEUER AND M. THIELSCHER, *Explicit and Implicit Determinism: Reasoning about Uncertain and Contradictory Specification of Dynamic Systems*, TR–96–009, ICSI Berkeley, CA, 1996.

[4] C. BOUTILIER AND R. I. BRAFMAN, *Partial–Order Planning with Concurrent Interacting Actions*, in Journal of Artificial Research 14 p.105–136, Access Foundation and Morgan Kaufmann Publishers, 4-2001.

[5] J. FERBER, *Multi-Agent Systems, An Introduction to Distributed Artificial Intelligence*, Addison-Wesley, ISBN 0-201-36048-9, Great Britain, 1999.

[6] N. GRIFFITHS, M. LUCK AND M. D'IVERNO *Cooperative Plan Annotation through Trust*, in Workshop Notes of UKMAS'02, Eds. P. McBurney, M. Wooldridge, UK Workshop on Multi-agent Systems, Liverpool, 2002.

[7] M. N. HUHNS AND L. M. STEPHENS, *Multi-Agent Systems and Societies of Agents*, in G. Weiss ed., Multi-agent Systems, ISBN 0-262-23203-0, MIT press, 1999.

[8] D. KINNY, M .LJUNDBERG, A. RAO ET AL. *Planning with Team activity*, 4th European Workshop on Modeling Autonomous Agents in a Multi-Agent World, LNCS 830, pp. 227–256, S. Martino al Cimino, Italy, 1992.

[9] L. LAMPORT *Time, clocks and the ordering of events in a distributed system*, ACM, vol. 21, no. 7, pp.558-65, 1978.

[10] P. R. WAVISH AND D. M. CONNAH, *Representing Multi–Agent Worlds in ABLE*, Technical Note, TN2964, Philips Research Laboratories, 1990.

[11] D. WEYNS AND T. HOLVOET, *The Packet–World as a Case to Investigate Sociality in Multi-agent Systems*, Demo presented at the Conference of Autonomous Agents and Multi-Agent Systems, AAMAS 2002, Bologna, Italy, 2002. Demo available at: www.cs.kuleuven.ac.be/~danny/aamas02demo.html

[12] D. WEYNS AND T. HOLVOET, *Look, Talk and Do: A Synchronization Scheme for Situated Multi-agent Systems*, in Workshop Notes of UKMAS'02, Eds. P. McBurney, M. Wooldridge, UK Workshop on Multi-agent Systems, Liverpool, 2002.

A Multi–agent System
for Dynamic Network Reconfiguration

Artur Maj, Jarosław Jurowicz, Jarosław Koźlak, Krzysztof Cetnarowicz

Department of Computer Science, University of Mining and Metallurgy
Cracow, Poland
arturamaj@poczta.onet.pl, jurowicz@poczta.fm,
kozlak@agh.edu.pl, cetnar@agh.edu.pl

Abstract. This paper presents a system for dynamic network reconfiguration based on intelligent agents and market–oriented methods. Reconfiguration encompasses routing changes as well as building new and removing unused connections between network nodes. The paper presents a short review of research background in network management methodologies, a description of the system's model and an overview of experimental results

1   Introduction

The number of Internet users and computers doubles every year. Recently, popular multimedia applications have stimulated the growth of the amount of data sent between the machines. Internet providers and e-commerce organizations are interested in the network quality improvement. Buying more bandwidth has usually solved this problem up to now. An alternative solution is to manage effectively the resources already possessed. The basic feature required from new generation networks is a *dynamic adaptation* to changing conditions, and it means:

- load optimization for making use of full potential;
- automation of configuration and administration processes;
- greater scalability;
- autonomous reaction in case of a failure or congestion.

Currently, most network management decisions needs participation of the man. This situation has the following disadvantageous consequences:

- data flow paths do not have to be optimal;
- centralization makes the „bottleneck" effect more likely;
- fixed routing is not applicable in case of breakdown;
- problems with management of large–scale networks;
- human factor is unreliable.

V. Mařík et al. (Eds): CEEMAS 2003, LNAI 2691, pp. 511-521, 2003.
© Springer-Verlag Berlin Heidelberg 2003

To some extent, centralized management of networks is in defiance of their nature – packet networks are decentralized. Regretfully, there are few methodologies taking this into account.

Multi-agent systems researches bring a really new quality to telecommunication networks management. A mobile agent can move thorough the network, gather the information on its state, exchange it with other agents met on the way and make changes to the network configuration. During the decision-making process, intelligent agents are able to analyze amounts of data much bigger than the man could take into account. Finally, one can obtain a system automatically self–adjusting to the load distribution and reacting instantly to faults and disturbances. A well–organized multi–agent system uses only local data; there is no need for global synchronization of decisions.

An effective method of intelligent agents coordination is market–oriented approach. Its usage brings three basic advantages: information propagation, optimization and opportunity to build a billing system for network services, costs and return of investment estimation and other market activities.

2   Research Overview

2.1   Network Management Methodologies

Network management systems (NMS) can be divided into a few general classes (after [3]):

- **centralized NMS** – there is one management interface to a whole network. Administration commands are mapped directly on protocol operations. This class includes commonly used SNMP.
- **weakly distributed hierarchical NMS** – agents installed on managed network devices use a predefined command set. This class consists of CMIP, RMON, SNMPv2.
- **strongly distributed hierarchical NMS** – decisions are made by an active and partly autonomous agent residing on a network device – and this reduces the load on the management station. This class includes active networks, mobile code as well as distributed objects systems.

     The basic idea of mobile code systems is execution of some computer program to the network agent set on a network device. *„Active networks enable their users to put custom programs into the network nodes."* [5]. These programs can process a data stream and alter it in some way (e.g. encrypt or compress). This idea breaks the sanctity of the higher-level data stream. Routing is not static, but it depends on the code execution result.

- **cooperative NMS** – based on using intelligent agents. In the cooperative approach, a manager gives an agent the problem to solve. The agent's task is to choose and execute proper actions which will lead to the solution. Agents move freely in the network, and thus the infrastructure has to be equipped with suitable mechanisms.

Market–based methods are successfully used in the network optimization. It is based on the assumption that microeconomic rules will lead the system to the equilibrium, which will be globally optimal, i.e.:

- resources are distributed accordingly to the requirements in different system areas;
- the most profitable configuration is chosen.

Market – based methods do not need a centralized management, all decisions are made on a basis of local knowledge. An agent makes decisions which maximize its profit. The competition between agents leads to self-regulation of the whole system [6].

2.2   Dynamic Network Management Systems

In [4], Minar, Kramer and Maes presented a dynamic routing management model using mobile intelligent agents.

The goal of agents, circulating in the network, is gathering information about existing connections and entering this information in routing tables on the network nodes. The measure of algorithm efficiency was the percentage of nodes having valid route entries vs. the one of the hosts designed.

The average efficiency grew rapidly to 0.8 at the 40th iteration, and then was oscillating between 0.73 and 0.84. The agents population can ensure a relatively high connection level in a dynamic changing network, and performs it in a very stable manner.

The most influencing parameter is the next node choice algorithm: when agents were choosing the most recently visited one, the average efficiency was 0.792; the system with agents traveling randomly has an efficiency value of 0.646. It is not any disqualifying difference – random agents can be useful in rapidly changing systems.

The system presented in [2] by Jennings, Gibney, Vriend and Griffiths manages the telecommunication network using intelligent agents and market–oriented methods. It consists of three layers: network infrastructure, multi–agent system responsible for routing and end–user interface. In the system there are three agent classes: link agents, path agents and call agents. Agents work on two markets: link market and path market. Offers and bids are matched by using the sealed bid auction mechanism.

Results of using a static routing are almost the same as those when using the market–based method (94,8 % and 95,4 % connections set together, respectively). More than a half of all calls were set by using the shortest path, and only 14 % by using the least effective way.

The authors created a routing mechanism, which can successfully compete with traditional static systems without centralized management. Thanks to load prediction the service is fast. Routing and load balancing algorithms are easy to implement. The system allows an instant calculation of the bill for a network service.

3   System Conception

Our goal was to create a computer-aided model of a telecommunication network which could get adapted without any external intervention to current traffic conditions through automatic routing reconfiguration and by adding and removing connections between the nodes. The intelligent agents have to analyze the network state and make the configuration changes. The system self-regulation is based on the microeconomic mechanisms.

To make our model more efficient and flexible, we gave up pricing at the most elementary level (as it is in [2]). Price changes on the basis of network traffic statistics are made by agents.

We also abandoned negotiations which would complicate and lengthen the routing process. We did not use auctions, because they usually give some number of "losers". In our model there must be no packets which cannot reach the target because of lack of money or get there with a significant delay.

The starting point in our work was the system described in [1]. From it we took the network architecture and packet movement basics. The major changes were made in the traffic organization and market rules. In [1], packets are directed via the shortest path – in our system they go by using the shortest path they can afford – when they lose all the money they go via the cheapest route. After reaching the target, the packet pays for the route beginning from the cheapest connection to the most expensive one. Each port has its own "accounting" for profit estimation. Incomes much lower than expected signal that the connection is too expensive. This solution is good for a simulation, but it does not allow to create a complete macroeconomic environment.

Agents work on behalf of the mother nodes and report only to them the information gathered.

The only departure from the distributed paradigm was in the creation of the centralized bank. In the real network, there should be at least one bank network, if not more.

The system was realized as a simulator. At the input, simulation regards the entry network and data streams definitions. The program imitates operations in the real network: packets and agents move, the network gets reconfigured. As an output, the simulator produces a new network structure, optimized to the given load.

4   The Model

4.1   Network Architecture

Network hierarchy. The network consist of two basic elements: host (alternatively called node) and line (connection between two adjacent nodes). Hosts are grouped in subnets. Each subnet has one host appointed as a gateway to the other subnets.

For the sake of standardization we troduced the higher-level subnet consisting of hosts representing subnets. E.g. host "BB" is directly connected with host B1, which is the gateway of subnet B and both hosts function as the two–interface router.

Hosts. In our model the term „host" means miscellaneous network entities: network server – data source; client computer; router.

Basic events and operations effected by host are: generation and routing of packets, agent emission, own configuration changes, building new and destroying unused connections.

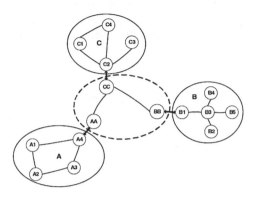

Fig. 1. Network architecture

Ports and lines. Hosts communicate by using lines, anchored in ports. Each port has two buffers: IN and OUT. The output buffer size is a few times greater than the line capacity and it has to prevent against short–time congestions. All traffic goes through the hosts interior, where the routing mechanism is. In a port there are also two separate buffers for agents. Each port charges packets coming out to the line. A port has two statistical agents collecting the data about packets traffic in and out.

The outgoing line has the following parameters: capacity (packets per simulation step), price for single packet transfer; length; maintenance cost and guaranteed capacity (it is the protection against network fragmentation). The decision on changing the line capacity or building a new line is made by a host.

Routing table. In each host there is a routing table. It includes entries about all adjacent hosts and some other hosts in the network.

The single record in the routing table looks as follows:

Destination address	Port	Time	Cost	Distance	Frequency

For the one host there can exist a few entries in the routing table differing from each other in time or cost. Beside specific records, there are default entries, consisting only of three fields: *source port, destination port and frequency*. All modifications of the routing table are made by agents specialized in network search and data stream analysis.

Packet traffic. Packets are generated in the hosts according to the specification given as a simulator parameter. Each host produces some amount of packets to some other host. The packet has the following attributes: a destination host identifier, a money amount, the history of a covered way and TTL – decremented with each line passed.

Passing the line, a packet writes in the way history - a record - which consists of the following fields: price, line length (geometric), bank account number to which it

5   Implementation

The functional project of the system was made by using UML. Then, there were created object classes corresponding to network architecture elements (host, port, line, packet, bank), mobile and static agents. Interactions between different classes were defined, too.

On the basis of this project, the program was realized in C++. Microsoft Visual C++ 6.0 was used as a compiler and developer environment. All the code has been written according to the ANSI C++ standard, which allows to adapt simply the work under different operating systems.

6   Results of Research

Our research on the system was made in two general areas: network traffic management and rebuilding network connections. Experiments were made by using two networks: network A was a one–piece local subnet consisting of 32 hosts. The other one (network B) was built from three local networks.

6.1   Network Traffic Management

We were interested in the analysis of time needed to reach the stable state by routing table and in the level accuracy of tables. The experiment was led with an option of building new and removing unused connections turned off. The network links bandwidth was set to the value so high that congestions should not occur. We carried out the experiment by using different routing table lengths. The percentage of packets reaching the destination was taken as an efficiency factor.

For the network A, the required routing table size was at least 8. At this value, the percentage of missed packets was about 1%. This value settles after 430 rounds. With the routing table size of 14, the efficiency grows to 99% almost instantly. That big routing table is required only for few key hosts, which transfer majority of traffic. We observed that the efficiency fell to 90 % after 840 rounds – it can be caused by periodic default gateway value changes.

Comparing results from networks A and B, we can remark how dividing the network into subnets improves the efficiency. It simplifies the routing and allows to reduce significantly. the routing table size. In the network B, when the routing table size is 0, the efficiency instantly reaches 90%; with size 3 it is 98%, and from 8 onwards it is 100%. This is caused by the fact, that when the routing table size is big, almost all hosts are in it, and packets do not use default gateway entries.

6.2   Network Structure Rebuilding

Network structure rebuilding experiments were made only on network A. At the beginning, all links have the bandwidth set to 300, and a guaranteed bandwidth set to 10, routing table size is 20, amount of money per packet is 5000. After 500 rounds the routing tables are settled, the traffic is often much lower than a bandwidth and profits do not surpass the costs. Of course, it is not optimal. We set the amount of money per packet to 1000. After 2500 rounds, the bandwidth is reduced almost on all connections.

After a fivefold increase of money amount per packet, 4 new links appear on relatively short and loaded routes. The fee for the link maintenance is in proportion to the square of the link's length, so the link cannot be too long. On the other hand, the static base fee prevents from creating too short links.

After increasing the amount of money per packet to 6000, and after   4500 simulator rounds, the topology of network graph was almost identical. It is by all means correct − it proves that the system runs stably. We expected some changes to be visible after a significant increase of money in the system. To check what the character of these changes would be like, we set the packet money amount to 10000. After 4500 rounds, 9 new links were built, even on long distances (they are marked with black solid arrows on figure 2.). The capacity of almost all other connections was reduced. Only few links remained intact.

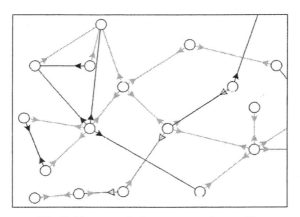

Fig. 2. The network fragment − packets traffic

All new links are profitable; in a few cases profits strongly exceed the costs, and this may makes one worry if the system works properly. On the other hand, new links are not built between all hosts. An other advantage, which cannot be read from figure 2, is the fact that the network shape settled between the 2000th and 2500th round and during last 2000 rounds; there were not any changes in it. It can attest to the system stability.

In the last experiment, the bandwidth on all links is set to 10, and this causes that the network is completely congested. The expected behavior should be similar to building the network from the basis. The money per packet amount is set to 10000.

In spite of similar initial values (except the connections bandwidth) like in the previous experiment, the number of new links is much greater than in the previous simulation. Marketing agents prefer to build new connections than to increase the bandwidth of the existing ones − in this case an agent does not take into account the loss of profits on the old connection.

6.3   Critical Remarks

Experimental results prove that system works according to assumptions in the area of routing management and network structure rebuilding. We should reconsider the way the new connections are built for making this process more flexible.

We found empirically that the routing systems cause chaotic creation and deletion of links in certain specific conditions.

The system should be optimized for computational efficiency. The standard simulation (5000 rounds) takes about 10 minutes on the PC computer with 600 MHz processor. It makes an effective testing hard to be carried out.

7   Conclusions

While designing our system, we referred to similar existing systems. The network architecture model is based on the one described in [1], but we have modified deeply the market elements of the system. The economical background was to achieve an optimal balance between computational efficiency and flexibility.

The simulator can be used to test various agent decision algorithms and marketing mechanisms in the research for the optimal self–configuring network. The side effects of the simulator work are optimally configured networks, and thus the system can be used in conventional network design.

The main values of our system are: proper modeling of the real telecommunications networks, possibility to change many parameters of the system configuration. Our system is of an innovative character.

Undeniable disadvantages are: huge computational complexity of the simulator, lack of the graphical interface, necessity of parameters adjusting by hand depending on the type of the network.

Our system in present form is complete, but it does not mean it cannot be expanded. These are a few most important changes possible to introduce:

- building links between any hosts from different subnets;
- coalitions of agents sharing a budget and goal;
- data trading, data mirroring;
- rebuilding charge system (for billing purposes).

References

[1] Krzysztof Cetnarowicz, Małgorzata Żabińska, Ewa Cetnarowicz. A Decentralized Multi-Agent System for Computer Network Reconfiguration.
[2] M.A. Gibney, N.R. Jennings, N.J. Vriend, J.M. Griffiths. *Market-Based Call Routing in Telecommunications Networks using Adpative Pricing and Real Bidding*. In proceedings of the 1999 Conference on Intelligent Agents for Telecommunications Applications, Stockholm, 1999.

[3] Jean-Philippe Martin-Flatin, Simon Znaty. *A Survey of Distributed Network and Systems Management Paradigms.* EPFL, SSC, Lausanne, Switzerland http://sscwww.epfl.ch, 1998.

[4] Nelson Minar, Kwindla Hultman Kramer, Pattie Maes. *Cooperating Mobile Agents for Dynamic Network Routing.* Mobile Computing and Communications Review, tom 3(2), 1999.

[5] D.L. Tennenhouse, D. Wetherall. *Towards an Active Network Architecture.* ACM Computer Communication Review, 26(2):5-18, 1996.

[6] Nir Vulkan, Chris Preist. *Automated Trading in Agents-based Markets for Communication Bandwidth.* http://www.hpl.hp.com/techreports/2000/HPL-2000-24.html, 2000.

A Highly Distributed Intelligent Multi-agent Architecture for Industrial Automation

Francisco P. Maturana[1], Pavel Tichý[2], Petr Šlechta[2],
Raymond J. Staron[1], Fred M. Discenzo[1], and Kenwood Hall[1]

[1] Rockwell Automation, Cleveland, USA
[2] Rockwell Automation Research Center, Prague, Czech Republic
{fpmaturana,ptichy,pslechta,rjstaron,fmdiscenzo,khhall}
@ra.rockwell.com

Abstract. In the 21st century, industrial automation will be greatly benefited by the advances in electronics, information systems, and process technology. However, these technological advances are still separate islands of automation. We believe that multi-agent systems will help the future of automation by providing flexible and scalable ways to integrate the different parts. This paper reports preliminary results of an ongoing research project that demonstrates advanced automation in a highly distributed architecture that is made of a synergy of intelligent agents, control, and physical devices. This was built to achieve the goals of reduced manning and improved readiness and survivability in US Navy shipboard systems.

1 Introduction

If we look at the internals of a shipboard system, we find several parallels with classical industrial environments. Therefore, it makes sense to consider the requirements of a shipboard system same as of a land-based factory. Nevertheless, the mission goals, human organization and operations, observe different but not too distant principles. Hence, the results of this work also apply to classical automation. The strategies and tools presented in this paper convey a substantial review to answer the requirements of the new century.

To successfully accomplish a ship's mission requires an intelligent evaluation of the conditions of the ship's subsystems and equipment. Here, highly distributed systems are understood as systems where the decision-making and execution components are physically and logically distributed. In a highly distributed intelligent shipboard automation system, autonomous agents carry out the required information processing in a perpetual manner. These agents use proactive and reactive behaviors to adapt the control system configuration to tasks and unforeseen conditions. A large population of intelligent agents is distributed among multiple automation devices and they carry out negotiation using common language. Novel properties of this architecture are high flexibility, survivability and diagnostics.

V. Mařík et al. (Eds): CEEMAS 2003, LNAI 2691, pp. 522-532, 2003.

The research community has proposed several definitions and interpretations of what intelligent agents are [1], [2], [3], [4], and [5]. According to the characteristics provided in Section 4, our definition is:

"An intelligent agent is an autonomous unit that encapsulates application knowledge and is able to interact with its environment in an intelligent manner."

In the past, our development of Intelligent Agent architectures was focused on experimental systems of reduced scale [6], [7], and [8]. Presently, the focus of research is to use the architecture to implement a survivable and reconfigurable system that will control a chilled water part of a shipboard automation for US-Navy vessels.

2   Shipboard Automation Architecture

To design a highly distributed shipboard automation system, four fundamental requirements are considered:

- Reduced manning: This is intended to create a system with less human intervention and more intelligent components capable of making decisions on behalf of the equipment and system goals.
- Flexible distributed control: This is understood as the capability of the system to adapt its components operations to respond to dynamically changing conditions without using predefined recipes. To achieve flexible distributed control, extensions to the control and network software is requisite to enable creation of component-level intelligence that increases robustness of the automation system.
- Commercial-off-the-shelf (COTS): This aspect addresses the cost reduction and system life cycle requirements of new shipboard systems. Under the COTS scope, a ship can be maintained at any friendly location in the world.
- Reliable and survivable operation: As the system becomes more autonomous and self-determined, it is required to augment the level of diagnosability of the components in a distributed manner.

The shipboard automation architecture is divided into 3 levels: 1) Ship, 2) Process, and 3) Machine, as shown in Figure 1. The Ship-level is concerned with ship-wide resource allocation. This level has direct communication with user-level (commander) interfaces. The Process-level is concerned with optimizing the performance of the components and ensuring the availability of services. The Machine-level is the lowest level in the hierarchy and focuses upon control, diagnostics and reconfiguration.

2.1   Chilled Water System

The CWS pilot system is based on the Reduced Scale Advanced Development (RSAD) model of the Auxiliary Machinery Controls and Automation Branch Carderock division in Philadelphia. The RSAD model is a reconfigurable fluid system test platform. The RSAD has an integrated control architecture, which includes Rockwell Automation technology for control and visualization. The RSAD model is presently configured as a chilled water system (see Figure 2).

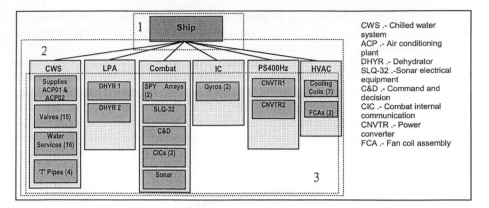

Fig. 1. Shipboard System

Immersion heaters provide stimuli for each service to model heat transfer. Essentially, there are 3 subsystems, plants, mains and services. There is one plant per zone (i.e. currently 2 plants). There are two types of services, vital (14) and non-vital (2). The physical layout of the chilled water system is a scaled-down form of the real ship.

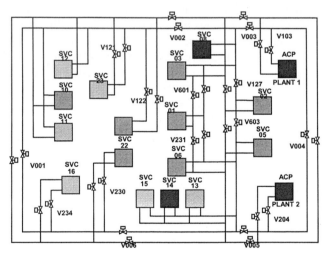

Fig. 2. RSAD Chilled Water System

3   Multi-agent System Architecture

The fundamental focus of the Multi-Agent System (MAS) is to instill methods for the creation of highly distributed control agents. The negotiation of agents is supported by fast auto-determination decision process. Auto-determination of agents corresponds to the degree of autonomy an agent has to build, commit, and carry out an action plan.

This behavior operates well in response-critical environments, where the intelligent agents expect synchronous responses, as opposed to pure MAS where asynchronous communication is the core mechanism. In this work, the agents operate in both domains, asynchronous and synchronous. The MAS architecture is organized according to the following characteristics:

- Autonomy: Each intelligent agent makes its own decisions and is responsible for carrying out its decisions toward successful completion
- Cooperation: Intelligent agents combine their capabilities into collaboration groups (clusters) to adapt and respond to diverse events and mission goals
- Communication: Intelligent agents share a common language for cooperation.
- Fault tolerance: Intelligent agents possess the capability to detect equipment failures and to isolate failures from propagating. This has special value in the detection of water leakage in CWS systems
- Pro-action: Intelligent agents periodically or asynchronously propose strategies to enhance the system performance or to prevent the system from harmful states.

Agent planning is carried out in three main phases: Creation, Commitment, and Execution. During creation, an intelligent agent initiates a collaborative decision making process (e.g., a load that will soon overheat will request cold water from the cooling service). The intelligent agents offer a solution for a specific part of the request. Then, the intelligent agents commit their resources to achieve the task in the future. Finally, the intelligent agents carry out the execution of the plans.

3.1   Automation Architecture

A primary requirement for new shipboard automation systems is the survivability of the control system. To fulfill this, we use a highly distributed control architecture, where the automation controllers are extended to enable creation of intelligent agents. Figure 3 shows the extensions to the automation controller firmware: 1) Distributed Control Agent (DCA) infrastructure and 2) Intelligent Agents. The DCA infrastructure glues the components via synchronized multithreads.

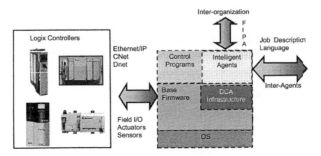

Fig. 3. Automation Control Device

The intelligent agents can contact any device in the network via a Job Description Language (JDL) message. The following description also applies to intra-device communication. JDL represents planning, commitment, and execution phases during the task negotiation. A second use of JDL is the encoding of plan templates. When an intelligent agent accepts a request, an instance of a plan template is created to record values emerging during the planning process. Information is encoded as a sequence of hierarchical actions with possible precedence constraints. If a part of the request cannot be solved locally, the agent sends a partial request to other intelligent agents as a sub-plan. The Contract Net protocol [9] is used to establish dynamic negotiations.

The intelligent agents can also emit messages outside of their organization via wrapping a JDL messages inside a universally accepted communication language. Presently, a commonly accepted language is the Foundation Infrastructure for Physical Agents (FIPA) Agent Communication Language (ACL) [10]. The FIPA standard uses a matchmaking mechanism to locate agents. Currently, our architecture includes a full implementation of Directory Facilitators (DF) that provides matchmaking and Agent Management Services (AMS) functionality.

Moreover, the architecture supports multiple DF agents. We developed dynamic hierarchical teamworks architecture to increase robustness of the system. The architecture offers the ability to create multiple global DF agents along with multiple local DF agents. Although, the user can predefine the structure at design time (solid arrows at Fig. 4), the system can automatically change its form at run time (dashed arrows). Robustness is increased using a heart-beating mechanism among DF agents. Breadth, Depth, and No knowledge propagation techniques have been implemented along with corresponding knowledge retrieval techniques. The Breadth propagation mechanism makes the knowledge global, the No propagation stores it locally, and the Depth propagates only up to global DFs.

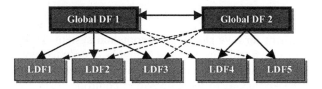

Fig. 4. Structure of Directory Facilitator agents - small scale example

During initialization time, each intelligent agent emits a registration message to its local DF. Then, the local DF registers the new agent in a database that is later used to match requests with the capabilities of agents. The DF agents exchange information automatically and seamlessly to create an open MAS enterprise.

3.2   Intelligent Agent Architecture

An intelligent agent exhibits goal-oriented social behaviors to be autonomous, cooperative problem-solving entities. The Ship agent originally emits a system goal. However, there are other system goals belonging to a group of agents or cluster [4]. Group goals emerge dynamically and these are agreed upon by the intelligent agents through negotiation. For instance, an intelligent agent that detects a water leakage problem in a pipe section establishes a goal to isolate the leakage, informs adjacent intelligent agents to evaluate the problem according to their data. This is the origin of what may become a group based goal, which is to isolate the section leakage. Figure 5 shows the intelligent agent architecture. There are four main components:

- Planner: This component is the brain of the intelligent agent. It reasons about plans and events emerging from the physical domain;
- Equipment Model: This component is a decision-making support system. The Planner evaluates configurations using models of the physical domain;
- Execution Control: This component acts as a control proxy and translates committed plans into execution control actions. It also monitors events from the control logic and translates them into response-context events to be processed by the Planner component; and
- Diagnostics: This component monitors the health of the physical device. It is programmed with a model of the physical device, where a set of input parameters is evaluated according to a model to validate the readings.

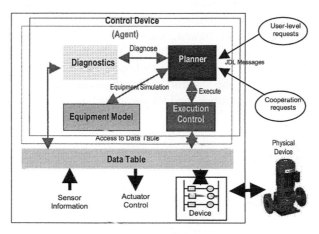

Fig. 5. Intelligent Agent Architecture

3.3   Distributed Diagnostics

The diagnostic component includes a suite of data acquisition, signal processing, diagnostic, and prognostic algorithms. These algorithms describe machinery and process health such as machinery fault detection, degraded operation, and failure prediction. The algorithms and models are organized into a multi-level structure [8]. This permits routines, such as bearing fault detection prediction algorithms, to be re-used in different agents. This architecture provides a mechanism for other agents to access information about a specific machine component.

The Diagnostic component of an intelligent agent can interrogate the diagnostic component of other agents to validate a fault hypothesis or to establish the viability of operating under extreme, possibly never anticipated, conditions. For example, a pump agent may sense a higher level of vibration and establish several fault hypotheses, such as a bad bearing or fluid cavitation. By employing corroborating information from the diagnostic components of the motor agent and valve agent, it may be determined that cavitation is occurring.

4   Development System

The Development Environment (DE) is a software tool that assists the user in programming the distributed application. The development environment introduces the following dimensions into the development phase:

- allow the user to specify the physical and behavioral aspects of the application in a manner completely independent of the control system;
- enable the user to specify a multi-processor control system in a manner completely independent of the application that is to run on it;
- assist the user in combining an application with a control system;
- generate the control code and behavior descriptions for each agent in the system;
- combine the code for all agents assigned to each processor in the system;
- augment each controller automatically to handle the communications to other controllers as a result of the program distribution; and
- communicate with all the controllers involved in an application, for their programming and configuration, and for subsequent monitoring and editing.

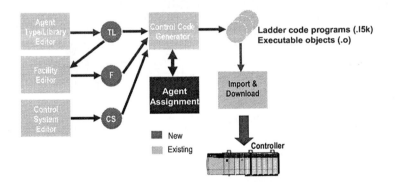

Fig. 6. Development Process

Figure 6 shows the general development flow through the system. One foundation for the DE is a library of components called the template library (TL). The library is editable by the user, and each template can contain both low-level control behavior (written in ladder diagram) and higher-level intelligent behavior (written in JDL and shown to the user as a function block diagram). The model for the control behavior supports an "object" view of the components in that, for example, inheritance is supported. The TL author can express, for example, that "A Radar is a type of CombatSystem". Each instance of Radar inherits all ladder data definitions and the CombatSystem logic.

The intelligent agent behavior, persistently stored as JDL scripts, is presented to the user as a function block diagram. The user creates a facility (F) from components of the template library and customizes their parameters. Next, the user establishes a Control System (CS) that describes all the controllers, I/O cards, and networks, plus their interconnections. After the TL, F, and CS parts are completed, the user generates and compiles the code. After the agent assignment, the user downloads the software into the controllers.

4.1   System Modeling

To establish an intelligent agent boundary, we consider the physical proximity of the devices (active and passive) and their function and relationships. There are cases in which it makes more sense to model an intelligent agent for a standalone device. In other cases, it makes more sense to group the devices under one intelligent representative. These design decisions have a direct effect on the size and complexity of the organization. We prefer a medium size population to keep the size of the population within practicable margins. In a large organization of intelligent agents high network traffic and saturation of the controllers' memory emerge as a problem.

4.2   CWS Partitioning

The water cooling plants (ACP plants) are modeled as a single intelligent agent each, and each includes pipes, valves, pumps, an expansion tank, and water-level, pressure, flow and temperature sensors. The main piping is partitioned as 'T' pipe sections. Load intelligent agents include a heat generator and a temperature sensor. Water Services intelligent agents include valves and flow sensors. There are standalone valves in the main looping for the supply and return lines. This partitioning gives us a total of 68 intelligent agents.

4.3   Multi-agent System Capabilities

Each intelligent agent is associated with a set of capabilities. Each capability is associated with a set of operations. The negotiation process is founded on local planning and negotiated planning (i.e., cooperation). For the local planning, the intelligent agents use their local 'world observations' to determine their next actions. The actions are translated into execution steps. The intelligent agents use the operations offered by the local capability. On the other hand, the negotiated planning is based on a capability discovery.

A chilled water system action is expressed as a chain of partial actions. For example, when a Load agent detects that it will soon overheat, it establishes an event for controlling the overheating. Since a Load agent does not have a cooling capability, it is required to ask for it as a cooling request (e.g. 'SupplyCooling'). The DF services provide the addresses of the agents that support such a capability. Water Service agents will be contacted to complete the request. However, since these agents only know how to supply water, they need to propagate the request as a more refined context. Next, the request emerges as a 'CoolWater' request that is directed to the

ACP Plants. Subsequently, the ACP Plant agents request for water regulators to transmit the water to the load.

5   Results

We built a prototype in the lab. at Rockwell Automation in Cleveland, Ohio. Once the intelligent agents were completed, a set of scenarios was tested to mimic the transactions of the shipboard system. Once the agent behavior and control logic were verified successfully, we transported the software library to the RSAD facility, where we carried out the instantiation of the intelligent agents using the real equipment. The Navy provided the team with a set of operations and desirable reconfiguration scenarios to be supported by the agent organization. In our lab., the team used the agent development tool to emit the agents automatically. This code contained agents and ladder algorithms. The team tested the code on the prototype and later the same code was used on the Navy facility.

In Figure 7, a UML sequential diagram shows the agents on the top. The vertical lines represent the time line. The horizontal lines represent inter-agent messages. CandD detects an overheating event and sends a message to its local DF (LocalDF1) to obtain possible candidates for 'CoolWater' capability. LocalDF1 sends an Inform message back to CandD with two possible candidates ACP01 and ACP02. CandD subsequently contacts them to obtain their bids for CoolWater capability.

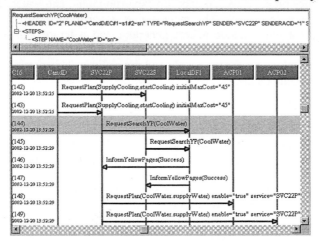

Fig. 7. Intelligent Agent Negotiation

Figure 8 shows the structure of the decision tree required to plan for a water route from a source to a consumer and vice versa. The figure shows the water route results to move water from ACP01 plant to SVC22S service. The figure contains both successful and unsuccessful paths.

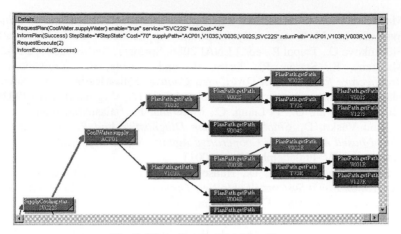

Fig. 8. Water Routing Decision Tree

6   Conclusion

This paper has accomplished a high-level description and use of a multi-agent architecture to a real-life control problem. The implementation of the architecture as a commercially available product is still work-in-progress. In this paper, the authors have presented the general use of the agents. The architecture will be prepared to operate on a Navy pilot facility within the next few months to fulfill a final deliverable. The architecture provides a simple manner to establish system functions and dynamically emerging relationships among the system components without preprogramming the relationships. The intelligent agents enable component-level intelligence that provides survivability and works with no human intervention. The architecture and tools are presently works-in-progress and subject to continuous improvement. The shipboard automation architecture provides a methodology to reduce manning onboard and to increase the survivability of distributed components through diagnostics and component-level intelligence.

References

[1] Brooks, R.A.: *A Robust Layered Control System for a Mobile Robot*, IEEE Journal of Robotics and Automation, 2(1), (1986) 14-23

[2] Christensen, J.H.: *Holonic Manufacturing Systems: Initial architecture and standards direction*, First European Conference on Holonic Manufacturing Systems, Hanover, Germany, (1994)

[3] Wooldridge, M. and Jennings, N.: *Intelligent agents: theory and practice.* Knowledge Engineering Review, 10(2), (1995) 115-152

[4] Shen, W., Norrie, D., and Barthès, J.P.: Multi-Agent Systems for Concurrent Intelligent Design and Manufacturing. Taylor & Francis, London, (2001)

[5] Mařík, V., Pěchouček, M., and Štěpánková, O.: *Social Knowledge in Multi-Agent Systems*. In: Multi-Agent Systems and Applications (Luck M., Mařík V., Štěpánková O., Trappl R., eds.) LNAI 2086, Springer, Berlin, (2001) 211-245

[6] Maturana, F., Staron, R., Tichý, P., and Šlechta, P.: *Autonomous Agent Architecture for Industrial Distributed Control*. 56th Meeting of the Society for Machinery Failure Prevention Technology, Sec. 1A, Virginia Beach, (2002)

[7] Chiu, S., Provan, G., Yi-Liang, C., Maturana, F., Balasubramanian, S., Staron, R., and Vasko, D.: *Shipboard System Diagnostics and Reconfiguration using Model-based Autonomous Cooperative Agents*, ASNE/NAVSEA Intelligent Ship Symposium IV, Philadelphia, PA, (2001)

[8] Discenzo, F.M., Rusnak, D., Hanson, L., Chung, D., and Zevchek, J.: *Next Generation Pump Systems Enable New Opportunities for Asset Management and Economic Optimization*. Fluid Handling Systems, Vol. 5, No. 3, (2002) 35-42

[9] Smith, R.G.: *The Contract Net Protocol*. High-level Communication and Control in a Distributed Problem Solver. In IEEE Transactions on Computers, C-29(12), (1980) 1104-1113

[10] The Foundation for Intelligent Physical Agents (FIPA): http://www.fipa.org

The Cambridge Packing Cell – A Holonic Enterprise Demonstrator

Martyn Fletcher[1], Duncan McFarlane[2], Andrew Lucas[1], James Brusey[2], Dennis Jarvis[1]

[1]Agent Oriented Software Ltd.
Mill Lane, Cambridge CB2 1RX, United Kingdom
{martyn.fletcher,andrew.lucas,dennis.jarvis}@agent-software.co.uk
[2]Institute for Manufacturing, University of Cambridge
Mill Lane, Cambridge CB2 1RX, United Kingdom
{dcm,jpb54}@eng.cam.ac.uk

Abstract. Many modern manufacturing systems are highly automated and are now requiring decentralised 'smart' architectures to control hardware and manage the flow of materials / knowledge, in order to provide responsiveness. This responsiveness is needed to satisfy an ever increasing consumer need for goods that satisfy their unique requirements and are delivered to market both quickly and economically. A key route to achieve this mass-customisation with distributed control is to apply the holonic enterprise paradigm, and one manufacturing process that exhibits a high potential for responsiveness is packaging. Therefore this paper presents some of the main features of such an enterprise – the Holonic Packing Cell demonstrator being built at Cambridge University's Institute for Manufacturing. It must be emphasised that this cell is constructed from state-of-the-art industrial strength facilities to demonstrate a spectrum of responsive manufacturing ideas – it is not built from Lego bricks.

1 Introduction

Traditional manufacturing control systems are hierarchical and are geared to mass production of low-variety goods. Often a schedule of the manufacturing operations on a given day is developed well in advance. As the schedule is executed, unexpected events, typical of many production, warehousing and supply chain environments, tend to invalidate the schedule and change how operations are managed. These events include introduction of rush orders, machine failures or handling of returned goods. Furthermore, in many of today's markets people want goods that are customised to their specific needs and they are not prepared to wait long lead times for delivery. For example, people want to specify how to mix and match constituent elements of a product via a web page and have it presented to their door next day.

V. Mařík et al. (Eds): CEEMAS 2003, LNAI 2691, pp. 533-543, 2003.

In other words, manufacturing businesses are being pushed, by market forces, to provide mass customisation of their product families and to react more quickly to consumer demands. This means frequent changes to production equipment function and layout. Meanwhile, the companies do not wish to throw away their existing factories or the investment they have made in hardware. Hence a new technological approach is needed to make, handle and transport products in a flexible fashion to cope with these 'one of a kind' demands. After investigating several UK and international manufacturing companies, we have come to the conclusion that one of the major processes in the manufacturing chain where flexibility is high, and therefore where there are good opportunities for mass customisation, is automated packaging. These opportunities exist because packaging is 'close' to the end-customer and so the demand for customisation is high. In this paper we describe a component-based approach to providing such flexibility in the 'pick and place' packing of Gillette gift boxes. Our model separates out resource dependencies (e.g. robot manoeuvres) from product requirements (e.g. a definition of desired grooming items to be placed in the gift box). The paper is structured so as to give a flavour of the design features and implementation experiences associated with our building of this holonic packing cell.

2   The Holonic Enterprise

In this paper we propose the holonic enterprise as a means of addressing the change requirements of today's manufacturing businesses. This section presents the generic features of a holonic enterprise and then presents a specific (and somewhat simplified) example of such an enterprise – the Cambridge packing cell.

2.1   General Features

The *Holonic Enterprise* is a distributed paradigm which is receiving increased popularity [1] to handle disturbances in the manufacturing business process and to cope with the demands of mass customisation, is. A Holonic Enterprise [2] covers a range of decision-making processes within both the manufacturing and business worlds. This decision-making aims to provide reconfigurable 'plug-and-play' manufacturing business systems. The entities making such decisions are called *holons*. The layers at which decisions are taken by holons are: supply chain management, planning and scheduling of production, and real-time control of intelligent machines.

As defined by Marik *et al* [3], "Holons are autonomous cooperative units which can be considered as elementary building blocks of manufacturing systems with decentralised control. Each holon usually contains:

(i)   a hardware/equipment part able to physically influence the real world (e.g. a device, tool or other manufacturing unit, transportation unit or storage facility etc), and

(ii)   a control part responsible for both the hardware/equipment part control and communications with the rest of the holonic community."

Interested readers are referred to the work of Chirn [10] and the papers edited by van Leeuwen [4] for an overview of the classic holonic principles and the current state of the art in applying these principles to a range of manufacturing control environments. In the context of this article, and Chirn's work, there are two classes of holons:

- Resource holons, which are self-contained system components which can perform operations on work-in-progress (WIP), such as fabrication, assembly, transportation and testing. Beside the visible physical part, a resource holon also contains an invisible control part which can perform its operations, make decisions and communicate with the aid of its plan library and knowledge base.
- Product holons, or order holons, which also contain a physical part and a control part. The physical part may include raw materials, WIP, finished goods, pallets and fixtures. Meanwhile the control part contains functions to manage routing, processes, decision-making and maintain production information.

The classification of these holons provides the potential for the holonic enterprise to be readily responsive. As a consequence of trying to use this body of research to develop a holonic enterprise demonstration, two critical technologies needed for making automated real-time decisions have been identified: Automatic Identification (Auto ID) systems, and agent-based and multi-agent systems [5, 6]. Auto ID systems (www.autoidcenter.org) are used to read/write information to tags via high frequency radio waves. These electronic tags can replace barcodes and uniquely identify goods, thereby enabling decisions to be made by the order holons representing them on an item-specific level and removing the line-of-sight requirement when reading.

Meanwhile agent systems represent the next major leap in functionality for computer systems. Agents are autonomous software entities that are aware of their situation and can reason about their behaviour to accomplish design objectives. They experience their environment (the larger system they 'live' in) through sensors and act through effectors. They are reactive, responding in a timely manner to sensed environmental change, and are also proactive, working towards their goals. Agents can also dynamically form themselves into teams, as humans do, and play different roles and collaborate in order to achieve their objectives. Intelligent agents have been successfully deployed into a number of real-world domains where decentralization, complexity and uncertainty are common.

Within the scope of this holonic enterprise, major aims of our ongoing research are:

- To demonstrate that holonic control can be integrated with the Auto ID infrastructure into open-loop control so the user has the ability to dynamically change how orders are made and managed [7].
- To show that flexible and robust operations can be achieved even when raw materials supply is random and varying, and order attributes regularly change.
- To illustrate interactive order adjustment, and dynamic modification of manufacturing operations in the case of errors and quality control failures.
- To fully exploit the potential responsiveness/reliability of the physical system [8].

Answers to these questions will help companies to be more cost effective, to respond more quickly, and to form closer collaborative networks with both customers and suppliers, i.e. creating a virtual enterprise that spans several organisations for the manufacture of customised goods. Yet the consequence of this strategy is that business models need updating and manufacturing processes must be re-engineered to cope with the added complexity that responsiveness demands. We define responsiveness in this context as 'the capability of the system, both in part and as a whole, to conduct business as usual in an environment where change is frequent and unpredictable'. To confront these challenges, the shop-floor needs to migrate away from a rigid centralised control philosophy to an open approach where hardware and knowledge resources can be easily and quickly added, removed or reconfigured. The predetermination of what products are to be made in a given manufacturing cell must also be relaxed – orders should arrive, identify what type of resources are needed and how to compose the product, and then control the machinery that is scattered across the factory as needed to make the goods while satisfying all the business criteria imposed on the organisation. This creates a range of complex decision-making problems (as seen in our example) that cannot be easily solved by conventional approaches due to the high degree of dynamics.

2.2   The Cambridge Packing Cell: A Holonic Enterprise Demonstrator

The goal is to design, develop and integrate a holonic packing cell to demonstrate how a holonic enterprise offers more responsiveness. The layout is shown in Figure 1 and the system is characterised by:

- **Business Problems:** To pack together consumable goods in a flexible way to meet specific and variable customer/retail needs. To efficiently and economically use intelligent warehouse, production and packing resources in the factory where uncertainty, failures and changes are commonplace. To get products to decide how best to make, manage and deliver themselves so that they are cost effective and satisfy the buyers' requirements.
- **Solution:** Holons are introduced onto the shop-floor to model both *resources* (e.g. conveyor shuttles, a robot, storage units) and *products* (gift boxes and items like razor blades). Every holon uses its own intelligence and interaction with others to determine how best to use facilities and get the orders packed effectively. The system enables the customer to select any three of four types of grooming product, pack them into one of two box styles, and change how their order is packed on the fly. This solution is now more robust to changes in order requirements than conventional packing lines.
- **Benefits:** The demand from customers for unique combinations of products to be packaged together has led to an examination of new control system technologies that will revolutionise the retail and production industries. Intelligent holons better utilise factory resources, make products more efficiently and so increase the reactivity of manufacturing businesses to changing market needs. Rush orders can buy packing services to get themselves made quicker, partially-packed orders can be broken down so that urgent orders can be made, resources can use market economies to ensure they are getting used optimally.

Fig. 1. The Cambridge Holonic Packing Cell

This cell comprises a storage unit to hold items, a Fanuc M6i robot to move items throughout the cell, a shuttle conveyor to transport batches of raw materials (items) and the boxes into which items are to be placed around the cell. The shuttles and their Montech track gives added responsiveness by controlling individual shuttles and assign transport tasks dynamically to them. The system schema is given in Figure 2.

Some of the responsive manufacturing scenarios that the cell demonstrates are:

- Introduction of batch orders whereby individual products (i.e. boxes) manage their own resource allocation. This allocation includes acquiring a suitable tray, shuttle and items to accomplish the goal of packing that box. Also included is negotiating with the docking stations to reserve a processing slot.
- Docking stations cooperating to evenly distribute workload at runtime.
- Handling of rush orders that must be packed earliest and how this influences the schedules of the docking stations and the other boxes to be packed.
- The interaction between shuttles and gates to ensure routing of shuttles around the track is both shortest time and gives highest priority to urgent shuttles.
- Failure of a docking station and how this resource change affects how and where shuttles are processed, fault tolerance and reconfiguration.
- Organising a storage unit when the robot is no longer busy so that items of the correct types or most frequently used are located at the head of each chute.
- Unpacking completed boxes so that urgent orders can be satisfied quickly.

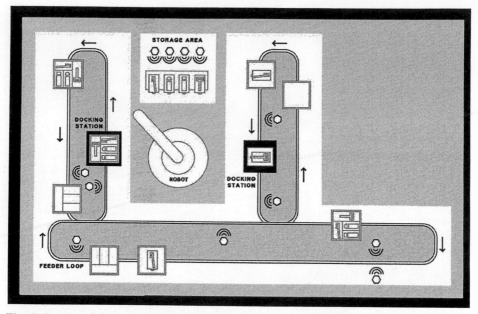

Fig. 2. Layout of the cell with three conveyor loops and independently controlled gates that guide shuttle navigation around the track. There are also two docking stations where shuttles are held so that the robot can pick and place items into the boxes that they carry. The system demonstrates many of the processes associated with responsive manufacturing

Regarding unpacking in more depth, a complete gift box could be unpacked of its items so that the items can be either:

- Put into a different box for a higher priority order or an order with a more pressing deadline.
- Replaced by a new item because either the existing one was incorrect (deduced by the quality control checking) or the customer changed the box configuration at packing time before the shipment left the factory.

Both situations can refer to either an individual box or the set of boxes in a particular customer's batch order. Consider the first situation, i.e. unpacking a box to satisfy other (more urgent) orders. A critical problem is to determine which complete gift box should be nominated as the candidate for having its items removed. One reasoning approach is for the order holon that managed the assembly of the box with the desired items in it to announce the deadline and price to other order holons in the community. Then the order holon whose box has the longest deadline and lowest price is selected. The box that has multiple items that are needed would also be viewed as the best candidate if several boxes met the initial criteria. To encourage the order holon to sacrifice its completion with only a probability (rather than a certainty) that it will now be delivered on time, the higher priority order holon must offer some electronic 'money' to the lower priority order holon to purchase his box. This lower priority order holon can then use this added money to ensure he is made by either being able to pay a higher price for use of resources (e.g. getting access to the robot as soon as possible) or for in turn buying other items to satisfy itself. Another issue is that if the packed box associated with the candidate order holon is buried at the bottom of a built-up pallet, the time to take the box off the pallet must also be considered as part of the purchasing (negotiation) protocol.

For the second case, the resource and order holons must cooperate to remove the damaged or invalid item from the gift box (while it is resident on the docking station) and deal with the item accordingly if it failed the quality check. If the box configuration is changed then the desired item must be removed from each box in that order and held (without further quality control work) in the storage unit. New items to replace the discarded ones must be acquired from either the storage unit or from a shuttle on the incoming conveyor. When an item is taken out of a box, it can be:

- Stored back into the storage unit which demands that the storage unit is not full.
- Held in the robot's tool. If the robot is to hold onto the item then no other picks and places can be done until the item no longer occupies the tool. This option also demands that for efficiency the shuttle with a new gift box arrives at either docking station as soon as possible.
- Placed into another box waiting on the other docking station. This option (most relevant for the high-priority replacement case) means that both docking stations must be assigned to holding boxes (one to be removed from and the other to be inserted into). Moreover, for efficient use of the available resources, the boxes should arrive at their respective stations simultaneously.
- Placed onto a shuttle that has its top configured to hold and transport items.

These scenarios have been demonstrated by a high-priority order arriving (say an empty red box), with a lower-priority filled box (in blue) being in the system at the same time. These two boxes have autonomous order holons associated with them that must interact effectively, and cooperate with available resource holons, to determine the best overall plan. The robot can then transfer the desired items between boxes.

3   Holon Building Framework

The primary entities in the cell are the orders and resources (that can be further classified into hardware control and knowledge serving). There are the following holon types in the system, with the number of instances shown in brackets:

- Hardware Control Resource Holons: Robot Holon (1), Docking Station holon (2), Gate holon (2), Reader holon (7)
- Knowledge Serving Resource Holons: Track holon (1), Box Manager holon (1), Storage holon (1) Production Manager holon (1)
- Product Holons: Order Manager holon (one spawned for each gift box that must be manufactured).

A frequent question asked of holonic or multi-agent system designs, is why have these holon or agent types been chosen. The answer in this case is that we first identified the types of separable physical hardware in the enterprise that must be controlled. Each of these entities (in the case of our Cambridge cell - robot, docking station and gate) has its own independent objectives and hence can make a variety of decisions. Therefore these entities should be modelled as resource holons. We can also identify that there may be other pieces of hardware that could be dynamically plugged into a physical system and must be controlled, process sensed information or make decisions upon their actions in an autonomous manner. These should also be treated as resource holons, and here this includes the Auto ID readers.

A trickier question is whether the entities in the control that do not have a one to one mapping with hardware are to be modelled as holons. The PROSA architecture uses staff holons to represent entities that do not neatly fit into the heterarchical view of the control system. We are faced with a similar challenge with our enterprise: there are several knowledge serving or processing entities that are neither resource holons nor order holons, yet provide a valuable set of services to the other holons. For example the track holon has the objective of monitoring where each of the shuttles is on the track loops in order to prevent too many shuttles being allowed into a given zone on the track. In the case of the cell, these entities are labelled as knowledge serving resource holons, for the want of a better term, and like the use of staff holons in PROSA point to a big problem with the resource/order holon architecture. Resolving this problem is a major topic of our future research. The objective of the order holon is to get itself made in a timely manner and so satisfy quality control. Hence it makes its decisions and orchestrates its interactions to fulfil each resource allocation goal in turn throughout its manufacturing recipe. We consider that all these autonomous cooperative holons interact to accomplish their goals via the structured exchange of messages. Styles of interaction include:

- Order holons and resource holons collaborate to ensure boxes and are packed speedily to the customers' specifications. This involves the order manager holon selecting plans for constructing a recipe of manufacturing operations from a XML-based representation of the desired product's attributes, identifying resource holons capable of supplying these operations, negotiating with them to secure necessary services and tracking the product's progress through the factory.
- Resource holons interact to compute their schedules based on maximising the payoff associated with executing their services, and they also co-operate to compensate for unexpected failures [9].
- Order holons coordinate to buy and sell goods (namely item and boxes), ensuring that customer batches are packaged effectively and shipped in a timely fashion. An example of this style of interaction is the unpacking scenario outlined above.

The aforementioned holons have been constructed using JACK Intelligent Agents™ platform. JACK was selected as the holon development environment over platforms like JADE or Grasshopper for several reasons including it has a rich set of graphical tools for agent design, plan editing and tracing, and it provides a native, lightweight communications infrastructure for situations where high performance is required. Moreover JACK supports a Belief/Desire/Intention (BDI) execution model. Therefore this means that the developer is not left on their own to develop all the software needed to build and run rational agents. This is beneficial for holon development because the BDI model has a very potential for reusing plans from within a plan library and has the possibility of sharing knowledge efficiently among agents using belief synthesis. Furthermore the use of agent intentions provides a basis to attain stability in the face of change by efficiently using the agent's manufacturing and data processing resources. Interaction between many low-level holons can result in a complex system behaviour which is difficult to understand, predict and control. The well-defined BDI model, and solid implementations of this model like JACK, helps tackle this complexity via using software engineering principles and flexible interaction strategies that can be easily comprehended, visualised and monitored at runtime. JACK agents execute their reactive and deliberative behaviours through pre-compiled plans. Which plan to execute is determined according to internal events that they post to themselves, external events (messages) that they receive from other agents, and knowledge that they have about themselves and the world. If a plan fails, other plans can be executed by the agent until the goal is achieved. The behaviours of the various holons described in the previous section were implemented using this classic BDI abstraction model, with some being encoded and traced using JACK's graphical tools. The interfaces that JACK agents have to the external world are implemented in Java as JACK *views*, which enable agents to interact with:

- A blackboard (in turn connected to a PLC that handles communication with hardware) to exchange sensor data and commands with shop-floor machinery.
- The Auto ID system (called the Savant), via Simple Object Access Protocol messages to gather data on which shuttle has just passed a reader and so forth.
- A server, also via SOAP, which provides knowledge on orders being placed etc.

A set of responsive manufacturing demonstrations have been run with these holons.

4 Summary

This paper described the features and implementation of a holonic packing cell to support a plethora of behaviours needed in responsive holonic enterprises, including unpacking of goods in, storage of WIP, sorting and retrieving of stored goods, packing batches of gift boxes based on customer choice, quality control of completed gift boxes, failure of redundant resources, manufacture of goods based on priority, and handling of rush orders. Such responsiveness can be seen as a measure of operational performance in the face of disruptions and is mainly influenced by the holons' algorithms. The main framework for building these behaviours is founded on the independence of orders from resources, coupled with the 'plug and play' philosophy for incorporating new hardware and the potential for sophisticated resource allocation and fault tolerance strategies. The JACK Intelligent Agents™ platform and its graphical development environment that was successfully used to build such an enterprise were also discussed. Our future work will explore methods, tools and philosophies associated with the design decisions that must be taken when building a holonic enterprise. So we are attempting to answer the following questions:

- How can agent-based holons be best integrated with manufacturing hardware to: (i) provide an increased range of manufacturing operations, (ii) be coupled together coherently at run time, and (iii) compensate for unpredicted failures?

- What types of algorithms are needed for: (i) scheduling and planning; (ii) routing of goods through and beyond the factory; and (iii) resource allocation, etc?
- How can holons be dynamically introduced, cooperated with and removed?
- How are quantitative measurements to be made on how the holons perform, both at both theoretical and implementation levels? We have commenced work in this topic, albeit from a qualitative focus, via a spidergram-based framework [11].
- What are the functional interfaces between holons and other (e.g. ERP) systems?

Developing holonic enterprise demonstrators, like the Cambridge packing cell, is valuable exercise because it provides us with a wealth of opportunities to test out new holonic models and ideas within the scope of a mini-factory environment where industrialists and academics can witness the benefits of responsive manufacturing.

References

[1]   "The Holonic Manufacturing Systems (HMS) project is an international industry-driven project addressing systematisation and standardisation, research, pre-competitive development, deployment and support of architectures and technologies for open, distributed, intelligent, autonomous and cooperating (holonic) systems on a global basis". Details at http://www.ims.org/projects/project_info/hms.html (2003)

[2]   Ulieru, M. (ed.): workshop on Holonic Enterprises at the 3rd International Symposium on Multi-Agent Systems, Large Complex Systems, and E-Businesses, Erfurt Germany, (2002)

[3]   Marik, V., Fletcher, M., and Pechoucek, M.: Holons & Agents: Recent Developments and Mutual Impacts, in Multi-Agent Systems and Applications, Springer Verlag, LNAI 2322, (2002)

[4]   van Leeuwen, E.H. (ed.): track on Multi-Agent and Holonic Manufacturing Systems at the 5th IFIP International Conference on Information Technology for Balanced Automation Systems in Manufacturing and Services, Cancun, Mexico, (2002)

[5]   Barata, J., and Camarinha-Matos, L.M.: Implementing a Contract-based Multi-agent Approach for Shop Floor Agility, 3rd International workshop on Industrial Applications of Holonic and Multi-Agent Systems, IEEE, Aix en Provence, France, (2002)

[6]   Martin, D., Cheyer, A., and Moran, D.: The Open Agent Architecture – A Framework for Building Distributed Software Systems, Applied Artificial Intelligence, vol 13,no 1, (1999)

[7]   Payne, T.R., Paolucci, M., Singh, R., and Sycara, K.: Communicating Agents in Open Multi Agent Systems, NASA workshop on Radical Agent Concepts, Greenbelt USA, (2002)

[8]   Brennan, R.W., Fletcher, M., and Norrie, D.H.: An Agent-based Approach to
      Reconfiguration of Real-Time Distributed Processes, IEEE Transactions on
      Robotics and Automation, vol 18,no 4, (2002)
[9]   Deen, S.M.: A Cooperation Framework for Holonic Interactions in
      Manufacturing, 2nd International Conference on Cooperating Knowledge Based
      Systems, Keele UK, (1994)
[10] Chirn, J.-L. and McFarlane, D.C.: A Holonic Component-Based Approach to
      Reconfigurable Manufacturing Control Architecture, 1st International workshop
      on Industrial Applications of Holonic and Multi-Agent Systems, IEEE,
      Greenwich, UK, (2000)
[11] Fletcher, M., Brusey, J., McFarlane, D.C., Thorne, A., Jarvis D.H.., and Lucas,
      A.: Evaluating a Holonic Packing Cell, submitted to the 1st International
      Conference on Applications of Holonic and Multi-Agent Systems, Prague,
      Czech Republic, (2003)

Towards Autonomy, Self-Organisation and Learning in Holonic Manufacturing

Paulo Leitão[1] and Francisco Restivo[2]

[1] Polytechnic Institute of Bragança,
Quinta Santa Apolónia, Apartado 134, P-5301-857 Bragança, Portugal, pleitao@ipb.pt
[2] Faculty of Engineering, University of Porto
Rua Dr. Roberto Frias, P-4200-465 Porto, Portugal, fjr@fe.up.pt

Abstract. This paper intends to discuss self-organisation and learning capabilities in autonomous and cooperative holons that are part of a holonic manufacturing control system. These capabilities will support the dynamic adaptation of the manufacturing control to the manufacturing evolution and emergency, specially the agile reaction to unexpected disturbances.

1. Introduction

The manufacturing systems are complex non-linear systems, since the occurrence of a disturbance causes non-linear impact in the system. As some of the effects of the disturbance can remain in the system after the resolution of the event that originated the disturbance, their occurrence may have severe impact in the performance of manufacturing systems. For this reason, it is necessary to measure the system performance also in terms of response to change and capability to learn.

The unpredictability of disturbances and the need to keep the system at work independently of their size and rate puts new requirements to manufacturing control systems, which have to handle them dynamically and to tell the difference between an occasional disturbance and the evolution of the system environment. Additionally, the assessment of potential impact of identified disturbances assumes a crucial factor.

Holonic manufacturing concepts and multi-agent systems implementations seem to have the capability to answer to these new problems, due to their decentralisation, autonomy and cooperation features.

This paper describes a manufacturing control architecture, designated by ADACOR, based in holonic manufacturing concepts, that aims to address the dynamic adaptation of the manufacturing control to the manufacturing evolution, specially the agile reaction to unexpected disturbances, by introducing the concepts of autonomy, cooperation, learning and self-organisation in each holon and in whole system.

V. Marik et al. (Eds): CEEMAS 2003, LNAI 2691, pp. 544-553, 2003.

2. Holonic Manufacturing and Multi-Agent Systems

The emergent requirements for distributed manufacturing systems, namely the dynamic adaptation to the manufacturing evolution and emergency, lead to the development of dynamic and adaptive manufacturing control systems based in new paradigms such as holonic manufacturing and multi-agent systems.

2.1 Overview of Multi-Agent Systems and Holonic Manufacturing Systems

The multi-agent system paradigm is characterised by decentralization and the parallel execution of activities based on autonomous entities, called agents. The definition of agent concept is neither unique nor consensual, existing some discussion in the scientific community about the issue, such as described in [1-3]. Despite the several definitions and interpretations for agents, a possible definition for agent is [4]:

An autonomous component, that represents physical or logical objects in the system, capable to act in order to achieve its goals, and being able to interact with other agents, when it doesn't possess knowledge and skills to reach alone its objectives.

Multi-agent system can be defined as a set of agents that represent the system objects, capable to interact between themselves, in order to achieve its individual goals.

The Holonic Manufacturing System (HMS) is a paradigm that translates to the manufacturing world the concepts developed by Koestler to living organisms and social organizations, mainly that complex systems are hierarchical systems formed by intermediate stable forms, being simultaneously a part and a whole [5]. The word holon is the representation of this hybrid nature, allowing that a holon can be part of another holon, e.g., a holon can be broken into several others holons, which in turn can be broken into further holons, which allows the reduction of the problem complexity. A holarchy is defined as a system of holons that can cooperate to achieve a goal or objective. A HMS is a holarchy, which integrates the entire range of manufacturing activities, where key elements, such as machines, products and robots, have autonomous and cooperative properties.

The agent-based and holonic manufacturing systems approaches are developed under the same principles of autonomy and cooperation, exploring the distribution and decentralisation of entities and functions. Although the similarity of the both concepts, there are some few differences that tend to be reduced, since at the moment the agent and holonic communities seem to be converging rapidly at the moment.

2.2 Open Challenges

In spite of the research developed using the holonic manufacturing paradigm, such as referred in [5-9], the holonic manufacturing paradigm presents some open questions on the design and implementation of manufacturing applications.

The first question is related to how it is achieved the global optimisation, since the holonic manufacturing approach is based in autonomous entities. In case of formation of hierarchies to achieve global optimisation, an open question is related to how temporary hierarchies are formed, managed and removed.

In order to be able to integrate different holarchies, other open question is related with the definition of common ontologies to support inter-operability and knowledge sharing during the interaction processes. This inter-operability has two different levels: inter-operability within the same control platform and a more complex inter-operability related to the integration of different (distributed) control platforms.

In order to adapt to disturbances, the implementation of self-organisation capabilities and the integration of planning, scheduling and plan execution functions, are yet far from trivial. The definition of how the learning capabilities of each holon should be improved to support the manufacturing evolution and emergency, also remains an open challenge.

At last, one drawback of holonic manufacturing paradigm is the few implementations using real industrial scenarios that can prove the advantages of the holonic approach.

3. ADACOR Holonic Control Architecture

The ADACOR architecture addresses the dynamic and agile adaptation to disturbances and the integration of all manufacturing functions, namely the process planning, the scheduling and the plan execution.

3.1 Architecture Entities

The architecture, based on the holonic manufacturing systems paradigm, is supported by a set of autonomous and intelligent holons, each holon being a representation of a manufacturing entity, such as a numerical control machine, a robot or an order. The ADACOR architecture considers four classes of manufacturing holons: the product, task, operational and supervisor holon [10]. Each product is represented by a product holon that contains all knowledge related to the product and process. Manufacturing orders to be executed in the factory plant are represented by task holons, which are responsible for the control and supervision of their execution. The operational holons represent the manufacturing resources, such as operators and robots, managing its behaviour and agenda according the resource goals, constraints and skills.

The product, task and operational holons are quite similar to the product, order and resource holons, presented at the PROSA reference architecture [5]. The supervision holon, not present in PROSA, introduces coordination and global optimisation in decentralised control approaches, coordinating several operational and supervisor holons. In normal operation, the supervisor holon supervises and regulates the activity of the holons under its domain, while when a disturbance occurs, these holons may have to find their way without the help of the supervisor holon. The supervisor holon is also responsible for the group formation, based in pre-defined clusters of holons, combining synergies, aggregating skills and offering the combined services to external entities in the manufacturing system. These groups can be formed to build a shop floor, a manufacturing cell, or a machine equipped with a set of tools, assuming the supervisor holon the control role of each group.

3.2 Fractal Holarchies

ADACOR architecture presents self-similarity features, since each holon possesses a structure and behaviour similar to the ones of the holon where it is encapsulated. An operational holon can be a set of several operational or supervisor holons, allowing to build holarchies upon fractal holarchies. As an example, a manufacturing cell can be represented by an operational holon that comprises several other operational holons, each one representing a manufacturing resource, and one supervisor holon representing the manufacturing cell controller. In this case the supervisor holon acts as the logic component, and the several operational holons act as the physical part of the holon. Additionally, each one of those operational holons that represent a manufacturing resource can comprise several other operational holons, such as the numerical control machine itself and the several tools stored in its tool magazine.

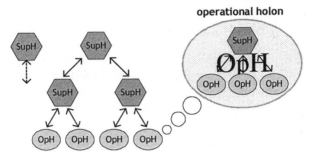

Fig. 1. Fractal Feature in ADACOR Approach

This fractal feature allows high flexibility in the organisation of the control structure, creating foundations to support the combination of global optimisation with agile reaction to disturbances. Additionally, it allows a modular development through the encapsulation of several functions or manufacturing components represented by holons in other holons.

4. Self-Organisation Capability

The industrial manufacturing systems are stochastic, volatile and dynamic environments. The heterarchical control architectures present good reaction to disturbances but degrade the global production optimisation; on the other hand, the hierarchical approach presents good global optimisation but weak reaction to disturbances. The challenge is to develop dynamic and adaptive manufacturing control approaches that improve the agility and reaction to unexpected disturbances without compromising the global optimisation.

The ADACOR architecture is neither completely decentralised nor hierarchical, but balances between one and the other [4], being the self-organisation crucial to reach the dynamic and adaptive control approach.

4.1 Autonomy Factor and Propagation Mechanisms

The self-organisation capability presented in all ADACOR holons allows the dynamic adaptation of each holon and the system as a whole to the emergent contexts and the quick reaction to the occurrence of unexpected disturbances. This capability supports the re-organisation into different control architectures more appropriated to the current situation. Self-organisation is supported basically by the autonomy factor and the propagation of re-organisation concepts.

The autonomy factor, α, associated to each operational holon is a parameter that introduces a fuzzy degree of autonomy in each holon, and evolves dynamically in order to adapt the holon behaviour according its goals and constraints and with the environment where it is placed. The autonomy factor is a continuous or discrete variable. Currently it is implemented using fuzzy logic, represented by the linguistic fuzzy sets {Low, High} and by a fuzzy-rule base. Normally, the operational holons have a {Low} autonomy factor, allowing the operational holon to follow the supervisor holon coordination [4]. The emergency triggers the change of the autonomy factor to {High}, the re-organisation into a heterarchical control structure, and the selection of one adequate behaviour to handle the disturbance.

The need for re-organisation, using pheromone-like techniques, is disseminated to the supervisor holons through the propagation and deposit of pheromone to the neighbourhood supervisor holons [10]. While spreading the need for re-organisation, the holon passes a parameter that reflects the estimated reestablishment time (τ), similar to the odour from the pheromone-like techniques, and that is calculated according with the type of disturbance and with the historic data. The holons associated to each supervisor holon receive the need for re-organisation by sensing the pheromone, propagating this need to neighbourhood holons. The dissemination of the need for re-organisation, allows the dynamic and continuous adaptation of the system to disturbances, reducing the communication overhead and improving the reaction to disturbances.

Table 1. Fuzzy Rule Behaviour for the Adaptive Mechanism

ρ	α	τ	New α	Action triggered
High	Low	-	High	Trigger selection behaviour.
High	High	Elapsed	High	Reload reestablishment time.
Low	High	Elapsed	Low	Re-organise into default DF.
-	High	Not Elapsed	-	-
Low	Low	-	-	-

The autonomy factor, the reestablishment time and with the pheromone parameter (ρ), that is concerned to the odour level of the pheromone or disturbance, jointly allow to regulate the adaptive behaviour of the operational holon. The adaptive mechanism determines the autonomy and the action to trigger according with Table 1.

In case that the action triggered be the selection of behaviour, it is necessary to know the disturbance type, the actual state of the holon and the historic data in order to select the appropriate behaviour and to estimate some required parameters.

4.2 Dynamic Production Control Structure Evolution

The production control is shared between the supervisor holon and the operational holons, in order to balance the control structure from a more centralised approach to a more flat approach, passing through other intermediate forms of control [4].

The proposed adaptive control splits the control evolution into alternative states: stationary state, where the behaviour of the system uses coordination levels and the supervisor role to get global optimisation of the production process, and the transient state, triggered with the occurrence of disturbances and presenting a behaviour quite similar to the heterarchical approach in terms of agility to react to disturbances.

In stationary state the autonomy factor of each operational holon is {Low}, allowing the operational holon to follow the schedule proposals sent by the supervisor holon. In this state, aiming the global production optimisation, the holons are organised in a federated architecture, with the supervisor holons interacting directly with the task holons during the operation allocation process. The supervisor holon, as coordinator, elaborates optimised schedule plans that proposes to the task holons and to the operational holons under its coordination domain [10]. The operational holons see these proposals as advices, having enough autonomy to accept or reject the proposed schedule. After the allocation of the manufacturing operations, the task holons interact directly with the operational holons during the execution of the operations, such as to ask for availability of space in the buffer.

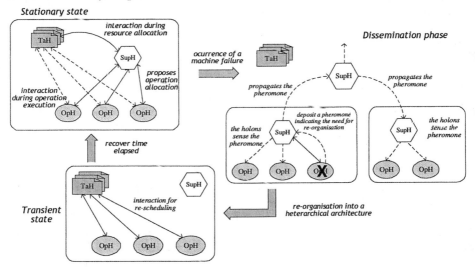

Fig. 2. Dynamic Re-organisation in Reaction to a Machine Failure

If, for any reason, the system deviates from planned, it is triggered a control system re-organisation, and it enters into the transient state. As illustrated in Fig. 2 for the case of a machine failure, the operational holon who detects the disturbance tries to recover locally the failure, but if it cannot recover from the failure, the operational holon increases the autonomy factor, disseminates the need for a re-organisation to the other holons in the system, and according with the type of disturbance selects an appropriate behaviour to handle the disturbance.

The other holons that sense the propagation, also increase their autonomy factor and re-organise themselves into a heterarchical structure. In this state, the task holons can interact directly with operational holons to re-schedule their operations, achieving a faster but not optimised schedule plan. The operational holons remain in this transient state during the reestablishment period, typically a short period of time. When the time is elapsed, they verify if the odour is already dissipated or remains active. In case that the pheromone remains active, the operational holons stay in the transient phase during an additional proportional reestablishment time, until the pheromone be dissipated.

After the disturbance recovery, the operational holons end the reinforcement of the pheromone, and the reestablishment and recover times are adjusted and tuned using appropriated learning mechanisms. The other holons don't sense anymore the dissemination, reducing their autonomy factor, returning the system to the previous control structure. The supervisor holon returns to its coordination function, re-scheduling the operations in an optimised point of view, and the optimised schedule to the operational holons.

5. Learning Capability

As an autonomous entity, an ADACOR holon is requested to take decisions about what actions it should perform. The introduction of learning capabilities in the holon behaviour intends to improve the holon and system performance.

5.1 Learning to Support the Emergency and Evolution

According to [12], learning in a multi-agent environment can help agents to improve their performance, namely to learn about the partner's knowledge and strategic behaviour, and to react to unexpected events by generalising what they have learned during a training stage.

Learning can be defined as a way to acquire knowledge and skills to adapt the behavioural tendencies, and it is crucial to respond to the dynamic evolution of the environment where it is placed and to improve the system ability to act in the future, by taking better decisions and performing better the required actions.

Learning is normally performed in result of a decision-making process allowing to adjust the decision parameters or even to update the behaviour rules. In the manufacturing control context, the learning mechanisms are triggered mainly in the following situations: when a process finishes (such as task allocation process and the end of the task holon life cycle), when the system configuration changes and when unexpected disturbances occur.

The ADACOR holons are self-optimised since they have the capability to continuously increase its performance using learning mechanisms. In spite of the wide range of learning techniques, such as described in [1, 11-12], the proposed learning mechanism in ADACOR uses simple and reliable techniques. The mechanism stores the decision taken and uses the posterior results to learn. In the decision-making process, holons use the new knowledge acquired from previous experience to support the following decision-making, which will probably lead to better decisions and actions.

Depending of situation where learning is used, different learning techniques are applied, such as rote learning (simple memorisation) and unsupervised learning.

5.3 Learning in the Prediction of Future Disturbances

To exemplify the application of learning mechanisms in ADACOR holons, it will be described how to apply learning to predict future disturbances. As previously referred, the occurrence of disturbances degrades the system performance. The control system should be able to analyse the unexpected events and decide when an unexpected event is a real disturbance or a normal situation. The objective is to use appropriated learning mechanisms to find patterns in the occurrence of disturbances, foreseeing the stochastic effects of industrial environment, making predictable the occurrence of future disturbances, preparing the system to support these events.

The proposed approach uses an unsupervised learning mechanism based in the statistical clustering technique [11], to predict the time interval between consecutive disturbances. Cluster analysis aggregates objects (a vector of n feature values) in clusters by analysing the similarity between them. A similarity metrics treats each object as a point in n-dimensional space, the similarity of two objects being the Euclidean distance between them in this space. The cluster formation is achieved such that the distance between any two instances in the cluster is less than the distance between any point in the cluster and any point not in it.

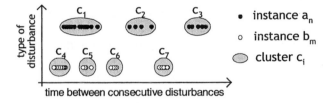

Fig. 3. Clustering of the Disturbances

The procedure involves, in a first step, the creation of groups of disturbances according to the similarities in the type of disturbances. In the next step each group is analysed individually, in order to find a pattern in the occurrence of that type of disturbance. In each group, obtained in previous step, the clustering algorithm described in [13] is applied, allowing to create clusters using the notion of a cluster diameter. This algorithm requires all data to be available prior to clustering, grouping the fault events in clusters, according to the similarities in the time between consecutive occurrences, as in Fig.3. In case that the distance between any two input pairs be the same, the location within the sorted list will be arbitrary and could lead to different classifications being produced.

After the detection of similarities between the historical disturbance events and the consequent creation of clusters, it is necessary to analyse all created clusters in order to detect the predominant cluster, which reflects the tendency of the disturbance sequence. A pertinent question is how to select the predominant cluster, since several parameters that characterize the disturbance sequence are not known in advance. The predominant cluster is selected taking in consideration the number of elements or the presence of the last disturbances. If the last disturbance events belong to the same cluster, that cluster reflects the tendency and it is considered predominant. Otherwise, the predominant cluster is the one whose contains the highest number of elements.

The last step is concerned to the analysis of the selected cluster and extraction of the predictability of occurrence of future disturbance, which based in estimation of the mean value of the cluster.

In order to validate the learning mechanism in the prediction of disturbances, its response was tested for several disturbance sequence inputs, as illustrated in Fig. 4.

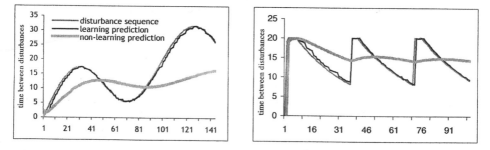

Fig. 4. Experimental Results

From the experimental analysis it is possible to verify that the proposed clustering mechanism presents a satisfactory precision in the prediction of the next disturbance, with precision over 95%. Comparing with a particular non-learning technique, the one that predicts based in an average of past events, it is possible to verify the improvement achieved by using the learning mechanism in this situation.

In opposite to some techniques that require initial training, the clustering dispenses this training, achieving faster a prediction value. However, the clustering technique presents low performance in case of fewer fault events and is highly dependent of the cluster formation and selection. In order to improve the performance of the prediction mechanism, in further research work it will be considered not only the values of the time between the disturbances but also the feedback related to the precision about the prediction, applying for example a reinforcement learning technique.

6. Conclusions

The manufacturing systems are complex non-linear systems, since the occurrence of a disturbance causes non-linear impact and some effects of the disturbance can remain in the system after the resolution of the event that originated the disturbance. The development of manufacturing control systems that handle efficiently and quickly to the occurrence of disturbances is an actual and open challenge.

The ADACOR architecture, based in holonic manufacturing paradigm, introduces the concepts of autonomy, cooperation, self-organisation and learning to support the agile reaction to unpredictable disturbances, such as machine failures and rush orders.

The self-organisation, based in the autonomy factor and propagation mechanism, allows to balance the control between different control structures, reaching an adaptive control approach that combines the agile reaction to disturbances with the global optimisation. The introduction of learning capabilities in manufacturing holons allows to improve the holon´s ability to act in future and to support the dynamic evolution of the environment where it is placed.

As ADACOR is an open framework based on holons that can be built upon several building blocks (similar to Legos® components), further work should focus on the application of learning mechanisms for the identified situations using more powerful learning algorithms.

References

1. Russel, S., Norvig, P.: Artificial Intelligence, A Modern Approach. Prentice-Hall (1995).
2. Wooldridge, M., Jennings, N.: Intelligent Agents: Theory and Practice. In: The Knowledge Engineering Review, **10** (2), (1995) 115-152.
3. Ferber, J.: Multi-Agent Systems, An Introduction to Distributed Artificial Intelligence. Addison-Wesley (1999).
4. Leitão P., Restivo, F.: Holonic Adaptive Production Control Systems. In: Proceedings of 28th Annual Conference of the IEEE Industrial Electronics Society, Spain, (2002) 2968-2973.
5. Van Brussel, H., Wyns, J., Valckenaers, P., Bongaerts, L., Peeters, P.: Reference Architecture for Holonic Manufacturing Systems: PROSA. In: Computers In Industry, **37** (3), (1998) 255-274.
6. Christensen, J.: Holonic Manufacturing Systems - Initial Architecture and Standard Directions. In: Proceedings of the First European Conference on Holonic Manufacturing Systems, Hannover, Germany, (1994).
7. Fisher, K.: Agent-Based Design of Holonic Manufacturing Systems. In: Journal of Robotics and Autonomous Systems, Elsevier Science B.V., 27, (1999) 3-13.
8. Bussman, S.: An Agent-Oriented Architecture for Holonic Manufacturing Control. In: Proceedings of 1st Workshop on the Esprit Working Group on IMS, Lausanne, (1998) 1-12.
9. Brennan, R., Fletcher, M., Norrie, D.: An Agent-based Approach to Reconfiguration f Real-Time Distributed Control Systems. In: IEEE Transactions on Robotics and Automation, **18**(4), (2002) 444-451.
10. Leitão, P., Restivo, F.: A Holonic Control Approach for Distributed Manufacturing. In: Marik, V., Camarinha-Matos, L., Afsarmanesh, H. (eds.): Knowledge and Technology Integration in Production and Services: Balancing Knowledge and Technology in Product and Service Life Cycle. Kluwer Academic Press, (2002) 263-270.
11. Kubat, M., Bratko, I., Michalski, R.: A Review of Machine Learning Methods. In: Michalski, R., Bratko, I., Kubat, M. (eds.): Machine Learning and Data Mining: Methods and Applications. John Wiley & Sons, (1996) 1-72.
12. Goldman, C.V. and Rosenschein, J.S: Mutually Supervised Learning in Multiagent Systems. In: Weiss, G. and Sen, S. (eds.): Adaptation in Multi-Agent Systems. Lecture Notes in Artificial Intelligence, Springer-Verlag, (1996) 85-96.
13. Hutchinson, A.: Algorithmic learning. Clarendon Press, (1994).

An Agent-Based Personalized Producer/Consumer Scenario

Christian Seitz[1] and Bernhard Bauer[2*]

[1] Siemens AG, Corporate Technology, Information and Communications
81730 Munich, Germany
Christian.Seitz@mchp.siemens.de
[2] Institute of Computer Science, University of Augsburg
86150 Augsburg, Germany
Bernhard.Bauer@informatik.uni-augsburg.de

Abstract. We present an agent-based Producer/Consumer scenario, that is the key element of manufacturing systems and therefore of utmost importance. We call it a MSWS-system, which is made up of a series of machines, shuttles, a warehouse and again shuttles. We applied a hybrid approach, i. e. which is a combination of a completely centralized and a totally decentralized approach. A controller supervises two MSWS-Systems and intervenes only in exceptional cases. On account of an increasing significance of the human factor in manufacturing systems, each machine operator is endowed with a user profile.

1 Introduction

The applicability of agents in the area of manufacturing has been studied very intensely in the last years. In this paper we focus on a small, but very important part of manufacturing systems, which we call a MSWS-System, a series of *M*achines, *S*huttles, a *W*arehouse and again *S*huttles. Such a system appears in any manufacturing system and often a MSWS-System is directly followed by another one. Since the productivity of people is in relationship with their motivation, we endow each operator and machine with a profile, which enables the production system to integrate the workers wishes in the manufacturing process. In order to guarantee, that all incoming orders are completed in time, each component is endowed with a load balancing mechanism. Coalitions of machines are formed to complete an order, with the consequence that a failure of a single machine harms less, because there is always a backup machine present.

Agent based manufacturing systems have been studied intensely in the literature in the last years. Design issues on agents and manufacturing system are illustrated in Bussmann *et al.* [2]. Shen and Norrie [9, 10] give a detailed overview of developed systems and mechanisms. Architectures of manufacturing systems are shown by Usher and Wang [11]. They differentiate between a hierarchical

---

* Former address: Siemens AG, Corporate Technology, Information and Communications.

V. Mařík et al. (Eds): CEEMAS 2003, LNAI 2691, pp. 554–563, 2003.

M: Machine Subsystem
S: Shuttle Subsystem
W: Warehouse Subsystem

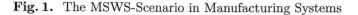

A)   B)

Fig. 1. The MSWS-Scenario in Manufacturing Systems

approach, where machines are supervised by a hierarchy of controllers and a *heterarchical* approach with a flat organization. We follow a hierarchical approach, but we only introduce one controller-layer. Manufacturing systems, which give the workers more competencies [5] are called human centered systems (HCS). In our system each worker has a user profile, which enables him to influence the system. There are several possibilities to control agent based manufacturing systems. Kis *et al.* [8] use a market mechanism and Chen *et al.* [4] apply negotiations and Bussmann and Schild [3] use auctions. We use a the contract-net for negotiation among the agents. Our primary goal is to conflate manufacturing systems and personalization.

The paper is structured as follows. In Section 2 we define our work. Section 3 gives an overview of the architecture of our system. Section 4 introduces the planning system. In section 5 we present some optimization aspects and section 6 concludes the paper with a summary.

2 Problem Definition

This section introduces the Producer/Consumer scenario. Furthermore, organizational aspects of manufacturing system are explained. The section concludes with some assumptions about the system.

2.1 Shop Floor Scenario

We focus on a small but very important part of manufacturing systems, which appears in every system. It is a Machine-Shuttle-Warehouse-Shuttle-(MSWS)-System (see figure 1A). A machine produces goods, which are transported by a shuttle[1] to a warehouse. If the products of the warehouse are needed for further production they are brought to another machine by a shuttle. The number of machines a M-subsystems consists of is not limited, but they all belong to the same machine type, e. g. a cutter or a CNC lathe. The same applies to the shuttle- and warehouse-subsystem. This small scenario is omnipresent in any shop floor and often a MSWS-System is followed by another one as depicted in figure 1B.

2.2 Preferences and Profiles of Humans and Machines

In manufacturing systems the humans working at the machines are often neglected. They do not have any possibility to intervene in the system. However,

---

[1] A shuttle is a kind of vehicle, which navigates autonomously in a shop floor.

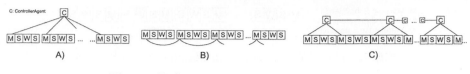

Fig. 2. Different organizational approaches

there is a tendency that the significance of humans in the production process will increase (see e.g. Choi and Kim [5] or Barbuceanu and Fox [1]). Giving a person more competencies, people are more motivated and this directly induces better work. Experience shows, that people defining their rest periods by themselves work faster after the break and make less errors. Therefore, we equip our manufacturing system with personalization aspects. Each worker is characterized by specific profiles for particular machines, like clock time, machine settings etc. Beyond machine specific profiles of a human, his preferences are taken into account, like break times or preferred working hours. Additionally, we associate a profile with each machine. The profile of a machine contains e.g. information about downtime, varying cycle times or production times. There are constraints regarding the entries in a machines' profile. An operator may not enter a cycle time in the machines profile with the consequence that the orders currently processed cannot be completed in time.

2.3   Organizations

There are three different approaches for the architecture of an agent-based manufacturing system. The first one is a totally centralized approach, depicted in figure 2A. A central controller agent (C) supervises all machines in the manufacturing system. This component is able to synchronize and coordinate all its subsystems and is able to perform a global optimization. But a breakdown of the central component disrupts the production and it is not easy or even possible to integrate rush orders in a running system, because replanning is too time consuming.

The opposite is a completely decentralized approach (see figure 2B). Each machine possesses its own local planner and performs local optimizations based on its local view of the world. The local planners communicate with other local planners of previous or successive machines. Thus, a machine can respond faster to local changes of the environment, since no coordinator is involved. However, if the system is complex and a problem occurs at the end of the assembly, the machines at the beginning do not know anything about the trouble. The longer the assembly line, the more time will elapse until information gets from one end of the line to the other.

The hybrid approach (see figure 2C), which we follow for the rest of the paper, combines the advantages and eliminates the disadvantages of the two previous mentioned methods. There are multiple coordinators, each responsible for a fixed number of machines. The coordinators communicate with each other to exchange information about their machines' behavior. The controllers enforce the communication between the machines and the local planners preserve flexibility. A breakdown of a single controller is less crucial in a hybrid system than in systems with only one coordinator.

2.4 Definitions and Assumptions

Before we describe our system in detail, some definitions and assumption are made. An order o consists of a product-id (pid), which specifies the product being made by a machine; the number of goods n which have to be produced, and a deadline t_d which specifies the time, the order must be completed. A *coalition* of machines is completing an order. A warehouse is made up of a fixed number of storage places, each capable of taking up a fixed number of goods. In a storage place only one type of product (same pid) is stored. We emanate from an shuttle surplus and we assume that shuttles will never break down. Finally, a profile of a machine is defined as follows:

Definition 1. *Let* M *be a machine. A profile **Prof(M)** of a machine* M *consists of a set of machine properties M_p, such that for each resource[2] type m_i, a set of PropertyNames N_{Prop}^i exist. The PropertyValues V_{Prop} are always (for each resource type) non-negative integers. A MachineProperty M_p of a machine* i *is a pair $N_p^i \times V_p$.*

Preferences PREF(U) of a user U are modelled as described in Kießling [7] and are a set of preference values V_{Prop} and preference attributes A_{Pref}^i. A relation $x \preccurlyeq y \subseteq V_{Prop} \times V_{Prop}$ is interpreted as, *a person likes y better than x*. With this, a user profile UP can be defined, using PROF(M) and PREF(U).

Definition 2. *Let $\{PROF(M_i)\}$ be a set of machine profiles M_i and U the users' preferences $PREF(U)$, a user profile $UP = \{\{PROF(M_i)\}, PREF(U)\}$.*

A workers' profile consists of one or more machine profiles[3] plus additional information about the users' preferences, e. g. duration of coffee breaks.

3 Architecture

In this section the architecture of the MSWS-System is described. It consists of a M-, S-, W-, and another S-subsystem. Each subsystem is made up of a fixed number of resources of the same type and a single machine is controlled by several agents, called the *Agent based Processing Unit*. Due to the hybrid approach, an additional control-layer, called the *Agent based Controller Unit*, is needed.

3.1 The Agent Based Processing Unit

The Agent based Processing Unit (AbPU), envisaged in figure 3A, consists of six agents. The *OrderAgent* OA is in charge of sending and receiving orders from

---

[2] We call a warehouse, a machine, and a shuttle resources for unification reasons.
[3] A worker does not always work with the same machine type and therefore for each type a profile is needed.

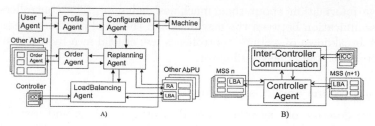

Fig. 3. Architecture of the Agent based Processing Unit (A) and the Agent based Controller Unit (B)

other subsystems. The received orders are administered by the OA in a priority queue. With the *ProfileAgent* (PA) the machine operator is able to change the profile of a machine and to transfer its own profile, residing on its UserAgent, to the machine. The *LoadbalancingAgent* (LBA) checks regularly the order queue to get information about the workload of the machine. This data is forwarded to all other LBAs. The *ReplanningAgent* (RA) is always informed when an exception occurs, e. g. a machine breaks down. The RA arranges the orders to make sure the order with the highest priority is served first. The *ConfigurationAgent* (CA) is informed when either the profile has changed or the machine breaks down. With the *UserAgent* a worker is able to edit his or the machines' profile and can transfer the profile to the PA. A profile is specified in XML according to the definition given above. The PA sends the changes of the profile to the RA. This agent tries to customize the machine. Only if all changes can be realized, the new profile is accepted, else it is declined.

The architecture of the shuttle- and warehouse-subsystem differs slightly. They do not contain a RA because it is not possible to transfer products from one storing place or shuttle to an other. However, the LBA is still present, but there is only a communication channel *to* the controller unit to forward availability bottlenecks.

3.2   The Agent Based Controller Unit

The agent based controller unit (AbCU) consists of two agents, the Inter-Controller-Communication-Agent (ICC) and the Controller Agent (CA) (see figure 3B). A AbCU is responsible for two MSWS-systems (see figure 2C) and it sends instructions only to the machine-subsystems. If a LBA detects, that all machines in a subsystem are too heavy loaded, the CA is informed by a LBA. The ICC communicates with all other AbCU in order to get information about the load situation in other subsystem. If necessary, the ICC informs the CA. The CA informs controllers of preliminary MSWS-Systems, in order to increase or decrease production, and informs successive controllers about the future developments of the orders. The coordinator intervenes only in exceptional cases, with the consequence that a breakdown of a AbCU is less crucial in hybrid system than in systems with only one controller.

3.3   Communication

Figure 4 depicts the messages sent by each subsystem. An order has its origin either from an ERP (enterprise resource planning) or from an previous MSWS-System. At first a coalition of machines must be found, able to complete the order in time. Either the order is released by a machine, or an order is requested by the OA of a single idle machine. In the former case, the subsystem releasing the order contacts all machines in a M-Subsystem. Each AbPU responds with the percentage of the order it is able to complete in the specified time. The machine, which is able to produce most of the pieces gets the complete order and is called m_w, the others m_{l_i}. If there is a draw, the machine, which has answered at first gets the acceptance of the bid. Now, at least one *collaborator* is needed. m_w initiates an *iterated contract net* protocol and invites all other machines to participate in producing the order. Each m_{l_i} returns the number it is willing to produce. The m_w evaluates the incoming messages and depending on the order size and due date, m_w chooses an appropriate (see section 5.2) number of supporting machines, which are finally informed by m_w. If the number of pieces produced by the other machines is insufficient, another iteration of the contract net must be started. In the first run the m_{l_i} only return the number of pieces they are able to produce without replanning. In the second run the m_{l_i} reorganize the queues of each OA. If even this is not successful the controller is informed, which starts a *Reorganization mechanism* (see section 4.2). Until the order is processed the LBA can change the number of pieces each coalition member has to produce. In the latter case - a single machine requests a new order on account of outrunning orders in the waiting queue - the machine gets the order and now the aforementioned negotiation-procedure is started.

If a shuttle is needed to transport a workpiece to the warehouse, the machine sends a request message to the shuttle pool. Because of an unlimited number of shuttles, the request will always be successful. The shuttle, transporting a product, has to find a storage place, where workpieces of the same product are stored. The shuttle contacts all storage places and if there is a storages place containing the *pid*, and it is not totally filled, the workpiece is transported' to this storage place, otherwise an empty one must be used. With each workpiece in the warehouse a *resting counter* is associated. Every time a new product arrives in

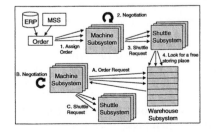

Fig. 4.   Communication in a MSWS-System

the warehouse the resting counter for each piece is increased. This enables the successive MSWS-system to identify the workpiece staying the longest time in the warehouse. If the number of free storage places falls below a threshold, the detecting LBA informs the controller, which is now responsible for either reducing the output of the producing machines or starting only orders, containing *pids*, already present in the warehouse. But more frequently, a machine of a successive MSWS-Systems sends a request to all storage places of the warehouse. Either the most urgent workpiece (deadline) or the workpiece spent the longest time is chosen. Now, the machine is able to continue its work and a complete MSWS-System-cycle is passed.

4   Exception Handling

In a manufacturing system exceptions may occur at any time. We differ between *local* and *global* errors. Local errors only affect one MSWS-System, then a *replanning* is started. In global errors at least two MSWS-Systems are involved, and a *reorganization* is initiated. A replanning is tried first and only if this action is without effect, a reorganization is initiated.

4.1   Replanning

The LBAs periodically examine the input-queues of their machines and if not all orders can be fulfilled or a machine is broken down, the RA is informed and a replanning process is started. Breakdowns of machines conform to a negative exponential distribution ($f(x) = \lambda e^{-\lambda x}$ with the mean value $\mu = \frac{1}{\lambda}$). According to statistical estimation theory a $(1 - \alpha)$-confidence interval is $[\frac{2n\bar{X}}{c_1}, \frac{2n\bar{X}}{c_2}]$. $\bar{X}$ is the average of all downtimes and n the number of breakdowns. The two constants c_1, c_2 are the $\frac{\alpha}{2}$ and $1 - \frac{\alpha}{2}$ values of a χ^2 distribution with $2n$ degrees of freedom. If a machine breaks down, we first estimate how long this might be. In case, the estimation results in a very short downtime, the replanning process needs not to be accomplished, because in spite of the incident all orders may be completed in time. The situation changes, when the estimated downtime exceeds an upper threshold and finishing an order early enough becomes impossible. In this case, the coalition members take over a little amount of extra work. However, it may happen, that the support of all coalition members is still insufficient. In such situations, the number of products, the broken machine ought to have made, must be transferred to another machine. This has the same effect as adding a completely new order to the system. In case of a breakdown there are four possible activities which might to be done:

1. No action has to be performed, if the estimated downtime predicts only a short-time failure.
2. The downtime is rated as too long, in this case parts of the order must be transferred to coalition members.
3. If all coalition members are unable to complete the order in time, a replanning is initiated.

4. If all aforementioned actions fail, a reorganization is started by the AbCU.

If the machine is reconfigured by changing its or the operators profile, the estimation step is omitted and only the two subsequent steps are executed.

4.2 Reorganization

If the behavior of two or more MSWS-Systems escalate, a reorganization procedure is started by the AbCU. There are two situations, when a reorganization is initiated. Either a preceding replanning was not successful or the LBA of any subsystem detects an error, from which a MSWS-System cannot recover by itself. The AbCU is always informed by the LBA about a machines load, properties and state. According to the received messages from the LBA, the AbCU may carry out a set of actions:

- Initiation of a replanning in other MSWS-systems.
- Increase or reduction of the output of an arbitrary MSWS-system.
- Information of MSWS-systems about orders in advance (e. g. rush-orders).

5   Optimization

This section describes how load balancing is achieved and how the optimal size of a coalition for an order is computed.

5.1   Load Balancing

Load balancing algorithms try to distribute the load equally among all system components [6]. In the AbCU the LBA, is in charge of distributing the load among all members of the subsystem. The LBA permanently observes the queues of the OA and decides whether orders are sent to other OAs.

At first, we calculate the time t_o, that is needed to complete the order o. It has to be taken into account, that a machine must be rebuild or may break down. These intervals must be additionally considered when calculating t_o.

$$t_o = t_{rb} - nt_p \cdot (1 + p_f t_{rep}) \tag{1}$$

t_o is the estimated time a machine needs to produce n pieces of an order o. p_f is the probability for the machine to break down and is defined as $p_f = \frac{\sum t_D}{t}$, i. e. the sum of all down times t_D during time t. The time, that is needed to repair a machine is t_{rep}. t_{rb} is the time, needed to rebuild the machine. t_p is the time needed to produce an workpiece and is subjected to change.

Let T_p^n be the set containing the last n ($|T_p^n| = n$) processing times t_p of the products being produced and $[\max\{t_{p_1}, t_{p_2}, \ldots, t_{p_n}\}, \frac{1}{\sqrt[n]{\alpha}} \cdot \max\{t_{p_1}, t_{p_2}, \ldots, t_{p_n}\}]$ the $(1 - \alpha)$ confidence interval for uniformly distributed data t_{p_i}. With this confidence interval we estimate $t_p^{est} = \min(T_p^n) + \frac{1}{2\sqrt[n]{\alpha}} \cdot (\max(T_p^n) - \min(T_p^n))$. Let t_{gap}^o be $t_d - t_o$, and let t_d be the remaining time to the deadline, t_{gap}^o specifies the time, when the execution of the order o must be started. With t^o_{gap}, an order o_i can now be associated with a priority $P_i = \frac{1}{t^{o_i}_{gap}}$. The larger the value of P_i the more important is the order. The orders i are queued according to their priority P_i, which must be recalculated each time step, because with proceeding time, P_i increases. In order to balance the load, the utilization $U_i(t) = \frac{t}{\sum_{t^i_d \le t} \frac{1}{P_i}}$ of the machine i is used, this is an indicator of the load of the machine at the time t. The value permanently changes. If a new order is added to the machine it increases and if a new piece is produced it decreases. The overall goal in the manufacturing system is, that all machines should have approximately the same utilization. In this case we talk about a *balanced system*. It is the LBAs task to control U of its machine and compare it with U_i's from other machines. If the U_i differ extremely, orders have to be shifted to other machines.

5.2   Determining the Coalition Size

In this section the optimal number n_{opti} of involved machines is determined. Let n be the number of available machines, t_{rb} the rebuilding time for a machine, s the number of pieces the order consists of, and t_p the time a machine needs to produce a workpiece. The time $t_o(n)$, that n machines need to complete the order, is given by equation 2 with the degree of parallelism p[4] ($(0 \le p \le 1)$):

$$t_o(n) = (n - np + t) \cdot t_{rb} + \frac{s}{n - np + t} \cdot t_p \tag{2}$$

Equation 2 only holds, if each machine produces the same amount of workpieces $\frac{n}{s}$ and the resetting of machines is not done completely contemporaneously. The last assumption is often true, because machines even if they start producing an order at the same time, do not complete it isochronously, because of breakdowns or variances in the cycle time. The optimal value n_{opti} is obtained by deriving equation 2. This leads us to $n_{opti} = \sqrt{\frac{t_p \cdot s}{t_{rb} \cdot (1 - p^2)}} - \frac{p}{1 - p}$. Finally, there are $\max\{2, \lceil n_{opti} \rceil\}$ machines in a coalition. If the number of pieces is not equally split among the machines, n_{opti} increases. Sometimes it happens, that n_{opti} exceeds the number of available machines. In this case, the negotiation needs not to be carried out, because all machines participate in completing the order.

6   Summary

In this paper we focused on a very important subsystem of manufacturing systems. It is a Machine-Shuttle-Warehouse-Shuttle scenario (MSWS-System). A product is produced by a machine M, transported by one of a set of autonomous shuttles S in warehouse W and eventually transported to another machine by another set of shuttles S. This paper shows the architecture of

---

[4] p equals 1, when an order is done completely parallel and it is 0, when it is done one after another.

a MSWS-System, composed of various agents, all having a well defined functional scope. A load balancing mechanism guarantees, that the load is equally split among all machines even in exceptional cases. Equipping the machine and its operators with profiles, results in a higher degree of self-determination at the working place.
We simulated a MSWS-system with data of from a real tyre factory. First promising results are available, but must not be published at present time.

References

[1] M. Barbuceanu and M. S. Fox. The architecture of an agent based infrastructure for agile manufacturing. In *Proc. of the IJCAI-95 Workshop on Intelligent Manufacturing*, 1995.
[2] S. Bussmann, N. Jennings, and Wooldridge. On the identification of agents in the design of production control systems. *Agent-Oriented Software Engineering, LNCS 1957*, pages 141–162, 2001.
[3] S. Bussmann and K. Schild. Self-organizing manufacturing control: An industrial application of agent technology. In *Proc. of the Fourth International Conference on Multi-Agent Systems*, pages 87–94, Boston, 2000.
[4] Y. Chen, Y. Peng, T. Finin, Y. Labrou, S. Cost, B. Chu, R. Sun, and B. Wilhelm. A negotiation-based multi-agent system for supply chain management. In *Workshop on Agents for Electronic Commerce and Managing the Internet-Enabled Supply Chain, Seattle, Washington.*, May 1998.
[5] B. K. Choi and B. H. Kim. Human centred virtual manufacturing system for next generation manufacturing. Technical report, Korea Advanced Institute of Science and Technology, Department of Industrial Engineering, VMS Lab., 1999.
[6] T. C. K. Chou and J. A. Abraham. Load balancing in distributed systems. *IEEE Transactions on Software Engineering*, 8(4):401–412, July 1982.
[7] W. Kießling. Foundations of preferences in database systems. *Proceedings of the 28th VLDB Conference, Hong Kong, China*, 2002.
[8] T. Kis, J. Váncza, and A. Márkus. Controlling distributed manufacturing systems by a market mechanism. In *Proc. of the 12th Europ. Conf. on Artificial Manufacturing Systems*, 1996.
[9] W. Shen and D. H. Norrie. An agent-based approach for dynamic manufacturing scheduling. In *In Workshop Notes of the Agent-Based Manufacturing Workshop at Autonomous Agents*, Minneapolis, 1998.
[10] W. Shen and D. H. Norrie. Agent-based systems for intelligent manufacturing: A state-of-the-art survey. *Knowledge and Information System, an International Journal*, 1(2), 1999.
[11] J. M. Usher and Y.-C. Wang. Negotiation between intelligent agents for manufacturing control. In *Proc. of the EDA 2000 Conference*, Orlando, Florida, 2000.

Application of Intelligent Agents in Power Industry: Promises and Complex Issues

Eleni E. Mangina

University College Dublin (National University of Ireland)
Department of Computer Science
Belfield, Dublin 4, Ireland
eleni.mangina@ucd.ie
http://www.cs.ucd.ie/staff/emangina/default.htm

Abstract. Agent-based systems have emerged in engineering applications dealing with increased uncertainty and dynamic complex environments. This paper describes how goal oriented software components have been used for data classification of partial discharge (PD) signals produced from a Gas Insulated Substation (GIS) chamber, for PD defects' diagnosis, which required data collection, data processing, classification and finally information extraction. The intelligent decision support required knowing how information from the data set is produced, measured and interpreted, in order meaningful conclusions to be produced from the agents. The knowledge repositories given contained the acquired data, while agents could be used for data analysis, integration and understanding of knowledge. Different issues will be discussed that appeared during the design and development of the multi-agent system, aiming to be usable by other similar agent-based applications and promote the networks of knowledge, with agents producing information for the decision making of diagnosis tasks in engineering applications.

1   Introduction

Power system problems are complex and this paper considers how intelligent agents might be used as a key element to tackle them with cooperative information technology environments, which are becoming widespread in utilities world-wide [1,3]. The ammount of data and the complex processes behind fault diagnosis indicates the need for an automated solution that views the problem as an interaction of software entities, for effective use of the available data, while the final outcome can be derived from the combination of the partial solutions provided by the components of the multi-agent system. The complexity of such processes can be managed using the hierarchical form of structure of the new software engineering paradigm, which includes interrelated software components and promises to broaden and deepen the scope of DAI systems in engineering.

V. Mařík et al. (Eds): CEEMAS 2003, LNAI 2691, pp. 564-573, 2003.
© Springer-Verlag Berlin Heidelberg 2003

Within this paper, the integration of intelligent systems techniques through COMMAS architecture [7] for data interpretation in electrical plant monitoring is discussed. This abstract layered architecture was the result of decomposing fault diagnosis' general tasks, while identifying the interrelationships among the various problem-solving components, so that they could be grouped together with identifiable high-level relationships and finally generating the simplified general model.

Data interpretation is of significant importance to infer the state of equipment by converting the condition monitoring data into appropriate information. The multi-agent system presented in this paper for the classification of partial discharge signatures from GIS, is the result of the agent-oriented decompositions. These have partitioned the problem domain, while the abstraction and software components' organisational relationships provide a natural means of describing it. The main challenges found within the described case study in this paper, include the development of integrated knowledge-intensive computation processes and structures capable of classifying data, integrating it with knowledge, transforming knowledge and learning from experience; although applied only for a certain parameter of the GIS chamber, the PD signals. The association of different functionality within interacting goal-oriented agents was the essence of successful decision-making.

This initial research suggests that the new approach may have a significant role to play in future engineering applications because it does not require a revolution in existing software systems and views the solution of a complex problem as a set of components, with each one having its own thread of control [5].

Within this paper, section 2 presents the case study of PD signal defects diagnosis, where the analysis of recorded signals can be simplified and automated through the application of classification tools and the use of intelligent agents. It analyses the different agent roles within the multi-agent system, as they were captured and identified within the problem domain specification. Section 3, finally draws some conclusions.

2   Case Study: GIS Chamber's PD Signal Defects' Diagnosis

Electrical utilities need to use their equipment closer to their design limits and require extending their operating life through automatic condition monitoring systems. Data interpretation is of high importance to infer the state of the equipment and is achieved by converting the data into appropriate information. This case study describes the use of agent-based technology for classification of partial discharge signatures of Gas Insulated Substations. The objective of this work is to take the next step and promote a decentralised, object-oriented, agent-based approach for data interpretation by making use of different artificial intelligence techniques embedded within intelligent agents, software entities as described in [14].

Gas Insulated Substations (GIS) are used in many power transmissions networks for switching and as transformation units for the control and management of electrical power. A GIS substation might be very large and complex in its design, as it is made of many chambers connected together through supporting barriers, corners and circuit breakers. The GIS chamber is a large coaxial transmission line with a central part consisting of a high voltage busbar. The enclosure is earthed and contains the pressurised SF_6 gas. The chamber is approximately 300 millimetres in radius. The busbar diameter is about 100 millimetres. Due to the proximity of electrodes, stresses within the chamber are very high and failure might occur due to small defects. For detection purposes the GIS has been equipped with sensors affixed to the chambers.

In extra high voltage gas insulated equipment, PD occurs when a defect enhances the local electric field. If the limit of the insulation medium is exceeded, this can lead to flashover and then breakdown. Various types of defects, depending on the type of equipment, may cause partial discharge activity. In GIS, PD can be initiated by free metallic particles or by sharp protrusions located on the electrodes, for example. For cost reasons, it is a necessity to avoid breakdown. Various techniques can be used to detect impending failures and monitor the problems on-line [11].

Continuous monitoring systems based on the principle of detecting the UHF signals emitted by partial discharges (PD) in SF_6, originally developed at Strathclyde University [10], are now installed at many substations world-wide and the technique is established as the most sensitive available for avoiding breakdowns and outages at critical nodes of the power transmission network. Interpretation of the parameters is complex but essential to assess possible performance deficiencies. By measuring these parameters on-line, the data can be gathered in a form that is ideal for the application of an intelligent agent-based condition monitoring system, which will diagnose potential faults using different techniques. Interpretation of the detected signals can lead to the evaluation of the cause of the PD, which currently is achieved based on expertise, and this introduces the need to look for methods to automate the process.

There are various types of defects that can cause PD. Commonly found defects fall into six main categories: free particles, busbar protrusion, chamber protrusion, floating electrode, surface contamination on insulating barrier and cavities in insulating barrier. Not only do the standard defects need to be monitored, but also external sources that can be detected by the actual system like communications noise, radar signals and motor noise and any other external source whose signal can be detected.

The PD monitoring system displays the detected signal in three dimensions: the phase-cycles-amplitude display as shown in Figure 1. The phase axis divides the AC cycle into equal phase windows, the cycle axis indicates the cycle number of the AC wave and the third axis is the actual amplitude of detected PD pulses. Signal patterns vary with respect to the type of source that created the discharge. Through experience, typical patterns are easily recognisable.

The objectives of this work are to investigate several methods of partial discharge classification embedded within intelligent agents and study the feasibility of integrating them into an agent-based condition monitoring system. The goal is to extract the meaningful information from the database of the PD signals supplied by the PD monitoring system, to evaluate the cause of the PD. The resulting classification program derived from redundant analyses based on computational intelligence techniques and their combination guaranteed a high level of confidence in the outcome.

The problems associated with monitoring GIS for PD signal defect identification include:

- There are a number of different diagnostic techniques (PD-detectors, chemical, optical, acoustic, electrical), which have individual advantages and disadvantages depending on the type of defect, where one type of defect remained totally or almost undetected. With these conventional PD-detectors no reliable results could be gained [2].

- The specialists must interpret the detected signal's 3D-display. The number of experts is limited and it is infeasible to monitor the GIS on a 24-hour basis.

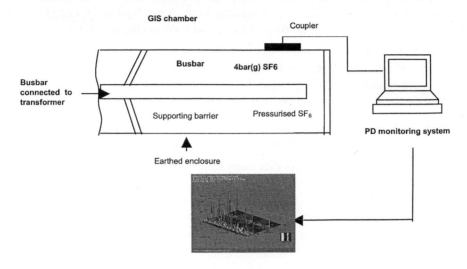

Fig. 1. GIS chamber and PD monitoring system producing 3D displays of PD signals

2.1   Why Use Agent-Oriented Approach for this Application?

Interpretation of the PD signals is complex but essential to assess possible performance deficiencies. The goal is to extract the meaningful information from the database of the PD signals supplied by the PD monitoring system, in order to evaluate the cause of the PD. This application required the tried and tested decision support tools to be integrated and extended with new functionality. The agent-oriented approach would allow the new autonomous computational entities to interact with the existing systems, while reasoning with different techniques. The parameters are measured on-line, and the data can be gathered in a form that is ideal for the application, enabling the use of several different problem-solving paradigms. The diverse range of activities that need to be performed mean there is no best problem-solving technique; for example Kohonen maps are required for classifying the data, whereas heuristic search is best for diagnosis. The experts' knowledge of interpreting the detected signal's 3D display for this case study could be captured and embedded within the multi-agent software system. In this domain a centralised decision support system would not be a viable option, as it would be too time consuming to maintain an up-to-date representation of the GIS chamber state to different type of users (engineers, researchers etc).

2.2   Multi-Agent System

Following the data preparation and the evaluation of different classification techniques, there could be identified cases where one individual method could not classify the type of defect accurately, or could identify only certain type of defect. Consequently, a number of software entities have been developed and form the hybrid solution for COMMAS-GIS (COndition Monitoring Multi Agent System for GIS) [7], the generic framework of which is given in Figure 2 and it covers the following activities:

- Receive the data
- Process the data available
- Detect the existence of a defect and determine the type of a defect
- Analyse the situation and inform the user

The different software agents, which interact in a dynamic way to support the required data interpretation functions include:

- *Kohonen-map agent*: classifies data using Kohonen maps [6]
- *Kmeans agent*: classifies data using Kmeans clustering algorithm [13]
- *C5.0_rule_induction agent*: classifies data using rule induction [13]
- Case Based Reasoning (CBR) agent: reasons based on past cases
- Meta-Knowledge Reasoning Agent (MKRA): final data interpretation
- *Engineering Assistant Agent (EAA)*: informs the user of the final result

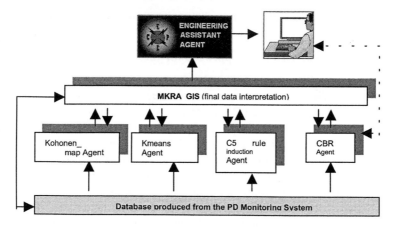

Fig. 2. COMMAS-GIS agents

2.3   Cooperative Diagnosis Based on Different Agents' Roles

The coupler within the GIS detects the signal, which is then sent to the diagnostic monitoring system. The "fingerprint" representation of the partial discharge record is based upon statistical analysis of the raw data. This reduces the amount of data to be stored, and picks out the salient features within the data. Within this application there were different cases in the database covering all distinct classes (types) of defect. The data provided to the software system are in the form of text files to be read and processed from the intelligent agents.

COMMAS-GIS could identify new cases based on the most appropriate classification technique by calling the different classification agents. The training of each algorithm has been implemented, and the accuracy of each method has been evaluated from the agents, which call the external programs responsible for testing. For each unidentified new case, the agents execute each method and the final result is the outcome of their combined interpretation (based on the "majority voting system") through the MKRA_GIS agent. Within each type of classification agents (Kohonen_map, K-means, C5.0_rule_induction) each clustering algorithm has been implemented to classify the data based on the classification role model as shown in Table 1. Although each classification agent is using a different method (by calling different external programs), they all belong to the same role model (as shown in Table 1), because the database has to be accessed and after training, the accuracy of ach algorithm to be calculated.

Table 1. Classification role model for COMMAS-GIS case study

Data Classification (Kohonen_map Agent, Kmeans Agent, C5.0_rule_induction Agent)	
Role Model: Classification	
Responsibilities:	Collaborators:
To read database (fingerprints)	-
To process information (application specific functions)	-
To inform another role	MKRA_GIS, EAA
External Interfaces:	
Read_Data, Training_Off_Line, Testing_On_Line Evaluate_Accuracy InformMKRA, InformEAA	
Prerequisites:	
Data to be provided in an appropriate format for the software.	

For the identification of each case the results are sent to the MKRA_GIS to be processed and the EAA informs the user of the procedure in detail. Figures 3, 4 and 5 show the general execution of each classification agent (Kohonen_map, K-means and C5.0 rule induction respectively). Each type of agent embodies the final vector of weights or rules from the training executed. The testing and the accuracy evaluation are accomplished on-line from each classification agent.

During discussions with the experts it was identified that there are certain characteristics of each type of defect that could be seen from the 3D display provided by the existing monitoring system. These allowed the expert to come up with a conclusion on which type of defect a case belonged to. For example, certain defects tend to appear at certain times, or phases.

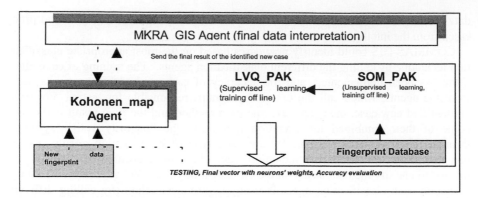

Fig. 3. Kohonen-map Agent

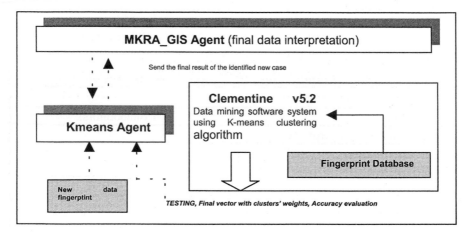

Fig. 4. Kmeans Agent

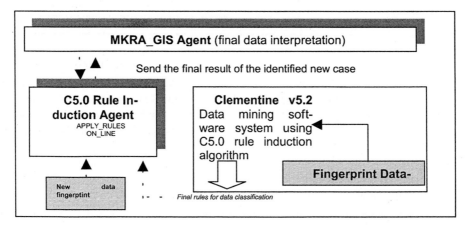

Fig. 5. C5.0 Rule Induction Agent

The expert would therefore look at parameters like time and phase dependency. Any symmetry that existed within the pattern on both the negative and positive cycle would provide information about the physical reality of the defect. To emulate the experts' reasoning, representative cases of each defect could be identified, which would then be provided to the user through the Case Based Reasoning (CBR) software agent within the COMMAS-GIS. Along with the fingerprints for each case, the 3D display from the raw data is stored to be used by the CBR agent, to display it to the user. This intelligent agent has been implemented using the case-based reasoning role model as shown in Table 2.

Table 2. CBR role model for COMMAS-GIS case study

Case-Based Reasoning (CBR_Agent) – ARA	
Role Model: Case-based reasoning	
Responsibilities:	Collaborators:
To read database (fingerprints)	-
To read the 3D display of each case (.gif files)	-
To process information (application specific functions)	-
To inform another role	MKRA_GIS, EAA
External Interfaces:	
Read_Data, Find_Most_Similar_Cases Retrieve_3D_Display_Of_Most_Similar_Cases Evaluate_Accuracy InformUser, Get_Feedback_from_User, ReEvaluate_Accuracy InformMKRA, InformEAA	
Prerequisites:	
Data to be provided in an appropriate format for the software.	

Based on the given images (as shown in Figure 6) the user will select which one is the most similar and will give feedback to the CBR agent along with the confidence factor representing the user's belief of the new case being of a certain type of defect. The result will be sent to the MKRA_GIS and the new case will be stored to the case memory of the agent and will be used for testing another new case in the future. The impact of the CBR agent to the overall multi-agent system is important, especially for cases where the software system cannot identify the class they belong to and there is the need for the experts' input. The feedback from the experts is then stored in the case memory as new cases and the knowledge can be reused and the accuracy of the system is increased over time.

3   Discussion

This paper has presented the analysis undertaken upon GIS PD monitoring data using clustering and classification techniques. The Kohonen maps could be used success-fully to classify most of the data classes by assigning a class identifier to each neuron in the map. The K-means clustering algorithm had a very good performance as it could accurately classify the input data according to which cluster the data is nearest. The C5.0 performance is comparable to that of the Kohonen map, where again certain classes could not be differentiated from the other classes and it provided rules, for future rule-based intelligent system implementation. For the decision combining, the majority voting was the first attempt, but there has been considered more advanced approaches for future development. The software system could be extended to monitor other parameters in association with other techniques. For example, different models of the GIS state could be specified, intelligent agents can be included to embed model based reasoning, or in case of optimisation problems to use genetic algorithms. Additionally, the development of CBR_Agent gave promising results for knowledge extraction from the experts and integrating the software system with learning abilities.

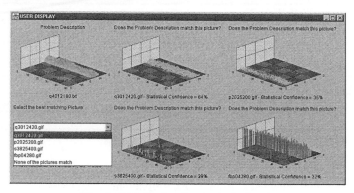

Fig. 6. CBR display for user's feedback

The agent-based approach offers a flexible architecture, which can be applied to any plant item. The distribution of the intelligence allows for scalability and ease of integration of new intelligent reasoning modules. It allows the reasoning to be performed across a number of processors at a number of locations. The main contribution of this research has been the industry-oriented application of agents with data mining scopes. The multi-agent software system has been designed and implemented using ZEUS agent building toolkit [9], in order to facilitate the communication and cooperation of the software components, which could process the data in different platforms through the network. Although the system has been implemented only for PD signal defect diagnosis, the same approach has been considered for practical use from industry for the evaluation of the plant health (GIS in this case), which would require monitoring more than one parameters.

The application described in this paper along with similar implemented in different domains [8], have proved several benefits. One of the key features of this system is that it can handle processing of different data types (raw data and 3D images) with different techniques. Based on this set-up, the final solution is the best suited to the given data. The implementation and standardization of such system for engineering applications in general remains a question. While different approaches have been proposed for different applications in power industry [4], clearly work will be required on developing a general implementation environment, due to the specific requirements of certain problem domains. In particular, identification of agents' role modelling, knowledge management, ontologies, communication between agents, identification of interdependent tasks, compatibility within existing software systems and presentation of information to users of different level of expertise are all issues to be considered in the future.

References

[1] Azevedo C. P., Feiju B., Costa M.: "Control centers evolve with agent technology", IEEE Computer Applications in Power, vol. 13, no 3 (2000) 48-53

[2] Boeck W.: "Sensitivity verification for partial discharge detection systems for GIS with the UHF method and the acoustic method", Task Force 15/33.03.05 on behalf of Study Committee 33, CIGRE (Paris), 1998

[3] Bussmann S., Jennings N. R., Wooldridge M. J.: "On the identification of agents in the design of production control systems" in Agent-Oriented Software Engineering (eds. P. Ciancarini and M. Wooldridge) Springer Verlag (2001) 141-162

[4] Corera J.M., Laresgoiti I., Jennings N.R.: "Using ARCHON, Part 2: Electricity transportation management", IEEE Expert, vol. 11, no. 6 (1996) 71-79

[5] Jennings N. R., Bussmann S.: "Agent-based control systems", IEEE Control Systems Magazine. (2003 to appear)

[6] Kohonen T. and Simula O.: "Engineering Applications of the Self-Organising map", Proceedings of the IEEE, Vol. 84, No 10, October 1996, (1996) 1358-1383

[7] Mangina E. E., McArthur S.D.J, McDonald J. R.: "COMMAS (COndition Monitoring Multi-Agent System)", Journal of Autonomous Agents and Multi-Agent Systems, Vol. 4, No 3, September (2001) 277-280

[8] Mangina E. E., McArthur S.D.J, McDonald J. R., Moyes A.: "A Multi Agent System for Monitoring Industrial Gas Turbine Start-up Sequences", IEEE Transactions in Power Systems, Vol. 16, Issue 3, August (2001) 396-401

[9] Nwana S. H., Ndumu D., Lee L., Collis J., ZEUS: A tool-kit for building Distributed Multi-Agent Systems, in Applied Artificial Intelligence Journal, Vol. 13 (1), pg. 129-186 (1999)

[10] Pearson J. S., Hampton B. F. and Sellars A. G., " A continuous UHF monitor for gas-insulated substations", IEEE Trans. Electrical Insulation, Vol. 26, No 3, (1991) 469-478

[11] Pearson J. S., Farish O., Hampton B. F., Judd M. D., Templeton D., Pryor B. M., Welch I. M.: "Partial discharge diagnostics for gas insulated substations", IEEE Trans. Dielectrics and Electrical Insulation, Vol. 2, No 5 (1995) 893-905

[12] Quinlan J.R., C4.5 programs for machine learning, Morgan Kaufman, (1993)

[13] Tarassenko L.: A guide to neural computing applications, Neural Computing Applications Forum, John Wiley & Sons Inc., (1998)

[14] Wooldridge M., Jennings N.R.: "Intelligent Agents: theory and practice", The knowledge Engineering Review, vol. 10, no 2 (1995), 115-152

Brokering in Electronic Insurance Markets

Luís Nogueira[1] and Eugénio Oliveira[2]

[1] Instituto Superior de Engenharia do Porto
Instituto Politécnico do Porto
luis@dei.isep.ipp.pt
[2] Faculdade de Engenharia
Universidade do Porto, LIACC
eco@fe.up.pt

Abstract. Almost all insurers now have a web site providing information on the company, its products and contact details, but the scope of insurance activities potentially affected by e-commerce is much broader than that, giving rise to a host of interesting issues. Also, customers buying over the Internet look for added value. This paper proposes a distributed multi-agent system for e-insurance brokering where customers are grouped together, exploiting user modelling and machine learning techniques, as an approach to better match customers and insurance product offers. Particular attention is paid to the interpretation of the generated communities. For this purpose, we use a metric to identify the representative insurance product configuration of each community. To improve broker's evaluation of received insurers' bids we propose the automatic construction of the customer's profile, reflecting its preferences on all the attributes of an insurance product.

1 Introduction

A recent comparative study [6], from Consumer Federation of America, of 25 web-based Internet sites offering comparative term life insurance information make evident that not all sites are useful for getting quotes. Some of them are too difficult to use and others are little more than referral services where the customer is put in touch with a human agent, something that customers, most of the time, do not need the Internet to achieve. Several of the existing quote services do not include no commission insurance companies, because many of these sites make money through commissions on sales and do not show these companies in their service since, it would reduce their incomes [6].

Most web sites offering online quotation and purchase of insurance products are implemented by insurers and sell directly to the customer, excluding the broker. Brokers, however, provide a valuable service and are widely used by both customers and insurers in traditional insurance. Yet, online brokerage is rare.

On the other hand, those sites which do offer a brokerage service, do so by drastically simplifying the problem: they standardise the products which insurers are permitted to offer through their sites. Broker's role is then reduced to

V. Mařík et al. (Eds): CEEMAS 2003, LNAI 2691, pp. 574–583, 2003.

collecting and presenting a standard set of information. This gives no advantage to any of the players, since customers are provided with a more limited choice of products, which may not meet all their requirements, insurers have limited flexibility in product design, targeting and pricing, and brokers lose their traditional role.

The system BIAS (Brokerage for Insurance - an Agent-based System) described in this paper presents a new approach to insurance products brokering and has the potential to improve the quality of customer service by ensuring that individual customer needs are reflected in the products offered.

2   Electronic Insurance Brokerage

Our model for the insurance brokering activities divides the interaction process aiming at solving the problem into the phases represented in figure 1. In the core of the provided brokering facility, we are using conceptual clustering procedures as an approach to better match customers' requirements and insurance product offers, providing a valuable add-on to both customers' and insurers' sides. Our insurance brokering system is then using COBWEB as a tool for grouping potential customers in meaningful classes we call *communities*. The question is whether there is any meaning in the generated communities, that is, if they associate users with a limited set of common interests. For this reason we use a metric to decide which preferences are most representative for each community. We try to construct a prototypical model, that we call *stereotype*, for each community, which is representative of its users and significantly different from other communities of users. This approach allows the insurance company to target product configurations at specific market segments, and avoids the need to ask all customers the same typically large number of product specific questions.

In phase 1, the user sends, trough its Customer Agent (CA), his personal characteristics and needs. The Broker Agent (BA), in phase 2, replies with the stereotype of the customer's community, indicating the representative preferences of its users. Based on this received stereotype the user defines the allowed range for the insurance product attributes' values. This definition includes attaching a degree of importance (weight value) for each one of the product's attributes (in a range from *low* to *high*) and the increasing order of preference for the attributes' values. The CA sends this request to the BA (phase 3).

In phase 4, the BA sends an announcement to each Insurer Agent (IA), starting a negotiation process. This negotiation process comprises several rounds, starting when the broker sends and announcement for all the insurer agents in the market. We have adapted the Q-Negotiation algorithm [13][12] to the insurance brokering problem. This algorithm uses a reinforcement learning strategy based in Q-learning for the formulation of new proposals.

Each IA replies with bids to BA, which are then evaluated according to customer's preferences, extracting relevant features from these bids (phase 5). These bids, plus relevant information, is sent to CA (phase 6). CA offers the

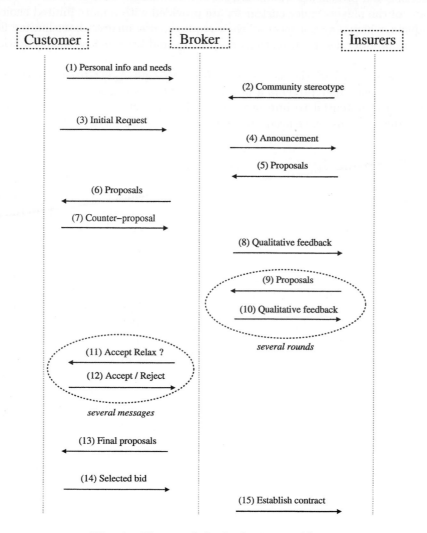

Fig. 1. Phases of the brokering problem

customer a flexible navigation tool that allows the exploration of the received proposals.

The customer has now the opportunity to define a counter-proposal and select the insurers he wishes to continue to negotiate with (phase 7). The broker helps insurers' agents on their task of formulating new proposals by giving them some hints about the direction they should follow in their negotiation space (phase 8). The response to proposed insurance configurations is formulated by the broker as a qualitative feedback, which reflects the distance between the values indicated in a specific proposal and the best one received so far, which can be classified in one of three categories: *sufficient, bad* or *very_bad.*

Insurer agents will use this feedback information to its past proposals, in order to formulate, in the next rounds, new proposals trying to approach the customer's preferences. At each negotiation round bids are evaluated and the one with the greatest evaluation value is considered the winner (phase 9 and 10).

When this negotiation process ends, BA starts a new interaction with CA. This interaction will ultimately direct the system to a suitable solution through a constraint satisfaction process (phase 11 and 12). This conversation takes the form of a sequence of questions whose aim is to reduce alternatives rather than simply sort them. This dialogue is detailed in [8].

If this conversation has produced a valid number of alternatives, BA initiates phase 13 by ranking selected proposals according to the user utility function results, and send them plus relevant information to CA. The user either rejects or agrees with one of the received proposals (phase 14).

If the user has selected one of the proposed insurance products, BA starts phase 15, establishing a contract with the winning IA.

3   Automatic Construction of Customer Communities

Like [9] we are interested in the identification of different user communities in a population, and not only in acquiring models of individual users interacting with a system, e.g. [1][2][11].

Customer communities can be automatically constructed using an unsupervised learning method. The branch of symbolic machine learning that deals with this kind of unsupervised learning is called *conceptual clustering* and a popular representative of this approach is the COBWEB algorithm [3]. A conceptual clustering algorithm accepts a set of object descriptions (in our case, customer data) and produces a classification scheme over the observations. These algorithms do not require a teacher (i.e., they are unsupervised) but they use an evaluation function to discover classes with "good" conceptual descriptions. A learning of this kind is referred to as learning from observation as opposed to learning from examples.

COBWEB is an incremental conceptual clustering algorithm that represents concepts probabilistically. The term *incremental* means that objects are incorporated into the concept structure as they are observed. An object is a vector of feature-value pairs. In our system, objects are user's characteristics. COBWEB is designed to produce a hierarchical classification scheme. It carries out a hill-climbing search through a space of schemes, and this search is guided by an heuristic measure called *category utility* [5].

The category utility of a partition is measured by the following equation:

$$CU = \frac{\sum_k \left(P(C_k) \left[\sum_i \sum_j P(A_i = V_{ij}|C_k)^2 - \sum \sum P(A_i = V_{ij})^2 \right] \right)}{k} \ . \tag{1}$$

Table 1. Population of observed customers

	Marital status	Children
U_1	single	no
U_2	married	no
U_3	married	yes
U_4	married	yes

where k is the number of categories or classes, C_k is a particular class, A_i refers to one of the I attributes and V_{ij} is one of the J values for attribute A_i.

COBWEB incorporates objects into the concept hierarchy using four clustering operators: placing the object in an existing cluster, creating a new cluster, combining two clusters into a new one (merging) and dividing a cluster (splitting). Given a new object, the algorithm applies each of the previous operators and selects the hierarchy that maximises category utility. Generated clusters represent customers communities.

Our insurance brokering system is then using COBWEB as a tool for grouping customers in meaningful classes (groups with similar characteristics) we call communities.

3.1   Example

The next example illustrates how the broker automatically constructs customers communities, using the population represented in table 1.

After observing the first three users, the broker has constructed community C_1, as represented in figure 2. Although there is differences in the attributes' values that describe each observed customer, there isn't, at this time, any distinguishable concepts associated with this three users.

However, adding customer U_4 to the existing hierarchy leads to the creation of community C_2, specialising the concepts associated with customers U_3 and U_4, as represented in figure 3. In this way, the broker, incrementally and automatically, constructs customers communities, grouping customers with similar characteristics.

4   Extracting Stereotypes

The clusters generated by COBWEB, should represent well-defined customer communities. But, besides the customer data used for incrementally build up customers communities, a customer is characterised by its own preferences and by the insurance configuration chosen in the negotiation process. In order to help customers defining their needs, the broker must associate a "typical" insurance configuration to each constructed community. Thus, the natural way to define meaningful stereotypes associated to the existing customers communities is by trying to identify patterns that are representative of the participating users'

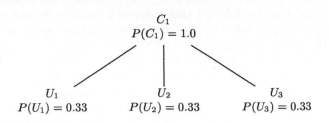

Fig. 2. Customers communities, after adding U_3

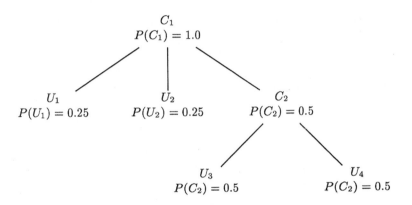

Fig. 3. Customers communities, after adding U_4

preferences. We try to construct a prototypical model for each community, which is representative of its users and significantly different from other communities of users.

Our system is using a metric to measure the increase in the frequency of a specific preference or negotiation result within a given community, as compared to the default frequency in the whole number of available observations [10]. In [9] and [4] the increase in frequency was used as an indication of the increase in the predictability of a feature (a given preference, for example) within the community. Given a component c (a user preference), with the default frequency f_c, if the frequency of this component within a community i is f_i, the frequency increase is defined as a simple difference of the squares of the two frequencies:

$$FI_c = f_i^2 - f_c^2 .$$

(2)

When FI_c is negative there is a decrease in frequency and the corresponding component is not representative of the community. A community's representative characteristic is found through $FI_c > \alpha$, where α is pre-established as the required threshold for considering that frequency increase enough relevant.

The quality of the generated descriptions for each community increases as we go down in the hierarchy constructed by COBWEB. Communities in lower levels are more concise and the extracted model has greater significance. Experiments, reported in [7], shows us that the insurance attributes chosen by either too few or too many users do not appear in the constructed community stereotype. In the former case the algorithm ignores them during learning and in the latter case, they correspond to such general interests, that they cannot be attributed to particular communities. Filtering out these two types of preferences is a positive feature of the used metric [10], greatly improving the quality of the generated stereotypes.

5   Implicit Learning of a Customer Profile

The customer approaches the broker with a requirement: he wish to buy an insurance policy to cover certain risks. This requirement will usually be incomplete and uncertain, and the customer will not be aware of all the options available. As such, if the broker's evaluation of the received proposals were only based on the attributes that the customer is able to specify the result might be very poor. We propose the construction of a user profile, induced from the set of selected proposals for the next negotiation rounds. This profile reflects the customer's preferences on all the attributes of an insurance product. The training set consists of the proposals that the user found interesting.

The task of constructing the customer profile involves judging whether an attribute of an insurance product is relevant or irrelevant for the user. It would be very frustrating and time consuming for a user to interact with an agent that starts with no knowledge but must obtain a set of positive and negative examples from user feedback. To reduce user evaluation burden, BIAS considers only examples that are interesting for the user (only positive examples).

Formally, a proposal is described as a vector $P = (atr_1, atr_2, \ldots, atr_n)$ of n attributes. The attributes can have binary, nominal or numerical values and are derived from the system ontology. The task of the learning method is to select the desired insurance configuration, based on a training set of m input vectors, that is, the selected proposals for the next negotiation rounds.

The construction of the customer profile is based on the correlation between the content of the selected proposals and the user's preferences as opposed to methods based on the correlation between customers with similar preferences. These preferences can be determined by using either explicit or implicit feedback. Explicit feedback requires the user to evaluate received proposals on a scale. In implicit feedback the user's preferences are inferred by observing user's actions, which is more convenient for the user. That's why we have adopted it in BIAS, despite the greater complexity in implementation.

In BIAS, insurer's proposals are represented as an n-dimensional vector, where each dimension corresponds to a distinct attribute and n is the total number of possible attributes. It's possible to extract a vector V_i from each proposal, $V_i = [x_1 : Fp_1, x_2 : Fp_2, \ldots, x_n : Fp_n]$, where Fp_i indicates how frequently an attribute-value pair x_i appears in a particular proposal. If the proposal does not contain x_i then Fp_i is set to zero.

Customer profiles can be represented just like documents by one or more vectors. The profile is represented as an n-dimensional vector, where n is the total number of possible attributes for an insurance product. Each dimension is represented by m vectors, where m is the total number of possible values for that attribute. In this approach a weight w_i is assigned to each value, based on how often the attribute-value pair appears in a particular proposal, Fp_i, and how frequently is occurs in the selected set of proposals, Fs_i.

$$Fs_i = \sum_{j=0}^{n} Fp_{ij} \ . \tag{3}$$

$$w_i = Fp_i * \frac{Fs_i}{n} \ . \tag{4}$$

We propose the algorithm 1 for the construction of the customer profile. The assumption behind this algorithm is that the more times a value appears in the selected set of proposals, the more relevant it is for the user.

Algorithm 1 Customer profile construction

---

  for each selected proposal **do**
    extract the vector V_i for this proposal
    combine V_i and the constructed profile V_{prof} in V_k, updating w_i
    sort the weights in the new vector V_k in decreasing order and keep the highest elements
  end for

This algorithm runs whenever a user selects a proposal for the next negotiation rounds. Thus, the customer profile is incrementally and continuously updated.

6 Conclusions

This paper proposes a distributed multi-agent system where customers are grouped together, exploiting user modelling and machine learning techniques. Changes in electronic insurance commerce, introduced in BIAS, are of benefit of both customers and insurers. By increasing the degree and the sophistication of the automation process, commerce becomes much more dynamic, personalised and context sensitive. From the customers' perspective, it is desirable to have software that could search all the available offers to find the most suitable one and then go forward through the process of actually purchasing the product.

From the insurer's perspective it is desirable to have software that could vary its own offering depending on the customer it is dealing with, on what its competitors are doing and on the current state of its own business.

The BIAS system, with its intimate knowledge of who the user is and what he wants, can shorten the time needed for finding an appropriate insurance product. Insurers can then use information automatically collected during negotiation to develop a more customer-directed kind of marketing strategy. Information about the customer can be used to find out what he is interested in and, therefore, a more personalised product could be offered.

Different communities of users can be identified and used to improve the exploitation of an insurance brokering service. The construction of those communities is achieved using an unsupervised learning technique. We also use a specific metric to decide which are the representative preferences of a user's community.

We propose the construction of a user profile, induced from the set of selected proposals for the next negotiation rounds. This profile reflects the customer's preferences on all the attributes of an insurance product.

We have also adapted an advanced negotiation protocol, suitable for multi-issue negotiation in electronic commerce activity. A learning capability was also included enabling agents to become more effective in a dynamic market by learning with past experience through the qualitative feedback received from their opponents.

References

[1] Marko Balabanovic and Yoav Shoham. Learning information retrieval agents: Experiments with automated web browsing. In *Proceedings of the AAAI Spring Symposium on Information Gathering from Heterogeneous, Distributed Resources*, pages 13–18, 1995.

[2] P. Chiu. Using c4.5 as an induction engine for agent modelling: An experiment for optimisation. In *Proceedings of the User Modelling Conference UM'97*, 1997.

[3] D. H. Fisher. Knowledge acquisition via incremental conceptual clustering. *Machine Learning*, 2:139–172, 1987.

[4] J.B. Weinberg G. Biswas and D. Fisher. Iterate: A conceptual clustering algorithm for data mining. *IEEE Transactions on Systems, Man and Cybernetics*, 28:100–111, 1998.

[5] M.A. Gluck and J.E. Corter. Information, uncertainty and the utility of categories. In *Proceedings of the 7th Conference of the Cognitive Science Society*, pages 283–287, 1985.

[6] J. Robert Hunter and James H. Hunt. *Term Life Insurance on the Internet: An Evaluation on On-line Quotes*. Consumer Federation of America, 2001.

[7] Lus Nogueira. Sistema multi-agente para mediao electrnica de seguros. Technical report, LIACC, University of Porto, December 2002.

[8] Lus Nogueira and Eugnio Oliveira. A multi-agent system for e-insurance brokering. In R. Kowalczyk, J. Mller, H. Tianfield, and R. Unland, editors, *Agent Technologies, Infrastructures, Tools, and Applications for e-Services*, volume 2592 of *Lecture Notes in Artificial Intelligence*, pages 263–282. Springer-Verlag, 2003.

[9] G. Paliouras, V. Karkaletsis, C. Papatheodorou, and C. Spyropoulos. Exploiting learning techniques for the acquisition of user stereotypes and communities. In *Proceedings of the International Conference on User Modelling (UM '99).*, 1999.

[10] G. Paliouras, C. Papatheodorou, V. Kakaletsis, C. Spryropoulos, and V. Malaveta. Learning user communities for improving the services of information providers. *Lecture Notes in Computer Science*, 1513:367–384, 1998.

[11] B. Raskutti and A. Beitz. Acquiring user preferences for information filtering in interactive multimedia services. In *Proceedings of the Pacific Rim International Conference on Artificial Intelligence*, pages 47–58, 1996.

[12] Ana Paula Rocha and Eugénio Oliveira. Adaptive multi-issue negotiation protocol for electronic commerce. In *Proceedings of The Fifth International Conference on The Practical Application of Intelligent Agents and Multi-Agent Technology (PAAM 2000),*, Manchester, UK, April 2000.

[13] Ana Paula Rocha and Eugénio Oliveira. Agents advanced features for negotiation in electronic commerce and virtual organisations formation process. *Lecture Notes in Computer Science*, 1991:77–96, 2001.

Modelling Electronic Organizations

Javier Vázquez-Salceda[1] and Frank Dignum[2]

[1] Departament de Llenguatges i Sistemes Informàtics
Universitat Politècnica de Catalunya
c/ Jordi Girona 1-3. E08034 Barcelona, Spain.
jvazquez@lsi.upc.es
[2] Institute of Information and Computing Sciences
Utrecht University
P.O.Box 80.089, 3508 TB Utrecht, The Netherlands
dignum@cs.uu.nl

Abstract. Institutions are established to regulate the interactions between parties that are performing some (business) transaction. One of the main roles of institutions is to inspire trust into the parties that perform the transaction.[1] The main focus of this paper is how an electronic organization[2] should be specified on the basis of the abstract patterns given by the institution on which the organization is formed, i.e., how can we define a (formal) relation between the (abstract) norms specified in the institutional regulations and the concrete rules and procedures of the organization such that the agents will operate within the organization according to the institutional norms or can be punished when they are violating the norms.

1 Introduction

When designing electronic organizations, the abstract regulations that are captured in the institution on which the organization is based have to be translated into implementable components. However, current approaches on *Normative Systems* in the agent community either work at a low level (policies and procedures) or at a very high level, formally specifying norms in, e.g., deontic logic. The low level approaches allow an easy implementation, but the problem arises when the correctness of the procedures and policies should be checked against the original regulations. High level approaches are closer to the way regulations are made, so verification is easier to be done. However, high level approaches usually use one or several computationally hard logics like deontic logic ([8, 11]). Although it is possible to capture the norms in this way and even give them a certain kind of semantics to reason about the consequences of the norms, this kind of formalization does not yet indicate how the norm should be interpreted within

---

[1] See [2] for more details on the roles of institutions.

[2] In our view, *institutions* consist only of the abstract patterns that regulate the interaction between the parties of a concrete *organization*, which is built as an instance that follows the institutional patterns.

V. Mařík et al. (Eds): CEEMAS 2003, LNAI 2691, pp. 584–593, 2003.

a certain organization. For instance, we can formalize a norm like *"it is forbidden to discriminate on the basis of age"* (when determining the best possible recipient for an organ) in deontic logic as $F(discriminate(x,y,age))$ (stating that it is forbidden to discriminate between x and y on the basis of age). However, the semantics of this formula will get down to something like that the action `discriminate(x,y,age)` should not occur. It is very unlikely that the agents operating within the organization will explicitly have such an action available. We claim that the level on which the norms are specified is more abstract and/or general than the level on which the processes and structure of the organization are specified. Therefore we need to *translate* the norms specifically to a level where their impact on the organization can be described directly.

In this paper we introduce HARMON*IA*, a framework that defines a multi-level structure, from the most abstract level of the normative system to the final implementation of the organization. It is composed of four levels of abstraction:

- the **Abstract Level**: where the statutes of the organization are defined in a high level of abstraction along with the first abstract norms.
- the **Concrete Level**: where abstract norms are iteratively concretized into more concrete norms, and the policies of the organization are also defined.
- the **Rule Level**: where concrete norms and policies are fully refined, linking the norms with the ways to ensure them.
- the **Procedure Level**: where all rules and policies are translated in a computationally efficient implementation easy to be used by agents.

The division of the system into these four levels aims to ease the transition from the very abstract statutes, norms and regulations to the very concrete protocols and procedures implemented in the system, filling the gap between theoretical (abstract) approaches and practical (concrete) ones.

In the remainder of this paper we will describe each of the four levels and their relationships in the next four sections. Then in section 6 we describe the role of policies, goals, role hierarchies and ontologies in the definition of e-organizations. We finish the paper with some conclusions and areas of further research.

2   The Abstract Level: Statutes, Objectives, Values and Abstract Norms

The *statutes* are the most abstract specification of the of the organization, as they indicate the main *objective* of the organization, the *values* that direct the fulfilling of this objective and they also point to the *context* where the organization will have to perform its activities. For example, the statutes of the National Organization for Transplants (ONT) [9] in Spain state the following:

> *The principal objective of the ONT is the promotion of donation and the consequent increase of organs available for transplantation, from which all its other functions result. The ONT acts as a service agency for the*

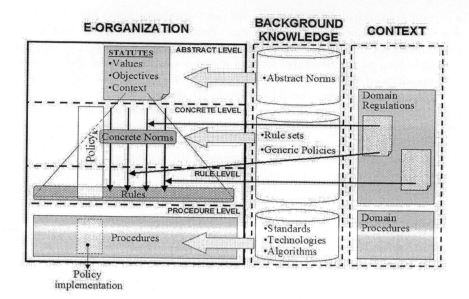

Fig. 1. The HARMON*IA* framework

*National Health System, works for the continuing increase in the avail-
ability of organs and tissues for transplantation and guarantees the most
appropriate and correct distribution, in accordance with the degree of
technical knowledge and ethical principles of equity which should prevail
in the transplant activity.*

In that statement we can find:

1. The *objectives*: the main objective is to increase the number of organs available for transplants. Another objective is to properly allocate organs.
2. The *context*: ONT states that it operates inside the Spanish National Health
   System, and such statement clearly defines the context of the organization.
3. The *values*: The latter part indicates the values according to which the
   ONT operates, e.g., to guarantee the most *appropriate, correct* and *equal*
   distribution among potential recipients. Where *appropriate, correct* and *equal*
   are vague terms defined by both technical (medical) and ethical standards.
   Implicitly it also says that ethical values are part of the organization.

At this highest level of abstraction, the *values* fulfill the role of norms in the
sense that they determine the concepts that are used to determine the value
or utility of situations. However, they do not tell us explicitly how we should
behave appropriately in any given social situation. This is the part played by
abstract norms, concrete norms (see section 3) and rules (see section 4).

In our framework the meaning of the values is defined by the norms that
contribute to this value. In an intuitive way we can see this translation process
as follows:

$$\vdash_{org} D(\varphi) \longrightarrow O_{org}(\varphi)$$

meaning that, if an organization *org* values situations where φ holds higher than situation where φ does not hold, then such value can be translated in terms of a norm (an obligation of the organization *org*) to fulfill φ. In our framework a norm *contributes to a value* if fulfilling the norm always leads to states in which the value is more fully accomplished than the states where the norm is not fulfilled. So, each value has attached to it a list of one or several norms that contribute to that value. The total list of norms (the ones in the abstract level plus the ones in the concrete level) together *defines* the meaning of the value in the context of the organization.

$$\vdash_{ONT} D(appropriate(distribution)) \longleftrightarrow$$
$$\{O_{ONT}(\text{"ensure an appropriate distribution"})\}$$

The *objectives* of the organization can be represented as the goal of an organization. As far as the organization has control over the actions of the agents acting within that organization, it will try to ensure that they perform actions that will lead to the overall goal of the society. See section 6 for more details.

Although the most abstract level of normative behavior in the statutes is determined by the values, we also include the abstract norms related to these values in this level. We define *ANorms* (the language for abstract norms) to be a deontic logic that is temporal, relativized and conditional, i.e., an obligation to perform an action or reach a state can be conditional on some state of affairs to hold, it is also meant for a certain type (or role) of agents and should be fulfilled before a certain point in time. For instance, the following norm might hold: *"The donor should consent to the transplantation before the transplantation can take place"*, which can be formalized as:

$$O_{hospital}(consent(donor) < do(transplant(hospital,donor,recipient,organ)))$$

The obligation is directed towards a hospital, assuming that the hospital is responsible for fulfilling it. I.e. it is the responsibility of the hospital to acquire the consent of the donor before (indicated by the "$<$") the transplantation is performed. In some sense this obligation has an implicit conditional. It only comes into effect if the hospital intends to perform a transplantation.

3 The Concrete Level: From Abstract Norms to Concrete Norms

In order to check norms and act on possible violations of the norms by the agents within an organization, the abstract norms have to be translated into actions and concepts that can be handled within such organization. Concrete norms pertain to actions that are described in terms of the ontology of the organization and from which therefore the meaning and effect is known or they pertain to situations that can be checked directly by the institute. The norms at this level are described in $CNorms$ (the language for concrete norms), which we assume for the moment to be equal to $ANorms$, but which might use different predicates. In addition we define a function $\mathbf{I}$: $ANorms \rightarrow CNorms$ which is a mapping from the abstract norms to the concrete ones. For each abstract norm $\mathbf{I}$ indicates how it can be fulfilled by fulfilling concrete norms within the context of this organization. This function is based on the counts-as operator as developed in [5].

There are several ways in which norms can be *abstract* and thus several ways to make them more concrete:

Abstract Actions: Norms often refer to an abstract action that can be implemented in many ways. For example: *"a living donor should consent to the donation of an organ"*. The translation in this case is a kind of definition of the abstract action in terms of the concrete actions. In the above case one could define this as follows:

$$sign(donor, contract) \cup carry(donor, codicil) \cup tell(donor, family) \Rightarrow_{ONT} Consent(donor)$$

i.e., *"to consent"* is performing either of the three more specific actions. Important to note is that this definition closes the way consent can be given.

Vague Terms: Norms use terms that are vague (have no precise meaning) and that have to be defined separately. E.g. *"the ONT should provide for an appropriate distribution"*. The term *"appropriate"* is so vague that there is a need to refine it in terms that are easier to check and/or implement:

$$O_{ONT}(ensure\_quality(organ)) \wedge O_{ONT}(ensure\_compatibility(organ, recipient))$$
$$\Rightarrow_{ONT} O_{ONT}(appropriate(distribution))$$

In this case the appropriateness has been refined, using the "counts-as" operator, in terms of two procedures: 1) to check that the organ has the minimum quality required to be transplanted, and 2) to ensure that the organ and the recipient are compatible[3]. See [5] for more about the "counts-as" operator.

Temporal Abstractness: Often there is an implicit deadline for obligations, which is implied by the fact that the fulfillment of an obligation is also the fulfillment of a condition for a permission. Returning to the appropriateness example, there is a missing temporal relation: the obligation of ensuring the quality and compatibility of the organ is limited by the temporal constraints of the assignation process (organs can only be preserved out of a human body for some hours), as the quality and compatibility tests should be performed before the assignation is made. We can then extend the formula as follows:

$$O_{ONT}(ensure\_quality(organ) < do(assign(organ, recipient))) \wedge$$

$$O_{ONT}(ensure\_compatibility(organ, recipient) < do(assign(organ, recipient)))$$

---

[3] As we will see in section 7, this refinement is imposed by the context of the ONT.

Agent and Role Abstraction: Norms abstract from the role or agent for whom the norm holds. The process to refine responsibilities is done as roles are refined in the *role hierarchy* (see section 6).

Actions or Situations not Directly Checkable: For instance, *"the decision of who is the best recipient for an organ cannot be based on the recipient's age"*. Although the norm is clear, it is impossible to check directly on which basis a decision is taken by an agent. This is an internal (mental) action. Therefore the organization has to devise some constraints and/or procedures that are checkable (or controllable) by the organization and which take care of the fulfillment of the norm. For example, the e-organization might withhold all information about age to the decision makers.

4   The Rule Level: Translating Norms into Rules

The translation from norms to rules marks the border among the *Normative System* in HARMON*IA* to the *Practical System*, from the normative dimension to the descriptive one. Such translation also implies a change in the language, from a deontic logic to a language more suitable to express actions and time constraints.

In [7], Meyer proposed a reduction from deontic logic to a Propositional Dynamic Logic. In this approach, deontic formulæ such as $O(\alpha)$, $F(\alpha)$ and $P(\alpha)$ are reduced to dynamic logic as follows:

$$O(\alpha) \equiv [\neg\alpha]\,V$$

Informally, it expresses that α is obligatory iff not doing α leads to a violation. An example of this kind of translation in the organ and tissue allocation problem is the following:

$$O_{hospital}(ensure\_quality(organ)) \equiv [\neg ensure\_quality(organ)]\,V(hospital)$$

Following this idea, norms can be translated for some part into restrictions on behavior and for the other part into triggers on unwanted behavior of the agents interacting in the e-organization. The main idea is that an e-organization cannot actually force agents to do an action (i.e. to pay for a good, as this is the autonomous decision of the agent), but it can control the fact that the agent cannot leave before the action is done.

Once the translation from norms to basic rules has been performed, these rules can be refined again. E.g. *ensure_compatibility(organ, recipient))* is defined in terms of donor-recipient compatibility rules[4]:

```
1- (age_donor >= 60) AND (age_donor < 74) AND (creatinine_clearance > 55 ml/min)
      -> (age_recipient >= 60) AND (transplant_type SINGLE-KIDNEY)

2- (age_donor >= 60) AND (age_donor < 74) AND (glomerulosclerosis <= 15%)
      -> (age_recipient >= 60) AND (transplant_type SINGLE-KIDNEY)
```

---

[4] These rules for the case of kidneys are a subset of the ones presented in [10].

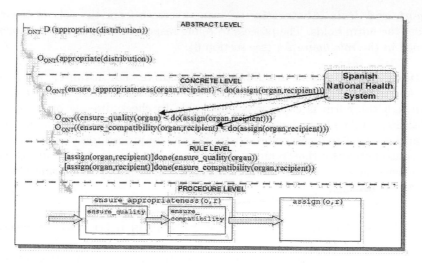

Fig. 2. An example of the refinement process, including the influence of context

5 The Procedure Level

The final step to build the e-organization is to implement the multi-agent system. There are two main approaches to implement the rules in the rule level:

- Creating a rule interpreter that any agent entering the e-organization will incorporate.
- Translating the rules into procedures to be easily followed by the agents.

Note that in both cases it is not ensured that the agents will follow those descriptions. The violations in the rule level should also be translated in some detection mechanisms to check the behaviour of the agents.

A system where all external agents blindly follow the protocols (as in IS-LANDER [4]) is quite efficient from a computational perspective but the agents have only the autonomy to accept/reject the protocol. A system where all external agents have to interpret rules could cope with these problems. However, such a system could not be applied to open environments, as there is a big assumption on the internal architecture of the agents and their way of reasoning.

The alternative is to be able to accept both kinds of agents. That means that the e-organization provides both the low-level protocols and the related rules. Those (standard) *Autonomous Agents* that are only able to follow protocols (expressed, for instance, in DAML+OIL), will blindly follow them, while the ones that can also interpret the rules (that is, the *Norm Autonomous Agents* or *Deliberative Normative Agents* [1][3]) will be able to choose among following the protocol or reasoning about the rules, or do both. With this approach the autonomy of the agents entering the e-organization is adapted to their reasoning capabilities.

In order to allow *Norm Autonomous Agents* to switch from following low-level protocols to higher level rules and norms, there should be a link from procedures to rules, and from rules to norms. An advantage of the HARMON*IA* framework is that those links are created by the designer in the process from abstract to concrete norms to rules to the final protocols by means of the successive translations that are made. Those links allow to track, for instance, which abstract norms are related to a given procedure. An example is depicted in figure 2. It is important to note here that the implementation of the rule can be more restrictive than the rule (e.g., it imposes the quality assessment to be done *before* the compatibility assessment). A deliberative normative agent will be able to detect an unusual delay of the `ensure_quality` procedure, and will break the protocol to cope with the abnormal situation, while keeping its behaviour *legal*.

6 Policies, Goals, Roles and Ontologies

Having defined the different levels we now turn to some elements of e-organizations that pertain to several levels at the same time:

Policies: In our framework policies are elements that group the norms and rules at different levels together around specific topics. E.g. an e-organization trying to fulfill the role of the ONT will have to define, at least a *Security policy* (imposed by the context, as we will see in section 7) for all the information about patients it manages. Hence, *policies* go from the abstract level (where goals and values are defined) to the rule level (where those values are described in terms of rules).

Goal/Role Hierarchy: As mentioned in section 2, the *objectives* in the organization's statutes can be represented in terms of goals (i.e., the *overall goal* of the society). The distribution of goals is defined by means of the *role hierarchy*. Figure 3 shows part of the role hierarchy for the organ allocation example. Even though roles are tightly coupled with goals, they are also tightly connected with the norms, rules and procedures defined in the e-Organization. As the refinement process is made, norms and rules are related to roles in the role hierarchy.

Ontologies: Ontologies are shared conceptualizations of terms and predicates in order to define a given domain. In our framework *Domain ontologies* define the vocabulary to be used by all the agents in the e-organization. They are defined in the abstract level and then extended in the following levels, as new norms and rules refer to new terms that are missing in the ontology.

7 Influence of the E-organization's Context

In section 2 we saw how statutes make reference to a certain *context* where the organization performs its activities. The context of an organization includes regulations that are applied to the organization's internal and/or external behaviour. Usually regulations define constraints in several levels, from the more abstract (*"do not discriminate because of race or sex"*) to the rule level and, even, at the procedure level, by defining protocols to be followed (*"in situation A first do α, then..."*).

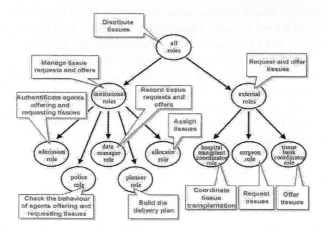

Fig. 3. An example of role hierarchy and goal distribution

An example are the ONT statutes presented in section 2. They state that the ONT operates according to the Spanish National Health system. Therefore ONT *inherits* the norms and values of this system as well and they restrict the ways in which the objectives of the ONT can be reached.

One of the **Values** inherited from the National Health System is that : *"Patients should not be discriminated because of race, social status, sex, economical issues, ideology or political affiliation"*(Article 10.1 LGS [6])

Some **Obligations** imposed to the ONT by the National Health System are about the allocation process, e.g., $O_{ONT}(Coordination\ of\ Organ\ and\ tissue\ allocation)$ or $O_{ONT}(Ensure\ equity\ in\ selection\ of\ recipients)$, some others about quality issues, e.g., $O_{ONT}(Ensure\ quality\ and\ safety\ of\ organs\ and\ tissues)$ and some about security issues, e.g., $O_{ONT}(Ensure\ security\ of\ patient\ records)$.

Figure 2 summarizes the example of the appropriateness of the distribution, and how it evolves through the different levels. In that example we already included the obligation $O_{ONT}(Ensure\ quality\ and\ safety\ of\ organs\ and\ tissues)$ as part of the refinement process, splitting the *appropriate* predicate in the Concrete Level into the *ensure_quality* and *ensure_compatibility* predicates.

The norms and values inherited from other organizations can be described at the top level of the e-organization explicitly. These norms have the highest priority and will *overwrite* any norms specified by the e-organization itself if they are contradictory. In our current work we are not considering those conflicting situations in the framework, but a quite simple solution to this scenario could be the use of a prioritized deontic logic, where default rules are used.

Another aspect of the context of an e-organization consists of the standards and available protocols and procedures for specifying its norms and procedures. An example is to design the search procedure to obtain a *"correct/fair distribution of organs"*. One possible option is to simply translate the current ONT procedure, which is *"appropriate"* but not *"efficient"* in time. An alternative would be to use *standards*, for instance, the FIPA Call-For-Proposals (CFP) protocol, in order to do a more efficient distributed search for recipients.

In our framework we propose to implement a repository where solutions used in the modelling of previous e-organizations could be used again to create new ones. This idea is depicted in figure 1, where the Background Knowledge is explicitly represented. A good example is security standards and policies.

8   Conclusions

In this paper we introduced HARMON*IA* , a framework to model electronic organizations from the abstract level where norms usually are defined to the final protocols and procedures that implement those norms. The main objective is to fill the existing gap in previous approaches, which work either at the level of norm formalization or at the procedural level. Some important parts of this model are formalized using multi-modal logics. Some parts of the model can make use of existing implementations (such as the ontology and procedure level). However, due to space limitations we defer a more detailed description of implementation issues to a next paper. A main area of further research is the formal description of the semantic relations between the levels. Another research issue is to formally define mechanisms such as Delegation of responsibility in our framework.

References

[1] C. Castelfranchi, F. Dignum, C. Jonker, and J. Treur. Deliberative normative agents: Principles and architecture, 1999.

[2] F. Dignum. Agents, markets, institutions and protocols. In F. Dignum and C. Sierra, editors, *Agent Mediated Electronic Commerce, The European AgentLink Perspective*, LNCS-1991, pages 98–114.

[3] F. Dignum. Autonomous agents with norms. *AI and Law*, 7:69–79, 1999.

[4] M. Esteva, J. Padget, and C. Sierra. Formalizing a language for institutions and norms. In J.-J.CH. Meyer and M. Tambe, editors, *Intelligent Agents VIII*, volume 2333 of *LNAI*, pages 348–366. Springer Verlag, 2001. ISBN 3-540-43858-0.

[5] D. Grossi and F. Dignum. Abstract and concrete norms in institutions. *Submitted to FAMAS 2003*, 2003.

[6] Ley 14/1986, de 25 de abril, general de sanidad. Boletín Oficial del Estado 102, 29 de abril 1986.

[7] J.-J. Ch. Meyer. A different approach to deontic logic: Deontic logic viewed as a variant of dynamic logic. *Notre Dame J. of Formal Logic*, 29(1):109–136, 1988.

[8] J.-J. Ch. Meyer and R.J. Wieringa. *Deontic Logic in Computer Science: Normative System Specification*. John Wiley and sons, 1991.

[9] Organización Nacional de Transplantes. http://www.msc.es/ont.

[10] J. Vázquez-Salceda, U. Cortés, and J. Padget. Integrating the organ and tissue allocation processes through an agent-mediated electronic institution. *LNAI-2504*, pages 309–321, 2002.

[11] G.H. von Wright. On the logic of norms and actions. *New Studies in Deontic Logic*, pages 3–35, 1981.

The Use of Adaptive Negotiation by a Shopping Agent in Agent-Mediated Electronic Commerce

Mihaela Oprea

University of Ploiesti, Department of Informatics
Bd. Bucuresti Nr. 39, Ploiesti, 2000, Romania
mihaela@upg-ploiesti.ro

Abstract. Software agents could help buyers and sellers to combat information overload and expedite specific stages of the online buying process. On the other hand, in a multi-agent system such as an agent-mediated electronic commerce, it is desirable that the agents try to adapt to the environment by learning or by an evolutionary process, thus doing an anticipation of the interaction with the other agents. The paper presents a shopping agent architecture, SmartAgent, whose role is to assist users when doing electronic shopping, in the Internet. The agent has a learning capability implemented by a feed-forward artificial neural network that allows him to model the other agent's negotiation strategy, thus doing an adaptive negotiation in order to make a better deal.

1 Introduction

The Internet and World Wide Web are becoming an important channel for retail commerce as well as for business to business transactions. At present, electronic purchases are still largely non-automated. While information about different products and vendors is more easily accessible, and orders and payments can be made electronically, a human is still in the loop in all stages of the buying process, which increase the transaction costs. In this context, the software agent technologies can be used to automate several of the most time consuming stages of the buying process. A software agent is personalized, continuously running and semi-autonomous. The literature reported several personal agents that assist the user with information processing needs by generating, filtering, collecting, or transforming information [1], [2]. On the other hand, internet stores are providing services customized by the needs and interests of individual customers. Such services can be viewed as *seller's agents* with the purpose to push merchandise and/or services on to the users. Therefore, there is a growing need for deploying *shopping agents* (i.e. the *buyer's agents*) whose goal is to best serve the user's interests and to make more informed purchasing decisions. Adaptability is an important issue that need to be addressed when designing flexible multi-agent systems. This property allows the generation of a model of the selection process within the system and thus results in internal representations that can indicate

V. Mařík et al. (Eds): CEEMAS 2003, LNAI 2691, pp. 594-605, 2003.

future successful interactions [3], [4]. The main purpose of adaptability in the case of a negotiation scenario is to improve the negotiation competence of the agents, based on learning from their interactions with other agents. In other words, to obtain an agreement and eventually, a better or even, the best deal. In this sense it is well known that multi-agent learning can be viewed as a mean to reach equilibrium. In the recent years several solutions were given to software agent adaptability implementation. Among these, the most used in the case of an agent-based negotiation are Q-learning, and Bayesian learning. We have proposed for the learning problem the solution of a feed forward artificial neural network that can be used by a seller/buyer agent to model the other agent negotiation strategy. The adaptive negotiation model was included in the architecture of a shopping agent, SmartAgent, that is under development at University of Ploiesti [5].

The paper is structured as follows. Section 2 presents the architecture of the shopping agent SmartAgent. The negotiation strategy learning problem and the adaptive negotiation model are described in section 3. Some preliminary experimental results are discussed in section 4. Finally, in section 5 we conclude the paper.

2   The Architecture of the Shopping Agent

The shopping agent will serve the interest of the user by understanding the user's goals and recommending products/services or suggesting modification to user queries or requirements that will be more likely to produce results at a higher level of user satisfaction. Also, the agent will be able to negotiate different issues (e.g. the price, the quality) regarding a specific product, in case the issues are negotiable. The consumer's initial choice or preference can be modified in the light of new information from rapidly changing marketplace (e.g. the latest options, deals, package offerings etc). The shopping agent must be able to track changing market conditions and to inform the user about interactions between stated constraints in queries and the prevailing market.

We have designed a shopping agent model, SmartAgent, whose architecture is described in figure 1. The shopper interacts with the user through a graphical user interface (GUI) based on the domain description. The agent is able to parse product descriptions and to identify several product attributes, including price and warranty. It achieves this performance without sofisticated natural language processing, and requires minimal knowledge about the domain of the products. The agent can extract information from online vendors by using an heuristic search, and an inductive learning technique [6].

The shopping agent may receive proposals from multiple seller agents. Each proposal defines a complete product offering including a product configuration, price, warranty, and the merchant's value-added services. The shopping agent evaluates and orders these proposals based on how they satisfy its owner's preferences (expressed as multi-attribute utilities).

The shopping agent has two main components: the learner (offline and online) and the buyer who has the ability to negotiate by using a specific negotiation strategy. For example, in the learning stage an offline learner creates a vendor description for each merchant, while in the buying stage a real-time shopper uses the vendors description to help the user decide which store offers the best price for a given product.

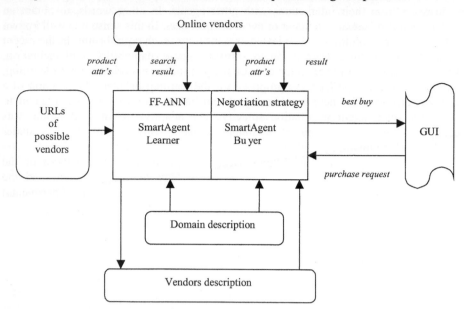

Fig. 1. The architecture of the shopping agent SmartAgent

Given the home pages of several online stores, SmartAgent autonomously learns how to shop at those vendors. After learning, the agent is able to speedily visit over a dozen software vendors, extract information and summarize the results for the user. The agent uses knowledge about different product domains. Also, the SmartAgent Learner allows the shopping agent to learn the other agent's behaviour through a learning capability implemented by a feed-forward artificial neural network (FF-ANN). For example, in the learning stage the online learner try to model the other agent's negotiation strategy and the other agent's reservation price, while in the buying stage the shopper uses the result of the first stage in order to make an adaptive negotiation and therefore, to increase the possibility of making a deal, the best one, if possible.

3   Adaptive Negotiation in Agent-Mediated Electronic Commerce

3.1   The Negotiation Strategy Learning Problem

Negotiation is a general process involving communication between two or more agents that attempts to find a way of mutually satisfying the separate agent's requirements by undertaking appropriate actions. In other words, negotiation involves determining a contract under certain terms and conditions. From the perspective of

CBB (Consumer Buyer Behaviour), the negotiation stage is where the price or other terms of the transaction are determined. For example, the negotiation used in commerce include stock markets, fine art auction houses, flower auctions, and various ad-hoc haggling (automobile dealership and commission-based electronic stores). As a coordination technique, negotiation enable to avoid deadlocks and livelocks in multi-agent systems. Negotiation is achieved through the exchange of proposals between agents. In this paper we shall limit the discussion to bilateral negotiation. The negotiation can be made over a set of issues and a proposal consists of a value for each of those issues and is autonomously generated by the agent's strategy. A way to enhance agent's autonomy in a dynamic environment such as an electronic market is to endow its architecture with learning capabilities.

Suppose we have two agents a and b that are negotiating over a set of issues that are represented by vector X. The negotiation thread at time t is the following: $X_{a \leftrightarrow b}^{t}$ $=\{X_{a \rightarrow b}^{1}, X_{b \rightarrow a}^{2}, ..., X_{a \rightarrow b}^{t}\}$. $X_{a \rightarrow b}^{t}$ [j] is the proposal made by agent a to agent b at time t for the issue j that is under negotiation. Each agent has a utility function U^{i}, $U^{i}:S^{i} \rightarrow R$. S^{i} is the state space relevant to agent i and R is the set of real numbers. The utility function order the states by preference. Each agent has some private and some shared knowledge. For example, each agent knows only its own utility function and can observe the other agent's actions, i.e. proposals. Also, each agent has some beliefs about the state that would result from performing its available actions. An agent can learn from observation of the interactions with the other agent. The proposals made by an agent are generated by his negotiation strategy that is specific to each issue under negotiation. The negotiation strategy is private to each agent. Let's consider the case of two agents, a seller and a buyer, that are negotiating the price of a specific product. Each agent knows its own reservation price, RP, which is how much the agent is willing to pay or to receive in the deal. A possible deal can be made only if there exists an overlapping zone between the reservation prices of the two agents. The agents don't even know if there is an agreement zone. The ideal rule to find if there is an agreement zone is the following:

if $RP_{seller} \leq RP_{buyer}$ then
              * The zone of agreement exists
              * Possible deal
else   * The zone of agreement doesn't exist
              * No possible deal

where RP_{buyer} is the maximum price the buyer is willing to pay for the product, and RP_{seller} is the minimum price the seller will accept to receive. Usually, it cannot be forecast if an agreement will be made between two agents that negotiate, so a learning capability would help to higher the percentage of deals that can be made in an electronic market. A learning agent makes his decision based on his own reservation price, on his a priori domain knowledge, and on the history of past price proposals that were exchanged. Through learning the agent will form a more accurate model of the other agent and could create some nested agent models [7].

3.2   Solutions

The main solutions that were adopted for the inclusion of a learning capability into an agent-based e-commerce system are the reinforcement learning with a special emphasize on Q-learning, Bayesian learning and model-based learning.

3.2.1   Reinforcement Learning

The reinforcement learning is a common technique used by adaptive agents in multi-agent systems and its basic idea is to revise beliefs and strategies based on the success or failure of observed performance. Q-learning is a particular reinforcement learning algorithm (an incremental reinforcement learning) that works by estimating the values of all state-action pairs. An agent that uses a Q-learning algorithm selects an action based on the action-value function, called the Q-function. $Q_j(s, a) = Q_j(s, a) + \lambda(r_j - Q_j(s, a))$, where λ is a constant, r_j is the immediate reward received by agent j after performing action a in state s. The Q-function defines the expected sum of the discounted reward attained by executing an action a in state s and determining the subsequent actions by the current policy π. The Q-function is updated using the agent's experience.

The reinforcement learning techniques have to deal with the exploration-exploitation dilemma. Some experimental comparisons between several explore/exploit strategies are presented in [8] showing the risk of exploration in multi-agent systems. In [9] it is demonstrated that genetic algorithm based classifier systems can be used effectively to achieve near-optimal solutions more quickly than Q-learning, this result revealing the problem of slow convergence that is specific to reinforcement learning techniques.

3.2.2   Bayesian Learning

Usually, Bayesian behaviour is considered as the only rational agent's behaviour, i.e. the behaviour that maximizes the utility. Bayesian learning is built on bayesian reasoning which provides a probabilistic approach to inference. The bayesian learning algorithms manipulates probabilities together with observed data. In [10] it is presented a sequential decision making model of negotiation called Bazaar, in which learning is modeled as a Bayesian belief update process. During negotiation, the agents use the Bayesian framework to update knowledge and belief that they have about the other agents and the environment. For example, an agent (buyer/seller) could update his belief about the reservation price of the other agent (seller/buyer) based on his interactions with the seller/buyer and on his domain knowledge. The agent's belief is represented as a set of hypotheses. Each agent tries to model the others in a recursive way during the negotiation process, and any change in the environment, if relevant and perceived by an agent, will have an impact on the agent's subsequent decision making. The experiments showed that greater the zone of agreement, the better the learning agents seize the opportunity.

3.2.3 Model-Based Learning

In [11] it is described a model-based learning framework that model the interaction between agents by the game-theoretic concept of repeated games. The approach tries to reduce the number of interaction examples needed for adaptation, by investing more computational resources in deeper analysis of past interaction experience. The learning process has two stages: (1) the learning agent infers a model of the other agent based on past interaction and (2) the learning agent uses the learned model for designing effective interaction strategy for the future. The experimental results presented in [11] showed that a model-based learning agent performed significantly better than a Q-learning agent.

3.3   The Adaptive Negotiation Model

We have extended the service-oriented negotiation model described in [12] with an adaptability component that is implemented by a feed forward artificial neural network. This negotiation model is based on a variation of two parties, many issues value scoring system presented in [13] and was used by generic negotiating agents for business process management applications.

Negotiation can range over a number of quantitative (e.g. price, cost, duration) and qualitative (e.g. type of reporting policy, nature of the contract) issues. Quantitative issues in negotiation are defined over a real domain (i.e. $x[j] \in D_j = [min_j, max_j]$). Qualitative issues are defined over a totally ordered domain (i.e. $x[j] \in D_j = <q_1, ..., q_n>$). When an agent receives an offer $X = (x[1], x[2], ..., x[n])$, where n is the total number of issues, it rates it by using a function that combines the scores of the different issues (by a linear combination):

$$V^a(x^t) = \sum_{1 \le j \le n} w_j^a(t) V_j^a(x^t[j]) \tag{1}$$

where $w_j^a(t)$ is the importance of issue j for agent a at time t.

Each agent has a scoring function $V_j^a : D_j^a \rightarrow [0, 1]$ that gives the score agent a assigns to a value of issue j in the set of its acceptable values D_j^a . For quantitative issues the scoring functions are monotonous. If the score of the received offer is greater than the score of the counter offer the agent would send at this point, then the offer is accepted. If the preset constant deadline (t_{max}^a) at which the negotiation must have been completed by agent a is reached, the offer is rejected by a. Otherwise, a counter offer is sent. Figure 2 describes the price negotiation context.

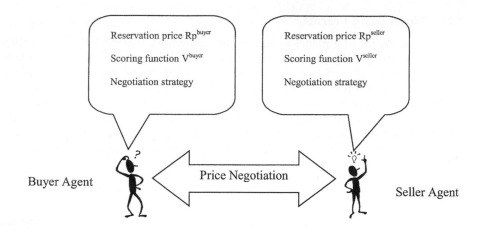

Fig. 2. The price negotiation between two agents - a buyer and a seller

If both negotiators use an additive scoring function, Raiffa showed that it is possible to compute the optimum value of X (the contract) as an element on the efficient frontier of negotiation. It has been demonstrated that negotiation convergence is achieved when the scoring value of the received offer is greater than the scoring value of the counter-offer the agent is intended to respond with. The aim of agent i's negotiation strategy is to determine the best course of action which result in an agreement on a contract X that maximizes its scoring function V^a. Each agent has a set of tactics that are used to build negotiation strategies. A new counter-offer is a combination of tactics and how this combination is made will be decided by the negotiation agent's strategy. In this service-oriented negotiation model several negotiation tactics could be applied in order to determine how to compute the value of an issue (price, volume, quality etc) by considering a single criterion (e.g. time, resources). Some time dependent tactics are Boulware and Conceder. While Boulware tactic maintains the offered value until the time is almost exhausted, whereupon it concedes up to the reservation value, the Conceder tactic goes quickly to the reservation value. Resource dependent tactics are similar to time dependent tactics and they model bounded rationality. Two types of such tactics are dynamic deadline tactics and resource estimation tactics. Finally, the behaviour-dependent tactics are relative Tit-For-Tat (the agent reproduces in percentage terms the behaviour that its opponent performed $\delta \geq 1$ steps ago – if n > 2δ), Random Absolute Tit-For-Tat (same as relative Tit-For-Tay but in absolute terms) and Averaged Tit-For-Tat (the agent computes the average of percentages of changes in a window of size $\gamma \geq 1$ of its oponents history when determining its new offer – if n > 2γ).

For simplicity, we have included so far in the negotiation model only one quantitative issue (i.e. only one attribute of a good that is under negotiation), the price of the good. The history of past price proposals exchanged between a buyer and a seller is given by:

$$X_{b \leftrightarrow s}^{t} = \{ X_{b \rightarrow s}^{1}, X_{s \rightarrow b}^{2}, X_{b \rightarrow s}^{3}, \ldots, X_{b \rightarrow s}^{t-2}, X_{s \rightarrow b}^{t-1}, X_{b \rightarrow s}^{t} \}.$$

This history of price proposals is a time series and the prediction of the next price proposal can be made by using a feed forward artificial neural network. Suppose that the seller agent has implemented the learning capability as a feed forward neural network. At time t (t>5) the seller has to decide the next price proposal of the buyer based on the past three buyer price proposals. The architecture of the neural network is 3×n×1 (see figure 3). The number of nodes in the hidden layer is set during the network training. The inputs set is Inp = $\{X_{b \to s}^{t-5}, X_{b \to s}^{t-3}, X_{b \to s}^{t-1}\}$, t>5. The output is $X_{b \to s}^{t+1}$. Based on the predicted buyer price proposal $X_{b \to s}^{t+1}$, the seller could become more flexible in order to make a deal more quickly and as convinient as possible from his utility function viewpoint. Sometimes a suboptimal solution could be accepted if a deal can be made. The learning capability is activated during the process of proposals and counterproposals exchanging and will influence the way in which the negotiation will evolve to an agreement. The seller agent will reason about the buyer agent based solely on his observations of buyer's actions.

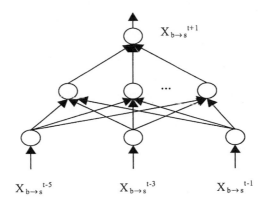

Fig. 3. The artificial neural network

Suppose at time t the seller will forecast the next price proposal of the buyer, $X_{b \to s}^{t+1}$, and based on this value and on the forecast of the buyer negotiation strategy, will decide which strategy to adopt. The core rule of the decision algorithm is the following:

If $V_j^{seller} (X_{b \to s}^{t+1}) \geq V_j^{seller} (X_{s \to b}^{t})$ then
   $*$ proposal of the seller is $X_{b \to s}^{t+1} + \varepsilon$
else
   $*$ proposal of the seller is $X_{s \to b}^{t} - \varepsilon$

where j is the price issue, ε is a domain-dependent value, X is the value of the price proposal, and the seller proposal is computed according to one of its tactics depending on the corresponding buyer strategy forecast.

$\varepsilon = |X_{s \to b}^{t} - X_{b \to s}^{t+1}| / d$, where d is the division number, d ∈ {2, 3, 4}. The seller agent chooses the divison number by using some heuristics that are dependent on the e-market domain.

Therefore, the seller try to adjust its negotiation strategy to the buyer's negotiation strategy by using the artificial neural network forecasts. The learning capability of the seller agent will give information about the overall negotiation style (e.g. the other agent is tough or compliant) and will provide some heuristic information regarding the buyer's reservation price. As a result of learning, the seller is expected to gain more accurate expectation of the buyer's payoff structure and therefore make more advantageous offers. The domain-specific knowledge could also help in order to make a better estimation of the other agent's reservation price. For example, in some businesses people will offer a price which is above their reservation price by a certain percentage, x%.

A very important observation that we have to make is that the proposed approach could be useful when there is plenty of time for negotiation, i.e. for medium and long term deadlines. The neural network will be adapted to different negotiation contexts. Because the training set is extracted on line, during negotiation, at the beginning of each negotiation, there will be a time window in which the neural network should adapt to the new context and so the learning capability cannot be exploited by the negotiation strategy during the first p proposals ($p \leq 5$). In order to keep the architecture of the neural network as simple as possible and also, to take into account the current behaviour of the buyer agent and to detect any change in his pricing strategy we have chosen a time window of size three, taken into account the last three buyer price proposals.

During negotiation, the seller can make predictions also about the reservation price of the buyer agent, by observing the price proposals that the buyer made. Taking into account the predicted reservation price of the buyer and the predicted next buyer price proposal, the seller could lower or raise its price over time by choosing a specific negotiation strategy.

4   Preliminary Experimental Results

So far, we have tested the learning capability of the shopping agent in different negotiation scenarios. As a testbed we have used an e-commerce market simulation (implemented in Jade) in which the price can be negotiated [14].

The two main components of the e-commerce market are:

- the marketplace engine (embedded in the Jade environment, where the agents "live" and make transactions),
- a user interface that handle all of the user interactions (the associated scripts are located on a web server).

The agent parameters include the good to sell/buy, the desired price to sell/buy for (the initial price which the agent will ask/offer), lowest acceptable price/highest offer (i.e. the reservation price of the seller/buyer agent), and the agent negotiation strategy with/without a learning capability. The parameters of an agent are defined by the user. In our simulations the list of goods to buy/sell was composed by several 2nd hand goods such as computers, mobile phones, books, printers, etc.

We have set experimentally the architecture of the neural network to three input nodes, three hidden nodes and one output node. The seller uses our adaptive negotiation model, while the buyer uses one of three simple negotiation strategies:

Table 1. Experimental results. Joint utility and number of exchanged proposals are monitored

	Type 1		Type 2		Type 3	
	JU	#p	JU	#p	JU	#p
ANN-agent	0.19	52	0.15	41	0.22	62
Q-agent	0.20	57	0.17	44	0.20	53

anxious, cool-headed and frugal (i.e. linear, quadratic and exponential functions). We have used a variable learning rate of the neural network. The weights initializations were in the range of [-0.1, 0.1]. Initially, ten different runs with different weight initializations were performed. Than, we made 20 runs with two different weight initializations and 10 different training sets. The initialization that gave the best result and that which was the closest to the average performance were selected as the two initializations in the actual 20-time cross-evaluation runs. After the pre-training step, we have used the neural network in different negotiation contexts to make the other training step and than we have used the trained network in the testing step.

The order of who begins the negotiation process is randomly selected (the agent which opens the negotiation process fairs better, irrespective of whether the agent is a buyer or a seller). The e-market was composed of two sellers (one that has the proposed adaptive negotiation model – ANN-agent, and one that has a Q-learning capability – Q-agent) and a number of buyers, randomly included in the e-market. We made a comparison between the performances of the two seller agents. The results are summarized in table 1. In all the experiments the zone of agreement was chosen as being not empty.

The three types of buyer agent's negotiation strategy are: type 1 – frugal, type 2 – anxious, type 3 – cool-headed. We have adopted the same joint utility as in [10] which is defined as: $(P^*-RP_{seller}) \times (RP_{buyer}-P^*)/(RP_{buyer}-RP_{seller})^2$, where P^* is the agreed price.

In table 1 we give the joint utility (JU) and the number of exchanged proposals (#p) The best performance is reached by the ANN-agent in the case of a cool-headed negotiation strategy of the buyer agent.

Table 2. Experimental results. Number of deals made in a specific time interval is monitored.

t (s) Seller	300	600	1800	3600	18000
ANN-agent	1	7	14	32	57
Q-agent	4	8	16	24	48

Also, we had run several simulations for short and medium-term deadlines with the following time limits (in seconds) of the e-market operation: 300s, 600s, 1800s, 3600s and 18000s and we have counted the number of deals made by the seller agents. The experimental results are summarized in table 2. In all situations, both agents, ANN-agent and Q-agent, were capable to make deals, the greatest number of deals being made by the ANN-agent (32 / 57, in comparison with 24 / 48 for the Q-agent) for the last two intervals of time (i.e. 3600s and 18000s), as expected. For the first interval, the Q-agent made a greater number of deals (4, in comparison with 1, made by the ANN-agent) , while for the second and the third, both agents made a similar number of deals (Q-agent – 8 / 16, ANN-agent 7 / 14). All the experimental results are related to the simulations data while in a real e-market things could be quite different, the next step of our work being the use of the ANN-agent in a real world e-market.

As the most successful tactics reported in the literature for long term deadlines are *linear*, *patient* and *steady*, we have included this set of tactics in the adaptive negotiation model of the ANN-seller agent. The linear tactic is a time-dependent tactic tactic (see equation (1) with β=1), while the patient and the steady tactics are resource-dependent tactics. All these tactics concede at a steady rate throughout the negotiation process.

The ANN-seller agent chooses a tactic from its set of tactics based on the predicted value of the buyer proposal at time t+1, according to the core decision rule of the adaptive negotiation model, explained in section 3.3.

5   Conclusion

With the rapid explosion of the electronic commerce stores, the consumer may be overwhelmed by the volume and diversity of information available on the net and may not have time to search the available information to make a judicious choice. Therefore, the solution offered by software agents could be adopted. In the context of

$$x^t_{s \to b}[j] = \begin{cases} \min {}^s_j + \alpha^s_j(t)(\max {}^s_j - \min {}^s_j), & V^s_j \text{ decreasing} \\ \min {}^s_j + (1 - \alpha^s_j(t))(\max {}^s_j - \min {}^s_j), & V^s_j \text{ increasing} \end{cases} \qquad (2)$$

an agent-mediated electronic commerce, the shopping agents can help the users to make better deals and to reduce transaction costs in a variety of business processes (e.g. industries such as gas, electricity, books etc). In this paper we have presented the architecture of a shopping agent, SmartAgent, that try to make an adaptive negotiation with the purpose of making a deal, a better or even the best deal, thus improving the buying process.

The main purpose of the work that is described in the paper was to study the usefulness of a connectionist approach as a learning capability implementation for a negotiating agent in the context of agent-mediated electronic commerce. The use of a feed forward artificial neural network as a learning ability of a negotiation model in the context of agent-based e-commerce is new. The preliminary experimental results obtained so far showed a good behaviour of the neural network in the case of medium and long-term deadlines. The e-markets that seems to be appropriate for our ANN-model are second-hand products selling (cars, computers, mobile phones, printers, etc), properties selling and so on. In such cases the negotiation time could be extended to a larger interval, in order to make a better deal.

References

[1]   Jennings, N.R., and Wooldridge, M.: Software Agents, IEE Review, January (1996) 17-20
[2]   Nwana, H.S.: Software Agents: An Overview, The Knowledge Engineering Review, vol. 11(3), (1996) 205-244
[3]   Oprea, M.: Adaptability and Embodiment in Agent-Based E-Commerce Negotiation, Proceedings of the Workshop Adaptability and Embodiment Using Multi-Agent Systems-AEMAS01, Prague, (2001) 257-265
[4]   Oprea, M.: Adaptability in Agent-Based E-Commerce Negotiation, tutorial notes of the 20th IASTED International Conference Applied Informatics AI'02 – symposium Artificial Intelligence Applications–AIA'02, February, Innsbruck, Austria (2002)
[5]   Oprea, M.: The Architecture of a Shopping Agent. Journal of Economic Informatics, **1** (2002) 63-68
[6]   Oprea, M.: Rule Generation Versus Decision Tree Induction, Proceedings of the 20th International Conference Applied Informatics AI'02, Innsbruck, Austria, ACTA Press, (2002) 395-398
[7]   Vidal, J., Durfee, E.: Learning nested agent models in an information economy, Journal of Experimental & Theoretical Artificial Intelligence, 10:**3** (1998) 291-308
[8]   Pérez-Uribe, A., Hirsbrunner, B.: The Risk of Exploration in Multi-Agent Learning Systems: A Case Study, Proceedings of the Agents-00/ECML-00 workshop on Learning Agents, Barcelona, (2000) 33-37
[9]   Sen, S., Sekaran, M.: Individual Learning of coordination knowledge, Journal of Experimental & Theoretical Artificial Intelligence, 10:**3** (1998) 333-356
[10]   Zeng, D., Sycara, K.: How Can an Agent Learn to Negotiate, Intelligent Agents III. Agent Theories, Architectures and Languages, LNAI 1193, Springer, (1997) 233-244
[11]   Carmel, D., Markovitch, S.: Model-based learning of interaction strategies in multi-agent systems, JETAI **10** (1998) 309-332
[12]   Faratin, P., Sierra, C., Jennings, N.: Negotiation decision functions for autonomous agents, Robotics and Autonomous Systems, **24** (1998) 159-182
[13]   Raiffa, H.: The Art and Science of Negotiation, Harvard University Press, Cambridge, MA, (1982)
[14]   Oprea, M: An Adaptive Negotiation Model for Agent-Based Electronic Commerce, Studies in Informatics and Control, 11: **3** (2002) 271-279

Agent Interaction Protocols for the Selection of Partners for Virtual Enterprises

Sobah Abbas Petersen[1] and Mihhail Matskin[2]

[1] Department of Computer and Information Science
Norwegian University of Science and Technology
N-7491 Trondheim, Norway
sap@idi.ntnu.no
[2] Department of Microelectronics and Information Technology
Royal Institute of Technology
SE-164 40 Kista, Sweden
misha@imit.kth.se

Abstract. A Virtual Enterprise can be described as an organisational form that emerges when individual entities form a team to achieve a specific goal. The ability to assemble the best team is key to the success of the Virtual Enterprise and this imposes strong demands on its formation. In this paper, we present an agent-based model of a Virtual Enterprise, where the partners of a Virtual Enterprise are represented by software agents. We show how this model can support the different processes that are used in selecting the partners. We do this by analysing the agent interaction protocols for the different partner selection processes and by adapting it to provide the necessary agent-based support. We also describe the contents of the knowledge base of a single agent and how it can be used in the selection processes.

1 Introduction

A Virtual Enterprise (VE) can be described as an organisational form that emerges when individual entities form a team to achieve a specific goal. An example of such a team is a project group. There have been several attempts at defining VEs from different research communities. A summary of these is given in [14]. We have reviewed these definitions to come up with a working definition: *a team of partners that collaborate to achieve a specific goal.* The partners may be human beings, organisations (or part of organisations) or software agents. Unlike traditional enterprises that are established and continue to exist over a long time, VEs are established to deliver a specific product or a service. VEs have a shorter life span and this means that the partners that participate in one VE may also be negotiating on a contract with another VE. Thus, there is a need to form VEs very quickly and frequently.

We believe that software agents, hereafter referred to as agents, are a suitable means of representing the partners of a VE. One important reason for this is that by delegating the agents to look for the next VE and conduct the negotiation on

V. Mařík et al. (Eds): CEEMAS 2003, LNAI 2691, pp. 606–615, 2003.

behalf of the partners, the partners would then have the time to do the actual work required in the current VE. Thus, we believe that agents could be used to represent the partners of a VE and to support the efficient formation of VEs. We consider the formation of VEs within the context of electronic markets, (see [11] for an overview), where the agents bid and compete to become the partners of a VE. The partners' bids are evaluated according to some criteria.

Industrial case studies have revealed a number of different processes and evaluation criteria that have been used to select the partners during the formation of a VE. We have analysed the different selection processes as agent interaction protocols, where an agent interaction protocol describes the sequence of communication between two agents and the contents of the messages. In this paper, we present an agent-based model for a VE and the model of a single agent in a VE. We describe how these models can be used to support the different agent interaction protocols and thus the different selection processes.

The rest of this paper is organised as follows: Section 2 describes the agent-based model of a VE; Section 3 describes the model of an agent; Section 4 describes how the different agent interaction protocols from the different selection processes are supported by our models; Section 5 reviews some of the literature related to this work and Section 6 discusses the conclusions and the work that is planned for the future.

2   Model of a Virtual Enterprise

We have developed an agent-based Enterprise Model of a VE by analysing the entities in a VE, their relationships and how they can be used in an agent context, [15]. An important contribution in modelling enterprises was made in [6] and this has been a source of inspiration for our model. In our model, the VE has a *goal* which is achieved by a set of *activities* which are performed by a set of *roles*. See Figure 1. The agents that fill these roles are the members of the VE and the agents are selected on the basis of how well they meet the requirements for the roles. For our work, we assume that the goals, the activities, the roles and their requirements are available before the VE is announced and that this information is used in the VE announcement.

The complete model of a VE is important in order to be able to understand how the different entities affect one another. For example, how does the selection of a particular agent affect the goals of the VE? Such a question can only be answered if we see the link from the agent to the goals of the VE. A complete model is also helpful in determining the kind of information that is flowing among the different entities. This in turn helps in designing the agents and the communication and collaboration among the agents.

The agents in a VE can be classified as:

VE Initiator (who may also be the customer), who takes the initiative to form the VE.

VE Partner (who may also be the VE Initiator), who are the members that form the VE.

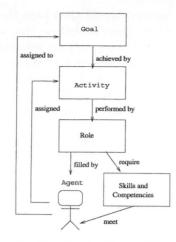

Fig. 1. Model of a Virtual Enterprise

A VE Partner evolves from someone that is interested in becoming a part of the VE to someone who is actually a part of the VE. We use the terms *Interested Partner*, one that is interested in becoming a part of the VE and submits a bid for the work, and *Potential Partner*, one that is considered for the VE and a contract is negotiated.

3   Model of an Agent

There are several agent architectures that uses a knowledge base of an agent, e.g. [8]. We have taken a pragmatic approach in designing our agent architecture to represent the knowledge that is required for the formation of a VE. Thus, we have only considered the basic components of the agent's knowledge base at this stage in our work. Each agent contains a set of goals, a set of activities and a set of capabilities, see Figure 2. The information that is represented by the goals, the activities and the capabilities of the VE Initiator and the VE Partners are slightly different. The VE Initiator agent represents the VE and thus the information represented by the VE Initiator reflects the VE whereas the information represented by the VE Partners reflects that particular partner. Table 1 summarises this. Although the information represented by the goals, the activities and the capabilities of the VE Initiator and VE Partners differ, we consider the same representation and structure for the different entities.

3.1   Goals

A goal can be considered from several points of view. e.g. strategic goal [17] and a product-oriented-view of goal [13] and [5]. In this paper, we have considered the product-oriented view of a goal and describe a goal or a subgoal

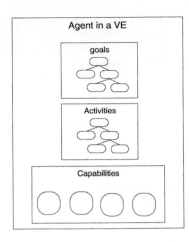

Fig. 2. Model of a Single Agent in a VE

using the following attributes: the name of the goal, product area (the area that the agent/VE intends to work on), deadline (the final date the agent/VE must deliver to the VE/customer) and cost (the amount of money that is associated with the work).

We consider the goal structure as a simple tree structure where a goal (or a subgoal) can have one or many subgoals, [3]. Any goal or a subgoal that does not have a subgoal is an atomic goal. An Interested Partner's goal is aligned with the goals of the VE if it matches one of the (sub)goals of the VE Initiator.

3.2   Activities

Similar to goals, the activities are also a tree structure where an activity (or a subactivity) can have one or many subactivities. An activity is performed towards achieving one or more goals. Activities are also defined by a set of attributes that describe the activity in terms of time constraints, resource requirements, relations to other activities as well as other related information, [6].

Table 1. Information Represented by the Agent Model

Entity	VE Initiator	VE Partner
Goals	Goals of the VE	Goals of the partner
Activities	Activities that need to be performed to achieve the goals of the VE	Set of *experiences* of the partner
Capabilities	Requirements (skills, time, costs, etc.) for the roles of the VE	Work that the partner is capable of doing in a VE

Fig. 3. Generic Agent Interaction Protocol

We consider the activities of a VE Partner as a set of experiences based on the activities that it has performed in the past. An agent bids for an (sub)activity in a VE to achieve one or more of its own goals and this (sub)activity is chosen based on the set of capabilities of the agent. By performing an activity in a VE, a new experience is added to its experience set. In this paper, we consider how the experience set can be used in the various selection processes used by VEs. Thus, we do not consider how it is updated every time the agent performs an activity in the VE.

3.3   Capabilities

The capabilities of an agent are a list of attributes, some of which may itself also be a set of attributes. The capabilities of a VE Initiator are the list of requirements for the roles in a VE. The requirements can be structured into different kinds of requirements, such as skills and experience related requirements, (e.g. set of required, skills, minimum no. of years of experience required, minimum level of skill), availability requirements and cost requirements.

The capabilities of a VE Partner is a set of attributes that meet the requirements of a VE and this is used in matching the Interested Partners to the roles in a VE.

4   Agent Interaction Protocols for Matching and Selecting VE Partners

4.1   Generic Agent Interaction Protocol

The interactions that takes place between the VE Initiator and the VE Partners are shown in Figure 3. VE is announced by sending out an invitation to bid. The Interested Partners respond to the announcement by proposing a bid. The bids are then qualified according to a set of criteria. The bids that do not meet the requirements are rejected and the VE Initiator then prepares to negotiate with the Potential Partners.

The agent interaction protocol presented above is a generic one that support the basic process of forming VEs. We are currently conducting a series of industrial case studies and we have identified the need for several agent interaction

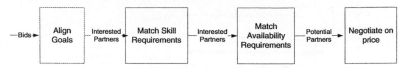

Fig. 4. Advanced Matching and Selection Process

protocols depending on the specific selection procedure chosen by the VE Initiator. For example, if a VE is formed to deliver something simple such as an intranet for a small company, the skills that are required are widely available and the degree of variation in the skills are not critical. So, a simple matching of required and available capabilities may be enough. However, if a VE is formed to deliver a more complex product such as a ship, the skills that are required are more specialised and not that widely available. In such a VE, the cooperative behaviour of the partners will also play a significant role. Thus, a more detailed set of requirements will be considered in the matching process. The general agent interaction protocol described above needs to be adapted to cater to the needs of a particular VE. For different selection processes, the agent interaction protocol will be different depending on the information that is communicated and the sequence of communication.

4.2   Advanced Matching Process

In a more advanced selection process, the VE Initiator may request for the information in several steps. For example, in one of our case studies, Business and Financial Consulting Group (BFS)[1], [1], uses the selection process shown in Figure 4 to select people to work on their projects. BFS has a pre-compiled database that contains the names and capabilities of people who have expressed their wish to work on BFS projects. So, when BFS needs to find people to fill the roles of a VE, it looks at the requirements of skills for the roles and finds a match from the database. They then check if the desired person fulfils the availability requirements and if s/he does, they then agree on a price for the work.

The information gathering and matching part of the agent interaction protocol shown in Figure 5 is an iterative process where the agent is first asked to submit its skills. The agent is asked to provide its availability only if the skills match the requirements. Similarly, the agent is required to provide how much it will charge for the work only if it meets the skills and availability requirements. Although the negotiation in this case is based on a single attribute, i.e. the price charged by the agent, the negotiation can also be based on multiple attributes.

The expression of interest to work with BFS on a specific project can be assumed as alignment of goals of the VE and the Interested Partner. BFS does not consider this step explicitly during the matching process. However, there

---

[1] BFS is a consulting firm registered in the Maldives that mans its projects by selecting resources from a pre-compiled database. BFS' project teams operate as a VE.

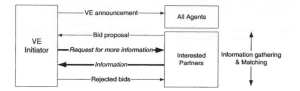

Fig. 5. Agent Interaction Protocol for Advanced Selection Processes

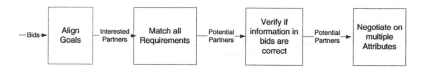

Fig. 6. Matching and Selection Process with Verification

may be situations where goal alignment is considered explicitly during the operation phase of the lifecycle of the VE. The information that is required for this multi-tiered matching process is based on the requirements for the roles of the VE, where the requirements are structured into skills requirements, availability requirements and cost requirements. The matching conditions and constraints can be defined to match the attributes of the agents to the requirements. For example, for matching the skills, the match could be based on string matching or, for availability matching, the start and end dates for an activity associated to a role can be defined as a set of constraints.

4.3   Verification of Information during Selection

During the selection process, the VE Initiator may chose to verify if the bid proposed by the Interested Partner contains information that is true, i.e. that the Interested Partner is not lying. See Figure 6. Case studies have revealed a more detailed and stringent selection process where different approaches have been used to verify the claims made in the bid. A common approach is to call in the Interested Partners for an interview if they meet the basic requirements.

Organisation Development Alliance AS (ODA)[2], [2], conducts detailed interviews with the Potential Partners to verify if they are actually capable of delivering. In addition to interviews, ODA often invites the Potential Partners to a workshop where the possible VE team is made to solve a problem collaboratively. This gives ODA an opportunity to judge if the Potential Partners have experience in collaborative projects.

Scenarios such as the one described above can be supported by requesting for additional information from the Potential Partners after the matching process.

---

[2] ODA AS is a Norwegian company that selects contractors (single or alliances of companies) for very large scale projects. The team of contractors operate as a VE.

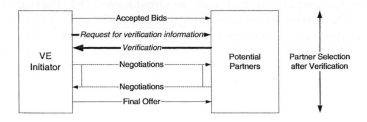

Fig. 7. Agent Interaction Protocol for a Selection Processes with Verification

See Figure 7. Note that the matching process may be multi-tiered as described in Section 4.2. In this case, in addition to matching the goals (implicitly or explicitly) and the requirements for the roles, the VE Initiator requests the Potential Partner to submit its activities (experience) structure to verify if the experience that is claimed can be matched to an activity in the experience tree of the Interested Partner. This process can also be strengthened by requesting the Potential Partner to submit additional material that could be checked electronically, such as authenticated references.

5   Related Work

An important contribution in modelling enterprises was made in [6] where a formal description of an enterprise was given. This work has since been developed to specify the structure of an enterprise and to support reasoning about an enterprise, [7]. Our model of the VE is inspired by this work. However, we do not provide a formal specification of the VE.

Most of the recent agent models employ a BDI-based model [16]. We have not underlined the BDI aspect of our model in this paper. However, the VE agents' goals, activities/experiences and roles/capabilities in our model can be expressed in terms of beliefs, desires and intentions as well. Our agent architecture can be related functionally to those implemented, for example, in PRS [12], IRMA [4] or in GRATE [8]. The parts of the knowledge base presented in these architectures are mostly focused on the agent's own self rather than the knowledge about the other agents, the acquaintance or the cooperation model, [9]. Our agent model is designed such that it can be enhanced to include the cooperation model and the set of rules.

Fischer et. al., [5], describe the selection of partners in a VE as a process of matching VE goals (or subgoals) to partial processes within the different enterprises that represent the partners of the VE. The matching process does not explicity consider the competency and skills requirements of the potential partners. In [13], the VE announcement is a set of n-tuples which represent the requirements as attributes and a reserve price. These examples consider a single agent interaction protocol and thus, do not describe the details of the contents of the messages between the agents. In [13], they distinguish between the Market

(VE Initiator) agent architecture and the Organisation (VE Partner) agent architecture. The Market Agent contains a goal descriptor and a VE selector while the Organisation Agent contains knowledge about the VE as well as individual knowledge. We use the same basic architecture for both the VE Initiator and VE Partner agents so that the VE Initiator can also be a VE Partner, i.e. it can initiate a VE, where it is a partner of that VE.

6   Conclusions and Discussion

In this paper, we have shown how an agent-based model of a VE can be used to support the different selection processes that are used in selecting the partners for a VE, where the partners of a VE are represented by agents. We do this by analysing the agent interaction protocols. We have shown how the models of both the VE and the agent itself fit well with the selection process, where the selection process takes into account the goals of the agents, their activities/experiences as well as their capabilities. We have also shown that the agent interaction protocols can be effectively adapted to the VE formation process.

The two cases revealed that matching the roles of a VE to agents is a multi-tiered process, where the requirements are structured into different categories and each of these categories are considered separately. Further, the selection process is made more stringent by adding a verification subprocess to the selection process. The verification subprocess takes into account the activity structure of an agent in addition to the goals and the requirements for the roles.

In the future, we plan to implement the ideas presented here using the AGORA multi-agent architecture, [10]. We also plan to extend the work on representing the experience of an agent and the verification of information during the selection process.

Acknowledgements

This work is partially supported by the Norwegian Research Foundation in the framework of the Information and Communication Technology (IKT-2010) program and the ADIS project. We would like to thank Rifaath Jaleel from BFS, Maldives and Edgar Karlsen from ODA, Norway for providing case studies.

References

[1] Business and financial consulting group pvt. ltd. http://www.consultbfs.com/.
[2] Organisation development alliance, as. http://www.oda.as/.
[3] M. Barbuceanu and W. Lo. A multi-attribute utility theoretic negotiation architecture for electronic commerce. In Carles Sierra, Maria Gini, and Jeffrey S. Rosenschein, editors, *aa2000*, Barcelona, Catalonia, Spain, June 2000.
[4] M. E. Bratman, D. J. Israel, and M. E. Pollack. Plans and resource-bounded practical reasoning. *Computational Intelligence*, 4:349–355, 1988.

[5] K. Fischer, J. P. Muller, I. Heimig, and A. Scheer. Intelligent agents in virtual enterprises. In *Proc. of the First International Conference and Exhibition on The Practical Applications of Intelligent Agents and Multi-Agent Technology*, U.K., 1996.

[6] M. S. Fox, M. Barbuceanu, and M. Gruninger. An organisation ontology for enterprise modelling: Preliminary concepts for linking structure and behaviour. *Computers in Industry*, 29:123–134, 1996.

[7] M. Gruninger, K. Atefi, and M. S. Fox. Ontologies to support process integration in enterprise engineering. *Computational and Mathematical Organisation Theory*, 6(4):381–394, 2000.

[8] N. R. Jennings. Specification and implementation of a belief-desire-joint-intention architecture for collaborative problem solving. *Intelligent and Cooperative Information Systems*, 2(3):289–318, 1993.

[9] N. R. Jennings. *Cooperation in Industrial Multi-agent Systems*. World Scientific, 1994.

[10] M. Matskin, O. J. Kirkeluten, S. B. Krossnes, and Ø. Sæle. Agora: An infrastructure for cooperative work support in multi-agent systems. In T. Wagner and O. Rana, editors, *Infrastructure for Agents, Multi-Agents, and Scalable Multi-Agent Systems, Lecture Notes in Computer Science,*, volume 1887. Springer Verlag, 2001.

[11] R. H. Guttman A. G. Moukas and P. Maes. Agent-mediated electronic commerce: A survey. *Knowledge Engineering Review*, 13(3), 1998.

[12] K. L. Myers. User guide for the procedural reasoning system. Technical report, Artificial Intelligence Center, SRI International, Menlo Park, CA, 1997.

[13] E. Oliveira and A. P. Rocha. *European Perspectives on Agent Mediated Electronic Commerce*, chapter Agents' Advanced Features for Negotiation in Electronic Commerce and Virtual Organisation Formation Process. Springer Verlag, June 2000.

[14] S. A. Petersen. Extended and virtual enterprises - a review of the concepts. Technical Report 2/02, Dept. of Computer and Information Sciences, Norwegian University of Science and Technology, Trondheim, Norway, 2002.

[15] S. A. Petersen and M. Gruninger. An agent-based model to support the formation of virtual enterprises. In *International ICSC Symposium on Mobile Agents and Multi-agents in Virtual Organisations and E-Commerce (MAMA'2000)*, Woolongong, Australia, December 2000.

[16] A. S. Rao and M. P. Georgeff. Modeling rational agents within a BDI architecture. In R. Fikes and E. Sandewall, editors, *Proceedings of Knowledge Representation and Reasoning (KR&R91)*, pages 473–484. Morgan Kaufmann Publishers: San Mateo, CA, 1991.

[17] M. Uschold, M. King, S. Moralee, and Y. Zorgios. The enterprise ontology. *Knowledge Engineering Review, Special Issue on Putting Ontologies to Use*, 13, 1998.

A Multiagent-Based Peer-to-Peer Network in Java for Distributed Spam Filtering

Jörg Metzger, Michael Schillo, and Klaus Fischer

German Research Center for Artificial Intelligence
Stuhlsatzenhausweg 3, 66123 Saarbrücken, Germany
{jmetzger,schillo,kuf}@dfki.de
http://www.dfki.de/

Abstract. With the growing amount of internet users, a negative form of sending email spreads that affects more and more users of email accounts: Spamming. Spamming means that the electronic mailbox is congested with unwanted advertising or personal email. Sorting out this email costs the user time and money. This paper introduces a distributed spam filter, which combines an off-the-shelf text classification with multiagent systems. Both the text classification as well as the multiagent platform are implemented in Java. The content of the emails is analyzed by the classification algorithm 'support vector machines'. Information about spam is exchanged between the agents through the network. Identification numbers for emails which where identified as spam are generated and forwarded to all other agents connected to the network. These numbers allow agents to identify incoming spam email. In this way, the quality of the filter increases continuously.

1 Introduction

One of today's greatest problems of email traffic is the lack of authentification of email servers and senders. Without the possibility to identify the sender of an email, there are people who take advantage of this security gap. They send spam email to a huge amount of people, who did not solicited them. The cost of sending spam emails is very low, giving an incentive to force a high number of users to spend time (and online fees) to filter unwanted messages. There are several ways to get email addresses. Spammers, the sender of spam email, scan mailing lists, homepages and forums. This is done with the help of spambots, programs which automatically scan the internet for email addresses. These lists of valid email addresses are sold to other spammers which use them for their own purposes. Statistics about the amount of spam received since 1996 have shown that in the last two years, the amount of spam email has increased exponentially [10]. These statistics are representative for most users of email accounts. There is no global legal protection from this problem. On the server side, the configuration of your mailserver can be configured to sort out email according to certain criteria and to block email from certain domains. For effective protection, regular reconfiguration of the server settings in necessary. There is also the risk of deleting email

V. Mařík et al. (Eds): CEEMAS 2003, LNAI 2691, pp. 616–625, 2003.

which is not spam. So this is not a satisfactory solution. For this reason, a lot of
software has been developed to recognize and filter spam email. An frequently
used approach is the creation of rules to filter emails. Programs like RIPPER
possess a database of rules [1]. It is difficult to adapt these rules to changes of
the email content and to keep them up-to-date. Other spam filters [6, 13] work
with algorithms developed for text classification. Although these filers delete
a huge amount of spam, they only work isolated from other filters. So they cannot give information about spam to other filters to upgrade their knowledge on
new forms of spam. There exists only one commercial distributed spam filter [12]
which exchanges spam information over a network in a distributed fashion. The
Vipul's Razor filter agents connect to servers which maintain a database with
identification numbers for spam emails. They identify spam emails with the help
of the identification numbers. Although this filter system is basically comparable with our spam filter network, it has several disadvantages. Our network has
no need of centralized servers. Instead, antispam agents are connected as nodes
of a peer-to-peer network which can communicate directly with each other to
exchange information. Furthermore, the Vipul's Razor filter agents cannot deal
with a new form of spam which more and more often appears.

With this work, we introduce a network of spam filter agents which combines the
power of text classification algorithms with a peer-to-peer network. The following section describes the basics of text classification and multiagent systems on
which we base our work. In Section 3 we introduce our spam filter network and
show how it has been implemented in Java. The paper closes with summarizing
remarks and future lines of research.

2   Basics

2.1   Support Vector Machines

Users of our filter network should have the opportunity to let the spam filter
classify incoming email into the categories *spam* or *nonspam* automatically. The
user can correct the classification result if needed. Today, there exits a huge
number of classification algorithms to choose from. Several comparisons of the
different methods have demonstrated that the classification algorithm Support
Vector Machines (SVM) outperforms most of the other algorithms (for example
Naive Bayes and k-nearest neighbor) [2, 5] and reaches rates of accuracy in classifying spam over 95 percent [11]. In order to classify text, its content has to be
represented as a feature vector. We choose a word as feature. The corresponding
vector is composed of various words from a dictionary formed by analyzing the
text contents. The weighting of the feature vector is constructed as follows. If
a particular word occurs in the content of the text, the corresponding value of
the feature is 1, otherwise 0. This is called the 'binary representation' of the feature vector. These vectors can be described as data points in an n-dimensional
space. The basic idea of SVM is to find a hyperplane which best separates the
data points into two classes. In this way, the number of classification errors is

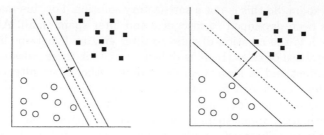

Fig. 1. SVM construct the hyperplane which maximizes the border between the two classes. The classifier on the right is the better one

minimal. Figure 1 shows the best separating hyperplane between the circles and squares in the two-dimensional space.

More precisely, the decision surface by SVM for linearly separable data points is a hyperplane which can be written as $w^T x - b = 0$. x is an arbitrary data point to be classified and the vector w (vector of the hyperplane) and the scalar b are learned from the training data. Let $D = \{(x_i, y_i)\}$ denote the training set with feature vector $x_i \in R^N$ and $y_i \in \{-1, 1\}$ be the classification for x_i ($y_i = +1$ if $x_i \in Spam$ and $y_i = -1$ if $x_i \in Nonspam$), the SVM problem is to find w and b that satisfy the following constraints

$$w^T x_i - b \geq 1 \quad if \ y_i = 1, \tag{1}$$
$$w^T x_i - b \leq -1 \quad if \ y_i = -1$$

and that the vector 2-norm of w is minimized (maximizing the separating hyperplane). Training examples that satisfy (1) are termed support vectors. The support vectors define two hyperplanes, which both go through the support vectors of the respective class. This quadratic optimization problem can be efficiently solved and a new vector x^* can be classified as follows

$$f(x^*) = sign\{w^T x^* - b\} \quad with \quad w = \sum_{i=1}^{N} v_i x_i \tag{2}$$

The course of the hyperplane is only determined by the positions of the N support vectors x_i with weighting v_i which the algorithm calculates.

2.2   Multiagent Systems and FIPA-OS

Multiagent Systems (MAS) consist of several autonomous agents, which work independently and distributed [14]. For that purpose several interfaces are defined. The MAS makes available basic services, where communication and interaction protocols are specified. The agent platform we use is fully implemented in Java.

The FIPA Open Source (FIPA-OS) platform [7] is continuously improved as an open source project and conforms to the agent standards set up by the Foundation for Intelligent Physical Agents (FIPA) [3]. FIPA-OS provides 'white pages' and 'yellow pages' services for the agents. The Directory Facilitator (DF) is a special agent which mediates between all agents on the platform. This includes tasks like registration, service information on other agents, deregistration etc. An index of the names of agents which are currently registered with the agent platform is maintained by the agent management service (AMS) and can be accessed by the DF. The Message Transport System (MTS) is responsible for the platform to platform transport and encoding of the messages. The agents of the MAS work together to achieve the common goal of spam filtering. In order to exchange information about spam, the agents must interact together at a semantically rich level of discourse. FIPA-OS provides an agent communication language (ACL) which describes a standard way to package messages, in such a way that it is clear to other compliant agents what the purpose of the communication is. These rules ensure that the semantic integrity of the language is retained. Negotiation, cooperation and information exchange are supported.

In the next section, we will show how the combination of multiagent systems and text classification leads to a functional distributed spam filter network.

3   Structure of the Distributed Spam Filter

In the following, we describe our novel approach on spam filtering based on the advantages of 'support vector machines' and multiagent systems. We explain the design and the implementation of a peer-to-peer spam filter network. Within the network, data concerning spam is exchanged between the agents. For each email, an identification number is created as described in Section 3.1. If the email is identified as spam by the classification algorithm, the corresponding number is sent to all other agents connected to the network. The antispam agents compare the identification numbers of all incoming email with those spam numbers collected from other agents. The concrete procedure of the antispam agents is described in Section 3.2. The last Section shows the interface in detail and the possibilities available for the user to influence the classification of email and to correct false decisions made by the spam filter.

3.1   Creation and Comparing of Hash Values

One of the necessary functions of the antispam agent is the ability to compare two different emails. For reasons of security, it is not desirable to send the plain text of the content of emails over to network to other agents and compare them word by word. The user certainly does not want other users to be able to reconstruct the contents of the received email from the data sent. Representations of the email content like word vectors cannot be sent over the network as well. Instead, a unique identification number for every email is generated locally and send to other agents if the corresponding email is spam. Therefore, it is impossible to conclude from this identification number (hash value) to the content of the corresponding email. Many procedures have been developed to deal with this issue. One popular solution is to hash the content of the email into a SHA-digest (secure hash algorithm) [9]. Although the SHA-digests which were created through hashing are easily to compare, they have a serious disadvantage. They cannot deal with a new form of spam. The content of this new form of spam is varied slightly from user to user, i.e. they contain details like the address of the receiver. So, although the email is from one sender and basically identical, the content of the spam message is slightly different for every user who receives it and hence, the SHA-algorithm generates a different digest for each message. Therefore, the SHA-algorithm cannot be used to compare the message contents. Our identification number generated for the content of emails follows a different idea.

For a certain amount of representative letters of the alphabet, the relative frequency of their occurrence in the content of the email is recorded. We line up the frequencies of these letters to a hash value. If we want to compare two hash values, the difference of the frequencies for each letter are formed and added up. The greater this value is, the more different are the frequencies of the letters and the more different are the two corresponding emails. This kind of identification number has several advantages:

- Emails with slightly different content are recognized as similar and spam email created in this way can be identified.
- Hash values of messages with the same content are equal to each other, their difference is zero.
- The hash value does not disclose any information on the contents of the emails to other users.

3.2   Spam Classification Procedure of the Antispam Agent

The principal unit of the spam filter network is the antispam agent. Every agent is assigned to a user. The agent is situated in the FIPA-OS platform treated in Section 2.2. The platform provides the antispam agent with a list of all other active agents in the network. This service is done by the Directory Facilitator. The agent stores the list of active agents in his own database, allowing the antispam agent to start communication with the other antispam agents. It sends them a request for new information about spam which the other agents have collected in the time where it was not connected to the network. Now, the other agent itself adds the sending agent to its database of active agents. The exchange of information is provided by the 'inform' communication act, part of the FIPA communication standard.

At the beginning of the classification process (cf. Fig. 2), the antispam agent downloads new messages from the mailserver of the user. The connection to a POP3 or IMAP server can be established using the Java Email Interface [4]. The configuration for the individual email account can be specified and saved by

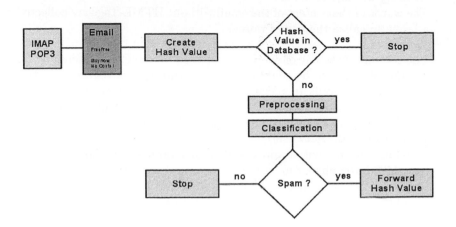

Fig. 2. Functionality of the antispam agent

the user. After downloading and optionally deleting the email from the server, the antispam agent generates hash values for each of the downloaded emails. The process of generating hash values is explained in more detail in Section 3.1. These values are compared with the hash value entries of spam in the local database of the agent. Note that the database only contains hash values of messages which where clearly classified as spam by the agent itself or by another agent which sent this spam hash value through the network. If the hash value of the new email matches with one in the database, the email is spam. In case the content of the two compared emails only differs slightly, the difference of the two belonging hash values is rather small. The more different the content of two emails is, the greater the difference between the hash values is. The user can specify a threshold value. Emails whose similarity to each other lies over this threshold are regarded as similar. With the help of this similarity measure, spam emails from the same sender which only differ in a few letters (e.g. personal address of the receiver) are recognized as equal and are filtered. The spam email is transferred to a specific folder for later review (optionally the email can be deleted directly). If the hash value is not sufficiently similar to one of the spam hash values, it has passed the first filter. It is forwarded to the classification algorithm. Before the SVM algorithm can start to classify, the text of the email has to be preprocessed. The necessary preprocessing steps are as follows:

– *Removing HTML-Tags*
  Because the Email will be classified with the help of word occurrences, all other parts of the email must be deleted. There is also the possibility that the tags contain (for the user invisible) information to mislead the classification algorithm. Therefore all HTML-Tags are deleted.

- *Creating the Bag of Words*
  The words of the content of the email without HTML-Tags are collected into a list, also called the bag of words.
- *Stemming*
  The content of the bag of words is processed by the Porter Stemmer [8]. The amount of words to be considered for classification is reduced by stripping all suffixes of words to receive their root forms, i.e. stripping the words 'introduction', 'introduced' to 'introduc'. The meanings of the words remain, but the number of words to be considered is reduced.
- *Using Stop List (optionally)*
  To reduce the amount of words further, general words without special meaning which often appear in texts can be cut off, i.e. words like 'the', 'of', 'on' etc. This method is not undisputed, some authors explain that using the stop list reduces the accuracy of the classification algorithm [2].
- *Representing Text as Attribute Vectors*
  The remaining words are mapped into an attribute vector. If the attribute (word) is in the bag of words, its corresponding attribute receives the value 1 independently how often the word occurs in the text. Otherwise this attribute gets the value 0. The created vector is called 'binary vector', because it only consists of $values \in \{0,1\}$. It is used in many text classification algorithms providing good classification results.

After the preprocessing, the actual classification is taken over by the support vector machines algorithm as a second filter. Before this algorithm can be applied, its classifier has to be trained based on training data. Training data consists of labelled email vectors, which have already been classified. The SVM algorithm builds up a training matrix from those classified vectors. Hereafter, the algorithm is ready to classify the unlabelled vectors of new emails. The preprocessed binary vector of the email is arranged either into the class 'spam' or the class 'nonspam'. The vector is classified using the matrix generated of training vectors. After the algorithm has arranged the email, the user has the possibility to change the classification judgement made by the SVM algorithm. Especially if the training matrix of vectors is small, there is a risk of misclassification. To increase the classification accuracy, the classified vector is taken into the local training matrix of the agent. With the growth of the matrix, the SVM algorithm quickly reaches a precision of over 95 percent [11]. Only if the email is classified as spam, its hash value is transferred to all other connected agents, which store this hash value in their local database. If they receive the same spam message, the recognize it at once, because the hash values generated from the newly received email is equal to the one received by the other antispam agent. Because it is impossible to infer the original content of the corresponding email from the hash value, the data transfer within the spam filter network preserves privacy, an important design objective. We explain why we do not send the classified email vectors through the network to antispam agents with a small amount of training vectors. This would power up their ability to classify emails correctly after a short time inside the spam filter network. But there are several big disadvantages which stand against sending vectors over the network. First of all, there is the possibility to recreate the content of the emails by analyzing the corresponding vector. This security gap does not appear when sending hash values which where created to guarantee security. Furthermore, malicious users could try to reduce the quality of the network by sending thousands of misleading vectors to other antispam agents.

3.3   Interface of the Antispam Agent

Figure 3 shows the user interface to the database of hash values from an antispam agent which is connected to the network. The hash value generated from the current email is displayed in the box below the list. This value is compared to all values of the database. The list of hash values is regularly updated by exchanging spam information with other agents. The similarity threshold for emails can be adjusted with the slider on the right from 70 % up to 100 %. The tab 'All Email' leads to the list of emails loaded from the server. The tab 'Classification' shows the result of the SVM algorithm in classifying the current email. The other agents connected to the network can be seen under the tab 'Agents'. This interface allows to easy control the classification activity of the user's antispam agent. This is important for the acceptance of such a tool.

4   Conclusions

In order to deal with the huge amount of spam received day by day, powerful email filters with high reliability are needed. We combined multiagent systems with text categorization to identify spam. Information about spam emails spreads over the network to all other agents. If one agent has classified a certain spam email, all other agents profit from the hash value sent to them. They recognize the same spam email with absolute reliability. Similar emails (with different personal address for example) are also detected and recognized. By the data exchange, agents which enter the network are quickly provided with actual information about spam. Newly created agents receive hash values from other agents of the network and set up quickly an up-to-date database with spam information. The second filter, support vector machines, greatly supports the antispam agents at the task of classification of incoming unknown email in order to create new hash values. Every user can influence the creation of his individual training matrix by changing the classification results of SVM. Thus, he can specify the email to be classified as spam to its own taste. A lot of advantages arise from the use of the MAS platform FIPA-OS. Agents can register and deregister with FIPA-OS on the fly without influencing the stability of the system. FIPA-OS enables the communication between antispam agents and allows simultaneous and asynchronous email classification. This form of spam filtering is attractive for both the normal user as well as enterprises.

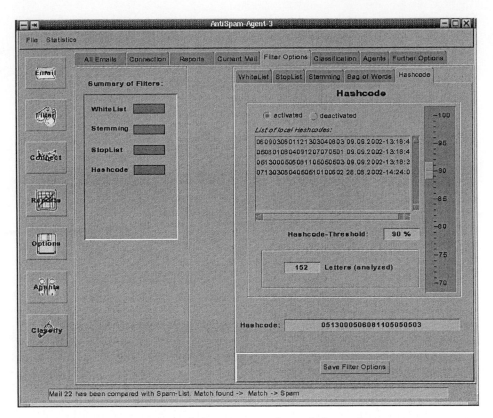

Fig. 3. Screenshot of the user interface of the antispam agent

5   Future Work

There are still two disadvantages within our spam filter approach. Firstly, a huge amount of data overhead is produced by the regularly exchange of hash values. Furthermore, it is possible for malicious users to flood our network with thousands of false hash values. In order to eliminate these drawbacks, we are currently working on a simulation platform of a distributed spam filter network with up to 100 agents where antispam agents will evaluate the hash values they receive and establish trust to agents which provide useful and correct hash values to identify spam. After exceeding certain thresholds, benevolent agents that receive the same spam mails will group together, exchange hash values within their group and use only hash values provided by trusted group members to identify spam. In this way, we will eliminate the two disadvantages mentioned above. The amount of data which is transferred over the network will be reduced by forcing the hash value exchange within the group of agents which receive the same spam. Malicious agents will be excluded from the groups of benevolent agents and will be prevented from flooding these groups with false hash values. Within the scope of the simulation platform, we will evaluate if the exchange of hash values within the network of antispam agents increases the total number of spam mails which are identified correctly.

With a few changes, our spam filter could also be used to assign emails to certain categories of interest. A user could sort emails about 'sports' or 'news' in the corresponding folders. Furthermore the filter network can be enhanced with several other components in the future. A whitelist filter which specifies a list of trusted email senders has already been included. Email from these people will never be classified as spam. Further filters can be implemented: Blacklists could be set up with addresses of people and organizations which sent spam email in the past. Their email could be blocked by the filter. The modular structure of the antispam agents with all modules written in Java provides space for additional identification methods for spam.

References

[1] W. W. Cohen (1996): Learning Rules that classify e-mail. Proceedings of the AAAI Spring Symposium on Machine Learning in Information Access 18–25, AAAI Press.

[2] V. Vapnik, H. Drucker, D. Wu (1999): Support Vector Machines for Spam Categorization. In: IEEE Transactions on Neural Networks, 10(5):1048 1054.

[3] Homepage of the Foundation for Intelligent Physical Agent (FIPA). http://www.fipa.org

[4] Java Mail (TM) API Design Specification. Sun Microsystems, Inc.: http://java.sun.com/products/javamail/JavaMail-1.2.pdf

[5] S. Shankar, G. Karypis (2000): A Feature Weight Adjustment Algorithm for Document Categorization. Proceedings of the Sixth International Conference on Knowledge Discovery and Data Mining (ACM SIGKDD 2000).

[6] P. Pantel and D. Lin (1998): SpamCop - A Spam Classification and Organization Program. Proceedings of AAAI-98 Workshop on Learning for Text Categorization 95–98, AAAI Press.

[7] Nortel Networks Corporation FIPA-OS Informations: http://www.nortelnetworks.com/products/announcements/fipa

[8] M. F. Porter (1980): An algorithm for suffix stripping. In: Program, 14(3):130–137.

[9] Secure Hash Standard (1995): Federal Information Processing Standards Publication 180-1. National Institute of Standards and Technology.

[10] Spam Statistic: http://www.raingod.com/angus/Computing/Internet/Spam/Statistics/index.html

[11] V. N. Vapnik, D. Wu (1998): Support Vector Machine for Text Categorization. AT&T Research Labs, http://citeseer.nj.nec.com/347263.htm

[12] Vipul's Razor Homepage. http://razor.sourceforge.net

[13] J. D. M. Rennie (2000): ifile: An Application of Machine Learning to E-Mail Filtering. Proceedings of the KDD-2000 Workshop on Text Mining, Sixth ACM SIGKDD International Conference on Knowledge Discovery and Data Mining.

[14] M. Wooldridge, N. Jennings (1995): Intelligent Agents: Theory and Practice. In: Knowledge Engineering Review 10(2):115–152, Cambridge University Press.

Engineering Web Service Invocations
from Agent Systems

László Zsolt Varga and Ákos Hajnal

Computer and Automation Research Institute
Kende u. 13-17, 1111 Budapest, Hungary
{laszlo.varga,ahajnal}@sztaki.hu
http://www.sztaki.hu/

Abstract. This paper presents a methodology that helps to bridge the gap between the theoretical foundations of agent technologies and their potential for industry-wide deployment. Agent systems are very often developed on top of a legacy system where agents have to be able to access the legacy system, usually web services, through a non-agent protocol and they have to be able to communicate with each other using an agent language. The methodology shows how existing web services can be integrated into agent systems. We have implemented tools to support the application of the methodology to mass amount of web service applications and a sample application to demonstrate the usage of the methodology and the supporting tools.

1 Introduction

Because the agent oriented approach is considered as one of the most important models for engineering complex distributed systems, research on methods for agent engineering [1] became important. Methods for engineering agent systems from scratch are well developed [2] and there are methods for creating agent systems from existing applications as well [3]. In most of the cases agent systems are developed on top of a legacy system [4] where agents have to be able to access the legacy system through a non-agent protocol and they have to be able to communicate with each other using an agent language. By developing methodologies for integrating existing systems into agent systems we help to bridge the gap between the theoretical foundations of agent technologies and their potential for industry-wide deployment.

Nowadays there are standards for these interfaces: agent communication is standardized by FIPA [5] and the web service interface [6][7] characterized by XML, SOAP, UDDI and WSDL is becoming widely used for accessing Internet applications, therefore it is promising to integrate existing systems into agent based systems using the FIPA and the web services standards. In this paper we discuss a novel methodology for engineering agent systems based on existing web services and present a code generating tool supporting the methodology.

V. Mařík et al. (Eds): CEEMAS 2003, LNAI 2691, pp. 626-635, 2003.
© Springer-Verlag Berlin Heidelberg 2003

2   Agent Architecture for Web Service Invocation

In agent systems based on web services there are agents, which invoke existing web services and utilize web service invocation results in agent interactions. The utilization of web services in agent systems gives the advantage of reusing existing applications and the rapid development of agent based systems. However web services do not have the autonomous and the proactive features required in agent based software engineering. In order to seamlessly integrate web services into agent based systems, the existing web services have to be extended with agent features. This extension can be done in two different ways discussed in the following.

The FIPA standard proposes the use of Agent Resource Broker (ARB) and wrapper agents for existing applications [8]. The ARB agent brokers a set of software descriptions to interested agents and client agents can ask from it what software services are available. In this paper we are not going to deal with the ARB, because we are investigating how the services of the existing application can be invoked. We will consider ARB aspects only when our design decisions have effect on how wrapper agent services can be found.

The wrapper agent of the FIPA standard performs a formal transformation of a non-agent interface to an agent interface without adding agent logic to it. The wrapper agent allows a client agent to request a dynamic connection to an existing software, invoke operations, get the results of the operations, query the properties and set the parameters of the software system, subscribe to events, manage the state of the existing software and terminate it. Because web services are usually provided by external service providers, the management of the state of the web service is not in the hands of the agent system. The main function of the wrapper agent is the invocation of service operations.

If we want to integrate the non-agent system into an agent system, then we have to add agent logic to the existing application as well, so we are going to investigate how agent logic can be included in the FIPA wrapper agent concept. Basically there are two different ways to do it: either the agent logic is integrated in the wrapper agent, or there are separate wrapper agents and a separate intelligent agent containing the agent logic and this agent invokes the wrapper agents which simply call the web services and return the results.

2.1   Architecture with Integrated Wrapper Agent

The agent architecture for web service invocation with integrated wrapper agent is shown in Figure 1. In this approach the wrapper agent has proactive and autonomous features and it may combine the results of one or more web service invocations.

The advantage of this approach is that the agent logic can efficiently be integrated with web service invocations. Web services are directly invoked from the wrapper agent, the results are processed within the wrapper agent and only the combined result is converted to FIPA ACL (Agent Communication Language). All conversions are done efficiently inside the wrapper agent code.

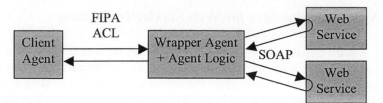

Fig. 1. Integrated wrapper agent converts SOAP protocol (Simple Object Access Protocol) into FIPA ACL (Agent Communication Language) and implements agent logic

The disadvantage of this approach is that agent logic is tightly integrated with the web services and if a given web service is utilized by several wrapper agents, then web service invocation has to be implemented in each wrapper agent. This approach reduces the reusability of wrapper agents.

2.2   Architecture with Separate Wrapper Agents

The agent architecture for web service invocation with separate wrapper agents is shown in Figure 2. In this approach the proactive and autonomous features implemented in a separate intelligent agent and there are separate wrapper agents for each web service. The wrapper agents provide the same functionality as the web services they wrap, but through a FIPA ACL interface.

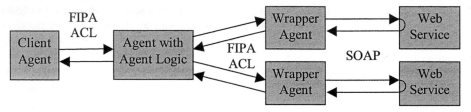

Fig. 2. Wrapper agent converts SOAP protocol into FIPA ACL and separate agent implements agent logic

The advantage of this approach is that agent logic and web service invocations are clearly separated, which makes the design, the maintenance and the reusability of the developed components easier. Different intelligent agents can use the same wrapper agents and combine the results of the same web service invocations in different ways to provide different intelligent agent services. The separate wrapper agents can also be handled separately by the ARB and other agents can dynamically discover and utilize the services of the wrapper agents.

The disadvantage of this approach is that the web service invocation results are first converted into FIPA ACL and they are combined into intelligent agent result later, which adds additional FIPA ACL communication between the web service and the intelligent agent. The price for the flexible architecture is slower operation.

Although the architecture with integrated wrapper agent gives an implementation with faster code, the architecture with separate wrapper agents is much clearer and flexible, therefore we recommend the latter one and we are going to discuss the engineering of this architecture in the rest of this paper. However many of our engineering results will be applicable to the architecture with integrated wrapper agents with the modifications of putting the agent logic into the wrapper agent.

3   Engineering Approach

Having defined the architecture for web service invocation from agent systems, we can concentrate on how this architecture can be implemented efficiently for mass amount of web services. The engineering approach of the implementation must build on the fact that web services have a well defined interface which allows the definition of patterns for web service invocation from agent systems. Once the pattern is defined, we can build tools to generate stubs or even full code for wrapper agents in order to facilitate the mass utilization of web services in agent systems.

In order to build the web service invocation pattern, we have to identify the software components in the web service invocation architecture. Basically we have the existing non-agent system and the agent system. On the web service side we have to grab the relevant parameters of web services. Web service instances are described in the Web Service Definition Language (WSDL) [9]. The important parameters of the web services can be extracted from the WSDL description, as it will be discussed in section 3.1. On the agent system side the most important software components are the ontology code for the FIPA ACL communication and the agent implementation code of the wrapper agent. These will be discussed in section 3.2.

3.1   Web Services

Web services are network services, which can be considered as a set of endpoints operating on messages containing either document-oriented or procedure-oriented information. Web services are described by WSDL documents in XML format.

A WSDL document defines abstract services, which are collections of network endpoints, called ports. For these ports a collection of operations are bound representing abstract actions, moreover for each operation input and output messages are assigned, which are abstract descriptions of the data being exchanged. Messages are further decomposed into parts whose data types are defined using the XSD (XML Schema Definition) type system [10]. Such abstract definitions of ports and operations are then bound to their concrete network deployment (such as internet location and communication protocol) via extensibility elements.

In WSDL there are abstract definitions, which are separated from their concrete network deployment. Although this allows the reuse of abstract definitions, in practice, when we want to connect an agent system to a concrete web service, we are interested in the concrete deployment.

In order to be able to use WSDL descriptions for agent system creation, we introduced an internal representation of concrete web services. The internal representation contains only the necessary, but complete information about the actual invocation of the web service as it is illustrated in Figure 3.

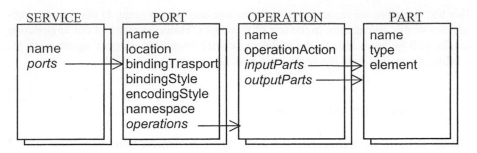

Fig. 3. Internal representation of concrete web services with location and protocol information

Parsing the WSDL and creating such an internal representation of web services allow us to grab and verify all the relevant information about the web service, moreover it provides an easier way to generate ontology and agent code (section 4.1) of wrapper agents.

3.2   Agent System Software Components

The two most important software components in agent system implementation are the ontology code and the agent code. The ontology code implements the way the agents encode, decode and interpret ACL messages. The agent code implements the actions taken by the agent. In the case of wrapper agents there are direct mappings from web service definitions to ontology code and web service invocation to agent code, because the wrapper agent converts the web service protocol to ACL messages and the only type of action it takes is the web service invocation.

The web service data types defined in the WSDL are mapped to ontology data types. The concrete mapping is discussed in the next section, where we deal with concrete agent platforms and data types. The web service invocation is mapped to an ACL message of FIPA REQUEST type corresponding to an agent action. The returned web service result is mapped to an ACL message of FIPA INFORM type corresponding to a predicate in the ontology.

The wrapper agent receives the FIPA REQUEST, interprets it according to the ontology, invokes the web service on the port defined in the WSDL, encodes the result of the web service invocation into a FIPA INFORM of the ontology and returns the result.

The intelligent agent, which adds agent logic to the wrapper agents, in communicating with its clients will use an ontology similar to the ontology used in communicating with the wrapper agents and probably a few other concepts, actions and elements, because the intelligent agent presents the web service results. The behavior of the intelligent agent also contains agent logic. Figure 4 shows how the agent system can be created for web service invocations.

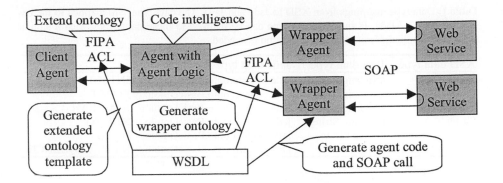

Fig. 4. Most of the code can be generated from WSDL, intelligence has to be added manually

Because the WSDL formally and completely describes the web services, and there is a direct mapping to the formal ontology and agent code, we can completely generate the code for the wrapper ontology and the wrapper agent code. Because the extended ontology and the intelligent agent contains agent logic, we can only generate a template for them and add the agent logic manually.

4   Engineering Tools and Methods

We have defined the agent system architecture for web service invocation and identified the necessary software components with the mapping from the web service definition. We are now in the position, where we can concentrate on the methods and the tools for generating and implementing the software code of the agent system itself. According to the survey of the Agentcities [11] world wide test bed of agent systems the market leader is Jade [12], a Java based agent platform, therefore we will elaborate the details of our method of software code creation for agents implemented in the Jade platform.

The methodology defines the way how the wrapper ontology code (section 4.1), the wrapper agent code (section 4.1) and the extended ontology template (section 4.2) are created, as well as a chart (section 4.3) describing the relations of these processes. These methods are implemented in the tools supporting the creation of agent systems for web service invocation.

4.1   Jade Ontology and Agent Code for Web Service Invocation

First we have to define how we map the XSD data types of the WSDL definition used in parameter passing to the Jade/Java data types for the web service invocation. The mapping is shown in Table 1 and it is general and valid for all web services. Note that we have to use Jade's internal types (e.g. BasicOntology.INTEGER) when registering an ontology in the platform, but on the other hand ontology codes have to be written in Java, where we must use native Java data types. The Jade-Java type mapping is defined in Jade documentation [13].

Table 1. Data type mappings from XSD to Jade and Java. The data types are mapped to the basic data types of Jade. If an XSD data type can be mapped to these data types, then a similar mapping is applied, if not, then a workaround is needed

XSD data type	Java data type	Jade data type
Integer	java.lang.Integer	jade.content.onto.BasicOntology.INTEGER
Float	java.lang.Float	jade.content.onto.BasicOntology.FLOAT
Boolean	java.lang.Boolean	jade.content.onto.BasicOntology.BOOLEAN
String	java.lang.String	jade.content.onto.BasicOntology.STRING
Date	java.util.Date	jade.content.onto.BasicOntology.DATE
HexBinary	byte[]	jade.content.onto.BasicOntology.BYTE_SEQUENCE

The ontology code of Jade agents has a standard structure as defined also in the Jade manuals [13]. This structure is used as a template and the concrete ontology code is generated using the parameters from the internal representation (see section 3.1) of the concrete web service. For each operation of the WSDL document a unique AgentAction-Predicate pair of classes is assigned representing the inputs and outputs of the web service invocation. This solution will allow the wrapper agent to decide which operation needs to be called on a request (by verifying the class instance of the incoming AgentAction message) and will determine the corresponding Predicate which will contain the result. The input parameters of the web service call, and its results are also wrapped in the related AgentAction and Predicate classes, respectively.

Figure 5 shows a part of generating the ontology code that produces the agent actions and the predicates. If there is an operation "Operation1" with "param1" input and "result1" output in the WSDL, then an "Operation1AgentAction" class with "param1" variable and an "Operation1Predicate" class with "result1" variable are generated. Generating the ontology instance to register the agent actions and predicates is done similarly from the internal representation.

The agents of the Jade platform extend the Agent class. The web service wrapper agent first registers in its setup method the ontology. Then the wrapper agent waits for incoming requests from clients in a blocking cycle. This is implemented as a behavior extending the CyclicBehaviour class. When a request is received, then the wrapper agent determines from the type of the request class the web service operation to which this request is related. The input parameters of the operation can be decoded from the request, and the web service operation can be invoked. The result of the web service invocation is encoded to the corresponding predicate class of the ontology, then the predicate is sent to the client as an inform message.

Because the above described algorithm has a template, the agent code for all web service invocations can be generated from the internal web service representation by substituting application specific values similarly as it is shown in Figure 5. Due to the limitations of this paper we cannot include the figure showing how the agent code is generated.

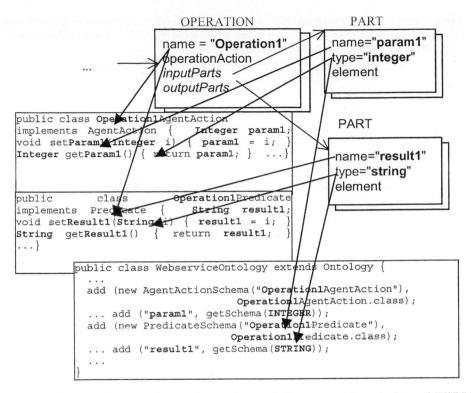

Fig. 5. A fragment of the ontology code. Ontology code is generated from the internal WSDL model using a template and substituting application specific values

4.2   Protégé Project Code for Extended Ontology Template

The ontology that we generated for the wrapper agent is good for implementing the wrapper agent, but it cannot be edited easily to create the extended ontology for the intelligent agent that adds agent logic to the wrapper agents. To support the creation of the extended ontology we introduced a methodology and implemented a program to create Protégé project code from the internal representation of the web service. Protégé [14] is a knowledge engineering tool for ontology creation and edition.

In order to generate the Protégé project code, first we have to define how we map the XSD data types of the WSDL definition to the Open Knowledge Base Connectivity (OKBC) data types of Protégé. This is a general mapping and valid for all web services. Using this mapping the frames in the Protégé project file can be generated.

Protégé has an extension to generate Java code for Jade agents, therefore if we generate an initial Protégé project code from the web service description using this mapping, then this initial Protégé project can be extended and the initial code for the intelligent agent for the web service can be generated as well.

Table 2. Data type mappings from XSD to OKBC. The data types are mapped to the basic data types of OKBC. If an XSD data type can be mapped to these data types, then a similar mapping is applied, if not, then a workaround is needed using facets

XSD data type	OKBC data type
integer	Integer
float	Float
string	String
all other types	String

4.3   Engineering Process

Now we are in the position to summarize how to create the agent system for web service invocation. The software components of the agent system of Figure 2 can be created using the process shown in Figure 6 below.

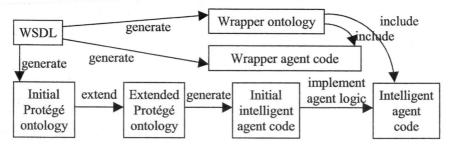

Fig. 6. The engineering process of agent system creation for web service invocation

We implemented the methodology described in this paper into a set of code generating tools and created a sample agent system based on existing web services. They are publicly available from our web site [15].

5   Summary and Acknowledgements

We have presented a methodology that helps to bridge the gap between the theoretical foundations of agent technologies and their potential for industry-wide deployment. The methodology shows how existing web services described in WSDL files can be integrated into agent systems. We have implemented tools to support the application of the methodology to mass amount of web service applications and a sample application to demonstrate the usage of the methodology and the supporting tools. Further work is required to extend the scope of the supporting tools as well as the agent platforms and knowledge engineering tools to a wide range of data types.

This publication is supported by IKTA4 grant 121/2001 and the implementation was carried out by the System Development Department of SZTAKI. The sample application to demonstrate the methodology was designed and implemented by Eric Pantera supported by an Agentcities student exchange grant. Our work was partly stimulated by similar work within the Integrating Web Services Working Group of the Agentcities project lead by Jonathan Dale from Fujitsu Laboratories of America as well as an initiative for a similar interest group of the World Wide Web Consortium. We are also thankful for Bernard Burg, Steven Willmott, Simon Thompson, David Bonnefoy and many other people for creating and maintaining the impulsive environment of the Agentcities world wide test bed in which the supporting tools are installed.

References

[1]   Zambonelli, F., Jennings, N. R., Omicini, A., Wooldridge, M.: "Agent-Oriented Software Engineering for Internet Applications" in Coordination of Internet Agents (eds. Omicini, A., Zambonelli, F., Klusch, M., Tolksdorf, R.) Springer Verlag (2001) 326-346.

[2]   Wooldridge, M., Jennings, N. R., Kinny, D.: "The Gaia Methodology for Agent-Oriented Analysis and Design" Journal of Autonomous Agents and Multi-Agent Systems 3 (3) (2000) 285-312.

[3]   Varga, L.Z., Jennings, N.R., Cockburn, D.: "Integrating Intelligent Systems into a Cooperating Community for Electricity Management", Expert Systems with Applications, Vol. 7, No. 4, Elsevier Science Ltd., (1994) pp. 563-579

[4]   Jennings, N.R., Corera, J., Laresgoiti, I., Mamdani, E.H., Perriollat, F., Skarek, P., Varga, L.Z.: "Using ARCHON to develop real-world DAI applications for electricity transportation management and particle accelerator control", IEEE Expert, Vol.11, No.6 (1996) pp. 64-86

[5]   Dale, J., Mamdani, E.: "Open Standards for Interoperating Agent-Based Systems" In: Software Focus, 1(2), Wiley, 2001.

[6]   Web Services, Executive and Technical White Papers at http://www.webservices.org/

[7]   UDDI, Universal Description, Discovery and Integration of Business for the Web, Executive and Technical White Papers available at http://www.uddi.org/

[8]   Foundation for Intelligent Physical Agents: "FIPA Agent Software Integration Specification", http://www.fipa.org/specs/fipa00079/, (2001)

[9]   Web Services Description Language (WSDL), http://www.w3.org/TR/wsdl

[10] W3C Working Draft "XML Schema Part 1: Structures", "XML Schema Part 2: Datatypes", http://www.w3.org/TR/xmlschema-1/, http://www.w3.org/TR/xmlschema-2/

[11] Willmott, S.N., Dale, J., Burg, B., Charlton, P., O'brien, P.: "Agentcities: A Worldwide Open Agent Network", Agentlink News 8 (Nov. 2001) 13-15, http://www.AgentLink.org/newsletter/8/AL-8.pdf

[12] Bellifemine, F., Poggi, A., Rimassa, G.: "JADE - A FIPA-compliant agent framework", In Proc. of the Fourth International Conference and Exhibition on the Practical Application of Intelligent Agents and Multi-Agents (PAAM'99), London, UK, (1999) pp. 97-108.

[13] Giovanni, C.: „Jade Tutorial: Application- Defined Content Languages and Ontologies", http://sharon.cselt.it/projects/jade/doc/CLOntoSupport.pdf

[14] Noy, N.F., Sintek, M., Decker, S., Crubezy, M., Fergerson, R.W., Musen, M.A.: "Creating Semantic Web Contents with Protégé-2000", IEEE Intelligent Systems, 16(2), (2001), pp. 60-71

[15] http://sas.ilab.sztaki.hu:8080/wsdltool, http://sas.ilab.sztaki.hu:8080/wsid

A Component Based Multi-agent Architecture to Support Mobile Business Processes

Habin Lee and John Shepherdson

Intelligent Systems Laboratory, BTexact Technologies
B62 MLB1/pp12, Adastral Park, Martlesham Heath, Ipswich, Suffolk, IP5 3RE, UK
{ha.lee,john.shepherdson}@bt.com

Abstract. Information as to the location of mobile workers plays a central role in tracking and co-ordinating teams in mobile business processes. This paper describes a multi-agent architecture for location based workflow management and team co-ordination. The architecture is based on reusable components that facilitate multi-agent interactions to produce services for locating and co-ordinating members of mobile teams and can be used as a generic approach, which is customised to support various kinds of mobile business processes. The details on the components and architecture for multi-agent systems are given and details of a case study, where an application based on the architecture was applied to a real mobile business process, are included to show its usefulness.

1   Introduction

Workflow management systems (WFMSs) have been considered a key technology to automate (or manage) business processes from the early 1990s. While there has been a lot of research on the use of WFMSs to support 'static' business processes (such as those executed within an office environment), relatively little research has been undertaken to automate 'mobile' business processes (mBPs).

A static business process is characterised by stable network connections, use of powerful computing devices, and easy access to various knowledge sources within the corporate Intranet. On the other hand, a mBP is centred around tasks which are performed outside of the office environment, where the network connection is low bandwidth and may be intermittent, and the mobile workers are provided with portable devices which have limited computing resources. These constraints place additional requirements on the development of a WFMS to support mBPs.

Firstly, mobile workers frequently travel between disparate locations (both to complete the various tasks necessary to fulfil a single Customer order, and to move on to the next Customer order); secondly, access to necessary electronic information sources can be problematic (because of the need to make a secure connection from anywhere in the field); thirdly, task duration is less predictable (due in part to

V. Mařík et al. (Eds): CEEMAS 2003, LNAI 2691, pp. 636-646, 2003.
© Springer-Verlag Berlin Heidelberg 2003

inaccurate travel-time estimation). As a result, some urgent Customer orders cannot be completed in time by the mobile worker originally assigned to them. Collaboration between mobile workers may be necessary in order to collectively re-balance work schedules to ensure that Customer orders can be completed in a timely fashion. Finally, tracking the location of mobile workers is crucial to ensure that appointment times with customers are met.

In this paper, a multi-agent system (MAS) approach is used to resolve the common constraints found within many mBPs. The use of a MAS has advantages for supporting mobile workers compared to other distributed systems, and as such has been the subject of much research in team co-ordination mechanisms. An autonomous intelligent agent can play the role of personal assistant for a mobile worker who is isolated from essential information sources on the Company Intranet and has difficulty getting real-time contacts with his/her colleagues. Furthermore, an autonomous agent is able to track the location of a mobile worker using a positioning system, such as a GPS (Global Positioning System) device, without the need to distract the mobile worker, and can autonomously provide whereabouts information to a central server agent for process tracking purposes (such as 'duty of care').

Not withstanding these advantages, the development of a MAS is considered difficult because of the reliance on message based communication. The creation and interpretation of a message requires an understanding of agent communication language (ACL), ontologies, and interaction protocols [1], which can be difficult for novice agent programmers to understand. The architecture proposed in this paper consists of re-usable and adjustable components which hide all the message composition and interpretation details from the user. The use of these components facilitates template-based, reliable message exchanges between agents. This feature is essential to support mBPs that have requirements over and above the common constraints mentioned above. The architecture can be used as an architectural pattern [2], which can be customised for mBPs that have different requirements by replacing (or customising) one or more of the proposed components.

This paper consists of four sections. The next section briefly reviews related work. Section 3 describes a framework which shows the relationship between components, architecture, and applications. Section 4 proposes a set of components and an architectural pattern that can be customised for the management of mBPs. Furthermore, the architectural pattern is customised to a real business process. Finally, section 5 summarises this paper.

2   Related Works

Multi-agent systems are used as a core technology in various applications, from information retrieval [3] to business process automation [4]. Most of the multi-agent system platforms are based on Java and must be run on 'heavyweight' (e.g. desktop or server) devices using Java 2 Standard Edition (J2SE) - examples include [5] and [6]. However, the Lightweight Extensible Agent Platform (LEAP) [7] is an exception, as it enables the key components of a multi-agent system to run on a wide range of devices, from PDAs and Smart Phones using either Java 2 Micro Edition (J2ME) or Personal

Java, to desktops and servers running J2SE. This paper favours LEAP as a MAS implementation platform as it enables the mobile worker to run a mBP-support application on a highly portable device (such as a PDA or mobile phone) in preference to a luggable laptop computer when working 'up poles and down holes' or on Customer's premises.

Agent technology has long been used for the development of WFMSs. Huhns and Singh [8] summarise the state of art on agent-based workflows. Shepherdson et al. [9] use a MAS for the co-ordination of cross-organisational workflows. Jennings et al. [4] insist that a MAS has the necessary features for the support of modern dynamic business processes and propose a suitable MAS architecture. Most of this research, however, is targeted at business processes that are executed within an office environment. One exception is the work of Alonso et al. [10] that suggests a workflow system architecture to support mobile clients where each one downloads tasks in batch mode before disconnection, and synchronises the state of the downloaded tasks later by reconnecting to the central workflow server. This utility of this approach, however, is limited in that the downloaded tasks are difficult to monitor from a central workflow engine during the period of disconnection.

The research on agent architectures can be classified into two categories: the internal architecture of a single agent and the architecture of a multi-agent system. Kinny et al. [11] consider a logical model, BDI (Belief, Desire, and Intention), as an architecture for a single agent. In MAS, the multi-agent architecture plays an important role in defining relationships and collaboration among agents [12]. The multi-agent architecture, as used in most MAS, is outlined in informal diagrams [12][13], which focus on implementation rather than the analysis, design, and evaluation of the architecture. Yim et al. [14] adopt a software architecture as the main concept for a multi-agent development methodology.

3   A Framework for Component-Based Multi-agent System Development

3.1   Informal Definition of Terminology

In this paper the term *business process* is defined as a set of tasks, control transitions between two tasks, resources used for the execution of tasks, and mapping relationship between a task and a resource (representing the resource used for the execution of the task). Sometimes, a set of business rules is attached to a control transition between tasks to represent conditional transition of control. A *task* represents work, which will be processed by a combination of resource (specified by participant assignment) and/or computer applications (specified by application assignment) [15]. A task normally has a set of pre-conditions and/or post-conditions attached to it. A pre-condition restricts the invocation of a task, whilst a post-condition restricts its completion. An *office task* is a task that is performed in an office environment. A *mobile task* is performed outside of an office environment. A *mobile business process* (mBP) is a business process which contains one or more mobile tasks. A *service* takes the form of computerised support for the execution of tasks. Finally, a *service component* (SC) is a replaceable component, which provides a service via interaction between multiple agents adopting an *interaction protocol*. We adopt the definition of interaction protocol given by [1] - viz an interaction protocol is a forced sequence of message exchanges among two or more of the role components that an agent has installed. The output of a task might be provided by execution of a SC.

3.2   The Development Framework

Fig. 1(a) shows a layered view of the framework used in this paper to develop a component-based multi-agent system. The framework consists of four layers. The foundation layer contains all the supporting functionality for a MAS, such as message transportation, ontology support, and language support etc. The implementation of this layer can be replaced with existing multi-agent systems platform such as Zeus, JADE, or FIPA-OS etc. The component layer consists of basic ontology and service components that are common across a number of mobile workforce applications. The ontology components are reusable ontology items such as Customer, Job, Shift etc. Each service component provides a standard mechanism for accessing a service such as work assignment, route planning etc. The ontology components are used by the service components to standardise and understand the contents of service request and response messages. Lastly, the architectural patterns layer is a set of pre-composed components (both of type ontology and service) to support generic business processes. At the application layer, a system is a customised collection of components from the layers beneath it.

Fig. 1(b) shows the internal structure of a SC. The two main building blocks are an interaction protocol and the role components. The interaction protocol defines the sequence of asynchronous messages sent between the role components, and the role components perform the actions necessary at each stage of the interaction protocol to achieve the service goal. The role components are installed into, and executed by, one or more agents. There are two generic role components for each SC - Initiator and Respondent. The Initiator component starts an interaction by sending a message and the Respondent component is activated when it receives a message from the Initiator component. These two generic role components can be specialised according to the requirements of a given SC. Each role component consists of an Interaction Protocol Scheduler (IPS), a Message Handler (MH), an Interaction State, an Action Pool (AP) and one or more Interfaces. Each role component is in effect a Finite State Machine, driven by internal state changes, and has a different set of internal states according to the role the component plays in the interaction protocol employed for a given SC. The IPS schedules and executes all the actions stored in the AP of a role component according to internal state changes. For this purpose, each role component maintains an Interaction State which is managed by the Interaction State Manager (ISM). The MH is responsible for validating outgoing messages and interpreting incoming messages. The role component provides a number of interfaces for customisation purposes. In this paper, an interface is defined as a set of method signatures. An interface must be provided with an implementation of the method signatures to be executed at run time. An Initiator role component has two kinds of interface: External and Internal (EI and II respectively). An EI (which has one method named 'execute') defines the input data and the service result which is returned to the service consumer.

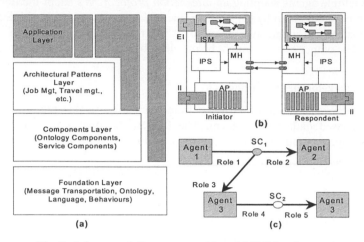

Fig. 1. A framework for component-based MAS development

An Initiator role component contains the implementation of the EI. The EI is a trigger for the entire SC. Calling the execute method in the EI activates the Initiator role component which activates all its other Respondent role components in order. An II is called by the role component itself, and an agent (which installs the role component) provides the implementation of that interface. For example, if a Respondent needs access to a knowledge source to get information to populate a response message, the developer should provide the Respondent component with an implementation of an interface when s/he installs the Respondent component in an agent. Then the Respondent component interacts with the application-specific interface implementation to retrieve the required information. The same is necessary for an Initiator component. From this, different mBPs can customise the same service component by providing different implementations of the interface, which reflect application specific contexts such as different knowledge sources, business rules, and legacy system APIs etc.

Fig. 1(c) shows the structure of an example architectural pattern. In this paper, the architectural pattern for a MAS is defined as a set of agents and service components employed for the interaction between the participating agents to achieve a business goal. The architectural pattern is based on a software architecture concept [16]. In the architecture each agent becomes a component, and a SC becomes a connector. That is, all the participating agents communicate with each other only via SCs. The pattern consists of four agents that use two service components (SC_1 and SC_2). Agent1, Agent2, and Agent3 participate with SC_1 by taking predefined roles for that component. Agent3 also participates with SC_2 to provide a service from SC_2 to SC_1.

Table 1. Identified generic service components

Domain	Service Components
Job Management	ReportCurrentLocation; AssignNewJob; UpdateJobState
Travel Management	PlanRoute; ReplanRoute; EstimateRouteCost; GetCurrentPosition
Knowledge Management	FindExpert; FindRelevantInformation; UpdateKnowledgeBase
Teamwork Co-ordination Management	RequestExpertise; MakeCollectiveDecision GiveJob; SwapShift

4   A Mobile Business Process Application

4.1   Identification of Service Components

A set of SCs have been identified and implemented which can be shared by a number of mBPs. Two separate mobile process domains were analysed to ascertain the common services. The resultant services can be classified in to four areas: 1) Job Management; 2) Travel Management; 3) Teamwork Co-ordination Management; and 4) Knowledge Management. Job Management services are used to manage jobs resulting from customer orders, such as assigning a job to an appropriate worker and updating job status etc. Travel Management services provide up-to-date information and guidance on travel planning. These service anticipate a mobile worker's travel needs, and provide guidance and time estimation so as to synchronise the movements of members of virtual teams. Decentralised Teamwork Co-ordination services empower individuals to collectively co-ordinate activities (e.g. by trading jobs, and automatically negotiating for additional work) using expressed personal preferences within an agreed policy framework. Knowledge Management services anticipate a mobile worker's knowledge requirements by accessing and customising knowledge (based for example on the mobile worker's skills, location, current job and device type) and provide access to collective knowledge assets in the team (e.g. by putting novices in touch with experts, as and when required). Table 1 shows the identified and implemented service components. Detailed descriptions of the SCs are not included for reasons of brevity.

4.2   An Architectural Pattern

Fig. 2 shows an architectural pattern that can be customised to develop a workflow management system for mobile business processes. The pattern consists of four types of agent. The WFControlAgent is responsible for managing workflow instances according to predefined workflow definitions, which specify the order of tasks and the role responsibilities for each task etc. When the execution of a task instance is finished, the WFControlAgent schedules the next task according to a predefined workflow definition and communicates with the TaskAgent, which finds a suitable mobile worker to take responsibility for the execution of the task, and puts the task into his/her job queue. For this, the TaskAgent accesses resourcing information to determine the most appropriate worker for a job considering skills, health and safety issues, and load balancing among workers etc. If the task is a mobile task, then the TaskAgent finds the corresponding PersonalAgent for the mobile worker and notifies it of the new job. The PersonalAgent's function is to support a mobile worker, and it typically runs on the worker's mobile device. A PersonalAgent is equipped with a SC that allows it to get its current location (GetCurrentLocation SC in Fig. 2). The PersonalAgent uses the location information to report to the TaskAgent for task progress checking and travel management purposes. The PersonalAgent is also equipped with the Initiator components for getting travel and job related information from the InformationAgents. Lastly, the PersonalAgent uses some of the Team Co-ordination Management SCs for job trading etc.

4.3   An Illustrative Example

The multi-agent architecture in the above section has been used to automate a real mBP (namely "Survey process for telecommunication service provision") of a telecommunications company in the UK. This process is executed by mobile workers, called Survey Officers (SOs). The function of the SOs is to provide relevant technical information when queries relating to provision of fixed telecom services for both residential and business customers arise. Each SO works within a fixed area (known as a 'patch') which covers the customer catchment areas of a number of telephone exchanges.

The overall flow of the process is as follows. First, a residential (or business) customer contacts a call centre to request installation of a new service or repair of existing equipment. A call centre operative creates a job for the order and places it in a job pool. Next, a computerised system dispatches the job to the appropriate SO's job queue, based on the location of the customer. Third, the SO downloads the job details and decides whether s/he can perform the job or whether s/he needs to dispatch it to a colleague. This decision depends on whether the SO has any higher priority jobs in hand. If the SO can perform the new job that day, s/he schedules a trip to the job location and performs the necessary tasks. Upon completion, the SO accesses the central job queue to update the job's status. Otherwise, s/he has to dispatch the job to a colleague – this frequently requires many phone calls and is very time consuming. If a colleague accepts the job, then the SO has to access the central job queue to change the ownership of the job. Fig. 2 also shows the customised multi-agent architecture that is used to automate the survey process. Firstly, a customised WFControlAgent was used to access an existing JobQueue system that contains all the customer orders.

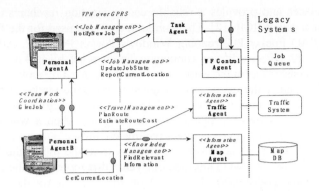

Fig. 2. An architectural pattern and its customisation for the survey process

For a new customer order, the WFControlAgent creates a workflow instance and schedules the necessary tasks according to a predefined workflow definition. The TaskAgent dispatches a job to an appropriate worker (taking into account a number of constraints, as previously mentioned). The GetCurrentLocation SC was customised to access a GPS device that had been added to a mobile device and the location information was passed to the TaskAgent to enable job progress monitoring. Second, four SCs were customised to support the SOs performing the "field survey" task. The GiveJob SC played a key role in the dynamic job re-allocation among team members. It employed FIPA Contract Net [1] as an interaction protocol. The Initiator component sends a call-for-bid (CFB) message to possible candidates (i.e. the PersonalAgents of the other SOs). The Respondent component of each PersonalAgent produces a bid message which indicates the willingness of its SO to take on the offered job, and the distance from its current location to the job to be re-allocated. To calculate the distance, the PrepareBid (an internal interface of the Respondent component of the GiveJob SC) executed the Initiator component of the EstimateRouteCost SC – the latter had been adapted to access a system that returned the distance between any two locations in the UK and the estimated travel time. At the next stage, the Initiator component of the GiveJob SC evaluated the bid received from the Respondent components. The most appropriate candidate was sent an acceptance message and the others rejection messages. In addition, the PlanRoute and FindRelevantInformation SCs were customised to support mobile workers. The "GetShortestRoute" interface (an internal interface provided by the Respondent component of the PlanRoute SC) was customised to return the shortest road route between any two locations in the UK. The main information source needed to determine how and where to modify the company's existing network was a server that holds the telecommunications network plant location and line routing maps. The FindRelevantInformation SC was customised by implementing the "KnowledgeHunter" interface (an internal interface provided by the SC's Respondent component) to access the map server, which resides on the company's Intranet.

All the service components were implemented using LEAP [7], a multi-agent platform which is unique in that it allows a FIPA compliant agent platform to run on lightweight devices and provides a reliable communication mechanism based on a wireless protocol called JICP [17]. The mobile device type used for the field trial was the Compaq iPAQ Pocket PC, running Windows Pocket PC 2002. All the devices were equipped with GPS cards, and communication was established over GPRS. Fig. 3 shows two screenshots from the workflow client that is used by mobile workers. The iPAQ on the left shows the list of jobs assigned to a mobile worker. Each job has a number of service activation buttons associated, and the list differs according to the job type. The figure shows the dialog box that appears when a worker clicks the "GiveJob" button. The dialog box receives parameters for the policies that are applied to the GiveJob SC (such as the maximum distance from the job to the location of a candidate worker, and the maximum time-out value that represents the time duration for negotiation with colleagues). The iPAQ on the right shows the screen that is displayed to a potential recipient of a job that was being traded via the GiveJob SC, giving the initiator of the service and the details of the proposed job.

5   Conclusions

The unique feature of a WFMS for mBPs is the use of mobile workers' whereabouts information to track the progress of workflow instances and assist in the co-ordination of mobile teams. This paper has described a component based multi-agent architecture for the development of WFMS for mBPs, and given details of a MAS based trial application that benefited from the tracking and co-ordination features (for example, in reduced communication costs, as a result of reduced transaction times and a feeling of empowerment for the Survey Officers). Furthermore, the component based approach allowed the MAS to be developed easily and quickly by maximising the reuse of SCs. The SCs, which abstract and implement reusable interaction patterns, hide the details on the creation and interpretation of messages, which makes is easier for novice agent programmers to adopt MAS technology. Ease of customisation of SC and speed of application development was further endorsed by the application of the architecture to another mBP (breakdown service provision) in Germany, in addition to the trial application described in this paper.

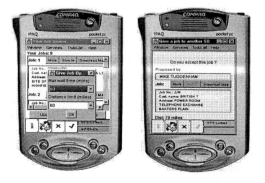

Fig. 3. Screenshots of the workflow client for mobile workers

References

[1]   FIPA: The Foundation for Intelligent Physical Agents. http://www.fipa.org/ (2002)

[2]   Buschmann, F. et. al.: A System of Patterns – Pattern Oriented Software Architecture. Wiley, ISBN 0-471-95869-71 (1996)

[3]   Klusch, M.: Intelligent Information Agents : Agent-based Information Discovery and Management on the Internet. Springer, Berlin-Heidelberg-New York, (1999)

[4]   Jennings, N. R., Norman, T. J., Faratin, P., O'Brien P., and Odgers, B.: Autonomous agents for business process management. Int. Journal of Applied AI 14(2), (2000) 145—189

[5]   Bellifemine, F., Poggi, A., and Rimassa, G.: JADE-A FIPA-compliant agent framework. In Proceedings of the 4th International Conference on Practical Applications of Intelligent Agents and Multi-Agent Systems (PAAM'99), London, UK, (1999) 97-108

[6]   Collis, J., Ndumu, D., Nwana, G., and Lee, L.: The Zeus Agent Building Tool-Kit. BT Technology Journal, 16(3), July (1998) 60-68

[7]   LEAP: Lightweight Extensible Agent Platform. http://leap.crm-paris.com, (2002)

[8]   Huhns, M.N. and Singh, M.P.: Workflow Agents. IEEE Internet Computing, 2 (4), (1998) 94-96

[9]   Shepherdson J.W., Thompson S.G. and Odgers B.: Cross Organisational Workflow Co-ordinated by Software Agents. WACC '99 (Work Activity Co-ordination and Collaboration) Workshop Paper, February (1999)

[10]   Alonso, G., Guenthoer, R., Kamath, M., Agrawal, D., El Abbadi, A., Mohan, C.: Exotica/FMDC: Handling Disconnected Clients in a Workflow Management System. In Proc. 3rd International Conference on Cooperative Information Systems, Vienna, May (1995)

[11]   Kinny, D., Georgeff, M., and Rao, A.: A Methodology and Modeling Technique for Systems of BDI Agents. LNAI 1038, Springer-Verlag, Berlin, Germany, (1996) 56-71

[12]   Brenner, W., Zarnekow, R., and Wittig, H.: Intelligent Software Agents. Foundations and Applications. Springer-Verlag, (1998)

[13]   Sycara, K., Decker, K., Pannu, A., Williamson, M. and Zeng, D.: Distributed Intelligent Agents. IEEE Expert, December (1996)

[14]   Yim, H.S., Cho, K.H., Kim, J.W. and Park, S.J.: An Architecture-Centric Object-Oriented Design Method for Multi-Agent System. ICMAS 2000, Boston MA, USA, (2000)

[15]   WFMC: The Workflow Management Coalition Specification. http://www.wfmc.org/standards/docs.htm

[16]   Garlan, D. and Shaw, M.: An Introduction to Software Architecture. I.J.Software Engineering and Knowledge Engineering, 1, World Science Publishing, (1993)

[17] Caire, G., Lhuillier, N. and Rimassa G.: A communication protocol for agents on handheld devices. In Proceedings of Workshop on ubiquitous agents on embedded, wearable, and mobile devices, held in conjunction with the 2002 Conf. On Autonomous Agents & Multiagent systems, Bologna, Italy, (2002)

Code Complexity Metrics for Mobile Agents Implemented with Aspect/J™

Jana Dospisil

School of Network Computing, Monash University
McMahons Rd., Frankston, Australia
jana.Dospisil@infotech.monash.edu.au

Abstract. This paper describes research in measuring the code complexity of mobile agent applications designed with aspect-oriented programming (AOP) as captured in the *Aspect/J™* language. The modularized code encapsulating agent interactions is characterized by class hierarchies which are shared structures. We observed additional subclassing leads to increase in entropic tendencies in the actual code. Our experience with fine tuning of protocols shows that the probability that a subclass will not consistently extend the protocol content of its superclass is increasing with the depth of hierarchy. The tools like *Hyper/J* and *Aspect/J™* support the separation of concerns thus allowing different approach to evolving the protocol implementation. In this paper we present the approach to assessing the complexity by measuring the entropy of the mobile agent application code designed with *Aspect/J™*

1 Introduction

Agents are viewed as the next significant software abstraction, and it is expected they will become as ubiquitous as graphical user interfaces are today. The decision making processes and interactions between agents will become very fast [12] and the agent applications will be characterized by fast growing complexity of the code. The new approach to development is separation of concerns and usage of relevant tools such as Aspect/J [13] or Hyper/J [17] which facilitate the development process [11,8].

The source of the problem in development of agent applications is that some kinds of behaviour or functionality *cross cut* or are *orthogonal* to classes in many components and they are not easily modularized to a separate class. Examples of such behaviour include the following: synchronization and concurrency, exception handling, event monitoring, and coordination and interaction protocols. Tarr and Osher [22] state that *"Done well, separation of concerns can provide many software engineering benefits, including reduced complexity…"*. To measure the quality of separation either in *N-dimensional* space or even the orthogonal separation only as seen in *Aspect/J*, the new set of complexity metrics is required.

V. Mařík et al. (Eds): CEEMAS 2003, LNAI 2691, pp. 647-657, 2003.

Layout of the paper: Section 2 provides a brief overview of negotiation protocols and complexity measures. Section 3 discusses the use of AOP in mobile agent design. Section 4 provides a brief overview of entropy metrics used to measure complexity of code. Section 5 contains experimental results.

2   Background

Negotiation and Protocols: Negotiation is a search process. The participants jointly search a multi-dimensional space (e.g. quantity, price, and delivery) in an attempt to find a single point in the space at which they reach mutual agreement and meet their objectives. For many-to-many coupling or interaction between participants, the market mechanism is used, and for one-to-many negotiation, auctions are more appropriate. The market mechanism often suffers from an inability to scale down efficiently [16] to smaller numbers of participants. On the other hand, one-to-many interactions are influenced by strategic considerations and involve integrative bargaining where agents search for *Pareto efficient* agreement.

Many different types of *contract protocols* (cluster, swaps, and multiagent, as examples) and *negotiation strategies* are used and have been experimentally implemented (18, 14 and others). Contracts in automated negotiations consisting of self-interested agents are typically designed as binding. In cooperative distributed problem solving, commitments are often allowed to be broken based on some local reasoning. Frequently, the protocols use continuous levels of commitment based on a monetary penalty method [e.g. 19, 18]. Unfortunately, the inflexible nature of these protocols restricts an agent's actions when the situation becomes unfavorable. The models which incorporate the possibility of decommitting from a contract with or without reprisals [20, 21] can accommodate some changes in the environment and improve an agent's gain.

The design and coding of these protocols is typically too rigid with respect to evolving, and accommodation dynamic requirements for improvement. This tendency is even more pronounced in mobile environment. According to our research, the complexity of these protocols and large number of exceptions which must be handled are the main reason why the resulting code shows entropic tendencies by deepening of hierarchies and extensive subclassing.

2.1   Overview of Entropy Based Complexity Measures

Entropy based complexity measures are based on theory of information. This is the approach taken by Davis and LeBlanc [5] who quantify the differences between *anded* and *neted* structures to provide an unbiased estimate of the probability of occurrence of event *m*. This measurement is based on chunks of FORTRAN and COBOL code (represented by nodes in the directed acyclic graph) with the same in-degree and the same out-degree to assess syntactic complexity. Belady and Lehman [4] elaborated on the law of increasing entropy: the entropy of a system (level of its unstructuredness) increases with time, unless specific work is executed to maintain or reduce it.

The use of entropy as a measure of information content, introduced by Harrison, has been around since 1992 [10]. This metric is intended to order programs according to their complexity and was tested on C code. However, it does not indicate the *"distance"* between two programs. It provides only the ordinal position thus restricting the way of usage. The work of Bansiya and Davis [3] introduces similar complexity measure – *Class Definition Entropy* (*CDE*) - replacing the operators of Harrison with name strings used in a class. The assumption that all name strings represent approximately equal information is related to the possible error insertion by misusing the string. The metric has been validated on four large projects in C++ and results have been used to estimate *Class Implementation Time Complexity* measure.

3   Utilizing AOP in Agent Design

In aspect-based design of negotiating agents, we separate two entities: *negotiation protocol* and *negotiation strategy*. *Negotiation strategy* can be seen as a private formalized strategy responsible for computation of appropriate actions and outcomes. The generated actions and outcomes depend on the role the agent assumes, the negotiation protocol used, and agent's relationship with other parties (e.g. cooperating self-interested agent). The *negotiation strategy* incorporates one or more *negotiation protocols*.

Aspects are used to localize or modularize cross cutting behavior or functionality that appears in multiple classes and / or methods. The behavior is not easily isolated into a single class or method for access via inheritance, delegation, or method calls. The functionality may also be temporary or transient; the developer may want to have the option to dynamically add or remove it from their application. A common implementation is behavior that is repeated in several classes or methods. Often if this behavior can be placed in a single component or method; it should be placed in an aspect when it can be dynamically added or removed. Placing the behavior in an aspect may also result in a simpler syntax and less lines of code overall (in the pre-woven code).

Aspect-based static agent design has been first proposed by Kendall [11]. She proposed role based design with aspects representing roles. In this approach, a role is a module equipped with rich interface that can be plugged in and out of an application, as needed. She used Line of Code measure to assess the final code complexity. Our experiments with contracting mobile agents (coded on aglets base [1]) indicate that such metrics are insufficient and lacking interpretation framework.

4   Entropy Based Metrics For Aspect/J

With *Aspect/J*™ specific features, we focus not only on improved maintainability and reusability but also on reduced complexity as the affect of splitting the control-flow to multiple streams [8, 7]. Control flow in a program is the order in which contained sequential units of code are executed. The local code within a unit (method) does not alter interaction between objects; therefore, it does not contribute significantly to complexity flow.

The entropy based metrics for AOP have been proposed and described in [7] and tested on an example of Java code. Data collection and extraction of symbols representing the control flow have been done with concern graphs and the FEAT tool [15] which displays the concerns as a collection of class trees. The structural metrics model is composed of different types of nodes and edges:

- *Symbol nodes si* are end nodes which correspond to global symbols in the class stream
- *Class nodes cj* are represented by the top structural units from which all derived nodes are sourced

Edges represent dependencies between

- *class nodes* and *aspects* thus describing the dependency between aspects and classes using the particular aspects. *Aspect dependency* refers to treatment of crosscuts.
- *symbols and nodes* which directly provide the source for symbol. *Symbol dependency* refers to dependencies relevant to processing logic.

Each symbol invocation requires V_s messages, one message for each symbol node. Since the structure is already known, the messages will traverse nodes in order of dependency edges. Source and destination *symbol nodes* denote each edge. We can describe the path of symbol s_i as follows:

$$\text{message}(\text{path\_to}(s_i)) = \{V_e(s_i), \text{node}_1, \text{node}_2, \ldots \text{node}_n\}$$

The entropy of the message describing a symbol node s_i is the sum of entropies (entropy of the total number edges which serve as information source to this symbol node and entropy of finding the edge destination if we know the symbol source). This is the *Path Entropy:*

$$H(P) = H(S) + \frac{V_e}{V_s + V_c} H(E)$$

Total number of edges is denoted by the sum of edges:

$$V_{e\_all} = \sum V_e$$

We divided our metrics proposal into two parts:

- Entropy based ordering of symbols within modules.
- Weighted entropy measures.

4.1   Entropy Based Ordering of Symbols

We consider the entropy for the aspect stream as the reduction in uncertainty for those edges that have some information "outsourced" to aspects. Aspects connect the classes (via symbols) which would not be connected otherwise.

$$I = H(E) - H(A)$$

The reduction in total entropy is then calculated as

Table 1. Definitions

$V_s = \sum_{i=0}^{I} s_i$	Total number of all **symbol nodes** in the graph. We assume that the number of symbol nodes is within the range 0 to I-1.
$V_c = \sum_{j=0}^{C} c_j$	Total number of class nodes range from 0 to C-1
$V_e = V_d + V_a$	Number of all **edges** in the graph (aspect edges - and symbol edges) relevant to the particular symbol and aspect.
$V_d = \sum_{i=0}^{I} e_i^s$	Total number of dependency edges in the class stream traversed to a symbol s *(for0<s<=S)*. Assumption: the symbol s may occur in multiple nodes.
$V_a = \sum_{a=0}^{A} e_a^c$	Total number of edges with aspects that have an entry in class c. ($e_a^c \rightarrow$ ath aspect edge associate with class c; the aspect is used by multiple classes)
$p(e_i) = \dfrac{V_d}{V_s}$	Probability that i^{th} symbol node is sourced by e edges
$p(e_a) = \dfrac{V_a}{V_d}$	Probability that a random symbol node i has an aspect associated with it
$p_e(d)$	Probability that the dependency edge has length d (the number of nodes needed to be traversed to reach the edge e is d)
$p(d)$	Probability that two random symbol nodes i will have d distance between them.
$H(S) = -\sum_{i=1}^{M} p(e_i) \log_2 p(e_i))$	Entropy of the total number edges which serve as information source to a symbol node
$H(E) = \sum p(d) \log_2 (V_s p(d))$	Entropy of finding the edge destination if we know the starting point (symbol source)
$H(A) = -\sum_{i=1}^{M} p(e_a) \log_2 p(e_a)$	Entropy of aspects

The probabilities have been computed as shown in Tab. 1. They can be also derived empirically from execution scenarios. Symbol ordering provides perspective on the complexity of each module and the usage of symbols.

4.2   Weighted Entropy Metrics

During our experiment with agent application we established that not all types of edges and nodes are equally important for given symbols. In order to distinguish the dependency edges according to their importance with respect to a given qualitative characteristics and their relationship to connecting nodes we have assigned to each edge type a non-negative weight proportional to its importance and significance. Weights of every edge type have an objective character representing the ratio of the objective probability that the edge path is the source of information for symbol s.

$$w(e_i) = -\frac{p(e_i)}{\log_e p(e_i)}$$

In this case we obtain the following expression for weighted entropy:

$$H(e) = \sum_{i=1}^{I} p(e_i)^2$$

In order to acquire more objective weights for different types of dependency edges, we have introduced finer granularity for edges, based on the information provided by the FEAT tool and execution scenarios. Each edge type can assume one of the subtypes in Tab. 2

Table 2. Symbol node classification and weighted assignment

Edge correspondence in FEAT	Description	Coupling measure as weight in % MOB-Trader
Calls, m_1, m_2	Method m_1 calls m_2	80
Reads m, f	Method m reads value of f	0
Writes m,f	Method m writes in f	50
Checks m, c	Method m checks class c	0
Creates m, c	Method m creates object of class c	30
Declares c, {m}	Class c declares method m	0
Superclass c_1, c_2	Class c_2 is the superclass to c_1	No – included in class nodes dependency

Weighted entropy measures provide a subjective view based on the associated failure risk and maintainability of each module. By introducing weighted entropy, we can distinguish between the quantitative uncertainty, related to the probability with which a symbol occurs, and the qualitative one, related to a given qualitative characteristic (anticipated failure risk factor or other property we want to measure). Furthermore, by balancing weights for observable and evolutionary changes (using empirical values) we can obtain sufficient foundation for prediction models.

5   Experimental Results

We have used ordering of symbols entropy metrics to estimate the complexity of mobile agent application *MOB-Trader* written for mobile agent platform – aglets [1]. The same application was implemented with and without aspects to compare entropy The application implements complex trading scenarios of multiple vendors (*Moderator* module) and mobile buyer agents (*Buyer* modules). In the *Buyer* modules, *Aspect/J* enhances the modularization by placing exceptions and handling of preconditions and post conditions in aspects instead of special classes and subclasses. Negotiation strategies range includes Contract Net Protocol (CNP), Constraint Satisfaction Problem based solutions, and market based models (game theoretical models).

In order to provide implementation flexibility, each negotiation strategy specific rules and exception handling are implemented as a set of interchangeable aspects.

```
1.  public aspect AspectForGetVendor{
2.          pointcut  getListOfVendor(ListManager   lMng,
      Message aMsg)
3.                :target(lMng)&&args(aMsg)&&call(public
      Hashtable ListManager.getVendor(..));
4.
5.          before(ListManager lMng, Message aMsg)
6.                  throws  InvalidRegisKeyException,
      InvalidBusinessException  :  getListOfVendor(lMng,
      aMsg){
7.        Hashtable buList = lMng.getBusinessList();
8.        Object infox   = aMsg.getArg("buType");
9.        String buType = infox.toString();
10.       System.out.println("Looking    for->"+buType+"
      in Hash size   "+buList.size());
11.   if(buType==null)              throw           new
      InvalidRegisKeyException("Null key");
12.   if(!buList.containsKey(buType))      throw     new
      InvalidBusinessException
13. ("No such that business");
14.   }
15. }
```

Fig. 1. Exception handling

Fig. 1 shows the example of code with aspects to handle two particular exceptions: '*InvalidRegisKeyException*' and '*InvalidBusinessException*'. Before *getVendor()* method (*ListManager* class) is called, the aspect *AspectForGetVendor()* is executed to validate the register preconditions: register key and business type. The aspect handles two exceptions: *InvalidRegisterKeyException()* and *InvalidBusinessTypeException()*.

The handler for each exception invokes additional submodule which provides customized exception handling.

AspectForStock () deals with negotiation mechanism implemented in multiple cooperating threads. The aspect is invoked after buyer agent reservation message is sent to vendor host. It starts a thread (code fragment in Fig. 2) to hold the reserved order until it receives a payment notification message from the buyer agent. If the response message is not received within expected time frame, the reserved order will be cancelled.

```
16. public aspect AspectForStock implements Runnable{
17.      private Vector resList = null;
18.      private Thread resTimer = null;
19.               pointcut     doQuotation(StockManager
     sMgr):target(sMgr)&&args(String)
20. &&call
21. (public Quotation StockManager.queryItemPrice(..));
22. ...some lines of code. . .
23.      after(StockManager sMgr) : doQuotation(sMngr){
24.           resTimer = new Thread(this);
25.           resTimer.start();
26.      }
27.      public void run(){
28.           resList  = sMgr.getStock();
29.           int index = (resList.size()-1);
30.           try { Thread.sleep(10*1000); ...........
```

Fig. 2. Aspect for dealing with threads

Several versions of each aspect have been implemented. The protocol improvement has been achieved by replacing the relevant aspects with new aspect code and repeating weaving process. The other classes and methods which implement remaining parts of protocol will stay unchanged.

Selected examples of the experiment results are in Fig. 3 , Fig. 4 and Fig. 5.

In Fig. 3, the *Moderator* module shows higher entropy for finding edge destination, path entropy (total entropy). Multiple versions of protocols implemented in aspects increased entropy of aspects. Entropy $H(A-1)$ was calculated for both modules implemented without aspects and no protocol modifications.

There are visibly higher weighted values for implementation for "run" symbol compared to its ordering values - Fig. 4.

Cumulative weighted entropy shows smaller values in both modules because many methods are simple "read" type with very low weights - Fig. 5.

6   Usability Remarks on Proposed Metrics

This paper has provided an overview of entropy based metrics used in object oriented mobile agent development. The entropy metrics are useful in ranking different modules and symbols with regard to their complexity. The single valued measure of complexity is appealing as quality indicator. However, as also discussed in Fenton's book [9] the results may not be suitable for use in prediction models or as guidance for improving the quality of the product. In our framework, we have introduced weighted entropic values to accommodate different quality aspects of software thus making them suitable for prediction models. In summary, the complexity ranking for protocol modules and weighted entropy for modules and symbols proved to become good indicators of even complexity spread across modules.

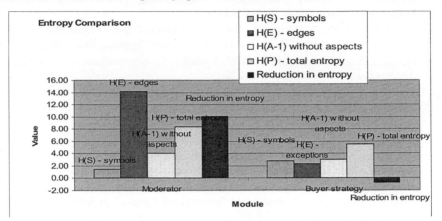

Fig. 3. Entropy comparison

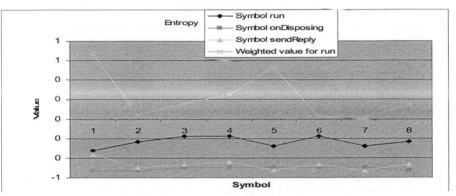

Fig. 4. Entropy values for selected symbols

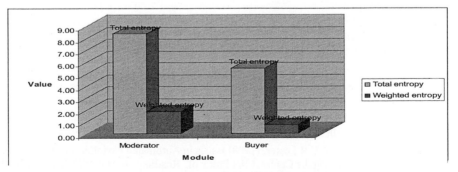

Fig. 5. Comparison of total and weighted entropy

References

[1]   Danny B. Lange, Mitsuru Oshima. (1998). Programming and Deploying Java mobile agents with Aglets, Addison-Wesley.

[2]   AspectJ Team. (2002). The AspectJ™ Programming Guide. Xerox Corporation, http://AspectJ/doc/progguide/printable.html.

[3]   Bansiya, J., Davis, C., Etzkorn, L. (1999). An Entropy-Based Complexity Measure for Object-Oriented Designs, Theory and Practice of Object Systems, Vol. 5(2), pp.11-118

[4]   Belady, L.A.and Lehman, M.M. (1976). A Model of a large program development. IBM Systems Journal, Vol 15(3), pp.225-252.

[5]   Davis, J.S., and LeBlanc, R.J. (1988). A Study of the Applicability of Complexity Measures. IEEE Transactions on Software Engineering, Vol 14(9), pp.1366-1371,

[6]   Decker, K. and Lesser, V. (1995). Analyzing the Need for Meta-Level Communication. Computer Science Department, University of Massachusetts, Technical Report 93-22.

[7]   Jana Dospisil. Jana Dospisil. (2003). Complexity metrics for Aspects. To appear in Proc. of IRMA'2003, Philadelphia, 19-22.5.2003

[8]   Dospisil, Jana.(2002). Dynamic weighted Entropy based complexity metrics for separation of concerns. In Proc. of the International Symposium Advances in Software Engineering, Baden-Baden, 1-4.8.2002.

[9]   Fenton, N. and Pfleger, S. L. (1997). Software Metrics: A Rigorous & Practical Approach. International Thomson Computer Press.

[10]   Harrison, W. An Entropy-Based Measure of Software Complexity. (1992). IEEE Transactions of Software Engineering, Vol. 18, No. 11, November, pp. 1025-1029

[11]   Kendall E. (1999). Role Model Designs and Implementations with Aspect Oriented Programming. Proceedings of the 1999 Conference on Object- Oriented Programming Systems, Languages, and Applications (OOPSLA'99), ACM Press, November.

[12]   Kephart, J. O., J. E. Hanson, D. W. Levine, B. N. Grosof, J. Sairamesh, R. B. Segal, and S. R. White. (1998) Dynamics of an Information-Filtering Economy. Proceedings of Second International Workshop on Cooperative Information Agents (CIA-98), Paris, July 4-7.

[13]   Kiczales, G., J. Lamping, A. Mendhekar, C. Maeda, C. Lopes, J. - M. Loingtier, and J. Irwin, (1997). Aspect Oriented Programming. Xerox Corporation, 1997. http://www.parc.xerox.com/spl/projects/aop/

[14]   Mass-Colell, A. Whinston, R. and Green, J.R. (1995) Microeconomic theory. Oxford University Press.

[15]   Murphy, Gail, C. Albert Lai, Robert J. Walker, and Martin P. Robillard. (2001). Separating Features in Source Code: Exploratory Study. Proc. Of the 23th International Conference on Software Engineering, Toronto, pp. 275-284.

[16]   Osborne, M.J., and Rubinstein, A. (1990) Bargaining and Markets. Academic Press.

[17]   Ossher, H., Tarr, P. (1998). Multi-Dimensional Separation of Concerns in Hyperspace: Position Paper, IBM T.J. Watson Research Center, New York.

[18]   Sandholm, T. (1993) An implementation of the contract net protocol based on marginal cost calculations. In American Association for Artificial Intelligence, 256-262.

[19]   Sandholm, T.W. and V.R.Lesser. (1998) Issues in Automated Negotiation and Electronic Commerce: Extending the Contract Net Protocol. Readings in AGENTS (ed. Michael N. Huhns & Munindar P. Singh), Morgan Kaufmann, 66-73

[20]   Sen,S. and Durfee, E. (1994) The role of commitment in cooperative negotiation. International Journal of Intelligent Cooperative Information Systems, 3(1):67-81.

[21]   Smith, R.G. (1980) The Contract Net Protocol: High-Level Communication and Control in a Distributed Problem Solver. IEEE Trans. on Computers C-29(12):1104-1113.

[22]   Tarr, P. Ossher, H. Harrison, W, and Sutton, Jr. (1999). N degrees of Separation: Multi-Dimensional Separation of Concerns. Proc. Of the 21st International Conference on Software Engineering, 1999

Author Index

Lecture Notes in Artificial Intelligence (LNAI)

Lecture Notes in Computer Science